Computer Systems Architecture
A Networking Approach

Pearson Education

We work with leading authors to develop the
strongest educational materials in computing,
bringing cutting-edge thinking and best learning
practice to a global market.

Under a range of well-known imprints, including
Addison-Wesley, we craft high quality print and
electronic publications which help
readers to understand and apply their content,
whether studying or at work.

To find out more about the complete range of our
publishing please visit us on the World Wide Web at:
www.pearsoneduc.com

Computer Systems Architecture
A Networking Approach

Rob Williams

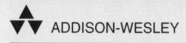

An imprint of **Pearson Education**

Harlow, England · London · New York · Reading, Massachusetts · San Francisco · Toronto · Don Mills, Ontario · Sydney
Tokyo · Singapore · Hong Kong · Seoul · Taipei · Cape Town · Madrid · Mexico City · Amsterdam · Munich · Paris · Milan

Pearson Education Limited
Edinburgh Gate
Harlow
Essex CM20 2JE
England

and Associated Companies around the world

Visit us on the World Wide Web at:
www.pearsoneduc.com

ISBN 0 201 64859 8

British Library Cataloguing in Publication Data
A catalogue record for this book can be obtained from the British Library.

Library of Congress Cataloging-in-Publication Data
A catalogue record for this book can be obtained from the Library of Congress.

10 9 8 7 6 5 4 3 2 1
04 03 02 01 00

Typeset by Ian Kingston Editorial Services, Nottingham, UK
Printed and bound by Ashford Colour Press Ltd, Gosport

Contents

A Companion Web site accompanies

COMPUTER SYSTEMS ARCHITECTURE:
A Networking Approach

by **Rob Williams**

Visit the Computer Systems Architecture Companion Web site at
www.booksites.net/williams
where you will find valuable teaching and learning material including:

For Lecturers:
- PDF files of all the diagrams from the text
- Phase tests

For Students:
- Lab exercises
- Links to resources on the web

Preface

Origins of this book

This book is based on a first-year degree course called Computer Systems Architecture (uqc104s1), which I have delivered for some years at the University of the West of England (UWE), Bristol. The course has expanded, contracted and expanded again, so it has been thoroughly shaken about and reorganized several times. Many of our graduates are recruited into the growing telecommunications industry, and interest in this subject area is very high. Therefore the course, and this book, reflect the shift in interest to encompass not only applied computer science but also data communication and networking.

Students

Whereas ten years ago students came into our first year with little in the way of computing qualifications or experience, now over half our new students have already successfully completed a two-year course (A level or BTEC) in the computing field. They have enrolled on a degree course in BSc Computer Science, BSc Software Engineering or BSc Computing for Real-Time Systems. The latter, in particular, attracts technical enthusiasts who are keen to progress into exciting new subject areas such as networking, Unix, embedded systems or real-time programming. With this more demanding audience in mind, I have attempted to inject new ideas and pursue fresh directions. The danger is always that such students will become bored and withdraw their commitment if they consider the course to be 'too easy' or 'out of date'. This book attempts to acknowledge and build on their existing experience.

Another worry often voiced by students concerns the place of mathematics within the course. Well, no advanced mathematics is needed. You will only occasionally be asked to use simple algebra and arithmetic. Common sense will be your most valuable resource! Also, we will do no soldering. This is not an electronics course.

Technological change

Keeping pace with technological change is an issue for all computing courses and texts, and I have taken up this challenge by basing the book on the Pentium processor, despite its daunting complexity. Systems which seemed capable of holding their advanced position within the market-place for several years, are now overtaken within months of launch. Software tools are being developed and adopted by commercial programmers long before universities have had a chance to obtain a copy. As a result, computing curricula are in need of continuous review in order to maintain their currency within the wider context. It is not uncommon for my students to return home to use their own computer systems because they are more advanced than those available in our undergraduate laboratories! But it is worrying to me how fashion-conscious the computing field has become. This can lead to rapid demotivation when the ideas and examples discussed during lectures, although academically and intellectually valid, are perceived as outdated. In this regard, I hope to have included enough contemporary material to maintain your interest!

Use of this text

We all learn differently, but the ability to use text effectively has been at the core of modern civilization for a long time. We all benefit so much from people's experience recorded on paper for others to read. Ignoring this vast resource is deliberately handicapping yourself. Life is difficult enough without conceding an unnecessary penalty! If anything, the introduction of the WWW has placed even greater literacy demands on everyone. Most Web pages presenting useful information still depend heavily on text. A picture may be worth a thousand words, but it is often the accompanying text that gives you a first glimmer of understanding.

At the start of each chapter you will see a graphic representation of the contents, modelled on the familiar Windows Explorer file browser. It enables you to see the subject context of all the chapters. It is not a contents list; rather, more an ideogram. Each chapter is supplied with a small set of questions for which answers are supplied at the back of the book. It goes without saying that you should make a serious attempt to answer the questions yourself before reading the answers! A full glossary is also included at the end of the book in an attempt to deal with the appalling jargon explosion that has taken place. We all bemoan this situation, but it does constitute part of the challenge of becoming a fully blown computer professional. It cannot simply be ignored.

Operating systems and programming languages

When presenting a course, or writing a text on computing, the choice of which language or operating system to use can be an emotional issue. Traditionally, university courses have tried to duck the question of commercial relevance and stick with the well-established academic favourites. I do find this frustrating, having once (twice?) tried to use Pascal for a commercial contract and then run up against all sorts of quite predictable problems which we had never honestly discussed with our students. With this experience in mind I have since always tried to use commercially viable tools in my teaching. The two operating systems that are universally seen throughout the world are Unix and Windows NT (in which we include Windows 2000). I expect you to have access to both systems for practical work. Linux is perfectly admirable for the Unix examples, although I have illustrated the text using Sun Microsystems' Solaris. As for languages, I assume that you are studying a programming language in parallel with this computer systems course, and so can quickly pick up the necessary level of C to understand my code fragments. I do not expect C++ expertise!

To further assist you in testing out the examples and trying the end of chapter questions, a student edition of the Microsoft Developer Studio Visual C++ is included with this text. The Appendix contains guidance notes to help you install the package and quickly start using it. Although we will only be using it for very elementary programming examples, you can continue to progress into C++, object-oriented programming and the use of MFCs (Microsoft Foundation Classes) if you are so minded! Source code examples and a very effective online system are provided to support your learning.

Practical course orientation

The course that you are following may be different from ours in many aspects. I plan on a 24 week schedule, splitting the work into two semesters. In this way, each chapter serves a week of the course. The order, and to some extent the content, is determined by the practical work that is carried out in the weekly lab sessions. I believe that it is principally the practical work which fully confirms technical understanding. I could never trust a software design that had not been tested by implementation! To reduce lab sessions, or decouple them from the theoretical discussion taking place in the lectures, can weaken our ability to understand and assimilate new ideas. We all learn differently. Some like to listen, some to read, and others to do. Personally, I have always found that practical activity drives home new concepts firmly and permanently.

'Listen and forget. Read and remember. Do and understand.'

For the tutor

The student readers

The typical readers that I have in mind have enrolled on a first year course in computing or a related subject area. They will be attending at least some of your weekly lectures, carrying out practical exercises, reading text books and talking to their friends about the work. They will also have regular access to the Internet, either at home or at their place of study. However, in my experience, no single one of these activities is sufficient to pass a degree course. In addition, it is unlikely that your students will only be studying computer systems and networking. In all probability there will be parallel courses in programming, systems design, mathematical methods and occasionally electronics. A successful course should help the student to integrate all these experiences and encourage cross-referencing from one discipline to another. This is precisely what this book enables them to do, since they will find links and road signs towards their other areas of study.

Our degree courses, like many, are integrated into a modular programme which offers the students some options in the second year. I find that many students require an introduction to these option subjects during the first year in order to make an informed decision. Systems administration, operating systems and networking in particular can be unknown areas for the students. This course is intended to fulfil this

'Foundation Course' function, as well as giving students a grounding in the practice and principles of computing systems.

Practical worksheets

I have made available on the Companion Web Site (www.booksites.net/williams) samples of the weekly worksheets that I use with my students. These focus on aspects of the theoretical material which has just been presented in the lectures. Often a worksheet also serves as an introduction to the assessed coursework assignment which follows. As you can see, we still closely link student lab work sessions to their classroom experience, something which is not always possible within a modular programme.

Assessment

Because of the practical orientation of the course, I set two assessed programming assignments. In the first semester it is currently an assembler exercise using the Visual C Developer Studio. This involves accessing the PC COM port for serial communications. The second assignment is a group exercise which builds on the first. It requires the production of software to support a packet-oriented ring network, again using the PC COM port. The second programming assignment is completed in the C language, and involves protocol negotiation and cooperative working. This is intended to prepare the ground for second year courses in networking and final year courses in distributed systems. As part of the coursework assessment, I ask the students to demonstrate their code and answer a couple of questions about the structure and functionality. This does take valuable time to carry out, but in my experience is well worth the investment.

In place of a single terminal exam I prefer to set several assessed class tests. These give the student regular useful feedback, and allow for corrective action by the tutors before it is too late! The questions listed at the end of each chapter offer some preparation for the tests and benefit from summary answers provided at the end of the book. Sample test scripts are available from the publisher's secure Web site.

Acknowledgements

Thanks to Phil Naylor for supplying the example administration script listed in Chapter 13 and, more significantly, maintaining our network of Sun workstations so well. I must warmly thank my colleagues Bob Lang and Craig Duffy for doggedly reading the early drafts and offering helpful comments. I would also like to mention the many students, past and present, on our very special BSc Computing for Real-Time Systems degree, whose good humour and determination often brightened long debugging sessions. The best reward for any teacher is to see students progress and develop their technical confidence, leading to successful graduation and rewarding careers.

As the book grew, my wife's initial scepticism changed to benign toleration and then, as the text spread across the living room floor, to alarmed disbelief. But despite heroic proofreading and executive editorial efforts on her part, all errors are mine, and I hope you will send me your comments and views (rob.williams@uwe.ac.uk).

I must also give praise to Brian Kernighan for his wonderfully small pic language, which I used to draft all the line diagrams throughout the text. The original text was edited with emacs and the formatting was all carried out using groff from Richard Stallman's GNU suite. It was here that I discovered the fun of using pic to code diagrams.

However, the most critical commentary was no doubt rendered by Cassie, our morose four-year-old cat, who regularly fell sound asleep straddling the monitor on which I was editing the text.

Rob Williams
Department of Computing
University of the West of England
Bristol
July 2000

The publishers would like to express their appreciation for the invaluable advice and encouragement they have received for this book from the following academics:

Hernk Corporaal
Delft University, The Netherlands

Peter Hood
University of Huddersfield, UK

Prasant Mohaptra
Michigan State University, USA

Henk Neefs
University of Gent, Belgium

Andy Pimentel
University of Amsterdam, The Netherlands

Mike Scott
Dublin City University

Bernard Weinberg
Formerly Michigan State University, USA

We are grateful to the following for permission to reproduce copyright material:

Figure 9.4 'Data sheet (p3) for a Harris 82C55A, Parallel Port I/O Chip', reproduced by permission of Intersil Corporation, © 2000 Intersil Corporation; Figure 12.4 from Hatfield, D. J. and Gerald, J. (1971) 'Program restructuring for virtual memory' *IBM Systems Journal*, Vol. 10, No. 3, p. 189, copyright 1971 by International Business Machines Corporation, reprinted with permission of the IBM Systems Journal; Figure 12.23 'A specification table for Maxtor hard disks', reproduced by permission of Maxtor Corporation.

While every effort has been made to trace the owners of copyright material, in a few cases this has proved impossible and we take this opportunity to offer our apologies to any copyright holders whose rights we have unwittingly infringed.

Trademarks

Adobe, Acrobat and PostScript are registered trademarks of Adobe Systems Incorporated.

Apple, AppleTalk, iMac and Macintosh are trademarks of Apple Computer, Inc..

Unix is a trademark of AT&T Company.

Atari ST is a trademark of Atari Corporation.

Winframe is a registered trademark of Citrix Systems, Inc.

Commodore PET is a trademark of Commodore Business Machines, Inc.

Cray is a registered trademark of Cray Inc.

Sound Blaster is a registered trademark of Creative Technology Ltd.

Alpha, AlphaServer and AltaVista are trademarks of DEC.

Centronics is a trademark of Genicom Corporation.

Hewlett-Packard is a registered trademark of Hewlett-Packard Company.

Quake is a trademark of id Software, Inc.

Celeron and Itanium are trademarks and Intel and Pentium are registered trademarks of Intel Corporation.

Lego is a trademark of The LEGO Company.

Microsoft, Developer Studio, Visual C++ and Windows are registered trademarks of Microsoft Corporation.

OS-9 is a registered trademark of Microware Systems Corporation.

Motorola is a registered trademark of Motorola, Inc.

Netscape and Netscape Navigator are trademarks of Netscape Communications Corporation.

NetWare is a registered trademark of Novell, Inc.

Polaroid is a trademark of Polaroid Corporation.

Psion is a trademark of Psion PLC.

MiniDisc and Digital Versatile Disc are trademarks of Sony Electronics Inc.

SPARC, UltraSPARC and SPARClite are registered trademarks of SPARC International, Inc.

Sun and Sun Microsystems are registered trademarks of Sun Microsystems, Inc.

Recommended lab sessions

It is expected that the majority of the readers of this text will be students pursuing a course called Computer Science, Computing, Software Engineering, or some similar title. Such courses normally include weekly lectures and practical work in laboratories. Thus the material covered in the following chapters represents only one component of your learning experience. The following practical worksheets are available for downloading and use (from www.booksites.net/williams), and have been planned to support and extend the principal ideas presented in each of the chapters. You may wish to read through them even if your own course demands that you carry out a different set of practical exercises.

Part 1

1. Videos with historic interviews and equipment
    Search engines
    Web sites with information about historic computers
    Investigate library catalogue

2. Introduction to the network
    Computing facilities, Unix and Windows NT
    Basic programmer's skills
    Revise binary numbers

3. Inside the PC
    Opening up the computer
    Identifying parts
    Reviewing component names and their function

4. Digital logic for the control unit
    Using truth tables
    Drawing simple circuits
    Understanding decoders
    Building traffic light controllers

5. Digital logic for the ALU
    Building a half adder
    Building a full adder
    Assembling a parallel adder/subtractor

6. Memory mapping
    Understanding the need for memory decoding
    Interpreting a memory map
    Writing a memory map from a hardware specification

7. Introduction to Pentium asm
    Online help
    Setting up a project on Visual Studio
    Writing and compiling C programs
    Including asm inserts

8. Subroutines
    Calling C functions
    Calling asm subroutines
    Passing parameters
    Stack frame preparation and scrubbing

9. Input and output methods using C routines
    Using the C library of IO routines
    Accessing COM1 and COM2 from C and asm

10. Inter-computer communications using RS232
    Packet data
    Flow control issues
    EOF problems

11. Memory performance
    Virtual memory swapping delays

PART 1

Basic functions and facilities of a computer

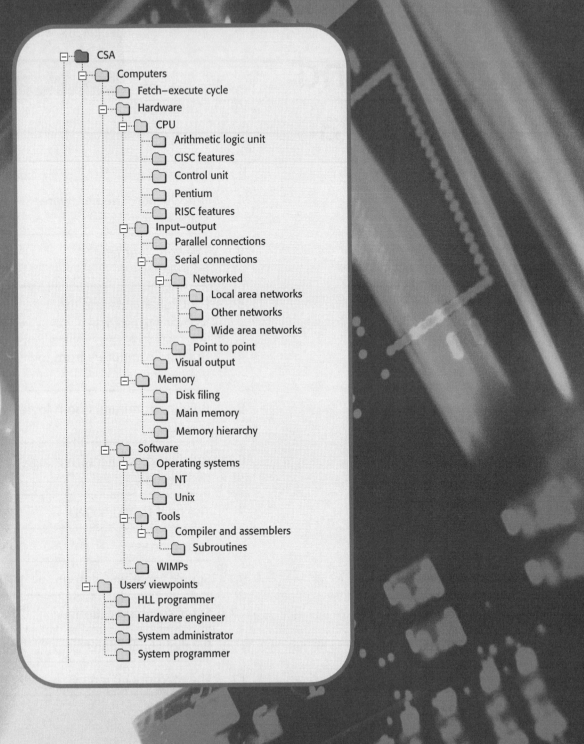

- CSA
  - Computers
    - Fetch–execute cycle
    - Hardware
      - CPU
        - Arithmetic logic unit
        - CISC features
        - Control unit
        - Pentium
        - RISC features
      - Input–output
        - Parallel connections
        - Serial connections
          - Networked
            - Local area networks
            - Other networks
            - Wide area networks
          - Point to point
        - Visual output
      - Memory
        - Disk filing
        - Main memory
        - Memory hierarchy
    - Software
      - Operating systems
        - NT
        - Unix
      - Tools
        - Compiler and assemblers
          - Subroutines
      - WIMPs
  - Users' viewpoints
    - HLL programmer
    - Hardware engineer
    - System administrator
    - System programmer

Introduction: the hardware–software interface

1

Overview

If you are just starting a new course at college or university, the first week can be confusing enough without having to cope with a scary new subject. So this introductory chapter will only try to explain what areas the subject of Computer Systems covers, the relevance of networking, and why you should study it. This text focuses on the interaction of hardware and software as it affects computer performance. Because it may not be a familiar or easy topic, some reasons will be presented why you should pursue this subject in some depth. These include: the need to maintain your own PC; the advantage of keeping up with the latest developments, including interconnectivity and the Internet; appreciating your windowing interface; and being prepared for the far-reaching changes in technology which will undoubtedly arise in the future. The astonishingly successful symbiosis established between hardware and software developers shows no sign of ending.

1.1   Computer systems – the importance of networking

College courses often have an introductory unit called 'Computer Systems Architecture' (CSA). But because there is not yet a universal definition of CSA, quite wide latitude exists for varying curricula and divergent interpretations (Fig. 1.1). Student confusion increases because commercial terminology can be even more creative! Sometimes CSA appears in the hardware orientation of digital electronics; at other times it takes on the guise of a unified software specification for a family of computers. Rarely is the central importance of network facilities, both to the computer designer and to the end user, sufficiently acknowledged, even though we are all aware of its growing significance in society. Indeed, more and more computer science graduates become involved in the data communications industry, and would therefore benefit from a grounding in this field. Thus an aim of this text is to place networks solidly within CSA.

It is clear that computers and networks require both hardware and software in order to work. But the historical academic separation of the two poses a difficult balancing problem when presenting such a course. Both are equally important and strongly espoused by their enthusiastic supporters. The distinction between hardware and software can be likened to the distant relationship between the formal team photograph, rigidly posed in front of the goalmouth, and the exciting unpredictability of the World Cup final. The static photograph of the players only vaguely hints at the limitless possibilities of the dynamic game. With the increasing sophistication of computer hardware, perhaps it is unfortunate that the dismantling and exploration of old computers is no longer encouraged. The tumbling prices of electronic components, added to the need to have modern equipment to run the latest games, has resulted, for the moment, in a salesperson's dream. Unexpectedly, this trend, although attracting many more people to use computers, has had an adverse effect on the fundamental level of knowledge among computing undergraduates on entry to university. Although we cannot turn the clock back to the self-build hobbyist days of home computing, knowledge of the interaction of **hardware** and **software** is still

Fig. 1.1
Computer
architecture.

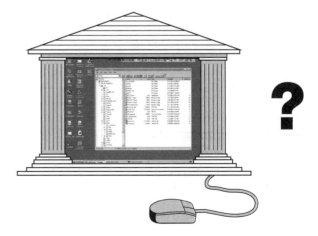

useful, if not necessary, for anyone wanting to be fully involved in the professional use of computers.

Curiosity about the computer systems which surround us, the Internet that frustrates us, and the mobile telephone networks that we increasingly rely on should drive us to investigate and question what is happening in the fields of software and electronics. The facilities that will become available to us in the next few years will depend largely on current developments in microelectronics and software design methodology. It is here that we can look for the future.

Throughout this text we will treat CSA as a study of the interaction of hardware and software which determines the performance of networked computer systems. We will also try to show that computers can always be viewed as hierarchical ordered systems which can be broken down into simpler component parts (hardware or software, as in Fig. 1.3) in order to fully understand their operation. Unlike other areas of study, such as physics or chemistry, complex ideas can always be split into simpler concepts which may then be understood more easily. This progressive decomposition approach is not only useful when studying computers, but can also be invaluable when designing and building new systems.

1.2   Hardware and software – mutual dependence

Although it is widely recognized that computer systems involve both hardware and software, it is still rare for college computer courses to require you to have a comparable understanding in both fields. Perhaps the analogy of only eating half a boiled egg is appropriate – you risk missing out on the yolk (Fig. 1.2). This demarcation, or specialization, has a number of serious negative results. When teams of developers are separately recruited as hardware engineers or programmers, the danger of an antagonistic split progressively opening up between the two camps is always present. Professional rivalry can arise through simple misunderstandings due to the different approaches and vocabulary used by hardware and software engineers. Problems, when they inevitably occur, can be blamed on the other camp and then take longer to resolve. Programmers sometimes find that unsuitable equipment has already been specified without consultation, and hardware designers can sit helplessly by as unsuitable software fails to exploit the performance advantages offered by their revolutionary new circuits.

Fig. 1.2
Both hardware and
software are needed.

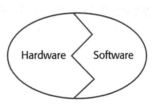

It has been claimed by some business analysts that hardware manufacturing will be of no great commercial consequence. The profit lies in programming: lead the world in the development of systems software! But it is now clear that in such a rapidly changing world, early access to new hardware designs gives the software industry an important marketing lead. The first software products to exploit some new hardware facility have a clear leadership in the market-place. The neglect of the hardware side of the computing industry has never delivered any long-term advantage. Understanding basic principles and appreciating their application by modern technology within a range of current products is a central aim of this text. Programmers neglect developments in hardware at their peril. The opposite situation, where software is overlooked, can lead to similar failures. Consider the much greater commercial success of the PC since running the Windows operating system, and the recent explosion in use of the **Internet** since the launch of the Netscape Navigator **browser**. Many excellent machines became commercial flops because of their sub-standard software. These well-rehearsed public examples can be added to and confirmed by thousands of private disasters which all underline the need to pursue hardware and software developments in concert. We now recognize that despite their technical superiority, computer systems can fail to win acceptance for many reasons, such as a poorly thought out user interface, a lack of applications software, or an inappropriate choice of operating system. Many recent developments have arisen from a simultaneous advance in hardware and software: windowing interfaces are only possible through sophisticated software and powerful graphics cards; network connections are supported by autonomous coprocessors working with complex driver routines; laser printers became universally popular when the xerography print engine was supplemented by the PostScript interpreter. Many such examples demonstrate the value of keeping abreast of developments in both hardware and software. An increasing difficulty with investigating the interaction of hardware and software is gaining access to the relevant facilities. With large, multi-user mainframe computers it was understandable that the ordinary programmer was denied access to the hardware and critical software to protect other users. However, with the introduction of Windows NT such security constraints have been introduced to single-user personal workstations, making it impossible to access the hardware directly. Only the operating system code (Fig. 1.3) has this privilege, while ordinary programs are forced to call 'trusted' system routines to read or write to any of the hardware.

1.3   Programming your way into hardware – VHDL, a language for electronic engineers

A remarkable empirical law describing the rapid growth of silicon technology was proposed by Gordon Moore, one of the founders of Intel. His eponymous rule, **Moore's Law**, states that the amount of circuitry (number of transistors) which can be

Fig. 1.3
Layers of software
above the hardware.

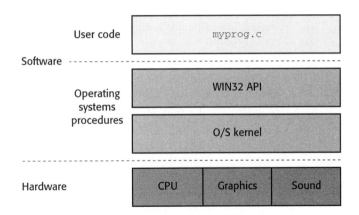

placed on a given chip area approximately doubles every two years. Figure 1.4 presents the data for some example circuits from previous decades. Notice that the vertical axis is not linear, so that the points cluster along a straight line. A circuit designed 24 months ago can now be shrunk to fit into an area of half the size. Intel's original 4004 processor involved 2300 transistors, while the Pentium has somewhere of the order of 5.5 million. The chip area has not increased by a factor of 2000! This capability to progressively shrink the size of electronic circuits could reduce the chip cost, because more circuits are processed on a single slice of silicon, but the technical advance has more often been exploited by enhancing the chip's functionality. Intel took this path

Fig. 1.4
Moore's Law of
technological
development.

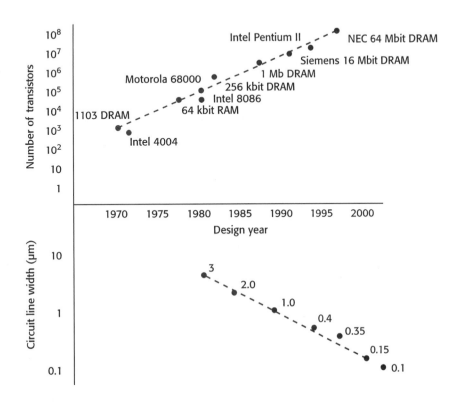

when it amalgamated the 8086 and the 8087, and again when it introduced the Level 1 (LI) cache.

Surprisingly, this law has held true since the early 1970s and is likely to stand well into the 2020s before the size of circuit elements become so small that quantum physics intervenes through Heisenberg's uncertainty principle. Already the on-chip circuit interconnections are only $0.25\,\mu$m wide and the insulating layers can be as thin as a couple of dozen molecules. However, Moore's Law remains somewhat of a mystery, given that the underlying variables responsible for the trend are as diverse as the ability to maintain ultra-clean factory environments, reduction of international trade barriers, development of increasingly high-resolution photolithography and the marketing success of games consoles!

Although the split between those concerned with hardware and those concerned with software is now well entrenched, there are developments which might reverse this trend. A programming language called **VHDL** (Very high speed integrated circuits Hardware Description Language) is beginning to be used to specify both the structure and function of hardware circuits. A fragment of a routine written in this language is presented in Fig. 1.5, describing the action of a decoder circuit. (We will return to decoders in Chapter 4.) As manufacturing techniques allow components to shrink in size, hardware engineers find it increasingly difficult to wire up 'breadboard' prototypes because the circuits they are building have grown too complicated. In any case, the performance of the large-sized components which they can handle easily in a traditional way is not identical to that of the miniature equivalents which will make up the final integrated circuit that is produced. The alternative approach, using VHDL, also supports computer **simulation** trials as well as providing input to automatic layout packages which arrange the final circuits. More and more, the job of the computer design engineer is becoming language-oriented: everything is specified by

Fig 1.5
A fragment of VHDL code specifying a decoder circuit.

```
ENTITY decoder8 IS
    PORT (sel: IN  std_logic_vector (2 DOWNTO 0); -- select i/p signals
          sig: out std_logic_vector (7 downto 0)); -- eight o/p signals
END decoder8;

ARCHITECTURE rtl OF decoder8 IS
BEGIN
    s <=  "0000_0001" WHEN (sel = X"0") ELSE
          "0000_0010" WHEN (sel = X"1") ELSE
          "0000_0100" WHEN (sel = X"2") ELSE
          "0000_1000" WHEN (sel = X"3") ELSE
          "0001_0000" WHEN (sel = X"4") ELSE
          "0010_0000" WHEN (sel = X"5") ELSE
          "0100_0000" WHEN (sel = X"6") ELSE
          "1000_0000";
END rtl;
```

writing programs, even the hardware. Perhaps in the future, computer scientists, even when trained only in software techniques, may find their code being used to produce new chips!

In the past there was a tendency for trained electronic engineers to migrate towards software, to pick up programming skills and to get involved in systems programming. Will this trend now be reversed? Programmers, software engineers, trained to deal with large systems and complex specifications, may take the opportunity of contributing to the hardware design by learning VHDL. This is another example of how hardware and software can come together through the tools and skills demanded by systems developers.

1.4 Systems administration – we all need to know

The popularity of the original IBM PC and all its subsequent clones has meant that many more ordinary computer users are now forced to be self-reliant and assume the role of **System Administrator** by carrying out their own repairs, upgrades and software installations, both at home and in the office. This contrasts with the earlier mainframe and minicomputers, which usually had teams of trained technicians to minister the necessary rituals. But such a luxury may be a thing of the past. Whatever the outcome, all these activities would certainly benefit from some fundamental understanding of Computer Systems Architecture. When trying to follow the impenetrable prose of a technical manual (apparently translated in an airport lounge) a clear, initial vision of what you are intending to achieve gives a massive advantage. Knowing where you want to go always helps when reading a map. All too often, inexperienced users are persuaded to buy more expensive hardware to improve the performance of their system, when a change to the software or even to the data organization would achieve more at no cost. Even simple problems, like printers failing to perform, can be diagnosed and solved if some elementary knowledge of CSA is available.

1.5 Voice, image and data – technological convergence

Modern computing has encompassed a wide range of activities in addition to the traditional area of commercial data processing. Gas bills, invoice generation and the Friday payroll have been superseded by the Internet, air traffic control and cellular telephones in the public perception of computing. Voice communications, video animation, publishing, broadcasting and music are some of the new areas which are now becoming completely reliant on computer technology. The separation of telephony and data processing, institutionalized in many companies by the dual posts of Telecoms Manager and Data Processing Manager, is fast dying out. Modern digital telephone switches, also known as Private Automatic Branch Exchanges (PABX), can now be described as computers with some dedicated input–output (IO) capability of handling the streams of digitized voice signals.

With some large telephone switches running a version of the Unix operating system, the traditional boundary between telecommunications and data processing has already become less distinct. When you understand that digital telephone switching equipment converts all the voice signals into digital form and then treats them much the same as any binary data, the mystery of **convergence** is somewhat reduced. The telephone switch schematic presented in Fig. 1.6 illustrates the central role of the controlling computer. All the new telephone facilities – call-back, camp-on, call redirect and conference calls – have all been programmed into the exchange software without any special alteration to the hardware. Truly this is a marketing dream!

Microsoft supplies a special telephone application programmer's interface (TAPI), with Windows, to work with a wide range of telecomms cards which are now appearing from many different sources. An interface standard for these cards, enabling them to exchange voice data streams independently of the PC bus, is called MVIP (Multi-Vendor Integration Protocol). The field of computer telephony (CTI) is currently expanding rapidly as organizations take the opportunity of building new types of system from these hardware and software components. Call centres, telephone answering services and information banks – all these depend on this new technology.

A more domestically familiar example of the merging of sound and data processing is the Sound Blaster card, so popular with PC games producers. **Multimedia** facilities have been the primary beneficiary of recent hardware developments, using DSP units (Digital Signal Processor) and Compact Disc grade **DAC**s (Digital to Analogue Convertors) to replay high-quality voice and stereo music. You can connect to a Web

Fig. 1.6
A telephone switch schematic showing the embedded computer.

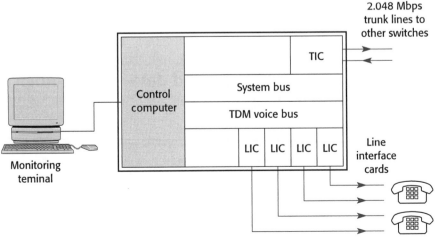
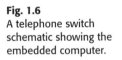

site, download sound files and listen to the music, reconstituted by the Sound Blaster card, through your stereo system.

Windowing interfaces – WIMPs

Students of computer science in the new millennium will probably only have encountered 'user-friendly' **WIMP** (Windows, Icons, Menus and Pointers) interfaces of which an example is shown in Fig. 1.7. These use the screen and graphics hardware to display rectangular windows for text and images. PCs running Windows, Unix with X, and the Apple Macintosh all provide such interfaces, but the original human–computer dialogue was completely text-based, depending on a Command Line Interpreter process, or shell, to decode the rather cryptic instructions typed into an ASCII keyboard, illustrated in Fig. 1.8. This situation is commonly referred to as running 'C >' (C forward-arrow), 'DOS prompt' or 'vanilla Unix'. The modern WIMP interface was a by-product of the microprocessor revolution, which allowed all users to have fast bitmapped graphics screens on their desks, and so enjoy the benefits of colour and images.

The penetration of the Microsoft Windows operating system into all aspects of our daily lives was clearly, but unfortunately, demonstrated to me when I approached my

Fig. 1.7
Windows NT Explorer used as a directory browser.

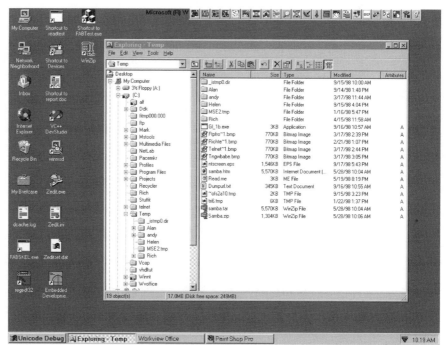

Fig. 1.8
Unix command line interface showing a
`.cshrc` file.

```
% cat .cshrc
umask 077
limit core 0
setenv TERM vt100
setenv PRINTER lw
set prompt = "'hostname' > "
set history = 25
biff y
mesg n
alias tt99 'setenv DISPLAY TT99:0'
set path = (./usr/ucb /usr/bin/X11 /bin /usr/bin /usr/local
set path = ($path /etc /usr/etc /usr/lang /usr/local
            $home/bin)
```

local bank ATM (Automatic Teller Machine) one morning on the way to work. Up on the screen was an unusual but nevertheless very disturbing error message:

```
        DLL initialization failure
     C:\WINNT\System32\KERNEL32.DLL
  The process is terminating abnormally
```

Despite the current success of WIMP interfaces, the old-fashioned **command line** schemes did have some advantages over the first windowing systems. They encouraged the user to set up **batch**, or command, files which could be saved to disk, thus avoiding having to enter the same commands repeatedly from the keyboard. The first windowing interfaces did not offer this facility, but Microsoft restored it with Windows NT. When you login to Unix the operating system will run your `.login` and `.cshrc` shell initialization scripts, as listed in Fig. 1.8. These are small batch files containing commands to set up your working environment. All the commands can be entered directly at the keyboard, but it is much easier, and safer, to store them in a file.

The joint pressure of user demands and emerging technological capabilities has provided the energy and financial drive which have pushed hardware performance from the 1 MHz 8 bit 8080 CPUs in 1974 to the current 1 GHz 32 bit Pentiums. In 20 years the cost of computing has fallen dramatically, while processing power and user expectations have risen. It seems that increased CPU power is quickly overwhelmed by new computational demands. The introduction of WIMP graphical interfaces removed most of the advantages provided by 16 bit processors, and the change to multitasking Windows has similarly soaked up much of the enhanced performance offered by the 32 bit processors. The likely application areas to benefit from future breakthroughs in hardware and software could be:

- Practicable voice input

- Better management of energy resources

- AI games with evolving storylines

- Graphical entertainment

- Video communications

- Interactive education

Recently there have been several commercial plans for online video delivery via the existing telephone network requiring the use of fast compression techniques, enormous database servers and high-speed modems. This is another example of the close interplay of hardware and software to provide new products and services.

1.7 The global Internet – connecting all the networks

The enthusiastic adoption of Netscape Navigator, and the other WWW browsers, giving easy access to the fabulous range of data available through the Internet, has focused the public's attention on computers, communications and software. The rapid expansion of the number of Web users is reminiscent of the change that occurred when telephone dialling displaced manual exchanges, enabling far more callers to get connected than ever before.

New facilities are being developed, such as network radio, Internet telephony, online shopping, remote surveillance. New enterprises are springing up to promote and exploit the services which have arisen from this creative synthesis of computing and communications. Just as railways, originating from the merging of steam-powered pump motors and transport engineering, revolutionized society by making cheap travel available to everyone, so easy access to the Internet could equally change our habits by reducing the need for travel, especially to and from the office.

As a first, not totally welcome step, commerce has only just started to exploit the new route into our lives for personalized promotional literature. The World Wide Web (WWW) arose from a similar synthesis of existing facilities (see Fig. 1.9). These included FTP (remote file access), archie (international subject database), hypertext (keyword inter-document referencing scheme), WIMP interfaces and network access capability (modems or LAN card). The linking together of large computers and local area networks (LANs) at the CERN nuclear research site in Geneva gave Tim Berners-Lee the idea for a more integrated approach to information storage and access. This grew beyond CERN and became the WWW, with sites from all around the world linking into this distributed information net. We will be looking in more detail at the WWW in Chapter 15. Perhaps in the future this may be judged the most outstanding technical achievement of the final decade of the century. If you have a PC and modem, it

Fig. 1.9
Influences on the World
Wide Web.

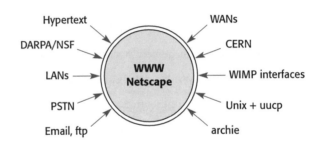

is easy to connect to the Internet by subscribing to a public **ISP** (Internet Service Provider), such as Compuserve, Demon or Virgin, and dialling into one of their ports using the local telephone network. The introduction in 1998 of free Internet subscriptions in the UK, led by Dixons' Freeserve and Tesco's TESCOnet, has massively increased the domestic use of email and Web browsers. There is, however, still no clear indication of the likely success, or otherwise, of Internet shopping. Not all commercial organizations have yet linked directly to the Internet. For security reasons many still prefer to dial into an Internet Service Provider only when necessary or continue to use direct modem connections to customers' computers. University staff and students can normally benefit from fast Internet access provided by governments to encourage research cooperation and academic development in Higher Education. Many schools have yet to connect, deterred by the likely increase in their monthly telephone bill!

The Internet is formed, as indicated in Fig 1.10, by interlinking thousands of local area networks (LANs) each having dozens of connected computers. This is similar to the way that the international road system can be seen as simply an interconnection of

Fig. 1.10
Connecting networks
into the Internet.

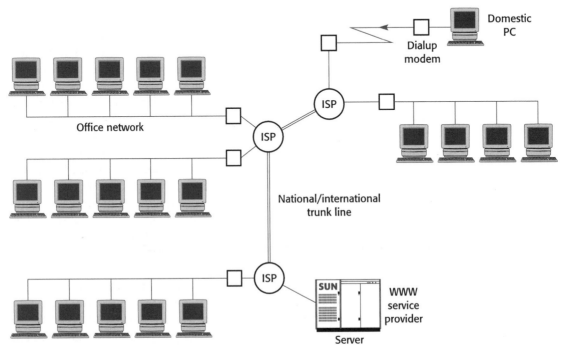

towns and cities. Thus millions of computers can exchange email, share data files and offer processing resources for others to use. The layout and complexity of everybody's local area network is different, but a typical configuration is provided in Fig. 1.11 in order to show the variety of technologies that may be employed.

One of the great technical achievements of recent years has been the establishment of the Internet. This has resulted from detailed negotiation and cooperation at national and international levels to enable the rapid and seamless distribution of data around the world. Internet transmissions are frequently initially dispatched along the local area networks and then transferred to the Internet through an ISP gateway (Fig. 1.11). Messages have to be divided up to fit into packets for transfer. Each packet contains important routing information as well as the data to be transferred.

The simplified data packet illustrated in Fig. 1.12 is based on the **Ethernet** standard, which can distribute data at speeds of up to 100 Mbps. In the same way that letters and parcels have to have destination addresses written on the front for postal workers to read, so every Ethernet packet contains a 48 bit destination address so that the packet can be read from the network by the correct machine and ignored by all the others. Section 14.4 explains in more detail how this arrangement operates, but a few more details might be of interest here. The Ethernet address for my Sun workstation is 42.49.4F.00.20.54, and although these 48 bit addresses are globally unique, the allocation being arranged by the hardware manufacturers, the problem of providing a worldwide routing directory based on them would be insurmountable. Imagine having to accept as your home telephone number the construction code that was allocated to the handset in the factory. Therefore a second configurable set of numbers was adopted for message routing in place of the static Ethernet numbers. These numbers are known as **IP** (Internet Protocol) numbers and every computer connected to the Internet has to be allocated a unique IP identifier. For instance, my workstation was given the number 2752186723. This format is unrecognizable to me because it is more normally presented as four-digit groups in base 256: 164.11.9.99. Check that they are the same value:

Fig. 1.11
A typical local area network.

$$(((((164 \times 256) + 11) \times 256) + 9) \times 256) + 99)$$

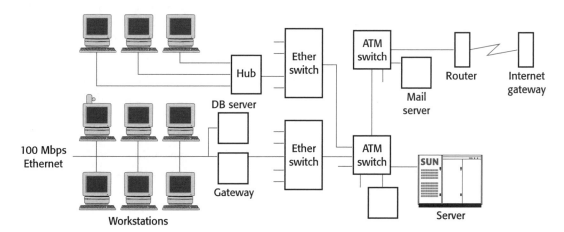

8 bytes	6 bytes	6 bytes		46–1500 bytes	4 bytes
Preamble	Destination address	Source address	Type	Data payload	Error check

Fig. 1.12
The internal structure of a LAN data packet showing the address fields.

Along with this IP number a unique name is also allocated to make the system more user-friendly. My Sun workstation is called 'olveston', after a local village to the north of Bristol.

You might think it rather strange that we have managed for more than 50 years with 10 digit telephone numbers, but were immediately judged incapable of dealing with 12 digit IP codes! In the event, the marketing advantage of having a recognizable Internet access name, whether email or WWW URL, has been quickly recognized by everyone.

1.8　Using the PC – a case study; more reasons to study CSA

If you still need to be convinced that CSA is an interesting and useful course of study, packed with relevant exciting ideas, then read the following account.

You decide to connect your home PC through the telephone network to either your work computer or a commercial service provider. This involves buying and inserting a modem card. You will also need to install the card and register it with the PC operating system and then load the correct device driver software. This may involve assessing what hardware is already installed and allocating different values for IRQ and port numbers. Several questions can arise:

- Do you understand the role and function of PC IRQs? Can two devices ever share the same IRQ?

- Establishing a dial-in terminal session with a host computer will require you to set various line transmission parameters: bits per word, parity, handshake CTS/RTS, buffer size and line speed. Can you recognize the symptoms if one of these is incorrect?

- It is recommended that you establish a PPP or SLIP session to allow Netscape Navigator to run in the PC Windows environment. What is the real difference between these two modes of operation and why are they better than character-based terminals?

- Certainly you will be using a WWW search engine such as Yahoo! or AltaVista to locate sites holding relevant data. But do you understand how they gather all their information?

- Why is your word processor program running so slowly when Netscape Navigator is loaded? Is the frantic disk activity anything to do with it? What is swap space? Is it an alternative to virtual memory?

- You think that a memory upgrade may be in order. But enlarging your PC memory to 64 Mbyte with more DIMM DRAM modules might be tricky. If you are using SIMMs, why do you need to buy two units, and why specify 60 ns access time? Would the cheaper 100 ns SIMMs still work just as well with your older 200 MHz Pentium?

- Do you understand how the Windows operating system 'knows' which icon you are pointing at with the mouse? How do several programs share a single computer, appearing to run at the same time?

- Have you been confused and frustrated by your Sound Blaster card refusing to work with different applications?

- How does Plug-and-Play work?

All these questions fall within the province of Computer Systems Architecture, and we will be visiting all these issues in the course of this text. An extraordinary challenge awaits us in the field of computer systems. This is due to the unbelievable pace of technological change. The original PC has witnessed a hundred-fold increase in speed and memory size within the twenty years of its commercial life. With this in mind, any computing course must take as a primary goal the anticipated intellectual demands of a career regularly buffeted by dramatic changes in technology and its application. By studying a variety of systems, analysing their action in terms of fundamental concepts, and taking account of historic trends in the industry, we can best prepare for the uncertain but exciting future.

You may like to read some history or watch the video accounts of the early electronic computers built during the 1950s and 1960s. This is a new area for archaeologists to investigate, but software engineers and systems developers, too, should not totally ignore previous experience. If you can avoid making a serious mistake in the development of a new computer system by reading a book, who would doubt the benefit of such an investment?

Review

- Computers and networks form an essential part of all our lives. Therefore we should study and understand them.

- In computers, hardware (electronics) and software (programs) work together to carry out the processing.

- Hardware is often seen as the bottom slice of a multi-layer system, with applications programs positioned on top of the stack. In the middle sits the operating system.

- Hardware evolution is on track to achieve further size, speed and cost improvements as predicted by Moore's Law.
- The methods used to develop software and hardware are now quite similar.
- The technologies found in broadcasting centres, telephone exchanges and computer units have converged to the point where everything can be viewed as data which requires collecting, processing and routing.
- The Windows graphical user interface rapidly opened up access to computers beyond the small clique of computer science graduates. It is an example of a closely interacting development of hardware and software.
- The Internet facilities started with a few interlinked computers running Unix, but has suddenly shot forward in popularity with the introduction of the World Wide Web. It is becoming the core of a major commercial and social revolution.
- We are now all systems administrators, so we need a better understanding of the interaction between hardware and software.

Practical work

The recommended practical work involves familiarization with the computer equipment, the available printer facilities, network access and operating systems. The library may have an online catalogue and reservation option.

Make sure you can send and receive email. Using a Web search engine (AltaVista), research the difference between the POP and IMAP email protocols. Find out which is available to you.

The historical summary videos suggested above may be available, or other similar documentary evidence.

Start building up a personal bookmark file containing the URLs of useful Web sites for use with Web browsers. You can copy this as a text file onto floppy disk and reinstall it when you next go online.

Exercises

1. How can the study of CSA assist you when buying a new PC?
2. What circumstances made the IBM PC so successful?
3. Can a digital telephone exchange distinguish between voice and data?
4. What do you use a Sound Blaster card for?
5. Does a Windowing interface give you all the facilities that a C > DOS shell provides?
6. What route do you use to connect through to the Internet?
7. Who is Tim Berners-Lee, and what is CERN?
8. Construct a sentence including the following words: subscription, 10, month, costs, Internet, pounds.
9. Why was Unix the preferred operating system for Internet hosts?

A. How long is an Ethernet address? How long is an Internet address (IP number)?

B. Name four commercial ISPs.

C. What is Moore's Law? Who is Gordon Moore? Why is Moore's Law relevant to programmers?

D. What do you understand by the term 'technological convergence'?

E. Sketch the physical layout of a local area network (LAN) that you know.

F. How many milliseconds (ms) are there in a second?

   How many microseconds (μs) are there in a second?

   How many nanoseconds (ns) are there in a second?

   What is one thousandth of a nanosecond called?

Answers and further commentary are at the back of the book.

Readings

- Find the computing section in your library. Appreciate the difference between long, medium and short loans. Check out the fining tariff!

- In the computing section of the library, find the magazines *Dr. Dobb's Journal*, *Byte* and *Personal Computer World*; find the video section, too. Look at the computing, engineering and business sections for books. Find out whether there is an online computer catalogue and help facility. This may also be accessible from computers outside the library.

- View the BBC Horizon video: The Dream Machine – Giant Brains.

- Inspect the recommended texts in your local bookshop. Familiarize yourself with the structure and contents list of several texts, such as the ones listed on pp. 645–6, so you will know where to look for particular subjects.

- Keep your eyes on the noticeboards for second-hand textbooks.

- Fire up Netscape Navigator and check out the following Web sites:

  - A good source of introductory information on many subjects:
    `http://webopedia.internet.com/`

  - The PC Guide is also often very useful:
    `http://www.pcguide.com/`

  - An online tutorial is available for the basics:
    `http://www.mkdata.dk/click/index.htm`

  - Microprocessor background information from:
    `http://www.vcnet.com/topcc/newversion/articles/history.html`

  - Building your own PC:
    `http://library.advanced.org/13714/interex3/parts.htm`

- Great CPUs and Microprocessors of the Past and Present (this really is worth browsing!):

  `http://www.cs.uregina.ca/~bayko/cpu.html`

- Intel news and products:

  `http://www.intel.com/intel/product/index.htm`

- Computer inventors, and their inventions:

  `http://inventors.miningco.com/education/inventors/library/`
  `blcoindex.htm?pid=2821&cob=home`

- Digital's wonderful search engine:

  `http://www.altavista.com/`

- For an indication of the extent of convergence of computing and telephony try:

  `http://www.mvip.org/Overview.htm`

- Some technical summaries for hardware devices:

  `http://www.tme-inc.com/html/service/general.htm`

- For an interesting slice of history try:

  `http://www.cranfield.ac.uk/ccc/bpark/colossus.htm`

- If you want to learning some more about lots of computing topics try:

  `http://www.programmersheaven.com/`

The tricky problem with recommending Web sites to other people is the possibility of the information being moved to a different position, or even withdrawn. There is no requirement to archive the information so that someone could request it at a later date, as you can with books and journals. Any change in their identifying **URL** (Uniform Resource Locator) can require you to carry out a search all over again. Sometimes you can quickly rediscover the site by using a **search engine**, such as AltaVista, because you now have a good 'key word'. You may even be able to guess a likely URL from information you already have. But if you get an error message similar to: 'requested URL could not be retrieved' do not give up immediately. It is the same as trying to find a particular book in a library. If it is not in the correct position on the shelf you have to look around to see whether it has been moved; then you try to track it down using the catalogue, and finally you ask someone to help. A similar text may provide an effective substitute: persistence can pay off! When you find a good site, set a bookmark so that you can easily return there. It is so much easier than writing down the URL. You can copy the bookmark file to floppy disk and carry it round for the next opportunity to browse the Web. Subjects like Computer Systems Architecture are changing so rapidly that sometimes the Web is the only widely accessible source of good technical information. There are several well-known undergraduate texts in this field, and I will be indicating the relevant sections at the end of each chapter, where they might be of interest and help to you. Full details of these books are given in the References (p. 645).

- Buchanan (1998)

- Hamacher *et al.* (1996)

- Hennessy and Patterson (1998)

- Heuring and Jordan (1997)

- Tanenbaum (1999)

The Web sites can be accessed via the Companion Web site for this book at:

`http://www.booksites.net/williams`

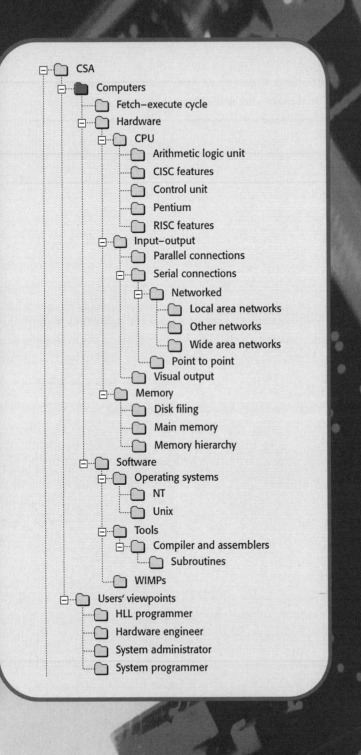

The von Neumann Inheritance

2

Overview

Computers are machines whose actions are governed by a program. A program is simply a carefully prepared list of instructions. All types of digital computer are fundamentally similar in this regard. This chapter introduces the basic technical principle of the fetch–execute cycle which the digital computer operates to execute a program. Instructions can only be understood by the computer if they are in a special binary form. Compilers are used to generate this binary format from programs expressed in a more convenient manner. Data also has to be manipulated and stored in binary format. For users, the personality of a computer depends more on the operating system software than the underlying hardware. Software systems are now often distributed between several computers attached to a network in a client–server configuration.

Fig. 2.1
...all under program
control.

2.1 Base 2 – the convenience of binary – 10110011100011110000

The fundamental structure of the current generation of digital computers, software and hardware, is credited to **John von Neumann**, while historians also insist on pointing out the contribution of Charles Babbage in 1830. Certainly, it was von Neumann's clear description and explanations which first captured the imagination of engineers and scientists during the late 1940s. The essential scheme (Fig. 2.1) – input–process–output – was all to be controlled by a special, custom-made program.

The first working electrical digital computer had already been constructed by Konrad Zuse in Germany during the late 1930s. He proposed the use of **binary** (base 2) for numeric representation, more suited to be implemented by electronic switches than the normal base 10 (see the note at the end of this chapter). However, the work in Germany came to nothing because Hitler's military ambition and optimistic forecasts overwhelmed his somewhat limited technical vision and the project was cancelled in favour of rocket-powered aircraft. In Britain, another important computing development from the war period was Colossus. This electro-mechanical computing machine was used to help decode encrypted radio transmissions, but it was built and hard-wired for a specific task, and did not have an internal store to hold instructions. Because of the secrecy surrounding military decryption activities, little information was made public until 1975. In the USA, other pioneering work was carried out by John Atanasoff in Iowa State College and George Stibitz in Bell Labs. Both these projects featured technological innovations well ahead of their time. Atanasoff used capacitive memory cells, a precursor to the present day DRAM chips. The use of binary for coding instructions and data was clearly established by 1950.

2.2 Stored program control – general-purpose machines

Von Neumann's original idea was that of an **executable program** controlling the action of a **general-purpose machine**. In this context, a program is a list of instructions used to direct a task, so music scores and knitting patterns are good examples of programs interpreted by humans but stored externally, whereas digital computers use their internal memory to hold both programs and data. At first sight this might appear

Fig. 2.2
Program store.

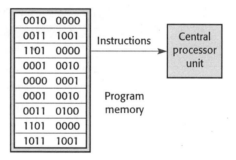

a recipe for disaster, because computers have no easy way of distinguishing data from instructions. Instructions and data are both represented by binary codes. A 16 bit instruction code could, in different circumstances, represent a number or two characters. If, due to an error, the computer starts bizarrely to execute data, or add up instructions, it will not immediately recognize the confusion. But most likely it will soon crash because the sequence of actions followed would be random, if not illegal.

The complex activities of a computer are only possible through a close interaction of hardware and software. While the software is stored in memory (Fig. 2.2), the **Central Processing Unit (CPU)** has the hardware which actually executes the program instructions.

Most computers employ general-purpose hardware, and so depend on different programs, rather than hardware, to produce the particular actions required. In order to store the program in memory and render it 'understandable' to the computer CPU the instructions and data have to be in a special coded form. A big step in developing the modern computer was the realization that the program could be stored in a fast access memory rather than on the original paper tapes.

Thus we could look on the **main memory** as necessary only because disk and tape storage are very much too slow. Later, in Chapter 12, the complex hierarchical structure of computer memories will be described in more detail. For practical and financial reasons, a single slab of main memory is not used in PCs, workstations or mainframe computers. You will probably now only see such a straightforward scheme inside your washing machine, and then only if it has an electronic microcontroller rather than a clockwork mechanism!

There is now a wide range of computer types (Table 2.1), many of which we regularly encounter in our daily lives. The processing power and production costs vary by a factor of 10^7 so it is remarkable that we can still recognize the close similarity between the extreme examples. As you can see, one of the original von Neumann concepts of a single model, general-purpose computer, serving all functions through a diverse library of programs, is not quite the contemporary commercial vision.

But von Neumann's specification of a computer containing an alterable program, held within a unified memory and governing the operational activities, has remained sound for 50 years. A slight variation, known as the 'Harvard architecture', has gained ground recently. This separates data from programs, requiring distinct memories and access buses. The intention is to increase transfer rates, improving throughput. In Chapter 21 we will see the need for such a change more clearly where RISC CPUs are

Table 2.1
Variety of digital
computers and typical
uses.

Computer	Application
Smart card	Telephone/credit card
Microcontroller	Washing machine controller
Games console	Interactive entertainment
Home PC	Web information browsing
Workstation	Design layouts for circuit boards
Office server	Central filing on local network
Mainframe	Corporate database
Supercomputer	Flight simulation studies

concerned, but another application of Harvard designs is the expanding range of Digital Signal Processing (DSP) chips, where the programs often need to handle large amounts of data at very high rates.

2.3   Instruction codes – machine action repertoire

Computers have a small fixed repertoire of instructions, known as the **machine instruction set.** Every manufacturer, such as IBM, Intel or Sun, designs and produces computers containing a CPU which has its own native instruction set. This typically includes between 100 and 200 instructions. There is no standard instruction set recognized by the industry in the way that the ASCII and Unicode data codes have been universally accepted.

With the number of instructions available varying from little more than a dozen to many hundreds, there was great enthusiasm for the development of standardized **High Level Languages** (HLL). Most people prefer to program using a high-level language such as BASIC or C because it is easier. But the HLL instruction codes still have to be translated back to the lower level machine codes in order to let the computer run the program. This translation typically expands each HLL instruction into 5–10 machine codes. An example for a line of C code is given in Fig. 2.3. A major problem that presented itself to the early pioneers when it came to testing the first digital computers was how to write a program, and then how to introduce it into the machine's memory. In fact, the programs were written by hand in binary, and manually entered into memory using a row of toggle switches. This excruciatingly laborious process underlines the enormous difference between the way human languages express ideas and intentions and the way computer instructions represent data processing activities. This difference has become known as the **semantic gap** (Fig. 2.3), a term which could upset linguistic scholars who perhaps might prefer to say the 'lexico-syntactic schism'. But the advantage to human beings of coding in a HLL need not be argued over!

It can be helpful to remember that all the machine instructions can be classified into a much smaller group of categories, as listed in Table 2.2.

Fig. 2.3
Equivalent HLL,
assembler and machine
code.

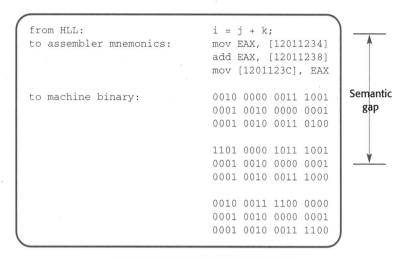

```
from HLL:                          i = j + k;
to assembler mnemonics:            mov EAX, [12011234]
                                   add EAX, [12011238]
                                   mov [1201123C], EAX

to machine binary:                 0010 0000 0011 1001
                                   0001 0010 0000 0001
                                   0001 0010 0011 0100

                                   1101 0000 1011 1001
                                   0001 0010 0000 0001
                                   0001 0010 0011 1000

                                   0010 0011 1100 0000
                                   0001 0010 0000 0001
                                   0001 0010 0011 1100
```

Semantic gap

Table 2.2
Machine instruction
categories.

1. Data transfer and manipulation

2. Input–output

3. Transfer of program control

4. Machine control

We will be dealing with these matters further in Chapters 7–10, so for the moment it is only useful to remember an outline explanation of these terms. The data transfer and manipulation group includes such instructions as: MOV, ADD, MUL, AND, OR and rotate/shift. These are the most commonly used machine instructions. Input–output instructions transfer data to and from the outside world. Oddly, this group does not exist in some CPUs, where all the ports to the outside world have to be addressed and accessed in the same way as internal memory. However, the Intel x86 and Pentium processors are provided with a separate IO space served by special IO instructions: IN and OUT. The transfer of program control group includes the branch, jump and subroutine call instructions: BRA, JMP, BSR and RTS. You may already know that academics avoid the GOTO instruction because it is seen as one cause of bad coding practice. Pity BRA and JMP in their position as poor relations of GOTO! The next, so-called 'dangerous', group of instructions, often forbidden to normal users, are in the machine control category. They can halt processing, alter interrupt masks or reset the hardware. You may be suffering machine code overload already, which is a good time to reflect on the manifest advantages of using HLLs!

2.4 Translation – compilers and assemblers

Thankfully, most programs are now written using a HLL such as C, C++, Java or BASIC. Programs called **compilers** translate the HLL instructions into machine code

Fig. 2.4
How executable code is
produced using
compilers.

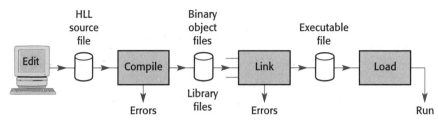

binary, capable of being executed directly on the computer. Compilers have become
critical components of computer systems, often determining how efficiently the hardware will be exploited by the programmers. Before HLL compilers were widely available, programmers used **assembler**. This also had the advantage of removing the need
to write programs directly in binary machine codes. In assembler language, each
machine code instruction is given a mnemonic name, such as ADD, SUB or MOVE. The
program is then written as a list of these mnemonics, which can easily be converted
into their corresponding binary machine codes. Because the translation of assembler
programs is, for the most part, a straightforward one-to-one operation, programs
were written to carry out this function. We can still occasionally find uses for assemblers, but generally HLL compilers have taken over.

The translation of HLL instructions into machine codes is now done automatically
by another program as outlined in Fig. 2.4. This translation can be done on-the-fly by
an **Interpreter** or beforehand by a **Compiler**. BASIC and Java both started with interpreters, but compilers then became available as well. Pascal and C are nearly always
compiled, but interpreters can be obtained. With the fast processors that are now
available, and the tendency to break large programs into semi-autonomous parts, the
disadvantage of waiting for compile-links to complete has largely disappeared. The
main benefit of interpreters has changed from reducing development delays to the
provision of a secure, uniform execution environment across several diverse
computers.

2.5 Linking – bringing it all together

Because programs have grown so big, requiring many years of effort to produce, they
are now divided, at the start of the project, into several separate parts or **modules**. In
order to produce a runnable program, each module has to be designed, coded and
compiled, and then all the resulting parts are joined together by the **linker**. This
linking-up process is not simply splicing together the pieces, but involves resolving
external references. When a large program is partitioned into modules there will be
frequent occasions when code in one module needs to reference data or subroutines
in a sister module (see Fig. 2.5). Compilers only translate one module at a time.

Fig. 2.5
Modules with external
references.

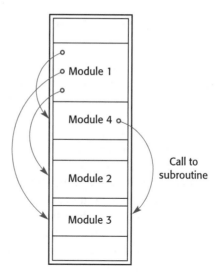

So when the compiler tries to determine a numeric equivalent for these symbolic references, it will discover that no values are available within the current module. The unresolved symbols are known as **external references** and remain symbolic (not numeric) until the linker gets to work, sorting out the references to items in other modules.

The linker phase is often overlooked by programmers because the compiler may automatically pass onto the linker with no user involvement. If you consider the Unix `cc` command, which compiles and links code, it is easy to read it as 'compile C', without adding 'and link, too, if possible'. The use of library routines always results in inter-module external references in need of resolution by the linker.

Library files, such as found in the Unix directories `/lib` and `/usr/lib`, hold the translated object code for many functions, but are only usable if linked into your code. By setting the correct linker options, you can ask for private (static) copies of the library functions, or agree to share a copy with other programs (dynamic). Such dynamic library modules (explained further in Section 8.9) are commonly referred to as **DLL**s by Microsoft programmers. When you buy a compiler, an important part of the deal is to obtain well-produced library routines for you to use with your code.

After all the object modules have been linked together, relocating libraries scanned for the required functions and all external references resolved, the program might be ready for loading at a specific memory address and executed. But, depending on the flags and parameter values given to the linker, the program may still need further address adjustment before becoming executable. If it is to run on a multitasking, virtual memory system, with interprocess protection and dynamic library binding, such as Windows NT or Unix, a further stage is needed to create system tables and install appropriate segment descriptors for the memory management unit when the code is loaded. But more of this later in Chapter 17.

2.6   Interpreters – executing high-level commands

Interpreters, such as used with BASIC and Java, offer an alternative way of running HLL programs. Instead of first translating all the HLL instructions into machine codes and creating an executable program, the **interpreter** reads the HLL instructions one at a time and carries out their orders using its own library of routines. In this way, the executable code is not generated from the source code, but is contained within the interpreter. The interpreter views the HLL source code as input data, which has to be analysed and the required processing carried out. The advantages offered by the interpreting node of dealing with HLL programs are rapid start-up and the apparent removal of the complexities of compiling and linking. Unfortunately, the disadvantage of interpreters is their slowness in operation; ready-compiled programs will always outpace interpreted software.

It is common for interpreters to convert the input instructions into an intermediate form, consisting of tokens, before deciding what action needs to be taken. In Fig. 2.6, each HLL instruction is read from the source file, checked for errors, and analysed for key words and syntactic structure. The abbreviated tokens are then passed to the decoder, which selects the appropriate routine for execution. Sometimes the interpreter is referred to as an example of a 'virtual machine' because it behaves in some regards like the computer hardware – it reads instructions one at a time and obeys them. Virtual machine interpreters are one way of narrowing the semantic gap

Fig. 2.6
Using an interpreter to translate and execute a program.

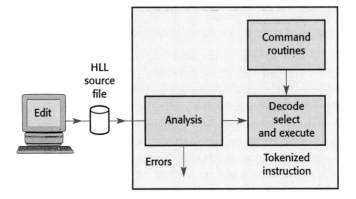

Fig. 2.7
Java uses compilers and interpreters.

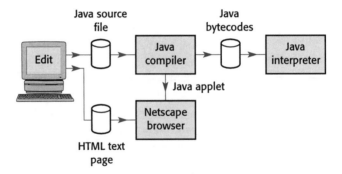

mentioned in Section 2.3, by raising the level of the execution environment towards the problem domain. Java has an interesting arrangement of compiling and interpreting. This is illustrated in Fig. 2.7.

The Java source file passes through a compiler and the resultant object file may either be executed as a traditional interpreted language program or loaded into a Web browser, such as Netscape Navigator or Internet Explorer, to provide additional functionality to a Web page.

2.7 Code sharing and reuse – let's not write it all again!

The financial advantage of reusing existing proven software when developing new systems has always been recognized. But this remains an elusive holy grail, yet to be fully attained. Every new fashion in software development claims to have broken through and achieved the goal of 'reusable software components'. I have long thought that the criterion of success in this regard should be the introduction by industrial distributers, such as RS Components in the UK or Avnet in the USA, of a catalogue volume dedicated to software modules. This may yet occur!

The many proposals to achieve effective code 'reuse', or code sharing, can be mapped onto the software development process as shown in Fig. 2.8. In the very early days of assembler programming, source-level subroutine and macro libraries were established. The intention was to take copies of the library routines, edit them into your new code and translate the whole together. The #include header files found in most C programs are a reminder of this era. Difficulties quickly emerged when the source code was transferred: who owned the code, how much could it be altered, who should maintain it?

To deal with some of these issues, pre-translated, relocatable binary libraries were introduced which could be linked into the new routines but not read or altered. The hope was to establish a software component market similar to that for electronic hardware. Although the technique of linking into relocatable object libraries is successful, and is still essential for all software developments undertaken today, it requires access to technical development tools and a good understanding of the methodology. The clear disadvantage is the need for each program to have a private copy of

Fig. 2.8
How code can be shared.

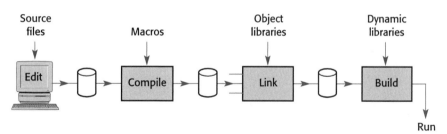

the subroutines, wasting valuable memory space, and swapping time, in a multitasking system.

Microsoft has promoted the method of **Dynamic Linking**. This allows a user to load a program which then uses 'public' routines already loaded into memory. The memory-resident libraries are mapped, during the build phase, through the memory management system to control access and avoid multiple code copies. Through the success of Microsoft's ActiveX standards, we may yet have witnessed the real dawn of a **software component** market-place!

2.8   Data codes – numeric and character

Since the early experimental days in the 1930s and 1940s, the advantage of using a binary representation for numbers stored within the computer has been universally accepted. This comes from the two-state, ON/OFF technology which is employed. So numbers have to be converted from base 10 (decimal) into base 2 (binary) before the computer can perform any arithmetic operations, or even store them. Perhaps unexpectedly, this transformation can be done by the computer itself using conversion routines. This is something like listening to French, but thinking in English. Binary numbers are laid out, as in decimal, using a limited number of symbols but extending their range by using 'positional significance'. Thus a '1' can represent 1, 2, 4, 8, 16, 32, 64 or 128 etc., depending on where it is written in the number.

4096	2048	1024	512	256	128	64	32	16	8	4	2	1	weighting
0	1	0	0	1	0	1	0	1	1	1	0	1	

The conversion from the binary format to a decimal equivalent is done by multiplying the weighting value by the associated digit (4096×0, 2048×1 etc.) and adding up the results. Because binary multiplication is disarmingly easy, we will simply write in the numbers:

$$2048 + 256 + 64 + 16 + 8 + 4 + 1 = 2397$$

Conversions in the reverse direction are not generally done in the same manner, for the obvious reason that it is more difficult.

1111101000	0001100100	0000001010	0000000001	weighting
2	3	9	7	

$$0010 \times 1111101000 + 0011 \times 0001100100 +$$
$$1001 \times 0000001010 + 0111 \times 0000000001 = 100101011101$$

A computer can manage such a sum very easily. But a more human-friendly method for converting decimal into binary is to repeatedly divide the decimal number by 2, writing down the remainder from each stage, either 0 or 1, from right to left. Try it out on a simple number first, as in Fig. 2.9.

Fig 2.9
Conversion of decimal numbers to binary by repeated division.

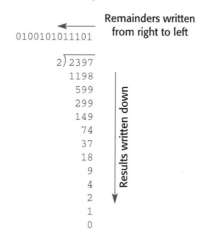

Later on in this book you will be encountering numbers, especially addresses, in hexadecimal (**hex**) format. This number base is only used as a shorthand to make it easier for humans to read long binary numbers. We do not carry out arithmetic in hex! In Table 2.3 the sequence of hex digits can be seen to carry on from 9, using the letters A to F. Throughout this book you can simply regard a hex digit as a representation of four bits.

Table 2.3
Equivalence of binary numbers to hexadecimal digits.

0	0000
1	0001
2	0010
3	0011
4	0100
5	0101
6	0110
7	0111
8	1000
9	1001
A	1010
B	1011
C	1100
D	1101
E	1110
F	1111

Humans frequently feed data into computers from keyboards. These now contain over 100 keys, and operating with the SHIFT and CTRL qualifiers, need more than 256 identifying codes. Thus the key codes were extended from 8 to 16 bits. At the same time, in similar manner, the well-established **8 bit ASCII** codes were abandoned as too limited for the display requirements of modern Windows-based word-processors. Also, with the global software market being established by companies like Microsoft, there was a need to handle international character sets. As a result of all these effects, the **16 bit Unicode** character code set was introduced with 7 bit ASCII as a subset.

With a 16 bit code, the Unicode character space can contain 65 536 characters. It is divided into 256 blocks containing up to 256 characters each, and the languages dealt with include: Arabic, Armenian, Bengali, Devanagari, Greek, Gujarati, Gurmukhi, Hebrew, Oriya, Russian, Tamil and many more! Have a look at the charts displayed at `http://www.unicode.org/` if you wish to see them all.

For many applications the 8 bit extension of the basic ASCII set (Table 2.4) is still adequate. However, the ASCII mnemonics can still be rather cryptic. Looking at Table 2.4, start by searching out BEL (coded as 07). When a binary pattern 0000111 arrives at your terminal the bell (or beep) should sound, nothing at all being printed on the screen.

Try the C program in Fig. 2.10, which sends the binary 0000111 to your screen. Insert a `for(;;)` loop to annoy your neighbours.

Any representation of numbers capable of supporting arithmetic manipulation has to deal with both integer and real values, positive and negative. **Integers** are whole numbers ($-1, 43, 747$), with no fraction part, while **real** numbers extend down beyond the decimal point (59.5, 0.101, −2.303). Standards have emerged for numeric representation in the same way that character codes were internationally agreed. Integers are generally 32 bits long. The enforcement of **two's complement** as a method of representing and manipulating negative integers was finally hammered home by hardware producers such as Intel, who supplied the microprocessors with it built in. Similarly, the **IEEE 754** standard for floating-point numbers was first introduced by the manufacturers of floating-point processors, who established a *de facto* industry standard for 32 and 64 bit formats. I will refer again to these matters in Chapter 5.

When you declare variables at the top of a function or program, you are telling the compiler to reserve the correct amount of memory space to hold the variable. Consider the fragment of C in Fig. 2.11.

The variable called `letter` will be 1 byte in size, being an ASCII character code. `count` is 2 bytes in size as a `short int`. The `uk_population` is stored as a 4 byte positive integer, while `world_population` is also 4 bytes long. The real number variables: `body_weight`, `building_weight` and `world_weight`, are 4, 8

Fig. 2.10
Ringing the terminal bell.

```
#include <stdio.h>

void main() {
    putchar (7);
}
```

Table 2.4
ASCII character codes.

bits 765			000	001	010	011	100	101	110	111
bits 4321	dec	hex	0 0	16 10	32 20	48 30	64 40	80 50	96 60	112 70
0000	0	0	NUL	DLE	SP	0	@	P	`	p
0001	1	1	SOH	DC1	!	1	A	Q	a	q
0010	2	2	STX	DC2	"	2	B	R	b	r
0011	3	3	ETX	DC3	#	3	C	S	c	s
0100	4	4	EOT	DC4	$	4	D	T	d	t
0101	5	5	ENQ	NAK	%	5	E	U	e	u
0110	6	6	ACK	SYN	&	6	F	V	f	v
0111	7	7	BEL	ETB	'	7	G	W	g	w
1000	8	8	BS	CAN	(	8	H	X	h	x
1001	9	9	TAB	EM	)	9	I	Y	i	y
1010	10	A	LF	SUB	*	:	J	Z	j	z
1011	11	B	VT	ESC	+	;	K	[	k	{
1100	12	C	FF	FS	,	<	L	\\	l	
1101	13	D	CR	GS	-	=	M	]	m	}
1110	14	E	SO	RS	.	>	N	^	n	~
1111	15	F	SI	US	/	?	O	_	o	DEL

NUL	Null	DLE	Data Link Escape
SOH	Start of Heading	DC1	Device Control 1
STX	Start of Text	DC2	Device Control 2
ETX	End of Text	DC3	Device Control 3
EOT	End of Transmission	DC4	Device Control 4
ENQ	Enquiry	NAK	Negative Acknowledge
ACK	Acknowledge	SYN	Synchronization character
BEL	Bell	ETB	End of Transmitted Block
BS	Back Space	CAN	Cancel
HT	Horizontal Tab	EM	End of Medium
LF	Line Feed	SUB	Substitute
VT	Vertical Tab	ESC	Escape
FF	Form Feed	FS	File Separator
CR	Carriage Return	GS	Group Separator
SO	Shift Out	RS	Record Separator
SI	Shift In	US	Unit Separator
SP	Space	DEL	Delete

Fig. 2.11
Variable declarations in
an HLL program.

```
char letter;

short count;
unsigned int uk_population;
long world_population;

float body_weight;
double building_weight;
long double world_weight;
```

and 16 bytes long respectively. Knowing the physical size of your variables can help to explain some types of problem, even errors, when they occur. The width of `int` variables in C programs used to be a frequent source of tricky errors when porting the code from one machine to another with differing hardware. But as the range of commercially available CPUs has been rationalized down to half a dozen, all adopting 32 bit widths as standard, such problems have ceased. The new Intel 64 bit Itanium could revive these issues!

<h2>2.9   The operating system – Unix and Windows</h2>

Although differences in hardware are sometimes noticed by the user, usually in a less than complimentary manner, it is the **Operating System** which provides the 'character' of the computer. It is the oddities of the operating system that the user must become familiar with from the outset. Because the computer hardware usually arrives with the operating system pre-installed on disk, many users have difficulty realizing that the operating system is only a program, not a hardware component. Although you may at the moment only recognize a few names, there have been quite a few developed over the past 40 years. The few that I can immediately remember are listed in Table 2.5. It doesn't mean that I have listed them all!

Some of these venerable creations will only be remembered by your grandparents if they happened to have worked with computers during the 1960s and 1970s, but surprisingly little has changed at the technical core. Only the introduction of windowing interfaces really distinguishes modern operating systems from many of the pioneering predecessors. In general, there are two ways that programmers are able to access the operating system facilities: Command line and System calls.

In the case of Unix, an operating system facility can often be invoked by either method listed in Table 2.6. An example which regularly occurs during introductory C

Table 2.5
Some of the better known operating systems.

AIX	OS/2	CDOS	Pick
CICS	PRIMOS	CMS	RSTOS
CP/M	RSX/11	MS-DOS	RTL/11
George	TDS	IDRIS	THE
ISIS	Unix	LYNXOS	Ultrix
MINIX	VERSADOS	MOP	VM
VMS	MVS	Windows NT and 95	BeOS
Multics	XENIX	OS-9	Linux

Table 2.6
Methods of accessing operating system facilities.

1. Command line interpreter (CLI), shell script or desktop selections
2. Function calls from within user programs (API)

Fig. 2.12
Unix command line instruction for 'raw' input.

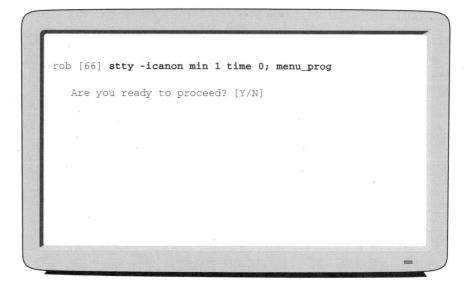

```
rob [66] stty -icanon min 1 time 0; menu_prog

     Are you ready to proceed? [Y/N]
```

programming sessions, involves keyboard input. If you are writing a character-based menu program, you may want to turn off the keyboard input buffer ready for direct 'Y/N' input. Normally you will have to hit the ENTER key after each Y/N keystroke, which may generate a problem with the CR character remaining in the buffer until the next keyboard read happens. This can create some confusion during the code testing! The Unix utility stty (Fig. 2.12) solves this problem by turning off character buffering and input editing, while still waiting for a single key to be pressed.

The second way to access operating system resources, as mentioned in Table 2.6, involves making direct calls to library functions, as shown in the C code fragment listed in Fig. 2.13. The request is then passed on to the operating system by the library code so that the keyboard input handler can be informed of the requested change. The equivalent example for the earlier menu program would now need the Unix ioctl( ) system call inserted to tell the operating system to accept 'raw' input.

It can be said that the main purpose of the operating system is to make the computer resources, hardware and software, more available to the user. The arrangement of multiple layers of software is often portrayed as concentric onion rings (Fig. 2.14), indicating the manner in which the dangerous complexity of the hardware is hidden from the user, or, more likely, how the sensitive core hardware is protected from ignorant or even malicious users! At the centre of the software, dealing directly with the hardware, are the device drivers, memory allocator and the process dispatcher. The user gains access through the CLI or desktop software.

To give the operating system a command it was once necessary to employ a Job Control or Command Language (JCL). Unix provides the **shell script** languages, the VAX had DCL, and even MS-DOS had a few commands! With the arrival of windowing interfaces, this activity has become more user-friendly, with the raw commands hidden by dialog boxes and pull-down menus. The underlying functionality is still the same, though. Pointing at little pictures (icons) with an arrow appears

Fig. 2.13
Unix system call for 'raw'
input.

```c
#include <errno.h>
#include <stdio.h>
#include <sys/termios.h>
#include <unistd.h>
#define TIMEOUT -1

extern int errno;
int sys_nerr;
extern char * sys_errlist[];

void setterm(void) {
   struct termios tty;
   int status;
      status = ioctl(0,TCGETS, &tty);
         tty.c_lflag &= ~ICANON;
         tty.c_cc[VTIME] = 0;
         tty.c-cc[VMIN] = 1;
      status = ioctl(0,TCSETS, &tty);
      if ( status == -1 ) {
           printf("ioctl error \n");
           perror(sys_errlist[errno]);
           exit();
      }
}
```

Fig. 2.14
Layers of software
wrapping the hardware.

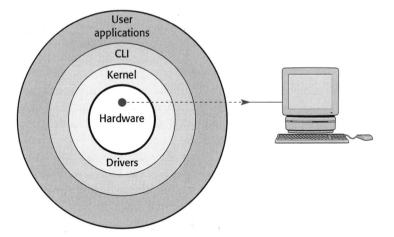

to be easier to understand and remember than a cryptic mnemonic such as `dir` or
`ls`. But the ability to store sequences of instructions in a 'command file' or 'script' is
essential for serious practitioners, in order to save time, reduce errors and provide
documentary evidence for the future. As this was not offered by the early WIMP interfaces it was considered a serious deficiency. Unix offers several command line interpreters, or shells, and users are encouraged to choose their own favourite. Table 2.7
lists some of the more common alternatives.

Table 2.7
Alternative Unix shells
(command line
interpreters).

sh	The original Bourne shell, still popular with administrators for scripts
csh	The C shell offers a more C-like syntax, and is better for interactive sessions
tcsh	Tenex shell, perhaps the most used interactive shell; emacs-like keying
ksh	Korn shell, normal issue with Hewlett-Packard workstations
bash	Bourne again shell; a freeware rework of several shells

Although you will have to wait until Chapters 17 and 18 to gain a full insight into the operating system, it is useful to remember that the main purpose of operating systems is to make the computer's resources, hardware and software, more available to the user. When the computer is shared between a number of tasks or users, this role would include the arbitration and resolution of contention disputes as well as the provision of system-software utility programs. Often the overall efficiency of a computer system is governed not by the crude power of the CPU but by the cleverness of the operating system routines which are responsible for managing the hardware.

2.10 Client–server computing – the way of the Net

Since von Neumann's original blueprint was published, many technical developments have produced quite dramatic changes to his vision. Perhaps the most far-reaching has been the introduction of fast information exchange across **computer networks**. Nearly all commercial PCs, workstations and mainframes are now linked to each other by a **local area network (LAN)**. Access to network facilities is also normally provided through the operating system. Novell developed remote file server systems for PCs, while Sun pioneered NFS (Networked Filing System) for its Unix workstations. Both endeavour to make accesses to local and remote resources indistinguishable to the end-user.

This networked architecture (Fig. 2.15) was introduced to provide printer sharing and central filing, but has been more fully exploited in order to redistribute processing loads across a group of machines. It is now common for programs running on widely separated computers to cooperate closely in the processing and display of information. The originator of the request is referred to as the 'Client', and the

Fig. 2.15
Client–server couplets
working across a
network.

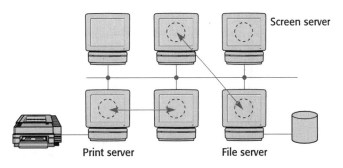

supplier of the service is designated the 'Server'. Local screens retained responsibility for display formatting, while more powerful central hosts offered database facilities, email distribution or Web services. It is a dramatic extension of multitasking programs, where the collaborating tasks are now distributed across different machines. This arrangement became known as **client–server** computing and was pioneered by the MIT **X Window** System. The final impact of this strategy is still not clear.

Client processes start the interaction off by sending a request message to the appropriate **server** (see Fig. 2.16). The response message may contain the required data, or simply an acknowledgement that the action has been taken. Further requests will then follow from clients to the server. The session illustrated in Fig. 2.17 concerns an aged Atari STE, bravely running X Window screen server software. It is already using the remote Unix host called pong to run the X Window manager, but is starting a remote login to a different networked host called milly. The Atari is in fact acting as an **X-terminal**, displaying text and graphics directed to it across the network. The real work is being carried out by the two other computers. In this way the processing deficiencies of the local machine are not so apparent.

Fig. 2.16
Timing of client–server interaction.

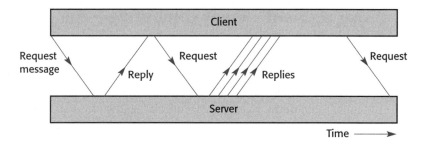

Fig. 2.17
Client–server operation across the network.

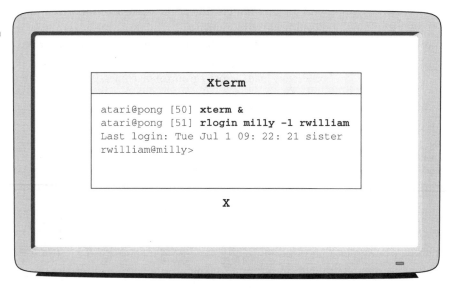

2.11   Reconfigurable hardware – an alternative to fetch–execute

Von Neumann's ideas on **programmability** from the 1940s must be put in the context of the technology then available. If the operation of a machine needed to be changed, the only option to change the functionality was to reconfigure extensive banks of switches or large patch-panels using hundreds of plugs and cables. His key idea was an easily replaceable program to control the machine activity. The possibility of a 'loadable' pattern which could set up the hardware to carry out a specific task was not even imagined.

This, however, is exactly what has now appeared in the guise of **Erasable Programmable Logic Devices** (EPLD). Such devices can be very quickly reconfigured by downloading initialization data, without even removing the chip from the equipment. In this way we can create completely different logic circuits, carrying out different functions, without changing any hardware. Perhaps if such techniques had arisen earlier, we would now be living in a world free from instruction sets and fetch–execute bottlenecks!

Review

- Digital computers follow the outline set down by von Neumann. This involves the machine (computer) loading a list of instructions (program) and obeying them one at a time (fetch–execute cycle).

- The advantage of having non-specific hardware, capable of carrying out any program of instructions, has been well exploited – the *same* PC could be calculating a payroll or monitoring water purification.

- Binary codes are used in computers for the convenience of being able to represent numbers by arrays of ON/OFF switches (transistors).

- Every computer has a primitive set of operations which it can carry out. All programs are made of these. Each has a unique binary code associated with it to trigger that particular operation.

- Writing programs using binary instruction codes is tedious and very error-prone. High-level languages allow programmers to write using more suitable terms, but compiler programs are then required to translate HLL programs back into binary machine code for the computer to understand.

- After the compiler has checked and translated the HLL source code, a linker is needed to bind together the various modules, including library functions. This all ends up as an executable program.

- Inside the computer, binary codes are also used to represent data, notably the ASCII set of character codes and binary integers.

- The operating system, such as Unix or Windows NT, is the software that provides users with the 'character and feel' of the computer as well as many convenient facilities.

- Software utilities and other resources can now be easily accessed across a network. This has led to the client–server programming paradigm which distributes the processing load between several computers.

Practical work

The recommended practical work demands more detailed encounters with the local operating system (Unix or Windows NT). This should involve managing personal directory space and checking and setting file access rights.

Identify the editor which you will use for general programming exercises later in the course. Try a 'hello world' program to test out the compiler and linker settings.

Revise your understanding of the binary number system to avoid any embarrassment later!

Exercises

0001. What does it mean to say that a computer 'understands' a program?

0010. List the name and number of five CPUs and their manufacturers.

0011. Compare translating French into English with translating C into machine code.

0100. What are meant by: assembler, binary executable, compiling, logging on, crashing?

0101. Get a knitting pattern and disassemble it, explaining its operation in plain words. Why is HLL coding preferable to assembler level coding?

0110. What are the common applications found for the following machines: IBM AS/400, Sun workstations, Cray processors, Psion Organiser, PC compatibles?

0111. What is a program? What are the special features that define a 'von Neumann architecture'? What is meant by 'Harvard architecture'?

1000. Construct a sentence including the following words: Ethernet, micro, bits, remote, windowed, LAN, per second, 10.

1001. What is hex (hexadecimal)? How is it different from binary?

1010. Examine the ASCII table in Table 2.3. Check that you can read 'A' as: 65, 41H or 1000001. What is 'a'? Write your first name in hex, in binary and in decimal. What does the ASCII pair $0A $0D do to a text Window (or VDU)? Use the minimalist program in Fig. 2.10 to send different ASCII codes to the screen. Change the 7 to "7" and see what happens.

1011. What is Unicode? Try a WWW search using http://www.altavista.com/.

1100. How many instruction codes does the Pentium recognize? Look back at the example in Fig. 2.3. Compare the machine code binary addresses with the assembler hex. Do they agree?

1101. Who or what is GNU? (Try Unix apropos gnu instead of AltaVista this time.)

1110. What is a linker, and when would you need it?

1111. What would you do if the following items ran too slowly?

(a)   a popular application program, such as Word

(b)   your maths computation assignment

(c)   a complex database query in SQL

(d)   a spreadsheet macro.

Readings

- What is the Computing section code for your library?

- Can you login remotely to the catalogue, look up a title and reserve it? Is it possible to renew a book loan from your terminal? This avoids penalty fines!

- ```
  if (today == thursday)
       { read the Guardian ONLINE section }
  else
       { flick through the latest Dr. Dobbs Journal }
  ```

- Find and look at the classic text Tanenbaum (1999).

- The Unicode home page:
  `http://www.unicode.org/`

- Everything about the fabulous GNU project:
  `http://www.gnu.org/`

- Online Glossary for Computing and Telecomms terms:
  `http://www.infotech.siu.edu/coc/glossary.html`

- A list of free compilers:
  `http://www.idiom.com/free-compilers/`

- Hennessy and Patterson (1998), Section 1.7.
  Heuring and Jordan (1997), Section 1.6.
  These are both historic overviews and commentaries.

- Tanenbaum (1999), Chapter 1. A wide ranging introduction to the subject.

- The Web sites can be accessed via the Companion Web site for this book at:
  `http://www.booksites.net/williams/`.

Note on base 11 counting

It has been accepted that we count in tens, to base 10, because we have 10 fingers, but this is not completely rational. Consider the electronic switch which led us to adopt base 2 for computing. It has two states: ON and OFF. Now, with a single hand, if we only allow one finger at a time, we can hold six states: NONE, Thumb, First, Second,

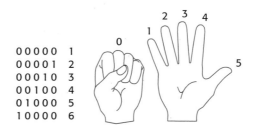

```
00000  1
00001  2
00010  3
00100  4
01000  5
10000  6
```
```

Third, and Fourth. Try it and see. Then, using two hands, we actually have eleven states, leading logically to humans counting to base 11!

Of course, if you were prepared to recognize as discrete states all the different up/down combinations of your 10 fingers there would be 2^{10} (1024) states to play with. But I am not ready for arithmetic to base 1024!

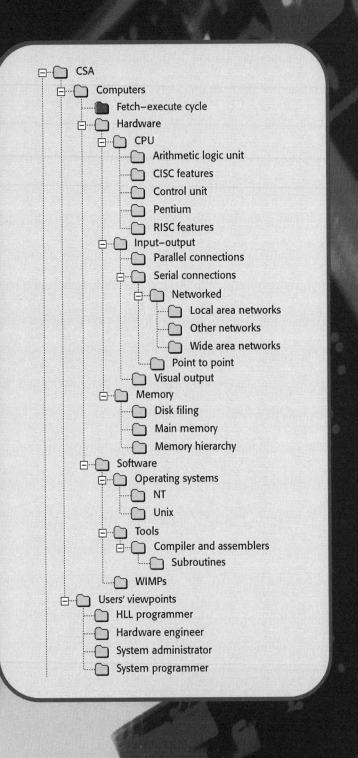

Functional units and the fetch–execute cycle

3

Overview

Taking a block diagram systems-level approach, the principal functional components of the digital computer can be identified: CPU, memory, input–output and interconnection bus. They all participate in the fetch–execute cycle, which is the fundamental unit of activity, allowing the computer to 'understand and obey' any program written in the correct language. This ability to follow a list of instructions can be seen as the novel idea behind all computers, distinguishing them from other machines. It is vital to maintain synchronization between these components, so a system clock signal is distributed to all the parts. The need to be able to access every location in memory has given rise to a rigorous addressing scheme. The parallel port is introduced as the simplest type of input–output unit.

3.1 The naming of parts – CPU, memory, IO units

Although digital computers can be described as having only three major hardware units (Fig. 3.1), when you open your PC the **motherboard** often appears much more complicated. This section aims to allow you to identify which part is which, and then to correctly associate the principal functions. The schematic plan of a modern PC motherboard, with the visible parts labelled, is shown in Fig. 3.2.

When you take the lid off a PC and look inside, the three units that you must try to identify on the motherboard are: **Central Processing Unit (CPU)**, **Main Memory** and **Input and Output** devices. These are the minimum set of components for a working digital computer; everything else could be classed as additional luxuries. Later in Chapter 12 we will have a look at disk drives, which can be the most significant part of an online data storage facility, but for the moment we will ignore them.

The CPU will currently be a **Pentium**, with large metal fins attached to dissipate the excess power and keep the silicon from overheating. There will also be a miniature fan fitted to assist this vital cooling. Figure 3.2 illustrates the CPU plugging directly into a 'Socket 7' on a motherboard. Inserting all 321 pins, required by this type of Pentium, into a push-fit socket would be tricky, so a ZIF (zero insertion force) unit is normally provided, allowing the Pentium to be dropped (carefully) into place and firmly clamped with a side lever. The newer Socket 370, which handles the increased number of Celeron pins (370!), operates in the same manner, but the Pentium II/III and AMD Athlon use a different arrangement involving another small circuit board holding the CPU, which is pushed into a motherboard slot.

Motherboards come in several sizes with slightly different organization of the chips. They are referred to as: AT, Baby-AT, ATX, ATX-mini and so on. Unfortunately, when attempting to exchange a motherboard unexpected problems can occur, such as the CPU cooler fan and the floppy disk compartment requiring the same space. Sometimes the only solution is to obtain a new-style case along with the motherboard. The most obvious memory will be in the form of small **DIMM** cards plugged into sockets. Sometimes these cards have memory chips mounted on both sides. Then there are a variety of IO devices which need connecting: keyboard, mouse, screen, printer and disk drives, not forgetting the front panel LEDs and reset switch! In Chapter 11 we will discuss how the **expansion slots** can be used for more IO connections. Now, though, you must try to see the devices in terms of their generic role. Appreciating the basic functions necessary for a computer to operate is more important in the long term than being able to distinguish the deluxe from the GTi model!

Fig. 3.1
The principal components of a computer.

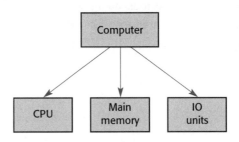

Fig. 3.2
PC-AT motherboard, showing the locations of the CPU, memory and IO card sockets.

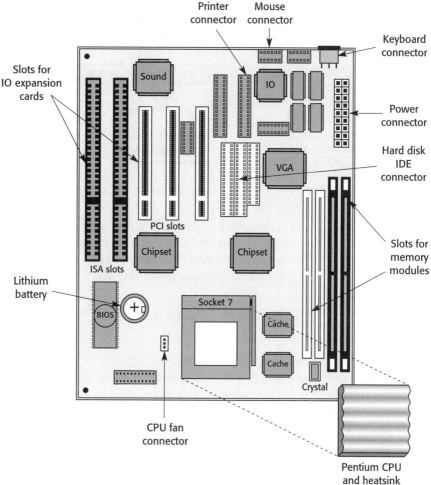

Computers can be divided into three principal subsystems, as represented in Fig. 3.1: the CPU, the main memory and the input–output units. Each of these subsystems is often made up of many components. On the motherboard, all the components are interconnected by signal highways, or buses. A **bus** is just a bundle of conductors, wires or tracks. The Intel 8086 had 20 shared address/data lines and a further 17 lines for control. With the Intel Pentium, the data bus was expanded to 64 lines and the address bus to 32 lines, while the next generation of processors will come with 64 address lines. Each hardware unit is connected to the address, data and control buses. This provides a simple way of building up a complex system in which each unit can communicate with all others. New units can be plugged in with little disruption and failed units can be swapped out for testing. When you open up a PC and look for the bus wires you may be disappointed. The card, or motherboard, on which the chips are fixed, can be multilayer, and is generally coated with opaque green varnish to protect the fine detail of the bus tracking. The bus interconnection scheme is often represented in diagrams as a wide pathway, rather than showing the individual wires (as in

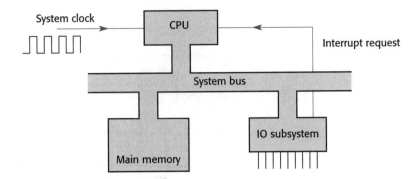

Fig. 3.3
System interconnection schematic.

Fig. 3.3). It is then assumed that the connected devices can have access to any signal line that they require.

Buses are not the only possibility. An alternative scheme which used point-to-point interconnection was tried, but led to an impossible tangle of wires when more than three units were involved. The number of pathways needed to link every possible pair of n units can be expressed mathematically:

$$\text{number of different pathways} = \frac{n(n-1)}{2}$$

Remember that each pathway will still require a full-width data highway, which could be 32 lines, and several (approximately 6) control lines. However, there is a benefit. Because the pathways are communicating point-to-point there would be no need for full-width address buses. Addresses serve the double purpose of specifying the destination device on the broadcast highway, as well as selecting the position within the device. The former would no longer be required with point-to-point pathways. Taking an example where the number of units to be linked, n, is 30:

$$\text{number of different pathways} = \frac{30 \times 29}{2} = 435$$
$$\text{number of wires} = 435 \times (32 + 6) = 16530$$

The number of 'wires' demanded by this interconnection scheme is unmanageable. You may like to check the method of calculating the required number of interconnection pathways by counting the lines in the simpler examples laid out in Fig. 3.4. Also shown for comparison is the much simpler bus scheme with six units.

So, taking into account the large number of devices which need to communicate with each other in a computer, the bus interconnection scheme rapidly won favour. However, there is a serious disadvantage to bus architectures. Because an electronic bus, like a railway line, can only transfer one item of data at a time, it leads eventually to a limit on the performance that can be achieved even when faster processors are available. This constraint is termed the **Bus Bottleneck**. So, very soon the transmission speed of signals on the bus becomes a critical parameter when considering how to

Fig. 3.4
Point-to-point escalation compared with simple bus interconnection.

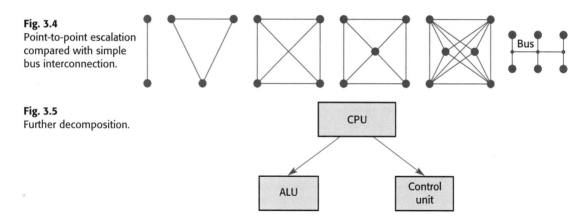

Fig. 3.5
Further decomposition.

increase system throughput. It is not possible to simply increase the **clock rate**, reducing pulse widths, to achieve faster transmission. The capacitance and inductance of the bus tracks place an upper limit on clock speeds. To get around this problem, wider data buses are being adopted for microprocessors. Since the early 1980s there has been an eight-fold change, from 8 to 64 lines. In addition, the more powerful computers employ several separate buses, thus allowing the computer to transfer many items of data simultaneously.

Concerns about the limitations imposed by maximum rates of data transfer will reoccur in Chapter 14 when we deal with networked computers. To further investigate the hardware, the CPU can usefully be divided into two functional sub-units: the **Control Unit** and the **Arithmetic and Logic Unit**. By attaching Fig. 3.5 to Fig. 3.1, you can see the whole structure developing.

3.2   The CPU fetch–execute cycle – high-speed tedium

The computer has to read and obey every program, including the operating system itself, one instruction at a time. This initially appears to be an incredible handicap to performance when compared with the myriad of simultaneous activities that living organisms can carry out. The basic operation, known as the **fetch–execute cycle**, is the sequence whereby each instruction within a program is read into the CPU from program memory and then decoded and executed. Only the phenomenal speed of electronic hardware makes this tedious cycle of repeated events of practical value. At any moment in the historic development of computers, one of the three units involved in the fetch–execute cycle, memory, bus and CPU, will be the limiting factor. This can affect both the design parameters which computer engineers have to work within and also the selection of algorithms for problem solving. For example, there are sometimes 'memory-intensive' methods available or 'compute-intensive' alternatives. If memory is fast and cheap then the former may be better; otherwise the latter will be chosen. Presently, DRAM chips used in **main memory** are not as fast as the

Table 3.1
Relative timings for
various activities.

ns	μs	ms
$\dfrac{1}{1000000000}$	$\dfrac{1}{1000000}$	$\dfrac{1}{1000}$
Fetch–execute 10 ns	Light 300 m/μs	Human reaction 300 ms
Logic gate delay 5 ns	TV line scan 60 μs	TV frame 20 ms
SRAM access 15 ns	Interrupt 2–20 μs	Hard disk access 10 ms
	Engine spark 10 μs	Car engine (3000 r.p.m.) 20 ms

CPU. Faster memory devices *are* available (SRAM) but at much higher cost, so they are only used in small, fast buffers, known as **memory caches**. These can help somewhat to reduce the main memory access delay by holding copies of current instructions and data. Chapter 12 will deal with this topic in more depth. To further reduce the negative effect of von Neumann's 'single stream' bottleneck, the new **RISC** generation (Reduced Instruction Set Computers) speeds up the fetch–execute rate by working on several (~5) instructions simultaneously by means of a push-through pipeline. This will be explained more fully in Chapter 21.

However familiar we become with computers, it seems impossible for us to really understand the incredible speed at which they operate. To attempt to bridge this gap in our understanding, Table 3.1 gives the speeds of various activities for comparison.

From Table 3.1 you can readily see the disparity in speeds between computer operations and the real world. Even something which appears to us to be very fast, like a single television scan line, is a thousand times slower than a CPU fetch–execute cycle.

As we have seen, computer programs are made up of binary coded instructions such as:

1011 1000 0000 0000 0000 0001

This is a Pentium instruction which would be expressed in assembler mnemonics as:

```
MOV AX,0x100
```

Or more recognizably in the C programming language:

```
ncount = 256;
```

This is a clear indication of the advantage gained from using programming languages (even the humble assembler!). This instruction will set the number 256 into the CPU accumulator register, AX.

The **fetch–execute cycle** is the process by which the CPU retrieves from program memory the next instruction, decodes it, and carries out its requested action. Fully describing the fetch–execute cycle for the Pentium CPU would go far beyond this

Fig. 3.6
Instruction pointer
register (IP) points to the
next instruction in
memory.

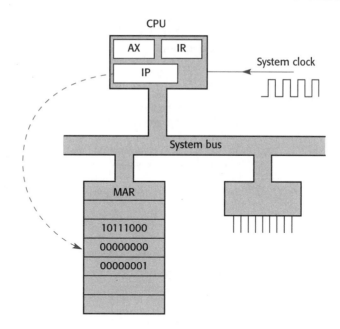

chapter, or even this book, but a summary can be given to help you appreciate that fetch–execute is actually made up of several separate phases of activity. In Fig. 3.6 can be seen the CPU with the **Instruction Pointer** (IP), **Accumulator** (AX) and **Instruction Register** (IR). Main memory holds the program, within which the single MOV AX, 256 instruction can be seen in binary form. The Memory Address Register is also represented because it is mentioned in the following description. Figure 3.7 illustrates the fetch phase and Fig. 3.8 the execute phase for the MOV AX, 256 instruction. Now try tracing out the sequence of actions which make up the fetch–execute cycle.

This schematic example is relatively straightforward when compared with the actual fetch–execute sequence of a modern processor such as the Pentium. Some instructions require an extra execute cycle to read in an address value from memory, which is then used to access the desired variable from memory to be operated on. It is not necessary to rehearse the fetch–execute cycle for every Pentium instruction. You are only expected to understand the principles, and apply them to the simpler instructions. Programmers will only come up against problems at this level if they are working with unproven prototype hardware – an experience best avoided!

To summarize: the fetch–execute cycle is the sequence by which each instruction of the program is read from memory, decoded and carried out. This may involve reading in further items of data from memory, so that an operation can be carried out, and writing result values back to memory.

Both Unix and Windows NT provide tools to watch the various activities as they happen. The Unix tool on Sun workstations is called **perfmeter**; on Linux it is **xsysinfo**; and on Windows NT it is the **Performance Monitor**. The Sun perfmeter display of the current CPU load is started with the command line

```
perfmeter -t cpu &
```

The peaks in activity in Fig. 3.9 were caused by capturing and processing the screen image for the diagram!

Fig. 3.7
The fetch phase of the fetch–execute cycle.

Fetch is identical for all types of instruction:

1. The address in the Instruction Pointer register is copied onto the address bus from where it is latched into the Memory Address Register: IP → MAR

2. Instruction Pointer is incremented ready for next cycle: IP++
Instruction Pointer now points to the next location in the program memory

3. Memory selects location and copies the contents onto the data bus: (MAR) → DBus

4. CPU copies the instruction code from the data bus into Instruction Register: DBus → IR

5. The decoding of the instruction in IR now starts.

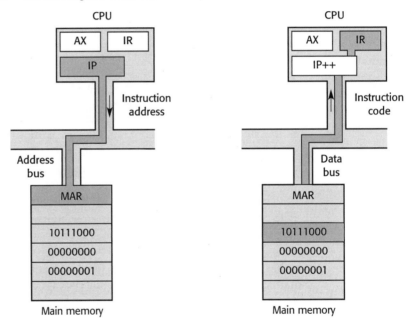

3.3   System bus – synchronous or asynchronous?

The signals sent out by the CPU along the system bus are separated into three distinct groups:

- **Data bus** – typically 32 bits wide, but will be increased to 64 bits

- **Address bus** – 32 bits wide, but will require more very soon

- **Control bus** – about 15 lines responsible for starting and stopping activities

Fig. 3.8
The execution phase of the fetch–execute cycle for `MOV AX,256`.

Execute varies with each type of instruction. For the Intel Pentium instruction `MOV EAX, 100` the sequence would be similar to:

6. IP is copied to address bus and latched into memory: IP → MAR
7. IP is incremented: IP++
8. The value selected in memory (100) is copied onto the data bus: (MAR) → DBus
9. CPU copies the value from the data bus into the EAX register: DBus → EAX

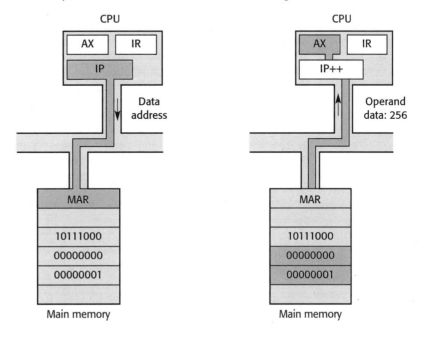

Fig. 3.9
Displaying the current CPU fetch–execute loading using Sun's perfmeter.

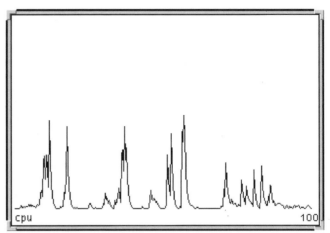

One of the control bus lines is the **System Clock**. It is generated by a high-frequency crystal oscillator which can be identified on the motherboard as a small silver cylinder, often situated close to the CPU. In most circumstances it is the CPU that starts an operation by sending signals along the bus wires to other units. These then respond by

Fig. 3.10
Synchronous bus fetch–
execute cycle timing
diagram (100 MHz).

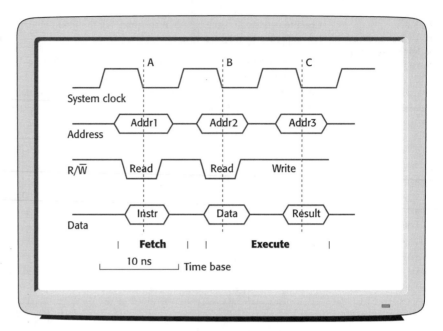

signalling back along the bus lines. Sometimes an action is triggered by a non-CPU unit, which may take control of the bus for a while at the expense of the CPU. The sequence of bus signals must follow a very precise timing pattern. If the timing is completely locked into the system clock signal the bus is termed 'synchronous'.

Synchronous buses require all attached units, memory and IO chips to operate at the same speed. This arrangement is quite simple to implement from the hardware viewpoint, but lacks the flexibility to easily accommodate a range of devices operating at a variety of speeds. The signal trace (Fig. 3.10), shows the timing relationships that operate on a synchronous bus. Note that 64 address lines and 32 data lines are collapsed onto single representative bus lines. The exact binary pattern carried is not relevant; you only need to know *when* there is a valid number on the bus. The figure represents an idealized screen from a four-trace oscilloscope. In real computers the actual voltage traces are much messier, and so quite difficult to disentangle. For a motherboard running at 100 MHz the clock period for a single cycle is 10 ns, while a 66 MHz clock has a period of 15 ns. Try to follow the fetch–execute cycle on Fig. 3.10. It starts with the address of the next instruction (Addr1) emerging onto the Address Bus from the IP register. The memory is told to carry out a 'Read' from this location by the R/W control line. The instruction code emerges from memory (Instr) onto the data bus and travels back into the CPU where it is saved in the IR register. The fetch cycle is now complete. The execute cycle requires two further bus cycles, the first to read in an item of data for processing, and the second to write out the result.

Asynchronous buses are more complicated, but also more flexible. They allow the CPU to adapt its cycle period to the speed of the unit with which it is actively

Fig. 3.11
Asynchronous bus cycle
timing diagram.

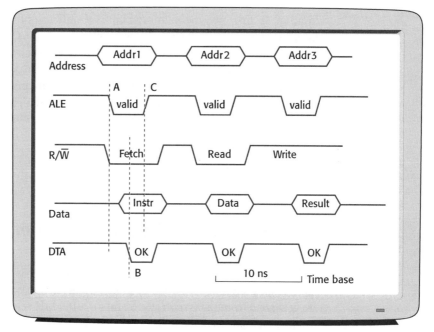

communicating. The important difference between the systems is the removal of the centralized system clock and the intoduction of ALE and DTA control lines (see Fig. 3.11). **Address Latch Enable** (ALE) is controlled by the CPU and is used to indicate to units on the bus when the address signal is valid. It actually fulfils part of the role of the system clock. The **Data Transfer Acknowledge** (DTA) signal does not emerge from the CPU, but is generated by the bus unit. It tells the CPU when the data write has been completed successfully, or when the data is valid for a read. If the memory needs more time it can delay activating the DTA signal and so delay the completion of the bus cycle. The ALE and DTA together are an example of a **handshake system** for data transfer.

Looking at Fig. 3.11, we can see that the sequence starts with the CPU putting an address value onto the address bus and then activating the ALE control line. The unit addressed responds by copying the addressed location back onto the data bus and activating the DTA line in response. When the CPU recognizes the DTA signal it will read the data bus and then deactivate ALE, removing the address too. The sequence follows the dashed lines A, B and C.

The distinction between synchronous and asynchronous working is relevant for all communication channels, including networks, so it is worth considering more fully here. The synchronous system distributes a clock signal from the CPU to all the components attached to the bus, which are then controlled by the downward falling edges, as indicated by the dashed lines in Fig. 3.10. Edge A tells the memory to copy the instruction code, from the addressed location, onto the data bus because the Read/Write signal is set for Read. Edge B then gets some data from memory, while edge C writes the result of the instruction execution back into another memory location. In this way, the memory chip is simply responding to the CPU control lines, but it has to act fast enough every time because the CPU has no way of telling whether the signals on the data bus represent valid data or are just random oscillations. If the memory cannot get an item of data out quickly enough, the CPU will carry on regardless until the erroneous data makes it crash! Now you see why the CPU can only run as fast as the slowest unit on the bus. This is a serious constraint when, as often happens, the system needs to use a few chips from a previous generation (legacy chips).

3.4   System clock – instruction cycle timing

It should now be clear, following Sections 3.2 and 3.3, that the fetch–execute cycle is not a single event but comprises a number of distinct phases, or **micro-cycles**. These are generated from the system clock, and for a 100 MHz clock the microcycle period would be 10 nanoseconds:

$$\text{period} = \frac{1}{\text{frequency}}, \quad t_{\text{micro}} = \frac{1}{100 \times 10^6}\text{s} = \frac{1}{100}\mu\text{s} = \frac{1000}{100}\text{ns} = 10\text{ ns}$$

The example shown in Fig. 3.12 has five micro-cycles within the full fetch–execute instruction cycle. Each micro-cycle is responsible for the completion of a particular operation. There is now a major difference between CISC and RISC computers in the organization of how the micro-cycles are arranged and implemented. We will be investigating this further during the following chapters.

As clock speeds rose to increase processor throughput, they were becoming too fast for memories to respond to within a single cycle. Yet more problems arose which involved the broadcast band for VHF FM radio, which rests at 90–100 MHz (Fig. 3.13). This was exactly the speed intended for the next generation of processor clocks. To make matters worse, the aerial length for FM broadcasts is of the same scale as the motherboard tracking, making them excellent emitters and receivers:

Fig. 3.12
Multi-phase instruction cycle.

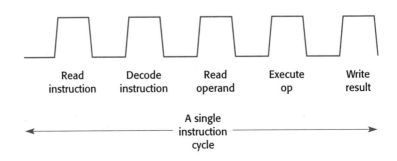

| Read instruction | Decode instruction | Read operand | Execute op | Write result |

A single instruction cycle

Fig. 3.13
Computers can emit
strong radio interference
in the FM band.

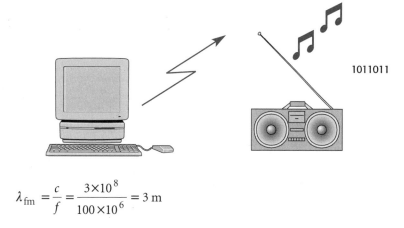

1011011

$$\lambda_{\mathrm{fm}} = \frac{c}{f} = \frac{3 \times 10^{8}}{100 \times 10^{6}} = 3 \text{ m}$$

Thus, a quarter of the full wavelength is 3/4 m, or 75 cm.

The microcomputer pioneers exploited this effect when testing out the original MITS 8080 microcomputer. It had been supplied with little in the way of input–output facilities, offering only a single row of eight LEDs and eight toggle switches. This demanded some ingenuity if anything approaching an impressive demonstration was required. Then it was noticed that a nearby transistor radio was inadvertently serving as an output device, so programs were quickly written to play tunes from the radio's loudspeaker! For a time, the radio emission problem was reduced by the use of clock doubling. This allowed the CPU to accept a lower frequency clock from the motherboard and then to synthesize a higher rate for use on-chip. For example, the 66.6 MHz system clock was doubled by the 150 MHz Pentiums. The much smaller dimensions of the CPU package reduced the quantity of VHF radio emission relative to the larger motherboard tracking. The long-term solution was to house computers in metal cases, which needed to be well earthed to screen away any radio emissions from inside. Current PCs have motherboard clocks running at 100 MHz, which for example are quadrupled by Pentiums operating at 400 MHz. Sometimes the motherboard clock is referred to as the **FSB** (Front Side Bus) clock because of the construction of the Slot 1 and Slot 2 CPU cards. The 'front side' connects to the main memory, on the motherboard, while the 'back side' connects to the cache memory held on the daughterboard itself. As the CPU is running 2, 3 or 6 times faster than the main system bus and memory, the need for faster on-chip cache memory suddenly became a keen requirement, and the move from CISC to RISC architecture became more urgent. Chapter 21 discusses the philosophy and advantages of RISC in more detail.

The maximum rate of signals in a computer is limited by fundamental electrical effects: resistance and capacitance. Although we have drawn the signals as sharp pulses with vertical edges, the physical resistance and capacitance of the wires and tracking have the effect of 'rounding the edges'. Problems start when a pulse 'tail' starts to overlap the rising edge of the next: see Fig. 3.14.

To increase the rate of pulses, which means the frequency of the clock, the computer hardware engineer needs to reduce the resistance and capacitance of the interconnecting bus wiring. This has been successfully achieved by miniaturizing

Fig. 3.14
Clock frequency limiting.

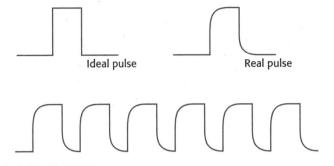

Ideal pulse   Real pulse

more and more of the circuits onto silicon chips. If the signal track or wire can be made with lower capacitance, it will need fewer electrons to charge it up to the required voltage (logic 1). Similarly, it will be able to discharge to the lower level (logic 0) much more quickly.

For many years, the voltage levels representing logic 1 and 0 have generally followed the standard set in 1970 by Texas Instruments for their TTL components. Logic 0 was indicated by a voltage less than 0.8 V and a logic 1 by a voltage greater than 2.5 V. This scheme works well with a 5 V power supply, but now, in order to increase clock speeds, a lower power supply of 3.5 V has been adopted by several chip manufacturers. This successfully reduces the transmission line charging and discharging delays, but demands tighter signal margins and less power supply noise. The latest voltage levels for fast chips are even lower (1.8 V). Another important factor constraining the CPU clock speed is the amount of heat being generated in the chip. Silicon transistors do not work so well when they are hot, and the faster the clock the more heat is generated. Pentiums can get so hot that they stop working, or require extra cooling equipment such as fans, to keep them running. There are also some intriguing experiments reported on using ice cubes to provide the extra cooling for CPUs. There is even a commercial refrigerator unit available to reduce chip temperatures to well below 0 °C which is sometimes used during CPU development work.

3.5   Pre-fetching – early efforts to speed things up

The fetch–execute sequence of micro-cycles (Fig. 3.12) can be made to run faster, but only within the limits of current technology. It was realized that the CPU was being held up at a number of moments during the fetch–execute cycle, principally because main memory DRAM was still working more slowly than the CPU. If the fetching of an instruction could be started before its predecessor had completely finished, overlapping each instruction cycle with the next, a big improvement could be engineered. Thus the **pre-fetch queue** was devised (Fig. 3.15), whereby instructions are continually read from main memory and held in a queue within the CPU, to be ready for decoding and executing. The architecture of the CPU was rearranged to support this

Fig. 3.15
CPU control unit with a
pre-fetch queue buffer.

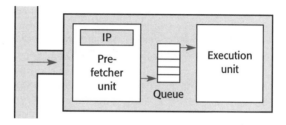

separation of function, and would eventually blend into the pipeline implementation of modern RISC processors.

The pre-fetch buffer is fed by the pre-fetch unit reading instructions from memory before they are actually needed by the execution unit. This overlapping of activities introduces some **parallelism** into the CPU operations, but will only work because much of the time taken for decoding and executing instructions does not involve any bus activity, leaving it open for pre-fetch transfers. (In the wider world it is normal practice to anticipate a sudden demand by stocking a store cupboard with groceries before the weekend rush occurs.) Overlapping activities has become a commonly used technique to speed up operations throughout the computer (Fig. 3.16), but problems arise in this case when the program implements a conditional branch or choice, as implemented by an if–else or switch–case statement. The pre-fetch buffer can only follow the instruction stream for one arm of a conditional branch. The alternative arm is left unread in main memory. Should the if-statement decide to follow the alternative 'else' route, the whole pre-fetch buffer has to be flushed and some time is lost re-reading instructions from the other program route. Is this the same as discovering that the weekend visitors are strict vegetarians, after you have bought in the salmon steaks? A return trip to the supermarket will be needed to fetch in some tofu. In Chapter 21 the techniques employed to anticipate, or guess, the outcome of such choice points and so be able to pre-fetch the correct route, will be discussed. But there always remains a time penalty should the guess be incorrect.

An interesting alternative architecture intended to speed up the fetch–execute cycle was tried by Fairchild with the F8 microprocessor family. The IP register was removed from the CPU and positioned in the program memory chip. In this way the bus

Fig. 3.16
Speed advantage of
overlapping fetch and
execute operations.

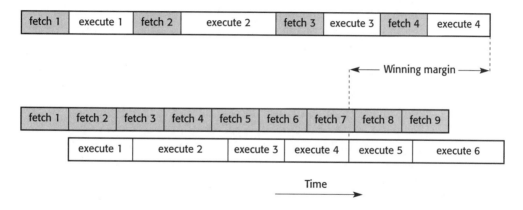

transfer delay associated with sending the instruction address off to memory every fetch cycle was eliminated. Clearly other problems appeared, such as what happens when you want to expand memory!

3.6   Memory length – address width

Main memory is central to the efficient running of a computer. The programs are stored here while instruction codes are fetched and executed. Also, associated data is normally loaded into main memory for speed and convenience. Selecting the type of memory for this role is critical because the speed of access to memory is a crucial parameter determining the rate at which the instructions can execute, and thus how rapidly the program can be completed. Theoretically, any technology would do: paper tape, magnetic disk, acoustic delay line, DRAM, SRAM and so on. At the moment, however, the universal choice is Dynamic RAM (DRAM). This can be mass manufactured and offers up to 64 million bits of read–write memory on a single sliver of silicon with access times as low as 50 ns.

An important parameter is the working size of **main memory**, but an even more significant value to the systems designer is the maximum possible length of memory. This is governed by the width (number of bits) in the CPU address registers, such as IP. It seems obvious that the address bus must also be wide enough to carry the largest address value, but the Motorola MC68000 originally had 32 bit wide CPU registers and only a 24 bit wide address bus. The reason for this odd decision was to reduce the packaging costs by limiting the number of pins! Intel dealt with the same cost problem on the 8086 processor by multiplexing the address and data bus signals onto the same set of pins. This solution, by which the address is sent first, followed by the data, along the same bus lines, does incur timing penalties and generally makes the motherboard electronics more complex because the signals have inevitably to be separated and demultiplexed before being used.

Look at Fig. 3.17 and understand the relationship between the address width and the memory length. Think of it like a postal address. If there are only two digits allowed for a house number, every road would be limited to fewer than 100 houses. It is important never to confuse memory width (data) limits with memory length (address) constraints. It might be worth committing to memory the four pairs of numbers: 16 – 64 kbyte, 20 – 1 Mbyte, 24 – 16 Mbyte and 32 – 4 Gbyte. These represent four generations of computer. It saves having to calculate them when you are doing a quick bit of estimating. Most computer system memories never actually reach fully populated status until near the end of the product life. So Z80-based computer boards ended up all supplied with the maximum 64 kbyte, and Atari enthusiasts bought extra RAM cards to get nearer to the physical 16 Mbyte limit. Currently, PCs with 0.5 Gbyte of DRAM installed are approaching the Pentium ceiling of 4 Gbyte!

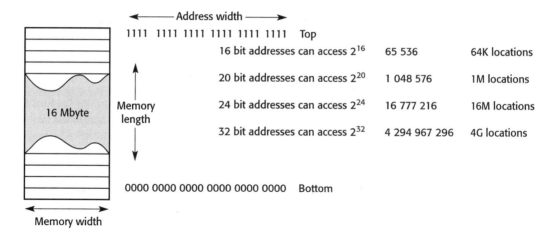

Fig. 3.17
Address width and
memory length.

While the early microprocessors accessed memory in units of one byte, this is not a universal standard. The old PDP-8 read 12 bit words from memory and its successor, the PDP-10, accessed 36 bit words. The Pentium reads 64 bit chunks at a time, disentangling them into 8 bit bytes, 16 bit words and 32 bit long words when they arrive at the CPU. Unfortunately the width of the external data bus is no longer a reliable indicator of the fundamental machine capability.

When you are dealing with memory addresses, hexadecimal notation is often used as a shorthand for binary. Thus a 32 bit address such as:

1010 0011 1101 0010 0101 1111 1110 0001

would be abbreviated to: A3 D2 5F E1.

The hexadecimal numbering system is listed underneath the decimal and binary equivalent symbols in Table 3.2. But the important thing to understand is that hex is a 'convenient' shorthand for binary.

It is worth mentioning here that modern operating systems support 'virtual memory' which is a technique allowing the main memory to overflow onto an area of disk. Although the Pentium can handle 4 Gbyte of physical addressing through its 32 bit address width, it also supports 64 Tbyte of virtual address space on disk through the virtual memory management unit. Although this obviously affects performance, because access to disk is very much slower than to main memory, there are other advantages in using virtual memory management in multitasking systems. The subject of virtual memory will be dealt with more fully in Chapter 18.

Table 3.2
Alternative
numbering systems.

dec	0	1	2	3	4	5	6	7	8	9	10	11	12	13	14	15
bin	0000	0001	0010	0011	0100	0101	0110	0111	1000	1001	1010	1011	1100	1101	1110	1111
hex	0	1	2	3	4	5	6	7	8	9	A	B	C	D	E	F

3.7   Endian-ness – Microsoft vs. Unix, or Intel vs. Motorola?

The arrangement of items of multi-byte data in memory follows one of two conventions set independently by Intel and Motorola. Very early on, Intel adopted the policy for 16 bit data of splitting it into two bytes, and storing the least significant (LS) first and the most significant (MS) next (**little-endian**). This had the advantage of common sense in its favour. Motorola eschewed normal logic and preferred to store the MS byte first and the LS byte next (**big-endian**). This did have the practical advantage of presenting the data in 'print order'. When stepping up through memory and dumping the data to a screen, the data appeared in the correct order for printing in the left-to-right writing sequence: MS – LS, MS – LS, MS – LS.

The different byte-ordering conventions are clearly shown in Fig. 3.18, where memory display windows from two debuggers (Intel Pentium and Motorola 68030) are reproduced. The region of memory being viewed contains three integer arrays holding bytes, words and ints. Each byte is presented as a pair of hex digits. So 01 represents 00000001 and FF represents 11111111.

Fig. 3.18
Differences in byte ordering in multi-byte numbers.

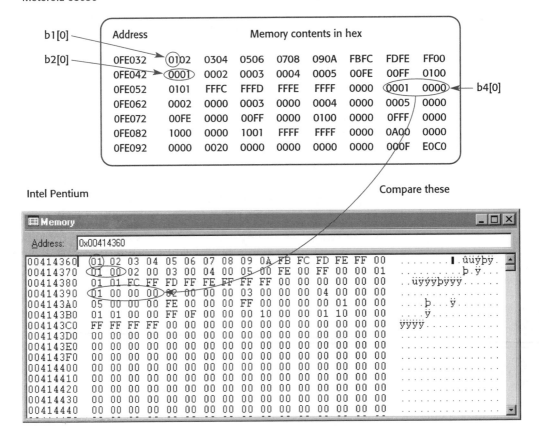

The C declarations for the three arrays are as follows:

```
unsigned char  b1[ ] = {1, 2, 3, 4, 5, 6, 7, 8, 9, 10, 252, 253,
                        254, 255};
unsigned short b2[ ] = {1, 2, 3, 4, 5, 254, 255, 256, 257, 65532,
                        65533, 65534, 65535};
unsigned int   b4[ ] = {1, 2, 3, 4, 5, 254, 255, 256, 4095, 4096,
                        4097, 4294967295};
```

By incorporating these declarations into C programs and compiling the code on both MC68030 and Pentium machines, it was possible to use debuggers to display the memory regions containing the three arrays. From Fig. 3.18 it can be seen that 8 bit integers (unsigned chars) are stored identically. The 16 bit integers (short) have upper and lower bytes in reverse order, as do the 32 bit integers (ints). Identifying the data was helped by using distinctive values!

It is worth underlining the point that if all the stored items were bytes (chars), there would be no ordering problem. Reading data from a file can also provide difficulties if it has been written under one convention and passed over to a computer operating under a different numeric regime. The conversion of files from big-endian to little-endian is straightforward if only one type of data is present – say, 32 bit integers. The byte positions can be quickly adjusted before access takes place. However, with a mixture of integer and char data the conversion is more complex. The integer words need their MS and LS bytes to be swapped, but the char string data should be addressed in sequence with no positional changes.

When transferring numeric data files from PC to Unix, there may arise the need to swap odd and even bytes, so Unix has a tool called dd with the power to swap bytes. This major disagreement means that if data files are transferred from PC to Sun they need to be converted. Sun follows the Motorola convention, after using the MC68000 for its early workstations, while Microsoft is tied to Intel processors, due to IBM selecting the Intel 8088 for its original PC.

A further difference commonly appears when transferring text files from Unix to PC, or vice versa. This involves the character used to mark the end of a line. PC applications often use ^M (CR, carriage return), while Unix prefers ^J, (LF, line feed). When you consider the intended meaning of these two ASCII control characters, you will see that *both* are actually required to move the cursor, or print head, back to the left margin and then down one line. In fact, to save some storage space it has been traditional to include only one of them in text files, relying on the screen driver to reinsert the companion code. Unfortunately, this simple choice left an opening for disagreement, and so it happened!

3.8   Simple input–output – parallel ports

The provision of a byte-wide **input port** is quite straightforward in hardware terms, as shown in Fig. 3.19. To the programmer, an input operation can appear the same as a memory read: the CPU simply takes a copy of the data which is obtained by reading at the designated port address. However, with modern multitasking operating systems, such as Windows NT and Unix, access to the hardware ports is strictly controlled and ordinary users have to ask the operating system to carry out port reading and writing on their behalf. We will return to this subject in Chapter 10.

An **output port**, such as the PC printer port (Fig. 3.20), is slightly more complex on the hardware side because there must be some way of remembering the last value of output data when the CPU is not actually writing to the port. In fact, the output port has to be provided with a single byte of memory, or **latch**, so that once the item has been written by the CPU, it will remain available in the port until another value overwrites it. In this way, an external device, attached to the port, can have valid data at all times. Of importance to programmers involved with controlling devices through such interfaces is the impossibility of reading values back from the output port. Once a value has been written to an output port it becomes inaccessible, so it is vital to retain a local copy, or shadow, for future reference and modification.

Fig. 3.19
Input port schematic.

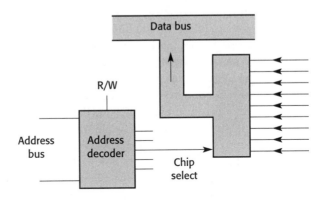

Fig. 3.20
Output port schematic.

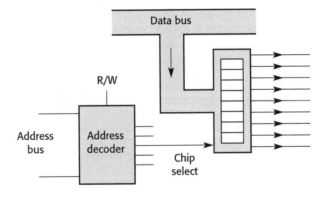

Review

- Digital computers comprise three functional parts: central processing unit (CPU), main memory and input–output units. These are necessary to carry out the fetch–execute cycle, which is the hallmark of a stored program machine.

- All these units are interconnected by parallel buses, which are seen as tracks on the PC motherboard.

- The CPU can be further separated into two parts: the arithmetic and logic unit (ALU) and the control unit (CU).

- The fetch–execute cycle is the fundamental activity which is repeated millions of times a second by a computer. During the fetch phase the next instruction from the current program is brought into the CPU. It is then decoded and carried out during the execute phase.

- Because the interconnecting bus can only carry a single item of data at a time, it gives rise to a performance bottleneck.

- The operations of all the units in a computer are synchronized by a central oscillator, or clock.

- Carrying out several things at the same time can increase throughput. This can be done by anticipating the need for instructions and pre-fetching them from memory.

- Maximum memory length is determined by the address width.

- When dealing with multi-byte data the ordering of the component bytes in memory needs to be ascertained.

- Simple input and output ports can appear to a program as single bytes of memory within the address space.

Practical work

The recommended practical work involves lifting the lid and looking inside a PC. The major parts should be identified and correctly named. Their function within the system should be discussed. Alternative part names and suppliers can be exchanged.

It is useful to use the Web at this stage to access further technical information, but try to avoid the 'sales hype' sites, where you can waste a lot of reading time and learn very little of value.

It may appear irrelevant, even odd, to provide the pin configuration for AT-style power sockets (Fig. 3.21). But if you are investigating the components of an older PC, one of the easiest ways to severely damage the

Fig. 3.21
AT power plug arrangement and voltages.

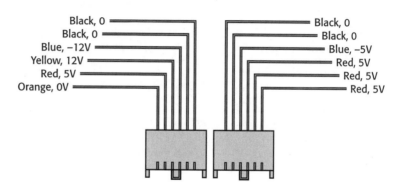

Black, 0
Black, 0
Blue, –12V
Yellow, 12V
Red, 5V
Orange, 0V

Black, 0
Black, 0
Blue, –5V
Red, 5V
Red, 5V
Red, 5V

equipment is to refit the power connector incorrectly. Because of its two-part construction, this is not impossible for those unfamiliar with the wiring colours. Most people simply remember that the black leads are positioned in the middle. The more publicized warnings concerning the effects of static electricity on VLSI circuits are really very much less significant than reversing the main power supply!

Exercises

1. Name the three principal component modules of a digital computer, and sketch a diagram with them interconnected. Insert a second IO unit.

2. What is the fetch–execute cycle, and why is it so significant? The fetch–execute cycle can be broken down into five sub-cycles. What are they?

3. How many Pentium 200 instructions may be completed during a single TV scan line? How long is a single clock period for a 200 MHz Pentium? Assuming you complete an instruction for every clock cycle, estimate how long would it take a 200 MHz Pentium PC to find a word in a 2 Mbyte array.

4. In what way do the data and address bus widths affect computer performance?

5. What is meant by the term 'bus bottleneck'? Suggest some schemes for avoiding the bus bottleneck.

6. What is the role of the system clock? Can you stop the clock without problems?

7. What is the essential feature of an asynchronous bus? Why is it considered superior to a synchronous arrangement?

8. How did Intel reduce the number of pins on the 8086 package? Was there any disadvantage to this strategy?

9. If the speed of an electrical signal is 1/3 the speed of light in a vacuum (3×10^8 m s^{-1}), how long does it take for a reset pulse to transfer across the PC motherboard? Put a VHF/FM radio on top of your PC and tune in.

10. Write a list of instructions to make a cake. Now tell a friend how to make a cake, over the telephone, one operation at a time. Perhaps their telephone handset is not in the kitchen!

11. How does the provision of a pre-fetch instruction buffer speed up execution? What is the disadvantage of having a pre-fetch buffer?

12. What advantage is there to having a CPU with on-chip (Level 1) cache? Why is off-chip (Level 2) cache less effective?

13. What is the difference between an IO port and a location in memory? What is the extra hardware requirement for an output port, beyond an input port?

14. How would the codes for 'Hello World' appear in a file on a Sun and on a PC? Now, repeat the exercise for a file containing the integers 0–9. When would you use the Unix command: `dd -conv=swab`?

15. What were the major changes in microcomputer software applications associated with the switch from 8 bit to 16 bit and from 16 bit to 32 bit?

16. Use the Windows NT Performance Monitor to watch the CPU loading: [Start] → Programs → Administrative Tools → Performance Monitor. Then you may need to start the CPU display: Edit → Add to Chart → Processor. Fire up Netscape Navigator or Microsoft Word, for example, and watch the loading change.

Readings

- Tanenbaum (1999) Section 2.1 introduces the fetch–execute cycle.

- Heuring and Jordan (1997) Section 2.4 is a detailed description of the fetch–execute cycle.

- There is a lot of interest on the Web in over-clocking CPUs:
  http://www.hardwarecentral.com/hardwarecentral/tutorials/134/5/
  http://www.tomshardware.com/guides/overclocking/

- Look at the details of the magnificent KryoTech CPU cooler on:
  http://www6.tomshardware.com/cpu/99q4/991115/

- Try reading through the steps described in 'Build your own PC':
  http://www.pcmech.com/build.htm

- The Web sites can be accessed via the Companion Web site for this book at:
  http://www.booksites.net/williams/

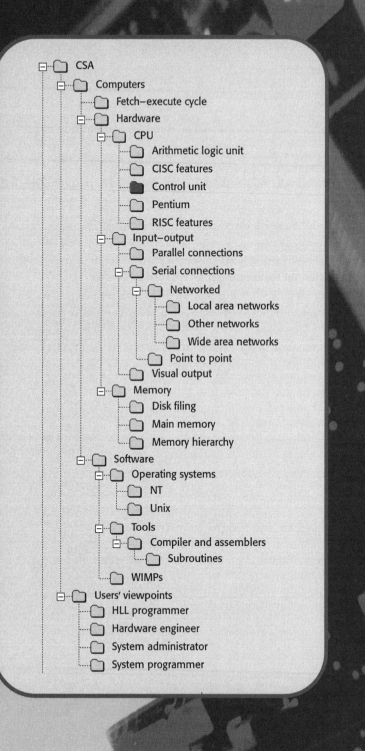

Building computers from logic: the control unit

4

Overview

The Control Unit, which comprises one half of the CPU, is the most important part of any computer, but is still constructed from logic gates. The basic activity of the CU is decoding instructions, which can be understood by looking at much simpler decoder circuits. Everyday examples are presented, such as traffic lights and washing machines. Thus we see that decoder and encoder circuits have a wide spread of applicability. The distinction between the newer RISC and older CISC CPUs is discussed in so far as it affects the Control Unit. When explaining the action of logic circuits we use truth tables. You will also find these useful during software design when input conditions become more complex.

4.1   Electronic Lego and logic – the advantage of modular units

This section is not intended to turn you into an electronic engineer! But learning about some basic **combinatorial logic** may help you to understand the operation of computers as well as how to program them. All computers are now built from **VLSI** (Very Large-Scale Integration) logic which can fit thousands of simple logic gates onto one small chip of silicon, 25 mm^2.

Using photographic reduction techniques, the conductor tracks on the surface of a modern chip are now less than 0.25 μm wide and beyond the limit of optical resolution, visible blue light having a wavelength of 0.45 μm. The production masks have to be manufactured using shorter wavelength X-rays or electron beams. Making circuits using VLSI techniques improves their reliability, speeds up circuit operation and reduces unit manufacturing costs. The first successful range of digital **integrated circuits** was produced by the Texas Instruments company and was called 7400 series TTL (Transistor–Transistor Logic). See Fig. 4.1 for a schematic diagram.

Because very clear design rules were specified with which other manufacturers complied, the expanding range of TTL chips became fundamental to the majority of computer developments for many years. The failure of software vendors to achieve a similar level of standardization has often been discussed and regretted. The advantage of having a range of trustworthy building blocks allowed hardware developers to move quickly forward to more complex designs. Because the growing problem of software piracy is now so significant, hardware designs are sometimes preferred, in place of a more convenient software implementation, to protect product copyright. Switching designs between hardware and software will become more common in the future as the Very High Level Specification Languages become more popular. Systems designers will set out their ideas using VHLSL, and then decide whether to implement in hardware or software. The 'program' which describes the system could be translated into a conventional HLL, such as C, for traditional software compilation, or into VHDL (see Section 1.3) to generate masks for VLSI production.

Fig. 4.1
Quad, dual input NAND
SN7400, TTL.

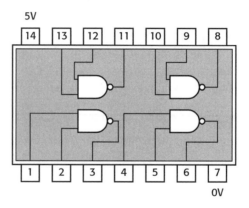

4.2 Basic logic gates – truth tables for AND, OR, XOR and NOT

Although there are more formal logic design methods available, such as Karnaugh maps, you can build simple digital circuits successfully using common sense and constructional methods similar to those suitable for Lego©. Only an understanding of the simple **Truth Table** is required for this work. A software engineer or computer programmer can appreciate the basic principles and learn practical skills without requiring sophisticated design methodologies.

Look at Fig. 4.2. Begin by reading the truth tables row by row. The left-hand side should display all possible input combinations, with the right-hand side holding the corresponding output value. Thus, for a two-input **AND gate** there will be four rows showing the possible combinations: 00, 01, 10, 11. In most cases it is very helpful to write the inputs in binary sequence down the table. It certainly helps with checking to ensure that all possible bit patterns are present.

AND and OR logic can be identified with simple domestic switch circuits. The AND is found when you plug a reading lamp into a wall socket: both switches must be ON to obtain light. The **OR** function is wired into car door switches for the courtesy light: the light comes on if any one or more of the doors is open. However, the staircase light, with switches at top and bottom, appears as an **XOR** (exclusive OR): the switches must be set differently for the light to come on. It is sometimes more useful to view the AND gate as a detector, signalling the 'all ones' condition, with the OR gate detecting 'all zeros'. By the judicious use of NOT inverter gates, any input pattern can be detected, as illustrated in Fig. 4.3.

Although we have drawn AND gates with only two or three inputs, any number of inputs is theoretically possible. An eight-input AND gate was routinely provided for building address decoder circuits. However, by wiring two AND gates into a third, it is always possible to synthesize a wider version. Perhaps the simplest useful application of a single dual input AND gate is to control the flow of data. In Fig. 4.4 the **data valve** allows one circuit to control the operation of another. The truth value of the data input can be 0 or 1. The logical AND relation can also be written: O = D AND X or O = D · X.

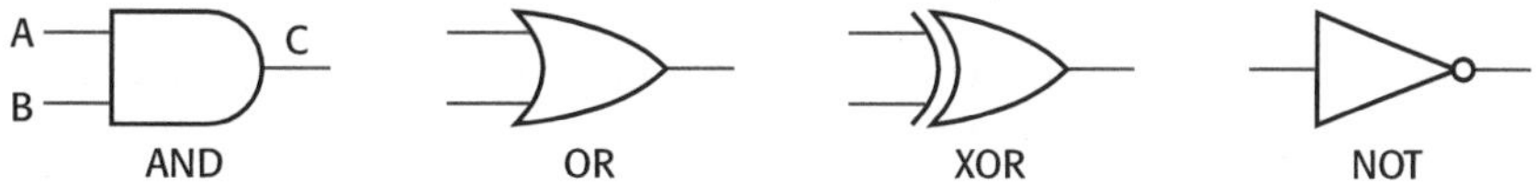

Fig. 4.2
Basic digital logic gates.

Inputs A B	C A AND B	Inputs A B	A OR B	Inputs A B	A XOR B	Inputs A	NOT A
0 0	0	0 0	0	0 0	0	0	1
0 1	0	0 1	1	0 1	1	1	0
1 0	0	1 0	1	1 0	1		
1 1	1	1 1	1	1 1	0		

AND   OR   XOR   NOT

Fig. 4.3
Using AND gates to
detect specific bit
patterns.

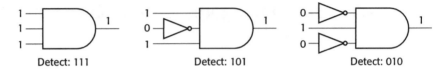

Fig. 4.4
Data flow control circuit.

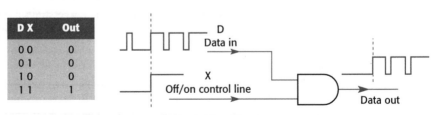

D X	Out
0 0	0
0 1	0
1 0	0
1 1	1

In this situation there is an alternative format for the truth table, as shown below.

D X	Out
d 0	0
d 1	d

Where the logic value of an input is not important, the value can be represented by a symbol, 'd', which can then be either 1 or 0. It may then appear in the output column in an expression, or singly as in this example.

4.3   Truth tables and multiplexers – a simple but effective design tool

Truth tables are powerful diagrammatic tools which can be used to describe the input–output relationship for any logical system or transformation. Both software routines and logic circuits can be designed from truth tables to produce the correct output value when any particular input pattern is applied.

A useful enhancement of the 'data valve' is the data selector, or **multiplexer**. Because we will need it later the circuit is presented here in Fig. 4.5 as an introduction to using truth tables.

Note how the truth table is written. The data inputs (A, B, C, D) are not specified as 1 or 0 because in this application it does not matter. All we need to know is which of the data inputs appears at the output. In its equation form, the logic relationship looks more complex:

$$O = (A \text{ AND } Z) \text{ OR } (B \text{ AND } Y) \text{ OR } (C \text{ AND } X) \text{ OR } (D \text{ AND } W)$$

The data selector circuit allows a control line, W, X, Y, Z, to select its associated data input for transmission through to the output. But unfortunately, this circuit will fail if

Fig. 4.5
Data selector circuit.

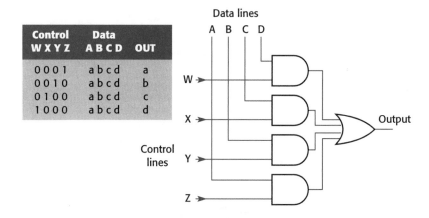

Control W X Y Z	Data A B C D	OUT
0 0 0 1	a b c d	a
0 0 1 0	a b c d	b
0 1 0 0	a b c d	c
1 0 0 0	a b c d	d

Fig. 4.6
A two-line decoder.

Selector Y X	Line d c b a
0 0	0 0 0 1
0 1	0 0 1 0
1 0	0 1 0 0
1 1	1 0 0 0

more than one of the control lines tries to select data at the same time. If we numbered the four inputs as 0, 1, 2 and 3, it would be convenient to be able to select one of the data streams by number. This involves the use of a decoder circuit.

The truth table for the required decoder is given in Fig. 4.6. Notice that there is only a single 1 in each output row and column, which makes the implementation simpler. We can use this circuit as a unit with the previous data selector to produce a better data multiplexer, shown in Fig. 4.7. The two-bit number presented at the XY control input will select one of the four data lines, A, B, C or D, for transfer to the output. This example also serves as an introduction to the **brute force** method of implementing a truth table in logic gates. Now, instead of only checking for an active 1 on the inputs, we will also check for the inactive 0s too. For the improved data selector, this can be written out as the logic equation:

$$O = (A \ \text{AND} \ (\overline{X} \ \text{AND} \ \overline{Y})) \ \text{OR} \ (B \ \text{AND} \ (X \ \text{AND} \ \overline{Y})) \ \text{OR}$$
$$(C \ \text{AND} \ (\overline{X} \ \text{AND} \ Y)) \ \text{OR} \ (D \ \text{AND} \ (X \ \text{AND} \ Y))$$

The bar over a symbol represents **NOT**, a logical inversion. Although this logic expression appears complex, it is made up of four similar terms. Each of these is responsible for one of the rows in the data selector truth table. In this way only one of the A, B, C or D data lines will get selected at any time. No incorrect selections are possible.

An alternative to the truth table is the **Signal Timing Diagram**, which we have already used in Chapter 3 to show the bus signals. Some hardware debugging tools display their data in this format, so it is useful to understand this display method as well as the truth table. The output trace in Fig. 4.8 can be inspected to see which of the

Fig. 4.7
Data multiplexer circuit
using a two-line
decoder.

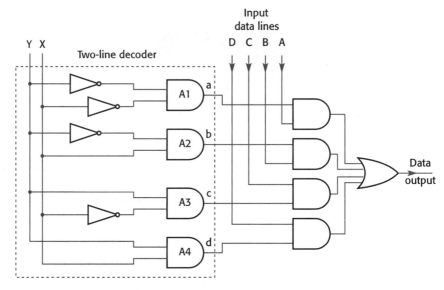

input data streams it is carrying at any time. You can see the multiplexer action as each
input stream, A–D, is selected one at a time by the control lines from the decoder, a–d.

When designing a logic implementation of a truth table it is possible sometimes to
reduce the final complexity by ignoring those rows which produce no output for the
output column under consideration. There is no need to specifically inhibit those
circumstances which would not produce an output!

Fig. 4.8
Signal timing diagram for
a four-line data selector.

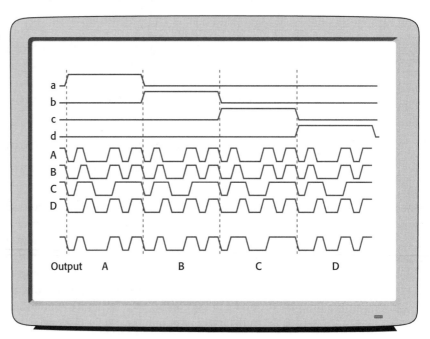

4.4   Programmable logic – reconfigurable logic chips

To help with logic implementation **PLDs** (Programmable Logic Devices) are available which provide all the gate resources needed to build a hardware logic circuit following the specification of a truth table. A PLD is capable of replacing the many separate logic packs that would otherwise be needed. There are several types for different uses, but very similar in their basic facilities. PLDs are logic chips which can be reconfigured internally by the user. This is sometimes achieved by the manufacturer actually providing too many pathway links, and requiring the user to remove the unwanted pathways by melting away in-line fuses. Only the needed pathways are then left in the circuit. An alternative technology 'enables' the wanted paths using a bit pattern stored in RAM or EEPROM memory (Electrically Erasable Programmable Read-Only Memory). These schemes have the advantage of allowing the user to reconfigure the circuit many times using the same chip. They are termed EPLDs (Erasable Programmable Logic Devices).

Programmable Logic Arrays (PLA) offer groups of AND–OR logic gates which ideally suit the implementation of truth tables. The PLA inputs (see Fig. 4.11), and the associated inverted twins, are connected to AND gates through fuse links. In the same manner, the connections to the OR gates are fused, allowing the circuit to be established by 'blowing' the unwanted wires and only leaving those that are needed. Thus, AND gates can be connected to any of the inputs and the OR gates can be connected to any of the AND gates. In this way each output can be 'programmed' to give a circuit (Fig. 4.9), to represent a 'sum-of-products' term such as:

$$O1 = (\bar{i}_3 \text{ AND } i_2 \text{ AND } i_1) \text{ OR } (\bar{i}_4 \text{ AND } i_3 \text{ AND } \bar{i}_2) \text{ OR }$$
$$(i_4 \text{ AND } \bar{i}_3 \text{ AND } i_2 \text{ AND } \bar{i}_1)$$

The expression 'sum-of-products' arises from the logic symbols favoured by mathematicians:

$$O1 = (\bar{i}_3 \cdot i_2 \cdot i_1) + (\bar{i}_4 \cdot i_3 \cdot \bar{i}_2) + (i_4 \cdot \bar{i}_3 \cdot i_2 \cdot \bar{i}_1)$$

Fig. 4.9
Implementing a sum-of-products logic equation.

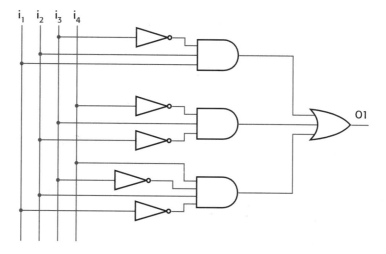

Fig. 4.10
The two-input NAND
gate (&) and its truth
table.

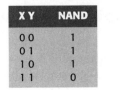

X Y	NAND
0 0	1
0 1	1
1 0	1
1 1	0

Any combinatorial logic function can be implemented using AND, OR and NOT gates. In fact you can get by with only NAND gates if you need to. This gate (see Fig. 4.10) behaves like an AND gate followed immediately by a NOT. It is important to remember that the inversion occurs *after* the ANDing. Perhaps it would have been better to have called it the AND*N* gate, but pronounciation confusions would inevitably have led to design errors! Section 5.1 will return to the subject of logic gate interchangeability.

When designing circuits in digital logic there are gate minimization techniques which can be applied. But these are rarely justified in real developments, where other constraints, such as gate costs, power consumption, signal-through-delay and the immediate availability or accessibility of different types of gate, are more pressing. For our purposes there is no need to rationalize or minimize your circuits.

A **PLA** (Programmable Logic Array) can act as a decoder. An example device is illustrated in Fig. 4.11. Here, an array of AND gates is connected directly to the inputs, or the inverted inputs. This can be described as the 'row detectors' in truth table-speak. Then the outputs from these AND gates are connected to the second array of OR gates which effectively behave as 'column generators'. All the connections can be altered by the programmer, making this device very flexible, but it is rather difficult to program. It is suitable for implementing all kinds of truth table.

An alternative approach to 'decoding' employs a **PROM** (Programmable Read-Only Memory). This might surprise you, because it is quite different from the normal role for memory as a store for programs and data. However, a PROM can be seen as a programmable logic device, too. In the same way that a PLA has a fixed pattern of inputs connected to AND gates, the PROM routes the address input lines to decoder circuits which select individual locations. This could be achieved by using AND gates set to detect each binary address. The PROM output patterns are provided, simply storing the correct values in memory locations.

A different logic device known as a **PAL** (Programmable Array Logic) offers fixed connections into the OR array, with the AND array being programmable. Using such a device, with a few extra circuits, you can set up a finite state controller!

4.5   Traffic light controllers – impossible to avoid!

There are some example systems widely used by teachers to introduce students to a particular subject or theory. Unsurprisingly, logic courses invariably include traffic

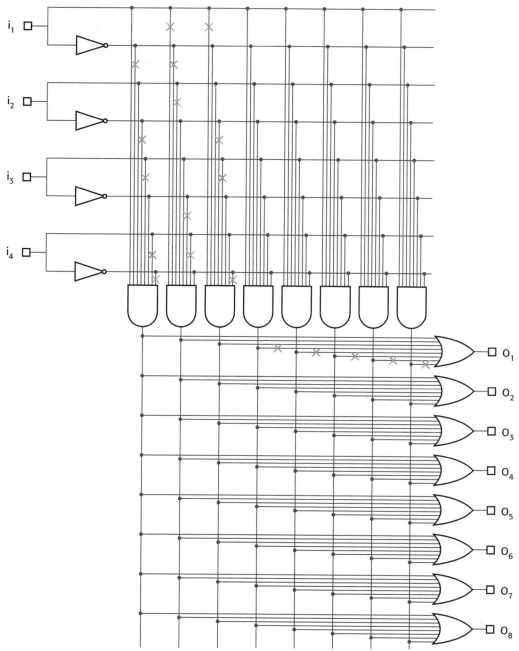

Fig. 4.11
Programmable logic
array implementing the
circuit in Fig. 4.9.

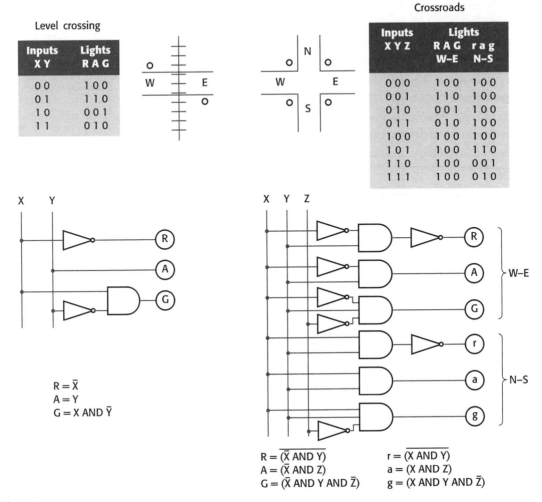

Crossroads

Level crossing

Inputs X Y	Lights R A G
0 0	1 0 0
0 1	1 1 0
1 0	0 0 1
1 1	0 1 0

Inputs X Y Z	Lights R A G W–E	r a g N–S
0 0 0	1 0 0	1 0 0
0 0 1	1 1 0	1 0 0
0 1 0	0 0 1	1 0 0
0 1 1	0 1 0	1 0 0
1 0 0	1 0 0	1 0 0
1 0 1	1 0 0	1 1 0
1 1 0	1 0 0	0 0 1
1 1 1	1 0 0	0 1 0

$R = \bar{X}$
$A = Y$
$G = X$ AND $\bar{Y}$

$R = \overline{(\bar{X} \text{ AND } Y)}$ $r = \overline{(X \text{ AND } Y)}$
$A = (\bar{X} \text{ AND } Z)$ $a = (X \text{ AND } Z)$
$G = (\bar{X} \text{ AND } Y \text{ AND } \bar{Z})$ $g = (X \text{ AND } Y \text{ AND } \bar{Z})$

Fig. 4.12
Traffic light controller circuits.

light controllers, so here goes! Consider the truth tables in Fig. 4.12 for the Red, Red/ Amber, Green, Amber, Red traffic light sequence found at British road junctions.

After reading this chapter you will appreciate that traffic lights controllers are simply another example of decoder circuits – closely related to the CPU control unit. For a long time commercial traffic light controllers were constructed from electro-mechanical relays, because they were considered more reliable than electronic components. Nevertheless, microprocessors running error-checking software have been enthusiastically accepted by road planners because of the much more sophisti-cated control sequences that they can offer. Integrated urban traffic management schemes, which are being installed in more and more city centres, depend on commu-nication links between the traffic light controllers and a central control computer. Simple digital logic circuits could not hope to include such a facility.

4.6 Circuit implementation from truth tables – some practical tips

When filling in a truth table, all possible input combinations must first be listed and entered into the left-hand columns. It is usually convenient to follow numerical order. Each row must then be completed with the correct output pattern in the right-hand columns. After each row of the truth table has been checked, the logic circuit design can begin. The technique employed depends on the circumstances, but there are several useful short cuts:

1. **Identical columns** By inspecting each column in turn, you may spot an easy solution when an output column is identical to an input column. Then you directly connect the input to output: no logic is required. The level crossing Amber output and Y input are in this category. Using algebraic formulation this can be expressed as:

    $$A = Y$$

2. **Nearly identical columns** An output can be generated by a simple logic function from only some of the inputs. Level crossing Red is simply the inverse of input X:

    $$R = \overline{X}$$

3. **Solo row** If an output column only has a single '1', use an AND gate to detect the input row pattern. All the Green outputs fit this category:

    $$G = X \text{ AND } \overline{Y}$$

    and with the crossroads:

    $$g = X \text{ AND } Y \text{ AND } \overline{Z}$$

4. **Inverted solo row** When an output column only has a single '0', use an AND gate to detect the input row pattern, and then a NOT inverter. Crossroads Red is nearly this simple: only the two rows need to be considered where X = 0 and Y = 1. Again, Z can be forgotten:

    $$R = \overline{(\overline{X} \text{ AND } Y)}$$

5. **Standard patterns** Sometimes it is possible to utilize an existing logic circuit, with minimum modification; XOR used as a 'difference detector' can be helpful, as you will see with the motor control output in the washing machine later in this chapter.

$$\text{Motor} = (\text{X XOR Y}) \text{ AND Z}$$

6. **Elimination** A slight short cut can be taken when considering the Crossroads truth table. Two rows contain X = 1 and Z = 1. Y can be 1 or 0, and appears to have no effect in determining the output if both X and Z are 1. In this circumstance it can be ignored:

$$a = \text{X AND Z}$$
$$A = \overline{\text{X}} \text{ AND Z}$$

7. **Sum-of-products** When these short cuts do not work out, the brute force method remains. This was used in Section 4.3, and involves running down each output column in turn and marking every row which contributes a '1'. Then set up an AND gate pattern detector for each marked row, remembering to use NOT gates on the inputs if a '0' is to be detected. Now allocate an OR gate to each output column. These have as inputs only the outputs from AND gates marked for their column. The following is an example for the level crossing problem:

$$R = (\overline{\text{X}} \text{ AND } \overline{\text{Y}}) \text{ OR } (\overline{\text{X}} \text{ AND Y})$$
$$A = (\overline{\text{X}} \text{ AND Y}) \text{ OR } (\text{X AND Y})$$
$$G = \text{X AND } \overline{\text{Y}}$$

It is worth understanding that the controller circuits we devised for traffic lights were only specially adapted versions of the decoders which are used so widely in computer systems.

4.7 Decoder logic – essential for control units and memories

The essential purpose of a decoder is to recognize a code number and invoke the corresponding action. This action may appear somewhat limited in its scope, consisting initially of only altering the logic level on a particular wire, but it is still very useful. In fact, it is essential to the operation of both memory and CPU control units. The schematic diagram for a decoder is a box with more output than input lines. It is important to understand that 'proper' decoders, like the 74F138 in Fig. 4.13, select only a single output line at a time. The one **selected** depends on the input number.

The ability to 'address' or 'select' something using a code number is a key concept in information theory. Although it might seem to be only a trick to reduce the number of transmission wires, it relates to a much more serious idea – **symbolic representation**. The printer receives a 7 bit ASCII code, recognizes it and selects the pattern of

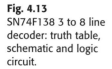

Fig. 4.13
SN74F138 3 to 8 line decoder: truth table, schematic and logic circuit.

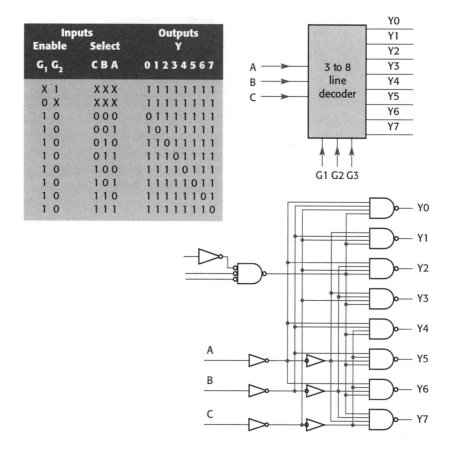

| Inputs | | Outputs | |
| Enable | Select | Y | |
G₁ G₂	C B A	0 1 2 3 4 5 6 7	
X 1	X X X	1 1 1 1 1 1 1 1	
0 X	X X X	1 1 1 1 1 1 1 1	
1 0	0 0 0	0 1 1 1 1 1 1 1	
1 0	0 0 1	1 0 1 1 1 1 1 1	
1 0	0 1 0	1 1 0 1 1 1 1 1	
1 0	0 1 1	1 1 1 0 1 1 1 1	
1 0	1 0 0	1 1 1 1 0 1 1 1	
1 0	1 0 1	1 1 1 1 1 0 1 1	
1 0	1 1 0	1 1 1 1 1 1 0 1	
1 0	1 1 1	1 1 1 1 1 1 1 0	

dots which we then interpret, visually, as a letter. This is further interpreted by our brain as part of a word, representing one of many possible ideas. Perhaps thinking is merely selection from a set of likely possibilities. Is decoding, then, the first step to consciousness? Probably not – more likely unconsciousness!

As discussed in the previous chapter, the truth table logic terms for each output column can be directly implemented by the brute force method which we will now demonstrate. The decoder in Fig. 4.13 has three inputs and eight outputs and could be modified to implement a binary to seven-segment display converter. The truth table is given in Fig. 4.14. Such devices are used to control the front panel display for cheaper equipment. The unit is constructed from seven LEDs (light-emitting diodes). Notice how we go for the inverted (OFF) conditions where there are fewer 0s than 1s in an output column. This reduces the length of the logical expression because fewer rows will be involved. In particular, $\bar{c}$ is much easier to specify than c!

The outcome for all the LED segments is:

$$\bar{a} = (\overline{W} \text{ AND } \overline{X} \text{ AND } \overline{Y} \text{ AND } Z) \text{ OR } (\overline{W} \text{ AND } X \text{ AND } \overline{Y} \text{ AND } \overline{Z}) \text{ OR}$$
$$(\overline{W} \text{ AND } X \text{ AND } Y \text{ AND } \overline{Z})$$

Fig. 4.14
Seven-segment
convertor.

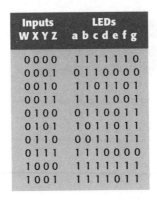

Inputs	LEDs
W X Y Z	a b c d e f g
0 0 0 0	1 1 1 1 1 1 0
0 0 0 1	0 1 1 0 0 0 0
0 0 1 0	1 1 0 1 1 0 1
0 0 1 1	1 1 1 1 0 0 1
0 1 0 0	0 1 1 0 0 1 1
0 1 0 1	1 0 1 1 0 1 1
0 1 1 0	0 0 1 1 1 1 1
0 1 1 1	1 1 1 0 0 0 0
1 0 0 0	1 1 1 1 1 1 1
1 0 0 1	1 1 1 1 0 1 1

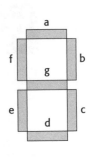

Fig. 4.15
Logic circuit for the 'a'
segment of a seven-
segment LED driver.

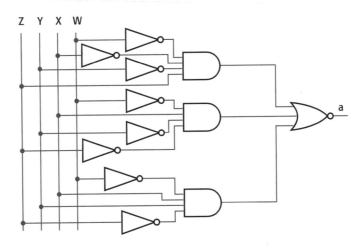

$$\overline{b} = (\overline{W} \text{ AND } X \text{ AND } \overline{Y} \text{ AND } Z) \text{ OR } (\overline{W} \text{ AND } X \text{ AND } Y \text{ AND } \overline{Z})$$

$$\overline{c} = \overline{W} \text{ AND } \overline{X} \text{ AND } Y \text{ AND } \overline{Z}$$

$$\overline{d} = (\overline{W} \text{ AND } \overline{X} \text{ AND } \overline{Y} \text{ AND } Z) \text{ OR } (\overline{W} \text{ AND } X \text{ AND } \overline{Y} \text{ AND } \overline{Z}) \text{ OR }$$
$$(\overline{W} \text{ AND } X \text{ AND } Y \text{ AND } Z)$$

$$\overline{e} = (\overline{W} \text{ AND } \overline{X} \text{ AND } \overline{Y} \text{ AND } \overline{Z}) \text{ OR } (\overline{W} \text{ AND } \overline{X} \text{ AND } Y \text{ AND } \overline{Z}) \text{ OR }$$
$$(\overline{W} \text{ AND } X \text{ AND } Y \text{ AND } \overline{Z}) \text{ OR } (W \text{ AND } \overline{X} \text{ AND } \overline{Y} \text{ AND } \overline{Z})$$

$$\overline{f} = (\overline{W} \text{ AND } \overline{X} \text{ AND } \overline{Y} \text{ AND } Z) \text{ OR } (\overline{W} \text{ AND } \overline{X} \text{ AND } Y \text{ AND } \overline{Z}) \text{ OR }$$
$$(\overline{W} \text{ AND } \overline{X} \text{ AND } Y \text{ AND } Z) \text{ OR } (\overline{W} \text{ AND } X \text{ AND } Y \text{ AND } Z)$$

$$\overline{g} = (\overline{W} \text{ AND } \overline{X} \text{ AND } \overline{Y} \text{ AND } \overline{Z}) \text{ OR } (\overline{W} \text{ AND } \overline{X} \text{ AND } Y \text{ AND } Z) \text{ OR }$$
$$(\overline{W} \text{ AND } X \text{ AND } Y \text{ AND } Z)$$

Using these logic expressions you can design a seven-segment display driver circuit
which accepts a four bit number and displays the decimal equivalent by illuminating
the correct set of LEDs. Figure 4.15 presents the driver for the 'a' segment. The design
of the other six circuits can be tackled on a rainy day!

4.8   CPU control unit – the 'brain'

The control unit (CU) is at the very centre of the computer. It performs the role of an orchestral conductor: setting the timing, initiating various activities when required, following the overall score and arbitrating conflicts. It also has the principal responsibility for fetching the program instructions from main memory, one at a time, and carrying out the coded instructions. It is responsible for controlling and coordinating the various activities of the computer. From the CU emanate control wires which start and stop the different functions: memory read, memory write, data input and output etc. Besides this external activity the control unit also orchestrates the complex sequences inside the CPU itself. In fact, the basic fetch–execute cycle is initiated and sequenced by the control unit.

The part of the control unit called the **decoder** is responsible for selecting the particular activity (ADD, SUB, MOV) requested by the current machine instruction held in the instruction register (IR). The CU decoder must select one activity out of the possible repertoire of machine instructions provided by the hardware designer. Often the machine instruction is subdivided into a few (of the order of five) constituent micro-cycles in order to simplify the design process. Thus, any instruction is split into micro-instructions which are executed one after the other in order to carry out the full machine instruction. The computer designer generally has a choice of two techniques when building the decoder – hard-wired decoding or microprogram decoding.

4.9   Washing machine controllers – a simple CU

To better understand the operation of the CU, it is worth considering how a simple washing machine controller could work. Our washing machine will only follow a single program: READY, FILL, HEAT, WASH, DRAIN, RINSE, DRAIN, SPIN, and back to READY as shown in Fig. 4.16.

The sequencing through the eight phases of the wash cycle will be carried out by a small, slowly turning motor which rotates a set of three cams fixed onto the motor shaft. The motor has to run very slowly because a full washing cycle is completed within a single, 360° rotation of the motor which in reality would take about 30 min. The profile of each of the three cams is detected, or 'followed', by a micro-switch which can only indicate 1 or 0. Thus the three micro-switches together provide a 3 bit number, or instruction, which is available to be decoded and executed. Really, we are building a 3 bit CU to regulate the action of the washing machine. For the moment we will dispense with temperature sensors, door locks, water level switches and other extra safety features.

If the washing cycle takes 30 minutes, then the sequencer motor must rotate at 0.55 mHz (millihertz, a thousandth of a revolution per second) as shown by the arithmetic:

Fig. 4.16
State transition diagram
for a washing machine.

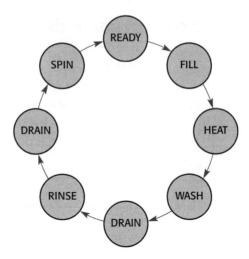

$$1 \text{ rev per } \frac{1}{2} \text{ hr} \rightarrow 2 \text{ rph} \rightarrow \frac{2}{3600} \text{ rps} \rightarrow \frac{1}{1800} \text{Hz} \rightarrow \frac{1000}{1800} \text{mHz} \rightarrow 0.55 \text{ mHz}$$

The washing machine contains some devices which have to be controlled: WATER VALVE, HEATER, DRAIN PUMP, MAIN MOTOR. The main motor has two speeds in order to allow it to wash and spin. The aim is to build some logic which will take the 3 bit instruction from the cam following micro-switches and decode it into dedicated control signals for each of the four devices. The truth table for the operation of this mechanism is given as part of Fig. 4.17.

An alternative way of 'decoding' the 3 bit instruction is to use a memory and an address register or program counter (PC). The number in the address register is used to access a location in memory which holds the pattern of control bits. This is basically the method used by microcoded CUs. Effectively, the instruction is used to form an address which accesses a memory in which are stored the control words. The washing machine would require a memory eight words long and five bits wide. During each of the eight phases of the washing cycle, the 3 bit instruction from the cam micro-switches would be sent to the memory, from which would emerge the new 5 bit control word to select the operations for that phase. Figure 4.18 illustrates the scheme.

This method of decoding, using a memory, is simpler to implement than discrete logic, and can be still further enhanced to support conditional jumping and looping. With the control word widened to contain an address field which can be loaded directly into the PC, there is the possibility of jumping to other memory locations. Such a scheme is illustrated in Fig. 4.19. In order that checks are included so that jumps can be conditional, we need a further field to be added, which contains status flag enable bits. Using one of these bits we can choose to test one of the input switches, indicating correct water levels or wash temperature. In our model, only one switch can be selected by the decoder, and if that switch is TRUE the new address will be loaded into the program counter. This is a conditional jump.

Unfortunately, the ability to handle subroutines is not provided because we have no mechanism for storing and reloading the return address. This is a problem which

Fig. 4.17
Schematic washing
machine controller unit.

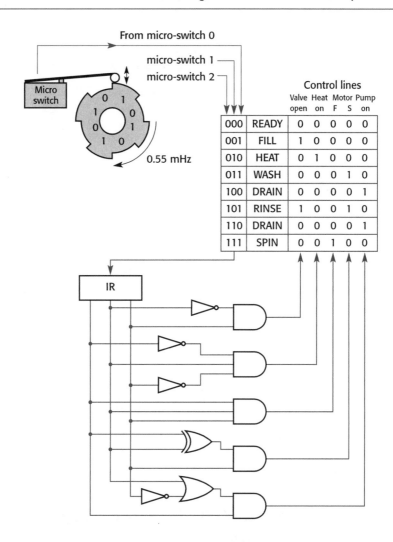

From micro-switch 0

micro-switch 1

micro-switch 2

Micro
switch

0.55 mHz

Control lines

		Valve open	Heat on	Motor F	S	Pump on
000	READY	0	0	0	0	0
001	FILL	1	0	0	0	0
010	HEAT	0	1	0	0	0
011	WASH	0	0	0	1	0
100	DRAIN	0	0	0	0	1
101	RINSE	1	0	0	1	0
110	DRAIN	0	0	0	0	1
111	SPIN	0	0	1	0	0

IR

Fig. 4.18
Using memory to
decode.

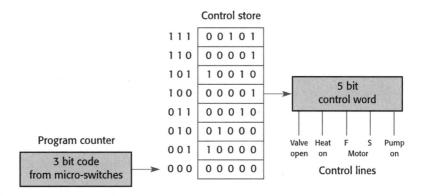

Control store

111	0 0 1 0 1
110	0 0 0 0 1
101	1 0 0 1 0
100	0 0 0 0 1
011	0 0 0 1 0
010	0 1 0 0 0
001	1 0 0 0 0
000	0 0 0 0 0

Program counter

3 bit code
from micro-switches

**5 bit
control word**

Valve open	Heat on	F Motor	S	Pump on

Control lines

Fig. 4.19
Schematic control unit with conditional JMP capability.

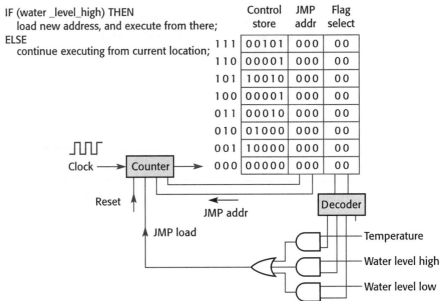

	Control store	JMP addr	Flag select
111	00101	000	00
110	00001	000	00
101	10010	000	00
100	00001	000	00
011	00010	000	00
010	01000	000	00
001	10000	000	00
000	00000	000	00

IF (water _level_high) THEN
    load new address, and execute from there;
ELSE
    continue executing from current location;

we will deal with in Chapter 8. But then, after all, we did only start with a washing machine! Perhaps this analogy is escalating out of control, so we had better not pursue it further. It should, however, give you a better understanding of how digital machines 'understand programs'.

4.10   RISC vs. CISC decoding – in search of faster computers

Recently there has been a split in the Computer Architects' Union: some advocate continuing to follow the VAX and 68000 by providing as rich and powerful an instruction set as possible (complex instruction set computers, CISC), while others have produced RISC machines (reduced instruction set computers) such as the Sun SPARC and the Power-PC. These have fewer, simpler instructions which can operate much faster than the more complex CISC instructions. This difference is most clearly manifested in the way in which the CU decodes the program instructions. A fuller presentation of the RISC philosophy will be given in Chapter 21, but it is appropriate to introduce the distinction here, within a chapter describing decoding techniques, because the two alternative methods are so different.

The hard-wired decoding method, as used in Fig. 4.17 for the washing machine, is the same technique as used by RISC processors and illustrated in Fig. 4.20. Although

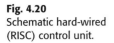

Fig. 4.20
Schematic hard-wired
(RISC) control unit.

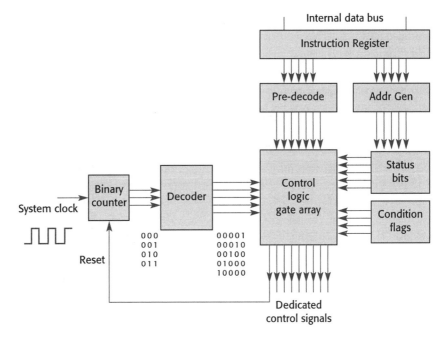

this represents little more than a glorified traffic light controller, it does involve the use of very complex decoder circuits to select a 'one-out-of-many' activity. This is sometimes referred to as using 'random logic', although, of course, it is all very carefully designed and tested. The current instruction code is read from memory and loaded into the Instruction Register. From here, the two parts (known as the opcode field and operand fields) are dealt with separately. The opcode value, which specifies the action to be carried out (ADD, SUB or MOV) is used as part of the input to a decoder array. Other inputs to this array include ALU status flags (see Chapter 5) and the current machine cycle number. As instructions can have different execution lengths, the machine cycle counter is reset to zero during the last machine cycle of each instruction, ready for the next fetch–execute cycle to begin. This is very streamlined and efficient, but incapable of coping with very complex instructions. For this reason programs are longer, requiring more instructions to carry out the actions required. This does not generally inconvenience the HLL programmer because it is the compiler that deals with the machine level instructions.

The alternative decoding strategy, outlined in Fig. 4.21, is known as microcoding, and is employed by CISC CPUs. It employs a fast 'inner processor', or nanocomputer, to carry out the machine level instructions. A very simple example of this method was given in Fig. 4.18, where the 3 bit washing machine code selected the next control word from a control store. As with the hard-wired method, the fetch–execute cycle is subdivided into several machine cycles. Each achieves part of the action, principally by accessing a large array of control words in the fast microcode store. The microcode words are wide, often 64–128 bits, and split into fields containing signal control bits and an address indicator. This latter directs the next access to microcode store. Thus we can implement looping and subroutine calls within the microcode. This can get

Fig. 4.21
Microcoded (CISC)
control unit.

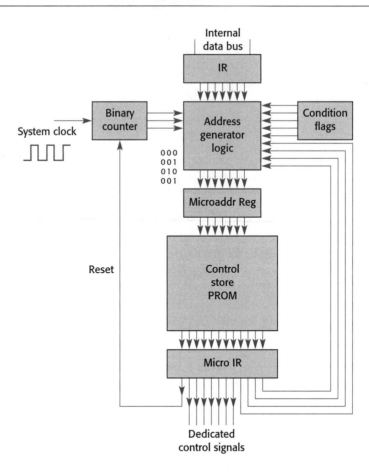

very tricky! Once again, variable length instructions are handled by resetting the machine cycle counter to zero for the start of the next instruction cycle.

Remember, it all comes down to sending a signal down the right wire at the right time to make something happen. During each micro-cycle a particular preset pattern of control signals is sent out to implement the micro-instruction.

In microcoded architecture these patterns of control signals are stored in the fast access memory known as the 'control store' or 'microcode memory'. This memory is short but fat: often 64 bits wide by 4 kbit long. Writing microcode for computers is difficult and a time-consuming nightmare (see Kidder, 1981). Few development aids are available and no generally accepted standards have yet emerged.

The Motorola 68000 16/32 bit microprocessor was microcoded, and IBM was able to exploit this by commissioning a new draft of the microcode to execute the IBM 370 instruction set for an advanced workstation. The PDP LSI-11 was also re-microcoded to directly execute Pascal P-codes. The interpreted language Forth had, for a very brief interlude, a bespoke microcoded CPU, the RTX2000. There is a microcoded AMD29000 in many PostScript laser printers. We await the high-speed Java interpreter in microcode from Sun Microsystems!

Some computers have RAM control stores which are accessible to users in order to allow dynamic alteration of the instruction set. This is a *dangerous* activity for normal humans. Using this facility we can make an IBM minicomputer execute Sun SPARC programs, without recompiling the code!

Review

- Digital logic is used to construct computers. Their modular construction and clearly defined interconnection rules assist engineers when designing complex circuits.

- The early logic units (referred to as TTL) have been replaced by highly integrated, complex circuits (VLSI) containing millions of switching transistors.

- The basic logic gates are: AND, OR and NOT, but XOR is useful for many applications, and a few NAND gates can be used to synthesize the basic functions.

- Truth tables can clearly express logic circuit functionality by displaying input–output relationships.

- Alternatively, signal timing displays are used on monitoring equipment and logic simulator software to show the relationships between circuit input and output.

- There are now logic devices which offer in-circuit reconfigurability: a boon for prototyping and even bug fixing!

- Decoder circuits, as exemplified by traffic light controllers, use an input binary number to select an output line, or several lines.

- Logic circuits can be implemented directly from truth table information. Some short cuts can be used to speed up the process. Logic minimization may not be the priority when building circuits.

- Decoders are widely used within the CPU Control Unit. The Control Unit reads a single binary instruction from the memory and uses decoders to activate the appropriate control lines in a timed sequence to carry out the required action.

- An alternative to hardware logic decoding (RISC) involves the use of a fast store in the CPU to hold the patterns of control line activities (CISC).

Practical work

The recommended practical work involves investigating digital logic circuits related to the control unit, the principal example being a decoder. The work can be done using breadboards or computer simulator programs, but an experience of both modes would be ideal.

To start the practical it is necessary to get the hang of drawing up truth tables and then using such tables to design a logic circuit. The use of elementary gates to produce the XOR element and the practical verification of de Morgan's Theorem (see Chapter 5) can also be carried out at this stage.

Exercises

01. Devise a circuit, using simple gates, for a security lock. It has 10 input switches, and so requires the user to remember a 10 bit number. To store the 'password' there are a further 10 switches inside the secure cabinet.

02. Write the truth table for a 2 → 4 line decoder. Then, using only simple gates, design the logic circuit.

03. What is a data demultiplexer? Draw up a truth table and then devise a logic circuit for a four-line demultiplexer.

10. How many keys are there on a PC keyboard? What type of circuit might be used to detect and communicate a keypress to the CPU?

11. If you are interested in digital logic, read about Karnaugh map methods and compare them with truth tables. Is there any advantage to Karnaugh maps?

12. How could a 256 bit ROM memory be used to test a byte for parity value?

13. Which has microcode, RISC or CISC?

20. If A = 1, B = 0, C = 1, what value will the following C statement deliver:

    ((Ā || B̄) && (A || B) && C

21. The C language does not have a logical XOR operator; i.e. the XOR equivalent of && and | |, which would be ^^, does not exist. How would you express IF (A XOR B) in the C programming language?

22. Why do some integrated circuit packs get hot while others remain cool, even while working well? How many watts does a Pentium dissipate?

23. Would you expect a C program compiled for a RISC CPU to be longer or shorter when recompiled for a CISC CPU?

30. A decoder circuit has 32 outputs. How many inputs are there?

31. What role does the CPU Instruction Register play in the decoding of machine instructions?

32. The MC68000 has instruction codes which are 16 bits long. Are you surprised that there are only about 100 opcodes available?

33. An optical scanner uses a 4 × 5 array of light sensors. How could an EEPROM (acting as a decoder) be used to distinguish between the images of the numbers 0–9?

100. What is the C statement which can be seen as the equivalent of a hardware decoder?

Readings

- Thewlis and Foxon (1983): a really basic introduction to logic.

- Heuring and Jordan (1997), Section 3.2: a quick comparison of RISC and CISC architectures; Section 3.3: an introduction to microprogrammed CUs.

- Hennessy and Patterson (1998), Appendix B: digital logic.

- Tanenbaum (1999), Chapter 3: digital logic again.

- Texas Instruments (1984): *The TTL Data Book*, known as the Orange Bible.

- Altera, Xilinx or Lattice Web sites for those logic designers who need them:
  http://www.altera.com/html/mktg/isp.html

  http://www.xilinx.com/

  http://www.latticesemi.com/

- Digital Works is a very useful simulator program, available for you to use from:
  http://www.dworks.co.uk/home.htm

- The Web sites can be accessed via the Companion Web site for this book at:
  http://www.booksites.net/williams/

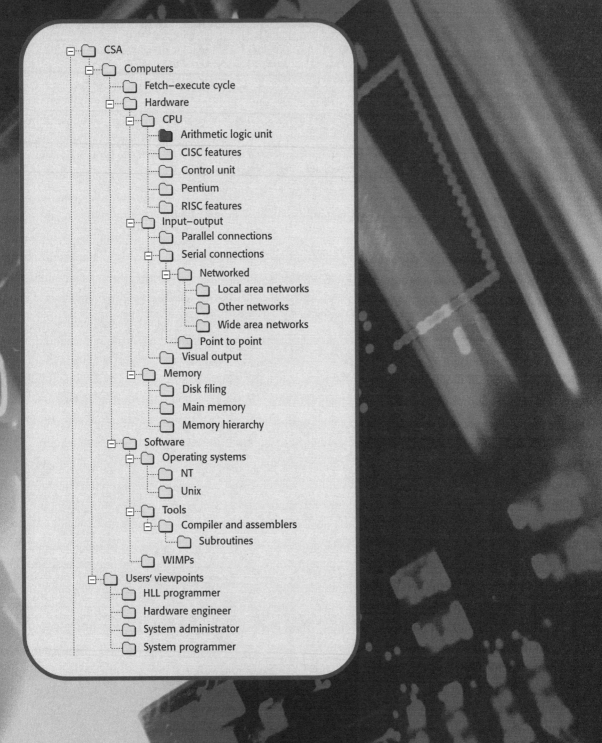

Building computers from logic: the ALU

5

Overview

The ALU part of the CPU is responsible for carrying out integer arithmetic and logical operations as requested by instructions from the program under execution. Adder circuits can handle both addition and subtraction if the numbers are represented in two's complement format. Integer multiplication is presented as repeated 'shift-and-add' operations. An introduction to the IEEE floating-point format shows the benefit to users of 'real' numbers.

5.1   De Morgan's equivalences – logical interchangeability

After drawing up truth tables and carefully selecting the correct combinations of AND, OR and NOT gates, it comes as quite a surprise to discover that it is possible to substitute AND for OR, and OR for AND. But this is precisely what **de Morgan's equivalence rules** allow us to do (Fig. 5.1). Because they appear so unlikely I suggest that you use a patch panel or logic box and try them out for yourself. Some ideas in science are just counter-intuitive!

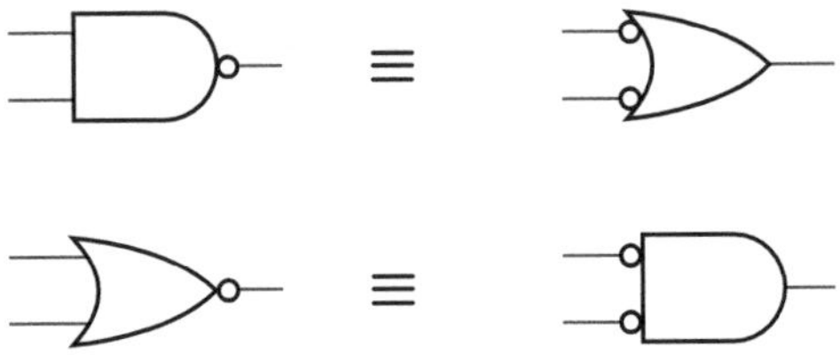

Fig. 5.1
De Morgan's equivalence relationships.

$$\overline{(X \text{ AND } Y)} \equiv (\overline{X} \text{ OR } \overline{Y})$$

$$\overline{(X \text{ OR } Y)} \equiv (\overline{X} \text{ AND } \overline{Y})$$

There is distinct relevance for programmers, too. Logical conditions in C code, such as:

```
while ( ! dog && ! cat )
{ plant_flowers( ) ;}
```

can be transformed to:

```
while (! (dog || cat ))
{ plant_flowers( ) ;}
```

which can make the loop exit condition clearer, at least for other people.

5.2   Binary addition – half adders, full adders, parallel adders

As already stated in Chapter 3, the **CPU** has two main components: the Control Unit (**CU**) and the Arithmetic and Logic Unit (**ALU**). The latter provides arithmetic and logical processing for the computer and can be understood in principle by studying adder circuits constructed from logic. A simple Parallel Adder, similar to that used in an ALU, can be constructed from relatively few basic logic gates. It serves as a useful example to help you appreciate the workings of a real ALU. Unfortunately, the actual circuits are obviously much more complicated, for a variety of reasons which are not important at this moment.

Fig. 5.2
Adder v.1.

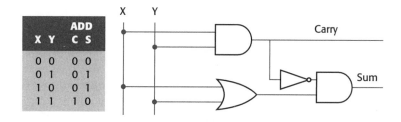

ADD			
X Y		**C S**	
0 0		0 0	
0 1		0 1	
1 0		0 1	
1 1		1 0	

Drawing up a truth table for 2 bit binary addition, as in Fig. 5.2, shows the need to provide two outputs: the Sum (S) and the Carry (C). Inspecting the Carry output may lead you to recognize the AND pattern. This follows the recommendation in Section 4.6, to look for standard logic patterns before adopting the brute force method. You may find it helpful to keep a crib set of AND, OR and XOR truth tables conveniently to hand when dealing with logic problems. In addition, the SUM output is nearly identical to the OR gate – only the double 1 row is incorrect. But by starting with an OR gate, this error can easily be eliminated by inserting a second AND gate on the output of the OR. This AND gate pulls the SUM output to 0 only when a double 1 appears, in the same way that the control line in the data flow control circuit (Fig. 4.4) operated. Thus we have used a couple of the tricks described earlier to design the logic for a one bit adder circuit. The truth table for an adder reminds us that there are two outputs – Sum and Carry.

There is frequently more than one way to implement a circuit. Another more common circuit for the adder is presented in Fig. 5.3. This is derived using the brute force method (Section 4.6). Take an output column and identify the rows contributing a 1. Write in an AND for each of these rows to detect the input pattern. Then lead all the AND outputs to an OR gate, whose output will give a column result.

An alternative circuit which uses different but fewer gates is given in Fig. 5.4.

If you are allowed to use the more complex XOR gate the adder is even simpler to build, as shown in Fig. 5.5.

The problem with all these otherwise excellent adder circuits becomes apparent when you consider the addition of multi-bit binary numbers. It also explains why they are often referred to as half adders.

Fig. 5.3
Adder v.2.

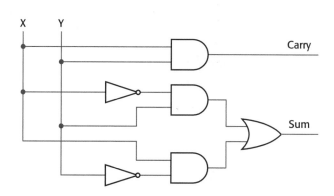

1011
<u>0111</u>+
1 0010

Notice that a 'carry 1' occurs when you add the two bits in the first column, which then needs to be added into the second column. It is clear that there is a need to cater for the carry-in value from the previous column. Thus we need an adder circuit with three inputs: a 3 bit full adder, not a 2 bit half adder. The full adder must deal with a carry-in from the previous stage, as well as its own two bits, and can best be assembled from two half adder units, as indicated in Fig. 5.6.

Fig. 5.4
Adder v.3.

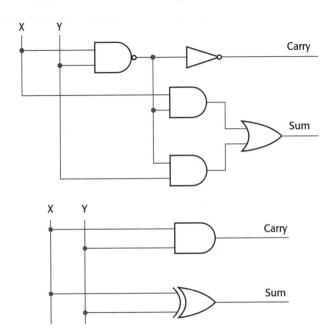

Fig. 5.5
Adder v.4, using an XOR gate for the Sum.

In Fig. 5.7 there are four full adders positioned next to each other in a row. They are each responsible for adding two bits from a 4 bit number. Note the **ripple-through** carry lines, taking the overflow bit across to the next stage. You may think that the right-hand stage could be trimmed back to a half adder to save some money, as there is no need for the C_{in} from nowhere, but this will soon be used to great advantage!

Fig. 5.6
Full adder.

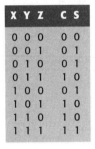

X Y Z	C S
0 0 0	0 0
0 0 1	0 1
0 1 0	0 1
0 1 1	1 0
1 0 0	0 1
1 0 1	1 0
1 1 0	1 0
1 1 1	1 1

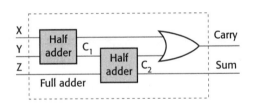

Fig. 5.7
Parallel addition for 4 bit numbers.

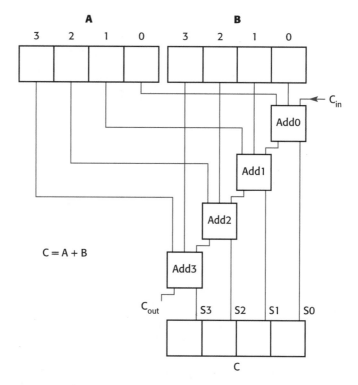

5.3 Binary subtraction – using two's complement integer format

Two's complement is a numerical convention which allows negative numbers to be stored in binary. An alternative is the sign and magnitude scheme, where each integer has one bit set aside to indicate positive (0) or negative (1). Although this latter method appears simple, the advantage of using two's complement to represent negative and positive integers is obvious to hardware engineers when building a circuit which can subtract as well as add numbers. Subtracting can be considered identical to addition if you switch the second number to its negative value. Thus you can use an adder to do subtraction. Conveniently, converting a two's complement binary integer to its negative value only involves inverting all the bits and adding a 1.

> Here is the problem: $8 - 7 = ?$
> Consider the binary equivalent: $1000 - 0111 = ?$
> Convert binary 7 into two's complement -7: $0111 \rightarrow 1000 + 1 \rightarrow 1001$
> Adding the two values: $1000 + 1001 = 0001$, the answer we expected.

Note that we are ignoring the carry-out overflow!

This manipulation needs to be tried out with paper and pencil if you are in doubt, but it means that the only alteration required to change our parallel adder (Fig. 5.7)

Fig. 5.8
Two's complement 4 bit
integers.

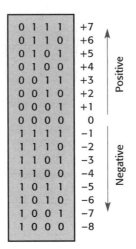

into a parallel subtractor is the insertion of inverters (NOT gates) on the inputs to the B port, and holding the primary carry-in (C_{in}) at logic 1. This is why we persisted in using the full adder for the LS stage.

Study the two's complement table in Fig. 5.8 for some time. The curiosity of one more number in the negative range than in the positive range may have escaped your initial glance. A sceptical approach may be in order, here. How do you know that 1100 represents –4? My favourite answer is to add it to +4 and hope for 0. Unfortunately, vigilant observers notice the overflow carry bit that is generated by that addition, which we seem to ignore. Practical applications of mathematics can be like that!

Now, if we also want to continue using the ALU for addition then the insertion of the invertors will have to be temporary. The schematic circuit in Fig. 5.9 achieves this by using XOR gates as **switchable invertors**. Check their truth table to make sure you understand this application of XOR gates. Computers need adder units for other functions besides arithmetic operations on numeric data. The IP register has to be

Fig. 5.9
Schematic ALU with
control lines.

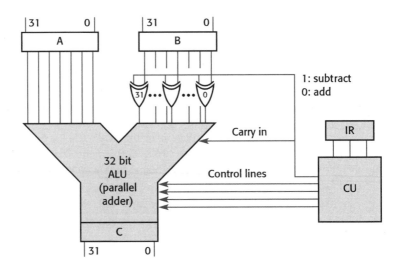

incremented by 1, 2 or 4 after each instruction cycle, as explained in Section 3.2, and there is a frequent need to build addresses from the values held in base and index registers.

Modern CPUs are supplied with several ALUs for integer, floating-point and address arithmetic. The integer ALU is designed to carry out all the usual arithmetic operations on positive and negative binary integers. These include ADD, SUB, MUL, DIV, CMP, AND and OR, as well as some more specialized operations such as shifting sideways and bit testing. Close by is a small block of fast memory called the CPU **registers**. These hold frequently used system variables or some program variables currently being processed. This ALU is only concerned with integer arithmetic, logical operations and bit manipulations. If the CU fetches and decodes an arithmetic instruction it will trigger the required action in the ALU through control lines.

The ALU, containing a more advanced version of our parallel adder circuit, is often represented as a big Y. The two numbers to be added (or whatever) enter at the top and the result emerges at the bottom.

5.4 Binary shifting – barrel shifter

The ALU often has to shift sideways a binary number or bit pattern as a contribution towards a more complex operation. In the next section we shall see how multiplication can be carried out by repeatedly adding and shifting a number. Because programmers sometimes need to request bit shifts explicitly, the C language offers the << and >> operators to carry out left and right movements. These two operators invoke the machine shift instructions, which can handle 8, 16 or 32 bit values. Although a left shift can also be carried out by simply adding a number to itself as often as is necessary, this is a slow technique. Subtraction does not achieve a shift in the reverse direction! Crosspoint switch units may be used to implement **barrel shifter** circuits as illustrated for a byte in Fig. 5.10. A crosspoint switch is a matrix of switches which are operated dynamically by control lines. They were originally intended for telephone routing (see Section 16.1) but have other applications too. By connecting all the switches on a diagonal, the input binary pattern can be routed onto the output bus with the required amount of sideways displacement. Both shifts and rotates can be carried out.

The C << and >> operators use the shift instructions, such as SHL and SHR. These introduce zeros into bit positions which have been freed, whereas if a rotational operator is used, such as ROR or ROL, the bits pushed off the end are wrapped round and reinserted at the opposite end, as shown in Fig. 5.11. The ALU hardware has to be able to provide both wrap-around rotation and zero insertion shifting, as selected by the instruction decoder.

Fig. 5.10
Crosspoint matrix used
as a bit shifter.

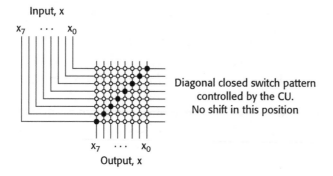

Diagonal closed switch pattern
controlled by the CU.
No shift in this position

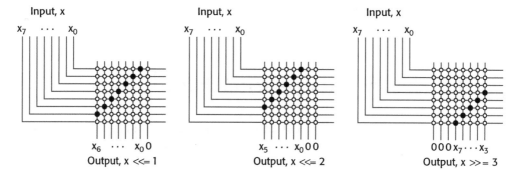

Fig. 5.11
Crosspoint matrix used
as a word rotator.

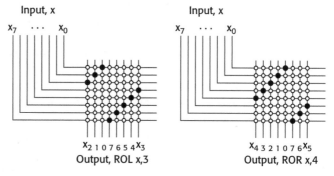

5.5   Integer multiplication – shifting and adding

The process of binary multiplication is the same as long multiplication in decimal:

```
  173                10101101
   57 ×              00111001 ×
 1211                00101101
 8650              00000000
 9861             00000000
                 00101101
                00101101
               00101101
              00000000
             00000000
              101000000101
```

This 8 bit multiplication, which delivers a 16 bit result, could be constructed from the parallel adder and the barrel shifter circuits. A software implementation of multiplication, making use of addition and shift operations only, is presented in Fig. 5.12.

Fortunately, the 'multiply, shift and add' method used in decimal long multiplication is simplified in binary arithmetic to: 'test, add and shift'. Although we find it easier to do all the adding at the end, the computer prefers to add up as it goes along. To understand the C multiply function in Fig. 5.12, you need to be able to recognize the addition operator: +, as well as the two sideways shift operators: << and >>. Note that these move the values a bit at a time, not a decimal digit at a time. So >>8 carries out a complete right byte shift. Using these operators, integer multiply can be coded as a test, add and shift loop. Taking only 8 bit numbers, so we can fit the description onto

Fig. 5.12
C function to multiply two integers.

```c
/* function to multiply two 16 bit positive integers
returning a 32 bit result, using only integer addition
and shift operators */

int multiply(int a, int c)
{
    int i;
        c = c << 16;

        for (i=0; i<16; i++)
        {
          if (a & 1) { a += c };
          a = a >>1;
        }
        return a;
}
```

the page, the integer multiply function can be traced through step by step (Fig. 5.13). Looking at the two registers needed, we see the accumulator (A), which holds both result and multiplier, and the multiplicand (C), which computes $45 \times 57 = 2565$.

Now check that 2565 really is 0000 1010 0000 0101! The conversion of 2565 to binary is described in Section 2.8.

You may have noticed the surreptitious introduction of CPU **registers** in this description of arithmetic operations. In Section 5.3 the registers A, B and C were used while explaining the operation of the ALU in its operation as an adder and as a subtractor. Most CPUs have more than three data registers, although the Pentium could be said to have only four. The ALU illustrated in Fig. 5.14 has a further eight data registers which are positioned in close proximity to the ALU so that they can offer fast support in supplying operands during arithmetic or logical operations.

The commercially available component ALU 74xx181, outlined in Fig. 5.15, is somewhat dated in technological terms, but serves as a useful example of a real device. It clearly shows the eight lines where the two input numbers, A and B, are entered, along with the carry-in bit from the previous stage, necessary if the devices are cascaded to deal with numbers larger than 4 bits. The result emerges on F (F for function) and C_{out}. The condition A == B is also signalled on an output line, which is a useful feature. Note that there are five control lines which select one of the 48 operations that it can execute. It may worry you that $2^5 = 32$, which is smaller than 48, and so could not possibly select one from 48. But note that the carry-in line is treated as another control line in this reckoning. Imagine the CU dispatching the 1001/0 bit pattern along these control lines to select an ADD operation, or 1011/1 for a logical AND operation. Although computer engineers may no longer be soldering 74xx181 chips into their latest computer boards, they will be selecting an equivalent VHDL module, of the same functionality, from the specification library, and installing it as a cell within their VLSI implementations.

5.6   Floating-point numbers – from very, very large to very, very small

Up until now we have assumed that all binary numbers represent integers: values with no fractional part and no digits after the decimal point. This, however, would not be popular with programmers, because it would make their job much more difficult. For example, storing very small numbers, such as the rest mass of an electron: 9.1×10^{-31} kg, or equivalently: 0.000 000 000 000 000 000 000 000 000 000 91 kg, is not possible in a standard integer format! Similarly, very large values, like the age of the Universe, present a difficulty to programmers. You can see that these numbers mostly consist of zeros, with only a few digits at one end or the other. The floating-point format for representing numbers exploits this by counting the number of zeros and storing that as the 'exponent', while keeping the significant digits separately as the 'mantissa'.

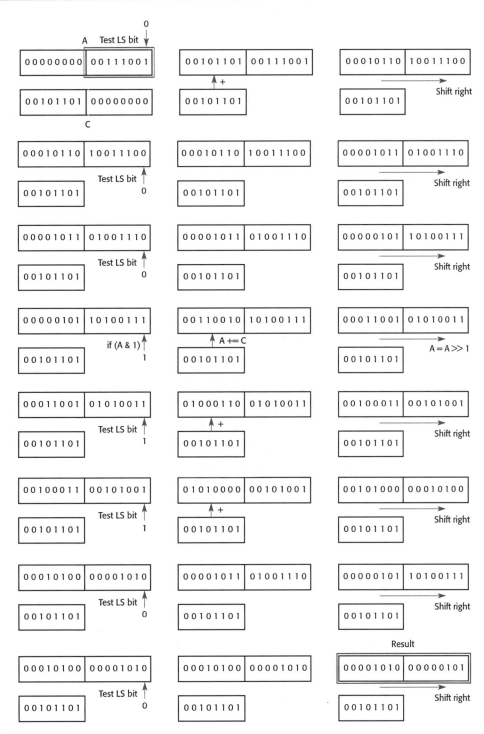

Fig. 5.13
Multiplication of 8 bit
numbers.

Fig. 5.14
Schematic ALU and CU
with CPU data registers.

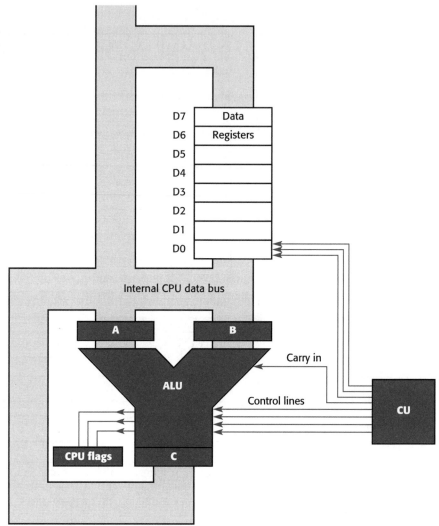

Floating-point arithmetic can be carried out by software routines which rely on the integer machine instructions and use the integer ALU. But now, more commonly, special-purpose hardware is provided to carry out floating-point arithmetic. This is known, predictably, as the **FPU** (Floating-Point Unit). While the Intel 80486 and MC68030 still had separate FPUs, fabricated on the same chip as the CPU, the Pentium has all these arithmetic operations fully integrated into the main CPU, but served by a dedicated ALU.

Originally the IBM PC had a socket provided for an optional floating-point unit, the Intel 8087, which later became incorporated onto the CPU chip. The common format for floating-point numbers is now the **IEEE 754**, for 32, 64 and 128 bit munbers. Interestingly, it took the mass production by Intel of the 8087 chip to enforce a single industry-wide standard for floating-point numbers and arithmetic.

Fig. 5.15
Control codes for the
74xx181 ALU.

S3–S0	M = 1 Logic	M = 0 Arithmetic	
		$C_{in} = 0$	$C_{in} = 1$
0000	$F = \bar{A}$	$F = A$	$F = A + 1$
0001	$F = \overline{A \text{ OR } B}$	$F = A \text{ OR } B$	$F = (A \text{ OR } B) + 1$
0010	$F = \bar{A} \text{ AND } B$	$F = \bar{B} \text{ OR } A$	$F = (A \text{ OR } \bar{B}) + 1$
0011	$F = 0$	$F = -1$	$F = 0$
0100	$F = \overline{A \text{ AND } B}$	$F = A + (\bar{B} \text{ AND } A)$	$F = A + (\bar{B} \text{ AND } A) + 1$
0101	$F = \bar{B}$	$F = (A \text{ OR } B) + (\bar{B} \text{ AND } A)$	$F = (A \text{ OR } B) + (\bar{B} \text{ AND } A) + 1$
0110	$F = A \text{ XOR } B$	$F = A - B - 1$	$F = A - B$
0111	$F = \bar{B} \text{ AND } A$	$F = \bar{B} \text{ AND } A - 1$	$F = (\bar{B} + A)$
1000	$F = \bar{A} \text{ OR } B$	$F = A + (B \text{ AND } B)$	$F = A + (A \text{ AND } B) + 1$
1001	$F = \overline{A \text{ XOR } B}$	$F = A + B$	$F = A + B + 1$
1010	$F = B$	$F = (\bar{B} \text{ OR } A) + (A \text{ AND } B)$	$F = (\bar{B} \text{ OR } A) + (A \text{ AND } B) + 1$
1011	$F = A \text{ AND } B$	$F = (A \text{ AND } B) - 1$	$F = (A \text{ AND } B)$
1100	$F = 1$	$F = A \ll 1$	$F = (A \ll 1) + 1$
1101	$F = \bar{B} \text{ OR } A$	$F = (A \text{ OR } B) + A$	$F = (A \text{ OR } B) + A + 1$
1110	$F = A \text{ OR } B$	$F = A + (\bar{B} \text{ OR } A) + A$	$F = (\bar{B} \text{ OR } A) + A + 1$
1111	$F = A$	$F = A - 1$	$F = A$

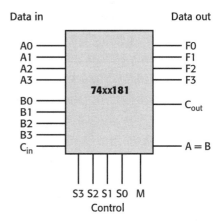

Up until that moment, every computer manufacturer seemed to take pride in introducing a new scheme for each new processor.

Although 32 bit integer arithmetic is the main activity of the ALU and central to the operation of the computer, application programmers frequently need to use so-called 'real numbers', with fractional parts, instead of integers. These floating-point numbers are stored in three parts which signify whether the number is positive or negative, the position of the decimal point, and the digits themselves. In C code the use of floating-point numbers can be recognized in the fragment contained in Fig. 5.16.

Before presenting details of floating-point arithmetic, it helps to review the storage method used by most software and hardware. This involves converting the more common format into scientific, or exponential form. In decimal this would be as shown in Fig. 5.17.

Fig. 5.16
Using floating-point
numbers in C programs.

```c
float net_cost, tot_cost, price;
float vat = 0.175;
int items;
    net_cost = price * items;
    tot_cost = net_cost + net_cost * vat;
```

Fig. 5.17
IEEE 754 floating-point
format.

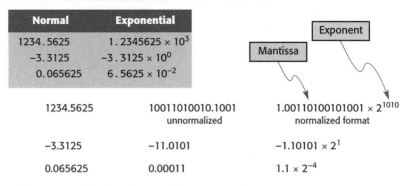

Normal	Exponential
1234.5625	1.2345625×10^3
−3.3125	$−3.3125 \times 10^0$
0.065625	6.5625×10^{-2}

Mantissa   Exponent

1234.5625	10011010010.1001	$1.00110100101001 \times 2^{1010}$
	unnormalized	normalized format
−3.3125	−11.0101	$−1.10101 \times 2^1$
0.065625	0.00011	1.1×2^{-4}

Floating-point numbers, in IEEE 754 32 bit format, appear in memory as:

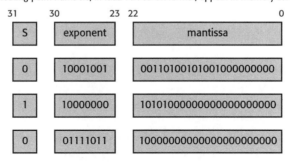

```
31   30        23 22                    0

 S    exponent        mantissa

 0   10001001   00110100101001000000000

 1   10000000   10101000000000000000000

 0   01111011   10000000000000000000000
```

Floating-point numbers are 'normalized' to a standard layout, or format, so that any routine or hardware knows what to expect (see Fig. 5.17). Normalization involves shifting the binary point sideways through the number, adjusting the exponent to maintain the correct value, until only a solitary leading 1 remains. The sign bit, out in front, clearly indicates whether the number is positive or negative; then the exponent field is followed by the mantissa. The exponent needs to span positive and negative values if the floating-point number is to be capable of representing very small, 2^{-127}, and very large, 2^{+127}, values. Two's complement would be a suitable scheme for expressing negative exponent values; however, an alternative 127 offset was adopted by the IEEE instead. This works by adding 127 to the true exponent value before storing it in memory. Thus, an exponent of 0 appears in memory as 127, and an exponent of –127 appears as 0. As 2^{-127} is really very, very small, quite nearly zero in fact, there is some attraction in identifying it as a number with an exponent field of 00000000 and a mantissa of 1.00000000000000000000000. However, when it comes to arithmetic operations the tidy normalized forms may have to be unpicked.

Manually converting a decimal float into a IEEE binary float is tedious but not difficult:

1. Convert the integer part into binary.

2. Convert the fractional part into binary, noting the 1/2, 1/4, 1/8, 1/16 pattern!

    ... 128 64 32 16 8 4 2 1 · 0.5 0.25 0.125 0.0625 0.03125 ...

3. Normalize by moving the binary point to produce the format 1.something with a positive or negative shift number.

4. Delete the leading 1, and extend the left bits with 0s to give a 23 bit mantissa.

5. Add 127 to the shift number to give the 8 bit exponent.

You can write a program to carry out the conversion and store the result in a file for later inspection. The C program in Fig. 5.18 writes the floating-point number 231.125 into a file called float_data, where you can view it using a file dump utility. This is shown in Fig. 5.19, where the Unix od command (octal dump) provides the information. In fact, od is much more useful than the name suggests, but the ancient origins of Unix do sometimes scare modern users! The byte-oriented microprocessor revolution pushed 3 bit octal into history. Check the Unix manual page (man od), which will describe how to get od to display the contents of a file in many formats including ASCII, integer, raw hex and scientific exponential.

Fig. 5.18
Program to store floating-point numbers in a file.

```
/* floatit.c - to write a real number into a file for
   viewing */

#include <stdio.h>

int main ( )
{
        FILE *fp;
        float f = 231.125;
          if (fp = fopen ("float_data", "w"))
          {
              fwrite(&f, 4, 1, fp);
          };
          return 0;
}
```

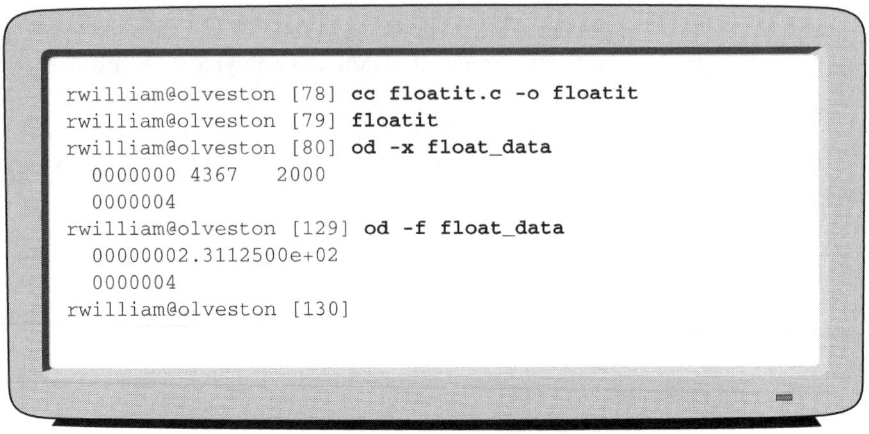

Fig. 5.19
Using the Unix od
(octal dump) utility to
inspect a data file.

```
rwilliam@olveston [78] cc floatit.c -o floatit
rwilliam@olveston [79] floatit
rwilliam@olveston [80] od -x float_data
  0000000 4367    2000
  0000004
rwilliam@olveston [129] od -f float_data
  00000002.3112500e+02
  0000004
rwilliam@olveston [130]
```

Table 5.1
Range and precision of
floating-point formats.

Range		Precision	
32 bit	8 bit	24 bit	$(1 \text{ in } 16 \times 10^6)$
64 bit	11 bit	53 bit	$(1 \text{ in } 8 \times 10^{15})$
128 bit	15 bit	64 bit	$(1 \text{ in } 16 \times 10^{18})$

The hex value 43 67 20 00 is the 32 bit floating-point number:

0 100 0011 0110 0111 0010 0000 0000 0000

sign   8 bit   23 bits of the 24 bit
bit   exponent   mantissa
        in 127
        offset
        format

The range and precision of the various floating-point formats are shown in Table 5.1.

You may have noticed that the mantissa field is 23 bits, but we have claimed 24 bit precision. Perhaps surprisingly, to save a single bit of storage, the leading mantissa 1 is suppressed and not explicitly stored. This anachronistic parsimony is only possible because floats are always normalized before storage, so that the mantissa always has a leading 1.

Review

- The ALU is part of the CPU which carries out the arithmetic and logical operations.
- Digital circuits can be redrafted to employ either AND or OR logic according to de Morgan's equivalence rules.

- The CPU can be further separated into two parts: the Arithmetic Logic Unit (ALU) and the Control Unit (CU).

- The simplest half adder circuit cannot handle the carry-in bit, so the full adder must be used when constructing parallel adders.

- Expressing negative numbers in two's complement form allows the use of adder circuits to perform subtraction.

- The ALU contains a sophisticated parallel adder. The Control Unit determines its operation after decoding the current instruction.

- Other operations which the ALU can carry out, such as shifting words sideways, assist with multiplication and division.

- The Pentium has a separate Floating-Point Unit to carry out arithmetic operations on real numbers (numbers with fractional parts).

- The IEEE 754 normalized format is used when storing floating-point numbers in memory.

Practical work

The recommended practical work continues the investigation of digital logic, but now switches to circuits related to the ALU. The principal example is an adder. Again, the work can be done using breadboards or computer simulator programs, but experience of both modes would be ideal.

The truth tables for half adders and full adders should be written down, and the circuits designed before attempting to construct them.

If several working units are available, a parallel adder can be assembled. This can be used to demonstrate subtraction using two's complement arithmetic.

Exercises

1. Reconcile the logic symbols used in this book (AND, OR, NOT) with those used on your maths course and in the C programming language.

2. Using simple AND, OR and NOT gates, design the logic for an exclusive-OR (XOR) gate. Remember to start by drawing up the truth table.

3. Use one 7400 (quad, dual input NAND gate pack) to build an XOR.

4. Does it matter whether you place an inverter before or after a gate? In other words: is 'NOT AND' the same as 'AND NOT'?

5. What are the disadvantages to the parallel adder circuit in Section 5.2?

6. Electronic car locks use 32 bit codes. If a trial takes 3 seconds, how long would an electronic 'black box' take to find the correct code by systematic search?

7. Devise a hardware logic circuit for a burglar alarm which takes four inputs from sensor switches and turns on the alarm if more than three are activated.

8. What is Texas Instruments famous for, besides Speak 'n' Spell?

9. What is the bit rate of a telephone call?

10. How long are the following C types: `char`, `long`, `int`, `float`, `double`, `unsigned char`?

11. Convert the 8 bit integer multiplication function in Fig. 5.13 to do integer division.

12. What is 'two's complement'? Write out a table for 5 bit two's complement numbers. Express the following numbers in 8 bit two's complement: 0, 1, −1, 127, −128, 15, −23.

13. Extend the diagram of the 4 bit parallel adder in Fig. 5.6 to 8 bit numbers, including the capacity to subtract B from A.

14. In the language C, what is the difference between an `int` and an `unsigned int`? When does this distinction become important?

15. Using the program `floatit.c` and the file dump tool `od`, described in Section 5.6, check your conversion of −123.625 into IEEE 754 32 bit floating-point format. Now try 0.00123625 and −0.0123625!

Readings

- Thewlis and Foxon (1983). This is a really basic, non-frightening introduction to logic.

- Texas Instruments (1984): *The TTL Data Book*, known as the Orange Bible.

- Heuring and Jordan (1997), Chapter 6: more advanced details on arithmetical circuits.

- Hennessy and Patterson (1998), Chapter 4: more theoretical treatment of computer arithmetic.

- Hamacher *et al.* (1996): rather a lot of hardware detail here.

- For more information about the hardware specification language VHDL, try: `http://www.doulos.co.uk/`

- The Web sites can be accessed via the Companion Web site for this book at: `http://www.booksites.net/williams/`

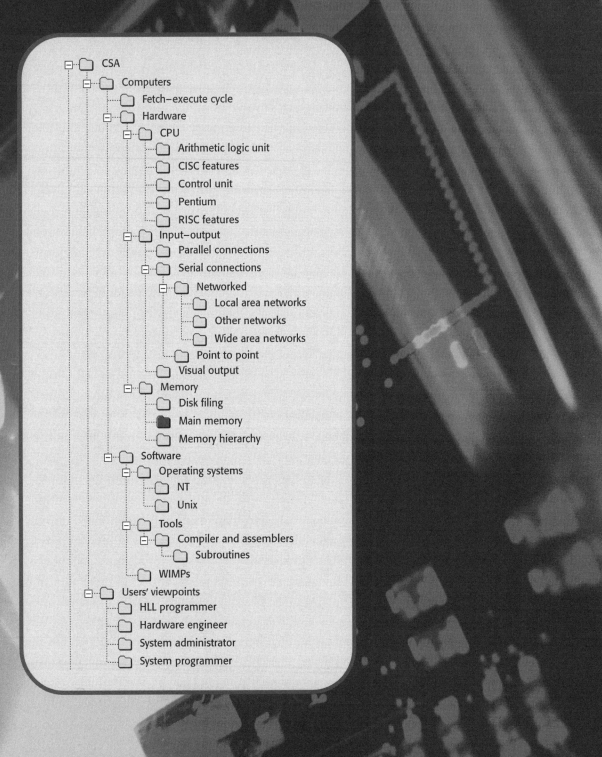

- CSA
  - Computers
    - Fetch–execute cycle
    - Hardware
      - CPU
        - Arithmetic logic unit
        - CISC features
        - Control unit
        - Pentium
        - RISC features
      - Input–output
        - Parallel connections
        - Serial connections
          - Networked
            - Local area networks
            - Other networks
            - Wide area networks
          - Point to point
        - Visual output
      - Memory
        - Disk filing
        - Main memory
        - Memory hierarchy
    - Software
      - Operating systems
        - NT
        - Unix
      - Tools
        - Compiler and assemblers
          - Subroutines
      - WIMPs
  - Users' viewpoints
    - HLL programmer
    - Hardware engineer
    - System administrator
    - System programmer

Building computers from logic: the memory

6

Overview

Fast access memory, to store data and program instructions, is a basic unit of the digital computer. It is currently built from silicon circuits, but it has not always been so. Each bit has its own cell which may be constructed in several ways. We will deal with SRAM and DRAM cells. Modern PCs have to go to some lengths to organize the DRAM chips to provide a fast enough service to the CPU. With so many memory chips, care has to be taken that the correct ones are activated during a memory access cycle. To the programmer, IO ports appear in many respects to be just locations in memory.

6.1   Data storage – one bit at a time

A simple form of memory cell requires at least two gates. This is not strictly true, but the circuit in Fig. 6.1 demonstrates why a single-gate memory cell has overwhelming disadvantages.

This single AND gate memory will remember a 0 after the input has returned to 1. It exploits the AND gate characteristic of always responding to a 0 at either of the inputs by asserting a 0 at the output. It is acting as a '0 detector'. If we wrap the 0 output signal back to one of the inputs, it has the effect of maintaining the output at 0 even when the other input returns to 1. It is rather incestuous as circuits go. The 'through' delay of the signal is very short, of the order of 4 ns (nanoseconds). Unfortunately there is a serious disadvantage to this scheme: there is no provision, short of turning off the power, for retraining! It is a one-shot memory. A second gate could be used to break the feedback link, but a better circuit using two NOR gates is more commonly offered as the basic **latch** shown in Fig. 6.2.

In this circuit, the NOR gate is used because it is a '1 detector'. When either of the inputs presents a 1, the output changes to 0. As before, with the never-forget AND circuit, the plan is to present a 1, which will generate a 1 at an output, which then gets wrapped back to the other input, thus maintaining the status quo when the original input changes back to 0.

The latch, or flip-flop, is a logic circuit which can **remember**. It does this by using a feedback link which strengthens and then substitutes for the input signal. This is possible due to the NOR gate characteristic which responds with a 0 output when either or both of the inputs are 1. So you can withdraw the 1 on the S input without affecting the Q output because the R input has now become 1 through the

Fig. 6.1
One bit storage.

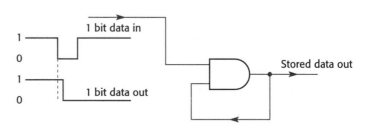

Fig. 6.2
Basic latch circuit.

Q_t	S_t	R_t	$\overline{Q}_{t+1}$	Q_{t+1}
0	0	0	1	0
0	0	1	1	0
0	1	0	0	1
0	1	1	illegal	
1	0	0	0	1
1	0	1	1	0
1	1	0	0	1
1	1	1	illegal	

Fig. 6.3
S-R latch signal timing.

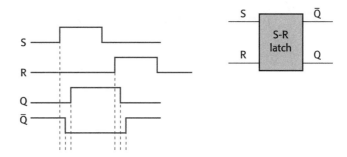

Fig. 6.4
Cat flap indicator.

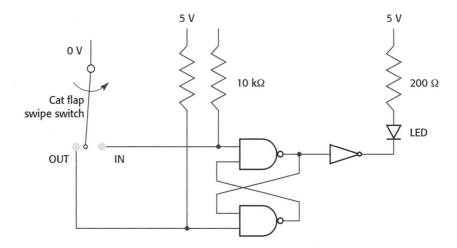

feedback link from the complementary output. The circuit works because there is a small delay time for the effect of input signals to pass right through the logic gates and alter the output status. Figure 6.3 presents the sequence of events as a timing plot.

As with all logic circuits, there are many alternatives and variants: R-S, J-K, D-type and T-type are all different flip-flop devices, each suited to a particular application. Latches respond to changes of the inputs at all times, while flip-flops are synchronized to a controlling clock pulse. But they all use cross-coupled gates, acting on each other through feedback links. As illustrated in Fig. 6.4, two NAND gates can also be connected to act as an R-S latch. This circuit can be used to make a cat-flap monitor which indicates whether your pet is safe at home or outside making trouble with the neighbours. Depending on the way you install the switches, the LED (light-emitting diode) will glow either when the cat is outside or when it is safe at home. Flap bounce could be a problem for the switches, requiring serious consideration, but the 10 kΩ 'pull-up' resistors make sure that the switch inputs are held at 5 V (logic 1) when the flap is not actually touching either of the IN or OUT contact points.

6.2   Memory devices – memory modules for computers

It is normal to explain that **RAM** stands for 'random access memory', and that **PROM** stands for 'programmable read only memory'. But these terms may not logically be used to distinguish between the functions of RAM and PROM because both devices are 'random access' memories. This then leaves RAM with no special characteristic. In fact, RAM should be known as **RWM** (Read–Write Memory) and PROM as **WORMM** (Write Once Read Many Memory).

There are different types of memory chips used for different applications, but all have random access capability. This means that access times are the same for all the stored items, irrespective of where the data is stored in the chip. Serial tape storage is very different because clearly the first blocks of data on the tape are quicker to read than the last blocks.

Table 6.1 lists some different types of memory that are used in computers, with an indication of their access speeds.

The EPROM illustrated in Fig. 6.5 shows the small quartz glass window, through which ultraviolet light can be shone to erase the memory before reprogramming it. This method of reprogramming, which requires that the memory chip be removed

Table 6.1
Types of memory.

RAM	50 ns	DRAM, Dynamic Random Access Memory – read and write, random access
	10 ns	SRAM, Static Random Access Memory
ROM		Read-Only Memory, factory written – random access
PROM		Programmable ROM – writable, but only once
EPROM	150 ns	UV erasable PROM, with a window in the package to admit the UV photons
EEPROM		Electrically Erasable PROM – useful for semi-permanent programming
FLASH		Similar to EEPROM – reprogrammable, non-volatile ROM

Fig. 6.5
Example memory packs.

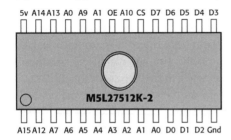

5v A14 A13 A0 A9 A1 OE A10 CS D7 D6 D5 D4 D3

M5L27512K-2

A15 A12 A7 A6 A5 A4 A3 A2 A1 A0 D0 D1 D2 Gnd

Mitsubishi, M5L27512K-2
64 kbyte EPROM
200 ns access time

3v D0 3v D1 0 D2 3v D3 0 3v WE CAS RAS CS B0 B1 A10 A0 A1 A2 A3 3v

MTC48LC8MA2-2

D7 0 D6 3v D5 0 D4 3v 0 DQ Clk Cke A11 A9 A8 A7 A6 A5 A4 0

Micron, MT48LC8MA2
8 Mbyte dynamic RAM
100 MHz operation

from the circuit, has now largely been replaced by in-circuit reprogrammable EEPROMs. These are erased by carefully imposing pulses at a higher voltage than would be operationally normal.

6.3   Static memory – a lot of fast flip-flops

SRAM (Static RAM) is constructed from thousands of flip-flop circuits. It is the fastest but most expensive of read–write memory used in computers, and is normally only selected for fast cache memory. There are SRAM circuits capable of responding to access requests within 10 ns, which makes them suitable for the fastest (LI) on-chip cache memory. Another advantage of SRAM is the low power consumption – making them ideal for battery-powered portable equipment and battery-backed CMOS RAMs. SRAMs are often made 'byte wide', meaning that each read–write access involves 8 bits of data. The layout of the package and pins frequently conforms to a JEDEC standard which ensures compatibility with EPROMs. Thus it is possible to unplug an SRAM and replace it with an EPROM, assuming it contains the correct program.

Curiously enough, in addition to acting as memory cells, flip-flops can also divide by two, as in Fig. 6.6. They can only demonstrate this remarkable achievement in a very particular situation. When a stream of pulses at a certain frequency is fed through a flip-flop, the output stream will be at half the frequency of the original. Although this is hardly exploitable for building ALU dividers, it is extremely useful when synthesizing the various system clock frequencies required in the CU and elsewhere around the computer. In Section 3.4 the important System Clock signal was introduced, while the circuit used to generate all the related lower frequencies depends on the flip-flop. There is also a circuit technique for synthesizing higher frequencies which is used by clock-multiplier Pentium CPUs. However, that method (Phase-Locked Loop) is way beyond the realm of this text.

Fig. 6.6
Using flip-flops as
frequency dividers.

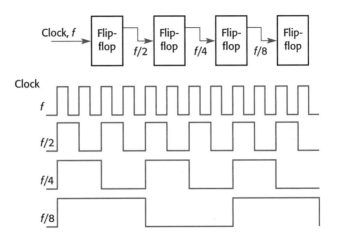

6.4   Dynamic memory – a touch of analogue amid the digital

DRAM (Dynamic Memory) employs a totally different approach to storing bits and only takes up 1/4 the area for the equivalent SRAM flip-flop storage. DRAMs exploit the tiny electrical capacitance of the gate connection to a **FET** (Field Effect Transistor). In Fig. 6.7, a single storage capacitor is arranged so that it can be selected using the Word line, and read (or rewritten) through the Bit line. Modern 64 Mbit DRAMs must work with capacitors of only around 20 fF (femtofarads – *femten* is Danish for 15); i.e. 20×10^{-15} farads. This is a magnificent achievement. A capacitor can hold electrical charge for a period of time, much like a bucket can store water. Unfortunately, in the case of DRAMS the bucket is leaky and needs to be refilled about 100 times a second! This is the same frequency as a fluorescent light tube. Another interesting problem involves random errors, which can be caused by nuclear particles, either resulting from cosmic rays or naturally occurring radioactivity. Statistical calculations suggest that a 64 Mbyte DIMM can expect such an error *probably* to occur once in 20 years of normal use. Despite these minor inconveniences the DRAM is an essential part of nearly all current computer systems because it is cheaper than the alternatives. DRAMs are rated by their storage capacity (1 Mbit–64 Mbit) and their **access** speed ranges from 150 ns to 50 ns. Memory access time is how long the chip takes to respond to a request to access one of its cells. We will discuss the **refresh** cycle in the next section. In most circumstances the larger the capacity the better, whereas in the case of access times, smaller values are considered better. PCs running with a 66 MHz system clock will require the faster acting devices which can respond within 60 ns. Another disadvantage of DRAMs is their need to 'rest' between read–write events. Although the access time of a DRAM may be 100 ns, it is not possible to read the device 10 million times a second. The minimum cycle time is likely to be greater than 160 ns, reducing the maximum access rate to 6 million times a second. The cycle time delay is caused by the need to pre-charge the bit lines to a constant voltage before the next read can take place. DRAM packages are offered in single bit and 4 bit widths, but more commonly you will buy DRAM already fitted into a SIMM or DIMM, providing

Fig. 6.7
A single DRAM memory cell.

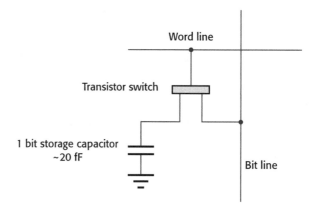

Fig. 6.8
A DRAM memory chip array.

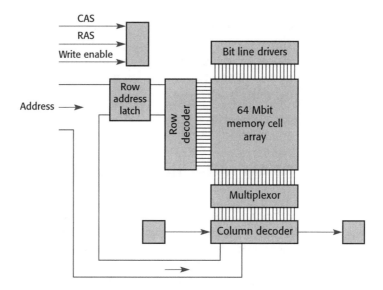

a 32 bit word read–write facility. The 64 bit Pentium data bus needs two SIMMs side by side to make up a 64 bit word.

Main memory is now built from arrays of DRAMs. The astonishing refinements achieved over the past two decades in the manufacture of these devices have meant that the size of the chips has shrunk, the price per megabyte has tumbled and the speed of access has steadily increased.

DRAM memory chips are organized as a two-dimensional array of capacitor memory cells (Fig. 6.8). The rows are made up of Word lines and the columns are the Bit lines. Thus the array provides random access to any of the cells. Row access is termed **RAS** and column access **CAS**. During a write cycle, a small charge of electricity, which represents a bit, can be routed along the Bit line and through the closed transistor switch, and will remain trapped on the capacitor when the switch reopens. A read cycle similarly involves selecting the correct row by activating a Word line and then reading the appropriate Bit line, which will give access to the required memory cell. It is normal to multiplex DRAM addresses, as shown in Fig. 6.9, by dividing the address into upper and lower parts: the row number and the column number. This reduces the size of the decoder circuits needed, and increases their speed. Such an arrangement is also necessary for the operation of burst access DRAMs, as explained in Section 6.6. To access a memory cell within the two-dimensional array, first the row

Fig. 6.9
DRAM address arrangement.

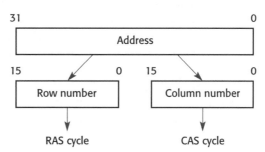

number is sent and written into the row latch by the RAS (Row Address Select) signal. Then the column number is sent along the same address bus to select the output from the correct column, CAS. The partitioning of the 32 bit address into two 16 bit numbers, one after the other on the multiplexed bus, is carried out by the DRAM controller.

6.5 DRAM refreshing – something else to do

Refreshing DRAMs takes time and requires extra circuitry to be included. This must include a hardware counter holding an address value which can be used when carrying out the special read–write refresh cycles. While the CPU is not accessing the memory itself, the refresh circuit executes a RAS cycle on the next row due, sending the upper portion of the address to the RAM. The rows are refreshed in order so that none are left out, resulting in data getting lost. The voltages on all the column bit lines are amplified and recycled back onto the storage capacitors. Thus a complete row of memory cells are refreshed at the same time. For a 64 Mbit DRAM this means a reduction from 64M to 64K operations every 10 ms.

Memory cards are designed with refresh circuitry included, increasing the hardware complexity and cost. The original IBM PC dedicated one of its four DMA channels simply to refreshing the DRAM, which now appears a wasteful use of resources. Newer PC memory systems do not rely on such a mechanism.

Interestingly, the Z80 CPU, found in SuperBrain and Sinclair computers, included DRAM refresh logic as part of the memory interface. This made it popular with systems designers, who were originally wary of the difficulties of building the DRAM refresh circuitry. The next generation of DRAM chips are being designed to auto-refresh without requiring external intervention.

6.6 Page access memories – EDO and SDRAM

Over recent years, there has been an increasing need to speed up memory access. CPUs have become faster, especially since the Intel 80486 and Pentium adopted on-chip clock doubling, tripling and quadrupling to speed up the CPU operations. So a clock tripling 200 MHz Pentium remains surrounded by memory and support chips driven by a 66.66 MHz system clock. This leaves the main memory running at the much slower external clock rate. Intel recognized this bottleneck and included 16 kbyte of fast SRAM cache on the chip, with the CPU. The Pentium II has been designed with the off-chip 256 kbyte secondary cache in close proximity to the CPU

Fig. 6.10
EDO DRAM timing
diagram.

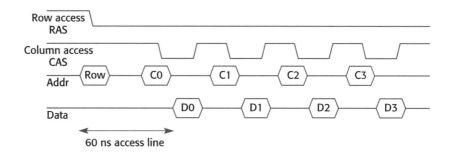

within a special cartridge pack. Motherboards are offering 100 MHz clock speeds, and the DRAM needs to run faster to keep up!

Besides the disadvantage of needing to be regularly refreshed, DRAM also has a recovery problem. After every access, the column, or bit, lines need time to recharge before the next cycle can take place. This delay is known as the **cycle time**. If it is possible to **interleave** accesses to the memory chips, this delay can be avoided. Imagine memory in two banks, with the odd memory addresses to the right and the even to the left. As the CPU steps up through memory fetching instructions it will be alternating left, right, left. In this way the chips will normally have two memory cycles to recover before another access is attempted.

Another technique, illustrated in Fig. 6.10, called page mode or **EDO** (Extended Data Output), carries out, in a burst, four access cycles on each read–write request. The first access of the sequence is normal, with the row address being latched in and the correct column selected, but then the next three columns are read in fast sequence, with only the column address changing. This reduces the cycle time by eliminating the RAS cycle from three of the accesses, so a four-word burst access can save 40% in time. In terms of bus clock periods, this four-phase burst takes 5–2–2–2, instead of 5–5–5–5. Perhaps it should be remarked that this gain in speed is possible only by sacrificing true random access capability: 75% of the data is accessed serially! Also, continuing the critical tone, it is never certain that the CPU will actually use the instructions or data contained in the following three locations. It may simply be ignored and then abandoned.

Further speed gains have been made with the current generation of Synchronous Burst DRAM, **SDRAM**s, where only the first location address is sent to the chip, which will then automatically cycle through the next locations using an on-chip CAS counter. This method of **bursting** allows the SDRAM to provide a 5–1–1–1 access performance, and even 3–1–1–1, in some devices. The major difference between EDO and SDRAM is the method of timing. EDO is controlled and timed by the RAS and CAS signal lines, while SDRAM follows the system clock in synchronous mode. To underline the distinction between asynchronous and synchronous operation, EDO performance is rated in terms of access response latency, while maximum clocking speed is given for SDRAMs. SDRAM also provides internal self-refresh facilities, and has selectable burst lengths, offering 1, 2, 4, 8 or even a full row of data for a single request. A faster generation of SDRAM chips will be capable of supporting burst rates of 1 Gbyte/s, allowing the motherboard to clock up to 200 MHz.

Bursting data to and from memory is thoroughly exploited when dealing with cache memory. We will cover this subject more fully in Chapter 17, but it is interesting to note that the Pentium cache is loaded in 32 byte bursts. This requires four bus cycles, each carrying 8 bytes, which fits well with the EDO DRAM sketched in Fig. 6.10. The challenge is to increase the access speed of DRAMs to match the current 100 MHz motherboards, without suffering cost or capacity penalties.

PC motherboards are now generally built to accept memory modules, illustrated in Fig. 6.11 and Table 6.2. These are small 100 mm × 20 mm cards with eight or nine DRAM chips. The ninth bit provides a parity error check on the other eight bits. According to the type of connector used the modules are called **SIMMs** (72 pin single in-line memory modules) or **DIMMs** (168 pin dual in-line memory modules). Memory modules can currently be bought in various sizes: 8 Mbyte, 16 Mbyte, 32 Mbyte, 64 Mbyte and 128 Mbyte DRAMS are currently available. For SDRAM DIMMS the burst access time is now 10 ns, matching the memory to the 100 MHz motherboard clock speed. It is worth noting the voltage rating – EDO SIMMs operated at 5 V, while the newer SDRAM DIMMs are made for 3.3 V.

Remember: $2^{20} = 1M$, so: $2^{22} = 4M$

Fig. 6.11
72 pin SIMM and 168 pin DIMM DRAM modules.

For my older PC, each of the 8 EDO DRAM chips on the 16 Mbyte SIMM stores four bits in its memory cells. As the SIMMs are mounted in pairs, this makes available 64 bits (16 × 4) in a single read–write operation. Their access time is rated at 60 ns, which suited the 66 MHz motherboard. As the Pentium 64 bit data bus can simultaneously transfer four instructions of 16 bit length, this means that instructions are available every 15 ns (60/4 = 15 ns). Furthermore, by using the access facilities of EDO DRAM, the three subsequent bus cycles can be enjoyed with only 30 ns delay between them giving, approximately, an instruction every 10 ns. Such estimates should be

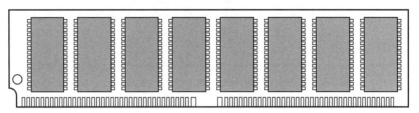

16 Mbyte, 50 ns access, 32 bit, 72 pin SIMM card

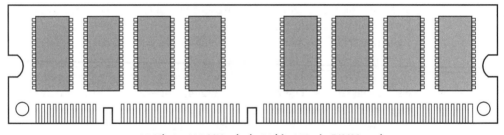

64 Mbyte, 100 MHz clock, 64 bit, 168 pin DIMM card

Table 6.2
Pin assignments for a
168 pin SDRAM DIMM.

1	Vss	43	Vss	85	Vss	127	Vss
2	DQO	44	NC	86	DQ32	128	CKEO
3	DQ1	45	C̄S̄2	87	DQ33	129	NC
4	D02	46	DQM2	88	DQ34	130	DQM6
5	DQ3	47	DQM3	89	DQ35	131	DQM7
6	Vcc	48	NC	90	Vcc	132	NC
7	DQ4	49	Vcc	91	DQ36	133	Vcc
8	DQ5	50	NC	92	DQ37	134	NC
9	DQ6	51	NC	93	DQ38	135	NC
10	DQ7	52	NC	94	DQ39	136	NC
11	DQ8	53	NC	95	DQ40	137	NC
12	Vss	54	Vss	96	Vss	138	Vss
13	DQ9	55	DQ16	97	DQ41	139	DQ48
14	DQ10	56	DQ17	98	DQ42	140	DQ49
15	DQ11	57	DQ18	99	DQ43	141	DQ50
16	D012	58	DQ19	100	DQ44	142	DQ51
17	DQ13	59	Vcc	101	DQ45	143	Vcc
18	VCC	60	DQ20	102	Vcc	144	DQ52
19	DQ14	61	NC	103	DQ46	145	NC
20	DQ15	62	NC	104	DQ47	146	NC
21	NC	63	NC	105	NC	147	NC
22	NC	64	Vss	106	NC	148	Vss
23	Vss	65	DQ21	107	VSS	149	DQ53
24	NC	66	DQ22	108	NC	150	D054
25	NC	67	D023	109	NC	151	DQ55
26	Vcc	68	Vss	110	VCC	152	Vss
27	W̄Ē	69	DQ24	111	C̄Ā̄S̄	153	DQ56
28	DQM0	70	DQ25	112	DQM4	154	DQ57
29	DQM1	71	DQ26	113	DQM5	155	DQ58
30	C̄S̄O	72	DQ27	114	NC	156	D059
31	NC	73	Vcc	115	R̄Ā̄S̄	157	Vcc
32	Vss	74	DQ28	116	VSS	158	DQ60
33	AO	75	DQ29	117	AI	159	DQ61
34	A2	76	DQ30	118	A3	160	DQ62
35	A4	77	DQ31	119	A5	161	DQ63
36	A6	78	Vss	120	A7	162	Vss
37	A8	79	CLK2	121	A9	163	CLK3
38	A10/AP	80	NC	122	BAO	164	NC
39	BA1	81	NC	123	All	165	SAO
40	Vcc	82	SDA	124	VCC	166	SA1
41	Vcc	83	SCL	125	CLK1	167	SA2
42	CLKO	84	Vcc	126	NC	168	Vcc

treated generously because other significant time delays are being ignored as they would take us further into the realms of electronic engineering.

A SIMM card is inserted into its socket at a 30° angle to the vertical, and then snapped upright into place. To remove it, the two metal clips have to be eased apart to allow the SIMM to fall forwards. DIMMs are more conventionally pushed vertically down into their sockets, but are ejected using the two end toggles.

6.7   Memory mapping – addressing and decoding

As explained in Section 3.6, the number of address lines coming out of the CPU determines the maximum length of memory which can be conveniently accessed: 20 lines for 1M memories, 32 lines for 4G memories. Although main memories (RAM) have grown cheaper with every new generation, the maximum memory addressing space is still rarely fully populated with chips. It would be too expensive for most users. The situation illustrated in Fig. 6.12 does not yet exist!

Extra decoder logic is needed to select the correct memory chip during a read or write cycle. When the CPU sends out an address, the low bits will be used inside the RAM to select the memory cell, but the upper address bits will be used by the system memory decoder logic to select the correct chip. If this is not done, all the RAM chips will simultaneously respond to all read–write requests from the CPU. It would be much as if when making a telephone call to 0117 987 654, the area code 0117 was ignored, and all the telephones in Britain with the number 987 654 were answered simultaneously.

Systems designers draw up **memory maps** to describe the location in address space of the chips that are to be installed. It is important to arrange the memory chips in an orderly fashion to avoid various problems when accessing the memory. If two chips respond simultaneously during a memory read cycle, the resulting value on the data bus will be invalid because it will be a mixture of the data coming from two different memory locations. This will create chaos for the CPU, which will probably crash. If

Fig. 6.12
Ideal configuration for a memory map.

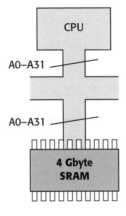

Device	Size	Pins	32 bit address bus	Address range
PROM1	1 Mbyte	20	0000 0000 xxxx ++++ ++++ ++++ ++++ ++++	0000 0000 – 000F FFFF
RAM1	16 Mbyte	24	0000 0001 ++++ ++++ ++++ ++++ ++++ ++++	0100 0000 – 01FF FFFF
RAM2	16 Mbyte	24	0000 0010 ++++ ++++ ++++ ++++ ++++ ++++	0200 0000 – 02FF FFFF
RAM3	16 Mbyte	24	0000 0011 ++++ ++++ ++++ ++++ ++++ ++++	0300 0000 – 03FF FFFF
RAM4	16 Mbyte	24	0000 0100 ++++ ++++ ++++ ++++ ++++ ++++	0400 0000 – 04FF FFFF

+ address line used directly for internal selection
x line ignored, indicates partial (degenerate) addressing
0 must be 0 for chip selection
1 must be 1 for chip selection

Fig. 6.13
Memory map for a
small computer
system.

the memory decoding is not thoroughly planned from the start, there may be 'holes' in the addressing space, requiring executable programs to be segmented. A quick disaster can occur if the CPU attempts a fetch–execute cycle at an empty location! An example memory map is given in Fig. 6.13, with the associated circuit schematic in Fig. 6.14.

An alternative layout for a PC memory map is given in Fig. 6.15, where the memory occupancy can be drawn to scale. This allows the small fraction of the potential 4 Gbyte used by the normal 64 Mbyte to be comprehended at a glance. It is quite a surprise the first time you realize the available memory space.

Building computers from simple logic gates is very difficult because of the vast number required. In order to satisfy hardware designers' needs for more and more logic gates, chip manufacturers now supply arrays of gates which designers can configure to suit their individual needs. These are called FGAs or PALs, and are widespread in consumer goods as well as high-performance computers. It is now possible to use the masks for the 68000 or 8086 and install a CPU in the corner of your own special chip. Thus the fundamental unit of design is rising far above the transistor or AND gate.

Memory chips come in several widths. DRAM chips are produced with cells 1, 4 or 8 bits wide, while SRAMs and EPROMs are normally 1 byte wide. As we have seen in Fig. 6.11, eight byte-wide DRAMs are stuck together to form a 64 bit DIMM to slot

Fig. 6.14
Memory schematic
showing the decoding
circuit.

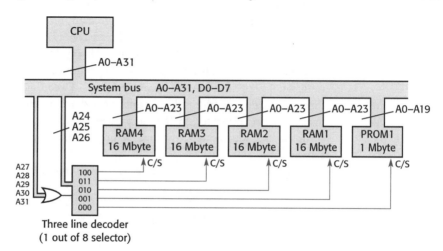

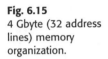

Fig. 6.15
4 Gbyte (32 address lines) memory organization.

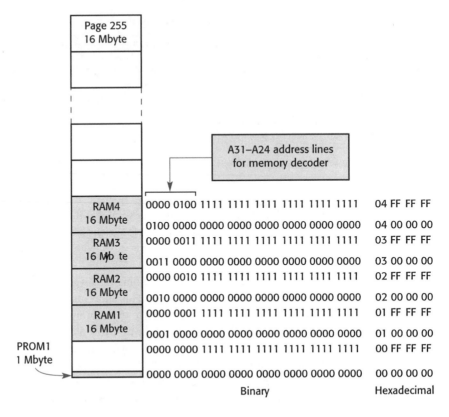

into the Pentium bus. For a simple computer system with a byte-wide data bus, each memory pack is connected to all eight data lines. This is not so with the control lines, where only the necessary few are connected. With regard to the address lines, starting with the lowest line, A0, only enough are connected to select one cell from the internal array. All packs also have a chip select (C/S) input which enables the chip and is frequently used to map the chips into their allocated address.

Memory chips, RAMs or ROMs, are not normally matched to the width of the address bus. This is not really feasible with so many different address widths on all the different computers. Hence memory chips have fewer address pins than the CPU address bus has lines: the CPU may send a 32 bit address, while the RAM packs can only directly receive 20 bit addresses. This requires some careful planning which results in the specification of a **Memory Address Decoding** circuit. This uses some of the remaining upper address lines, which are fed into a separate decoder. The decoder lines are then connected to the Chip Select (C/S) pins on the memory packs to complete the addressing. Any unused upper address lines can be left for future expansion.

It is quite common not to fully decode the address space. This results in multiple images of memory packs within the address space. This does not generally give any problems if everyone understands the situation and does not try to insert further devices in the 'occupied' locations.

Fig. 6.16
Memory layout for a
memory-mapped IO
scheme.

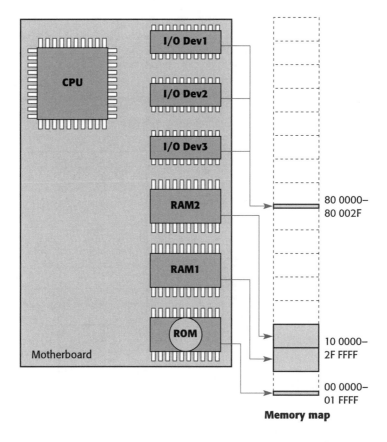

Memory map

Some computers have their IO ports inserted into the main memory map. Figure 6.16 illustrates this situation. It can lead to an inconvenient segmentation of the programmer's address space. The decoding circuitry can be much more complex and bus cycle timing becomes more critical because of the routine differences in access times between memory and port chips.

Drawing out the memory areas on a scaled chart does bring home very clearly the inefficient use of address space resulting from many decoding schemes!

6.8 IO port mapping – integration vs. differentiation

The memory maps so far discussed have included IO ports within the same addressing space as memory chips. This method is known as **memory-mapped IO**. Other computers, notably the Intel Pentium, split the addressing into two regions serving memory and IO separately, as indicated in Fig. 6.17. To implement this scheme, the CPU has to provide special instructions, e.g. IN and OUT, to transfer data between CPU and IO ports and different bus signals are required to implement the IO

Fig. 6.17
Memory and IO layout
for an IO-mapped
scheme.

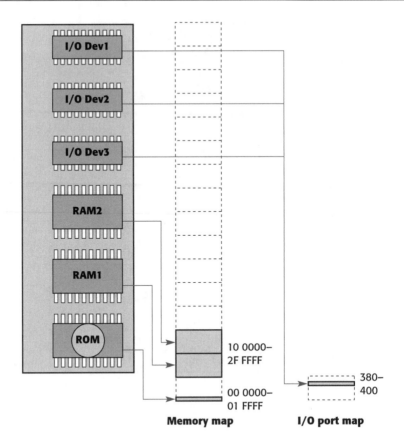

10 0000–
2F FFFF

00 0000–
01 FFFF

Memory map

380–
400

I/O port map

transfers. This is termed **IO mapping** because the ports are seen in a different address space to memory. With the Pentium, the memory space is much larger than the IO space, 4 Gbyte as compared to 64 kbyte, so the memory addresses are 32 bits long while the IO addresses are only 16 bits long. The two different schemes have advantages and disadvantages which need to be debated. Where IO ports and memory are kept separate, it is easier to maintain memory as a single contiguous block which programmers prefer. However, the range of IO instructions and compatible addressing modes is usually much less than the normal memory-oriented group, making programs slightly longer. Nevertheless, the implied advantage of using the wider range of memory-oriented instructions to handle IO operations should not be taken at face value. Many of the seemingly suitable machine instructions which set or clear individual bits within a memory byte, may not be usable on peripheral chip registers. This is because such registers are not infrequently 'write-only', making the use of read–operate–write instructions impossible. Such a limitation would apply to the following group of MC68000 instructions:

```
ori.b #bmask,OP_reg   ; logical OR a mask to set a port bit
andi.b #$f7,OP_reg    ; logical AND a mask to clear a port bit
asl.b (a5)            ; shift port bits left for display purposes
```

```
not.b OP_reg           ; shift port bits right for display purposes
bclr #1,OP_reg         ; test a port bit and leave it 0
bset #2, (a2)          ; test a port bit and leave it 1
```

All these instructions work by reading the data at the indicated location back into the CPU, modifying it as required, and then writing it back to the original memory location. With 'write-only' hardware registers this is not possible. Compilers will use such instructions when dealing with normal data variables, but unfortunately neither assemblers nor compilers are able to spot the difficulty when accessing memory-mapped peripheral chips and a nasty run-time bug may result.

It is not unusual for IO bus cycles to need to be longer than the equivalent memory cycles, perhaps due to the use of less modern fabrication technology for IO chips. Having different IO bus signals makes this easier for hardware engineers to implement. When the early 8 bit microprocessors first appeared, it was often said that programmers preferred Motorola and electronic engineers preferred Intel! Sometimes, low level debugging is easier on a differentiated system because breakpoints or error traps can be imposed more generally. Then any wayward access to an output port can be immediately noted and corrected if necessary. Finally, it will be apparent, after discussing the technical justifications for the change to RISC CPU architectures in Chapter 21, that any unnecessary, extra instructions further complicate the CU, and introduce overall performance penalties. Hence by mapping IO ports into the memory the execution of all the remaining instructions may be speeded up.

Review

- The simplest practicable 1 bit memory cell can be constructed from two cross-coupled NOR gates. This is known as an S-R latch. It is related to the circuit used to build SRAM, which is found in cache memories.

- A variety of technologies are used to manufacture memory packages with different characteristics: DRAM, SRAM, EPROM, Flash RAM and EEPROM. The main memory in current digital computers is made up of SDRAM (synchronous DRAM) chips.

- Dynamic RAM uses small integrated capacitors to store electrical charge to represent a binary 1. Unfortunately, the capacitors leak and have to be regularly refreshed.

- DRAM is usually obtained as modules (DIMMs) which plug into slots on the motherboard. The access time and cycle time need to be matched to the system clock speed. To improve overall memory access, data is now read and written in bursts rather than single bytes.

- Memory mapping is required when the total address space (defined by the address width) is not fully occupied. The unused upper address lines are then used to select the correct memory module.

- IO ports may be memory mapped or installed in a separate IO address space. Here they will require special instructions for access.

- Carrying out several things at the same time can increase throughput. This can be done by anticipating the need for instructions and pre-fetching them from memory.
- Maximum memory *length* is determined by the address *width*.
- When dealing with multi-byte data the ordering of the component bytes in memory needs to be ascertained.
- Simple input and output ports can appear to a program as single bytes of memory within the address space.

Practical work

The recommended practical work involves the understanding and design of new memory maps. This could lead on to the design of decoder circuitry for those with an interest in the electronics side of microcomputers.

Exercises

1. What is the difference between a CPU data register and a location in memory?
2. What happens during a write cycle if two RAM chips respond to the address?
3. What is the maximum size of the Pentium physical memory? What is the maximum size of the Pentium virtual memory?
4. How many address lines are needed to access a byte-wide 24 Mbyte memory?
5. How many lines are used to access a 200 Mbyte disk?
6. What is the minimum pin count for a 1 Mbit PROM pack?
7. Sketch a possible 2 Mbyte PROM card using such a chip.
8. The Atari cartridge port had two banks of ROM space supplied with address lines A0–A15. What was the maximum size for a plug-in games program?
9. My Sun UltraSPARC workstation has 64 Mbyte RAM. What is the minimum address bus width to serve this memory space? How many more pages of 64 Mbyte DRAM could the 64 bit SPARC CPU cope with?
10. How can the physical memory range of a processor be extended beyond the maximum set by the width of the program counter?
11. With DRAM, what is the relation between 'access time' and 'cycle time'? What technique is commonly used to avoid the 'cycle time' delay?
12. How much would it cost to fully populate the memory space for a CPU with a 32 bit address bus? (A 60 ns, 16 Mbyte SIMM currently costs about £20.00.)
13. State the advantages and disadvantages of using synchronous or asynchronous memory access cycles.
14. Why do DRAMs require refreshing, and how often? How is this done on a standard PC? Estimate how many electrons are stored on a single DRAM cell. ($Q = V \times C$; $q_e = 1.6 \times 10^{-19}$ coulombs; assume $V = 1.2$ volts.)

15. How many pages of size 64 Mbyte can you fit into a 32 bit address space?

16. A 64 Mbyte memory is divided into four 16 Mbyte pages. What address lines would be used to select the separate pages?

17. On a Pentium, how big is IO space as a fraction of the memory space? What are the advantages of a CPU offering a separate IO addressing space?

Readings

- Tanenbaum (1999), Section 3.3: introduction to memory components.

- Heuring and Jordan (1997), Section 7.2: RAM structure, SRAM and DRAM.

- Hennessy and Patterson (1998), Appendix B.5: memory elements.

- For more technical information about the manufacture of memory chips try:
  `http://www.micron.com/resources/semi_history.htm`

- Tom's Hardware Guide also has some useful practical details:
  `http://www7.tomshardware.com/guides/ram.html`

- The Web sites can be accessed via the Companion Web site for this book at:
  `http://www.booksites.net/williams/`

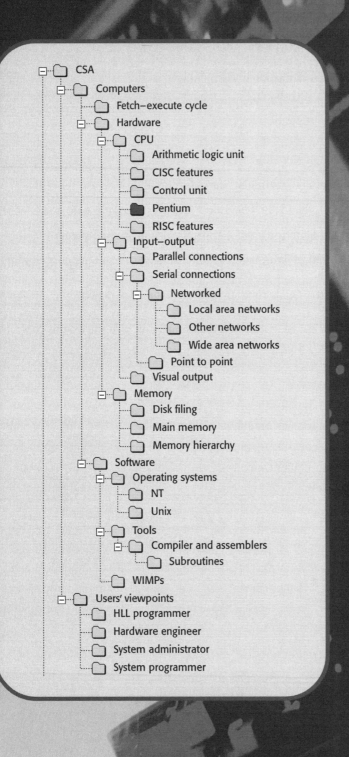

The Intel Pentium CPU

7

Overview

The Pentium microprocessor provides the processing power for most PC equipment. The programmer can benefit from understanding some aspects of the internal structure of the CPU. The CPU registers, basic instruction set, status flags and addressing modes are discussed, as they can all affect the efficiency of HLL programs. The necessary directions to write assembler routines using Microsoft Developer Studio are presented because programming at this low level is the best way to understand the operation of computer systems.

7.1   The Pentium – a high-performance microprocessor

It is preferable to introduce new subjects with simple examples, but in the case of microprocessors this is becoming increasingly difficult because they are being designed with more and more sophisticated circuits in a never-ending search for improved performance. Rather than use a simplified, 'idealized model' we will attempt to discuss the Pentium itself, despite the extra complexities involved, by dealing only with those aspects of most importance to programmers. Because it is used in all new PCs, with examples and variants manufactured by Intel, IDT, AMD and Cyrix, it has become by far the most commonly encountered processor. Indeed, Intel has run a high-profile advertising campaign for the latest Pentium processor on peak-time television! Historically, the **Pentium** is only the latest CPU in the Intel 80x86 family, which, in its register structure, still retains some similarity to the original Intel 8080 microprocessor from 1975. In this regard, it has been somewhat unfairly referred to as the very fastest 8 bit processor!

A large change that has occurred over the years has been the packaging and cooling of microprocessors. Whereas the 8080 was encapsulated in a 40 pin dual-in-line (DIL) plastic package, the Pentium chip is housed in a much larger, square pin grid array sprouting some 300 pins from the bottom (Fig. 7.1). It needs to dissipate around 12 watts of heat, which for a surface of only 25 cm^2 area puts it way ahead of my domestic radiators – 750 W/m^2 for the radiator, compared with 12 W/25 $\times$ 10^{-4} m^2 = 4.8 kW/ m^2 for the Pentium. To deal with this excess heat there has been a remarkable development of miniature cooling fans.

Throughout the decades since 1975, Intel has espoused a policy for its microprocessor products of binary backward compatibility. This means that existing programs should be able to run on new processors without any requirement to recompile the source code. Originally this facility had appeared somewhat irrelevant, because in the

Fig. 7.1
Socket 7 IDT 200 MHz
MMX Pentium, pin grid
array package.

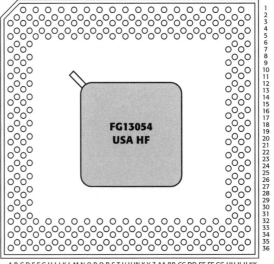

FG13054
USA HF

early days of microprocessor applications everybody wrote their own software. This meant that they retained control of the source code, enabling them to carry out recompilations for any new processor that emerged onto the market. But the situation has completely changed. Now with many PC users acquiring an extensive library of application software in binary format, with no access to the source code, the cost of repeatedly replacing such a library would be a major consideration when deciding whether to upgrade the processor. Thus it makes good marketing sense to offer backward binary compatibility. For a manufacturer of CPUs any potential source of resistance to hardware upgrades could be financially disadvantageous.

With the progressive change from the CISC 8086 to the Pentium, Intel has attempted to include some beneficial aspects of current RISC technology without relinquishing binary compatibility with the earlier members of the x86 family. For example, the simpler machine instructions are now decoded by hard logic, which is faster than the microcode technique used within the x86 CPUs. The fact that it was possible for Intel to include a microcode engine in addition to twin hard logic decoders (see Fig. 7.4), gives some indication of the recent advances in VLSI fabrication techniques. So the Pentium CU still handles the more complex i486 instructions using microcode. In this way, Intel has tried to benefit from RISC but maintain the flexibility of CISC.

The first Intel 8088 processor, which was used inside the original 1980 IBM PC, worked at a clock speed of only 4.77 MHz. The contemporary main memory DRAMs were well capable of responding within the four clock cycles then required by the bus controller (839 ns = $4 \times 1000/4.77$). However, since those days, processor clock speeds have increased by a factor of 100, while DRAM access speeds have improved by a factor of only 4. This means that if a modern microprocessor were to read data or instructions directly from main memory, it would have to wait up to 25 clock cycles to receive the requested data back from memory. Such delays are clearly undesirable! A possible solution would be to replace the DRAMs with faster SRAMs, but this would raise the price too much and also increase the board area needed because SRAM cells are bigger than DRAM cells.

Most high-performance, modern computers, including the PC/Pentium combination, achieve a compromise between cost and performance. We saw in Chapter 6 that DRAM was cheaper but considerably slower to access than SRAM. By providing a relatively small amount of SRAM as a cache memory, the slow access times of the much larger DRAM main memory can be effectively hidden. Although we will be dealing more thoroughly with the organization of computer memory in Chapter 17, the basic layout of the Pentium memory is presented here for reference.

The Pentium address bus remains 32 bits wide, but the main data bus has been widened to 64 bits, with an internal CPU bus providing widths of 128 or 256 bits. Widening the data pathway allows slower memory to deliver enough data to prevent the CPU stalling. Wide, slow channels do, however, require sufficient data buffering at the receiver end. This is similar to high-volume, low-speed transportation schemes, such as ocean steamers, where suppliers rely on warehouses to 'smooth out' the peaks and troughs in delivery. The Pentium CPU is provided with a very fast on-chip memory cache, known as the Level 1 cache, which is organized as two separate 8 kbyte buffers. One is dedicated for data and the other for instructions. The cache also has a special 'burst access' facility to speed up data transfers. Using four consecutive EDO DRAM bus cycles, 32 bytes of data are moved to or out of the cache. Such a chunk of data is known as a 'Cache Line'.

Having 8 kbyte of instructions held in very fast SRAM fabricated on the same silicon die as the CPU provides a substantial improvement in performance. Similarly, the 8 kbyte data cache, holding variables, will speed up the handling of data. The previous i486 processor only had a single, unified cache. With a RISC-style pipelined decoding arrangement, there will inevitably be access demands on the cache SRAM from two stages of the pipeline simultaneously. By separating the cache into two parts the Pentium reduces the number of such access clashes, and the associated delays. Unfortunately, most programs compile into code which is very much bigger than the 8 kbyte offered by Level 1 cache, so all recent PC systems now include a second level of SRAM cache, called Level 2 cache, positioned between L1 CPU cache and main memory. The Pentium II 'secreted' this L2 cache with the CPU inside the Slot 1 package in order to gain better performance. However, it is possible that the distinction between L1 and L2 will disappear in the future, when the size of L1 has been sufficiently increased to remove the need for L2 provision.

Some of the project names that Intel uses for internal purposes have leaked out (Table 7.1). Celeron is one of these, and referred initially to a PII CPU Slot 1 processor

Table 7.1
Pentium processor development names.

Name	Processor
P24T	486 Pentium OverDrive, 63 or 83 MHz, Socket 3
P54C	Classic Pentium 75–200 MHz, Socket 517, 3.3 V
P55C	Pentium NWX 166–266 MHz, Socket 7, 2.8 V
P54CTB	Pentium MMX OverDrive 125+, Socket 517, 3.3 V
Tillamook	Mobile Pentium MMX 0.25 μm, 166–266 MHz, 1.8 V
P6	Pentium Pro, Socket 8
Klamath	Original Pentium II, 0.35 μm, Slot 1
Deschutes	Pentium II, 0.25 μm, Slot 1, 256 kbyte L2 cache
Covington	Celeron PII, Slot 1, no L2 cache
Mendocino	Celeron, PII with 28 kbyte L2 cache on die
Dixon	Mobile Pentium IIPE, 256 kbyte L2 cache on die
Katmai	Pentium III, PII with SSE instructions
Willamette	Pentium 4, L2 cache on die
Tanner	Pentium III Xeon
Cascades	PIII, 0.18 μm, L2 cache on die
Merced	P7, First IA-64 processor, L2 cache on die, 0.18 μm
Kinley	1 GHz, improved Merced, IA-64, 0.18 μm, copper interconnects
Foster	Improved PIII, IA-32
Madison	Improved McKinley, IA-64, 0.13 μm

Fig. 7.2
Intel Celeron Pentium II
CPU module.

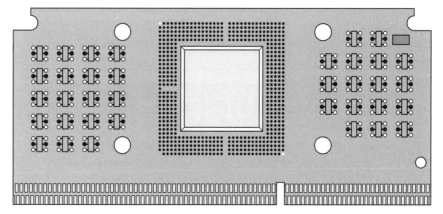

board built without L2 cache (Fig. 7.2). This was intended as a cheaper product for the domestic market which had been dominated by AMD, with its K6-2. Later, Intel introduced the Mendocino version of the Celeron CPU with clock frequencies of up to 333 MHz and crammed 128 kbyte of L2 cache onto the CPU chip. The performance was much better than expected because the bus between CPU and L2 cache ran at full processor clock speed. With the Slot 1 processor board only supporting the CPU, Intel decided to revert to sockets and give up on the more expensive PII slots. This new larger socket for the enhanced Celerons is called Socket 370 (Fig. 7.3). AMD has now produced the K6-3 which has 64 kbyte of L1 and 256 kbyte of on-chip L2 cache.

Perhaps more impressively, the Pentium has included, on chip, the circuitry for both segmented and paged memory management. Further details of these will be provided in Chapter 12. However, it might be useful to remember, when we come to look at the virtual memory management scheme, that the addresses used to access the cache memory are real 32 bit physical addresses.

The Pentium also supports Branch Prediction Logic (**BPL**), with an associated look-up table, as shown in Fig. 7.4. This will be further discussed in Chapter 21, but for the moment it can be understood as detecting any conditional instructions, such

Fig. 7.3
Intel Socket 370 Celeron
processor.

Fig. 7.4
Block diagram of
Pentium CPU.

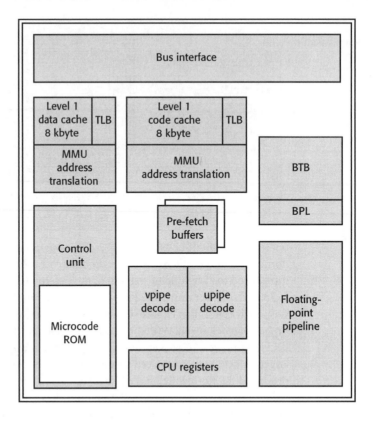

as IF...ELSE or CASE statements, as they enter the decoder pipeline, and trying to guess which route the program will eventually choose. Because the Pre-fetch Unit is reading instructions ahead of time, it is important to read in the correct ones!

7.2   CPU registers – temporary store for data and address variables

As indicated earlier, the Pentium is a clever compromise between the speed advantages following the newer RISC architecture and the backward-compatible CISC scheme. The complex arrangement of special-purpose registers clearly relate to the 8086's CISC origins. We will see in Chapter 21 that pure RISC designs offer many more CPU registers, but with few special designations. The basic Pentium CPU register set has remained unchanged since the 80386. Industrial archaeologists may be interested to identify the shadowed outline of the original 8080 registers still made visible by the low rays of the setting sun! Such detailed knowledge of the CPU register set, and how it is used, is certainly not required for HLL programming. But it is essential for students of computer architecture who are trying to understand the reasons

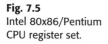

Fig. 7.5
Intel 80x86/Pentium
CPU register set.

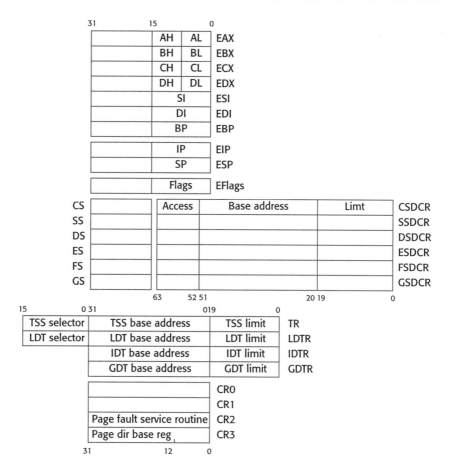

for the different grades of performance found in various computers to have a clear view of this level of operational activity.

The CPU registers displayed in Fig. 7.5 do not include the floating-point registers or the newer MMX (Multi-Media Extension) group. These will be discussed later in Section 20.8. Although we have not yet fully introduced the Pentium instructions, here are some example instructions expressed as assembler mnemonics to show how the CPU registers might be used. Note that the Intel assembler mnemonics represent data transfers by following the HLL assignment rule: from right to left. (This can be confusing, because the Motorola and Sun assembler mnemonics are written in the reverse direction.)

EAX: This is still sometimes called the Accumulator, and is used as a general-purpose data register during arithmetic and logical operations. Some instructions are optimized to work faster when using the A register. In addition, A is involved with all the data transfers to and from input–output ports. It can also be accessed in various ways as 8, 16 or 32 bit chunks, referred to as AL, AH, AX or EAX. For multiply and divide instructions it has an 'implied' role, which simply means that it is actively employed without being specifically mentioned in the instruction. Such a limitation is really only of interest to assembler-level programmers or compiler writers.

```
MOV EAX,1234H  ; load constant value 4660 into 32 bit accumulator
INC EAX        ; add 1 to accumulator value
CMP AL,'Q'     ; compare the ASCII Q with the LS byte value in EAX
MOV maxval,EAX ; store accumulator value to memory variable 'maxval'
DIV DX         ; divide accumulator by value in 16 bit D register
```

EBX: The Base register can hold addresses to point to the base of data structures, such as arrays in memory.

```
LEA EBX,marks    ; initialize EBX with address of the variable
                 ; 'marks'
MOV AL,[EBX]     ; get byte value into AL using EBX as a memory
                 ; pointer
ADD EAX,EBX      ; add 32 bits from EBX into accumulator
MOV EAX,table[BX] ; take 32 bit value from the 'table' array using
                 ; the value in BX as the array index
```

ECX: The Count register has a special role as a counter in loops or bit shifting operations.

```
      MOV ECX,100  ; initialize ECX as the FOR loop index
      ...
for1:              ; symbolic address label
      ...
      LOOP for1    ; decrement ECX, test for zero, JMP back if
                   ; non-zero
```

EDX: The Data register can be involved during input–output data transfers or when executing integer multiplication and division. Otherwise it is generally available for holding variables.

```
IN AL,DX      ; input byte value from port, with 16 bit port
              ; address in DX
MUL DX        ; multiply A by value in D
```

ESI: The Source Index register is used as a pointer for string or array operations within the Data Segment.

```
LEA ESI,dtable  ; initialize ESI with memory address of variable
                ; 'dtable'
MOV AX,[EBX+ESI] ; get word using Base address and Index register
```

EDI: The Destination Index register is used as a pointer for string or array operations within the Data Segment.

```
MOV [EDI],[ESI]      ; moves a 32 bit word from source to destination
                     ; locations in memory
```

EBP: The Stack Base Pointer register is used as the stack frame pointer to support HLL procedure operations. It is taken as an offset within the Stack Segment.

```
ENTER 16             ; saves EBP on stack, copies ESP into EBP, and
                     ; subtracts 16 from ESP
```

EIP: The Instruction Pointer (Program Counter) holds the offset address of the next instruction within the current Code Segment.

```
JMP errors           ; forces a new address into EIP
```

ESP: The Stack Pointer holds the offset address of the next item available on the stack within the current Stack Segment.

```
CALL subdo           ; call a subroutine (subdo), storing return
                     ; address on stack
PUSH EAX             ; save 32 bit value in accumulator on stack
```

EFLAG: The Flag register holds the CPU status flags, implicated in all of the conditional instructions.

```
JGE back1            ; tests sign flag for conditional jump
LOOP backagin        ; tests zero flag for loop exit condition
```

CS–GS: These 16 bit Segment Selector registers were originally introduced to expand the addressing range of the 8086 processor while maintaining a 16 bit IP. This was done by adding a Segment Register to the IP to extend its addressing range. Because the new segment registers were also only 16 bits wide, they were first left shifted by 4 bits to give a 20 bit addressing range (2^{20} = 1 Mbyte). However, each of the separate segments – Code, Stack, Data and three extra data segments – remained limited by the 16 bit IP to a maximum size of 64 kbyte. This unwelcome constraint, which was misguidedly built into the MS-DOS operating system, forced programmers into years of addressing contortions long after the introduction of full 32 bit hardware. For the Pentium processor, the Segment registers can now be seen as part of the expanded memory management group, helping to divide the main memory space into segments when the Pentium is running in protected mode. The Segment Selector registers are no longer segment base pointers, and so do not contribute directly to forming the Effective Address. They now point to relevant entries in one of the Segment Descriptor Tables (GDT and LDT). The selected entry is then read into the associated

64 bit cache register (CSDCR), from where the base pointer can be read to form the effective address with the EIP.

CSDCR–GSDCR: These registers are invisible to the programmer, but they are vital to the operation of the MMU. During normal Protected Mode operation, the 64 bit Code Segment Descriptor Cache Register holds the current Code Segment Descriptor, which includes Base address, size Limit and Access permissions. The Segment Descriptor is obtained from either the Global or Local Descriptor Tables held in memory. Because these values need to be used for each memory access it is important to provide fast, easy access. Every effective address emerging from the CU will be added to the appropriate Segment Base Address, having the Limit and Access permissions checked at the same time.

TR: The Task Register holds the 16 bit segment selector, the 32 bit base address, the 16 bit size limit and the descriptor attributes for the current task. It references a TSS descriptor in the Global Descriptor Table (GDT). When a task switch occurs, the Task Register is automatically reloaded.

IDTR: Interrupt Descriptor Table Register holds the base address and size limit of the current Interrupt Vector Table (IVT). It is a 48 bit register, with the lower 16 bits dedicated to the size limit value, and the upper 32 bits holding the IVT base address. This allows the Pentium to relocate the 1 kbyte IVT from the default starting location at 0000 0000. Such a facility can be useful during development, and enables Windows NT to offer multiple 'virtual machine' environments simultaneously.

GDTR: The Global Descriptor Table Register holds the segment descriptors which point to universally available segments and to the tables holding the Local Descriptors.

LDTR: Each task can use a Local Descriptor Table in addition to the Global Descriptor Table. This register indicates which entry in the Local Segment Descriptor Table to use.

CR3: This Control Register points to the directory table for the Paging Unit.

CR2: This Control Register points to the routine which handles page faults which occur when the CPU attempts to access an item at an address which is located on a non-resident memory page. The service routine will instigate the disk operation to bring the page back into main memory from disk.

MM0–MM7 (not displayed in Fig. 7.5; see Fig. 20.20): These are the eight extended data registers used by the MMX instructions (Multi-Media Extensions). The Pentium II has around 50 MMX instructions aimed at speeding up arithmetic operations by carrying out several simultaneously. The MMX data registers are 64 bits wide so that

Fig. 7.6
The original Intel 8080
CPU register set.

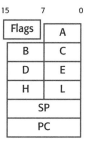

In contrast, the register set for the original Intel 8080 from 1975 looks rather puny (Fig. 7.6).

four 16 bit integers can be loaded and then processed by a single instruction. This can assist with graphical computations using matrices.

FP0–FP7: These 64 bit registers are not displayed in Fig. 7.5. They are dedicated to the FPU ALU so that floating-point (real) arithmetic can be carried out more rapidly.

In contrast, the register set for the original Intel 8080 from 1975 looks rather puny (Fig. 7.6).

Can you see the origins of the Pentium general-purpose registers in the 8080? Compare Fig. 7.6 with Fig. 7.5. You may be surprised. Although the 32 bit extensions to these registers have made the Pentium much more versatile, it is clear, when you compare the two register sets, that most of the development effort has gone into memory management systems. There will be more on this topic in Chapter 12.

7.3 Instruction set – introduction to the basic Pentium set

All computers have a set of machine instructions which carry out a variety of actions to manipulate data and control the operation of the hardware. You have already met several instructions from the Pentium set in the previous section where they were used to expose the use of the CPU registers. In fact, the Pentium has over 200 distinct instructions, with several addressing modes to extend this wide range of operations further. The binary codes representing these instructions are not of fixed length and vary in length from 1 to 15 bytes which helps to reduce the length of programs because 'popular' instructions are assigned the shorter codes. Having a variety of instruction code lengths has now fallen into disfavour with the shift to RISC architectures and the reduction in concern about memory size limitations.

Each machine instruction can be classified into one of the five categories listed in Table 7.2.

The data movement group can also sometimes be used for input–output operations. This is the case with the Motorola 68000, where the only instruction intended specifically for data IO is MOVEP. This is really only provided to assist with byte-wide

Table 7.2
Categories of machine
instructions.

1.	Data movement (copying)
2.	Data input–output operations
3.	Data manipulation
4.	Transfer of control
5.	Machine supervision

peripheral ports, and is not terribly useful. Intel chose to provide special IO instructions, `IN` and `OUT`, for its processors, including the current Pentiums. Data manipulation instructions include the bitwise logical operations `AND`, `OR` and `NOT`, in addition to the more commonplace `ADD`, `SUB`, `MUL` and `DIV`. Transfer of control refers to any instruction that can alter the steady increment of IP values that accompany the normal fetch–execute sequence. An abrupt change in IP indicates a jump to a different part of the program, due to a procedure call or even a rare `GOTO`. Instructions such as `JP` and `CALL` effect such actions. Machine supervision instructions are often the most dangerous ones to experiment with. The `HLT` instruction may require a hardware system reset to retrieve the situation, while a change of interrupt threshold can starve the system of necessary input data. Even inappropriately altering the Global Descriptor Table in memory could crash the system.

When starting a new language the size of the unknown vocabulary can be daunting. In Table 7.3 you will find a short list of basic Pentium instructions which will allow you to understand our examples and get started with assembler programming for yourself. You can even cut this abbreviated offering down to a meagre 14 if you find 18 too many!

Table 7.3
Basic 'starter'
instructions for the
Pentium.

MOV	copies data from location to location, register or memory
LEA	load effective address
CALL	calls to a subroutine
RET	return from a subroutine
PUSH	push an item onto the stack, possibly as a subroutine parameter
POP	pop an item off the stack
INC/DEC	increment or decrement
ADD	arithmetic integer addition
SUB	arithmetic subtraction for 2s complement integers
CMP	compare 2 values, a subtract with no result, only setting flags
AND/OR/XOR	logical operators
TEST	bit testing
JZ	conditional jump
LOOP	implements a FOR loop by decrementing the CX register
ENTER	sets up a subroutine (procedure) stack frame
LEAVE	cleans up a stack frame on exit from a subroutine
JMP	a dreaded jump instruction
INT	software interrupt to get into an operating system routine

Table 7.4
Machine instruction
functional components.

1	The action or operation of the instruction
2.	The 'victims' or operands involved
3.	Where the result is to go

7.4 Structure of instructions – how the CU sees it

Once an instruction is fetched from memory and inserted into one of the instruction pipelines, the CU has to decode the binary pattern and start the necessary activities at each stage. This is not carried out by a single decoder circuit as outlined in Chapter 4, but requires a more complex arrangement because of the need to carry out the operations in a phased sequence, through five steps. Most instructions need to contain the three pieces of information listed in Table 7.4.

To specify these three distinguishable parts, machine instructions are planned with distinct bit fields to contain information about the operation required, the location of operands and results, and the data type of the operands. Pentium instructions can be anywhere from 1 to 15 bytes long, depending on the operation required and the addressing modes employed. The prefix field has a major role in determining the length of the current instruction. But whatever length, all instructions will have to specify action and operands. The Pentium instruction format is presented in Fig. 7.7.

The first 6 bits of the opcode byte identify the basic operation (ADD, AND, MOV etc.) The D bit specifies whether the following REG field refers to the source or destination operand. The W bit distinguishes between byte and word operations, but distinguishing 32 bit from 16 bit words requires the inclusion of a prefix byte which sets the DB bit in the relevant segment descriptor. Including the 'optional' prefix byte allowed the 80386 to maintain backward binary compatibility with its simpler predecessors. The MOD field identifies whether one of the operands is in memory, or both are in registers. In the latter case, the R/M field holds the second register identifier; otherwise R/M is the Memory Access Mode field.

Specific examples of the coding structure of some of the simpler instructions are provided in Fig. 7.8. You can use the Developer Studio debugger to check out the binary values listed for any of the instructions.

7.5 CPU status flags – very short-term memory

In the Pentium, as in all digital computers, there is a set of status flags, organized in a single CPU register, to record the outcome of various operations and events. Some CPUs will only alter the flags after an arithmetic or logical operation. Intel has arranged it so that data moves (MOV instructions) do not affect any of the flags. The

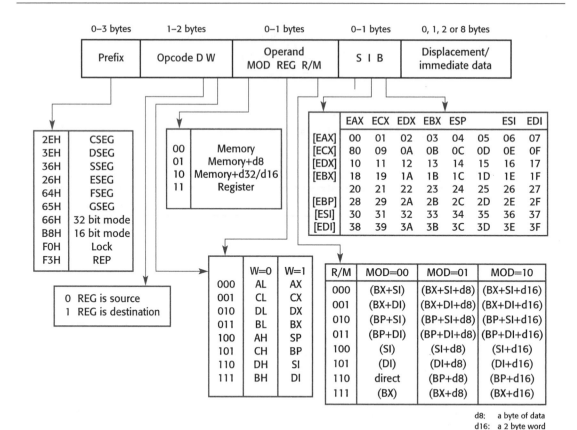

Fig. 7.7
The five fields within a
Pentium instruction.

Status register is sometimes referred to as the Eflags because it was extended from 16 to 32 bits with the introduction of the Pentium.

The CPU status flags, as presented in Fig. 7.9, play an essential role in the operation of all digital computers. As the von Neumann architecture is essentially sequential, one instruction following another, there is an implicit requirement for communicating the result from one instruction to the subsequent instructions. Should the result be a data item there is no problem, because the value is placed in a register or memory location. But if the effect of an instruction is only to test a number to see whether it is zero, there would be little point in writing the result of the test to another register, as that value would then have to be tested, and so on!

In the example illustrated in Fig. 7.10, the CMP instruction is used to check whether a letter variable held in the A register is 'q' or not. The CMP instruction works like a subtraction, but with the numeric result being ignored. Hence only the (secondary) side effect of setting or clearing the CPU flags remains after its execution. In this case, if the variable in AL happened to be 'q' the CMP instruction would leave the Z (zero) flag set to 1 because 71H – 71H = 0 (the ASCII code for 'q' is 71 in hex, 0111 0001 in binary). When the next conditional instruction which tests the Z flag executes, its operation will be determined by the previous CMP instruction. This assumes that no

Fig. 7.8
The bit fields within
Pentium instructions.

03 C3   ADD AX,BX

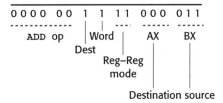

0 0 0 0 0 0 1 1 1 1 0 0 0 0 1 1
------------ | | ---   -------   ------
     ADD op | Word   AX   BX
           Dest
           Reg–Reg
           mode

                Destination source

Another example:

66 6B 00 00 00 00 00 00 12 00 MOV EAX,12H

0 1 1 0 0 1 1 0   1 0 1 1   1   0 0 0   0000 0000 0000 0000 0000 0000 0001 0010
-----------------   ------- | ------   --
  32 bit prefix   MOV op Word AX   Immediate data

Again:

3C 71   CMP AL,'q'

0 0 1 1 1 1 0 0 0 1 1 1 0 0 0 1
-------------- | -------------------
CMP A op   Byte Immediate data

31   0

| | | | | | | | | | ID |VIP| VI |AC|VM| R | | N |IOP| O | D | I | T | S | Z | | A | | P | | C |

ID   Identification flag or CPUID availability
VIP   Virtual interrupt pending
VI   Virtual interrupt active
AC   Alignment check
VM   Virtual 8086 mode active
RFR   Resume task after breakpoint interrupt
NT   Nested task
IOPL IO privilege level
O   Arithmetic overflow error
D   Direction of accessing string arrays
IE   External interrupt enable
T   Trap, single-step debugging, generates an INT #1 after each instruction
S   Sign, MS bit value
Z   Zero, result being zero
A   Auxiliary carry, used by BCD arithmetic on 4 LS bits
P   Parity, operand status
C   Carry, indicates an arithmetic carry or borrow result

Fig. 7.9
CPU status flags.

Fig. 7.10
How CPU status flags
operate.

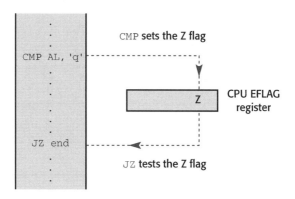

intervening instruction has altered the Z flag status, wrecking the link between CMP and JZ. Assembler-level programmers can spend many happy hours tuning such sensitive interactions to gain speed or size advantages.

Thus the CPU Status Flags are central to the operation of a programmable machine. In effect they 'glue' the simple machine instructions together, allowing one instruction to leave behind a bit of information to guide the action of subsequent instructions. CPU flags can also be seen as a means of communication between the ALU and the CU. The ALU sets the flags, and the CU tests them.

7.6   Addressing modes – building effective addresses

To extend the use of machine instructions, making the instruction set more flexible and easier to use, CPUs generally support several addressing modes. These represent different ways of forming the operand addresses and can thus better support the needs of HLLs when they need to manipulate large data structures. The MOD field has a central role to play in specifying the active addressing modes that are used by the CPU to access the operands. Note that if an instruction has two operands it also incorporates two addressing modes, which need not be the same.

Data Register Direct

    MOV *EAX,EBX*

This is the fastest to execute and easiest to understand. An item of data is copied to or from a CPU register. This example has two Register Direct operands. The machine instruction identifies which register by having a 3 bit operand field. On execution the data item is transferred to or from that register depending on whether it is a source or destination operand.

Immediate Operand (IP Indirect)

```
MOV EAX, 1234
```

In this case the constant data value 1234 is included as part of the program and stored immediately after the instruction. In this way, as the instruction pointer (EIP) is incremented during the fetch–execute cycle, it conveniently points to the data, which can then be easily read back from memory. Thus Immediate Mode could also be known as IP Indirect Mode.

> The assembler distinguishes 1234 from [1234]; so must you!

Memory Direct

```
MOV EAX, [var1]
```

Frequently you need to access a variable stored in memory. This mode builds on the Immediate Mode by storing the variable's *address* immediately after the instruction. The IP is again used to point to the memory location which is holding the address, which is then read back into a temporary register within the CPU. From here it is redespatched back to memory to select the item of data required. This is read back into the CPU. This is a surprisingly complex and time-consuming operation simply to read a memory variable!

Address Register Direct

```
LEA EBX, var1
```

This uses Immediate Mode to load a memory address into a register and is commonly used to initialize pointers which can then reference data arrays.

Register Indirect

```
MOV EAX, [EBX]
```

Here, a register holds the memory address of a variable. It is said to 'point at the data'. The instruction only has to copy this address from the register to memory to receive the data back. This is a fast and efficient process.

Indexed Register Indirect with displacement

```
MOV EAX, [table+EBP+ESI]
```

It is not necessary to employ two registers. The symbol 'table' in this example is the address of the array base. This mode can also be written in an alternative way which is easier to interpret when dealing with one-dimensional arrays if you are familiar with HLLs:

```
MOV EAX, table[ESI]
```

7.7   Execution pipelines – the RISC speedup technique

In Section 3.5 it was explained that overlapping operations in a continuous processing sequence provides immediate performance benefits. This technique is exploited in RISC architecture CPUs by organizing the pre-fetch buffer as a production line. In other words, the pre-fetched instructions, rather than just sitting in the queue awaiting their turn to be decoded and executed, are subjected to partial decoding and execution as they progress through the queue. This is known as pipelining, and delivers a fantastic improvement in performance. A schematic diagram to illustrate the structure of a pipeline is given in Fig. 7.11. The new instructions are read in from memory by the pre-fetcher and held in the buffer before entering the pipeline. As an instruction passes through the pipeline it is processed, stage by stage. For a given clock rate, say 100 MHz, a CISC control unit may use 5 cycles to complete each instruction, reducing it effectively to 25 MHz performance, while the pipelined RISC completes an instruction every clock cycle, giving it a ×5 speed advantage.

A five-stage pipeline would have the sections committed to different decoding tasks in a manner similar to that shown in Fig. 7.12. During any clock cycle the pipeline should complete the execution of an instruction and read in another instruction at the front end.

Pipelining can be seen as a form of multiprocessing, with several actions taking place simultaneously. The CPU hardware is necessarily more complex to be able to manage such parallelism with some duplication of circuitry involved, but the improvement in performance easily justifies this penalty.

So far we have only proposed a single stream of instructions, dealt with through a single pipelined decoder, but to further improve the performance of the Pentium, the Intel designers implemented a dual pipeline scheme (Fig. 7.13) so that, theoretically, two instructions could be completing every clock cycle. In the computing industry this technique is known as 'superscalar' processing to distinguish it from the multiple

Fig. 7.11
CPU Control Unit with pipelined decoding.

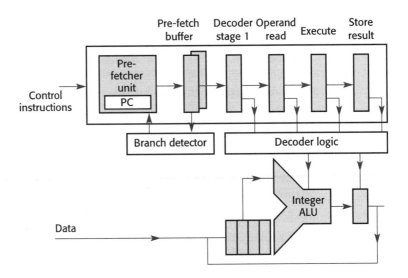

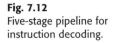

Fig. 7.12
Five-stage pipeline for
instruction decoding.

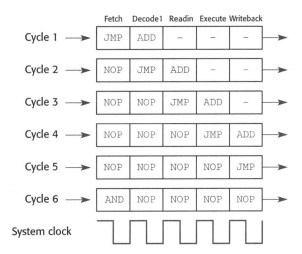

instruction 'vector processors' and the basic, single instruction 'scalar' units. The twin five-step instruction pipelines, U and V, can complete the decoding process for two instructions per clock cycle but only non-floating point instructions are eligible for this parallel treatment. There is a third pipeline for floating-point operations! Currently, pipeline V is not so well provided with hardware as pipeline U, and the eight-stage floating-point pipeline is not fully capable of running in parallel with integer operation. So there is still room for hardware improvement!

Given the right conditions, two integer instructions can be completed in the same clock cycle. The performance of the floating-point unit is improved beyond that of the earlier Intel 8087, but unfortunately shares some of the logic of the U pipeline, somewhat reducing the opportunity for parallel operation.

Fig. 7.13
The Pentium triple
decoder pipeline fed
from the L1 cache
memory.

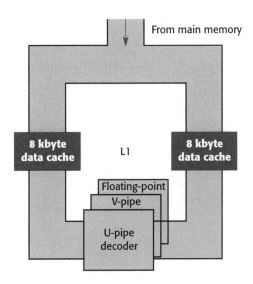

7.8   Microsoft Developer Studio – using the debugger

A debugger tool is often supplied packaged with the compiler and linker. It appears to be rarely used by normal programmers, who prefer to isolate errors in their programs by inserting temporary print statements to reveal where a variable becomes corrupted. The same job could be done more elegantly with a debugger. Perhaps this situation has arisen because of the perceived difficulty of learning the repertoire of debugger commands. Having one more learning task when you are already struggling with a new workbench environment, editor commands, language syntax and application logic is not welcome. However, students of computer architecture can also use the debugger to get a convenient low-level view of the software operations within the CPU.

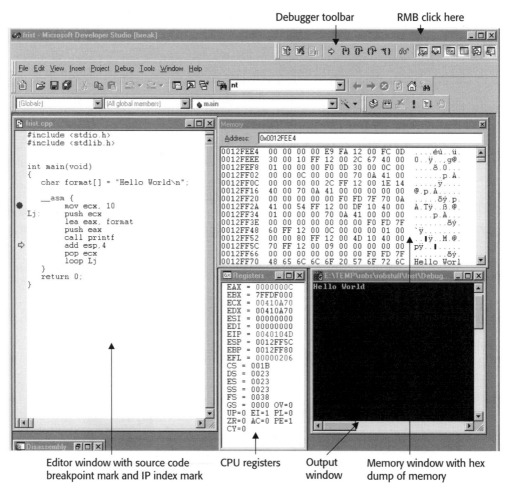

Fig. 7.14
The Microsoft Developer Studio debugger in operation.

The Developer Studio debugger allows the programmer to watch a program while it is executing (Fig. 7.14). The system manages this by running the debugger and the target program simultaneously, swapping from one to the other in order to display the contents of CPU registers and memory locations as required. For our purposes the most useful facility is **single stepping**. This allows you to execute the program one instruction at a time, giving you plenty of opportunity to check the result of each instruction. By pressing the F10 key a single instruction will be executed and the resulting changes to CPU flags, registers and memory locations can be seen.

Before you can use a debugger it is normal on most systems that a special compile and link operation has to be carried out to provide the extra information that such sophisticated debuggers require. In Microsoft Developer Studio, this debug option is set by selecting [Build] → [Set Active Configurations] → [Debug]. Remember to rebuild the executable code every time that you edit the source file.

It is best to start by using straightforward hand-crafted assembler routines. The output from HLL compilers can be quite mysterious for the novice, and even the expert! To save the need to buy and install a separate assembler, I have used the in-line __asm facility offered by the VC++ compiler. Other compilers offer equivalent possibilities. The assembler code example used in Fig. 7.14 is listed more clearly in Fig. 7.15.

The HLL control structures (SEQ, IT and SEL) are directly supported by special instructions in the machine set. For example, the FOR counting loop is implemented by the LOOP group. These decrement-branch instructions can test 2 conditions when deciding whether to continue in the loop, or exit. After decrementing ECX by 1, LOOPNZ checks whether the count value has reached 0, OR if the CPU Z flag (ZF) is

Fig. 7.15
Example use of __asm directive.

```
/* demonstration of the use of asm instructions within C prog*/
#include <stdio.h>
#include <stdlib.h>

int main (void)
{
char format[] = "Hello World\n"  //declare variables in C

__asm {                        ;switch to inline assembler
        mov ecx,10             ;initialize loop counter
Lj:     push ecx               ; loop count index saved on stack
        lea eax,format
        push eax               ;address of string, stack parameter
        call printf            ;use library code subroutine
        add esp,4              ;clean 4 byte parameter off stack
        pop ecx                ;restore loop counter ready for test
        loop Lj                ;dec ECX, jmp back IF NZ
}                              ;back to C
return 0;
}
```

Table 7.5
Useful keyboard shortcuts within the Developer Studio debugger.

F1	Help
F4	Go to next error
^F5	Run the program
F7	Build executable code
^F7	Compile only
F9	Set breakpoint
F10	Single step (over functions)
F11	Single step into functions
ALT+TAB	Toggled windows backwards/forwards

set, either condition will stop the loop. Otherwise a JMP back to the top of the loop occurs. Interestingly the ECX decrement itself does not affect Z, leaving it available for other instructions within the loop to use as an abort flag.

Debuggers can be very confusing, so reduce the number of display windows to a minimum. I recommend that you start with only four: the editor, CPU registers, data output, and sometimes also the memory window. The debugger tool bar allows you to open and close these displays.

In Microsoft Developer Studio there are some useful keyboard shortcuts which relieve the mouse of regular trips around the mat. These are presented in Table 7.5, and will save you time in the long run.

The **debugger tool bar** holds the key to opening the various debugger view windows, so a summary is given in Fig. 7.16. If you get lost, a useful pull-down menu is available by clicking the RMB on the grey background towards the top right-hand side of the Developer Studio display. There are five windows provided by the debugger (listed in Table 7.6) which can be seen in the screenshot of Fig. 7.14.

When you have the Register and Disassembly windows in view, you can configure the displays using the right mouse button to reveal pull-down menus. It is generally not necessary to show the floating-point registers, so I turn them off to get more room on the screen.

When you get more adventurous you might try using the disassembler to display the assembler mnemonic code produced by the compiler for one of your C/C++ programs!

Finally, the keystrokes listed in Table 7.7 are common to all Windows applications. You may find them useful while developing programs.

Table 7.6
Microsoft Developer Studio debugger display windows.

1.	CPU registers
2.	Program memory with labels and disassembled mnemonics
3.	Data memory with ASCII decode table
4.	Output screen for your program under test
5.	Stack, but only for the return addresses

Fig. 7.16
Microsoft Developer
Studio debugger tool
bar.

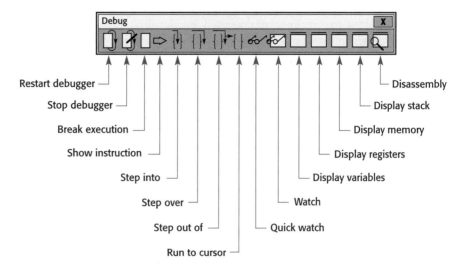

Restart debugger
Stop debugger
Break execution
Show instruction
Step into
Step over
Step out of
Run to cursor
Quick watch
Watch
Display variables
Display registers
Display memory
Display stack
Disassembly

Table 7.7
Keyboard shortcuts for
Windows NT.

^ESC	Open the Start Menu on the Taskbar. You can then open applications.
Tab	On the desktop, this switches between desktop, Taskbar and Start menu. If you already have the Start menu, Tab switches between Applications.
Alt+F4	Terminate current application. This can also terminate Windows if you are on the desktop!
Alt+Tab	Switch to next window.
Shift+Alt+Tab	Switch to preceding window.
ESC	Sometimes cancels the previous action.
F1	Display the online help for applications.
Shift+F1	Context-sensitive help.
F2	If an icon is highlighted you can change its name.
F3	Open Find window.

Review

- The best-known CPU is the Pentium microprocessor. This is used in all modern PCs. Many different versions are manufactured by Intel, AMD and Cyrix.

- To improve performance, fast cache memory (L1) has been included on the processor chip. Now the Celeron 370A also has L2 cache on-chip.

- Although the Pentium is a CISC CPU, it has adopted pipeline decoding from RISC design. This enables it to decode several instructions simultaneously, like a production line.

- The Pentium CU is equipped with twin decoder pipelines to enable it to process two streams of instructions simultaneously where they do not mutually interfere.

- ■ The CPU registers retain some dedicated functionality, such as ECX handling the loop counting. This appears to be very CISC, and even relates to the original Intel 8 bit microprocessors.

- ■ The primitive instruction codes can be separated into fields, as the CU will have to do, in order to understand the decoding process.

- ■ CPU status flags act as messengers between instructions in the program sequence.

- ■ Accessing data, in memory or the CPU registers, can be achieved using a variety of modes.

- ■ The pipeline decoder speeds up the CPU by overlapping operations.

Practical work

The recommended practical work involves gaining familiarity with the Microsoft Developer Studio IDE (Integrated Development Environment) and starting to develop and run short assembler routines, within HLL programs written in C, using the __asm directive. The CD-ROM included with this text has a student edition of the Developer Studio for your use. An installation guide and some ideas for your first program can also be found in the appendix at the back of this book.

Exercises

1. How many data registers does the Pentium CPU have? How many bytes of storage does this provide the programmer?

2. List the five categories of machine instruction type and allocate the following Pentium instructions to the correct category:

```
MOV AX, count
OUT port1,AL
ADD EAX,20
CMP AL, 'Q'
JMP DONE
CALL doit
INT 21H
HLT
```

3. Explain the addressing modes used in this instruction: ADD EAX, [SI]. In what circumstances might a compiler utilize this instruction?

4. Give three different ways to clear AX.

5. What is the principal advantage of Register Indirect addressing?

6. Which addressing mode do you consider to be the fundamental mode? Why?

7. How many addressing modes could be used in the execution of a single Pentium instruction? Explain the term 'effective address'.

8. What addressing modes are used in the six following instructions:

```
mov DX, [countx]
```

```
lea ESI,array1
add EAX,[SI]
cmp EAX,target
call doneit
mov result,EAX
```

9. Explain the use of the Pentium LOOPZ instruction. If you wanted to loop 10 times, what would be your initial and final loop counter values?

A. Explain the action of the Pentium CMP instruction.

B. What is the difference between the JZ and JNZ instructions?

C. What role do the CPU status flags play during program execution? In what way could they be seen as a means of communication between the ALU and the CU?

D. What is or are the Pentium equivalents of the dreaded HLL goto instruction? Why are you more likely to use these instructions than the HLL goto?

E. Consider the asm code in Fig. 7.15. What is the parameter list for printf( )? Why does adding 4 to ESP make it disappear? Replace "add esp,4" with an alternative line of code.

F. What do each of the following six Pentium instructions achieve:

```
LOOP strout, MOV AL,123H
MOV DX,[count], PUSH AX
MOV CX,0AH, LEA EBX,NAME1
```

Readings

- Messmer (1995)

- Anderson and Shanley (1995)

- Intel (1997)

- There is detailed information at the following site, but allow yourself a lot of time!
  http://developer.intel.com/design/pentium/manuals/

- Online *Intel Technology Journal*, with past issues available from:
  http://developer.intel.com/technology/itj/

- For current discussion on processor performance:
  http://amtguide.com/

- Try this for assembler-oriented descriptions and explanations:
  http://cs.smith.edu/~thiebaut/ArtOfAssembly/ArtofAsm.html

- A must for real programming enthusiasts:
  http://www.programmersheaven.com/

- The online help which comes with Microsoft Developer Studio provides some good descriptions and technical explanations.

- Heuring and Jordan (1997), Section 2.2: Instruction sets.

- Tanenbaum (1999), Section 5.5.8: Pentium II instructions.

- The different Intel processor sockets (4, 5 and 7) are described in:
  `http://www.powerleap.com/tn-006p.html`

- The Web sites can be accessed via the Companion Web site for this book at:
  `http://www.booksites.net/williams/`

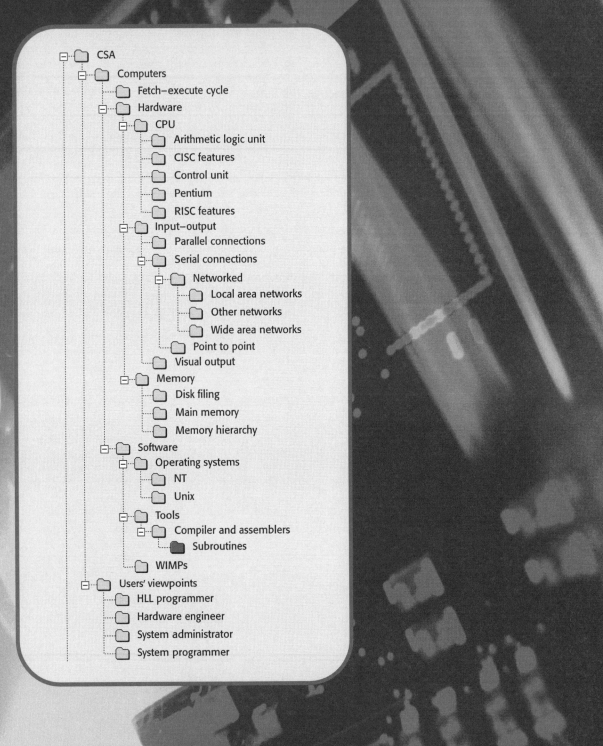

Subroutines

8

Overview

Subroutines, procedures, functions or methods are all the same thing. They are blocks of code which may be accessed repeatedly from many different points in (possibly) many different programs. The efficient support of subroutining comprises an important part of CPU functionality. Passing parameters into the subroutine, managing local variables and supervising the return, are all assisted by special hardware facilities within the CPU.

8.1   The purpose of subroutines – saving space and effort

Programmers now generally use High-Level Languages (HLLs) to write their programs. This gives advantages of efficiency and accuracy and hides much of the underlying complexity. **Subroutines**, referred to as **procedures** in Pascal and **functions** in C, are chunks of code which are repeatedly used as the program executes. Thus, using subroutines was originally seen simply as a method of sharing code, so as to reduce the size of programs. Special machine instructions, such as BSR or CALL, are provided which overwrite the address value in the IP so that the target of the fetch–execute sequence is switched to the subroutine code. Changing the IP in this way is effectively a 'jmp' or 'goto' operation, but the CALL instruction carries out some additional actions which will be discussed in the following sections to allow control to be returned to the place which did the call.

The use of subroutines within a single program results in the need to resolve the question of 'where to return to' or 'where did I come from?' when a subroutine is completed. This is illustrated in Fig. 8.1, where the subroutine average( ) is invoked at different moments from two different places in the main program. The question of where to go back to has to be answered every time a subroutine finishes.

Further problems emerge when subroutine code is to be shared by several programs which will be executing concurrently under the control of a multitasking operating system such as Unix or Windows NT. In this situation, as illustrated in Fig. 8.2, the subroutine will be entered into a public Dynamic Link Library (**DLL**) which has to be loaded into memory along with the client programs. The 'where to return to' question becomes more complex because several programs may be simultaneously executing the same subroutine code! In addition, it becomes vital that none of the user programs have the opportunity to modify the shared code or interfere with variables set up by the other users.

Using subroutines does slow down the program execution speed, but this is no longer considered a serious issue for HLL programmers to worry about. You will find

Fig. 8.1
Where did I come from?

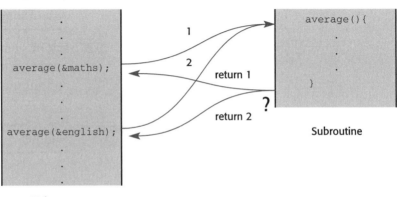

Main program

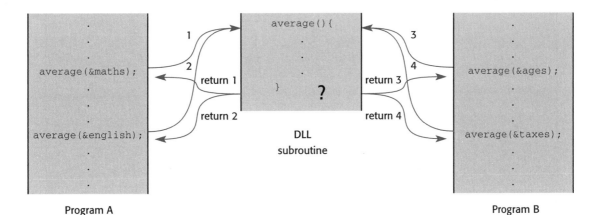

average()

average(&maths);

return 1

average(&english);

return 2

}   **?**

DLL
subroutine

average(&ages);

return 3

average(&taxes);

return 4

Program A

Program B

Fig. 8.2
Who did we all come
from?

out the reason for this delaying effect later in the chapter. It is true that programmers now expect the compiler optimization phase to minimize the run-time of their code, but if the results are still too slow, why not buy a faster CPU?

A more important aspect of subroutines is the way they **encapsulate**, or package, a particular activity. When a programmer designs and writes a subroutine it is good style to identify and isolate a specific action or processing job for the subroutine to carry out. This makes it suitable (after it has been thoroughly tested) for entering into a library for others to use. Subroutine libraries are available with HLL compilers, graphics environments, operating systems interfaces, Internet support packages and many, many more. As we discussed in Section 2.5, the linker brings together compiled files to create an executable program. To speed up the linking process, subroutines are compiled into object form and then entered into a library. Linkers normally scan through several such libraries while trying to find the correct subroutine to use. So, although programmers started using subroutines to reduce code size, their more significant modern role is that of providing easy access to tried and tested code. This assists with keeping down costs and speeding up the production of reliable software systems.

8.2 Return address – introducing the stack

A fundamental problem for all digital computers involves the use of shared code or subroutines. When you transfer control from one piece of program to another, during a CALL to a subroutine, how do you 'remember' where you came from when you want to go back? It might be suggested that the **return address** be stored in a specially dedicated memory location, or even a spare CPU register. This would work initially, but when a subroutine itself needs to CALL a second subroutine the problem reoccurs because the special memory location or register is already occupied. More

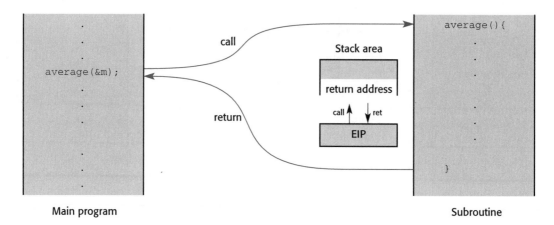

Main program   Subroutine

Fig. 8.3
Using the stack to
hold the subroutine
return address.

return registers would be needed, but how many is unknown until the program actually runs.

   This tricky dilemma is now elegantly solved by storing return addresses on a **stack**,
in memory, before jumping to the subroutine, and then recovering the address at the
end of the subroutine. Figure 8.3 shows how this can be done. The CALL instruction
now has two jobs to do, firstly copy the address from EIP to the stack (PUSH), and
then put the required subroutine address into EIP (JMP). When terminating the
subroutine, the RET instruction simply POPs the last 32 bit item off the stack, trusting
that it will be the return address, and stuffs it back into EIP. Should the 32 bit item
popped off the stack into EIP not represent a valid address, a nasty crash occurs!

   Because of this fundamental importance and frequent use, a special register, called
the Stack Pointer (ESP), is provided within the CPU to point to the area of main
memory which has been chosen as the stack. It is important to understand that the
stack is a data area in memory which is located by the address in the ESP register in the
CPU.

   As illustated in Fig. 8.4, system stacks usually start at the top of memory and grow
downwards. But this is only a convention. It is important not to confuse 'queue' and
'stack' data structures. The queue is operated in a democratic, first in, first out (**FIFO**)
mode, while the stack offers the very different regime of last in, first out (**LIFO**). Note
also that the stack data is only valid if it is above the stack pointer. If it is below, it
might still be readable using a debugger, but from the program's point of view it is
stale and unreadable.

8.3   Using subroutines – HLL programming

All processor instruction sets, such as for the Pentium or MC68000, have a group of
special instructions to support the use of subroutines. It is these instructions that the
compiler will select when it encounters a procedure or function name in the HLL

Fig. 8.4
Stack Pointer Register (ESP) points to top of stack.

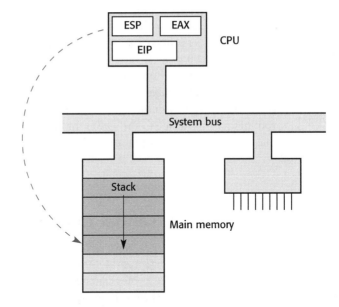

program being translated. An example code fragment in C (Fig. 8.5) shows the use of a library function, `printf( )`, and a user-defined function, `average( )`.

Notice that the function `average( )` is used more than once and in different parts of the program. The compiler will translate the `main( )` and `average( )` functions into machine codes. The function `printf( )`, which is also used more

Fig. 8.5
The use of functions, or subroutines, in a C program, `average.c`.

```c
#include <stdio.h>
#define NCLASS 10

        int maths_scores[NCLASS];
        int tech_scores[NCLASS];

float average(int x, int*y){
    int i;
    float av;
    for (i=0; i<x; i++){
        av += *y++;
    }
    return av/= x;
}

void main (void) {
    int i;
.....

printf("Average of maths=%3.1f\n", average( NCLASS, maths_scores));
.....
printf("Average of technology=%3.1f\n", average( NCLASS, tech_scores));
.....
}
```

than once, is supplied in the C library and so does not need to be compiled again, only linked to the user program before loading. Another important feature of subroutines is the declaration of local variables. These appear automatically when a function is entered and disappear immediately the function finishes. The variables i and av are examples of local variables inside the function average( ). An assembler program shows the use of subroutines at a lower level, with direct access to operating system routines for outputting to the screen. In Section 8.5 you will see the assembler code that the compiler produced for the average.c program.

8.4   The stack – essential to most operations

A stack is also used as a temporary store for variables. If two variables need the same CPU register, such as ECX, they can use it in turn by employing the stack as a 'scratch-pad' temporary store. The machine instructions PUSH and POP copy items onto the stack and then remove them when required later, as shown in Fig. 8.6. These explicit stack operations use the stack pointer register ESP to hold the address of the item which is currently at the head of the stack.

The PUSH instruction works by first decrementing the address in ESP by the size of the item, and then using the ESP address to write the item into memory. This is an example of the 'register indirect pre-decrement' addressing mode. The POP instruction works in the reverse way, an item is read using ESP as a pointer to memory, and then ESP is incremented by the correct amount to remove (invalidate) the item from the stack. This demonstrates the 'register indirect post-increment' addressing mode. Sometimes the stack pointer has to be adjusted up or down the stack explicitly by the programmer:

```
ADD ESP,4           ; knock a longword off the stack
SUB ESP,256         ; open up 256 bytes of space on stack
```

The Pentium, like a lot of other computers, will not PUSH or POP single bytes. If only a byte is involved it will be handled as a complete word.

Some computers have the stack area inside the CPU for greater speed. Others have very few CPU registers and rely on the stack to hold all arithmetic operands.

Fig. 8.6
Using PUSH and POP stack instructions.

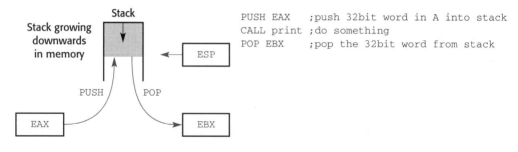

```
PUSH EAX    ;push 32bit word in A into stack
CALL print  ;do something
POP EBX     ;pop the 32bit word from stack
```

Table 8.1
Common uses of the
system stack.

1.	To save the **return address** during procedure calls
2.	To pass **parameters** into procedures
3.	To allocate **local variable** storage space (stack frame)
4.	As temporary **scratch-pad** storage for register values

A computer can operate with a single stack, but this will not offer any opportunity to separate user programs from more privileged system code. In order to achieve this level of security it is necessary to swap between user and system stacks. Such a feature can be extended for multitasking systems, to the point where each task is allocated its own private stack. Only one is active at any moment, with the ESP pointing to its top item. The MC68000 actually offered two stack pointer registers in the CPU to assist with switching between user and supervisor modes. The Pentium provides a further security feature to protect items in memory by dividing it into distinct **segments**. In this way, memory is split into a Code Segment, Data Segment and Stack Segment. To ensure that only valid actions are performed on the stack it can be initialized within a separate Stack Segment. If this arrangement is adopted, fetch–execute accesses are only allowed into the Code Segment, and PUSH and POP will only work in the Stack Segment. Modula-2, C, Pascal and ADA compilers all use the stack area of memory for Procedure CALL/RETURN sequences, temporary variable storage and some other activities as well. Table 8.1 lists the four principal jobs involving use of the stack.

Some interesting and subtle errors can occur when the stack handling is unbalanced. Programs may test out fine, and even run for long periods, until the stack error makes itself apparent through a system crash due to the stack running off the top of memory, or overwriting the code, or delivering an illegal return address. During HLL programming, the compiler ensures that all parameters, local variables and return addresses are PUSHed and POPped correctly.

8.5 Passing parameters – localizing a subroutine

Most subroutines require some **parameters** to tell them exactly what to do at each evocation. printf( ) would be particularly useless without parameters! Subroutines which do *exactly* the same each time they run are not terribly helpful. Parameters particularize, or localize, the action of a subroutine. For us, it is important to know how the calling program hands over parameter values, and how the subroutine sends back a result. The simplest method of passing items of data into a subroutine is to copy the value into an available CPU **register** before jumping off to the subroutine. The value will still be in the register when you arrive! The same technique can be used to return a value. In fact, C functions normally do return their value in a data register, EAX in the case of the Pentium.

Using only the CPU registers to pass parameters into a subroutine would be too constraining. And so the **stack** is employed for parameter passing, too. Thus the compiler depends heavily on the stack for the whole subroutine CALL-PASS-RETURN sequence. When a subroutine is to be invoked, first the parameters are pushed onto the stack, then the return address is pushed, and finally space is allocated for any local variables (see next section) declared within the subroutine. In all, the stack is used like a communual letterbox. Passing a **value parameter** into a subroutine is similar to the paper-boy or girl throwing a newspaper over the garden fence. It may be welcome – even expected – but the provenance may be uncertain! If you need to get back in touch with the newsagent it is useful to have a telephone number, or an address. This is where a **reference parameter**, or address, comes in. Instead of pushing the value of the variable onto the stack as a parameter, its address is pushed instead. In C functions you can recognize this by the & that prefaces the variable name. This allows the subroutine to modify the original variable, considered dangerous by the more cautious.

The Microsoft Developer Studio window presented in Fig. 8.7 is the **disassembly** display holding C source lines and Pentium assembler mnemonics. The debugger reads the executable machine code and reverse-translates the binary codes into assembler mnemonics. It also interleaves the original C source code at the appropriate points, thus clearly showing you what the compiler produced for each HLL instruction. Inspecting this type of output can be fascinating for the technical enthusiast!

The small arrow on the left margin indicates the current fetch–execute position, or where EIP is pointing. The screenshot was captured just after a CALL to the average( ) function was executed. If you look towards the bottom of the display the function call can be identified (n = average(NCLASS, maths_scores);).

Notice the following two instructions (PUSH maths_scores and PUSH 0AH). These are the two parameters declared for the function average( ) (0A is 10 in hex) being entered onto the stack for passing into the subroutine. The instruction following the CALL is ADD ESP,8, which raises the Stack Pointer eight bytes, thereby formally removing our two parameters from the stack by invalidating them. Such action is known as stack scrubbing and is needed to prevent the stack growing bigger and bigger as the program runs. This can be a cause of the phenomenon termed **memory leakage**, when the PC appears to suffer from an ever-reducing RAM size. In fact, it is brought about by programs which acquire memory resources but do not dispose of them correctly when finished with.

Such disassembly listings are packed with intriguing information, so we will return to Fig. 8.7 in the next section when dealing with local variables and stack frames.

In Fig. 8.8 the snapshots of the register display and the memory display windows were taken at the same moment as Fig. 8.7. The memory display has been focused on the stack area of memory to allow us to keep a watch on function CALL/RETURN activities. It has also been sized down to 4 bytes wide to make it easier to separate 32 bit items. The stack pointer (ESP) is indicating the current top-of-stack position; note that the stack is growing *upwards* on this display. Items that are already on the stack sit at the higher addresses, *below* the arrow. We can see our two subroutine parameters and the return address:

Fig. 8.7
Microsoft Developer
Studio debugger
disassembler display for
`average.c`.

```
Disassembly                                                          _ □ X
  5:      int tech_scores[] = {11,12,13,14,15,16,17,18,19,20};
  6:
  7:            |
  8:      float average(int x, int * y) {
  00401020   push       ebp                    ⎫
  00401021   mov        ebp,esp                ⎬ setting up the stack frame
  00401023   sub        esp,8                  ⎭
  9:      int i;
  10:     float av;
  11:     for (i=0; i<x; i++) {
⇨ 00401026   mov        dword ptr [i],0
  0040102D   jmp        average(0x00401038)+18h
  0040102F   mov        eax,dword ptr [i]
  00401032   add        eax,1
  00401035   mov        dword ptr [i],eax
  00401038   mov        ecx,dword ptr [i]
  0040103B   cmp        ecx,dword ptr [x]
  0040103E   jge        average(0x00401056)+36h
  12:          av += *y++ ;
  00401040   mov        edx,dword ptr [y]
  00401043   fild       dword ptr [edx]
  00401045   fadd       dword ptr [av]
  00401048   fstp       dword ptr [av]
  0040104B   mov        eax,dword ptr [y]
  0040104E   add        eax,4
  00401051   mov        dword ptr [y],eax
  13:     }
  00401054   jmp        average(0x0040102f)+0Fh
  14:     return av /= x;
  00401056   fild       dword ptr [x]
  00401059   fdivr      dword ptr [av]
  0040105C   fst        dword ptr [av]
  15:     }
  0040105F   mov        esp,ebp
  00401061   pop        ebp
  00401062   ret
  16:
  17:     int main( void) {
  00401063   push       ebp
  00401064   mov        ebp,esp     ← clearing down the stack frame
  00401066   push       ecx
  18:         float n;
  19:         n = average( NCLASS, maths_scores);
  00401067   push       offset _maths_scores(0x00415a30)
  0040106C   push       0Ah
  0040106E   call       @ILT+0(_average)(0x00401000)
  00401073   add        esp,8
  00401076   fst        dword ptr [...]
```

```
73 10 40 00      return address      ▲
0A 00 00 00      NCLASS              │ Stack growing
30 5A 41 00      maths_scores        │
```

Look back to Fig. 8.7 and make a note of the address of the instruction which immediately follows the call to our function, `call @ILT+0(_average)`. You can see
that it is the very same address saved on the stack: `00401073`. There is a bit of a
nuisance with the bytes being displayed in reverse numerical order in the memory
display, but it is a small inconvenience to suffer in order to have the privilege of
watching the Pentium stack doing its thing!

The order that parameters are pushed onto the stack is a point of disagreement
between Pascal and C compilers. C pushes starting from the right-hand parameter in

Fig. 8.8
Microsoft Developer
Studio debugger stack
and register display for
`average.c`.

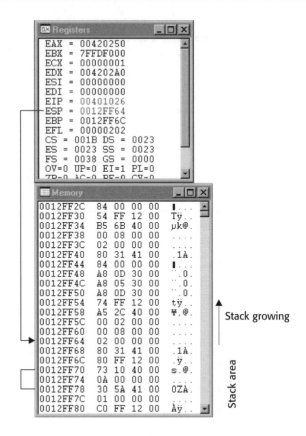

the list, while Pascal choses the left-hand parameter to be pushed first. This can give rise to a real mess if you try to employ library routines produced under the alternative regime.

8.6   Stack frame – all the local variables

The area of the stack used by a procedure is known as the **Stack Frame**. It holds the return address, procedure parameters, and local variables. Because there is always the possibility of nested procedure calls, there is the requirement for a marker to indicate the top of the current stack frame and the bottom of the previous frame. This is done using a CPU register designated as the **Stack Frame Base Pointer**. With the Pentium, EBP is usually reserved for this role. While ESP may commute up and down during the execution of a procedure, the value given to EBP will remain unchanged. But there is only one EBP, so when another stack frame is allocated, due to a call to another procedure, the value in EBP is pushed onto the stack to free EBP to point to the new stack frame. The stack for a CPU running compiled code would look something like Fig. 8.9 during a procedure call.

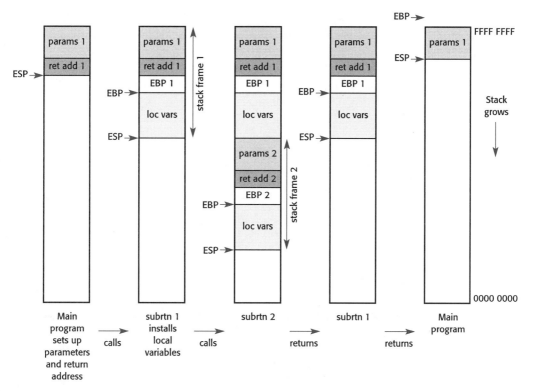

Fig. 8.9
Using the stack for local variables.

On the stack the saved value from the Stack Frame Base Pointer (EBP) is sometimes referred to as the **Environment Pointer** because it points to the previous stack frame. Now, in languages such as Pascal or ADA these earlier stack frames are termed 'in-scope' and the local variables contained are still accessible through the Environment Pointer. It is worth mentioning that C does not allow this practice, as it forbids the declaration of functions within each other. Pascal compilers can predict the run-time arrangement of frames on the stack by looking at how the procedure declarations are nested in the source code.

Seen together on the stack, and accessed in an identical manner through the frame pointer, local variables and parameters are closely related. In fact, procedure parameters could be seen simply as local variables which have been pre-initialized with useful values.

Referring back to Fig. 8.7, you can see the parameters and local variables being set up in the stack frame. Parameter handling for the call to average( ) has already been discussed in Section 8.5, but now look at the first three instructions inside average( ) at the top of the figure. Here you can see the frame base pointer value being saved on the stack (PUSH EBP), a new frame pointer being initialized (MOV EBP, ESP) and the space established for two local variables (SUB ESP, 8). Moving forward to Fig. 8.8, you can see these items on the stack:

02 00 00 00	space for av – current Head of Stack
80 31 41 00	space for i
80 FF 12 00	old EBP value

Stack growing

Fig. 8.10
A common error when using C pointers on the stack.

```c
#include <stdio.h>

char* getname(void) {
  char nstring[25];
      printf("Please type your name: ");
      gets( nstring);
      putchar( '\n');
  return nstring; //SERIOUS ERROR IN THIS PROGRAM
}

int main(void) {
  char* myname;
  myname = getname();
  printf("%s\n", myname);
return 0;
}
```

Because the stack frame is invalidated after the return at the end of the subroutine, no further reference should be made to those local variables. However, by using a debugger it may still be possible to inspect the area of memory used for the stack and see the old data before it gets overwritten by the next items to be pushed onto the stack. If the stack area gets unintentionally overwritten, or the stack grows too big, the run-time errors can be quite unpredictable and difficult to trace.

Assembler-level programmers retain control over all stack handling, which can lead to some major snarl-ups at run-time when errors get through unnoticed. The assembler provides no error checking at this level. Code generated by HLL compilers does benefit from some syntax checking, but even so, pointer operations regularly continue to mess up our code when not used correctly. The example listed in Fig. 8.10 should be a warning to us all. It passes through the compiler without a blink, but will produce serious run-time failures some of the time.

The function getname( ) in Fig. 8.10 inputs a string using gets( ), saves it in a local variable, nstring[ ], and returns the start address of the string as a pointer to the caller. But local variables are no longer valid after the subroutine has been terminated and the return has taken place. Unfortunately, when the calling program attempts to use the pointer myname to access the data it will not be stopped by error handlers. Although the data string is now below the stack pointer, indicating that it is 'stale', it may still be readable. Despite this fatal flaw, the program runs the serious risk of sometimes working because the memory area containing the string data will only get overwritten when another item has been pushed onto the stack. Try it and see, then insert another function call between getname( ) and printf( ) to overwrite the area of stack containing the stale local variable nstring[ ].

8.7 Supporting HLLs – special CPU facilities for dealing with subroutines

With all CPUs, procedure calls and returns are carried out by a special CALL/RET instruction pair. These are fundamentally the same as jump instructions, which work by inserting new address values into the program counter (EIP). As explained in Section 8.2, the CALL instruction also pushes the current EIP value onto the stack, as the return address, and then loads the subroutine start address into EIP, thus effecting a jump to the subroutine code. To speed up the return from subroutines, the Pentium has an enhanced 'RET n' instruction. This returns control to the calling program after deleting any parameters from the stack. Such an action conforms to Pascal compiler conventions, while C compilers insert stack scrubbing code to remove parameters not in the subroutine but immediately after the CALL instruction. Thus parameters are inserted and removed in the same block of code. Strangely enough, Windows adheres to Pascal conventions, which include pushing the parameters onto the stack in reverse order to C. Pascal compilers push parameter lists from left to right, C pushes right to left!

The Pentium offers another useful pair of instructions, ENTER and LEAVE, to open and close stack frames for the local variables. In the special case of Pascal-like HLLs, where it is necessary to access in-scope variables held in previous frames, higher up the stack, the ENTER instruction can copy down environment pointers from previous frames already on the stack. These pointers give fast access to in-scope variables. A group of environment pointers is known as the Display Frame. Without the Display Frame, the only way to access in-scope stack variables would be to walk back up the stack from frame to frame using the environment pointers, until the correct frame is reached – not a convenient operation.

8.8 Interrupt service routines – hardware-invoked subroutines

Although **Interrupt Service Routines** (ISR) are similar to ordinary subroutines, in that they contain code to carry out an operation on behalf of the system, they are given a completely different status by programmers. They are discussed in hushed reverential tones, and more often than not totally ignored by general programming courses. Maybe this is due to their critical functionality or the traditional practice of hand coding them in assembler! The major distinction is that ISRs are never entered using a normal CALL instruction. They are executed only when a hardware interrupt signal (Fig. 8.11), or a special trap instruction, sometimes referred to as an **exception**, occurs. An interrupt could come from a disk drive wanting to tell the CPU that it has finished transferring data, or from a mouse indicating movement, or from the memory signalling a fatal error. Alternatively, trap instructions can be used to request

Fig. 8.11
Interrupts as hardware-
invoked subroutines.

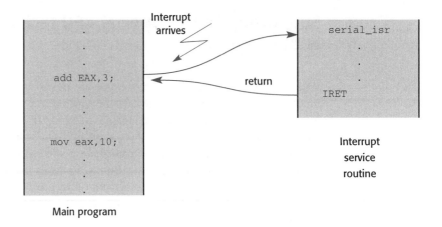

resources or actions under the control of the operating system. Interrupts are considered to be totally unpredictable. So what is the problem? When the interrupt occurs, the CPU quickly swaps to the ISR code, but to execute this code it needs to use several CPU registers. However, there are no CPU registers reserved for only the ISRs to use, which means that they may already contain important data from the preempted program – so here is the problem: how can we protect the existing program and data from corruption when an interrupt occurs?

The solution is to PUSH the contents of any register that the ISR will be using onto the stack – execute the ISR – then POP the registers back just before returning to the main program. This excellent solution, however, is of no use to the HLL programmer who cannot directly access PUSH and POP instructions. Standard HLLs do not offer statements which simply compile into PUSH or POP. Thus another clear distinguishing feature is revealed: ISRs need to be coded in assembler.

The same return mechanism – using the stack to hold the return address – is used as described in Section 8.3. But there are major differences when developing code for ISRs rather than subroutines.

Because hardware interrupts may arrive at any time, without any warning, the programmer has to plan for every eventuality. Another major difference between interrupt service routines and normal procedures is their complete lack of parameters. Because the interrupt can occur at any time, it is impossible to prepare a parameter list. Similarly, there is a problem in returning a result, which often means that the only effect of an interrupt routine is to update some global variables in memory. This gives rise to further difficulties which will be described in Section 9.5.

8.9   Accessing operating system routines – late binding

There is much theorizing in computing circles about the correct moment for address binding: should we defer binding or not? Now binding is the action of establishing a physical address for something so that we can access it, and the discussion becomes of practical significance when considering how to get at operating system facilities, or shared library modules which are already loaded into memory. If the compiler does not know exactly where the entry points will be it is impossible to insert the correct address into the CALL instruction. Considering the following code fragment which uses the normal CALL instruction it is clear that the compiler or linker can compute the correct address for filter1 and insert it into your executable program.

```
call filter1
```

There can be no doubt: the compiler determines the subroutine referenced, and the linker fixes up the address. This is early binding. However, with the following code fragment:

```
lea esi,filter1
...
call [esi]
```

the subroutine to be called is only determined at run-time by the address loaded into the ESI register. By loading different addresses into ESI, several alternative subroutines might be called depending on the preceding code. This is known as late binding. The provision of register indirect addressing makes such dynamic referencing possible. This is the situation that Windows finds itself in when trying to link code with an application program CALL to a function offered by a DLL (Dynamic Link Library). The Windows operating system needs to pass to the caller program the entry address of the DLL function so that access can be obtained.

In MS-DOS, and other operating systems, an alternative approach is taken which is supported by a particular instruction: the software interrupt, INT. The very concept of a software-invoked interrupt is rather strange. Interrupts are meant for unpredictable external events. But here we have an instruction, within the ordered run of a program, asking for an interrupt to occur. In fact, it is really only used in place of a CALL instruction, temporarily transferring control to a service routine. The important advantage of using the INT version of calling is that the location of the service routine is entered into the Interrupt Vector Table (IVT), which is situated at a fixed position in memory. Thus if the operating system has to move the entry points to handler routines, it only needs to update the address entries in the IVT. The application programs can remain unchanged.

In addition, it is worth remembering that an interrupt will alter the CPU priority level, because normally all ISRs are owned by the operating system. Funnelling operating system calls through an interrupt doorway allows the operating system to control access to critical resources.

Review

- Subroutines, functions and methods are chunks of code which can be invoked many times within one program. They save memory space and programmer effort.

- Because they can be called from several places, there has to be a mechanism to remember where to return to at the end of the subroutine.

- The Pentium, like most processors, uses the stack to hold the subroutine return address. This is a convenient technique because it also deals with nested subroutine calls.

- Data is only written and read from one end (head or top) of the stack. These manoeuvres are called PUSH and POP. Stacks frequently grow downwards in memory.

- Parameters are passed into subroutines by placing them on the stack before leaving the calling segment of code.

- Local variables, declared in a subroutine are given space on the stack underneath the parameters. This area is then called the stack frame.

- Parameters can be seen as pre-initialized local variables.

- Several common but serious errors occur due to passing pointers as parameters into subroutines.

- Libraries of subroutines are provided with compilers. They are bound to your code by the linker.

Practical work

The recommended practical work involves using the subroutine CALL/RET instructions and viewing the stack area of memory using the debugger memory window. Passing parameters into the subroutine can also be tried in CPU registers and on the stack. Calls to C language library functions can be used at both HLL and asm levels.

Exercises

1. In computing, what is meant by the 'Where did I come from?' problem? Give some solutions which might be viable.

2. Explain the difference between the terms 'local variables' and 'function parameters'.

3. Why is the stack so important for HLL programmers? What use is the Pentium RET n instruction?

4. Why is the stack pointer contained in the CPU while the stack itself is in memory?

5. How do C functions return their value to the calling program? How can a function return an array variable?

6. When might the compiler choose to use the PUSH/POP instructions?

7. Explain the difference between value and reference parameters in assembler terminology.

8. Where are HLL global variables held?

9. What does a linker program actually do?

A. Check the assembler equivalents for various HLL variable declarations: `char`, `int`, `array of char`.

B. What is the role of the stack during a C function call? Use the debugger to single-step the program in Fig. 8.11. Watch the stack area and how the returned pointer becomes 'invalid'.

C. How do computers with no system stack manage the procedure call/return activity? What about the parameters?

D. Why are local variables accessed through the Frame Pointer, rather than simply using the Stack Pointer?

E. How can some subroutines, such as `printf( )`, have a variable number of parameters?

F. What are the disadvantages of relying on globally declared data instead of using parameter passing when invoking subroutines?

Readings

■ Heuring and Jordan (1997), Section 3.3.4.

■ Tanenbaum (1999), Section 5.5.5: procedure call instructions; Section 5.6.3: comparison of subroutines to coroutines.

■ Hennessy and Patterson (1998), Section 3.6: hardware support for procedure calls.

■ The Web sites can be accessed via the Companion Web site for this book at:
   `http://www.booksites.net/williams/`

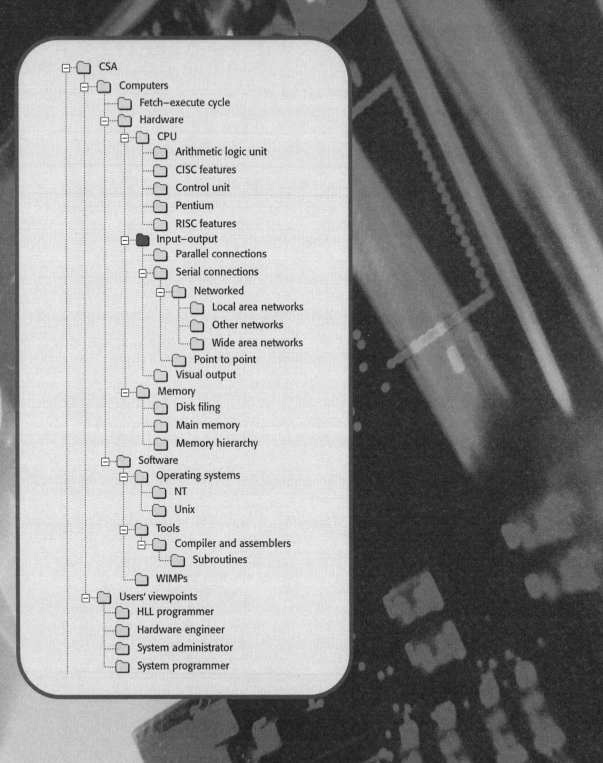

- CSA
  - Computers
    - Fetch−execute cycle
    - Hardware
      - CPU
        - Arithmetic logic unit
        - CISC features
        - Control unit
        - Pentium
        - RISC features
      - Input−output
        - Parallel connections
        - Serial connections
          - Networked
            - Local area networks
            - Other networks
            - Wide area networks
          - Point to point
        - Visual output
      - Memory
        - Disk filing
        - Main memory
        - Memory hierarchy
    - Software
      - Operating systems
        - NT
        - Unix
      - Tools
        - Compiler and assemblers
          - Subroutines
      - WIMPs
  - Users' viewpoints
    - HLL programmer
    - Hardware engineer
    - System administrator
    - System programmer

Simple input and output

9

Overview

The three techniques used by computers to transfer data to and from the 'outside world' (polling, interrupts, DMA) are introduced with example applications. An important distinction is drawn between 'intermittent' and 'dedicated' polling. The three categories of register found in IO chips (status, command, data) are explained from the programmer's viewpoint. Some aspects of interrupt servicing are exposed, and the various uses of interrupts discussed. This introduces the problem of critical data, or data corruption due to concurrent access. The appropriate use of DMA facilities is also discussed. The important role of interrupts in supporting multitasking operating systems is introduced.

9.1   Basic IO methods – polling, interrupt and DMA

The very simple, byte-wide parallel ports introduced in Section 3.8 are still widely used to transfer data into and out of computers. The Centronics printer port is basically such a byte-wide parallel port, and has been provided on all PCs from the very beginning. But serial ports are equally useful, often being referred to as COM ports or modem ports. It is worth noting that the local area network interface is essentially a fast serial port giving access to a high-bandwidth network. This requires greater hardware support in order to deal with the much faster bursts of data. The new USB (Universal Serial Bus) standard is intended to provide an alternative means of interconnecting devices to a computer without needing to invest in the complete networking paraphernalia. More details of serial communication links will be discussed in Chapter 10, while Chapter 11 is dedicated to parallel buses and interfaces.

Whether dealing with serial or parallel ports, there are three principal software techniques used to transfer data through a computer IO port, as listed in Table 9.1.

We will discuss each method in greater detail later in this chapter. All require so called software **driver** routines to work closely with their IO hardware units. These routines are normally part of the operating system and not infrequently written in assembler. In the PC market-place, extension card suppliers provide such driver routines on either floppy disk or CD-ROM along with the hardware, so that they may be installed by the user. It is also increasingly common to have access to driver routine libraries via the Internet. Following the pioneering example of Unix, modern operating systems are written as far as possible in HLL, probably C. In this way, porting the operating system to a new processor is faster and more reliable – once a good C compiler has been obtained! Windows NT has defined a specific hardware interface layer of software, HAL (Hardware Abstraction Layer), which acts as a **virtual machine** layer to aid porting to new processors. The traditional view of software as a hierarchy of intercommunicating layers is presented in Fig. 9.1. Each layer has a specific data processing role with adjoining layers exchanging messages.

HAL hides many of the specific hardware differences between the Pentium, Alpha and MIPS processors from the main part of the operating system code, making it easier to port and maintain the system code. Although direct access to the IO hardware is still possible with Windows 98, Unix and Windows NT strictly deny this possibility for security reasons. Such a limitation does not concern most application programmers, who only ever access IO facilities by calling library procedures provided with the HLL compiler, such as `getc( )` and `putc( )`. These procedures may also then call operating system code, sometimes stored in PROM or FLASH RAM to gain access to the actual hardware.

Table 9.1
Different input–output techniques.

1	Dedicated and periodic **polling**
2.	**Interrupt** driven
3.	Direct Memory Access (**DMA**)

Fig. 9.1
Software access to
hardware.

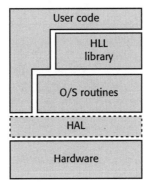

9.2 Peripheral interface registers – the programmer's viewpoint

If you need to address the IO ports directly, assuming the operating system security controls will allow this, you will have to know the base address of the IO chip in the memory map and the layout and function of its internal registers.

In this situation, a copy of the technical datasheet from the chip manufacturer and some helpful application notes are invaluable, if not essential. When confronted with such literature, programmers, not being electronic engineers, have to quickly learn the art of selective reading, paying attention only to those aspects of relevance to programming; see Fig. 9.2 for an example page from such a datasheet (the full version of which can be found at `http://www.intersil.com/data/FN/FN2/FN2969/FN2969.pdf`). Programmers would certainly need the information to include the port addresses of the internal registers and their function. Reading the hardware user's guide for a peripheral interface chip, despite the initial appearance of complexity, is no more difficult than reading a text on programming. The majority of IO chips contain only three types of register, as listed in Table 9.2. There may be none or several of each type. IO registers are often accessed as bytes rather than words, and sometimes each bit corresponds to a separate feature or facility. When reading technical datasheets about IO chips it is advisable to start by identifying these three register types.

The purpose of **Command Registers** is to allow the programmer to specify more exactly the action of the IO chip. There may be a wide range of options provided, such as transmission speeds, buffer sizes and error handling techniques, all to cater for different circumstances and a variety of applications. This allows the chip manufacturer to supply a single product which can be set up, using the Command Register, to fit in with a variety of applications. The particular choice is made during system

Table 9.2
Categories of peripheral
chip register.

1.	Command registers
2.	Status registers
3.	Data registers

Fig. 9.2
Datasheet (p. 3) for a
Harris 82C55A parallel
port IO chip.

82C55A

Functional Description

Data Bus Buffer

This three-state bi-directional 8-bit buffer is used to interface the 82C55A to the system data bus. Data is transmitted or received by the buffer upon execution of input or output instructions by the CPU. Control words and status information are also transferred through the data bus buffer.

Read/Write and Control Logic

The function of this block is to manage all of the internal and external transfers of both Data and Control or Status words. It accepts inputs from the CPU Address and Control busses and in turn, issues commands to both of the Control Groups.

(CS) Chip Select. A "low" on this input pin enables the communcation between the 82C55A and the CPU.

(RD) Read. A "low" on this input pin enables 82C55A to send the data or status information to the CPU on the data bus. In essence, it allows the CPU to "read from" the 82C55A.

(WR) Write. A "low" on this input pin enables the CPU to write data or control words into the 82C55A.

(A0 and A1) Port Select 0 and Port Select 1. These input signals, in conjunction with the RD and WR inputs, control the selection of one of the three ports or the control word register. They are normally connected to the least significant bits of the address bus (A0 and A1).

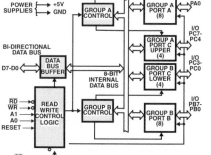

FIGURE 1. 82C55A BLOCK DIAGRAM. DATA BUS BUFFER, READ/WRITE, GROUP A & B CONTROL LOGIC FUNCTIONS

(RESET) Reset. A "high" on this input initializes the control register to 9Bh and all ports (A, B, C) are set to the input mode. "Bus hold" devices internal to the 82C55A will hold the I/O port inputs to a logic "1" state with a maximum hold current of 400μA.

Group A and Group B Controls

The functional configuration of each port is programmed by the systems software. In essence, the CPU "outputs" a control word to the 82C55A. The control word contains information such as "mode", "bit set", "bit reset", etc., that initializes the functional configuration of the 82C55A.

Each of the Control blocks (Group A and Group B) accepts "commands" from the Read/Write Control logic, receives "control words" from the internal data bus and issues the proper commands to its associated ports.

Control Group A - Port A and Port C upper (C7 - C4)

Control Group B - Port B and Port C lower (C3 - C0)

The control word register can be both written and read as shown in the "Basic Operation" table. Figure 4 shows the control word format for both Read and Write operations. When the control word is read, bit D7 will always be a logic "1", as this implies control word mode information.

82C55A BASIC OPERATION

A1	A0	RD	WR	CS	INPUT OPERATION (READ)
0	0	0	1	0	Port A → Data Bus
0	1	0	1	0	Port B → Data Bus
1	0	0	1	0	Port C → Data Bus
1	1	0	1	0	Control Word → Data Bus
					OUTPUT OPERATION (WRITE)
0	0	1	0	0	Data Bus → Port A
0	1	1	0	0	Data Bus → Port B
1	0	1	0	0	Data Bus → Port C
1	1	1	0	0	Data Bus → Control
					DISABLE FUNCTION
X	X	X	X	1	Data Bus → Three-State
X	X	1	1	0	Data Bus → Three-State

initialization by writing the appropriate bit pattern to a Command Register. Sometimes the hardware makes Command Registers appear as 'write-only', which makes for further programming difficulties if some bits in the register need to be updated.

On the other hand, **Status Registers** are provided so that the software can keep a watch on the IO chip by reading and testing the contained status flags. These registers may be 'read-only', which is not a great source of inconvenience.

The **Data Registers** are the 'letterboxes' through which the data actually passes during its journey into or out of the computer. Generally you expect to write to an output port, and read from an input port, but sometimes the opposite, too, is allowed.

The Programmable Peripheral Interface (8255) was originally produced by Intel as a member of the family of IO support chips intended for the 8080 microprocessor. Despite its ancient origins back in the 1970s, it is still found on PC IO cards offering three byte-wide parallel ports for interconnecting equipment to the computer. The data sheet circuit diagram in Fig. 9.2 shows three bidirectional ports, which are referred to as A, B and C. Port C has various alternative functions and can be split into two 4 bit sections under certain conditions. From the addressing table in Fig. 9.2, the two address lines, A_0 and A_1, can be seen to select one of the ports, while the READ and WRITE control lines determine whether the current access is an input or output activity. The advantage of using a 'programmable' IO device comes from the flexibility that it offers. For example, the program initializes major aspects of the functionality, including whether it is acting as an input or an output port. The Control, or command, Register must be set up correctly before any data can be transferred. There are three modes of action:

- Mode 0 – basic byte-wide input and output ports

- Mode 1 – bytes passed by strobed (asynchronous) handshake

- Mode 2 – tri-state bus action

The three byte-wide ports, A, B and C, can operate simultaneously under differing modes of activity. Figure 9.3 presents the function of the individual bits within the Control Register, and offers a fragment of C code to initialize the 8255 for routine IO operation.

Fig. 9.3
Control Register functions for the 8255 PPI.

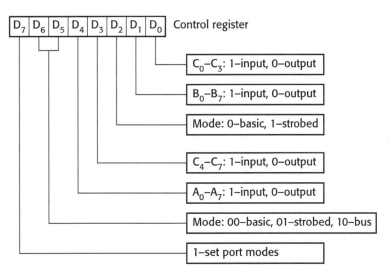

```
// win-98. Initializes 8255 at 0x1F3: Port A IN; B OUT; C OUT
outp((short)0x1F3, 0x90); //Initialize 8255 Command Register
```

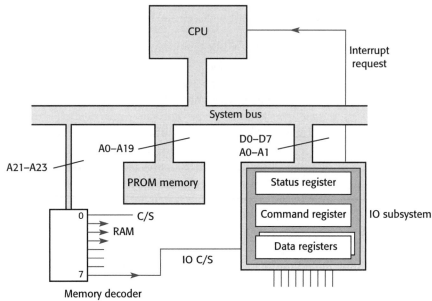

Fig. 9.4
Accessing registers in memory-mapped IO. Copyright Intersil Corporation, reproduced with permission.

The PC uses the separate 64 kbyte port address space provided by the Pentium, which is accessed using the IN and OUT machine instructions. The C language is extended to incorporate these codes with the inp( ) and outp( ) functions. Other processors do not have this distinct address space, so all the IO ports have to be mapped into the memory address space alongside the RAMs and ROMs.

The IO chip in the example system illustrated in Fig. 9.4 is memory-mapped. This means that it is accessed in the same way as memory – there is no need to use special port-in and port-out instructions. The MOV group of machine instructions can operate with memory-mapped ports as well as locations in memory. In this case the registers are located at the following addresses:

```
E00000H – command register
E00001H – status register
E00002H – receive data
E00003H – transmit data
```

When you study the memory decoding circuit in Fig. 9.4, you can see that the total address space of 16 Mbyte is split into eight 2 Mbyte pages by the most significant three address bits. The top memory page is reserved for the input–output devices, while the lower seven are available for RAM or ROM. The formal memory map table is given in Fig. 9.5. Note that because we have not applied full decoding, the IO chip would act promiscuously and respond enthusiastically to each block of four addresses in the upper page, giving 524,288 equivalent addresses for the same chip. This unwelcome aliasing effect would make it impossible to install any other devices in the top 2 Mbyte page without modifying the memory decoding circuit.

Device	Size	Address pins	Address bus	Address range
PROM1	1 Mbyte	20	000x ++++ ++++ ++++ ++++ ++++	00 0000–0F FFFF
RAM1	2 Mbyte	21	001+ ++++ ++++ ++++ ++++ ++++	20 0000–3F FFFF
RAM2	2 Mbyte	21	010+ ++++ ++++ ++++ ++++ ++++	40 0000–5F FFFF
RAM3	2 Mbyte	21	011+ ++++ ++++ ++++ ++++ ++++	60 0000–7F FFFF
IO	4 byte	2	111x xxxx xxxx xxxx xxxx xx++	E0 0000–E0 0003
				E0 0004–E0 0007
			aliases {	E0 0008–E0 000B
				E0 000C–E0 000F
				. . .

Fig. 9.5
Memory map for the system in Fig. 9.4.

In summary, the Command Registers contain writeable bit flags. These allow the programmer to control the activity of the chip, which is usually done by writing to the register during the initialization phase, whereas the Status Registers contain readable bit flags which indicate chip activities and errors. The Data Registers, usually designated as input or output, are the window through which data items pass to and from the external device.

9.3   Polling – single-character IO

For the Motorola MC680x0, the fundamental method of reading data from an input port into a CPU register is the simple execution of a MOVE instruction. As with the Pentium's MOV, this must have source and destination arguments to route the data correctly. The MC68000 requires all IO ports to be installed to look like memory locations, as explained in Section 6.8, while the Intel Pentium, because it offers a separate IO map for ports, has to use distinct IN and OUT instructions.

An example of input by programmed **polling** is presented in the Pentium assembler code fragment listed in Fig. 9.6. This would only work on a system running MS-DOS or Windows 98 because Windows NT and Unix expressly deny direct access to hardware in this fashion for security reasons. Under NT, the operating system code handles all the IO operations, so the IN and OUT instructions are hidden inside NT or Unix device driver code. The receive ready flag (RXRDY) in the Status Register is repeatedly checked in a tight polling loop until it has been set to 1 by the hardware, indicating that a new item of data has arrived in the data Receive Register. The loop then drops through and the byte is read from the data Receive Register and checked for zero. A value of zero would indicate the end of the current data transfer. If it is non-zero, the item is saved into the data array using a pointer, and the loop continues.

It is also very important to understand that IO port hardware, detecting the action of somebody reading data from the data register, RXDATA, clears down the RXRDY flag in readiness for the arrival of the next item of data.

At this point, if C code is of no particular interest to you, please feel free to JMP GASP (p. 188) and so avoid a worse headache!

Fig. 9.6
Example input polling
loop in assembler and C
code.

```
Loop:     IN AX, STATUS        ;read status port ◄─────────────┐
          TEST AL, RXRDY       ;test device status  Polling loop │
          JZ LOOP              ;if no data go back again ─────────┘  ⚑
                                                                      RxRDY

DATAIN:   IN AX, RXDATA        ;get data from Rx port & clear RXRDY flag
          OR AL, AL            ;test for end marker
          JZ COMPLETE          ;jmp out if finished
          MOV [DI], AL         ;save character in data buffer
          INC DI
          JMP LOOP             ;back for more input
COMPLETE: ....                 ;character string input complete
```

For a memory-mapped I/O system, the C equivalent of this code might look something like this:

```
do {
  while !(*(BYTE*)RXSTATUS & RXRDY) { } ;\*wait until data arrives *\
} while (*pch++ = *(BYTE*)RXDATA) ;       \*check data for a NULL *\
```

Which of the two code fragments in Fig. 9.6 is judged as less cryptic may be a close call, depending rather more on dogmatic principle than objective evidence. The C code is certainly shorter. Perhaps some explanation, or justification, for this odd C fragment is required. Sometimes with C, a problem can arise when constant definitions, like RXSTATUS and RXDATA, are referenced. As #define constants, they default to the integer type, which confuses the compiler. Thus, the (BYTE*) casting is required to coerce the type from integer to pointer-to-BYTE (a BYTE is only another name for an unsigned char). The second, leading * de-references the pointer, delivering the desired byte value from the memory-mapped port register. If this is not done, good compilers will throw up a warning message, which could annoy those among us with an inquiring disposition. To avoid this we are confronted by the need to employ the curious *(BYTE*) type casting construct.

Another point related to C compilers which programmers might appreciate is the rare opportunity to apply the type qualifier **volatile** to the status and data register declarations. This may be necessary because compilers can decide to optimize the final code after having noticed that the variables RXDATA and RXSTATUS are read but not written. Thus they appear as constants to the compiler, which may then decide to adjust the generated machine code to run more efficiently. So we must tell the compiler that although RXDATA and RXSTATUS may appear to be constant, they are in fact being altered by some other action which is invisible to the software: hence the 'volatile' qualification.

GASP:
The complementary version which *output*s data is nearly identical, except that the TXDATA flag in the Status Register is polled until it changes to 1, indicating that the Transmit Data Register is available. The next data item is then moved from memory into TXDATA, the Transmit Register. At this point the loop starts all over again.

Table 9.3
Relative speeds of
operation.

System buses operate at	500 Mbyte/s
Blocks of characters can be moved at	100 Mbyte/s
Ethernet transfers data at	10 Mbyte/s
Telephone call needs	8 kbyte/s
Serial lines frequently run at	1 kbyte/s
Epson printers operate at	100 byte/s
Keyboards send at	4 byte/s

Because the CPU operates so much faster than the peripheral devices and their human attendants, if a computer depended solely on this method (called spin polling) to communicate with peripheral devices it would spend most of its time in *wasteful* polling loops, testing each device in turn to see if they are ready and require service. It is like a telephone with a broken bell: *making* a call is perfectly all right, but the only way to *receive* a call would be to regularly pick up the handset and check by listening to determine whether anyone is on the line. The likely frequency of occurrence of events, and the seriousness of any penalty which befalls should any be missed, needs to be determined before choosing which IO technique to employ. In Table 9.3 the widely differing rates of commonplace activities are presented for consideration.

Devices may be polled at a regular timed interval, which is referred to as **Intermittent Polling**. This is found in many embedded systems around the home, in environmental monitoring equipment or in traffic counting systems. The polling interval is chosen to suit the needs of the application. It could be once a second (1 Hz) or faster. Sometimes a quite ancillary requirement determines the cycle timing, such as the need to reduce front panel display flicker to a minimum. By only polling the device intermittently, the time lost in spin polling is avoided. Such a method works well and avoids the complexity of interrupt processing. This suggestion is slightly disingenuous, because to achieve a 25 ms intermittent polling rate would require the assistance of an interrupt-driven clock tick, so we have simply swapped one interrupt requirement for another! However, it is useful to distinguish clearly between **dedicated** (spin) and **intermittent** (timed) polling (Fig. 9.7) when discussing the merits of the different techniques.

Some equipment, such as radar echo processing systems, require such a fast reaction to incoming data that even an interrupt response is too slow. In these circumstances only a fast dedicated polling loop might suffice.

Fig. 9.7
Comparing dedicated
and intermittent polling.

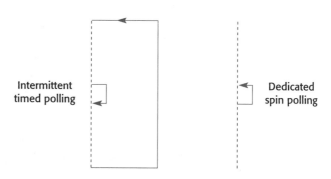

Intermittent
timed polling

Dedicated
spin polling

```
/* io.h 68k header file with h/w definitions */

/* messages */
#define PAPER_OUT       -1
#define DE_SELECT       -2
#define YES             0
#define NO              -1
#define OK              0


/* address, offsets and setting for M68681 DUART */
#define DUART       0XFFFF80    /*base address */
#define ACR         9           /*aux control reg */
#define CRA         5           /*command reg A */
#define MBA         1           /*mode reg A */
#define CSRA        3           /*clock select A */
#define SRA         3           /*status reg A */
#define RBA         7           /*rx reg A */
#define TBA         7           /*tx reg A */
#define RXRDY       1           /*bit mask for rx ready bit */
#define TXRDY       4           /*bit mask for tx ready bit */

/*Settings for the Motorola M68230 Parallel Interface Timer
   These only deal with mode 0.0, and for ports B and C
   No details about the timer.
*/

/* PI/T offsets and addresses, PIT registers are all on odd addresses */
#define PIT         0XFFFF40    /*address OF PI/T */
#define BCR         0XF         /*offset for port B cntrl Reg*/
#define BDDR        7           /*offset for B data direction*/
#define BDR         0X13        /*offset port B data reg */
#define CDR         0X19        /*offset port C data reg */


/* Parallel port settings masks and modes */
#define MODE0          0X20     /* mode 0.0, 2X buff i/p, single buff o/p */
#define MODE01X        0X80     /* mode 0.1X, unlatch i/p, 1X buff o/p */
#define OUT            0XFF     /* all bits output: 0 - 1/p, 1 - o/p*/
#define STROBE_MINUS   0X28     /* strobe printer -ve */
#define STROBE_PLUS    0X20     /* strobe printer +ve */
#define PRINT_ST       1        /* paper out pin 00000001 */
#define PAPER_ST       2        /* paper out pin 00000010 */
#define SELECT_ST      4        /* paper out pin 00000100 */
```

Fig. 9.8
Header definition file for 68k single board computer.

When attempting to read in data from a device, it is important to ascertain from the start whether you intend to **block** on the read or not. This refers to the situation where you commit the program to wait until some data is available. In an HLL program it will involve a call such as scanf ( ), which will not return until it has a satisfactory parameter to deliver back. The host operating system handles the complex details of IO within a multitasking environment, but it does still feel like a dedicated polling loop to the programmer. Such single-minded perseverance may not be to your liking when your program has many other things to do. A simple solution is to make sure that there is some data waiting to be read before going into a blocking read such as

Fig. 9.9
Example C program,
using polled IO directly
to the hardware.
(Continued on p. 192)

```c
/*Initialization and data transfer routines for 68k SBC */

#include "io.h"

/* set up Mc68681 DUART serial port A only */
void dinit() {
    register char *p;
    register int i;

        p = (char *)DUART;
        *(p+ACR) = 128;/* set baud rate */
        *(p+CRA) = 16;/* reset Rx */
        *(p+MRA) = 19;/* no modem, no PARITY,  8 bits */
        *(p+MRA) = 7;/* no ECHO, no modem cntrl, 1 STOP */
        *(p+CRA) = 5;/* enable Rx & Tx */
        *(p+CSRA)= 187;/* Rx & Tx at 9600 */

        p = ( char *) PIT;/* set to base address of PI/T */
        *(p + BCR ) = MODE0;/* mode 0.0 */
        *(p + BDDR ) = OUT;

        for(i=0; i != 1000; i++) ;/* init delay */
}

/* set up 68230 PIT for print out on port B */
void pinit() {
    char *p;
        p = ( char *) PIT;/* set to base address of PI/T */
        *(p + BCR ) = MODE0;/* mode 0.0 */
        *(p + BDDR ) = OUT;
}

/* get char from serial port A   returns character */
char get()  {
    register char *p;

        p = (char *)DUART;
        while ( !( *(p+SRA) & RXRDY )) {};  /* block here */
        return *(p+RBA);
}

/* put character c to serial port A */
void put( char c) {
    register char *p;

        p = (char *)DUART;
        while ( !( *(p+SRA) & TXRDY )) {};  /* block here */
        *(p+TBA) = c;
}

/* put string to serial port A using put routine */
void puts(char* p) {
        while( *p )
                put(*p++);
        put('\\n');
}
```

scanf( ). The same situation can occur for a write using a call such as putc( ). If the output device is not ready to despatch data, perhaps because it is still busy transmitting the previous data, it will block your write request and not return your call until it is free to service it. To avoid the situation of a program blocking on every input and output function, operating systems are capable of carrying out an availability check. There are several useful functions, such as kbhit( ) or GetInputState( ).

Fig. 9.9
continued

```
/*put character to parallel port */
int print (int c) {
  register char * p ;

    p = (char *) PIT;
    while ( *(p + CDR) & PAPER_ST) )
    {
        if ( !( *(p + CDR) & PAPER_ST) )
            return (PAPER_OUT) ;
        if ( !( *(p + CDR) & SELECT_ST) )
            return ( DE_SELECT);
    }
    *(p + BDR) = c;              /*send data */
    *(p + BCR) = STROBE_MINUS;/* strobe positive */
    *(p + BCR) = STROBE_PLUS;/* strobe negative */
    return OK ;
}
```

Unfortunately, these status-checking functions are not part of the standard set of C library calls. Each operating system has its own status checking functions.

A clear distinction can be drawn between intermittent and dedicated polling, as illustrated in Fig. 9.7. Although dedicated polling wastes much CPU time when the peripheral runs much more slowly than the CPU, the alternatives of interrupt-driven IO and autonomous DMA are more demanding in terms of hardware and software support. Polling is normally considered as a first option because it is readily implemented and straightforward to test and debug. Figures 9.8 and 9.9 list some C code which handles data IO directly through polling the hardware status flags.

The code fragments listed in Figs. 9.8 and 9.9 illustrate the use of polled IO with access directly to the hardware. The two points in the code where the operation will block if the IO device is not ready are marked with comments. Normally such code is hidden within the operating system. Working on bare hardware, shown in Fig. 9.9, is now only found when dealing with microcontroller developments, where the size of the application does not justify the provision of full operating system functionality, such as a filing system or user password management.

9.4 Interrupt processing – service on demand

As we mentioned in Section 8.8, it is possible to arrange for a specially written subroutine to be invoked by an externally triggered **interrupt** signal. Most CPUs are provided with one or more interrupt request lines which play an important part in keeping the

Fig. 9.10
Telephonic interruptions.

computer system on its toes and maintaining a service to all its customers. Think of interrupts working like the telephone bell (Fig. 9.10). It sounds when you are engrossed in some serious dish-washing activity. Putting down the sponge, you run to the telephone and take up a conversation with a friend. When this reaches its end, you put the handset back in the cradle and resume the dish-washing where you left off. The dishes are totally undisturbed by the interruption. Alternatively, the operating system may intervene and not hand control back to the originally interrupted task. If it was your mother reminding you to send a birthday card to your sister, you might decide to swap tasks after the telephone call, deferring the dishes to a later time, when the priorities have settled back.

So the interrupt signal arriving at the CPU forces it to stop executing the current program and change to another routine, known as the Interrupt Service Routine (ISR). When the ISR is complete, the CPU **resumes** the interrupted program. The way an interrupt works is quite simple, though the start-up initialization that needs to be carried out can be more complex.

Systems often have multiple sources of interrupt, as in Fig. 9.11. This raises the difficulty, when an interrupt occurs, of determining which device has requested the interrupt. There is also the difficulty of devices firing requests simultaneously. Then a decision has to be taken as to which to service immediately and which to defer until later.

Hardware can be employed to **prioritize** the incoming interrupt signals, as illustrated in Fig. 9.12. The Pentium **PIC** (Programmable Interrupt Controller) chip allows through a single **IRQ** from the most urgent device (see Fig. 9.13). Even then, the CPU may still not accept the request because it has disabled all interrupt processing, As shown in Fig. 7.9, the Pentium has a flag which indicates whether the CPU is prepared to respond to interrupts or not. To control this, there are a pair of

Fig. 9.11
Connection of interrupting devices to the CPU.

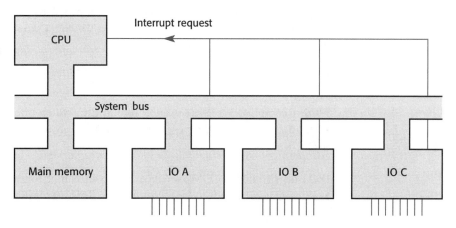

Fig. 9.12
Interrupt prioritization
hardware.

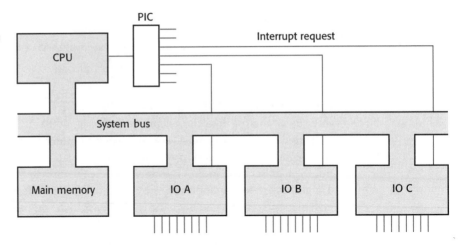

instructions to set and clear the interrupt flag: `STI` and `CLI`. However, these instructions are only available to privileged users!

Once an interrupt is accepted by the CPU there remains the problem of identifying the source of the request and then locating the correct ISR in memory. The PIC identifies which IRQ was responsible for the interrupt. However, when asked by the CPU for the identification it does not return the IRQ number, but an 8 bit number, known as the vector. This is used by the CPU to access the correct entry in the **IVT** (Interrupt Vector Table) held in memory. The IVT data table holds the addresses of the entry points for all possible ISRs. Every source of interrupt has a unique entry in the IVT.

The relatively small number of interrupt lines available on the PC would seem to be a major disadvantage when trying to add further devices. But so far people have got by, often by disabling existing devices or even unplugging boards in order to share an IRQ. Suffering an IRQ conflict is a common problem when installing new cards.

IRQ1 has the highest priority and IRQ15 the lowest. Not all IRQ lines are mapped through to the ISA and PCI expansion buses.

IRQ0 – committed for the principal system timer. This generates the ticks which enable the operating system (Unix, Windows 95/98/NT) to regain control from any process at the end of its allocated time slot.

IRQ1 – committed to the keyboard controller.

IRQ2 – committed to the cascaded second PIC, which offers IRQ8–IRQ15. IRQ9 takes on the role of IRQ2 inputs, but is not commonly used to avoid the possibility of conflict.

IRQ3 – designated as COM2 serial port, but widely used for modems, internal as well as external, which leads to frequent conflicts. This may be avoided by relocating the

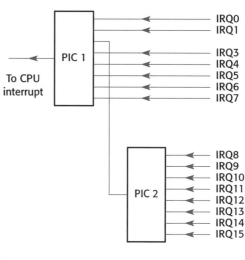

Int Number	Function	Source
77	Hard Disk2	IRQ15
76	Hard Disk1	IRQ14
75	8087	IRQ13
74	PS/2 Mouse	IRQ12
73	Soundcard	IRQ11
72	Network	IRQ10
71	Redirected	IRQ9
70	RTC	IRQ8
...		
18	BIOS/TOD	INT
17	BIOS/softboot	INT
16	BIOS/print	INT
15	BIOS/KBD	INT
14	BIOS/comms	INT
13	BIOS/disk	INT
12	BIOS/msize	INT
11	BIOS/check	INT
10	BIOS/Video	INT
0F	LPT1:	IRQ7
0E	FDC	IRQ6
0D	SoundCard	IRQ5
0C	COM1:	IRQ4
0B	COM2:	IRQ3
0A	...	IRQ2
09	KDB	IRQ1
08	System Timer	IRQ0
07		
06		
05	Screen dump to printer	
04	Numeric Overflow	
03	Breakpoint	
02	NMI, Power fail	
01	Single Step Trace	
00	Integer Divide Error	

Fig. 9.13
Part of the PC Interrupt Vector Table and related PIC connections.

modem to an unused IRQ, or disabling the COM2 activity in the BIOS setup parameters. Sometimes a sound card may try to take on this IRQ, which adds to the confusion. An extra problem is that unfortunately COM4 is designated to this interrupt as well.

IRQ4 – committed to COM1/mouse, an RS232 port which is often dedicated to serial mouse activity. Like the COM2/COM4 situation, this interrupt is shared with COM3, which is unfortunate because modems are often preconfigured to COM3, thus guaranteeing a conflict with the serial mouse! A solution to this is to use a PS/2 mouse (if your system can use one); alternatively, you can use a bus mouse.

IRQ5 – designated as LPT2, a second parallel port initially for another printer, but now more commonly used for the Sound Blaster card. Not many PCs have a requirement for two printers, but the parallel port can also be interfaced to other plug-in devices, so conflicts may still occur.

IRQ6 – committed to the floppy disk controller (FDC).

IRQ7 – committed to LPT1, the parallel printer port.

IRQ8 – committed to a hardware timer for real-time programmers.

IRQ9 – often used for network cards and other PCI-based devices

IRQ10 – available and often used for network cards, Sound Blaster or SCSI adapters. Available for the PCI bus.

IRQ11 – available as for IRQ10.

IRQ12 – committed to PS/2 mouse if it is provided, otherwise much the same as IRQ10 and IRQ11.

IRQ13 – committed to the maths coprocessor unit (8087).

IRQ14 – committed to the first IDE disk controller.

IRQ15 – committed to the second IDE controller.

Windows NT has a useful administration tool which allows you to inspect the IRQ allocation, as well as some other interesting parameters. To fire it up select the following:

Start → Programs → Administrative Tools (Common) →
   Windows NT Diagnostics → Diagnostics → Windows NT Resources → IRQ

Figure 9.14 shows the IRQ listing for a Windows NT machine. The Properties button is worth trying if you need more details. Later in this chapter you will return to view the alternative DMA display.

For external IRQ interrupts, the Pentium CPU is only told which interrupt line is active. This may be insufficient information to **identify** the requesting device if there are several tied to that IRQ line. Each of the devices would be capable of causing an interrupt at that priority level. A solution is to resort to direct polling code within the ISR to check each suspected device until the culprit is discovered. But this is not an ideal plan when time is precious. A better scheme, used by the MC68000, is where each device holds its own **interrupt vector**, instead of centralizing that responsibility within the PIC. Now, during the interrupt acknowledge cycle, the CPU requests the device to identify itself. The CPU broadcasts an interrupt acknowledge signal which asks any device of that priority level which has an active interrupt request pending, to

Fig. 9.14
Displaying PC IRQs using
Windows NT.

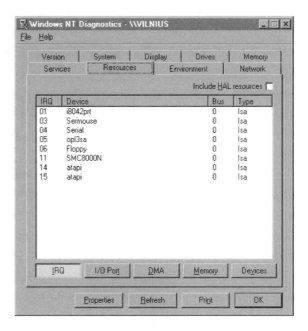

own up. The response, which is an 8 bit interrupt vector, is arranged to be an IVT offset value, indicating the appropriate ISR entry address. Holding the 8 bit interrupt vectors inside the peripheral chip does mean that they have to include a vector register in order to participate in the game of vectored interrupts. Not all IO chips do.

The situation for the Pentium, PIC, IVT and peripheral device is illustrated in Fig. 9.15. The ritual of asking for a vector number, indexing into an address table and jumping to an address appears somewhat laborious. Why could not the PIC simply return the full 32 bit address of the ISR to the CPU? There are probably historic reasons, but they elude me. Back in the 1970s, the PIC was built to respond to an interrupt acknowledge signal by jamming a full CALL instruction, complete with ISR address, onto the bus. This forced the 8080 CPU into the appropriate ISR. This method, involving a 3 byte 'interrupt fetch' by the CPU from the PIC rather than main memory, was abandoned as too inflexible. But the current PC interrupt scheme is still generally judged as very restricting.

On entering an ISR the first job to be done is to protect those CPU registers that will be used in the ISR from **corruption**. This simply involves PUSHing the contents onto the stack, from where they will be restored at the completion of interrupt processing. Then the source of the interrupt has to be verified, perhaps by testing a peripheral device flag bit, and the cause of the interrupt removed. Until this is done there is the danger of suffering a repeated interrupt from the same source, even though all the processing has been completed. It may then be necessary to **reinitialize** the peripheral device to ready it for another interrupt request, although sometimes this is not required. The end of the ISR is marked by POPing the saved registers and the execution of an rte instruction to restore the PC value.

The 8086 required the interrupt vector table (IVT) to start at 0000. But the facility to relocate the IVT anywhere in main memory was introduced with the 80386

Fig. 9.15
Locating the interrupt
service routine.

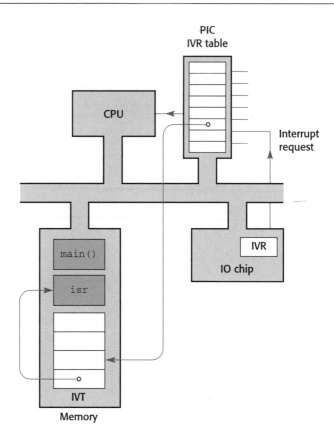

through the provision of the Interrupt Descriptor Table Register (IDTR). To move the IVT you simply copy the contents, with any needed revisions, into the new position and point the IDTR to the base of the new table.

If a device requires only occasional attention then the interrupt method works fine: the peripheral just demands CPU help when it needs it. Using interrupts does require special hardware to be installed, and the changeover from main program to ISR and back again is a wasteful activity which often takes several microseconds each time to complete.

Most peripheral devices can be configured to use the CPU interrupt facility, but if there are many such devices triggering interrupt requests there will be extra problems to be considered. When several requests arrive at the same time there is a need to prioritize the devices and queue the requests until they can be serviced. The identification of the source of the interrupt may require explicit device polling if the hardware is unable to return an interrupt vector. Locating the appropriate interrupt service routine in memory is normally straightforward using the VBR and the IVT.

The various sources of interrupts may be put into six categories, listed in Table 9.4.

Some small microcontrollers do not allow interrupt processing itself to be interrupted. The ability to accept and honour interrupts at any time is known as interrupt nesting. In this situation, a high-priority device, such as a hard disk, could break into a low-priority service routine without delay.

Table 9.4
Possible sources of
interrupts.

1.	IO data transfer request
2.	Software TRAP (SVC)
3.	Machine failure
4.	Real-time tick
5.	Run-time software error
6.	System reset or watchdog

A further important use of modern interrupt facilities has been introduced by the implementation of access modes. By allocating CPU facilities and memory segments either 'User' or 'Privileged' status, the system can protect its core functions from ordinary users, reserving the more risky capabilities for 'root' (or super-user). This is illustrated in Fig. 9.16, with the privilege levels represented as concentric spheres. Such access control is essential for modern multi-user operating systems and depends on all interrupts switching the CPU into Privileged Mode.

Thus interrupts provide a small entry window to the system facilities which can be policed by ISR code, which is now included as part of the operating system. This could be seen as the most significant use of the software interrupt or TRAP instruction.

There is an extra problem when trying to debug systems running interrupt routines. With ordinary subroutines, the programmer should be able to tell exactly when each subroutine will run, taking into account the variation from moment to moment of IF-THEN-ELSE statements which may test changeable environmental conditions. In fact, some subroutines may never run at all because it happens to be a leap year, or Sweden doesn't recognize Euro-travel Passes, or whatever. The role of Interrupt Service Routines (ISR) is to run when the CPU interrupt signal gets activated by a circumstance which is not always under the control of the programmer. Thus we say that subroutines are predictable and synchronous, while interrupt service routines are asynchronous and unpredictable. This makes debugging software systems where several interrupts are likely to fire at any time much more demanding, especially when the debugger software confuses the situation by using the trace interrupt for its own ends!

Using the interrupts on digital computers has been criticized as dangerous because of the unpredictability of their occurrence and the resulting difficulty in thoroughly testing the system. Thus programmers building embedded computer systems for life-

Fig. 9.16
How interrupts assist
operating system
security.

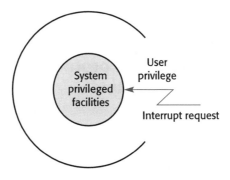

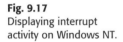

Fig. 9.17
Displaying interrupt
activity on Windows NT.

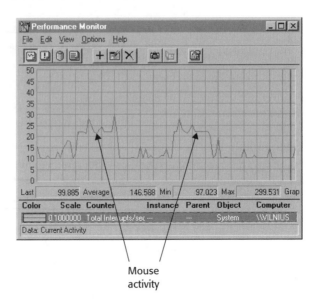

Mouse
activity

critical applications often try to avoid relying on interrupt facilities. But when considering less risky areas, hardware interrupts can offer an efficient technique to introduce some measure of responsive multitasking to the system. Windows and Unix provide helpful viewer tools which enable you to watch the rate of interrupt processing as it occurs on your machine. Unix has perfmeter, which was introduced in Section 3.2, while Windows NT offers Performance Meter which is illustrated in Fig. 9.17.

This useful administration tool allows you to inspect the IRQ allocation, as well as some other interesting parameters. To fire it up select

Start → Programs → Administrative Tools (Common) →
   Performance Monitor → Edit → Add to Chart → Interrupts/sec

In Fig. 9.17 the interrupt activity is displayed as a running average taken during 0.1 s intervals. When the mouse is oscillated from side to side it generates a burst of interrupts which show up as a rise in the average value. Such an increase would also result if the keyboard were to be used, or any other device which is tied into the PC interrupt system.

9.5 Critical data protection – how to communicate with interrupts

As we started to discuss in Section 8.8, there is a particular problem with passing data back from an ISR. Consider the situation shown in Fig. 9.18 of a time-of-day (TOD) program which has two parts. There is a real-time clock (RTC) ISR being triggered

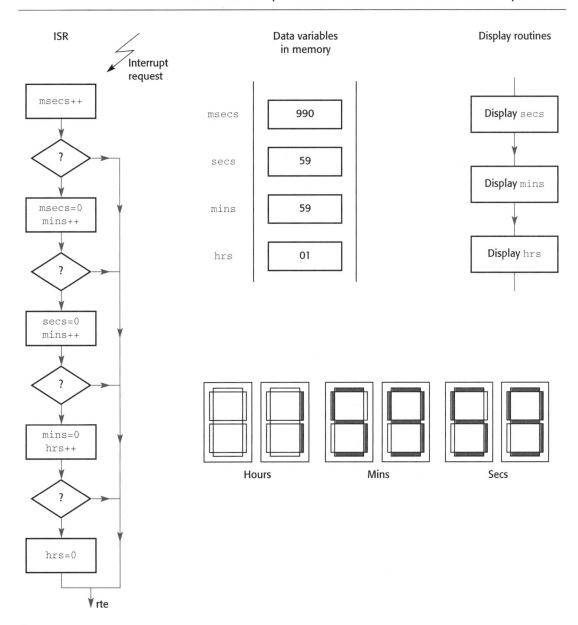

Fig. 9.18
Real-time clock and
time-of-day display.

every 10 ms to increment the seconds, minutes and hours values, and there is a display routine to refresh a set of front panel digits showing the TOD. The msec, sec, min and hrs data is held in memory. The routine which refreshes the display runs regularly, about twice a second as a low priority task, perhaps in the main processing loop. It takes the current seconds value, converts it to seven-segment format and writes it to the display. Then it does the same for minutes and then for hours.

The RTC ISR is more urgent and will break into any main process so that it can update the clock data in main memory. Now, what happens if the display is being refreshed when an RTC interrupt occurs? Consider the situation 01:59:59, with the

Table 9.5
Alternative solutions to protecting a critical resource.

1.	Disable interrupts
2.	Serialize the access
3.	Use a semaphore

display refresh having just written new values for secs and mins, and being poised to read the hrs from memory – and just then the RTC ISR occurs. It will rollover increment msec to 00, then sec to 00, then min to 00, then hrs to 02. Having completed the 'tick' it returns control to the main program. This happens to be right on the point of refreshing the hrs display. Which it does, leaving the incorrect value 02:59:59 for all to see. The false value will remain visible until the next display refresh occurs to correct it. In this example, the clock values in memory have not been corrupted, so no lasting damage is done (unless you missed your train). If the display update routine also served a network connection, there would be scope for a larger disaster.

The problem described arises from the complexity of the data being processed and the need for simultaneous unsynchronized access by two or more processes. In a more general form you may encounter the same problem when programming a multitasking application for Unix or NT. It is known as the **critical resource** problem. In this case, it is worth noting that if time was simply stored as a 32 bit integer there would be no problem, because the value would always be valid: interleaved update and display operations could not result in corrupted data unless the computer had multiple processors!

There are several solutions which can be tried to clear up the difficulty, as listed in Table 9.5.

If the interrupts were disabled to block the RTC interrupt request on entry to the display update routines, and then re-enabled at the completion of the display refresh, the display would remain coherent but would progressively go wrong. When the system receives an RTC interrupt its response would be delayed if the interrupts are disabled, so there is a risk that the TOD would become out of true. This is a more significant issue when the ticks occur more rapidly than 100 Hz. In fact, turning off all of the interrupts is far too drastic, because it would interfere with other interrupt-driven activity, such as IO transfers. This solution is only acceptable for small microcontroller systems, where interrupt deferment would not be too disruptive.

A better solution in this clock example would be to serialize access to the critical data region, as presented in Fig. 9.19. This means moving all the code across from the RTC ISR to the main program flow, just before the display refresh routines. This makes it impossible to read partly updated data. But now the RTC ISR must indicate to the main program through a flag or simple integer that a tick has occurred since the last display update. A check on the value of the RTC flag will determine whether a clock increment needs to take place.

It should be recognized that the tick flag is a critical resource in itself which could also be in danger of corruption. To assist with this the Pentium has a special non-interruptible mode for a small group of instructions, including BTS, BTR and BTC (Bit-Test-and-Set, Bit-Test-and-Reset, Bit-Test-and-Complement). These are useful for testing and resetting single bit flags and, when preceded by the LOCK instruction,

Fig. 9.19
Using a tick flag.

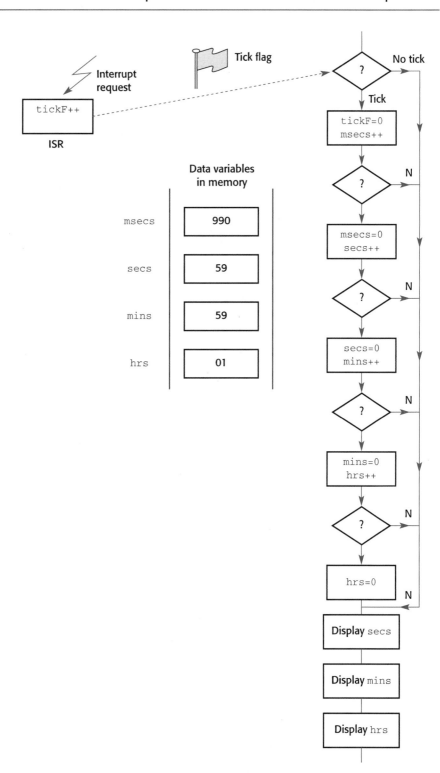

are guaranteed to run to completion even if an interrupt or DMA request is received half way through execution.

9.6 Buffered IO – interrupt device drivers

When computers are furnished with sophisticated multitasking operating systems, neither simple hardware polled IO nor interrupt routines are directly accessible to the application programmer. The former would be hugely inefficient, while the latter is prevented because of the risks involved in allowing ordinary users control over the interrupt system. All the data transfers into and out of the computer have to be handled by the trusted operating system routines known as **device drivers**. In both Unix and Windows NT these routines run in privileged mode and are responsible for the direct hardware interface. This includes flow control and error trapping when necessary. Frequently they also include software data buffers to smooth out any hiccups in the flow of data. In Chapter 17 we will find out how the IO interrupts and the device driver service routines are essential components in the wider process scheduling scheme. Application programmers gain access to the device driver routines either through HLL library functions such as printf( ) or putch( ) or through specially provided library functions which need to be explicitly linked into the code. Figure 9.20 presents the outline structure and action of interrupt device drivers. You can see that the device driver code is split into two parts: the front end and the interrupt service routine. Between them is the data buffer, where data is temporarily stored before moving onward.

Consider a data output operation, illustrated in Fig. 9.20. The application program calls an output function with the data item as a parameter (putc( )). Control then passes to a library routine, which in turn calls an operating system routine. This

Fig. 9.20
Using buffered interrupt-driven IO.

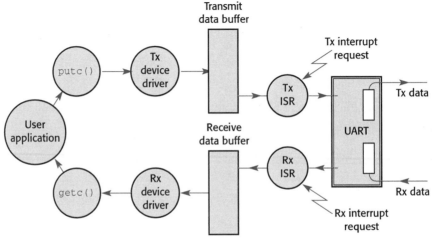

checks to see whether there is space in the transmit buffer associated with the specified device. If there is space, the item is entered at the back of the queue, the queue pointers are updated and control returns to the original program. If there happens to be no space in the buffer, perhaps due to a failure of the link, an error status code is returned to the program. The data will hang about in the transmit buffer for a moment before it gets transferred to the output port by the Transmit ISR. This is triggered by the port hardware when it is ready to receive more data. So an application program may appear to have satisfactorily written some data out to a device, when it actually got no further than the transmit buffer.

The sequence of operations is similar for the receive channel. Data arrives at the receive port and triggers an interrupt which invokes the Receive ISR. This moves the data into the receive buffer, from where it may be read by an application program.

9.7 Direct memory access (DMA) – autonomous hardware

For large quantities of data, or high-speed transfers, the Direct Memory Access (**DMA**) method is preferred. In this case, data is moved from source to destination, along the bus, without passing through the CPU. Indeed, the CPU is not even responsible for carrying out the individual data transfer cycles. A separate DMA controller unit has to be available to manage each data transfer, but the overall operation is still instigated by the CPU. Such autonomous activity has the advantage of greatly reducing the processing load imposed on the CPU. The DMA controller can independently manage read–write bus cycles, generating addresses and toggling the control bus lines – everything that is required to move data from source to destination. However, in order to do this they need to 'borrow' the whole bus from the CPU by using the Bus Request facility. There is a danger that DMA activity may delay normal CPU fetch–execute cycles, but it can also be cleverly timed to take over the bus only when it is not required by the CPU. The PC has suffered from rather outdated 8 bit DMA facilities provided by two venerable i8237 controllers. Faster 16 bit Ultra DMA has now displaced the original 8 bit facilities. Discrete components have been redrafted inside a VLSI system chip, along with the APIC and other system support devices. The PC DMA devices (Table 9.6) each provide four independent channels, but because the two devices are cascaded only seven are useable. Channel 4 is occupied with connecting the second device.

The CPU is still responsible for initiating the data transfer by loading several registers inside the DMA controller to start the activity.

Data is frequently transferred from IO units to memory as in Fig. 9.21, or vice versa, but memory-to-memory transfers are possible, too. The DMA controller needs to know the addresses of source data and destination array, and the quantity of data to be transferred. Because the DMA data transfer can proceed concurrently with main CPU

Table 9.6
Designation of the PC
DMA channels.

Channel	Function	Width
0	DRAM refresh	8 bits
1	Sound Blaster	8 bits
2	Floppy drive	
3		
4	Cascaded to second DMA controller	
5	Sound Blaster	16 bits
6		
7		

activity, the CPU does not automatically know when the transfer has finished. So the DMA controller uses an interrupt to inform the CPU of the completion of the data transfer task. With the two previous methods, all the input–output data has to pass through the CPU registers. But DMA passes data directly along the bus from source to destination, missing out the time-consuming detour through a CPU data register. This seems to be a good idea, since it frees the CPU for other activity. However, fundamental problems need to be resolved in systems that support cache memory and virtual addressing. These facilities will be introduced in more detail in Chapter 12.

Commercially available DMA controller chips normally offer multiple channels, allowing concurrent data transfers. Rather curiously, on the IBM PC one DMA channel is reserved for DRAM refresh duties. DMA operations require bus time which is taken in competition with the CPU and any other DMA controllers. Time can be allocated in blocks of cycles, known as bursts, during which periods the CPU is totally excluded from accessing main memory. Alternatively, time can be accrued on a cycle by cycle basis. This fits the DMA memory accesses in between CPU activity, thus avoiding any

Fig. 9.21
Using DMA to transfer
data.

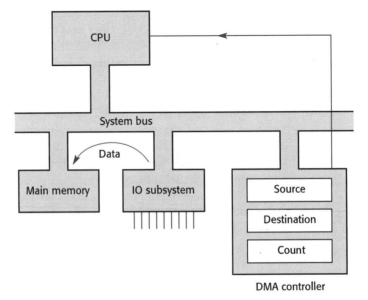

DMA controller

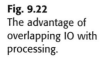

Fig. 9.22
The advantage of overlapping IO with processing.

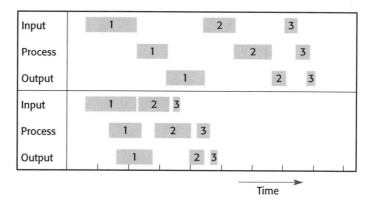

serious disruption to the main processing. With the Pentium, the bus contention problem is ameliorated by the L1 cache, which allows the CPU to continue fetching and executing as long as it can be satisfied with the instructions held locally in cache.

To further free the main CPU from slow IO tasks, more powerful channel processors were developed with autonomous capabilities, including device polling, channel program execution (including code conversion), interrupt activation and direct memory access for data and instructions. By plotting input, processing and output times on a bar graph, as in Fig. 9.22, the advantage of overlapped operations is easy to see.

Channel processors are semi-independent processors communicating with the main processor only occasionally. They can now be seen as one type of a growing class of dedicated coprocessors: floating-point processors, LAN interface processors, graphics processors etc. Two principal categories of channel processors can be identified: Selector Channels and Multiplexer Channels. With Selector Channels, each channel may serve a number of IO devices, with their associated controllers. They would normally be concerned with fast data streams such as from a hard disk drive. During data transfer, the channel is dedicated to the selected device and excludes all others until the transfer is accomplished. When slower devices are being considered, a Multiplexer Channel would be appropriate because this supports transfers from several devices simultaneously by byte-interleave or multiplexing the data streams with no loss of efficiency.

This sharing by devices of a single channel processor leads to a hierarchical bus structure, with the main bus joined to the IO bus through the dual-ported channel processors.

9.8 Single-character IO – screen and keyboard routines

When you first try to write a program with menu input, requiring a sequence of single characters from the keyboard, a problem reveals itself which neatly demonstrates how

Fig. 9.23
Keyboard input.

```
#include <stdio.h>

int main(void) {
      int answer;
do {
      printf("please enter a single letter: ");
      answer = getchar();
      putchar('\n');
      printf("%c\n",answer);
      } while (answer != 'E');

return 0;
}
```

the operating system software handles your program's IO requests. The code fragment listed in Fig. 9.23 will initially run as expected, but on the second iteration of the input loop a phantom input seems to happen and the menu is printed a second time with nothing required from the keyboard – see Fig. 9.24. This is not what the client asked for!

When this code is run, the user will discover that the program blocks on the call to getchar ( ) until the ENTER/RETURN key is pressed. Then the first character 'A' is processed correctly. Unfortunately the second 'B' is preceded by a strange event, a kind of phantom keystroke. The reason for this hiccup can be traced back to the way the input data from the keyboard is temporarily held in a low level buffer before it gets

Fig. 9.24
Demonstrating input buffering problems.

```
please enter a single letter: A
A

please enter a single letter:        ←          ?

please enter a single letter: B
B

please enter a single letter:        ←          ?

please enter a single letter:
```

Fig. 9.25
Exposing the hidden
character.

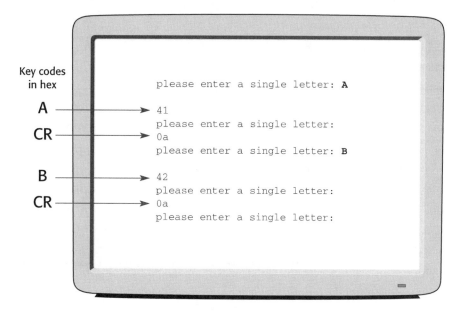

```
                       please enter a single letter: A
Key codes
  in hex
    A                  41
                       please enter a single letter:
    CR                 0a
                       please enter a single letter: B

    B                  42
                       please enter a single letter:
    CR                 0a
                       please enter a single letter:
```

passed onto the user program. This arrangement allows the system to provide line-editing facilities and control character trapping. Entering ^C (control-C) while the program is waiting, will abort the process. In fact, the program will not see any characters until the ENTER/RETURN key is struck. Then the contents of the whole buffer, including a CR, is sent to the program for processing. In the case of the code in Fig. 9.23, this would mean that the 'A' is followed closely by the CR code: 0AH. This can easily be checked by running the debugger, or by simply substituting '%x' for the '%c' in the printf( ) statement, which has been done to produce the screen dump shown in Fig. 9.25. This will reveal the numeric code of the character to be printed, even if it is an invisible character.

One solution for Unix has already been presented in Section 2.9. An alternative solution to this problem, suitable for PCs as well, is for the user program to 'consume' the CR character before it does any harm, as presented in Fig. 9.26.

The extra getchar( ) is only there to read the trailing CR from the buffer and then forget about it. Another way is to use scanf( ) instead of getchar( ). scanf( ) can read more that one character at a time, and the format string can be set up to forget characters, too. Instead of the two getchar( ) instructions, use the following:

```
scanf("%c%*c", &answer);
```

The %*c reads in a single character without referring to any variable. This is the shortest way to solve the problem of intrusive CR characters.

Fig. 9.26
Single-character
keyboard input without
hiccups.

```c
#include <stdio.h>

int main(void) {
      int answer;
do {
      printf("please enter a single letter: ");
      answer = getchar();
      getchar( );
      printf("%c\n",answer);
      } while (answer != 'E');

return 0;
}
```

Review

- There are three basic IO methods: polling, interrupt and DMA.

- Peripheral devices have registers which need to be referenced when carrying out IO. Sometimes the operating system forbids ordinary application code from doing this. In such circumstances, there will be system calls to device driver routines which will handle the IO for you.

- There are usually Status, Command and Data Registers inside IO devices. In memory-mapped systems these registers will look just like a location in memory. However, if it is an IO-mapped system there will have to be special instructions provided beyond the normal HLL set.

- Polling can be wasteful as it ties up the CPU in waiting for an event. Intermittent polling is better than dedicated (spin) polling.

- The interrupt line allows devices to demand attention from the CPU. The CPU stops its current processing and jumps to a specially designated routine (ISR) to deal with the interrupt. If there is more than a single source of interrupts, identification and prioritization mechanisms have to be available. After processing the interrupt, the CPU may return to the interrupted code.

- The PC has only 15 interrupt lines (IRQs), which causes some difficulty when installing new hardware. Sharing interrupt lines requires a specially written ISR.

- Interrupt service routines are located in memory through the IVT (Interrupt Vector Table), which holds the starting addresses of all the installed ISRs.

- Because interrupts may come in at any time, there is a danger of data corruption. This is termed the critical data problem.

- DMA can relieve the CPU of some IO activity, usually the disk or LAN interface. The DMA controller hardware can be initialized to move blocks of data within the computer.

Practical work

The recommended practical work involves using the input and output routines supplied as part of the C function library. Data can be sent to the COM1 or COM2 serial ports using `fputc( )` and read in from the same ports using `fgetc( )`. Use a terminal emulator, such as Hyperterminal, to send and receive text messages.

Exercises

1. What three types of register might be found in a peripheral IO chip? What are they used for? Can they only be accessed using assembler routines?

2. Give one example from the PC for each IO method: polled, interrupt, DMA.

3. What does the term 'blocking' mean to a programmer? Under what circumstances does the `putch( )` function block? How would you prevent your PC C program blocking on a `getchar( )` call? Try looking up `kbhit( )` in the Microsoft Developer Studio online help.

4. Estimate the minimum polling rate that you might recommend for the following:

    car accelerator pedal position and car engine inlet manifold pressure, both for the engine control unit

    washing machine front panel buttons

    living room thermostat

    supermarket barcode scanner (12 digits, 4 bars each)

    roadway vehicle detector for traffic lights

5. Which IO technique would you use with the following applications:

    coffee vending machine front panel keyboard

    LAN interface card

    fire alarm smoke detector

    credit card reader

    PC mouse

6. How does a computer keep track of the time of day, even when it is turned off?

7. What important function is served by the real-time clock tick? Where do RTC ticks come from? What is the normal range of frequencies for system ticks? What role did RTC chips play in the Y2K scare?

8. What is the main criticism of dedicated flag polling as a means of IO? If polled IO is so bad, why is it employed so often? What situation might require dedicated polling?

9. How can you use interrupts from within an HLL program?

10. How does the CPU identify the source of an interrupt? What happens to the interrupt threshold when an interrupt occurs? Where would you find rts and rte instructions?

11. List the operations which need to be carried out within an ISR.

12. In what circumstances would a critical region appear when using interrupts? What are the possible programming solutions to this problem?

13. What does DMA stand for? Where and when would you expect your PC to employ DMA? If DMA is used to routinely update a large array of data, what precautions would a programmer need to take?

14. What happens to the program in Fig. 9.22 if you inadvertently put in a leading tab or space character? Can you explain the confusion?

15. What is the purpose of providing data buffers for IO channels? Are there any disadvantages to using buffering?

Readings

- Heuring and Jordan (1997), Chapter 8: input–output processing.

- Buchanan (1998), Chapter 5: interfacing; Chapter 8: interrupt action.

- Tanenbaum (1999), Section 5.6.5: using interrupts.

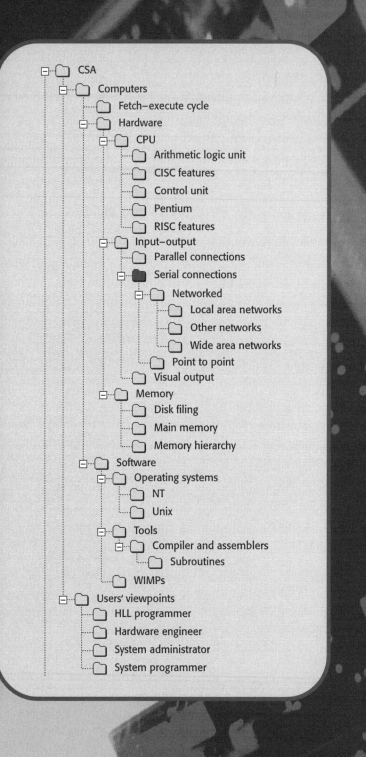

Serial communications

Overview

Data is frequently exchanged between equipment using a single-bit-wide channel. Many of the technical issues which we will later encounter with networking can be studied more easily with only two machines interconnected. These problems include receiver synchronization, error detection and data flow control. The different types of modem are presented and their use for data transmission along analogue telephone lines.

10.1   Serial transmission – data, signals and timing

Digital data transmission has progressed from the straightforward connection between a computer and its peripherals to complex, international networks of communicating computers. But there are still many useful lessons to be learnt from the simpler, point-to-point link, often referred to as **RS232** after the Electronic Industries Association standard (Fig. 10.1). It is useful to note that serial communications present a different set of problems from those arising from the parallel buses used inside computers.

Although parallel transfers are faster, most of the transmission of data between computers is carried out serially to reduce the cost of the cable and connectors. There are also physical limits on the distance that a fast parallel bus can work over. Whatever technology is on offer, there will always be a need to reduce the cost and make better use of the available resources. With serial communication, data is sent one bit at a time and, despite the seeming inefficiency of this arrangement, the whole of the Internet depends on such channels. These normally operate at transfer rates of between 10 Mbps and 150 Mbps. Despite the mature age of RS232 serial communications technology, plugging a COM1 PC port into a different computer for a quick file transfer can still run into unforeseen difficulties and take several days to sort out, exposing layers of unimagined software complexity. As in many areas of computing, the initial impression of complex hardware becomes totally forgotten when you become involved in a practical application. It is a common experience that the really tricky difficulties, in nearly all circumstances, relate to poorly understood software!

From a somewhat academic viewpoint, all communication activities must involve three aspects, as listed in Table 10.1.

So we are effectively already starting to study networks by looking at point-to-point serial transmission. Although much simpler, RS232 exhibits many of the problems we will encounter with networks in Chapters 14–16. The issues of synchronizing receiver with transmitter, detecting accidental errors and controlling the rate of flow of data are all problems for the Internet as well as the PC COM ports. There is, however, a major distinction between point-to-point serial and networking schemes, which is the routing of data. If there is only one place to go, the possibility of exercising any routing

Fig. 10.1
Point-to-point serial communications using an RS232 cable.

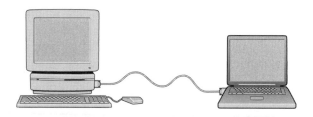

Table 10.1
Fundamental components of communications.

Data	Compression and coding schemes, quantity
Timing	Synchronization of sender and receiver; frequency and phase
Signalling	Error handling, flow control and routing

choice is seriously restricted! If a mismatch occurs in any one of the areas listed in Table 10.1, the data transfer will eventually fail. Communications engineering tries to anticipate such failures and put in place recovery measures.

10.2 Timing synchronization – frequency and phase

The difficulty for a listener of synchronizing with a speaker is often only apparent to humans when they are learning a foreign language. Then the problem of distinguishing one word from the next and establishing the integrity of important phrases can be a real frustration. We often start with a rather poor low-level strategy of matching our meagre vocabulary of words to the stream of sound coming in at us, but then move on to a much more sophisticated conversational approach in which the meaning and intention of the speaker play a greater part. We also find that it becomes easier if we take more control of the situation by asking questions and interrupting the speaker's flow.

Some mechanism is always needed to allow the receiver to sample the centre of the incoming bits reliably. Receivers must know the width of the bits and their starting point (see Fig. 10.2). This may be expressed as the receiver needing to know both the frequency and the phase of the data stream. If the fundamental bit clocks of the transmitter and receiver can be locked together, it would ensure perfect synchronization, but this arrangement is not always possible. In Fig. 10.3 the transmitter is writing a bit on the rising edge of the clock while the receiver is sampling the line half a clock period later, in the middle of the bit, using the falling edge. However, in this illustration, the frequency of the receiver clock is 1% lower than the transmit clock. Such a situation leads to a gradual drifting apart, until the moment is reached, after 25 bit periods in this case, where the sampling point is hovering dangerously over a transition. The crystal oscillators used in PCs to generate clock frequencies are generally rated as working to an accuracy of 20 parts per million (p.p.m.), or 0.002%. As we can see, an error will occur when the transmit clock is half a clock period misaligned with the transmitter. At a transmission rate of 9600 bps, a bit is approximately 0.1 ms wide, so there will need to be a period of time lasting 25 000 bits, or 2.6 s, before the crystal drift results in receive errors. To avoid any danger of this happening the receiver must

Fig. 10.2
Receiver attempting to sample the middle of a bit.

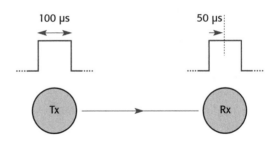

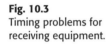

Fig. 10.3
Timing problems for
receiving equipment.

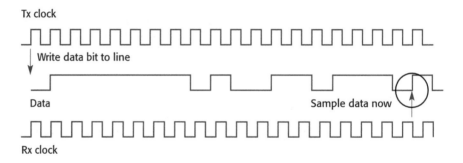

Tx clock

Write data bit to line

Data   Sample data now

Rx clock

regularly resynchronize at the bit level. For other reasons, the starting point of character, packet and message components must also be resynchronized regularly.

The number of bits transmitted per second is normally referred to as the 'bps', but the older term 'baud' can still be found. Strictly speaking, the baud rate is the fundamental clock frequency, which means that baud and bps are synonymous for straightforward transmission techniques. Later we will encounter methods of squeezing several bits into a single clock cycle, so that the number of bps can be greater than the associated baud rate.

Agreeing a common frequency, or bit width, can require a manual intervention to set 'Line Speed' on an initialization menu. Alternatively, a semi-automatic process during the login sequence demands that the user taps the RET key several times to enable the receiver to guess the correct line speed, knowing that if it does not recognize the bit pattern as a RET character it should try a different line speed. Other systems specifically send clock signals along with the data, in much the same way that the GMT pips are broadcast on the hour to allow clocks to be set correctly all over Britain. If the receiver and sender share a common system clock they are said to operate in **Synchronous Mode**, whereas if they have separate clocks (of identical frequency) they must operate in so-called **Asynchronous Mode**. The latter is common when using COM1 and COM2 on the PC.

Because of the availability of very accurate crystal-locked oscillators, providing a good, stable frequency source is no longer a difficulty. But receivers still need to determine the middle point of each incoming bit to read the data reliably. In asynchronous mode the transmitter does *not* send a clock signal along with the data. Rather, it inserts a pseudo-clock pulse, known as the Start bit, in front of each transmitted byte. Thus each ASCII character is dealt with as an independent transmission, with Start, Stop and Parity bits appended (Fig. 10.18). The line speed is set manually before the session begins. For phase information, the receiver has to detect the onset of the Start bit. Significantly, to allow this scheme to work there has to be a period of 'quiet' between the characters, which is imposed by the trailing Stop bit. If you wanted to, you could view the Start bit as a synchronizing pulse sent by the transmitter to the receiver. It is technically possible to program a microcontroller to work as a serial communications device and measure the width of every Start bit as it arrives. In this way the receiver could obtain both frequency and phase information from the transmitter, working in a quasi-synchronous manner.

In Synchronous mode characters are transmitted in rapid succession, without Start and Stop bits. To give the receiver a chance to synchronize on the data, the message block is preceded by special Synch characters, which are detectable by the receiver hardware. They are also transmitted continuously by the transmitter units when there is no data available. Synchronous mode transmissions can use clever modulation schemes, relying on extra hardware, transfer data and clock information along the same pair of wires. This is the method used by Ethernet, known as Manchester encoding, but for short distances it is easier and cheaper to use separate conductors for clock and data. The incoming clock signal will provide accurate bit frequency and phase information to the receiver, which then knows when it is safe to read the incoming bits.

An alternative synchronous method for faster serial transmission is used for non-character, bit-oriented data. This technique allows faster data rates and was a precursor to the development of Ethernet. Known as HDLC (High-level Data Link Control) it again uses a special bit pattern (01111110) to enable the receiver to lock onto the start of the message. Should that particular bit sequence occur naturally in the data stream it is deliberately disguised by stuffing in a 0 to form: 011111010. The inserted 0 is removed at the receiving end.

There is a small problem in describing these methods, as the term 'Async' is not applied consistently with other areas of computing. For example an 'asynchronous bus' implies an interlocked handshake governing the transfer of data items. The same is true for the Centronics parallel port and SCSI bus. Who is correct? Does 'asynchronous' simply mean 'no shared clock', or does it imply the more significant complexity of a 'receipted' handover? I think the latter makes more sense. Then the real distinction between the two modes depends on the ability of the receiver to communicate back to the transmitter, via a signal line, that the transfer has taken place successfully and the transmitter can now terminate the current cycle and proceed to the next one. Thus asynchronous links allow communicating equipment to operate at different processing rates without danger of losing data, or having to reduce the clock rate of the faster player throughout the session.

Similar synchronization problems also exist for the higher software levels. When you switch on the radio, how do you recognize the start of your programme so that you can then pay more attention? You can understand all the words being spoken but are they contributing to a political debate, which precedes your favourite comedy review, or have you missed the start and come in on the panel session already? There is a need for clear markers to be transmitted between elements in order to help the receivers handle this difficulty. If you refer to the ASCII table in Section 2.8 (Table 2.4), you will now be able to appreciate the reason for some of the stranger codes: SYN, SOH, STX, ETX, EOT and ENQ. They are signalling codes, sent to 'synchronize' the receiver at the data frame and message levels. IBM used them for the early BiSync protocol, where 8 bit character codes were transmitted, together with a bit clock signal. This was a 'synchronous' protocol, with transmitter and receiver sharing the same bit clock, so there was no difficulty in synchronizing at the bit level. These codes dealt with the frequency/phase problem at the byte, frame and message levels. In more detail these codes represent:

SYN – a special flag byte to assist the receiver with byte-level synchronization. Only used when the channel is operating in Synchronous mode.

SOH – Start of a message header.

STX – Start of message text block.

ETX – End of message text block. Messages could therefore be split into multiple text blocks.

EOT – End of message transmission.

The sender needs to insert these codes at appropriate points in the outgoing data stream so that the receiver can know where it has got to in an incoming transmission.

We have mentioned that Async lines are quiet when no data is being sent. This is not so for BiSync communications, where the line is kept continually busy by the insertion of SYN characters between data transmissions. This is to maintain synchronization with the receiver at all times. It allows clock signals to be sent along the data lines, and recovered by special hardware circuits at the receiver end, thus saving a separate wire.

10.3 Data codes and error control – parity, checksums, Hamming codes and CRCs

Errors can arise when using a circuit connection which suffers from electrical interference. Fluorescent strip lighting, large electric motors being switched on and off, and vibrating thermostats are classic sources of such 'noise', as illustrated in Fig. 10.4.

The vicious inductive spikes radiate energy which can be picked up by nearby wiring behaving in the same way as a television aerial. As the operating voltages used in computer systems are reduced to improve speed and packing density, the significance of noise pickup increases. So computer cabinets are built to exclude such electrical disturbances. Even the mains power connection may be carefully filtered to protect the computer circuits. However, once out into the world the error rates can increase by a factor of a million. This sounds terrible, but the probability of an accidental error within a computer is very low, being estimated at around 10^{-18}. Even when you are dealing with data at 10^9 bps, as in the Pentium, this would mean waiting

Fig. 10.4
Electrical noise burst.

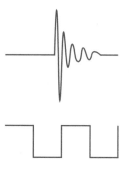

for 10^9 seconds before an error was likely. I make that about 30 years, or once in a lifetime of playing Doom and Tomb Raider!

Although modern communication channels are increasingly reliable, especially the optical fibre variety, the application of error-detecting and correcting techniques has been revitalized by the introduction of CD-ROMs and DVDs. Surface blemishes would quickly render these unusable if it were not for error detection/correction techniques. There are several methods worth studying (Table 10.2). All error detection methods incur a cost in the transmission of non-essential data. The obvious example is where the receiver echoes a copy of the incoming data back to the transmitter. This uses twice the original bandwidth, which has to be paid for! Alternatively, a second copy of the data could be transmitted after the original, so that the receiver can do the comparison. The former (echo) method has the extra bonus of simultaneously providing a flow-control mechanism, should you wish to use it. We will return to this topic in the next section.

All error trapping systems rely on so called redundant (non-essential) data. Very often data is encoded prior to transmission. We have already met ASCII and Unicode character code sets in Chapter 2. This can help with detecting errors if some bit patterns are actually illegal for that chosen code set. Should a receiver detect an illegal code coming in it may do something to rectify the situation, or just throw the corrupted data away.

Parity is the most often discussed error detection method for protecting serial transmissions involving ASCII coded characters. You could think of the single parity bit in this way: it doubles the size of the code set, but renders half of the possible binary patterns illegal. The 'distance' between valid code numbers is called the Hamming distance. So, if you take a number with a single parity bit, it enjoys a Hamming distance of 2, because changing a single bit will result in an illegal value (situated in the 'gulf' between valid numbers), while changing two bits will inevitably deliver a neighbouring valid number. This is the principle of error detection: to dig a wide Hamming ditch (distance) around each valid code, into which the errors will fall!

Table 10.2
Error detection and correction techniques.

Parity bits	Simple to apply, not very secure
Block checksums	Simple to apply, not very helpful
Polynomial division	More complex to compute, good security

Fig. 10.5
Using XOR to compute parity.

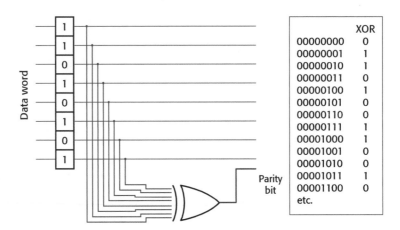

All three techniques listed in Table 10.2 are still widely used in data storage application areas as well as serial data transmission. The technique always involves the transmitter/writer (Fig. 10.5) taking some of the data, computing some sort of signature value, and then transmitting both the data and the signature. When the message arrives, the receiver/reader will again have to compute something using the data, and then compare the new signature with the value just received. If the signatures do not tally, an error has occurred. The parity bit technique is applicable to any length of binary data. An extra bit is appended to each word, as a signature, to adjust the parity status of the total word to ODD or EVEN. An ODD word contains an odd number of 1s, while an EVEN word has an even number of 1s. Computing parity is normally done using the XOR function, as illustrated in Fig. 10.5.

Hardware circuits to carry out single-bit parity insertion prior to transmission, followed by parity checking on reception, are included in all UART devices (see Section 10.5). However, as you can see from Fig. 10.6, a single parity bit, unimpressively, would only guard against a single bit error. Any two bit errors will cancel out the check and get through undetected – so it can be judged as a pretty insecure technique in a noisy environment where an electrical spike burst is more than likely to

Fig. 10.6
Error detection using single appended parity bit.

Data to be sent	Parity is computed and appended to make even for transmission	Transmit	New parity value computed and compared	
0110 0111	0110 0111 1	No errors	0110 0111 1	No error detected
0111 0110	0111 0110 1	Errors ↓ 0111 1110 1	0111 1110 0	Error detected
0111 0100	0111 0100 0	Errors ↓ ↓ 0111 1101 0	0110 0101 0	**No error detected!**

Fig. 10.7
Triple parity bit
assignment.

$$p1 = d1 \; XOR \; d3 \; XOR \; d4$$
$$p2 = d2 \; XOR \; d3 \; XOR \; d4$$
$$p3 = d1 \; XOR \; d2 \; XOR \; d4$$

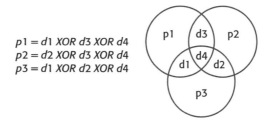

damage multiple bits in a word. It all depends on the speed of the transmission (width of the bits) and the frequency of the noise burst.

If you do detect an error, there is not always a need to do something about it. Perhaps it can be ignored without too devastating a penalty. This might be the case if the data corrupted represented a single pixel in a million pixel frame of a real-time video stream. Waiting for the next frame to come along within 15 ms seems to be the best bet in the circumstances. Alternatively, if you had agreed a re-transmit scheme, a fresh copy could be requested from the sender. The ideal solution would be to take responsibility yourself and sort out the damaged bit or bits. This is termed 'error detection and correction' or **Forward Error Control** (FEC). As you can see from Fig. 10.6, a single parity bit will never offer much security or be able to identify the exact position of an error within the word. It will only indicate that an odd number of errors have occurred, somewhere.

However, by appending more than one parity bit, the error location can be identified. This is known as a **Hamming code**. Figure 10.7 illustrates how a 4 bit nibble of data can be error detected *and corrected* with the addition of only three parity bits. Each parity bit looks after three data bits. Such a scheme would be a real bargain. Even if you sent the whole four bits twice, to allow the receiver to confirm their validity, if the two versions disagreed there is no way to establish the correct value of a bit. You would have to send three copies (12 bits), allowing a vote to be taken on the correct value, before you could get error correction from the system.

But in the scheme illustrated in Fig. 10.7, if there is a single error in d1 or d2 or d3 then two parity bits will be affected. This allows the culprit to be identified. An error in d4 affects all three parity bits, and so can also be tracked down. Similarly, if a single parity bit is in error, it can be recognized by the lack of corroborating evidence from the other parity bits. Once the offending bit is identified, it simply remains to invert it! Such a scheme can be formalized and extended to longer data words. However, the correct positioning of the parity bits is the key to implementing an elegant scheme.

To appreciate the way the Hamming code calculation works, it is important to understand the way in which the parity bits are inserted into the data word. This is illustrated in Fig. 10.8 for four bits of data, but clearly we are interested in longer words. The trick is to allocate all the bit positions which are powers of 2 to parity bits:

Fig. 10.8
Assigning parity bits to
longer words.

8	7	6	5	4	3	2	1
p4				p3		p2	p1
P	d4	d3	d2	P	d1	P	P

1, 2, 4, 8, 16 and so on. The other bit positions are used for data. Now we look at the numeric values to which the parity bits contribute.

Bit 1 is present in every other number, the ODD ones: 1, 3, 5, 7, etc.
Bit 2 is present in 2, 3, 6, 7 etc.
Bit 4 is present in 4, 5, 6, 7 etc
Bit 8 is present in 8, 9, 10, 11 etc
Bit 16 is present in 16, 17, 18 etc.

So bit positions 3, 5, 7, 9 etc. are checked by p1 (position 1), and bit positions 3, 6, 7, 10, 11 etc. are checked by p2 (position 2), while positions 5, 6, 7, 9, 10 etc. are checked by p3 (position 4).

It is possible to tabulate the number of data bits which can be dealt with by any given number of parity bits to achieve single-bit error correction. Figure 10.9 shows the method and the paired numbers of data and parity bits.

The values for each of the parity bits are calculated using the assigned data bit. From Fig. 10.10 you can see that it is possible to develop a selector matrix which does the operation using matrix multiplication. Although it looks wonderfully complex, it is quite simple for a computer to do and produces a really elegant technique.

Consider the example of the data item 1 0 1 1 in Fig. 10.10. This needs to be coded up with the correct value of parity bits inserted: 1 0 1 p3 1 p2 p1. This is best done by using the selector operator to calculate the three parity values, which are set to 0 initially.

The highlighted bits in the matrix act as parity bit selectors. With the parity values inserted into the designated positions in the data word, repeat the matrix multiplication; the answer should come to (0 0 0), indicating that all is correct with the data.

Now for the fun. We really must see what happens when we artificially introduce an error into the data word, then reapply the operator. The result obtained is known as the syndrome. For example, let's zap bit 5, which then becomes an erroneous 0 in the data word (Fig. 10.11).

Fig. 10.9
Numbers of data and parity bits to achieve single-bit error correction.

Number of parity bits	p	1	2	3	4	5	6	7	8
	2^p	2	4	8	16	32	64	128	256
Number of data bits	d	0	1	4	11	26	57	120	247

$$d = 2^p - (p + 1)$$

4d–3p

Fig. 10.10
Calculating a 4d–3p syndrome (transmitter).

$$[1 0 1 0 1 0 0] \times \begin{bmatrix} 1 & 1 & 1 \\ 1 & 1 & 0 \\ 1 & 0 & 1 \\ 1 & 0 & 0 \\ 0 & 1 & 1 \\ 0 & 1 & 0 \\ 0 & 0 & 1 \end{bmatrix} = [0 0 1]$$

7 6 5 4 3 2 1
d d d p d p p

So p3 = 0, p2 = 0, and p1 = 1
giving [1 0 1 0 1 0 1] for *transmission*

Fig. 10.11
Calculating the 4d–3p
syndrome (receiver) with
error present.

Error here

$$1\ 0\ 0\ 0\ 1\ 0\ 1 \quad \times \quad \begin{matrix} 1 & 1 & 1 \\ 1 & 1 & 0 \\ 1 & 0 & 1 \\ & 0 & 0 \\ 0 & 1 & 1 \\ 0 & & 0 \\ 0 & 0 & \end{matrix} \quad = \quad 1\ 0\ 1$$

Table 10.3
Single error correction,
double error detection
by multiple parity.

	No error	Single error	Double error
p0	Agrees	Error	Agrees
Syndrome	0	Non-zero → error	Non-zero confused

Hey presto, the syndrome is an amazing 5 (in binary of course). It has not only detected the error, but figured out its position in the data word, too. All we have to do is get in there and flip it back and so correct the transmission error. If you think that is a mathematical trick, you are probably right. But it sure impresses me! Unfortunately, the magic does not encompass double bit errors, so it is now common practice to include a single overall parity bit, p0, which has the responsibility of helping out when there are two bits in error. In this situation the syndrome is not 0, but confused, as described in Table 10.3. Such a scheme is referred to as 'double error detection, single error correction'.

The 64 bit memory word used by the Pentium requires the inclusion of 7 parity bits: p0–p6, inserted into bit positions 0, 1, 2, 4, 8, 16, and 32. This achieves the double detection level of protection, which for some systems, like Air Traffic Control computers, is considered a necessary precaution.

If you have not yet covered matrix algebra, as used above, complain to your maths tutor. Computers are very good at it, and it can actually be useful in graphics programming.

Another method commonly used to detect transmission errors is the **Block Checksum**. This first needs the data to be cut into blocks, so that a checksum number can be computed and appended prior to transmission. The method of generating a checksum is simply to add all the data in a block, and truncate the resulting sum. Often the sum is limited to a single byte value, truncating to less than 256. You may prefer to think either of adding the data into an 8 bit accumulator, and ignoring the overflow, or of carrying out a modulo 256 division. Either way you are throwing away the most significant bits! The checksum is then inverted and transmitted after the data. The job of the receiver is to add up all the data items as they arrive, including the final checksum. If no error has occurred the resulting sum will come to zero. If it is not zero some data corruption has occurred, and the data block has to be retransmitted. No correction is possible. Well-known examples of checksums are the Motorola S record format, or the Intel Hex record equivalent. These were devised in the early days of microprocessor development, when less than reliable paper tape readers were standard equipment. When attempting to read in a long paper tape, only a small paper

Fig. 10.12
Motorola S record format
with trailing checksum.

2 bytes	2 bytes	6 bytes	< 256 bytes	2 bytes
Type	Length	Address	Data	Checksum

```
S0 03 0000 FC
S2 24 010400 46FC26002E7C000808006100005E610000826100033C46FC270023FC00010678 6B
S2 24 010420 O00C011023FC00010678000C011423FC00010678000C011823FC00010678000C 6D
S2 24 010440 O11C610003A4303C271053406600FFFC46FC21006100057A4E4B000000004E75 3B

. . .

S2 24 012200 0968584F4878004C4EB900010928584F206EFFFC524810BC0004602248790001 7D
S2 24 012220 21CA4EB900010968584F487800484EB900010928584F206EFFFC524842104E5E 84
S2 08 012240 4E750000 D1
S8 04 000000 FB
```

Fig. 10.13
Example fragment of
a Motorola S record
format file.

tear was needed to cause an error. It was then possible to stop the reader, back up a short length of tape and re-read the offending data block, thus averting much frustration and some strong language.

The data in Motorola S records and Intel Hex files is all in ASCII format. Before transmission, each byte is split into two nibbles which are then converted to an ASCII representation of hex digits (0–F). This explains why a single-byte checksum suddenly appears as two bytes in Fig. 10.12.

Fig. 10.13 is an example fragment of a Motorola S record file which has been artificially spaced out to help you identify the fields. You should now confirm the checksum arithmetic. Choose one of the shorter data records (S2 Type) – the penultimate is convenient – and add up, in Hex, the Length, Address and Data fields. Some calculators have Hex mode, so try to borrow one:

08 + 01 + 22 + 40 + 4E + 75 + 00 + 00 = 12E
Forget the 1 as overflow, leaving 2E (0010 1110)
Invert the bits: 1101 0001 (D1) – the checksum!

A more complex checksum implementation is the **Bose–Chaudhuri–Hocquenghem** (BCH) method which can detect multiple bit errors and also identify their position. A technique with such a title deserves to be cherished, not least because it was successfully used to protect time and date information on car parking tickets. When microprocessor control was first applied to vending ticket equipment (Fig. 10.14), the punched hole codes were too vulnerable to damage during energetic shopping sessions, and the rejection rate would have been unacceptably high. By including a BCH error-detecting and correcting code, valid numbers could be retrieved from the vast majority of tickets. The brave salespeople would, by way of demonstrating the effectiveness of BCH coding, rip tickets in half, casually feed both halves into the reader, and complete a valid transaction. Exciting stuff for mathematicians!

Another well used error detection method is the **Cyclic Redundancy Check** (CRC). This is a powerful error detection method, but the location of the offending bits is not revealed. As with all the other ideas for error control, the CRC method computes a checksum value, but this time by using arithmetic division. The data to be sent is

Fig. 10.14
Parking ticket using BCH
error correction coding.

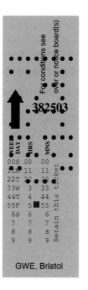

divided by a number specially chosen for its relationship to a suitable polynomial. In essence it is a way of grouping bits together to be associated with a redundant bit. The division is carried out using modulo-2 arithmetic, which bans carry through, making the computation the same as XOR again! Figure 10.15 uses the data value 11001, which is divided by 101 to give a remainder. This acts as the signature and is transmitted after the data.

The positions of the 1s in the divisor number, can be seen as implementing the same selection process achieved by the Hamming operator in the earlier method. Both use binary mask patterns, applied to the data, to select groups of bits. The CRC goes on to repeatedly shift and apply the same short mask over the full width of the data, while the Hamming method employs several full-width masks instead. The data and remainder are transmitted. The quotient (result of division sum) is discarded. The receiver, as you would expect, recomputes the division and hopes that the remainder will be the same. If it is not, the only recourse is to ask for a retransmission.

Fig. 10.15
Calculation of a CRC at
sender and receiver for
data item 11001.

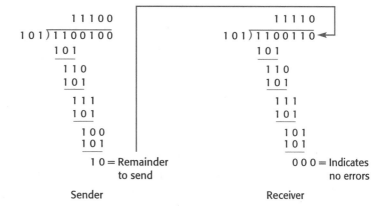

Fig. 10.16
CRC generation using
shift registers and
XOR gates.

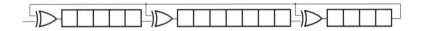

The power of this method is impressive. A CRC generating a 16 bit remainder will detect the following:

1.   All error bursts of 16 bits or less

2.   All odd numbers of bits in error

3.   99.998% of all error bursts of any length.

Computing CRCs in hardware can appear much easier than the software approach using long division. In Fig. 10.16 the arrangement of shift registers and XOR gate feedback circuits is given for a 16 bit data word.

10.4   Flow control – hardware and software methods

Protocols are needed to control the transfer of data, especially over complex networks or into large computer systems. **Flow control** is usually necessary to prevent overrun errors where the receiver cannot deal with the incoming data fast enough. If the first data is well received, but cannot be processed fast enough, subsequent data arrives and overruns the earlier items in the receive buffer. When a transmitter can supply data faster than the receiver can process it, a means of flow control is required to prevent the receiver suffering data overrun.

Note that this has *nothing* to do with baud rate incompatibility. Initially, the receiver handles the data fine, with no errors. It is only after the input buffer has completely filled up that the incoming data starts overwriting the earlier arrivals, and overrun errors then appear. As you might recognize, the input buffer operates in bath tub overflow mode. As long as the incoming data arrives, on average, at a rate lower than the tub is being emptied, no overflow will occur. However, when a large burst of data arrives, it runs a higher risk of filling the buffer and then overwriting previous entries – unless, that is, the receiver has the power to request the transmitter to stop sending data until the buffer has been emptied. Such a facility is called flow control, and is essential for nearly all communication links.

The techniques listed in Table 10.4 are not usually left to the application programmer, but implemented at much lower levels within the operating system's device drivers and manager routines. We have already encountered the use of 'echo' to detect a transmission error in Section 10.3. This can also be used in a flow control role. When you are typing into an editor, the characters appear on the screen within a text buffer window. These are the 'echo' sent back to you by the receiver, the computer. If you overwhelm the system with your fast typing (not very likely in my case) the computer will stop echoing and the screen will no longer display what you

Table 10.4
Flow control techniques.

Echo back
Hardware control lines: RTS/CTS
Software control codes: ^S/^Q
Frame-based handshake codes: ACK/NAK

are typing. An unresponsive screen seems to stop most people from typing, giving the system time to empty its input buffer and so catch up with you. It will then restart echoing your keystrokes, and you can continue typing. The keys that you hit when the screen was not echoing will have been stored in the keyboard buffer and will not have been lost. The provision of large storage buffers can assist in situations where the long-term average data rate is manageable for the receiver. The problem is the bursty nature of the transmissions, with periods of high activity interspersed by long, quiet inter-ludes. Buffering is certainly the standard solution to this scenario. Hardware control is particularly relevant to the RS232 serial link, which is introduced in the next section. Software controls do not require any extra hardware to operate. They can be imple-mented in software and need only to occasionally send special code values along the data channels. They work in much the same way as a human telephone conversation. Generally the participants take turns at talking, though simultaneous exchange can occur! If you miss some information you say 'pardon?' and hope for a retransmission. If the other person is talking too fast you might say 'just a minute...'. We have a wide and rich set of words and phrases which act as conversational control codes. Computers are a bit more limited: control-S (^S) for STOP and control-Q (^Q) for CONTINUE. These codes are frequently referred to as Xon and Xoff. If you have access to Unix you can try these out from the keyboard. It is not uncommon for novices to hit ^S by mistake and freeze the screen, without understanding what has happened.

A programmer will have to understand and perhaps use, at different times, both of the principal methods of flow control illustrated in Fig. 10.17.

A more sophisticated flow control scheme is implemented on fast, synchronous lines and networks so that a transmitter may continue to send data for a period of time even when no acknowledgement has yet been received. The intention is to keep the channel fully occupied and not wastefully block the transmitter. This is referred to as **Window Flow Control**. The transmitter maintains a buffer to hold transmitted items which have not yet been acknowledged. Thus a retransmission can be initiated by

Fig. 10.17
RS232 flow control techniques.

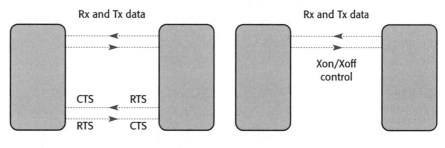

Hardware handshake   Software handshake

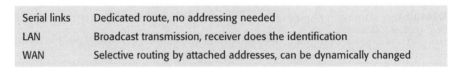

Table 10.5
Data routing methods
for serial
communications.

Serial links	Dedicated route, no addressing needed
LAN	Broadcast transmission, receiver does the identification
WAN	Selective routing by attached addresses, can be dynamically changed

reception of a delayed request to retransmit, or indeed in the event of a timeout. Items are deleted from the transmit buffer when they are fully acknowledged by the receiver.

As proposed in Table 10.5, with any scheme beyond simple point-to-point connection there is also a need to transmit **routing information** (source and destination addresses). Long messages are usually cut into submessage components and high bandwidth channels are frequently shared to reduce costs. Thus the data from different sources needs to be distinguishable to allow demultiplexing and reassembly. You can appreciate that the signalling protocols can become very complex!

The topic of signalling can also encompass the need to route data across large networks. While on a point-to-point serial line the opportunity for choosing routes is not often available, when it does happen it is often dealt with as an equipment control issue. For example, we might have to send special escape codes to a switch box in order to select a particular exit port. In Table 10.5 we have stated the three approaches to routing, and we will return to this subject in the next two chapters.

10.5   The 16550 UART – RS232

At the lowest, hardware, level the common standard used to connect equipment is a serial data link known as the RS232 or V24. This employs a 25 or 9 pin D-shaped plug and socket with often only three interconnecting wires. A '1' bit is transmitted as approximately −9 volts (called mark) and +9 volts is recognized as a '0' (space). Figure 10.18 sketches the voltage plotted from an RS232 transmission of the ASCII code for 1 (one): 31H or 0110001B.

The pins on an RS232 D-type are fixed in two ways for DCE (data communication equipment, now understood as computers) or for DTE (data terminating equipment, now understood as terminals or printers!). Because the original 25-way connector was often only active on three pins (to save money you may buy 25-way D-type plugs with only three pins inserted) a new 9-way D-type standard has been introduced (Fig. 10.19).

Usually the CTS control input is simply a hardware gate beyond the programmer's influence, unless equipped with a suitable paper clip to force CTS into the correct state to permit the computer to transmit data. By connecting the RTS output directly into

Fig. 10.18
RS232 voltages
representing ASCII '1'.

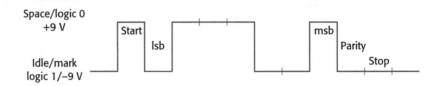

Fig. 10.19
RS232 9-way D-type pin
functions (COM1 and
COM2).

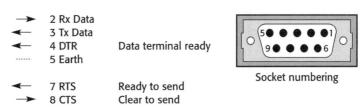

DCE (9 pin D-type) IBM COM 1 modem port

→ 2 Rx Data
← 3 Tx Data
← 4 DTR   Data terminal ready
‥‥‥ 5 Earth

← 7 RTS   Ready to send
→ 8 CTS   Clear to send

Socket numbering

the CTS input using the aforementioned paper clip it is possible to subvert the normal hardware flow control system! If you fire up the Hyperterminal program on a Windows NT system there is a serial port setup screen (Fig. 10.20) which allows you to reset some of the basic parameters.

The line speed (bit width), parity mode, flow control method and several other parameters are under your control from the keyboard. Now try plugging the COM1 port of one PC into the COM1 port of another. You will need the correct crossed-over lead in order to pass information between the computers. Whereas connecting a terminal to a computer needs a 'straight through' lead, if you are linking two computers, you need a 'crossed lead', sometimes called a 'null modem'. As in all things, D-type plugs come in two sorts: male and female. Unlike human society, this merely doubles the problem. Take a good look at the COM2 socket before you go out to buy a lead!

The outline programs presented in Fig. 10.21 show how the PC COM ports can be accessed directly using functions really intended for file access. Note that the constant EOF is defined as –1 in the `stdio.h` header file. Before experimenting with such an arrangement, it is advisable to run Hyperterminal, or similar terminal emulator, on both machines to check that the connection is functioning correctly and that data can be sent reliably. Although the data items are handled as 32 bit `int`s within the program, when they are transmitted through COM2 this is reduced to the lower byte – the higher bytes are not transmitted. When entering data from the keyboard the Control-Z key serves to supply an EOF for the receiver to detect.

Fig. 10.20
Setting COM1 port
parameters with
Hyperterminal.

COM1 Properties

Port Settings

Bits per second: 9600
Data bits: 8
Parity: None
Stop bits: 1
Flow control: Hardware
  Xon / Xoff
  Hardware
  None

Restore Defaults

OK   Cancel   Apply

Fig. 10.21
Exchanging messages
across the RS232 link on
a PC.

```
/* Transmitter.c */
#include <stdio.h>

int main(void)
{
FILE *dp;
int c;
       if ((dp = fopen("COM2", "w")) == NULL)
       {
           printf("fail to open COM port\n");
           return 1;
       }
        while ((c=getch()) != EOF)
       {
        fputc( c, dp);
        fflush(dp);
       }
       return 0;
}
============================================================
/* Receiver.c */
#include <stdio.h>

int main(void)
{
FILE *dp;
int c;
       if ((dp = fopen("COM2", "r")) == NULL )
       {
           printf("fail to open COM port\n");
           return 1;
       }
       while ((c= fgetc(dp)) != EOF)
       {
        putch( c);
       }
        return 0;
}
```

Any new communication interconnection is a potential source of frustration and anguish. *Beware*: tread carefully and logically. Often, with new hardware, the only way of getting the necessary information is by bravely opening the hardware circuit diagram and turning to the serial interface section. This requires either nerves of steel or a good friend. If you are using the trial and error method of tracking down a problem, keep notes and drawings of the test configurations for future head-scratching.

The interface chip used to convert the internal parallel data to external RS232 serial format is known as a Universal Asynchronous Receive and Transmit device (**UART**). It is connected to the bus as any other device: all computers that offer serial ports for modem or terminal connection have UARTS.

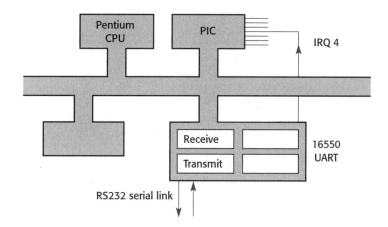

Fig. 10.22
Attaching a UART serial
line interface.

The UART is a data protocol converter, interfacing the internal parallel bus to an external serial line, as shown in Fig. 10.22. For this reason it has been referred to as a SIPO/PISO, meaning Serial in, Parallel out/Parallel in, Serial out. UARTs can also carry out some low-level error trapping. Typically, they can help by detecting an incoming character which is of the wrong length or the wrong parity, or which arrives too soon, overwriting the previous item.

The 8250 UART supplied with the original PC was never very popular with programmers, having a reputation for hardware bugs. Its contemporary alternative, the Intel 8251, certainly had some problems with responding correctly to the CTS line! Interestingly, the new higher performance, National Semiconductor 16550A UART has short, 16 byte, push through FIFO (first in, first out) buffers on both the transmit and receive channels. This reduces the timing constraints on the CPU, because it allows up to 16 characters to be received before the CPU must grab the data from the UART and store it away safely in main memory. On the PC, an IRQ4 interrupt is generated to warn the CPU of the arrival of data requiring servicing. With a 16 byte input buffer, the interrupt rate is reduced by up to a factor of 16. This is significant because if the CPU response is not fast enough, the data in the UART will get corrupted by more incoming data overrunning the earlier bytes in the receive buffer. With a block of 16 bytes to transfer, it might even be worth considering the use of a DMA controller to completely eliminate direct CPU intervention all together.

The outline programs presented in Fig. 10.23 transfer data from a file on one PC to a file on a second PC, connected through their COM2 serial ports. There is however a problem with extending this COM port example to more interesting examples if you are using Windows NT. The code listed in Fig. 10.23 'blocks' at the fgetc( ) function call. This means that if no incoming data is present at the port, the program stalls, waiting for data to arrive. This can be an undesirable feature when you have other ports to check or screens to update. Under Windows NT there is a useful status checking function, kbhit( ), which allows you to 'look at' the keyboard device before committing to a blocking read, but no such function is available for the COM ports. A workable alternative is to use the SetCommTimeouts( ) function which can limit the blocking time down to 1 ms, or whatever. This means that the ReadFile( ) function

```
/* Filetrans.c */
#include <stdio.h>
#include <conio.h>
#define CNTRLZ 0x1A

int main(void)
{
FILE * fp
FILE * dp;
int c;
if ((fp = fopen("C:\TEMP\text.dat", "rt")) == NULL)
{
        printf("fail to open data file\n");
        return 1;
}
if ((dp = fopen("COM2", "wt")) == NULL)
{
        printf("fail to open COM port\n");
        return 1;
}
while ((c = fgetc(fp )) != EOF)
{
 fputc( c, dp);
}
fputc(CNTRLZ, dp);
fflush(dp);}
fclose(fp);
return 0;
}


/* Filereceive.c */
#include <stdio.h>
#include <conio.h>
#define CNTRLZ 0x1A

int main(void) {
FILE *fp;
FILE *dp;
int c;
    if ((fp = fopen("C:\TEMP\text.dat", "w")) == NULL)
    {
        printf("fail to open data file\n");
        return 1;
    }
    if ((dp = fopen("COM2", "r")) == NULL)
    {
        printf("fail to open COM port\n");
        return 1;
    }
    while ((c= fgetc(dp)) != CNTRLZ)
    {
     fputc( c, fp);
    }
    fflush(fp);
    fclose(fp);
    return 0;
}
```

Fig. 10.23
Accessing COM2 –
slow inter-PC file
transfers.

Fig. 10.24
Using COM2 in non-
blocking mode.
(Continued on p. 236)

```c
#include <stdio.h>
#include <conio.h>
#include <windows.h>
#include <winbase.h>
 HANDLE hCom;
 char inpacket[16], outpacket[16];
 BOOL fSuccess;
/////////////////////////////////////////////////////////////////
// Initializes PC COM2 port to non-blocking mode
//
void initcomm(void)
{
 COMMTIMEOUTS noblock;
 DCB dcb;

 hCom=CreateFile("COM2", GENERIC_READ | GENERIC_WRITE,
                      0, NULL, OPEN_EXISTING, 0, NULL );
 if (hCom == INVALID_HANDLE_VALUE) {
     dwError = GetLastError();
     printf("INVALID_HANDLE_VALUE()");
 }
 fSuccess = GetCommTimeouts(hCom, &noblock);
     noblock.ReadTotalTimeoutConstant = 1;
     noblock.ReadTotalTimeoutMultiplier = MAXDWORD;
     noblock.ReadIntervalTimeout = MAXDWORD;
 fSuccess = SetCommTimeouts(hCom, &noblock);

 fSuccess = GetCommState(hCom, &dcb);
     if(!fSuccess) printf("GetCommState Error!");
         dcb.BaudRate = 9600;
         dcb.ByteSize = 7;
         dcb.fParity = TRUE;
         dcb.Parity = EVENPARITY;
         dcb.StopBits = TWOSTOPBITS;
         dcb.fRtsControl = RTS_CONTROL_HANDSHAKE;
         dcb.fOutxCtsFlow = TRUE;
 fSuccess = SetCommState(hCom, &dcb);
     if(!fSuccess) printf("SetCommState Error!");
     else  printf("Comm port set OK!\n");
 }
```

can be used to get characters from COM with no inconvenient blocking delay when data is not available. Useful functions are listed in Fig. 10.24.

10.6 The serial mouse – COM1 rodents

There are two varieties of mouse available: bus mouse and RS232 (or serial) mouse. The latter is an unusual case of 'standards exploitation' which bears consideration. Most mice work with mechanical components which register the physical movement of the mouse across the table-top. The rubber ball, rolling on the table-top, rotates two slotted disks, as shown in Fig. 10.25. The disks signal the X and Y mouse movements, with black spokes interrupting infrared beams as the wheel rotates.

Fig. 10.24
continued

```
////////////////////////////////////////////////////
// Reads COM2, single character
// IF no char at COM2 it returns 0, ELSE it returns ASCII char
//
char readcomm()
{
        char item;
        int ni;
fSuccess = ReadFile( hCom,
                  &item
                  1,
                  &ni,
                  NULL
  );
  if (ni >0 ) return item;
  else return 0;
}
////////////////////////////////////////////////////
// tests and reads keyboard
// IF no char at kbd lt returns 0, ELSE it returns ASCII char
//
char readkbd()
{
 if (kbhit() ) return _getch();
 else return 0;
}
```

Initially, the use of interrupts would seem appropriate to deal with the button press and the pulsed outputs from the four optical sensors used to detect X and Y movements in the two wheels. The disk sectoring gave 100 pulses for each complete rotation of the 80 mm circumference rubber ball. Moving the mouse at 40 mm/s would deliver pulses at a rate of 50 per second. Although there are four such sensors, they operate in pairs, so requiring the system to deal with only 100 pulses/s, in addition to

Fig. 10.25
Optical disk direction
and speed sensing.

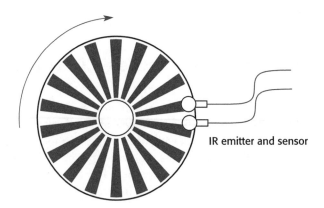

IR emitter and sensor

Fig. 10.26
Arrangement for a PC
serial mouse with UART.

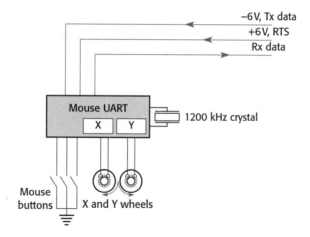

the occasional button press. A pair of beams and sensors for each slotted disk is necessary to give direction as well as speed information.

This event load is easily manageable using interrupts, but in fairness, could equally be handled by polling. The processing load on the CPU from regularly polling the mouse would be around $100 \times 50 = 5000$ instructions/s. The modern microprocessor is capable of 200 million instructions a second. We see that mouse polling would present a CPU loading of 0.0025%.

The parallel mouse, now termed the bus mouse, directs the seven switch inputs to a parallel port, which makes the status information available to the main processor. An alternative arrangement is used on some models, where the mouse is dealt with simply as an extension of the keyboard, being scanned by the keyboard microcontroller. This scheme also reduces the main processor loading.

The serial mouse, which plugs into a COM port, works the same way but transmits the information differently. It could be termed more intelligent in that it counts the X and Y movement pulses coming from the IR beam receivers, incrementing and decrementing internal registers. It then converts the signed integer values into serial bytes and transmits the serial data, at 1200 bps, to the RS232 COM port of the PC. Thus the mouse is equipped with its own specialist UART! The schematic circuit is shown in more detail in Fig. 10.26.

10.7   Serial ports – practical tips, avoiding the frustration

When plugging equipment together for the first time the equipment may fail for a number of reasons. Sorting out the obvious situations can reveal more subtle and mysterious problems. For serial line interfaces the source of the difficulty can be any one, or more, of the suggestions in Table 10.6.

Table 10.6
Tips and hints on serial
connection failure.

Hardware issues

Plugs and sockets don't fit: 25 pin vs. 9 pin, sockets vs. pins

Tx and Rx pins confused – crossed vs. uncrossed lead

Different plug configurations

Incorrect wiring of hardware flow controls (CTS/RTS)

Reversed internal IDC ribbon cables

Incorrectly assembled IDC ribbon cables

Incorrectly installed interface card (IRQ, DMA, port number)

Serial port hardware not initialized

Incompatible transmission formats

ASCII vs EBCDIC or Unicode

Line speed setting: 1200, 2400, 9600 bps

Error checks: odd/even/none parity

ASCII character length: 7 vs. 8 bits

Number of stop bits

User-defined packet lengths

CR-LF line terminator differences in files

Tab vs. multiple SP differences

Word processor control characters (Word)

EOF problems

Flow control failure

CTS input uncontrolled by receiver

RTS/CTS talking to Xon/Xoff

Intermediate buffers on end-to-end flow control

Unread echo characters on serial lines

RAM buffer threshold problems

Software problems

Sending/receiving data through wrong channel

Incorrect device driver installed

Uninstalled device driver

10.8   USB – Universal Serial Bus

A consortium of computer manufacturers met together in the early 1990s to discuss
the problem that suppliers and users experienced when attaching new devices to PCs.
It was decided that there was an opportunity to develop a new industry standard for

Fig. 10.27
USB sockets.

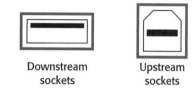

Downstream   Upstream
sockets   sockets

serial interfacing. This was intended to be suitable for slower speed peripherals, and was designed from the start for straightforward interfacing from the user's point of view. Thus there was to be no need for manual device configuration or rebooting the computer, no extra PCI card for each device, a single style of universal connector and cabling, and no external power supply required. The overall USB port bandwidth is 1.5 Mbyte/s, shared by all the attached devices, of which there is an upper limit of 127 set by the address width. The four-wire cable uses two wires for data transmission and the other pair for power (5 V and 0 V).

Differing master and slave plugs are provided to assist with correct interconnection, as shown in Fig. 10.27. The connection arrangement is through a tree topology with hub routers at the nodes, as shown in Fig. 10.28. To accommodate this hierarchical scheme, USB devices are often equipped with further sockets to accept plug-ins from more USB devices. There are three unit types defined: USB host, USB hub and connected function unit. The host is generally a PC. The hub may be a standalone unit or incorporated into a peripheral device which is also providing the required function.

USB operates on a master–slave protocol. The root hub addresses all the attached devices every millisecond (1 kHz) with a synchronizing frame. This marks out a communication slot, within which the master may be sending data down to a device, the hub may be requesting data, or a device may be returning data back to the hub. There are four types of frame as listed in Table 10.7.

A frame can encapsulate several packets of data, which can be input or output directed. Every frame starts with a Start-of-Frame (SOF) packet, while data packets may contain up to 64 bytes of data. Every packet starts with a synchronization byte and ends with an error-detecting CRC byte.

Fig. 10.28
USB connectivity.

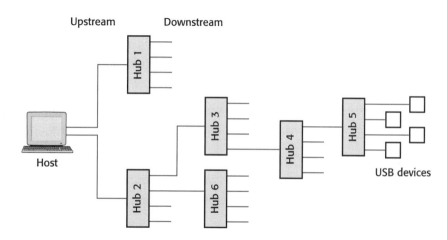

Table 10.7
Different USB frame
types.

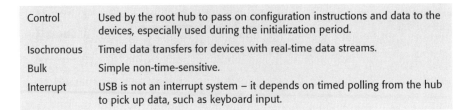

Control	Used by the root hub to pass on configuration instructions and data to the devices, especially used during the initialization period.
Isochronous	Timed data transfers for devices with real-time data streams.
Bulk	Simple non-time-sensitive.
Interrupt	USB is not an interrupt system – it depends on timed polling from the hub to pick up data, such as keyboard input.

Data is transmitted serially at a rate of up to 12 Mbps. The standard is intended to be used for the interconnection of the host PC to many peripherals, without the traditional difficulties associated with inserting new ISA or PCI cards. Up to 127 devices are addressable in a hub-tree topology, which should provide sufficient expansion capability and flexibility to deal with all the 'low-speed' devices. The USB software has been designed for dynamic detection, so that devices can be added or removed while the PC is operating, and the required software modules will be automatically loaded or unloaded. Addressing and system resource assignments are also automatic, so that the end user will not need to get involved with arcane IO addressing problems or IRQ assignments. Suitable devices would be mice, keyboards, joystick, digital telephones, and digital cameras.

USB cables can only be up to 5 m long, so it is intended for peripherals, not communication networks. Usefully, some power can be drawn from the four-core cable to avoid the need for batteries or extra mains power supplies in most cases. The cables used to connect devices to hosts or hubs have a different connector at each end – an 'A' type plug at the end toward the host PC, and a 'B' type plug at the end toward the peripheral device. USB devices may provide further sockets for other devices to plug into 'downstream'.

The typical host PC system unit has two 'A' type sockets so that a pair of peripherals can be directly attached to the PC. Alternatively, a hub can be attached to increase the number of sockets to four. Note that for current implementations, if the PC has two ports they are part of the same logical bus.

As yet, enthusiasm for the USB standard has been rather muted among equipment manufacturers. Intel have produced a special version of its i8251 microcontroller, which includes a high-speed UART for USB interfacing.

The i8x931 illustrated in Fig. 10.29 uses a **PLL** (Phase-Locked Loop) clock synthesizer to synchronize the local bit clock with the incoming data signal. Each frame is preceded by a special **SOF** (Start-of-Frame) byte to synchronize at the byte level. The input and output channels are supplied with 16 byte FIFO buffers to reduce the number of interrupts generated by the device and reduce the danger of data overrun. Assistance with routing of frames to and from the downstream devices is also offered by the hardware.

The Apple iMac was the first serious attempt to exploit the standard, and was not initially well understood by the high street suppliers, leading to problems with the wrong device drivers being installed.

Fig. 10.29
Intel 8x931 USB
peripheral
microcontroller.

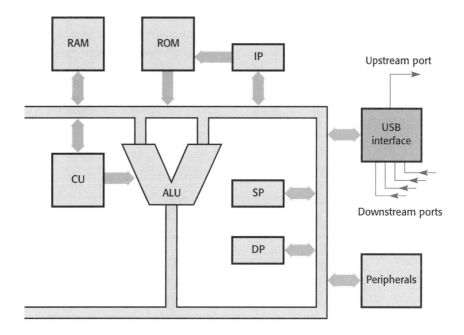

10.9   Modems – modulating carrier waves

Telephones and data communications have been associated for many years. Dial-up connections, using a modem (Fig. 10.30), allow computers to exchange data over long distances. The typical telephone modem offers communication rates from a range: 300, 1200, 2400, 9600, 14 400, 19 200, 28 800, 33 600 and 56 000 bps.

The term 'modem' is an abbreviated form of 'modulator–demodulator'. At one time, it was possible that modems would be rendered obsolete as the telephone system converted completely to digital technology. But this looks unlikely now, and a new generation of modems have been developed for use with neighbourhood cable networks and the forthcoming DSL standard (see Section 16.6).

The difficulty of transmitting binary computer data along telephone lines intended for analogue signals is well recognized, and the normal solution is to install a modem between the computer and the telephone socket. This is shown in Fig. 10.30. Modems convert the computer logic levels 1 and 0 into distinctive tones, or whistles. You may have heard them when you mistakenly dialled a wrong number which had a modem or fax machine attached. The frequency of the tones must be within the normal speech range (300–3500 Hz) for transmission along telephone channels. Figure 10.31 illustrates two possibilities which might be used. The first sends a tone to represent a 1, but nothing to represent a 0. A more reliable technique, known as **FSK** (Frequency Shift Keying), uses different tones to represent 1s and 0s. Because the final subscriber link is usually two wires, serving communication in both directions, there is a real need to consider whether such an arrangement would work in full duplex mode, transmitting

Fig. 10.30
Using modems to
transfer data across the
telephone network.

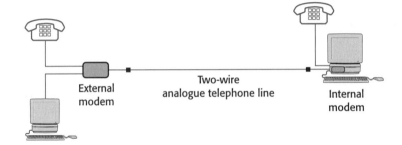

and receiving simultaneously. To satisfy this important requirement, four tones are designated, two for each direction.

Further difficulties include the voltage standards, noise levels and bandwidth constraints. While the RS232 COM port uses +9/–9 V voltages, normal subscriber telephone links run at 0/–50 V. In addition, telephone voice channels are electronically limited to a maximum frequency of 3.5 kHz, while a computer COM port regularly transmits at 9.6 kbps, which superficially requires a 19.2 kHz channel. Another problem to be resolved is the conversion of the two wire subscriber line interface to the four line equivalent normally required by terminal equipment. Sending and receiving on the same wire, through the same port, can be tricky. Traditional telephone technology was also able to tolerate electrical interference, which introduced pops and crackles into our conversations. The new digital age, although potentially offering more 'noise immunity', does require sophisticated error detection and correction facilities. Modems play an important role in solving all these problems.

There are internationally agreed modem standards, as partially listed in Table 10.8. Modern modems can normally be initialized using a group of commands drawn from the Hayes AT set (see Table 10.9). The most common configuration string is ATZ, which is the hardware reset command. Initialization commands are sent to the modem from the PC, but there are also internally stored configurations that can be accessed by using the ATF1 command. It is also now common to build a processor into the modem unit. This handles the initialization dialogue and offers an optional data compression facility to improve the data transfer rate and capacity. The most popular is MNP-5,

Fig. 10.31
Frequency modulation
technique.

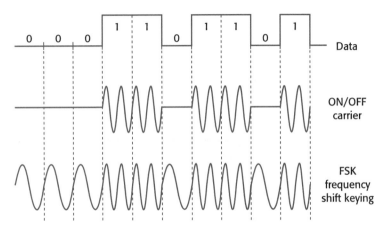

Table 10.8
Modem standards and
coding schemes.

ITU category	Capacity	Type
V.21	300/600 bps	Frequency shift
V.22	1200 bps	Phase shift
V.22bis	2400 bps	Amplitude and phase shift
V.29	9600 bps	Phase shift
V.32	9600 bps	Amplitude and phase shift
V.32bis	14.4 kbps	Amplitude and phase shift
V.17	14.4 bps	Fax
V.34	28.8 kbps	Amplitude and phase shift

developed by Microcom Corp. and adopted with improvements by the ITU as V.42bis. This can achieve a 3:1 compression of plain text using a Lempel–Ziv–Welch (LZW) algorithm. The more advanced modems, offering to transfer at 38.4 kbps or 56 kbps along the normal 4 kHz bandwidth-limited telephone lines, rely on effective data encoding and compression to achieve these high data rates. If the data is already compressed, there is a consequent reduction in the effective data transfer rate.

Figure 10.32 shows how the carrier frequency required to transmit a fixed rate of data can be reduced by encoding several bits into a single cycle. This is usually exploited not by reducing the carrier frequency but by increasing the bit rate. So a 2400 Hz modem carrier frequency can be used to transfer 2400 bps, 9600 bps, 19200 bps or higher, depending on the coding scheme which has been chosen.

The ability to discriminate quickly between different phases of the same frequency depends on the use of **DSP** (Digital Signal Processor) technology. DSP chips provide the necessary arithmetic processing speed to track the carrier waves and detect the sharp changes in phase which signal the data values. Whereas previous circuit

Table 10.9
Some of the Hayes
modem AT command
set.

Command	Function
ATA	Answer incoming call
ATDnnn-nnnn	Tone dials the phone number nnn-nnnn
ATL	Redials last number dialed
ATPDnnn-nnnn	Pulse dial nnn-nnnn
ATW	Wait for dial tone
ATH0	Hang up
ATM0	Speaker off
ATM1	Speaker is on until a carrier is detected
ATM2	Speaker is always on
ATO0	Puts modem in data mode
ATO1	Takes modem out of data mode
ATY0	Disable disconnection on pause
ATY1	Enable disconnection on pause

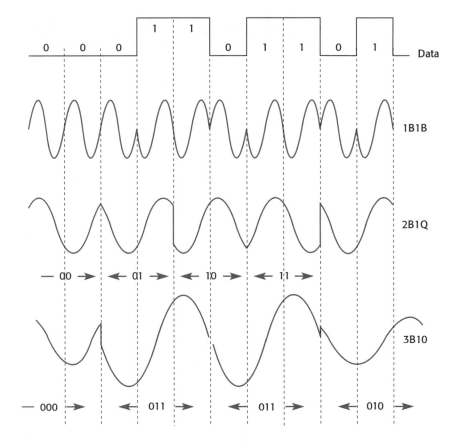

Fig. 10.32
Phase modulation increases the bit signalling rate.

techniques could distinguish phase changes of $\pi/2$ (90°), the newer techniques can work reliably with phase differences as small as $\pi/8$ (22.5°). The DSP chips are also coded to carry out echo cancellation. This allows the modem to work in full duplex mode over a single pair of wires. This requires the effective separation of the transmitted and received data by subtracting the strong outgoing signal from the combined incoming signal.

The amplitude–phase diagrams in Fig. 10.33, sometimes referred to as constellation plots, show some examples of the use of phase modulation techniques employed in modern modems. So-called QAM modems use a single-frequency carrier which is varied in both phase and amplitude. The first represents a simple phase shifter which signals a binary 1 by transmitting a frequency burst for a set period, and a binary 0 by switching the phase by π. The second plot illustrates simultaneous variation of phase and amplitude to enable the sender to transmit four bits in each time slot. It does this by having four distinguishable variations of the carrier wave: high amplitude + zero phase, low amplitude + zero phase, high amplitude + 180° phase shift, low amplitude + 180° phase shift. The third scheme is known as QAM (Quadrature Amplitude Modulation). The carrier amplitude is held constant, and the phase has four distinguishable values: 45°, 135°, 225° and 315°. Finally, the most sophisticated method offers 32 distinct variations of the carrier wave by using four amplitudes and eight phase settings.

Fig. 10.33
Amplitude–phase
diagrams illustrating
some modulation
schemes.

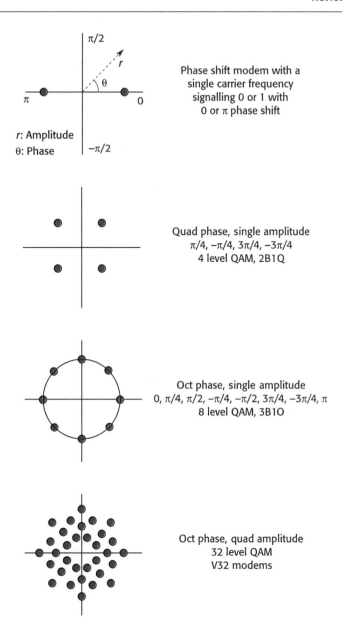

Phase shift modem with a
single carrier frequency
signalling 0 or 1 with
0 or π phase shift

Quad phase, single amplitude
$\pi/4$, $-\pi/4$, $3\pi/4$, $-3\pi/4$
4 level QAM, 2B1Q

Oct phase, single amplitude
0, $\pi/4$, $\pi/2$, $-\pi/4$, $-\pi/2$, $3\pi/4$, $-3\pi/4$, π
8 level QAM, 3B1O

Oct phase, quad amplitude
32 level QAM
V32 modems

Review

- The Internet is based on serial communications between computers. The two PC COM ports allow direct point-to-point connections using the RS232 standard.

- Communication involves three important aspects: data, timing and signalling.

- Receivers need to recognize the centre point of each incoming bit so that an accurate reading can be taken. This involves knowing the width of a bit (bps, baud rate) and the start point of a bit (phase information).

- Asynchronous transmission requires the transmitter to insert a pulse (start bit) in front of each byte to alert and synchronize the receiver. Synchronous transmission is used at higher speeds. Here the transmitter will send a continuous clock signal alongside the data. This fully synchronizes the receiver.

- Errors can occur during transmission. Error detection and even correction is possible if extra redundant information is transmitted with the data. A single parity bit is the most common example of error detection.

- Multiple parity bit Hamming codes can detect and correct errors.

- Block checksums can detect storage and transmission errors, and are simple to implement. However, the CRC is more effective and commonly found in many applications.

- A system of flow control is required to prevent fast sources overwhelming slow receivers; otherwise, overrun errors occur in the receive buffer. For RS232, there are hardware (CTS/RTS) and software (Xon/Xoff) techniques available.

- Routing the data is not an issue with simple point-to-point serial communications.

- A UART is an IO interface chip which converts data between parallel and serial formats. It can also handle parity-based error checking and RS232 flow control.

- The COM port mouse has a special UART inside it.

- USB is a new high-speed serial transmission standard for device interfacing.

- When transmitting serial data across traditional analogue telephone lines, modem units are needed. These use an audio carrier wave, modulated to represent the data.

Practical work

The recommended practical work involves using the COM port on several PCs to implement a primitive packet-passing ring network. Unless you limit the experiment to only a pair of PCs, a special cable will have to be made up. The initialization, input and output routines use Win32 functions. This brings into focus the extra problems which come with networked broadcasting, rather than the previous chapter's point-to-point arrangement. Consideration must be given to avoiding the blocking system calls.

Exercises

1. What is the difference between asynchronous and synchronous communications? Are the following synchronous or asynchronous?

   Television broadcasts

   Fax transmissions

   Ethernet

CD-ROMs

Explain why.

2. Sketch out the bit pattern for an RS232 transmission of the letter 'A', using 8 bits, EVEN parity, 1 stop bit.

3. What is the bit rate of current fax modems? How long would it take a Group III fax scanner to transmit an uncompressed A4 page? Group III operates at 1142 lines, each holding 1728 black/white pixels. Assume a 9600 bps transmission.

4. What is the principal advantage of digital data transmission?

5. Explain the signals CTS and RTS. What was their original function with modems, and how are they now used when transferring data directly between computers along a serial line?

6. Why is some form of flow control always used in data communications? Will the provision of an input buffer remove the need for flow control?

7. Is cable television digital or analogue?

8. How long does it take to transmit 2500 characters down a telephone line?

9. When receiving data at 19 200 bps, how often would the system need to service interrupts when the receive buffer is enabled?

10. Try computing one of the checksums in the S record file from Fig. 10.13.

11. Introduce a different bit error into the Hamming code example in Section 10.3. Apply the operator and reassure yourself that the syndrome is correct

12. Look back at Fig. 4.8 and identify the data carried by the four input streams.

Readings

- Heuring and Jordan (1997), Section 8.5: error control methods; Section 10.2: serial communications.

- Tanenbaum (1999), Section 2.2.4: error-correcting codes.

- Anderson (1997)

- PC mouse information:
  http://www.hut/~then/mytexts/mouse.html

- For more technical information and application examples for the USB interface, try:
  http://www.intel.com/design/usb/

- An introduction to modem terminology can be found at:
  http://www.physics.udel.edu/wwwusers/watson/student_projects/scen167/thosguys/

- The Web sites can be accessed via the Companion Web site for this book at:
  http://www.booksites.net/williams/

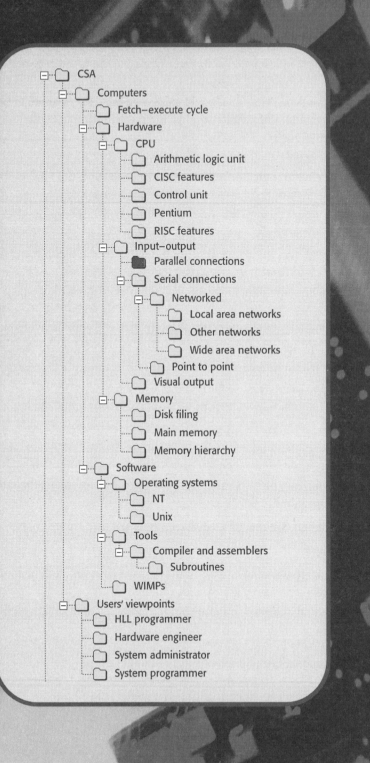

Parallel
connections

Overview

The transfer of data along buses inside the computer is carried out in parallel mode. That means that many bits are transmitted along clusters of wires simultaneously. The generally used technique of asynchronous handshaking during a data transfer is introduced for the Centronics printer port. The SCSI and IDE interconnect buses are presented as important standards which allow other devices to be attached to the PC with some confidence.

11.1   Parallel interfaces – better performance

Inside the computer, data is transferred along parallel highways called **buses**. The data, address and control buses 'tie' the computer together. As discussed in Section 3.6, the *width* (number of lines) of the address bus is a critical parameter when designing new computer systems. Each generation of microprocessors, since the 1970s, has widened the address and data buses to improve performance. Currently, the Pentium uses a 64 bit external data bus to loosen the stranglehold exerted by the 'bus bottleneck'. Two longwords can be transferred simultaneously to or from memory. While within the CPU itself, the data bus may be 128 bits wide to further improve transfer rates.

Generally, devices such as printers or screens, which use parallel connections to the computer, are not attached directly to the system bus, but require an **interface** circuit to manage the connection. The difference in voltages, timing and control signal make a direct connection problematical. The simplest parallel interface was presented in Section 3.8, but often considerably more functionality than an 8 bit **latch** is needed to translate the control bus into a form that is compatible with the device control lines. The likely need to make the connection work in both directions, to support input and output operations, also complicates the issue.

In general, one of the most significantly troublesome areas for users and programmers is still the connection of peripheral equipment to computers. It seems that this remains unpredictable even with all the standardization, Plug-and-Play and years of experience in mainframe, mini- and micro-computing.

11.2   Centronics – more than a printer port but less than a bus

Multi-wire parallel links, such as the Centronics printer interface, can transfer all 8 bits of an ASCII code simultaneously. This generally works at up to 100 kbyte/s over short distances (10 m), but offers only a point-to-point master–slave service. This means that it should not properly be referred to as a bus, because an essential feature of a bus interconnection is its ability to offer a service to more than two devices. There are three standards for this interface currently available with different capabilities. These are summarized in Table 11.1.

Table 11.1
PC parallel port (Centronics) standards.

SPP	Standard Parallel Port	100 kbyte/s	Output	Software-operated
EPP	Enhanced Parallel Port	1 Mbyte/s	Input–output	Hardware handshake circuits
ECP	Extended Capability Port	5 Mbyte/s	Input–output	DMA with FIFO

Fig. 11.1
The Centronics standard interface (SPP).

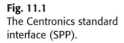

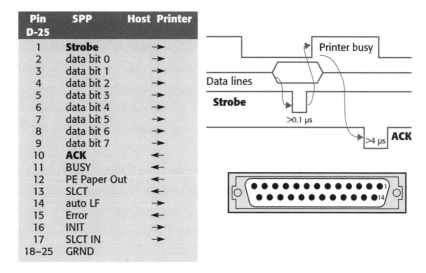

Pin D-25	SPP	Host	Printer
1	**Strobe**		→
2	data bit 0		→
3	data bit 1		→
4	data bit 2		→
5	data bit 3		→
6	data bit 4		→
7	data bit 5		→
8	data bit 6		→
9	data bit 7		→
10	**ACK**		←
11	BUSY		←
12	PE Paper Out		←
13	SLCT		←
14	auto LF		→
15	Error		←
16	INIT		→
17	SLCT IN		→
18–25	GRND		

The Standard Parallel Port was intended simply for data output and was provided with only the few input lines necessary to carry out an asynchronous handshake. The transfer speed was limited because all the testing and setting of control and status pins was carried out by software. The hardware was really a simple byte-wide parallel port with an upper transfer limit of around 100 kbyte/s.

To send data to the printer, the computer sets the eight data lines by writing to the port data register. It then waits a short time, as indicated in Fig. 11.1, for the signals to settle (>50 ns) and pushes the Strobe down for at least 0.1 μs. The printer uses this Strobe as an indication of 'data present' and immediately reads the data port if it is free to do so. Having completed the read the printer responds to the computer with a 4 μs pulse on the ACK line to indicate that the transfer was successful. A separate BUSY line, back from the printer can be used to block further transmissions from the computer when the printer is unable to keep up with the computer. But the implementation of flow control is usually left to the ACK signal. An alternative description, using a sequence diagram, which is more familiar to programmers, is given in Fig. 11.2.

This is an example of an **asynchronous handshake** scheme. Data is only transmitted when the receiver is ready, which allows the transmitter and receiver equipment to use widely different clock rates and to actually operate internally at different speeds.

Parallel connections would seem to offer substantial bandwidth advantages over serial links. It immediately begs the simple question of why use serial links at all when they are eight times slower? The answer lies in the realm of electrical engineering. When all eight bits are simultaneously transmitted along parallel wires they suffer from an electrical signal degradation known as 'skew'. This is where the differing resistances and capacitances of the separate wires introduce slightly differing transmission delays, making the pulses go out of alignment with each other. Engineers become worried by this kind of thing and eventually signals on a parallel bus can skew badly enough to corrupt the received data value, which concerns even programmers!

Fig. 11.2
Sequence of events
within a Centronics data
transfer.

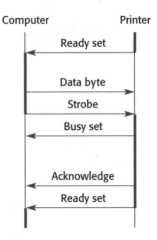

The Centronics standard has been extended to include the bidirectional EPP and
ECP modes. These allow the data lines to be used for input as well as output. In addition, four of the status lines are redeployed for other purposes, as listed in Table 11.2.
The change to bidirectionality was necessary to support Plug-and-Play devices, where
the host computer needs to interrogate the device which identifies itself during the
boot-up phase.

Table 11.2
The Centronics
enhanced interface
(EPP/ECP).

Pin D-25	EPP	Computer	Printer
1	Write	→	
2	data bit 0	←→	
3	data bit 1	←→	
4	data bit 2	←→	
5	data bit 3	←→	
6	data bit 4	←→	
7	data bit 5	←→	
8	data bit 6	←→	
9	data bit 7	←→	
10	Interrupt	←	
11	Wait	←	
12	user def	←	
13	user def	←	
14	Strobe	←	
15	user def	←	
16	Reset	→	
17	Addr Strobe	←→	
18–25	GRND		

Table 11.3
How to prevent delays
caused by printing.

1.	Fitting a large memory buffer inside the printer
2.	Installing a print spooler on the computer to run in the background
3.	Use a full multitasking operating system (e.g. Unix, Windows NT, Windows 98)

With an asynchronous data transfer, the handshake supports a variable data rate to suit the slowest of the pair, which can be frustrating if you are waiting for the printing to finish. This inconvenience can be avoided in a number of ways, as listed in Table 11.3.

Most computer workstations are now running multitasking operating systems which are built to handle printers without interfering with the interactive foreground activities. Less sophisticated computer systems may be enhanced to provide this facility by loading a print driver as an interrupt routine. This takes the data to be printed and passes the characters out to the printer, sometimes as an extra activity of the keyboard scanning routine or the real-time clock update. In this way the slow printer can be supplied with characters at a fast enough rate to keep it busy, but without seeming to affect the main foreground activities.

Using the Centronics printer port in other roles, such as accessing security **dongles**, or as an interface to writeable CD drives, has been a problem in the past. The SPP mode limited the hardware to support only data output, even though the actual chips used were often capable of bidirectional activity. This has now been altered so that the 'printer port' can serve a wide range of other functions when in EPP or ECP mode. These faster modes are served by extra hardware which can carry out flow control handshaking, relieving the software of this testing and timing activity. All the program has to do is write a byte of data to the output port. The port hardware will then check to see whether the printer is not busy, and send a strobe pulse. These modes commonly do not check the ACK line.

Recently there has been a new burst of interest in this facility, stimulated by the introduction of Windows NT into laboratories. Manufacturers of interface cards were often not prepared for the dramatic change from DOS to NT, and found that their DOS software no longer worked under the more secure NT regime. A quick solution was to move their special equipment outside the computer, using the only easily available parallel port!

11.3 SCSI – the Small Computer Systems Interface

The SCSI parallel interface offers a fast asynchronous, byte-wide bus (5 Mbyte/s) connecting up to eight devices. The host adaptor, which on a PC would be an ISA or PCI expansion card, is allocated '0' as a SCSI address, which is set using miniature on-board switches. As host adapters are simply SCSI units, there is the possibility of several PCs connecting to the same SCSI bus. This is one method of implementing a disk sharing arrangement. The other attached devices can have any of the other addresses. Unusually, addresses are passed in decoded form on the data bus by

Fig. 11.3
Sequence of phases
within a SCSI transfer.

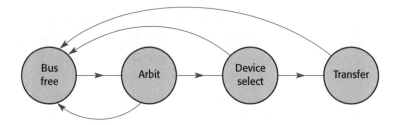

activating the appropriate bus line. So address 0 corresponds to bus line 0, address 2 to bus line 2, and so on. In this way several target devices can be addressed simultaneously. When connecting new units to the SCSI bus it is vital to use a different address. SCSI is intended for hard disk drives, CD-ROMS or tape units. It is an example of a secondary bus, the use of which can improve the performance of a computer by reducing the traffic on the main bus. Subsequent variants of the first 5 Mbyte/s standard have improved the transfer rate by offering a double speed, 10 Mbyte/s synchronous transfer mode (Fast SCSI) and the 40 Mbyte/s variant with a 32 bit data bus (Wide SCSI).

There are three principal phases to a SCSI communication event: bus seizure, device selection and information transfer. As illustrated in Fig. 11.3, a good way to understand the way a SCSI transfer takes place is to express the phases in a state diagram. The initiator, which starts the communication, and the target, which replies, exchange data packets. Because each device is allocated a unique bus address (0–7) several 'conversations' may be interleaved at the same time. The PC host adapter card does not have to be the initiator. Any device can start communications with a nominated target device. As mentioned, this multiple bus master capability enables the SCSI bus to be used as an interprocessor communication highway on multiprocessor computers.

A communication session begins with the initiating master device checking to see whether the bus is available by inspecting the BSY line and then taking control of it. The hopeful master will copy its 8 bit ID onto the data bus while asserting the BSY control line. If no higher priority device responds (0 – low, 7 – high priority) the bus has been claimed successfully and the data transfer sequence can proceed. The new master sends an inquiry packet containing a code, as indicated in Table 11.4, to the target device with which it intends to establish communications. The target must acknowledge with status information before the data transfer can proceed.

You may be interested to note from Fig. 11.4 that the byte-wide data bus is protected by a single parity bit, so Section 10.3 has some relevance here! The SCSI control lines, listed below, can operate an asynchronous handshake to pass data across the bus.

$\overline{\text{BSY}}$ – Busy indicates that someone is currently using the bus.

$\overline{\text{SEL}}$ – Select is used by the initiator to select a target and by the target to resume an interrupted session.

Table 11.4
SCSI message codes.

Group 1			
00	Test unit ready	13	Verify
01	Rezero unit	14	Recover buffer
03	Request sense	15	Mode select
04	Format unit	16	Reserved unit
05	Read block limits	17	Release unit
07	Reassign blocks	18	Copy
08	Read	19	Erase
0A	Write	1A	Mode sense
0B	Seek	1B	Start/stop
0F	Read reverse	1C	Receive diagnostic
10	Write file mark	1D	Send diagnostic
11	Space	1E	Lock media
12	Inquiry		
Group 2			
25	Read capacity	30	Search data high
26	Extend addr rd	31	Search data equal
2A	Extend addr wr	32	Search data low
2E	Write 7 verify	33	Set limits
2F	Verify	39	Compare
		3A	Copy and verify

Fig. 11.4
Small Computer Systems Interface (SCSI) and command packet.

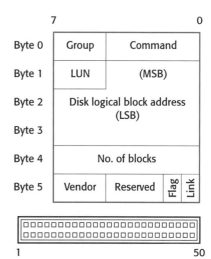

Pin		Master	Slave
2	data bit 0	←→	
4	data bit 1	←→	
6	data bit 2	←→	
8	data bit 3	←→	
10	data bit 4	←→	
12	data bit 5	←→	
14	data bit 6	←→	
16	data bit 7	←→	
18	PARITY	←→	
32	ATN	→	
36	BSY	←	
38	ACK	→	
40	RST	→	
42	MSG	←	
44	SEL	→	
46	C/D	←	
48	REQ	←	
50	I/O	←	

$\overline{\text{C/D}}$ – Control/Data is controlled by the target to indicate whether control or data items are being transferred on the data bus.

$\overline{\text{I/O}}$ – Input/Output allows the target to define the direction of the data transfer.

$\overline{\text{ACK}}$ – Acknowledge is used to confirm a request.

$\overline{\text{ATN}}$ – Attention is used by the master to tell the slave that data is available on the bus.

$\overline{\text{MSG}}$ – Message, activated by the target during the message phase of transfer.

$\overline{\text{REQ}}$ – Request, used by the target device, signals to the master that data can be transmitted. It is part of the REQ/ACK handshake pair.

$\overline{\text{ACK}}$ – Acknowledge, controlled by the initiator to confirm a transfer.

$\overline{\text{RST}}$ – Reset bus, forces all attached devices to stop activity and reset the hardware.

The command packet structure is given in Fig. 11.4. Because there are several size command packets, each starts with a packet size code, Group 0 using 6 bytes and Groups 1 and 2 using 10 bytes.

The 50-way IDC ribbon cable is connected in daisy-chain fashion, looping from card to card for up to 6 m in length. It must be correctly terminated at both ends to avoid disruptive electrical reflections, and all signal lines are paired to ground lines, which makes for cleaner transmissions. When connecting a new device it is vital to allocate a unique bus address (1–7) and set it correctly on DIL switches or PCB jumpers. Two devices answering to the same address would be chaotic! The SCSI bus does offer high performance, speed and capacity, but at a higher cost than the IDE alternative. Although relatively rare on PCs it is still common on larger systems. It does offer the useful advantage, very relevant for PC systems, of only needing a single interrupt (IRQ) for up to seven disk drives, which would otherwise demand an impossible 4 IRQs with IDE units. To add to the cost of the drive, SCSI controllers are rarely offered as standard equipment on the motherboard, so a new controller card is also required. These can incorporate a fast DMA controller and RAM buffer so that data transfers are made more quickly than with the standard PC DMA controllers.

There is a specific advantage to using SCSI disks when burning CD-R disks. These, as we will see in Section 12.9, must have an uninterrupted inward flow of data (300 kbyte/s for ×1 speed units), or else the burn will fail with an 'underrun error'. This is not an uncommon problem when relying on IDE disk drives, but SCSI controllers support queued requests, thus reducing the time delay between the completion of one data block read and the start of the next.

As ×4 and ×8 CD-R/CD-RW drives become popular, needing faster input data streams, the advantage of the SCSI bus may again be more widely recognized.

11.4 IDE – Intelligent Drive Electronics

The **IDE** interface, which is a simplified version of the ISA bus, was introduced to deal with the growing size and speed of PC hard drives. The earlier IBM interfaces for the ST412/506 disk drives required separate boards full of electronics to separate the data from the clock signal and organize the head movements across the platters. Only the motor controller was sited on the disk drive itself. Besides the problem of keeping abreast of all the different drives and controller cards which flooded on to the market, not always mutually compatible, the rate of data transfer along the interconnecting ribbon cable became a problem. The signals emerging from the disk drive were nearly raw and very susceptible to interference and degradation. By including more electronics with the disk drive, the IDE signals could be partly processed before transmission down to the computer bus. By integrating controller electronics and drive mechanics, both the transmission and compatibility problems are resolved. The command set of around 30 instructions used to communicate with IDE devices was defined by the AT attachment standard (ATA) set out by a Common Access Method (CAM) group of manufacturers in 1989.

So Intelligent (or Integrated) Drive Electronics was introduced to allow PC users to upgrade their hard drive without also needing to upgrade an expensive, complex interface card. The standard was quickly accepted for the cheapest and most popular disk drives available. The essential controller electronics are included on the drive, and the 40-way IDC ribbon connector plugs directly into the AT bus. Each cable can serve only two drives, one designated as Master and the second as Slave. A jumper link is normally used to impose this significant distinction. Nothing much works if both drives on a cable are set to Master! Although the drives are physically different in track and sector specification, the interface makes them respond like the traditional ST506 drives. Thus the 40 sector tracks were translated to appear like 17 sector tracks. An upper size limit of 1024 tracks, 8 platters (16 heads) and 63 sectors was set by the original IDE standard, amounting to a maximum disk size of 504 Mbyte. Strangely, the head limit was not due to field width limitations set within the drive registers but resulted from the low-level driver routines (BIOS). Thus with an enhanced BIOS this was increased to 7.88 Gbyte simply by changing the 4 bit head number field to 8 bits (not dissimilar to the Y2K problem!). The newer **EIDE** standard can access 65 536 tracks, 256 platters and 63 sectors, amounting to a maximum disk size of 128 Gbyte.

There is also dual level formatting. The primary track and sector formatting is completed in the factory and cannot easily be repeated. Only the secondary formatting, to set the partitions and directory structures, need be carried out by the user.

Routines to access data on an IDE disk are now provided within the operating system. Special device driver software for a particular manufacturer's units are not generally required. Rather like the SCSI description, there are three phases, or cycles, of the IDE bus. First the CPU writes parameters into the IDE command registers. Then cylinder, head and sector information is loaded. A data block can then be transferred.

For some time it was arranged for the CPU to handle all the actual data transfers as well as setting up the initial commands. Because the latest technology had been applied to the design and manufacture of the CPU, but not yet to the peripheral components, the DMA controller handled the same task more slowly. So all the data was accessed in polled mode. However, with the new availability of DMA-33, the situation has changed, and the IDE drives now use the DMA facilities to transfer their data.

The original IDE interface standard has been enhanced to the EIDE (Extended Integrated Drive Electronics). Control of the drive is achieved by writing a sequence of control codes to the command registers. This is the responsibility of the device driver routines which are accessed through HLL function calls such as `open( )` and `fprintf( )`.

11.5   AT/ISA – a computer standards success story

The original IBM PC 62 pin expansion bus provided an 8 bit data bus and a 20 bit address bus. This is still found on old interface cards, such as that illustrated in Fig. 11.5. As the Intel 8088 processor operated at 4.77 MHz, the expansion bus followed suit. In the first generation of PCs, the ISA bus was an extension of the main bus, providing interface control signals. Nowadays it has been downgraded to a peripheral bus, requiring incoming data to pass through two gateway devices before reaching the main motherboard bus! This is further explained in Section 11.6.

The ISA bus was quickly upgraded to the AT bus (Fig. 11.6), with an extra 36 pins, allowing 16 bit data transfer and 24 bit addressing. This was accepted as the basis for the ISA bus (Industry Standard Architecture bus) and the maximum speed was increased to 8.33 MHz. Since then the processor and main motherboard have further increased their speeds, but in order to retain compatibility with the slower interface chips the ISA bus clock was limited to 8.33 MHz. This bus is run *synchronously* from

Fig. 11.5
An 8 bit PC/ISA bus
printer interface card.

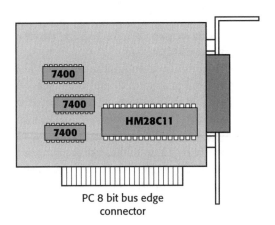

PC 8 bit bus edge
connector

Fig. 11.6
An extended 16 bit PC/
ISA bus parallel IO card.

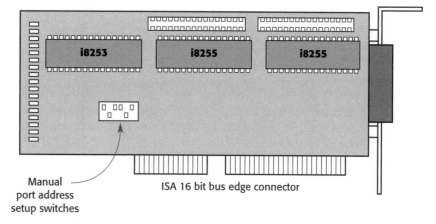

Manual port address setup switches

ISA 16 bit bus edge connector

the main system clock. When a slow device is to be accessed, extra WAIT states are inserted by the CPU to waste time and so match the slower partner. This can result in a noticeable degradation in system performance.

The dimensions of a full-length EISA/AT card are 13.2 in × 4.8 in, with two edge finger connectors, the original 62 pins and the additional 36 pins for the AT bus extension (Fig. 11.6). Modern PC cabinets are sometimes unable to accept a full-length ISA card, even when equipped with ISA slots on the motherboard.

The historic 8.33 MHz speed ceiling and the 16 Mbyte addressing limit soon became serious disadvantages for the ISA standard. When the much faster Pentium CPU arrived, with a 64 bit bus, the performance disadvantages grew more obvious. Nevertheless, there is still a thriving market in both 8 and 16 bit ISA expansion cards catering for the lower demands of simple IO operations. If we consider the difference between the peak data transfer rates of the main bus (800 Mbyte/s) and ISA bus (16 Mbyte/s), the penalty of transferring bulk data over the ISA bus becomes obvious. The technical problem of bus width mismatch, where an 8 byte Pentium bus has to communicate with a 2 or even 1 byte ISA bus, is taken care of by the bus controller. The four BE (Byte Enable) CPU bus control lines switch on the requested data lines and route the bytes through, rather like a train shunting yard.

Look at the pin labels in Fig. 11.7 and identify the groups of lines which make up the address, data and control buses.

The next bus standard was the Extended ISA (EISA) which permitted a 33 MHz transfer rate. But the newer PCI bus rapidly became the most popular choice for higher-performance Pentium systems.

11.6 PCI – Peripheral Component Interconnection

Although the ISA bus was enhanced to carry 16 bit data, the fundamental speed limitations and the need to maintain backward compatibility were always likely to seal its

Fig. 11.7
ISA bus connector
layout.

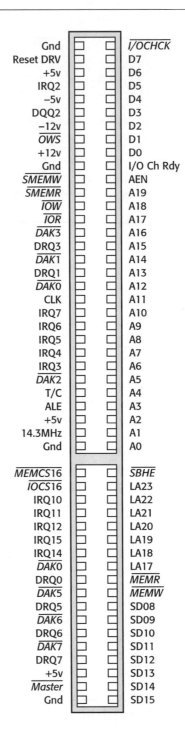

Gnd	$\overline{I/OCHCK}$
Reset DRV	D7
+5v	D6
IRQ2	D5
−5v	D4
DQQ2	D3
−12v	D2
$\overline{OWS}$	D1
+12v	D0
Gnd	I/O Ch Rdy
$\overline{SMEMW}$	AEN
$\overline{SMEMR}$	A19
$\overline{IOW}$	A18
$\overline{IOR}$	A17
$\overline{DAK3}$	A16
DRQ3	A15
$\overline{DAK1}$	A14
DRQ1	A13
$\overline{DAK0}$	A12
CLK	A11
IRQ7	A10
IRQ6	A9
IRQ5	A8
IRQ4	A7
IRQ3	A6
$\overline{DAK2}$	A5
T/C	A4
ALE	A3
+5v	A2
14.3MHz	A1
Gnd	A0

$\overline{MEMCS16}$	$\overline{SBHE}$
$\overline{IOCS16}$	LA23
IRQ10	LA22
IRQ11	LA21
IRQ12	LA20
IRQ15	LA19
IRQ14	LA18
$\overline{DAK0}$	LA17
DRQ0	$\overline{MEMR}$
$\overline{DAK5}$	$\overline{MEMW}$
DRQ5	SD08
$\overline{DAK6}$	SD09
DRQ6	SD10
$\overline{DAK7}$	SD11
DRQ7	SD12
+5v	SD13
$\overline{Master}$	SD14
Gnd	SD15

eventual fate. The recent success of the PCI bus in capturing the market for graphics cards and plug-in modems has quickened the demise of ISA. ISA cards are now referred to as 'legacy products' (bequeathed by an ancestor?). As shown in Fig. 11.8,

Fig. 11.8
Relationship of the PCI
bridge to main bus.

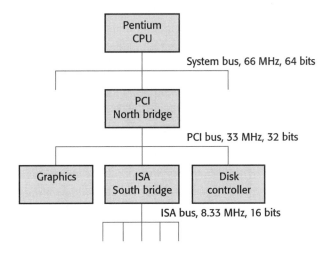

The PCI bus is isolated from the main bus by a **bridge** device, such as the i82443. This is commonly referred to as the 'North Bridge' to distinguish it from the PCI to ISA bridging device, such as the i82371/PIX4 which has been named the South Bridge. Isolating both the PCI and ISA buses from the main system bus was required because of their difference in transfer rates. While the motherboard is following the 66 MHz system clock, the PCI runs at half that speed. But because it has a 32 bit data width it can achieve a 132 Mbyte/s transfer rate. A 64 bit version is also available which doubles this rate to 264 Mbyte/s. While PCI designers have been widening the bus to improve throughput, motherboard clock rates have also been increased from 66 to 133 MHz, and they will continue to increase to 200 MHz. As occurred with its predecessor, the ISA bus, a new standard for the PCI bus may soon be required. Referring to PCI as 'legacy' does seem somewhat premature. Its inventors may object. Perhaps we now need to coin a new term referring to 'disgarded' rather than 'bequeathed' products. May I offer 'littered products' for possible adoption? This might adequately capture the ephemeral nature of our technological achievements and the need to consider more seriously our approach to product recycling!

The PCI bus can operate in two modes:

- **Multiplexed mode:** a single 32 bit bus is shared by address and data information. This increases the effective bus width, but reduces the data rate.

- **Burst mode:** this is the same trick that EDO DRAM employs. After an address has been sent, several data items will follow in quick succession. The bridge is capable of assembling 'packets' of data and bursting it through to the PCI bus when ready.

As illustrated in Fig. 11.9, the PCI bridge requires two internal buses and four data buffers to handle the simultaneous loading and unloading that it attempts to carry out. This decouples the PCI bus from the system bus, with great advantage to both

Fig. 11.9
The PCI bridge.

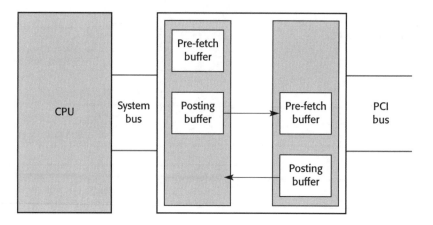

sides. The two internal buses within the PCI bridge enable the separation of system-side activity from PCI-side activity. The twin buffers on each side allow for data to be transferred within the bridge while both sides are also handling external bus transfers.

Figure 11.10 shows a PCI socket.

11.7   Plug-and-Play – automatic configuration

Plug-and-Play was introduced by Microsoft in order to simplify the installation and configuration of new devices. It allows the operating system to recognize new hardware when it is attached, select the correct configuration parameters for it and install the appropriate device driver software. Special BIOS routines are needed to carry out the boot-up query sessions. The alternative manual procedure has always been a source of trouble for the less experienced user, with ample frustrating opportunity for crashing the system. The Plug-and-Play scheme was released with Windows 95, but Windows NT is not wholly compliant; full support arrived with Windows 2000.

The essential difficulty for the operating system is to find what hardware is present and then obtain suitable software drivers to access it correctly. Unfortunately there has been no real discipline imposed on hardware suppliers. They have been free to use port addresses and IRQ lines as they choose. Incompatibilities between cards from different manufacturers are commonplace. Given this situation, there was a severe problem when trying to establish an enquiry protocol which the operating system could deploy during boot-up. The method of operation requires that all expansion slot cards respond in the correct way to a coded initiation key written to a particular, known, port. The cards will then start competing with each other to win the attention of the configuration program. This is done by each card outputting in bit sequence its unique 70 bit serial number. This is made up of the manufacturer's code number (MID) and the individual product code number (PID). Some examples are listed in

Fig. 11.10
PCI socket.

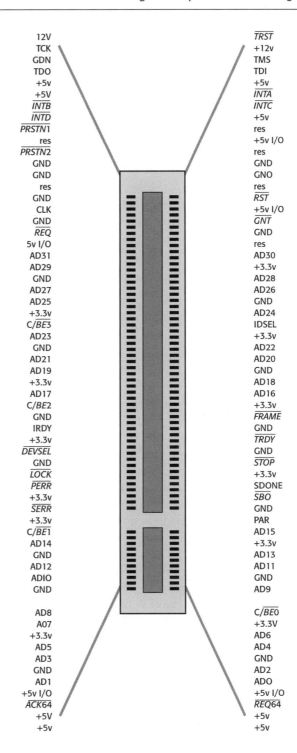

12V	$\overline{TRST}$
TCK	+12v
GDN	TMS
TDO	TDI
+5v	+5v
+5V	$\overline{INTA}$
$\overline{INTB}$	$\overline{INTC}$
$\overline{INTD}$	+5v
$\overline{PRSTN}1$	res
res	+5v I/O
$\overline{PRSTN}2$	res
GND	GND
GND	GNO
res	res
GND	$\overline{RST}$
CLK	+5v I/O
GND	$\overline{GNT}$
$\overline{REQ}$	GND
5v I/O	res
AD31	AD30
AD29	+3.3v
GND	AD28
AD27	AD26
AD25	GND
+3.3v	AD24
$C/\overline{BE}3$	IDSEL
AD23	+3.3v
GND	AD22
AD21	AD20
AD19	GND
+3.3v	AD18
AD17	AD16
$C/\overline{BE}2$	+3.3v
GND	$\overline{FRAME}$
IRDY	GND
+3.3v	$\overline{TRDY}$
$\overline{DEVSEL}$	GND
GND	$\overline{STOP}$
$\overline{LOCK}$	+3.3v
$\overline{PERR}$	SDONE
+3.3v	$\overline{SBO}$
$\overline{SERR}$	GND
+3.3v	PAR
$C/\overline{BE}1$	AD15
AD14	+3.3v
GND	AD13
AD12	AD11
ADIO	GND
GND	AD9
AD8	$C/\overline{BE}0$
A07	+3.3V
+3.3v	AD6
AD5	AD4
AD3	GND
GND	AD2
AD1	ADO
+5v I/O	+5v I/O
$\overline{ACK}64$	$\overline{REQ}64$
+5V	+5v
+5v	+5v

Table 11.5
Example Plug-and-Play
identity numbers.

Manufacturer	MID	PID
Adaptec	9004	36868
Compaq	1032	4146
Creative	10F6	4342
Cyrix	1078	4216
Epson	1008	4104
Hewlett-Packard	103C	4156
Intel	8086	32902
Matsushita	10F7	4343
Mitsubishi	1067	4199
Motorola	1057	4183
NCR	1000	4096
Toshiba	102F	4143
Tseng Labs	100C	4108

Table 11.5. Because all the cards are asserting the single bus line simultaneously there will be chaotic contention. A device outputting a 1 will get overridden by its neighbour, which is outputting a 0. Any device trying to get a 1 accepted, if it reads back the line status and sees a 0, must withdraw from the competition. If a device has a serial number made up of all 0s (illegal), it would always get through to the final round. As each card battles through to win one of the elimination stages, it will be interrogated by the operating system, remotely configured and told to withdraw from the Plug-and-Play identification competition. Eventually all the devices will have been identified, configured and correctly installed by the operating system. This involves allocating the necessary resources to each device, without allowing any conflicts to happen. Base addresses, IRQ numbers and DMA channels have to be organized to everyone's satisfaction – a tall order for a mere computer! The success sequence is given in Table 11.6. Imagine that the serial number bits are stepped out in the A → H reverse binary order, 0 always beating a 1. The winner withdraws and leaves the previous losers to play again. The winner of any stage will be the number with the longest initial run of 0s. Then after the first 1, again the longest run of 0s. When all players output a 1 nobody gets eliminated.

Table 11.6 exemplifies what happens when the 15 cards output their 8 bit serial numbers in sequence. Rounds A to D achieve no eliminations because the card serial numbers are all 0. Then round E eliminates cards 8–15 because they offer a 1. Round F leaves only 1, 2 and 3 in contention. Finally round G sees 2 and 3 eliminated, leaving 1 as the sole remaining card, which will have transmitted its serial number correctly after the next unopposed round. The second play-off will not include the earlier winner and will result in cards 2 and 3 testing each other in rounds G and H. Round G will be a draw because they both offer a 1, but round H will see card 3 eliminated.

Table 11.6
Plug-and-Play sequence.

Card	Serial number
	A B C D E F G H
1	0 0 0 0 0 0 0 1
2	0 0 0 0 0 0 1 0
3	0 0 0 0 0 0 1 1
4	0 0 0 0 0 1 0 0
5	0 0 0 0 0 1 0 1
6	0 0 0 0 0 1 1 0
7	0 0 0 0 0 1 1 1
8	0 0 0 0 1 0 0 0
9	0 0 0 0 1 0 0 1
10	0 0 0 0 1 0 1 0
11	0 0 0 0 1 0 1 1
12	0 0 0 0 1 1 0 0
13	0 0 0 0 1 1 0 1
14	0 0 0 0 1 0 1 1
15	0 0 0 0 1 1 1 1

11.8 PCMCIA – Personal Computer Memory Card International Association

After you have tried to hold a conversation about PCMCIA cards you will be pleased to hear that it has now become acceptable to abbreviate the name to PC Card!

The standard specifies the PC interface, bus and card size. It was originally intended only to provide extension memory modules for laptop PCs. The cards are credit card size (85.6 mm × 54 mm), with miniature 68 pin connectors set on one of the edges. However, the format has been adopted by manufacturers for a diverse range of IO functions. A second connector was installed on the opposite edge, and you can now obtain PCMCIA modems, parallel ports, Ethernet interfaces, ISDN ports, video conferencing systems, hard disk drives and many more. To encompass such a diverse selection of needs, there are three card standards progressively offering more circuitry through increasing thickness: 3.3, 5.5 and 10.5 mm, all having the same length and width. Because the connector socket remains the same, the thinner cards can be inserted into one of the thicker slots, but not the reverse. The interface is designed to allow for 'hot swapping': removing and inserting cards without switching off the power or even rebooting the computer.

The address bus on the card is 26 bits wide, giving an addressing range of 64 Mbyte. There is a 16 bit data bus. The addressing of memory or IO ports cannot be done

Fig. 11.11
PCMCIA interface.

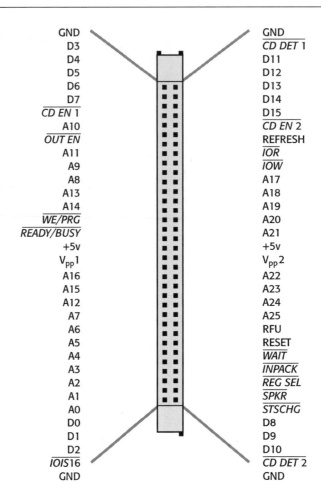

directly. All on-card addressing is handled by a PCIC controller, such as the i82365SL. This works through the PCI bus and is responsible for mapping the address range offered by the card into the main memory or IO map, a limited sort of virtual memory management. The mapped regions are termed 'windows', and the start and end addresses of the mapping windows are held by the PCMCIA control registers.

The PCMCIA card is inserted into a special socket, which acts like an IO unit, regardless of whether there is a PCMCIA card inserted or not. When a card is inserted, it is automatically configured with IO address, IRQ, memory-mapped address and DMA if required.

When a PCMCIA card is inserted into the socket (Fig. 11.11), the PCIC controller can detect its presence using the CD DET input lines. The V_{pp} lines are used for programming the flash RAM cards. If the PCMCIA card sports a Write-Protect switch its state is read through the IOIS16 input. Surprisingly, the SPKR pin allows the card to connect directly to the audio system!

Review

- The hardware units within computers communicate using parallel buses. Buses are 'bundles' of wires. A data bus may be 8, 16, 32, 64 bits or whatever, wide. The wider the bus, the higher the throughput, or bandwidth.

- Interface circuits are required for external devices to translate their signals to the equivalent counterparts on the system bus.

- The Centronics port is an 8 bit parallel interface with an asynchronous control handshake. There are now three standards for the Centronics printer port. Although it is termed a bus, it is only fit for point-to-point communications.

- The SCSI bus can handle eight connected devices. PCs require a SCSI PCI/ISA interface card. SCSI can operate in either asynchronous or synchronous mode. It was intended for disk or tape units, but can be used for any device equipped with a SCSI interface. It has the advantages of fast operation, internal data buffering, simultaneous activities through interleaved transactions, transaction queuing, dedicated DMA controller.

- IDE disk drives include on-board controller electronics. PCs generally offer the possibility of four IDE drives, connected in pairs to two motherboard sockets.

- The 16 bit ISA bus has developed from the original PC expansion card sockets. It operates in synchronous mode at 8.33 MHz, requiring wait states to be inserted when dealing with slow devices.

- The 32 bit PCI operates at half the motherboard frequency, but is decoupled from the main bus by a buffered gateway chip. It is currently the preferred expansion bus for the PC.

- Plug-and-Play is a scheme which manages the self-configuring of hardware. It involves special BIOS routines which run at boot time. New devices should be automatically recognized during boot-up and the correct software drivers installed.

- The PCMCIA (PC card) standard for expansion cards is intended for laptop computers, but has a wider relevance in mobile equipment.

Practical work

The course work assignment will be reviewed in class by the lab tutor, with practical demonstrations of the code.

Exercises

1. Separate the following Centronics printer port signals into those originating at the computer and those coming out from the printer:

   STROBE, ERROR, SELECT, AUTO_FEED, OUT_OF_PAPER, BUSY, SELECT_INPUT, INT, ACK

How many of them are really essential? Describe the handshake exchange that takes place as each byte is transferred.

2. In what aspect is the Centronics interface superior to the serial COM ports?

3. The Ultra-SCSI standard offers a 16 bit wide data bus and is capable of operating at up to 20 MHz. How many units may be connected to it? How can the SCSI subsystem carry out more than one transaction at a time?

4. Does Centronics provide for detection of errors during transmission? How many devices can be connected to a Centronics port? Does the Centronics interface work with 16 bit Unicode?

5. The SCSI bus works with a wide range of devices. Would you expect the bus to be synchronous or asynchronous? What data transfer rate can be achieved using SCSI?

6. What is the difference between IDE and SCSI? Why are SCSI drives still considered faster when they both share the same motherboard bus?

7. The AT/ISA bus has an industry-agreed maximum clock rate. What is it? How long would it take to transfer an SVGA screen image across the ISA bus?

8. What is the PCI bridge? In what way can it speed up data transfer?

9. A Sound Blaster card is delivering pairs of 16 bit words at a rate of 44.1 kHz. Can this fit onto the slower ISA bus?

10. Explain the interrupt structure on the ISA and PCI buses.

11. With optical fibre being used in roles which previously had been the province of parallel buses, is there a hint that wide, unwieldy buses have had their day?

12. How does Plug-and-Play determine the presence of new hardware, prior to selecting the correct driver routine?

Readings

- A short introduction to the topics in this chapter with links to other sites can be found at:
  http://www.webopedia.com/

- A short summary of Centronics operating modes can be found at:
  http://whatis.com/eppecp.htm

- Tom's Hardware Guide is a good start for basic and current commercial information:
  http://www7.tomshardware.com/storage/97q3/970728/hdd-06.html

- Some useful tutorial documents including SCSI and IDE material can be found at:
  http://www.hardwarecentral.com/hardwarecentral/tutorials/

- The PCMCIA standard is discussed more fully at:
  http://www.pc-card.com/pccardstandard.htm

- The Web sites can be accessed via the Companion Web site for this book at:
  http://www.booksites.net/williams/

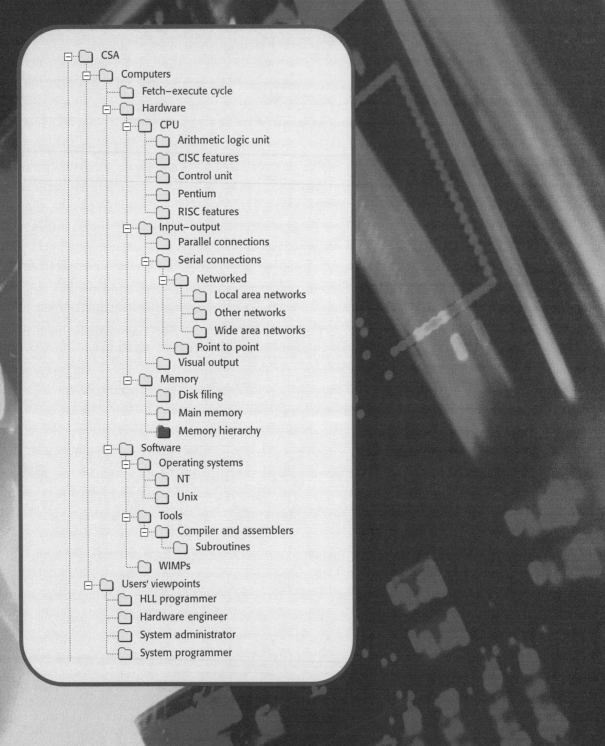

CSA
  Computers
    Fetch–execute cycle
    Hardware
      CPU
        Arithmetic logic unit
        CISC features
        Control unit
        Pentium
        RISC features
      Input–output
        Parallel connections
        Serial connections
          Networked
            Local area networks
            Other networks
            Wide area networks
          Point to point
        Visual output
      Memory
        Disk filing
        Main memory
        Memory hierarchy
    Software
      Operating systems
        NT
        Unix
      Tools
        Compiler and assemblers
          Subroutines
      WIMPs
  Users' viewpoints
    HLL programmer
    Hardware engineer
    System administrator
    System programmer

The memory hierarchy

12

Overview

A balanced provision of all the different kinds of memory – CD-ROM, hard disk, main memory DRAM, cache SRAM, CPU cache and CPU registers – helps to improve the system throughput. At any moment data and instructions are being moved up or down through this storage hierarchy to satisfy the demands from the higher levels, and ultimately the CPU. This scheme relies on the fact that programs tend to progress sequentially and access data within a locality. Because of this characteristic, blocks of instructions and data can be moved up and down the memory hierarchy to improve efficiency.

12.1   Levels of performance – you get what you pay for

The CPU could be furnished with enough main memory to fill its complete address space (as defined by the width of the address bus). Memory read–write access times would have to be chosen to match the system clock. This would mean that 500 MHz Pentium PCs would have a 4 Gbyte (2^{32} bytes) DRAM chip installed, which would then be rated at 2 ns access delay (Fig. 12.1). This is certainly not yet practicable, and even if it were it might not be an efficient solution. It is perhaps worth remembering that when a CPU family is approaching the end of its commercial life, the main memories *are* fully populated and this rarely leads to any substantial improvement in system performance. Often, software demands have already outstripped the available memory, and other methods have to be employed to cater for the overspill. In the meanwhile, to optimize performance and keep costs within reasonable bounds, most computers are provided with a layered hierarchy of memory devices in an attempt to keep up with the demands of faster CPUs and to cope with ever-expanding software.

The **storage hierarchy** (Fig. 12.2) has the fastest CPU registers at the top, and the slowest tape drives at the bottom. In between are arranged the magnetic disks, main memory DRAMs and SRAM caches. There are a lot more locations in main memory than CPU registers because the cost of providing space on the CPU chip is very high compared with that of locations in DRAM. The relative price of each type of memory facility actually determines how much can be offered. Thus the hierarchy can look more like a pyramid, with a narrow peak and a wide base.

But comparing the real cost of storing data in each type of memory is a complex issue because of the 'hidden extras' which need to be accounted for. Power supplies, cooling fans, controller chips, driver software, maintenance contracts and even desktop space can change the balance of cost. A major saving in not having to refurbish an aged air-conditioning plant could fully cost-justify many disk upgrades! Similarly, the floor space saved in a city centre office when cupboards are no longer required can convince accountants to invest in document scanners and a CD-RW unit!

The selection and use of the various types of storage depend on several parameters. Cost and speed of operation are obviously critical, but power consumption, volatility of storage, physical size, convenience of use, security of operation and other less important factors, such as fan noise, can be important. Table 12.1 lists the current approximate costs for the various components. The final column carries the interesting figures: cost per byte.

Fig. 12.1
Fully populated main memory.

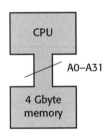

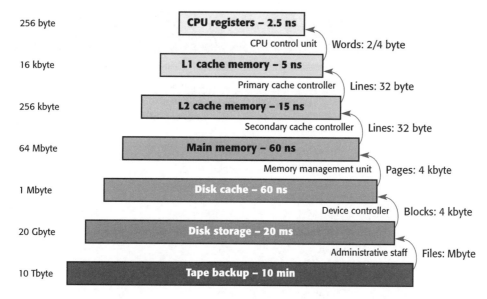

Fig. 12.2
Memory performance and storage hierarchy.

By considering only the **access speed** we can organize all memory in a **performance hierarchy.** Data is then transferred between adjacent layers when required. Interestingly, the unit size of data transferred between the layers is not the same for all the layers (see Fig. 12.2), reflecting the differing setup times required to start up a data transfer. Also, the control of data transfers between layers is not centralized, being under the supervision of three separate units which operate under completely different regimes. It is another example of how the close interaction of hardware units and systems software can bring about a revolution in performance and commercial applicability. The memory hierarchy acts as a supply pipeline, queuing blocks of data and code as they are moved closer and closer to the CPU, until they are loaded into the Level 1 cache ready to be accessed by the CU. The principal aim of the management of these transfers is to respond to a request for data as quickly as possible. Usually the unit of data transferred is bigger than requested, in anticipation that nearby locations will be accessed sometime in the immediate future. This is an example of **pre-fetching** in an attempt to anticipate the need before it occurs.

12.2 Localization of access – exploiting repetition

An important, but not unexpected, characteristic of computers is their tendency to spend periods of time accessing the same locality of memory. This arises from the basic structures supported by programming languages: SEQ, IT and SEL (see Chapter 13), and such an immensely useful feature of executing programs has been recognized and employed to enhance computer performance. The habit of dwelling on particular areas of data, and revisiting sections of code over and over again is partly due to the

Table 12.1
Memory costs.

Facility	Size	Device	Unit cost (£)	£/Mbyte
DRAM	64 Mbyte	SDRAM 168 pin DIMM	40	0.6
	32 Mbyte	EDO 72 pin SIMM	50	1.6
SRAM	256 kbyte/10 ns	SRAM chip	2	64
SCSI	PCI card		180	
Hard disk	10 Gbyte	IDE	110	0.01
	10 Gbyte	SCSI	250	0.025
CD-ROM	650 Mbyte	32× IDE	60	0.12[R]
CD-RW	650 Mbyte	2× IDE	200	0.3[R]
	WORM	disk	0.75	
	RW	disk	2.50	
Jaz	1 Gbyte	drive	200	
	1 Gbyte	disk	65	0.25[R]
Zip	100 Mbyte	drive	60	
	100 Mbyte	disk	15	0.75[R]
DAT	4 Gbyte	SCSI drive	350	
	4 Gbyte	tape	2.5	0.09[R]
Floppy	1.4 Mbyte	drive	15	
	1.4 Mbyte	disk	0.5	11[R]

programmer clustering related data items together in arrays or records, and partly due to the compiler attempting to organize the code in an efficient manner. Whatever the cause, this **Localization of Memory Access** can be exploited when setting up a memory hierarchy. Only that portion of code, and data, which is actually being attended to by the CPU need be loaded into the fastest memory nearest the CPU. Other sections of the program and data can be held in readiness lower down the access hierarchy.

Figure 12.3 is an actual plot, over a period of time, showing which memory address is being accessed at any moment. It is clearly not a random distribution, but shows localization of access, with abrupt changes probably resulting from calls to subroutines for particular services, such as input or output. If you know where in memory particular routines are loaded, you can follow their activity by studying this kind of plot.

Programmers can take account of the memory architecture if they want to avoid some of the worst performance hiccups. Looking at the relative access times, it is obvious that any access to disk is to be avoided if at all possible, and asking the Computer Officers to mount up a special data tape might not get a fast response on a busy Monday morning! Anyway, when dealing with data processing applications which involve 'file bashing', programmers try to read the complete input file into an

Fig. 12.3
Memory access plot, showing locality effects (from Hatfield D. and Gerald J. (1971). *IBM Systems Journal*, **10**(3)).

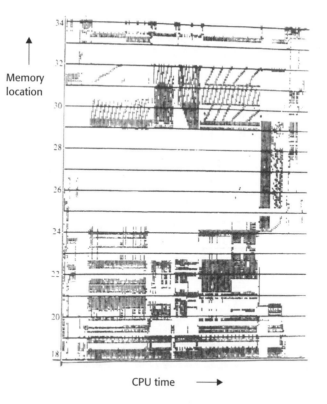

Memory location

CPU time ⟶

array at the start of the program, to improve run-time performance. Similarly, the output data can be assembled in an array and finally written out to disk at the completion of the program. Such explicit strategies are fine, but the underlying memory management operations of the operating system can still intervene and disrupt your planning. If the data file is very large it will undoubtedly be moved out onto the swap area of disk by the memory manager. Although this is a transparent operation, and offers convenience to the programmer, it certainly reduces the hoped for speed advantages of the carefully chosen, array-based algorithm.

The programmer may also lay out the data and design the code in such a way as to try to minimize memory management activity. To demonstrate this, compile and run the C program listed in Fig. 12.4, which simply adds up all the elements in a 1000 × 1000 two-dimensional integer array. Study the run times resulting from the two parts. You will see that the first part, accessing the array row by row, is twice as fast as the second, which accesses, without any other change, column by column. Figure 12.5 illustrates the way that an array or matrix would be stored in memory.

On my Sun workstation, with 64 Mbyte main memory, 256 kbyte cache and 4 Gbyte of local disk, the results from running the test program are given in Fig. 12.6. I also repeated the two conditions in reverse, as a check against an ordering effect, and found little difference. The function `times( )` delivers the length of time that the process has been running in system clock ticks. My system ticks 100 times a second.

The run times for the two test loops from Fig. 12.4 are 150 and 310: quite a difference for a small rearrangement of accesses to data. So where does the 150 ms time

Fig. 12.4
Demonstrating cache
action.

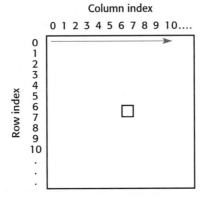

Row 0	Row 1	Row 2	Row 3	Row 4

Fig. 12.5
Array indexing with
memory layout of array
data.

```c
#include <stdio.h>
#include <sys/times.h>
#include <limits.h>
#define MAX 1000

clock_t times(struct tms* b);

main () {
int i, j;
int big[MAX] [MAX];
int sum, start, middle, end;
struct tms tbuff;
   times( &tbuff); start = tbuff.tms_utime;
   for(j=0; i<MAX; i++) {
       for(j=0; j<MAX; j++) {
           sum += big[i][j]; /* <------------ i, j here */
       };
    };
   times( &tbuff); middle = tbuff.tms_utime;
   for(i=0; i<MAX; i++) {
       for(j=0; j<MAX; j++) {
           sum += big[j][i]; /* <------------j, i here */
       };
    };
   times( &tbuff); end = tbuff.tms_utime;
   printf("First run time is %d\n", (middle - start)*1000/CLK_TCK);
   printf("Second run time is %d\n",(end - middle)*1000/CLK_TCK);
}
```

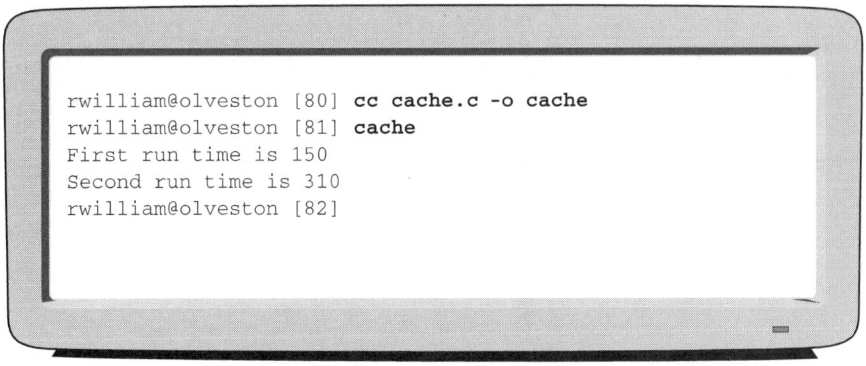

Fig. 12.6
Results from the cache test.

```
rwilliam@olveston [80] cc cache.c -o cache
rwilliam@olveston [81] cache
First run time is 150
Second run time is 310
rwilliam@olveston [82]
```

period come from? The two nested `for(;;)` loops execute 1 million times, which means that the workstation is taking 140 ns per circuit. By obtaining an assembler code dump (Fig. 12.7) we can check the number of machine instructions actually contained within the loop. Looking at the code listing in Fig. 12.7 we can see that there are 21 insructions in the inner loop and a further 13 in the outer. We will assume a 200 MHz CPU, with an instruction cycle period of 5 ns.

$$21 \times 5 \text{ ns} \times 10^6 + 13 \times 5 \text{ ns} \times 10^3 = 105 \text{ ms}$$

There is still an unaccounted 45 ms, but as the process has been timed out and restored this may be due to this scheduler activity. The larger discrepancy remains the difference between 150 ms and 310 ms, when the same number of instructions are executed each time but in a different sequence. It should be noted that the size of the executable code file is 23 340 bytes, which makes six pages in virtual memory and 730 cache Lines.

The cause of this 100% difference is the difficulty incurred while accessing the 4 Mbyte data array. Although the 64 Mbyte main memory is big enough to hold such an amount of data, so it may not get swapped to disk, the 256 kbyte cache memory is certainly not big enough. When the accesses are sequential, down through the data array, as in the first part of `cache.c`, the memory management systems have little difficulty in organizing the data cache. However, the second version requires large steps to be taken down through memory, which results in much movement of data up and down the memory hierarchy. This can be seen diagrammatically in Fig. 12.8.

Instruction and data caches – matching memory to CPU speed

Consider a Pentium CPU with a clock speed of 400 MHz. It needs to access program memory, on average, every 2.5 ns just to fetch instructions, and even more often when

Fig. 12.7
A fragment of assembler code output from the SPARC compiler for `cache.c` in Fig. 12.4.

```
! 19    for(i=0; i<MAX; i++) {
               mov0,%10
               st%10,[%fp-8]
               ld[%fp-8],%10
               cmp%10,1000
               bge.L118
               nop
               ! block 2
  .L119:
  .L116
! 20    for(j=0; j<MAX; j++) {
               mov0,%10
               st%10,[%fp-12]
               ld[%fp-12],%10
               cmp%10,1000
               bge.L122
               nop
               ! block 3
  .L123:
  .L120
! 21    sum += big[i][j];
               sethi%hi(-4000016),%10
               or%10,%lo(-4000016),%10
               ld[%fp+%10],%14
               sethi%hi(-4000012),%10
               or%10,%lo(-4000012),%10
               add%fp,%10,%13
               ld[%fp-8],%10
               sll%10,12,%12
               sll%10,5,%11
               sub%12,%11,%12
               sll%10,6,%11
               sub%12,%11,%11
               add%13,%11,%12
               ld[%fp-12],%10
               sll%10,2,%11
               add%12,%11,%10
               ld[%10+0],%11
               add%14,%11,%11
               sethi&hi(-4000016),%10
               or%10,%lo(-4000016),%10
               st%11,[%fp+%10]
! 22    };
               ld[%fp-12],%10
               add%10,1,%10
               st%10,[%fp-12]
               ld[%fp-12],%10
               cmp%10,1000
               bl.L120
               nop
               ! block 4
  .L124:
  .L122:
! 23    };
               ld[%fp-8],%10
               add%10,1,%10
               st%10,[%fp-8]
               ld[%fp-8],%10
               cmp%10,1000
               bl.L116
               nop
               ! block 5
  .L125;
  .L118;
```

Fig. 12.8
Alternative access
patterns for a two-
dimensional array.

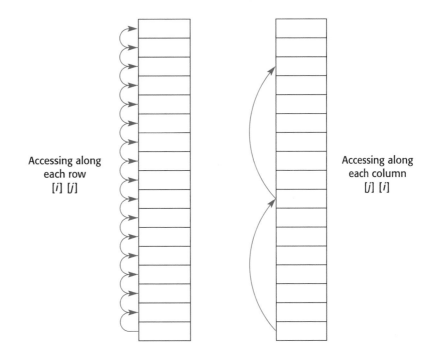

Accessing along
each row
[*i*] [*j*]

Accessing along
each column
[*j*] [*i*]

the requirement to access data variables is also considered. EDO DRAMS are only capable of responding within 60 ns, so there is a serious speed imbalance to be resolved! If the CPU only had DRAM to store program code the system would run 24× slower. This mismatch in component performance is behind a lot of the complexity found in modern computers.

Over the past fifty years there has been a see-saw development with regard to the relative speed of CPUs and memory devices. At certain times memory was capable of handling faster CPUs, while at others the CPUs could outstrip memory. Currently, Pentium and Alpha processors running at 500 MHz and above are well ahead, and some clever systems design is needed to prevent the CPU wasting most of its life waiting around for the memory to respond to its requests. This is why the cache level of the memory hierarchy was introduced. **Cache** helps only because it is built from the more expensive SRAM chips which can operate faster than DRAM. Ideally, the access speed of cache memory should be matched to the system clock speed, allowing the CPU to access data and instructions without incurring any extra delays. Most CPUs do, however, still need to wait for slower devices to carry out an operation, so the CPU bus controller is able to insert **Wait States** into any read–write bus cycle to deal with this situation.

Cache memory, and its **CCU** (Cache Controller Unit), are inserted between the CPU and main memory (Fig. 12.9) where they can intercept all memory requests emerging from the CPU. The aim is to maintain in fast cache the currently active sections of code and data. All memory read–write requests from the CPU are directed at the cache in the hope that a fast response will be forthcoming. The CCU checks the addresses to see if the item requested is currently lodged in the cache. If it is, the CPU

Fig. 12.9
Cache memory and
controller unit.

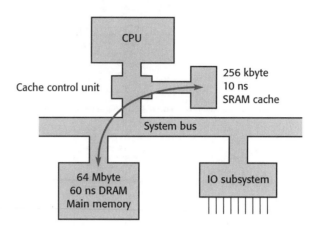

is satisfied immediately, else the controller has to bring in the item from main memory, which incurs a considerable time delay. This obviously speeds things up well if a program is executing a short loop of instructions, all of which can fit into the small cache memory. However, it can also work well with sequential, linear code if the cache controller is able to 'read ahead' and keep the cache stocked in anticipation of the CPU's requests. Some compilers manage this by inserting special instructions which stimulate the CCU to do this.

When new items are being introduced into cache memory, there is usually the need to make a decision about what existing item has to be sacrificed to make room for the new entrant. A further delay may result from having to write back into main memory any data which has been altered during its residency in the cache.

The distinction between **Level 1** and **Level 2** cache is geographic. On the MC68040 and the original Pentium, the fastest cache is closest to the CPU and integrated onto the CPU chip. This is referred to as Primary or Level 1 (L1) cache, and benefits from its privileged position by tremendous speed advantages, but suffers from a limitation in size because of manufacturing constraints. For the Pentium, with a 16 kbyte L1 cache, Intel decided to split it into two separate halves, one for data and the other for instructions. Differentiating a memory in this way is not in the von Neumann tradition, but does allow simultaneous instruction fetching and access to variables if the data bus is also doubled-up. With a pipeline decoder, as described in Section 7.7, dual buses are also required to prevent bus contention happened when two or more pipeline stages require to transfer items at the same moment. This was technically possible for the on-chip cache, but not for the off-chip cache.

The more distant, Level 2 cache can be constructed as large as necessary (typically 512 kbyte) if it is located off-chip on the motherboard, but it will always run slower because of the delays involved in driving signals off the chip and across the system bus. To improve this situation, Intel introduced the Pentium II, where the L2 cache is isolated, together with the CPU, inside the Slot 1/Slot 2 package. This includes a local bus, dedicated to the CPU and L2 cache, operating at 200 MHz, a great deal faster than the 100 MHz system bus on the motherboard.

As explained in Section 7.1, Intel has now successfully integrated an L2 cache of 128 kbyte on the Celeron CPU chip, alongside the L1 cache and operating at the same speed. AMD offers the K6-3 CPU with 256 kbyte of cache integrated on the CPU chip.

It is worth noting in Fig. 12.2 that the unit of data transferred between cache and main memory is known as a **line**, which can be 256 bytes long, although the Pentium uses a 32 byte line which is equal to four bus cycles of 8 bytes each. This fits in well with EDO DRAM, with its ability to rapidly access four locations in sequence (see Section 6.6). The speed that lines can be moved about the memory hierarchy is very important when trying to improve system performance. Employing a wide bus and transferring lines of data as **bus bursts** allows the system to keep up with the CPU. The movement of data around the various memory units can be understood as following the motorway café style of service. Here, groups of tourists arrive in coaches every 15 minutes, to wait in queues for coffee or toilets. Both these facilities are being utilized 100% of the time despite the 15 min arrival intervals. Such a system relies on buffering the customers in queues and then managing embarkation fast enough to avoid a traffic jam. In the case of the CPU, buffering data and instructions is simply a matter of including the necessary registers, but the embarkation problem is solved by memory offering 16 RAM chips simultaneous access to designated bits on the 64 bit bus.

12.4　Cache mapping – direct or associative

The use of an SRAM memory cache that is considerably smaller than the main DRAM memory exposes a problem which recurs at several different points within computer systems. How do we map a large address space into a smaller working space? Although the theoretical mapping for a PC requires the 4 Gbyte address space to be mapped to 512 kbyte of motherboard L2 cache and then further to 16 kbyte of L1 cache, in practice there is often only 64 Mbyte of main memory active. There are at least three technical solutions, listed in Table 12.2, which could be used to solve the 'many → few' address mapping problem.

Hashing is really only included for completeness' sake. It is not used for cache address mapping because of the time delay that it would incur, but it has been used in a similar role for virtual memory page mapping. We will discuss that topic in Section 12.5.

Organizing the cache by the **Direct Mapping** technique divides main memory into cache-sized pages. Each page is further divided into **lines**. If we consider a Pentium Level 2 cache, with 32 bit address, 512 kbyte of cache and 32 byte cache lines, the address can be segmented into three fields. The lower 5 bits (A0–A4) address bytes within the 32 byte line. The next 14 bits (A5–A18) address the line slots within the cache, while the remaining upper 13 bits (A19–A31) specify the page in main memory from which the line has been obtained. A simpler example with an 10 bit address width and 8 line cache is presented in Fig. 12.10.

Table 12.2
Mapping addresses from
main to cache memory.

1.	Folded address space, also known as direct mapping
2.	Associative (content addressable) memory
3.	Hashed mapping

Each line is mapped to a **slot** in the cache by the address bits A5–A18. When a new line of data is copied into its cache slot the upper five address bits are written into the associated location in **Tag** memory. Thus when the cache controller accesses a slot in cache, it also has to check the relevant page number in Tag memory to establish which page of main memory the Line came from.

When an address emerges from the CPU the cache controller uses the middle part of the address to access the correct slot. It compares the associated Tag memory entry with the upper part of the address and it uses the least significant bits to slide along the line to pick up the data word required.

As long as the current program is not referencing data within lines from different pages mapped to the same slot, this scheme would work quite well. But the risk of slot collision, where two active lines are mapped to the same slot, cannot be eliminated and results in a big reduction in performance.

In a more realistic system, every 0.5 Mbyte memory page is considered to have 16 384 lines of 32 bytes. When considering a 64 Mbyte memory, there will be 128 lines of main memory mapped to each cache slot. The probability of an undesirable slot collision then depends on the size of the program and the structure of its data.

Fig. 12.10
Address folding for direct
mapped cache.

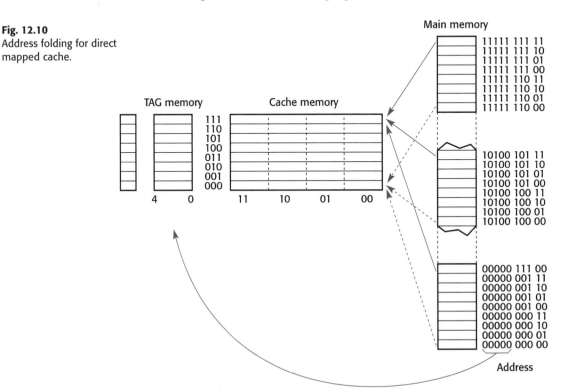

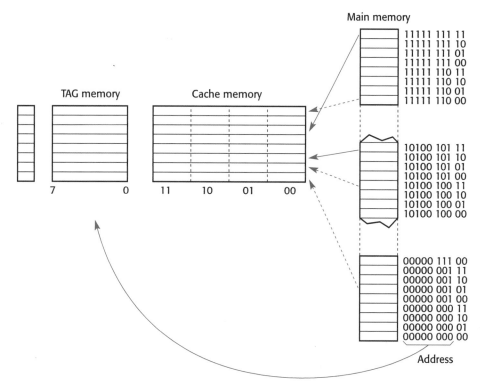

Fig. 12.11
Associative cache.

An alternative scheme, **Associative Mapping**, is shown in Fig. 12.11. It allows lines of data from main memory to be copied into any cache slot, and main memory is not divided into pages, only lines. Following the previous example of a 10 bit address and a 32 byte cache Line, Tag memory would have to be 8 bits wide.

Again, the upper bits of the line main memory address are entered into the Tag memory when a new line is entered into the cache. But now the cache controller has to check all the Tag memory locations (8192) to find the correct slot. Such a search, if it were carried out sequentially, would be hopelessly slow, so associative cache systems have a lot of extra hardware to do this address checking. You may be pleased to recognize the XOR gate again in Fig. 12.12.

The array of 8 XOR gates decides whether the upper bits from the incoming address match the value in that Tag register or not. Each cache slot will have its own comparator circuit, allowing all these checks to be carried out in parallel. Although fast and flexible, the circuitry is expensive. In practice, a combination of these two techniques, known as **Block-Set-Associative**, is normally used, which is the case for the Pentium. Block-set-associative mapping allows more than one line of data to be held in the same direct mapped cache slot. It does this by simply having two or more cache memories for the cache controller to work with! Thus the chance of a slot collision is considerably reduced. The upper address bits direct the application to an 'extended slot' where a much simpler comparison is done to see if either of the two Tag registers matches the incoming value.

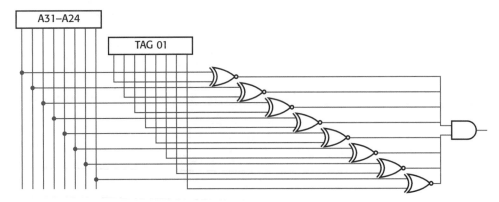

Fig. 12.12
Checking the address in associative memory.

A general issue to be resolved with any caching scheme, where copies of data are used, is how to maintain **data consistency** after a write operation. One strategy is called **Cache Write-Through**. Every time an item of data in cache is written to, the original version in main memory is also updated. Because this incurs some time delay, an alternative, known as **Cache Write-Back**, delays writing to main memory until the cache Line in question is replaced, to make room for another. This write-back is only carried out if a marker flag indicates that the line has been modified since entering into cache. Thus each cache line has to be provided with a **Dirty Bit flag**, which gets set if a data write occurs and gets cleared when a new line is loaded.

Another policy decision which affects system performance is what to do with a full cache when the cache controller signals a miss. A **cache miss** occurs when an address is requested that is not currently present in the cache. Clearly something has to be sacrificed. A random choice is surprisingly effective, but the **LRU** (Least Recently Used) method, where the line which has been accessed least over the preceding period is replaced, seems more logical! Generally, cache misses occur under three circumstances: when the program is first run, if the cache does not currently hold the required line and when a direct mapped conflict occurs (Table 12.3).

The correct sizing of cache memory is a tricky business, depending on the mix of applications running and relative performance of the other memory components in the hierarchy. Often it is easier to use an online performance monitor to provide evidence of where and when the actual cache misses are happening, rather than attempting to predict the bottleneck.

It might have struck you that a possible technique to further improve the cache hit rate would be to try to pre-load lines into cache before they are actually required. This would reduce the number of cache stalls following a miss and so keep the CPU running more smoothly. Some progress has been made to implement such a technique, usually by simply bringing into cache the line from main memory following that containing the current instruction. This anticipates the point of execution

Table 12.3
Causes of cache misses.

1.	On start-up of a new program
2.	When the cache is too small to hold the active execution set
3.	Cache line conflict in a direct mapped cache

stepping forward through the sequence of code. Unfortunately, this does not always happen, and the danger of unfortunately choosing to replace the next required line is always present!

12.5   Virtual memory – segmentation and demand paging

The operation of **Virtual Memory** systems was developed at a time when main memory was expensive, scarce and not so fast. It provided a convenient expansion of main memory by 'overflowing' data and program code onto magnetic disk (Fig. 12.13). The area on disk reserved for this purpose is known as the **Swap Space** and is managed by the operating system. The application programmer does not normally worry about such things and simply leaves it all to the Virtual Memory Management services.

Before this technique became widely available, the only option when your code grew too big to fit into main memory was to cut it into several segments and 'chain' them together. The first segment was loaded into main memory from disk and began execution. When it finished it would load in the second segment and pass control to it. Thus each segment of code also had to load in the next segment when it completed. The application programmer had the responsibility for organizing this rudimentary memory management scheme.

Magnetic disk storage units are now considered to be essential peripheral devices for business data processing applications. In addition, many industrial and most personal systems are using hard disks for auxiliary storage in order to take advantage of the good capacity/cost ratio. Despite rapid improvements in the performance of large semiconductor memories, the disk manufacturers have always managed to keep ahead in price per byte.

Fig. 12.13
Virtual memory scheme for main memory overflow.

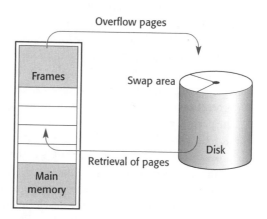

Modern multi-user operating systems with virtual memory management enable each user to write programs as if they were the sole user and not sharing the system with many others. This was achieved at first by multi-user operating systems simply swapping complete programs in and out of memory as needed. Such a heavy-handed approach to resource sharing was time-consuming and very inefficient. The next approach involved organizing programs into **segments**, similar to the CODE, DATA and STACK segments still apparent in the Intel x86 family. The possibility of swapping only segments, not whole programs, in and out of memory reduced the overheads and maintained the 'sole user' illusion. Segments can be positioned anywhere in memory because they are each located by dedicated **Segment Base Registers**. These address registers have to be set up to point to the first location of a segment when the segment is loaded into memory. Such a scheme offers advantages of flexibility and run-time security because the access to different types of segment can be controlled by hardware.

However, because of the variable size of segments the memory manager had tremendous difficulty in reusing the memory efficiently. Sometimes a large proportion of main memory grew inaccessible after the computer had been running for some time due to **fragmentation** problems. Our university car park has no parking bays painted on the ground. The different widths of cars (and skills of their respective drivers!) means that during the day, as cars come and go, the parking arrangement becomes disorganized and inefficient, with wasteful gaps occurring between cars. Large vehicles leave and smaller cars arrive to occupy the same space. This is simply another example of resource fragmentation. A dedicated attendant could go around organizing the cars, allocating spaces as appropriate, so achieving a more efficient parking arrangement. Hence, by giving big spaces to big vehicles and combining small spaces together, more useful parking space would be freed up. In fact, some computing operating environments do have such a facility, known unkindly as the **Garbage Collector**. Straightforward variable size segmentation will eventually lead to the situation where a considerable percentage of memory space is cut up into tiny portions which are no longer usable. To avoid this, the successful virtual memory management schemes cut the program segments up into identical sized pages, which then become the swap units. As all pages are the same size (typically 4 kbyte) there is no longer any significant fragmentation problem. Only the considerable complexity of such a scheme remains as a challenge to hardware and systems designers!

When microprocessors were developed, and RAM became cheaper, the personal workstation might have heralded the demise of complex virtual memory systems, but perhaps surprisingly they remain an important feature of nearly all current computers, from desktop PCs upwards. This situation may partly be attributed to the **protection** and **security** features that such operating systems offer. Besides managing the page swapping, the isolation of processes and their data is ensured by a memory segmentation scheme. Because virtual memory enables the programmer to develop programs without concern about whether they will fit into the available main memory, much larger systems have emerged, notably in the areas of graphics and communications. Similarly, enormous data arrays can be declared regardless of RAM size limits, which helps with the development of large database systems.

A modern virtual memory system, like Unix or Windows NT, works by dividing main memory into **frames**, often sized at 4 kbyte. The executable program is similarly divided into frame-sized chunks known as **pages**. When a program is invoked not all the pages are loaded into main memory, only sufficient to get it started. The rest are copied into the disk area known as the swap file dedicated to virtual memory support. As the program runs, the moment will arise when the fetch–execute cycle requires an instruction from a page not yet resident in main memory. This situation is termed a **page fault**. A page fault interrupt is triggered and the operating system intervenes in order to load the next page from disk. If no frames are empty the decision has to be taken to free up the least used frames to allow the new pages to be loaded. This is termed **swapping**.

A reference made to a variable within a user program will be in the form of a 32 bit logical address. If we are dealing with a 4 kbyte page system, the lower 12 bits can be seen as the 'within page' address, with the upper 20 bits serving as the 'page number'. The **page table** provides a look-up, whereby the logical page number can be exchanged for the physical frame number. When the operating system loads all or part of a program into physical memory it must also amend the page table entries.

It is assumed, when source programs are compiled to run on multitasking, virtual memory machines, that the code will start executing from address 0000. All the internal address references to functions and variables are set up on this basis. Clearly this cannot happen in reality. Not every program can be loaded at the same place! The mapping of logical to physical addresses solves this difficulty by repositioning the pages at the convenience of the operating system. Because the position and sequence of the program pages as they are loaded into main memory frames cannot be specified at compile/link time, an address translator is required to sort out the jumble that results. The **MMU** (Memory Management Unit) is set between the CPU and memory, including the cache memory. It maps the references to variables and functions which had been set by the compiler into physical references to frame numbers and offset addresses, as required by the computer hardware. This translation from virtual to physical address is carried out in real time for each read–write access to memory by the MMU. The relationship between logical and physical addresses is illustrated in Fig. 12.14. The MMU uses an array, the **page table**, to map the logical page references to the physical frame addresses. In practice, the page table is too big to fit into the MMU, so only information about the most recently used pages is held in the MMU. If a reference is made to an item in a page not listed in the MMU table, a memory read has to take place to update the MMU array from the full page table. Figure 12.15 shows the location of the virtual memory management unit.

Because of the inevitable delay introduced by this conversion process, the MMU is supplied with a fast cache buffer to hold active entries from the page table. This cache is commonly known as the **TLB** (Translation Lookaside Buffer) which obviates the need to access the full page table in main memory on *every* memory access so as to carry out virtual memory address translations. But the Pentium, like some other processors, retains the earlier segmentation facilities, and so needs to add in the segment base address offsets too.

Fig. 12.14
Virtual memory logical
page into physical frame
address translation.

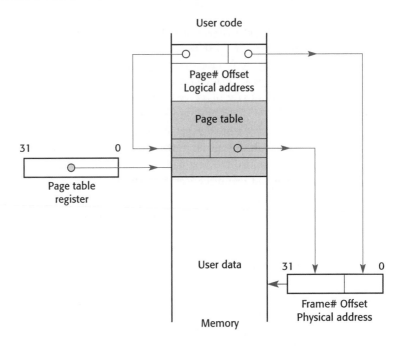

Although segments were originally introduced by Intel to expand the addressing range of the CPU, their role also encompassed memory access control. This aspect can still be exploited by operating systems to police multitasking environments, but now some of this functionality is actually duplicated by the paging mechanism, and Windows NT uses the latter. The process where every memory access is corrected for segment offset, checked against the segment bounds registers and passed on to the paging unit to obtain the equivalent physical address, appears impossibly slow; segmented paged virtual memory is really only workable thanks to the fast TLB cache.

Fig. 12.15
Location of the virtual
memory management
unit.

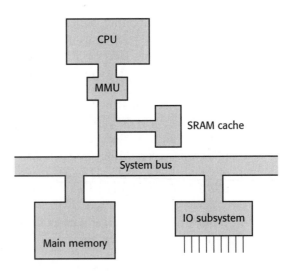

This complex **demand paged** virtual memory scheme has now completely displaced the earlier chaining and swapping schemes. There is still a small loss of memory availability in the use of main memory. The final page of each program will probably not completely fill the allocated frame. Thus one semi-unused frame per process is the penalty. The remaining doubt surrounds the time wasted in moving pages from disk to memory and back. Furthermore, a pathological condition known as **thrashing** can still occur if there is an over-demand for memory frames. The memorable error message from PRIMOS:

```
sorry, too busy to run 'logout'
```

might be striking evidence of such a serious situation where a low priority task can never obtain sufficient resources to execute to completion.

12.6 Address formulation – when, where and how much

The units of transfer between disk and main memory, between main memory and cache, and between cache and CPU, are not identical. The consideration of such issues is sometimes referred to under the term **granularity**. Disk units feed 4 kbyte pages into main memory, cache asks for 32 byte Lines, and the CPU fetches a couple of instructions at a time from the cache. The size of this final unit of transfer is determined by the width of the data bus, so the Pentium can handle 8 bytes, which could be as many as four instructions, at a time.

You will encounter several terms used in texts when referring to addressing: logical, virtual, effective and physical. Often they overlap in meaning, which does not help in establishing a clear distinction when one exists. Figure 12.16 contains a summary explanation.

A **Logical Address** is a programmer's term for the idealized space in which the program is written. It often involves several separate segments, each starting with address 0 and often simply assumed to extend to infinity! Which segment is active is determined by the type of access taking place. So, all fetch–execute cycles are directed to the CODE segment, reading and writing variables to a DATA segment, and stack operations to the STACK segment. A logical address comprises the segment identifier and the offset within the segment. The programmer also assumes that there will only be the one program running on the system, even if it is a multitasking environment.

The idea of a **Virtual Address** arises from the need to map independent segments into a single linear address space. Segments are positioned one after the other within the virtual space. Each segment is allocated a base register to hold its start address. Every user has an independent virtual address space. The loader program is responsible for allocating the virtual address space for an application program. A virtual address can be seen as an implementation of its logical counterpart.

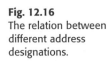

Fig. 12.16
The relation between different address designations.

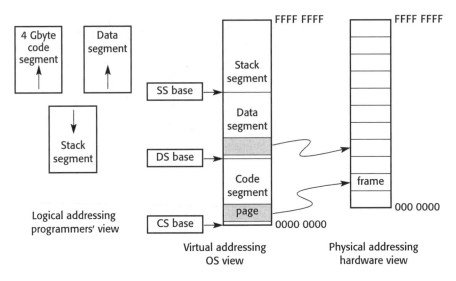

Logical addressing programmers' view

Virtual addressing
OS view

Physical addressing
hardware view

Effective Addresses are constructed in the CU as the instructions are executed. For example, the programmer may have specified that a data structure should be accessed using a base address (array name) and offset value (index). The CPU, however, needs to build a unitary address before it can read a memory location. This address is known as the effective address. The range of effective address space is governed by the width of the CPU address registers, or the address bus if this is narrower.

The **Physical Address** is the actual 32 bit or 64 bit number which is dispatched to the cache controller and thence to main memory to select the next item. If a virtual memory management system has been activated, this physical address is obtained from the effective address after a translation process. This may be a straightforward offset addition to move the logical space up from zero, or it may involve the more complex page table lookup process. Whatever the method, the maximum size for the physical address space is determined by the width of the address bus. However, it is more commonly limited by the amount of DRAM that has actually been installed. There is no point in sending 32 bit addresses up the bus to empty slots! This technique allows virtual addresses to spill over the top of physical RAM onto a disk area. The maximum extent of virtual addresses is thus determined by the size of the disk area (swap file) dedicated to this function.

12.7   Hard disk usage – parameters, access scheduling and data arrangement

IBM introduced the Winchester drive (3340), with aerodynamically 'flying' heads, to improve the performance of its DASD units (Direct Access Storage Device). The heads and arms are sealed into the platter housing to reduce the problem of dust. As

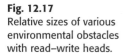

Fig. 12.17
Relative sizes of various
environmental obstacles
with read–write heads.

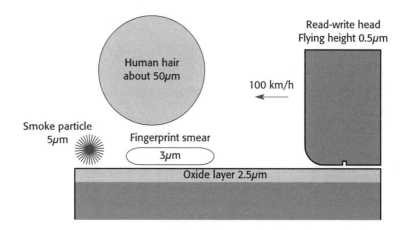

you can see from Fig. 12.17, a collision with a smoke particle would be quite threatening, while a human eyelash would be disastrous! The heads are only intended to land on the surface when the platter stops rotating. There are specially reserved head parks set aside for this purpose. Should a head scrape the surface it would permanently damage the stored data and render the area unusable in the future. This is the notorious **head crash**. These high-capacity hard drives have significantly contributed towards many of the developments in modern computing: large databases, virtual memory operating systems, WWW servers and telephone voice-messaging. Any application that requires fast, online access to large data sets would not be viable without the gigabyte disk packs that are now available.

Looking back, the first PC was equipped only with floppy drives, but the popularity of the later PC-AT was partly due to the ST506 hard disk being installed as standard. Subsequently, the Intelligent Drive Electronics (IDE) disk units from Compaq had much greater capacity and better performance. This development also removed the need for a separate AT interface card. At the same time the Small Computer System Interface standard (**SCSI**) was becoming more widely accepted by minicomputer users. This interface has now been adopted for other devices in addition to hard magnetic disk units, but is more complicated and expensive than the IDE interface.

From Fig. 12.18 it can be seen that the read–write head is attached to a swinging arm so that it can be positioned over any track. When the disk is powered down, the arm quickly swings in, landing the head on a safe area of disk. The mechanism used to push and pull the arm is similar to that of a loudspeaker coil. A small electrical coil in a large magnetic field will physically move when a current is passed through it because of the interaction between the two magnetic fields. This is a conveniently rapid effect, but provides no exact positioning information. To overcome this disadvantage, one surface in the drive is permanently written with track information and is not used for data. This provides an alignment signal for input to a positional feedback servo supplying current to the positioning coil. Such a dedicated servo loop has the advantage of automatically compensating for any temperature effects and it allows for some clever 'micro-stepping' techniques to better find lost tracks.

Fig. 12.18
Schematic diagram of
hard disk unit.

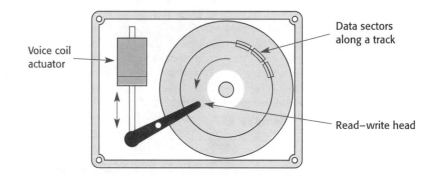

Voice coil
actuator

Data sectors
along a track

Read–write head

Typically, hard disks had 17 sectors per track and 980 tracks per surface. The maximum storage capacity is given by:

drive capacity = No. of surfaces × No. of tracks × No. of sectors × size of sector

Tracks are sometimes called cylinders' because when several disks are mounted on the same spindle, spinning together, the same tracks on the different surfaces appear as a single extended track, or cylinder.

To allow time for the computer to deal with the fast flow of data from the disk read head, it is now common to use sector interleaving. Thus sectors 1, 2, 3, 4, 5 etc. will not be arranged in simple order, but as something like: 1, 6, 2, 7, 3, 8, 4, 9, 5. This gives the system a sector interval to deal with the data before the next sector in numerical sequence arrives under the read head.

Access to disk data is carried out by telling the disk controller which cylinder, head and sector to access. This is known as **CHS** (Cylinder, Head, Sector) accessing, representing the lowest physical level of disk control. Moving a head across to a cylinder takes time. Waiting for the correct sector to rotate to the critical position under the head takes more time. Finally the flow of data from the disk, up into the head and down into a data buffer will take time. All these factors have to be considered by disk drive manufacturers. There are some relevant technical parameters made available by the suppliers through their advertising and data sheets so that performance estimates can be made. Top of the list is the total storage capacity of the hard drive unit. Currently the smaller IDE drives, suitable for PCs, are rated at more than 8 Gbyte. The price seems to increase symmetrically: both smaller and larger drives cost more. It is a mass product market, and the prices reflect that. You can obtain less popular items, but it will cost you! The next parameter is head movement speed, or **seek time**. Here, two parameters are quoted: track-to-track and random seek. A random seek is intended to be a statistically average value and is equated to moving the head one third of the maximum distance. There is a need to take into account the large difference between picking up data from a file, where the items are stored in an orderly, sequentially manner, and the much less efficient situation which older, fragmented disks find themselves in, where data files can be broken up and scattered all over the place. The speed of rotation is often given as a **rotational latency** figure. This is computed as half

Table 12.4
A specification table for
Maxtor hard disks (taken
from Maxtor Web site:
http://
www.maxtor.com/).

Disk performance specification	
Track to track seek	1 ms
Average seek	< 9 ms
Maximum seek	20 ms
Average latency	5.77 ms
Rotation	5400 r.p.m.
Controller overhead	< 0.3 ms
Start time	7.3 s
Computer interface rate	< 66.7 Mbyte/s
Media read–write rate	< 27.8 Mbyte/s
Sectors per track	266–462
Cylinders (tracks per surface)	17 549
Bytes per sector	512
Data zones per surface	16
Integrated buffer size	2 Mbyte
Memory type	SDRAM

Model	90650U2	90845U	91020U3	91360U4	92040U6	92040U8
Capacity (Gbyte)	6.5	8.45	10.21	13.61	20.42	27.23
Heads	2	3	3	4	6	8
Disks	1	2	2	2	3	4

the rotational period because, on average, the head has to wait half a rotational period for the data to come round for accessing. Knowing how much data there is in a single track will also give you the data rate: data has to flow straight off the head into the memory buffer – there can be no hiccups or the read will fail.

Consider the performance estimate outlined in Fig. 12.19. More up to the minute drive parameters are given in Table 12.4, but as the rate of progress in this field is still rapid, you should download the latest values from the Web site.

Such estimates are not very reliable due to software effects, such as competition from other processes or operating system disk scheduling. This involves queuing up disk access requests and reordering them so as to improve some performance metric. Such schemes are open to debate: should we try to give a fair chance to all processes, or favour a few? It would appear sensible to group all access requests for data on a certain cylinder together. In this way, only one head movement will be incurred. But deliberately delaying the departure of the bus until all the passenger seats have been taken might not be a popular strategy! Clever algorithms have a habit of unexpectedly disadvantaging some section of clients, who may not understand why their service has suddenly become so poor.

Figure 12.19
Estimating hard disk
data retrieval time.

```
A computer system having 2 Mbyte of RAM has hard disks with the
following characteristics:

Rotational speed:                           3600 r.p.m.
Track capacity:                             16384 byte
Heads/cylinder:                             10
Head movement time, track to track:        20 ms
Average seek time:                          50 ms

How long does it take to dump memory onto disk? Assume the disk is empty.

3600 r.p.m. = 60 r.p.s.
Rotational period = 1/60 s = 1000/60 ms = 16.66 ms = 17 ms
Latency = 8.5 ms

Data rate = 16 kbyte/17 ms = 1 Mbyte/s
Flow time for 2 Mbyte = 2000 ms = 2 s

2 Mbyte needs 128 tracks or 12.8 cylinders, i.e. 13 head movements

Total time = head movement (seeks)+ rotational delays (latencies) + data flow time
           = 1 × 50 + 12 × 20      + 13 × 8.5                      + 2000
           = 2314 ms
```

12.8   Performance improvement – blocking, caching, defragmentation, scheduling, RAM disk

Data is not transferred to and from disks in bytes. For such small items it would hardly be worth moving the head! Instead, blocks of data, typically 512 bytes long, are moved between the disk and a RAM buffer. So, all disk accesses are made through this transfer buffer organized by the disk controller. A performance benefit to **Blocking** only comes if the data is being accessed in a sequential manner. We know that program code runs like that, so that is no problem. If the data is not sequential, there is clearly a penalty, due to the need to read 512 bytes when only 1 is required. This technique is sometimes extended by declaring a much larger (1 Mbyte) **Disk Cache** area in main memory. Of significance to file-basher programmers is the essential need to 'flush the buffers' before terminating a program: there may be important data held in the disk cache, as yet unwritten to disk. With gigabyte main memories a growing possibility, the issue of disk caching will become more important. If the disk cache is set *larger* than the active disk, which is possible, the whole of the file system could be run from the RAM cache. Such a situation can lead to the disconcerting circumstance of 'successfully' accessing a disk pack after it has been unplugged! The Unix command sync is recommended before system shutdown, so that a full disk cache flush is carried out.

On smaller systems, perhaps not provided with local hard disk units, the possibility of installing a **RAM Disk** facility can be investigated. These are programs which reserve a large chunk of main memory and install themselves with the operating system to respond to device access requests. They pretend to be a disk. Certainly the earlier generation of Amiga and Atari home computers and the floppy disk PCs, demanded the use of such a fast access pseudo-disk to make HLL compiling a tolerable activity. The problem of transferring all important data from the files held in RAM disk must be attended to before turning off the power or rebooting the system.

When a task makes a request for data held on disk, the disk handling routines in the operating system could simply offer a **first come, first served** (FCFS) response. The data requests would be queued up, waiting their turn to be executed. This would lead to very inefficient arm movements, with the read–write head scurrying back and forth across the disk surface to action the immediate requests. Imagine a postman who works by blindly picking a letter from his bag and immediately setting off to deliver it! When there is a lot of work to do, it would be much better to sort the requests and plan the route first, so reducing backtracking and repeated visiting. With modern multiprocessing computer systems there can be dozens of large disk units attached, offering terabytes ($\sim 10^{12}$ bytes) of online storage and serving many users concurrently. This will lead inevitably to request queues building up for access to the disk packs. As soon as you see a service queue develop, with a variety of demands, the possibility of rescheduling the requests should be considered. When only a small system is involved, the default strategy of FCFS may be appropriate, but for the vast corporate database, 'disk farms', a more sophisticated approach is adopted. The requests may be reordered so that the quickest are dispatched first. This would probably mean that those requiring the least arm movement, **shortest seek time first**, would gain advantage. The danger with this approach is that those users with data stored at the distant, less popular, reaches of the disk surface will be unfairly treated, and end up waiting more than other users.

Another approach is modelled on the delivery of mail. A fixed scan path is established for the head, which normally progresses in sequence from track to track across the disk, servicing the read–write requests as they are possible. New requests can be inserted into the queue to benefit from the current position of the head on its journey. This is a bit like mail being faxed into our postwoman in mid-round so that she does not have to return to the sorting office: ever! This method is called the **SCAN** strategy and has much in common with the algorithms used by companies who install office lifts (elevators). The SCAN method results in a more predictable access time, but has to be modified if all the accesses are limited to a few neighbouring tracks. There is really no point in cycling to the end of our village, visiting all the houses, when there is no more mail to deliver. The result is the **LOOK** method, where disk access requests are initially sorted by locality and then serviced in track order. In Fig. 12.20 the movement of a read–write head is mapped out under the different regimes, all servicing the same initial queue. The difference in performance is quite obvious (Fig. 12.21) in this case, with the SCAN strategy winning easily.

A particular problem with all read–write storage is the **Fragmentation** of the available free space. This has been discussed in another context in Section 12.5. A different problem arises with disks, though. It is not that the elements of free space are unusable – they are all the same size already, so this is not a problem. Rather, it is the much lengthened access times experienced with files whose blocks are not written contiguously but

Fig. 12.20
Disk access scheduling
techniques.

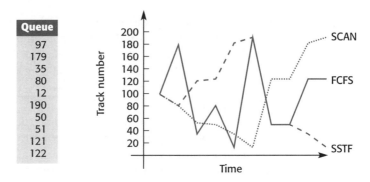

Fig. 12.21
Comparison of disk
scheduling techniques.

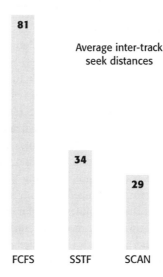

Average inter-track
seek distances

are unfortunately scattered all over the disk pack. To access such a file, the head would be moving to a new track for each block: not a good situation. If the delays become unacceptable, a 'defragger' utility program can be employed to rearrange the blocks of data. Basically it rewrites all the files as if to a fresh, clean disk so that the data is now neatly arranged in linear order. Defragging is a time-consuming activity.

12.9   Optical discs – CD-DA, CD-ROM, CD-RW and DVDs

Optical disc storage started with compact discs as a digital replacement for plastic LPs in the music industry. They are manufactured from a metal master unit by mechanically pressing out the polycarbonate copies. The single spiral track (Fig. 12.22) can hold 74 minutes of stereo music, twin track, 16 bit encoded, at a 44.1 kHz sampling rate. Bits are represented as physical pits in the groove which scatter the laser beam, reducing the intensity of the reflected light. The data stream for high-quality music

Fig. 12.22
CD data spiral and
magnetic disk concentric
tracks.

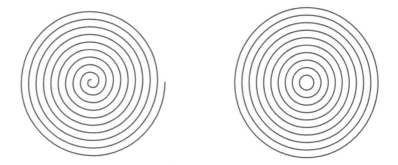

from a CD drive is 150 kbyte/s, supplying new values every 22.7 μs. For good reason, the pressing is done from one side, while the reading is carried out from the reverse. The laser has to traverse the full thickness (1.2 mm) of the polycarbonate disc to 'see' the pits (Fig. 12.23). Accidental surface damage, making the disc unreadable, is much more likely by scratching the thinner top surface lacquering than the entry surface for the laser. As the lacquer is only applied at 10 μm thickness, and the pits are of the order of 0.1 μm deep, there is ready opportunity for scratch damage on the top surface. The reason for directing the laser up through the bottom surface of the disk is to reduce the effect of surface blemishes at beam entry. This is possible because at the point of entry into the disk the beam is not focused on a small area; thus any scratch will be less disruptive.

The organization of data on a CD-DA (Digital Audio) was planned with prolonged serial access in mind. The spiral track is divided into 270 000 blocks, each holding 2 kbyte. The blocks have 12 byte headers and index numbers. These are arranged as three pairs of BCD (Binary-Coded Decimal) digits which refer to the expired play-time: minutes, seconds, sector. So there are 75 sectors to a second, 60 seconds to a minute and 60 (74!) minutes to a disc. The extra 14 minutes of playing time comes from a reduction in the space taken by ECCs (Error-Correcting Codes). The ECC chosen was a very powerful Hamming-type code, known as Reed–Solomon. A 288 byte checksum can be appended to every 2 kbyte block. A rule of thumb was that 1 minute of uncompressed CD music demanded 10 Mbyte of storage.

Fig. 12.23
Optical disc read head.

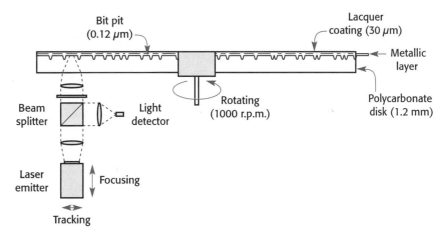

When the CD-ROM manufacturing techniques and playback units were adapted for computer data storage, the only significant changes necessary were to improve error detection and correction. Whereas music CDs are supplied with a basic CRC (see Section 10.3), which was sufficient for delivering a signal where drop-out errors could be interpolated without too much difficulty, with computer data a single error could be a serious, fatal occurrence. To improve the error trapping, the data was blocked together, as done with magnetic media, and a secondary CRC applied to each block. The blocks are typically 2 kbyte in size, and the appended ECC takes 280 bytes. This amounts to nearly 10% of the storage capacity, reducing the total usable space to 650 Mbyte. The CD is, however, now considered suitable for secure backup storage and long-term archiving. It is interesting to remember that they are formatted in a spiral pattern, which runs for about three miles, should you wish to unravel it! The disks are also read from the centre outwards, the opposite way to vinyl LPs.

Factory-manufactured optical CD-ROMs were accepted for distributing games software, but their impact was muted until disc writing equipment became available. Then limited copies could be conveniently produced without industrial press facilities. The so-called CD-WORM (Write Once, Read Many), or 'single shots' were used for software distribution and long-term archiving, and have begun to displace tape technology from these markets. Compared with magnetic hard disks they have the advantage of being removable and reliably compatible between different machines. However, they still suffer from much slower access speeds than magnetic disks. The CD-WORM drives worked by using a higher powered laser to punch little holes in a fine metallic layer sandwiched in the polycarbonate disk. This irreversible process was satisfactory because the blank discs were reasonably cheap, and mistakes could be tolerated. An alternative scheme, using a chemical dye layer, enables lower powered lasers to carry out the writing. However, the ability to erase the data and reuse the disc was still desirable. Two alternative schemes to achieve this are available: the magneto-optical disc and the phase-change CD-RW.

Magneto-optical discs, also known as MiniDiscs, again use a high-power laser to heat up a metallic layer embedded in the disc. This metal film has been selected for its magnetic properties, but like all magnetic substances, it loses its magnetic ordering when heated above a specific temperature, known as the Curie point. While it cools down, however, it is especially susceptible to any magnetic field that is present. So the CD-MO drive is provided with electric coils to set up a magnetic field at the point where the laser is focused on the disk. By reversing the magnetic field direction and firing the laser, the magnetic domains at that point can be reversed, thus storing a 1 or a 0. The read-back technology is even more sophisticated. The light from a low-powered laser is polarized so that when the beam is reflected off the magnetic film, it will have the plane of polarization affected by a complex interaction of light and electromagnetic fields known as the Kerr effect.

The next type of reusable optical disc to be developed was the phase-change CD-RW, which provided full rewritable capability but without relying on magnets. It employed a chemical substance which can exist in either an ordered crystalline state or a chaotic amorphous state. The heat generated by the high-powered laser beam can 'melt' the crystals, which then cool back into either an identical crystalline state or the disordered amorphous state, depending on the time allowed for the cooling process.

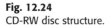

Fig. 12.24
CD-RW disc structure.

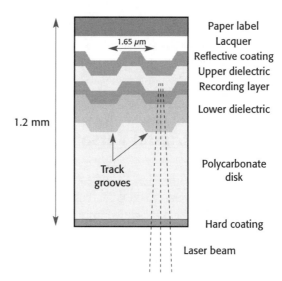

A slower change is imposed by turning off the laser over a longer period. In order to read back the stored data, it must be possible to distinguish between the two states using the light reflected off the surface. This is achieved thanks to the different reflectivity exhibited by crystalline and amorphous films. As shown in Fig. 12.24, a spiral track is physically embossed on the top of the polycarbonate disc during manufacture. Further layers are then deposited to produce the 'switchable' reflectivity that provides the write–read capability. The embossed track offers a good means of guiding the head as it is steered in and out, accessing data.

Unlike magnetic disks, the size of the bits on the inner tracks is the same as that for the outer tracks. This is due to the magnetic disk bits being written by constant length pulses, whereas CD-ROMS are pressed out mechanically. Thus the magnetic disks hold the same number of bits on any track, while the CD-ROM has 3× more bits on an outer arm of the spiral. Given this situation, to maintain a constant data rate for the music CD, the speed of rotation is varied according to where the read head is positioned on the spiral. As the head moves outwards, the disc is slowed down. For a 2× drive the inner track rotates in 55 ms, while the outer track takes 150 ms to maintain a constant bits/s read rate. This is known as CLV (Constant Linear Velocity) a technique which was also used by Apple for its original Macintosh floppy drives. This allows the outer tracks to have more bits stored than the smaller inner tracks. Controlling the speed of rotation gets too difficult for higher performance drives, where CLV is dropped in favour of the simpler CAV (Constant Angular Velocity) technique, which is the same as normal hard drives.

A continuing problem exists with the use of CD-R drives on PCs. While writing a data file to the disc, the data stream must be continuously available or the operation will fail irrevocably. There is no possibility of having a second go at writing a block onto the spiral track. The disk has to be thrown away. This was not so much of a problem with the single speed drives, but as technology improves, and 2×, 4× and 8× versions become available, the danger of data underrun is more likely. To counteract this threat, manufacturers of CD-R drives include 2 Mbyte RAM buffers to smooth out any hiccups in the supply of data. A 2× drive, requiring 300 kbyte/s of data, should be able to survive a 6 s gap if supplied from such a buffer.

12.10   DVD – Digital Versatile Disc

Digital Versatile Discs, or Digital Video Discs as they are sometimes called, are starting to take over the CD-ROM and CD-RW role in microcomputer storage. As with CD-ROM, DVD has benefitted from the ability to serve both as an entertainment media and as computer bulk storage. The read-only versions appeared first, intended to offer playback for full-length feature films and extended graphic computer games. Lately, rewritable DVD-RW disks have become widely available for audio applications.

DVD extends the CD-RW technology by allowing multi-layer recording and double-sided discs. A single-sided, single-layer DVD offers a storage capacity of 4.7 Gbyte, compared with the 650 Mbyte for a CD. Double-sided, dual-layer DVDs can offer as much as 17.0 Gbyte!

The basic manufacturing process for DVD and CD-ROMs is very similar. Injection moulded polycarbonate discs are stamped out ready for their reflective coatings. DVDs will require two such discs, which are then bonded together. For the dual-layer discs, a semi-reflective layer is deposited which allows the laser beam to focus on either layer and so choose which to read or write. The DVD laser assembly offers higher resolution than the earlier CD design, allowing reliable working with smaller bit pits. The minimum pit length of a single-layer DVD is $0.4\,\mu$m, while that for a CD is $0.83\,\mu$m. In addition, the DVD track pitch is reduced to $0.75\,\mu$m, half that of a CD.

Because it only takes an instant to refocus a lens from one reflective layer to another, the layout of data on a DVD may begin to emulate the multi-platter hard disk 'cylinder' model. It has also been arranged that data can be read in either direction: inwards towards the hub, or outwards towards the edge, which will provide for the introduction of some interesting new scheduling strategies!

The application of DVD technology for computer storage began with DVD-ROM, providing 3.9 Gbyte, and DVD-RW providing 2.6 Gbyte (single-sided) and 5.2 Gbyte (double-sided). Read and write speeds are currently the same as CD-ROM and CD-RW.

12.11   Floppy disks – waiting to be redeveloped

Floppy disks have somewhat been left out of the recent frenzy of technological development. When other memory media (DRAMs, hard disks and CD-ROMs) were surging ahead in capacity, speed and popularity, the 1.4 Mbyte diskette was left alone to grow small and slow by just remaining the same. It was not always so. When microprocessors first emerged on the market floppy disks were very significant in the development of affordable, personal computers. The original 128 kbyte 8 inch floppy disks were introduced by IBM as a convenient way of loading microcode into large minicomputers. They were seized on by the microcomputer fraternity as the ideal secondary store to fit in with the new microprocessor CPUs. The US firms IMSAI and Altair quickly produced home computers with Intel 8080 CPUs, S100 buses and floppy disk drives.

The smaller 3.5 inch disk systems thankfully superseded the more expensive and less reliable 5.25 and 8 inch drives. Typically the 3.5 inch disks have 80 tracks and 9 sectors of 1 kbyte, giving 1.4 Mbyte storage. Unlike hard disks, the read head is in direct contact with the magnetic surface of the disk at all times, which does give some problems with wear, even at the rather slow rotational speed of 300 r.p.m. At variance with the rest of industry, the original Apple floppy disk mechanism allowed for variable rotation speed. The disk spun at 300 r.p.m. when accessing the outer tracks and 600 r.p.m. when accessing the inner tracks. This gave a constant bit density, avoiding longer bits on the outer tracks. The technique of variable-speed drives has been revived for use in CD-ROM units.

The 1.4 Mbyte floppies used to transfer files around usually contain a small MS-DOS FAT file system which either Unix or Windows NT will accommodate. This is a useful vehicle for data exchange where networks are not available, but it is rapidly losing its role as common file sizes grow way beyond 1.4 Mbyte.

Review

- Computers rarely have fully populated address spaces because of the expense. To improve performance a memory hierarchy is provided in an attempt to match processor requirements.

- Layers of storage devices with differing performance characteristics are used, with the operating system transferring data between the layers as required.

- The ability of such a hierarchy to work effectively depends on the fact that memory accesses tend to dwell for periods of time in the same region (localization of function).

- Programmers should understand the structure and function of the storage hierarchy so as to optimize their code.

- Cache memory lies between main memory and the CPU. It is small and fast compared with main memory. For the best performance, cache may reside on the same chip as the CPU.

- A main memory overflow, or swap area, is allocated on disk. This forms the basis of virtual memory, where all programs are split into fixed size pages for mapping into available spaces in main memory. The MMU is responsible for this address translation process.

- By combining hardware facilities (MMMU) with operating system functionality, virtual memory can be segmented to provide access control for defined areas of memory.

- Disk performance is specified by the parameters access time (speed of head movement), latency (rotational speed), and data rate (track bit density). Fragmented files take longer to read because of the need for more head movements.

- Hard disk units are sealed up in clean rooms to avoid contamination from dust. The heads 'fly' aerodynamically on a thin layer of air pulled round by the spinning disk.

- Requests to access hard disks for read–write operations may be queued and rescheduled by the operating system to minimize overall head movements. Different algorithms are available.

- Optical discs store more data and are not volatile, but as yet are slow to access.

Practical work

The recommended practical work involves the investigation of memory performance differences. It is possible to design programs to incur (or not to incur) virtual memory swapping penalties. It is also desirable to design programs to run efficiently with the cache memory available.

Exercises

1. Obtain prices for memory modules and IDE disk units from the WWW. Calculate the cost per bit of SRAM, DRAM and disk storage. Then calculate the cost of the access bandwidth in bits/s per penny for each of these storage media.

2. Why did Intel introduce two levels of SRAM cache into the PC arena?

3. How does localization of access benefit PC performance?

4. What does DRAM stand for? Why is it called that? In what way has DRAM recently become less random access? How are SDRAM DIMMs interfaced to PC L2 cache?

5. Amend the program in Section 12.2 so that the data is written back into the array.

   ```
   sum += big[i][j];
   big[i][j] = sum; /* <---add in this line */
   sum += big[j][i];
   big[j][i] = sum; /* <--- and this line */
   ```

   How does this change the caching situation?

6. Intel separated the L1 cache into two sections for code and data. What is the problem of employing a unified cache?

7. Under what circumstances would you expect to suffer cache misses? Can a programmer do anything to reduce the rate of cache misses?

8. Repeat the calculation shown in Fig. 12.19 for one of the disk units chosen from Table 12.4, but make main memory 64 Mbytes.

9. What is the difference between DVD and CD-ROM?

10. Calculate how much uncompressed data (kbyte) a music CD carries for 74 min playing time. What is the highest frequency accurately reproduced using this scheme? Can you play a music CD on your PC?

11. CD-ROM drives are currently offering much slower access times than hard disks. Why is this? Can you imagine any changes that might improve this situation?

Readings

- The PC Guide is good for technical information on disks and CD formats:
  `http://www.pcguide.com/ref/cd/`

  See also:
  `http://www.mkdata.dk/click/index.htm`

- Heuring and Jordan (1997), Chapter 7: memory design; Section 9.1: disk systems.

- Hennessy and Patterson (1998), Chapter 7: the memory hierarchy.

- A fascinating read for the off-centre curious at the following site is Subject [7-8] 'How do CD-Rs behave when microwaved?':
  `http://www.fadden.com/cdrfaq/faq07.html#[7-8]`

  But the other more regular FAQs are very interesting, too.

- The Web sites can be accessed via the Companion Web site for this book at:
  `http://www.booksites.net/williams/`

Networking and increased complexity

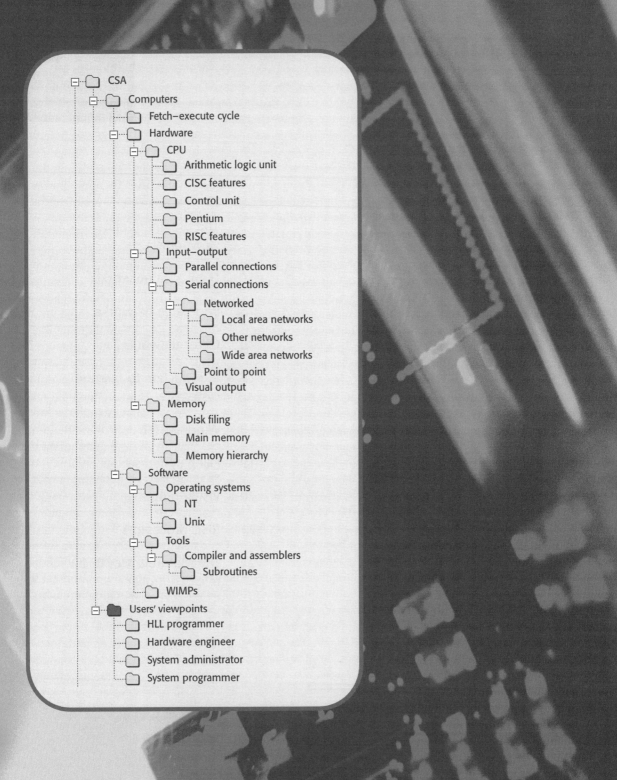

- CSA
  - Computers
    - Fetch–execute cycle
    - Hardware
      - CPU
        - Arithmetic logic unit
        - CISC features
        - Control unit
        - Pentium
        - RISC features
      - Input–output
        - Parallel connections
        - Serial connections
          - Networked
            - Local area networks
            - Other networks
            - Wide area networks
          - Point to point
        - Visual output
      - Memory
        - Disk filing
        - Main memory
        - Memory hierarchy
    - Software
      - Operating systems
        - NT
        - Unix
      - Tools
        - Compiler and assemblers
          - Subroutines
      - WIMPs
  - Users' viewpoints
    - HLL programmer
    - Hardware engineer
    - System administrator
    - System programmer

The programmer's viewpoint

13

Overview

The computer can be analysed from any number of different viewpoints. Hardware engineers and programmers certainly describe the same equipment very differently. But even those concerned mainly with software have very distinctive ways of dealing with the functional capabilities of computers. This chapter presents the viewpoints of different users to help you to understand other people's needs. An initial investigation of the diverse facets of the computer introduces the abstract technique of layering, which assists the reader to better subdivide the complex functionality of computers. The concept of virtual machines is introduced and the need to understand the facilities which underpin the increasing popularity of networked applications is discussed.

13.1   Different viewpoints – different needs

When dealing with computers, being able to understand some of the technical details of the underlying hardware and operating systems software can be useful. But in reality most computer users do not often require this level of knowledge to carry out their job. They actually use a much reduced **abstract model** of the computer which represents only the structures and information which are relevant for a particular task. Experience teaches you what information is essential and what is, for the moment, of only academic interest. Dealing with colleagues and clients who have a different viewpoint (Fig. 13.1) can be a real challenge! Sometimes you find that the terminology used to refer to commonplace items is different. A program is called an application, a data file has become a document and a directory is a folder. Such changes of vocabulary seem to be instituted as often to mystify as to simplify. Unfortunately, that is the current nature of a rapidly changing, highly competitive business.

The different viewpoints and approaches to problems can be exemplified by the case of the slow-running spreadsheet. When faced by a large spreadsheet that was taking 40 min to update, the Hardware Engineer suggested a processor upgrade to speed up the fundamental machine cycle. At best this might halve the run time. The Application User was convinced that the poor performance was due to the legacy software product and suggested that a new fully featured spreadsheet package should be tried. When this was done, the update took 60 min. A Systems Administrator whipped up a Unix awk script to carry out the same calculation in 10 min. But it could only perform the specified calculation. The HLL Programmer read the user manual and discovered that by disabling screen refresh, which was taking place after every calculation, the processing time was reduced to 4 min. The Systems Programmer experimented with accessing the data array using pointers, rather than cell indexing, and succeeded in reducing the update time to 40 s!

An aspect of software which is increasingly influential in our lives is the spectacular development cost. Billions are spent every year on producing new software, much of which is never successfully commissioned. Software remains a labour-intensive **craft**. This cost factor has led to software systems sometimes exerting an unexpectedly conservative influence on society due to the prohibitively high investment needed to fund replacement work. The Y2K scare resulted mainly from very old programs,

Fig. 13.1
Different jobs, different viewpoints.

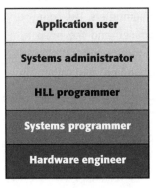

never intended to last more than a couple of years, which were still being maintained 30 years later. No programmer could have imagined that their mainframe COBOL program, written in the early 1960s, would still be running in 1999.

13.2 Application user – office packages

It can be depressing for computer scientists that the vast majority of computers are only used for routine word-processing, spreadsheet and email applications. Lotus 1-2-3, Microsoft Word and various email programs provide the familiar daily work environment for most people. Perhaps understandably they are not much interested in how the software works, and are so unconfident at the thought of hardware that they are alarmed by the prospect of plugging in a printer. As has often been said, this technological alienation, or disempowerment, cannot be good for the individual or the organization for whom they are working. A more thorough appreciation of the functioning of hardware and software would be to everyone's benefit.

The viewpoint of someone using a word processor package is often limited to a schematic file system (Fig. 13.2), screen, printer, keyboard and mouse. The **WIMP** (Windows, Icons, Menus, Pointer) interface, when introduced in the mid-1980s, was intended to make computing more accessible to those people without a university degree in computer science. In this regard it has been an amazing success. The Windows **GUI** (Graphical User Interface) immediately provides the application user with many facilities through the 'drag-and-drop desktop metaphor', considered by

Fig. 13.2
Graphical representation
of a PC directory using
Explorer.

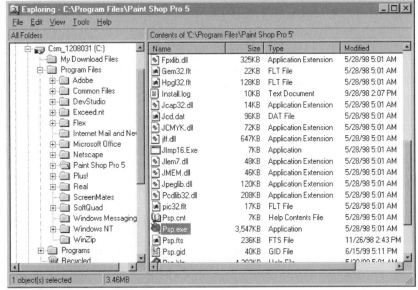

Fig. 13.3
Traditional text-only Unix
directory listing using `ls`.

```
rob@milly [80] ls -alt
total 6702
drwx--x--x  76 rob csstaff    7168  Aug  7  17:57
drwx--x--x   3 rob csstaff    3072  Aug  7  15:55
-rwx------   1 rob csstaff   42544  Aug  6  14:57 #testparam.c#
-rwx------   1 rob csstaff   42545  Aug  5  14:55 sort.c
-rwx------   1 rob csstaff    9505  Aug  5  14:35 jeffsm.c
-rwx------   1 rob csstaff    9525  Aug  5  14:31 jeffsm.c
-rwx------   1 rob csstaff    5144  Aug  5  14:31 a.out
-rwx------   1 rob csstaff   17851  Aug  3  14:31 ch_9c.txt
-rwx------   1 rob csstaff   17890  Aug  3  14:30 ch_9c.asc
-rwx------   1 rob csstaff   21180  Aug  2  17:28 ntime.c
rob@milly [81]
```

most users to be much more friendly than the previous character-based interfaces, as shown in Fig. 13.3.

An additional complexity has been introduced into the office computing environment with the desire to interconnect all equipment through a local area network. This development was originally driven by the hope that accessing a shared laser printer or a central file server would reduce costs. But now the need to exchange email and access the wider Internet has taken over as the driving motive. Both Unix and Windows NT offer support for remote resource access which makes it appear to the user no different from local access. The large and diverse networking requirements of offices have pushed forward the development of these facilities.

Now, software packages are identified by **desktop icons** and they are started simply by positioning the screen pointer and clicking the mouse button. How the pointer moves on the screen in sympathy with the mouse is not questioned. The only understanding of the way the software works is inferred from the keystroke functionality. Abbreviated online help is the user's only source of information. Even knowing the size of the program has become unimportant with recent reductions in the price of RAM and disk hardware. To maintain this veneer of simplicity, an enormous effort is expended by suppliers of software in order to hide the intricate complexity of their products. All good intentions inevitably backfire when some unanticipated sequence of events throws the system into confusion, requiring, once again, intelligent human intervention to sort out the mess. As software becomes more sophisticated, perhaps a good knowledge of computer systems architecture will eventually become an essential survival skill for office workers!

To support the development of application-level programs the Windows interface offers a wide library of routines, accessible through the API (Application Programming Interface), which can be used to provide a convenient repertoire of 'interactions' for the end-user: tracking mouse movements, supporting menu selection, window resizing and refreshing, and organizing the appropriate responses to mouse button clicks. But the **API level** belongs to the domain of the programmer, not the user.

13.3 Systems administration – software installation and maintenance

Systems administrators generally look after *existing systems*. Their view of computer systems is similar to a warehouse keeper, worrying about the availability of stock or of empty space to accept new deliveries. They do not often need to write programs from scratch. Much of what they do has been done before, and programs, or tools, have been made available by the system suppliers or user groups. The abstract model, or viewpoint, used at this level includes the file system hierarchy, as described above, but also maps the files to physical disk drives. Now the size of files is significant, and which disk drive is actually holding them, too. Systems can fail if there is not enough free space available on disk.

When processing files, the data is often represented a bit like water flowing around the system. **Data streams** get passed from one program, or process, to another to accomplish a task, such as the text formatting example in Fig. 13.4. Although systems administrators, for the most part, will also interact with the computer through a GUI, they also require a console or command window. This accepts 'old-fashioned' typed commands which are directed to a shell or **CLI** (Command Line Interface) program, providing a wider repertoire of controls than the GUI.

The Unix operating system, especially, offers systems administrators a higher level of systems building using shell scripts and ready coded **tools**, such as sort, grep and sed. These tools can be 'plugged' together using **pipe** facilities which allow the data output from one program to be routed directly into another program without needing to be stored in an intermediate disk file.

The simple process pipeline in Fig. 13.4 was used to print Chapter 7 on my local PostScript laser printer. The first part of the pipe concatenates (sticks together) the header file with the file containing Chapter 7 (third version) before passing the data through a series of **filters** (programs), plugged together in a pipeline. These accept special formatting commands, embedded in the text, before finally creating a Post-Script file ready for printing. lp is the Unix line printer command, but it can also

Fig. 13.4
A Unix process pipeline to format and print text.

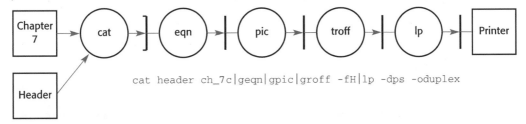

```
cat header ch_7c|geqn|gpic|groff -fH|lp -dps -oduplex
```

service the newer laser printers, as in this case. The instruction 'duplex' is a request to carry out double-sided printing.

The data flows between the different processes are mediated by **pipes** which are technically similar to the storage buffers used to hold data coming from and going to disk. Each process in the pipeline is running as independently as is possible when relying on other processes for the essential input data. When no data is available the process will block. When more data arrives it can proceed as fast as it can until an EOF (end of file) marker is received. Pipelines can also include a program written by you in C, or some other language. Such a program may be saved and used later in other pipelines, thus becoming a tool!

The previous pipeline example employed 'anonymous' pipes in that they did not have explicit names. There is an alternative form, 'named' pipes, which you can demonstrate using the Unix 'mknod p' or 'mkfifo' command. This will create a pipe buffer in your directory, as shown in Fig. 13.5.

A distinctive feature of this level of interaction with computer systems is the use of scripts or **command files**. These simply contain keyboard sequences which can be 'replayed' whenever required. Because they have been found to be so useful, the scripting languages have now been extended beyond what is possible to run directly at the keyboard, and have evolved into elaborate, and sometimes rather quirky, programming languages (sh, csh and Perl). Because they are line-by-line interpreted, not compiled, the execution is slower and less efficient than ordinary HLL programs, but they are still preferred for this kind of application. As you will see from the example given in Fig. 13.6, shell scripts make heavy use of other tools, which they call rather like functions to carry out specific jobs on their behalf. Interestingly, the debugging support for scripting languages is much worse than for C, Java or BASIC. Does this reflect the greater expertise of system administrators or their professional arrogance?

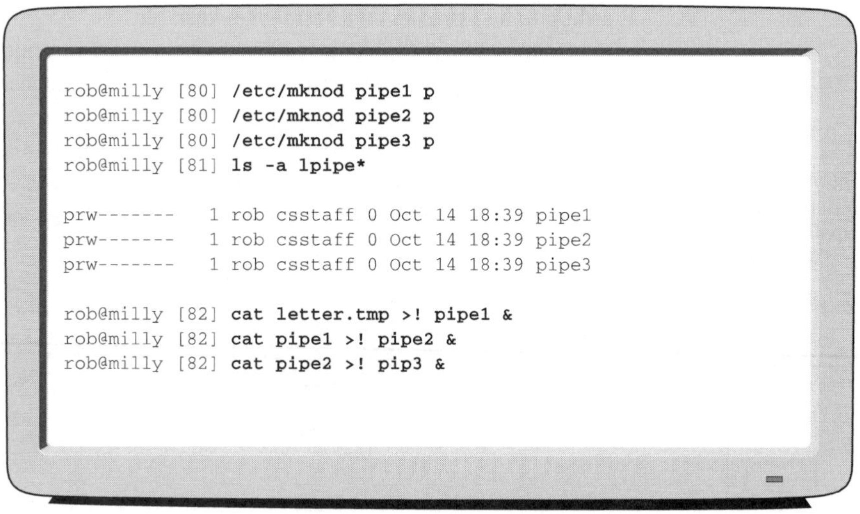

Fig. 13.5
Demonstrating Unix named pipes.

```
rob@milly [80] /etc/mknod pipe1 p
rob@milly [80] /etc/mknod pipe2 p
rob@milly [80] /etc/mknod pipe3 p
rob@milly [81] ls -a lpipe*

prw-------   1 rob csstaff 0 Oct 14 18:39 pipe1
prw-------   1 rob csstaff 0 Oct 14 18:39 pipe2
prw-------   1 rob csstaff 0 Oct 14 18:39 pipe3

rob@milly [82] cat letter.tmp >! pipe1 &
rob@milly [82] cat pipe1 >! pipe2 &
rob@milly [82] cat pipe2 >! pip3 &
```

The example listed in Fig. 13.6 is a Unix administration script written for the Bourne shell (sh). It uses sar (System Activity Reporter) to take the system performance logs, written to files normally positioned in the directory /var/adm/sa/, filters them and produces more useful graphical output. At the start, there are several procedures defined. These are used in the main section of the script. The procedure remclutter( ) uses a pipeline of grep processes to filter out all the unwanted lines from the data file. Commonly, grep rejects lines not containing the target item, but grep -v *rejects* lines containing the target.

The example administration script presented in Fig. 13.6 displays many of the features which distinguish Unix scripts from normal HLL programs. Scripts regularly use other tools, such as cat, grep, sed, sar and tr within process pipelines, to carry out jobs. Variables need not be declared before use. Files are read and written using the process IO redirection. It may now be clear that the construction of a script does not follow the best 'structured code' guidelines. All these features are distinctive, and special to scripting languages.

Fig. 13.6
A Unix administration script to assemble performance statistics.
(Continued overleaf)

```
#!/bin/sh
#
# Script converts sar data into graphs - PJN 20/10/1998
#
# Extend the PATH to include gnuplot
PATH=${PATH}:/usr/local/bin ; export PATH

# Procedure to remove non-data lines from log file.
remclutter() {
grep : | grep -v free | grep -v % | grep -v / | grep -v restarts
}
# Procedure to pad numbers with zeros to 2 digits.
padnum() {
NUM=$1
while [ `/bin/echo "${NUM}\c" | wc -c` -lt 2 ]; do
    NUM="0${NUM}"
done
echo $NUM
}
# Procedure to convert time of day timestamps to decimal days.
parsetimes() {
DAY=0
OLDHOUR=23
while read TIME DATA; do
    if [ "$DATA" = "" ]; then
        DATA="0 0 0 0 0 0 0 0 0 0 0"
    fi
    HOUR=`echo $TIME | cut -f1 -d:`
    MIN=`echo $TIME | cut -f2 -d:`
    if [ $HOUR -lt $OLDHOUR -a "$MIN" = "00" ]; then
        DAY=`expr $DAY + 1`
    fi
    PTIME=`expr \( \( \( \( $HOUR \* 60 \) + $MIN \) \* 100 \)/1440`
    PTIME=${DAY}.`padnum $PTIME`
    echo "$PTIME $DATA"
    OLDHOUR=$HOUR
done
}
# Procedure to get data from a named column.
getcol() {
tr -s ' ' '^' | cut -f1,${1} -d\^ | tr '^' ' '
}
```

Fig. 13.6
continued

```
# Determine the i/p and o/p files (for last week's data).
WEEK=`date +%W`
WEEK=`expr $WEEK - 1`
if [ $WEEK -eq -1]; then
   WEEK=52
fi
WEEK=`padnum $WEEK`
DATAFILE=/var/adm/sa/sa$WEEK
OUTFILE=/tmp/$$.graphs

# Process virtual memory data from sar log.
echo "VM usage"
sar -f $DATAFILE -r > /tmp/$$.sar
cat /tmp/$$.sar | remclutter | parsetimes > /tmp/$$.sar-f
rm /tmp/$$.sar
cat /tmp/$$.sar-f | getcol 2 > /tmp/$$.freemem
cat /tmp/$$.sar-f | getcol 3 > /tmp/$$.freeswap
(cat << EOF
  set term postscript
  set time
  set xtic 0, 0.5
  set title "`hostname` virtual memory usage"
  f(x) = (x * 512 ) / 1048576
  g(x) = (x * `pagesize` ) / 1048576
  plot [0:7] []\
  "/tmp/$$.freemem" thru g(x) title "Free RAM (Mb)"with lines,\
  "/tmp/$$.freeswap" thru f(x) title "Free Swap (Mb)"with lines
  EOF
) | gnuplot > $OUTFILE
rm /tmp/$$.freemem /tmp/$$.freeswap /tmp/$$.sar-f

1p -d ps $OUTFILE
sleep 60; rm $OUTFILE
exit
```

Perl, a newer scripting language, incorporates many of the facilities only previously offered by several, separate utilities, and because it is also available on many different operating systems in addition to Unix, it is displacing the use of the traditional 'cat | sort | grep | awk' pipelines and shell scripts. Many programmers applaud this as a genuine advance in rationalizing so many disparate tools. But it could be observed that replacing traditional bricks by bigger concrete slabs did not improve urban architecture – many of the high-rise constructions have already been demolished as unmaintainable. Is small always beautiful? On the other hand there would be a tremendous advantage to have a single scripting language available for all computer systems. More and more programmers are working with Windows NT, and the convenience of such a unified scripting facility is clear.

Nowadays computers are frequently connected to a network. An increasing responsibility of systems administrators is network management. Thus, the scope has changed from a single isolated computer, to a group of interlinked workstations, often with a unified, shared file system. This radically changes the viewpoint, especially if the network is part of a larger, corporate structure.

13.4 HLL programmer – working with Java, C++ or BASIC

We will spend a bit more time and space in describing the viewpoint of the high-level language programmer because it involves a closer understanding of Computer Architecture, although with computers running sophisticated operating systems there is little chance of gaining direct access to the underlying hardware, unless you are very determined or are employed to design the next generation of Talking Toaster. These, as yet, are not running Unix. Almost all programs for PCs are now written in C or C++ due to the influence of MS Windows. This is the type of programming we are now considering.

It has been claimed that programmers, on average, can only produce five lines of working, fully debugged and documented code within a day. This estimate can even appear a trifle optimistic to many old hackers! But the curious outcome is that the language employed does not influence the final number. Thus, using Pascal or C will always be 5–10 times more efficient than assembler, because compilers translate each line of HLL code into 5–10 lines of machine code. Perhaps this revelation is unsurprising, but the simplicity of its expression is rather breathtaking. Nevertheless, the message has got across, and most programmers strive to employ the highest level of language to express their solutions.

The view of HLL programmers will focus on the problem to be solved, the **algorithm** and methods to be used (Fig. 13.7), and finally the vocabulary and syntax of the available languages. Some HLL compilers require a fixed code format. Pascal needs the data declarations and code sections in a particular order, FORTRAN demanded careful tabulation, and BASIC used line numbers. The structure of HLL code now generally follows the Sequence, Iteration and Selection guidelines (SEQ, IT and SEL), and HLLs offer support for these with WHILE, FOR and REPEAT loops and IF and CASE switches, as illustrated in Fig. 13.8.

As already mentioned, the **file system** of most computers is arranged as a hierarchical tree, which allows the user to organize program and data files in related subject groups. This is reminiscent of the traditional library scheme used to catalogue books. Most HLL programmers ignore completely the technical details of disk data storage, but rather think in navigational terms of wandering around inside the file system. This can sometimes feel like driving across London with only the memory of a 10-year-old map for guidance! 'Find' tools can be invaluable. On large computers, even the simple parameters: 'file size' and 'free capacity' are now ignored, to the eventual detriment of all users. With the arrival of gigabyte drives for personal computers, the

Fig. 13.7
Example HLL algorithm –
bubble sort.

```c
#include <stdio.h>

int bsort (char* pc[ ], int n ) {
   int gap, i, j;
   char* pctemp;
for (gap = n/2; gap > 0; gap /=2)
   for (i = gap; i < n; i++)
      for(j = i-gap; j>= 0; j -= gap) {
      if (strcmp (pc[j], pc[j+gap]) <=0) break;
      pctemp = pc[j], pc[j] = pc[j+gap]; pc[j+gap] = pctemp;
   }
}

void main(void) {
   int i;
   char* names[ ] = {
       "Monday", "Tuesday", "Wednesday", "Thursday",
                 "Friday", "Saturday", "Sunday"};
   i = bsort(names, 7);
   for(i=0; i<7; i++) {
       printf("%s\n", names[i] );
   };
}
```

sensible practice of routinely deleting old files to release more space has practically disappeared.

HLL programmers view the main memory as providing slots or pigeon holes to store program variables. This is where data items can be written, read and updated. The amount of space taken by the variables is not usually considered – only the declared type is relevant to a successful compilation and execution. Variable types entail the set of operations which the compiler considers 'legal'. An attempt to compile code which contains unauthorized combinations of variables and operators will generate a compile-time error. Some of the built-in data types for C++/C are listed in Table 13.1.

The exact position in memory of variables or function code is rarely thought about. And as for CPU registers – never! Some HLL programmers have initial difficulty distinguishing local and global variables, which occasionally leads to unexpected run-time errors. This confusion would never occur with assembler level programming!

Programmers who are developing code for small microcontroller applications still have to worry about the size of their programs, but fortunate Unix and Windows NT users are completely freed from this constraint by the virtual memory facility as described in Chapter 12.

Data IO is rarely given a second thought by HLL programmers. When they do, it is to imagine data passing through a channel, similar to those mysterious airport gateways where relatives and friends wave and disappear behind a security screen. They

Fig. 13.8
Structure chart
representations of SEQ,
IT and SEL.

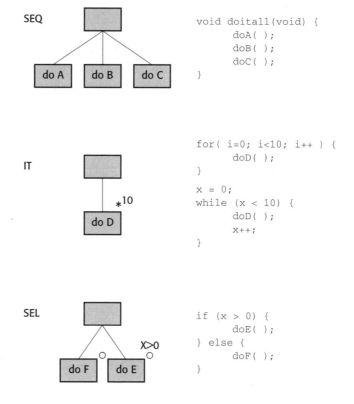

```
void doitall(void) {
    doA( );
    doB( );
    doC( );
}
```

```
for( i=0; i<10; i++ ) {
    doD( );
}
x = 0;
while (x < 10) {
    doD( );
    x++;
}
```

```
if (x > 0) {
    doE( );
} else {
    doF( );
}
```

also tend to reappear suddenly, frequently at the wrong time and accompanied by strange luggage. The HLL IO instructions normally make heavy use of operating system routines to carry out the various operations. This makes it easier for HLL code to be independent of the underlying hardware, but means that compilers generally cannot produce code for bare-board computers. Also, because of this dependency,

Table 13.1
Data types for C and
C++.

bool	unsigned 1 bit value
char	unsigned 8 bit value
wchar	unsigned 16 bit value
byte	unsigned 8 bit integer
short	signed 16 bit integer
word	unsigned 16 bit integer
int	signed 32 bit integer
long	signed 32 bit integer
unsigned	unsigned 32bit integer
dword	unsigned 32 bit integer
float	IEEE 32 bit real
double	IEEE 64 bit real

changing the operating system can lead to the same tricky problems as changing the hardware platform.

Being able to use the same HLL, irrespective of the actual computer hardware, is very helpful. C is usually the first HLL compiler to be written for a new microprocessor. Because the language constructs relate to the problems requiring solution, and not to the CPU or memory addresses, programmers are able to focus more on the problem and less on the technology. Often the distinction between intrinsic instructions and external library procedures can be forgotten.

Operating system facilities are often far more useful than expected, and there is a temptation for more advanced programmers to exploit the extra commands when access is provided by HLL compilers. These go beyond the necessary, standard, language to make the full range of the operating system calls accessible to the programmer. In fact, with Pascal, this is probably essential just to stop the system crashing when routinely running the program! But using extra operating system facilities makes porting the code even more of a problem, and so should be avoided as far as possible.

13.5   Systems programming – assembler and C

This low-level work is now mostly the elite preserve of experienced programmers. It might involve writing a driver routine to interface a new device, optimizing a graphics algorithm, or squeezing code into a small microcontroller. As we have pointed out already, the productivity advantages of using an HLL should never be neglected. However, when the aim is to learn more about the hardware–software interface there is no better way than experimenting with low-level programs. Perhaps only programs intended for the performance-sensitive and highly competitive games market are now fully written in assembler. It is more common now to code the bare minimum in assembler, and call it, when required, as a procedure from the main HLL program. In this way a critically important section of code can be hand-crafted to maximize performance, without losing the advantage of using an HLL for the majority of the code.

One other benefit from using assembler is the ability to access all the hardware resources. HLLs cannot immediately be adapted to fit in with every new feature or facility that becomes available with each new CPU released. However, the assembler can access any new registers or special instructions immediately. Also, to fully understand the relationship between HLL code and the hardware, we really have to consider the intermediate assembler code level. Each line of HLL source code is checked and translated by the compiler into a sequence of several executable machine instructions. Some compilers also give the option of printing out an intermediate assembler code file, which for educational and serious debugging activities can be very useful. For similar reasons, we saw, in Section 7.8, how to embed assembler instructions inside a C program when using the Microsoft Developer Studio.

HLL computer programs use various data structures to represent situations and sequences of events (e.g. arrays, stacks and queues). These structures are sometimes specially supported by hardware provision or particular groups of machine instructions intended to make the implementation or execution more efficient. The assembler file will contain all the details of these data structures in a machine-oriented manner: how many bytes are required for the array, which CPU register is used as a data pointer to your record and how long the executable code will be.

There are no strict rules governing the format of assembler code, only conventions. However, because programmers are aware that such a liberal regime can quickly lead to chaos, the local conventions are often strictly followed. To implement the IT or SEL structures in an assembler program will require status flags to be explicitly checked and a conditional branch instruction to be used to jump back to a label. A single IF loop will require several interacting instructions. FOR loops normally count down to zero for more efficient coding. IF branches require target labels to be inserted in the code.

The example code fragments in Fig. 13.9 are in Pentium assembler mnemonics. They are presented here only for you to compare with the C examples in Fig. 13.8.

Fig. 13.9
Flow chart representation of SEQ, IT and SEL.

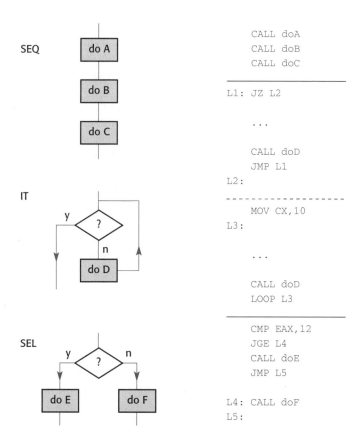

```
         CALL doA
         CALL doB
         CALL doC
         ──────────────
    L1:  JZ L2

          . . .

         CALL doD
         JMP L1
    L2:
         - - - - - - - - - - - - - -
         MOV CX,10
    L3:

          . . .

         CALL doD
         LOOP L3
         ──────────────
         CMP EAX,12
         JGE L4
         CALL doE
         JMP L5

    L4:  CALL doF
    L5:
```

When programming at the assembler level, disk accesses are usually done through calls to operating system routines, in the same manner as with HLL programming. However, there are extra initialization operations to be carried out before the data can be transferred. The data buffer areas have to be explicitly reserved and declared. Mistakes and programming errors can be more serious.

Variables can be treated as bytes, words or longs, and data registers within the CPU are used as temporary stores for the variables. Normally, however, a memory location is reserved for each data variable and a name designated for each location. Occasionally programmers have to know the physical address of these locations, but usually the assembler will handle the translation from location label to location number with no problem.

All the CPU registers are referred to by name: R0, D1, EAX etc. In Chapter 7 we met the Pentium register set. While writing assembler code, the programmer has to keep track of how all the CPU registers are being used at all times as the program executes. There is no assistance available for this task, and it can be the source of tricky bugs.

The stack is the centre of many difficulties encountered by systems programmers. The stack pointer, SP, may need to be explicitly initialized in order to start the stack at the correct position in RAM, and then checked after a procedure call/return. The most troublesome aspect is handling the parameters, which have to be explicitly pushed onto the system stack in the correct order, before calling the subroutine, and then removed from the stack on return. The system stack is also very important because it will hold all the local variables, procedure parameters and return addresses. Stack overflow is one of the less uncommon errors with new software!

Memory addresses can be very important for assembler programmers, who may need to spend some time pondering over the start address and length of their code. But with modern relocating linkers this is not so common. Nevertheless, physical addresses, when they occur, are still expressed in hex! If the code is to be installed in PROM there will be further complications in distinguishing the address ranges for PROM and RAM. A recurrent difficulty in learning assembler programming is the method of referring to data variables. This can involve complex addressing modes which must be mastered right at the beginning. A further problem for beginners stems from the confusion in the use of hex, numerical addresses and symbolic labels. More of this later.

When IO is required, as it often is, the absolute port addresses for the interface chips may have to be discovered, as well as the function of all their internal registers. You should be warned that ascertaining port addresses in the absence of any useful documentation can mean looking at the hardware circuit diagram and deducing the port address from the hardware decoder circuit. As systems grow in complexity, operating systems, such as Unix and Windows NT, try to prevent any direct access by programmers to the IO chips. IO operations are then done by calling operating system functions with the correct set of parameters and waiting for the transfer to happen. There was a situation when I was attempting to port a program to a new platform, and no suitable compiler was yet available. Noting that the new hardware had a very similar CPU and UARTs to the old platform, I took the original binary executable file and searched through it using a hex editor for all the port IO operations. These were actually limited to the `getch( )` and `putch( )` IO functions, and so were easy to discover. Patching new port addresses directly into the binary file was all that was needed to obtain a successfully ported program. Such a low-level approach to portability was only possible because there were no outstanding operating system calls to throw a spanner in the works.

Not every single assembler mnemonic has to be memorized! However, a minimum subset of CPU instructions and addressing modes will have to be learnt before starting assembler programming. The rest can be picked up as you go along, like any language. Each CPU has similar instructions and modes, but they are sufficiently different to cause problems. The complexity of assembler level programming really comes from the need to consider the application algorithm and the machine architecture at the same time.

Understanding the role of the CPU status flags cannot be avoided by assembler level programmers. Within the CPU is a group of status bits, some of which record the outcome of various ALU operations. They are used to 'bind together' the machine instructions, to provide a short-term memory for activities which span several machine instructions. Programmers sometimes explicitly use these flags, but mostly they are implicitly involved in the operation of conditional instructions. Here lies a principal difference between HLL and assembler programming: a single machine instruction often achieves nothing.

Start-up initialization remains a crucial responsibility for assembler code. All the software initialization may be left to an assembler routine, sometimes called `cstart.asm`. There are some activities which just cannot be done in HLLs, such as setting up the stack and starting the interrupt system.

Interrupts remain, for the most part, the hallowed province of the assembler programmer because all direct references to CPU registers have to be made at the assembler level. However, some specialist languages, such as ADA, do incorporate facilities to provide the HLL programmer with access to interrupts.

Until recently all operating system calls were primarily specified for assembler programs, with HLL libraries provided to launder the parameter list conventions. This is no longer true, and manuals now primarily give the interface protocol for C calls.

The use of the assembler, linker and loader programs may appear to be more difficult than equivalent HLL compiler suites, but this is only due to the efforts made by compiler suppliers to hide the complexity of their products. When something goes wrong, the complexity quickly reappears.

13.6 Hardware engineer – design and hardware maintenance

Computers have matured as products to the point where the day-to-day operational hardware can be very reliable, reducing the need for support engineers. Also, with the internationalization of the IT market-place there are now relatively few engineers

Fig. 13.10
Circuit schematic
diagram.

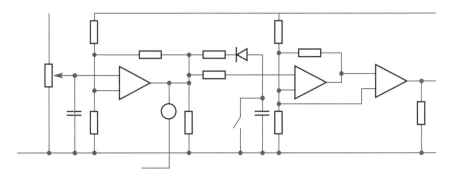

employed in the design and development of new models. However, many more are still required for the installation and maintenance of customer equipment. Whereas designers have to be able to visualize the computer at the digital logic level, the maintenance engineer is more likely to partition the computer into removable units, such as plug-in cards or disk drive packs. In this situation it is more useful to think of complex units exchanging information flows rather than tracing individual signals, with their characteristic parameters: voltage levels, pulse widths and rise times.

There are still hardware engineers who do deal with the component devices and gates, as represented in Fig. 13.10, but more often than not these are buried in the surface of an integrated circuit, invisible to the human eye. Hardware designers rely on CAD (Computer Aided Design) packages to design and layout their circuits and computer simulation programs to test their ideas. Breadboarding prototype circuits will soon be an historic activity undertaken only by students! Hardware design engineers, as we commented in Section 1.3, are often using very similar tools to their programmer colleagues. Certainly, the computer screen is now more important than the drawing board. Such an interesting change has not benefitted the hardware maintenance engineer, who has been required to abandon all attempts to diagnose and identify the failed component. Fault-finding activity is commonly reduced to a procedure of board swapping, which unfortunately does not deliver the same problem-solving satisfaction to the individual.

13.7   Layered virtual machines – hierarchical description

The close mix of hardware and software which makes a computer system can be represented by layers of functionality. Each layer accepts commands from the neighbour above, translating them and passing on the equivalent instructions in a reduced language to the next layer down. Ideally, we would want to submit requests in plain English at the top and obtain the correct actions from the hardware at the bottom. We are still quite far from such a dream! Hierarchies of interpreters, or servers, are also used in other contexts to help partition and organize complex systems. We will meet a layered model again in Chapter 15 when considering TCP/IP networking protocols.

Fig. 13.11
A multi-level computer.

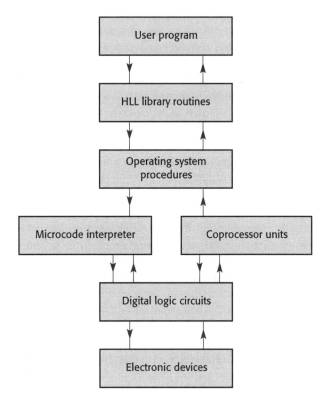

Looking at the computer system, as illustrated in Fig. 13.11, as a pile of 'virtual machines' also encourages us to consider the possibility of relocating functionality within the pile. Questions can be asked, such as 'Which is the best layer for floating-point operations?' or 'Where should the disk access routines be positioned?'. In the past, with the previous generation of CISC computers, such as the VAX-11 and MC68000, it was popular to 'migrate downwards' frequent activities in order to speed up execution times. Thus, some activity might be first implemented as a HLL procedure. An example might be the manipulation of a graphics entity, such as a games sprite. After this phase it would be recoded in assembler for better performance. Then, the systems programmer might be asked to include the routine as part of the next release of the operating system, which would allow other users to access it. To improve performance again, the routine could be implemented in microcode inside the CPU and become a machine instruction, with its own binary code and assembler mnemonic. But for ultimate speed, the final step would be the design of special hardware to carry out the activity. For a graphics operation this would probably involve the production of a secondary processor to work exclusively on the graphics images. Some compilers even allow you to select which version of floating-point arithmetic you wish to use: private HLL library routines, publicly shared operating system routines, floating-point coprocessor instructions or main CPU floating-point instructions.

More recently, with the introduction of RISC processors, functionality was migrated back up the layers again. But we will explain the justification for this counter-intuitive development in Chapter 21.

An additional responsibility of each layer, besides accepting commands from above and passing back information from below, is start-up initialization (booting). When electrical power is applied, the bottom layer might wake up ready to run, but the higher layers often need help to initialize and get ready to work correctly. The operating system code is usually stored on disk, and so must first be loaded into memory. Compilers and assemblers are rarely immediately available, although the original IBM PC was supplied with a BASIC interpreter in ROM! Computer systems can be thought of as being woken from the bottom layer upwards.

In the event of an error or failure to complete an action, a virtual machine layer will return an error code to the requesting layer. This means that all requests must also have associated with them some scheme of error recovery. All too often programmers try to forget about this responsibility until the principal portion of the code is being tested and some real failures have to be handled.

13.8   Assemblers – simple translators

Assemblers have four principal jobs involving translation. These include the translation of:

1.   Instruction mnemonics into binary codes

2.   User-defined symbols into constant numbers

3.   Numbers from base to base, normally decimal to binary

4.   Symbolic position labels into physical addresses.

Assemblers, when they are translating the pre-defined command mnemonics into binary codes, employ a three-column array called the **Symbol Table**. This is initially set up with all the standard mnemonics and their numeric values ready for the assembly process. Also, as the source code file is processed by the assembler line by line, each new user symbol is also entered into the symbol table with the associated numeric value. Thus, the `start` label will be written into the symbol table against a suitable physical address, computed as an offset from the start of the code segment. If there are other references to `start`, the correct numerical address value can then be read out immediately.

In the event of a reference to a symbol being encountered for the first time before its value has been entered into the symbol table (Table 13.2), known as a 'forward reference', the assembler may act in either of two ways. It may continue with reading the file and updating the symbol table with values. On reaching the end of the program, all

Table 13.2
Symbol table entries.

Symbol	Type	Value
ADD	opcode	$FF
ADDA	opcode	
SUB	opcode	
MOVE	opcode	
start	defined	
exit	undefined	
loop1	defined	
spx	defined	
sprite	defined	

the values should be discovered, so a further pass through the source file may be undertaken to finalize the earlier unresolved forward references. Alternatively, to avoid a second pass, the assembler can insert pointers into the symbol table in place of values, so that when the value is at last resolved a quick trip back through the file can be taken to paste the values into the code.

After the assembly process, the symbol table is usually disposed of, but it can be explicitly preserved for later use with a symbolic debugger.

The facility to translate between number bases allows programmers, if they should so wish, to enter binary values when dealing with status registers, hex when referring to addresses and decimal when doing arithmetic. The assembler can also translate ASCII code values, saving the programmer the trouble of looking them up in a table.

13.9 Compilers – translation and more

Compiling a C program is a multi-pass process, as shown in Fig. 13.12. The textual pre-processing is carried out to deal with header file insertions (#include <stdio.h>) and constant definitions (#define TMAX 100). Then the more complex lexical analysis, syntactic analysis and code generation are carried out in sequence. Lexical analysis involves the segmentation of each source file statement into several primitive tokens. These tokens are either pre-defined by the language or declared by the user during the course of the program. The tokens are represented by short code numbers and placed into a table in the order of occurrence. At the same time a symbol table is produced, as with the assembler, to assist with identifying the numerical value for logical symbols.

The next phase of syntactic checking and analysis is also called parsing. The parse attempts to identify ordered groups of tokens which represent an action to be carried out when the program runs. The output uses an intermediate code format, which is not targeted at any particular CPU. This intermediate code is taken by the next phase,

Fig. 13.12
Stages of compilation.

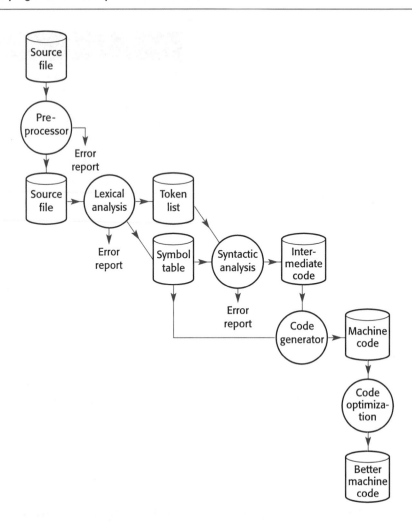

code generator, and translated into the specific machine code required for the target CPU. Often a further stage of processing is included to optimize the final executable program, either for speed of execution or code size. Compilers recognize flags or command line parameters whereby the best optimization technique can be selected by the programmer.

It has often been observed that the principal problem with implementing computer systems is the vast gulf between the manner in which users express their needs and the language acceptable to computers. Users speak English, or whatever, but a computer CPU only understands binary codes. To help with this situation there are translator programs which take one language and convert it to another. Compilers convert HLL to machine code. But even current HLLs are a far cry from natural language, with all its wonderful subtlety and expressiveness. Compiling is only one way to bridge the 'semantic gap' between what we want to happen and how we need to communicate the instructions to a computer.

Review

- Computers are used by many different people for many different tasks. Each has a different viewpoint and specialized vocabulary. The computer scientist must have some understanding of all these perspectives and how they interrelate. Presenting the computer as a layered system may be helpful in organizing this analysis.

- Application users have a very abstract model of the computer system and the interconnected network. The Windows interface reduces their need to understand or at least remember technical details.

- Computer systems administrators maintain existing systems. They are increasingly concerned with networking issues. They frequently write short script programs to help with the daily drudgery of upgrading, installing, restarting and rebooting.

- HLL programmers create new application programs.

- Systems programmers worry about device drivers and efficient algorithms to improve network performance.

- Hardware engineers, if involved in computer design work, generally target VLSI chips. Their work could involve the use of a HLL, such as VHDL, to specify the circuit, and would certainly require intensive simulation testing before implementation.

- The layered hierarchy which is commonly used to describe a computer can encompass both hardware and software.

- HLLs are translated by compilers, whereas the lower level of assembler mnemonics require an assembler program to carry out the translation.

Practical work

If this is the first practical of the new semester, it will be worth your while to review last semester's worksheets and refamiliarize yourself with the Developer Studio environment. Try locating some of your programs and resuscitating them. After that, the recommended practical work involves carrying out some scripting on Unix. The first examples will be pipelines built up on the tcsh command line.

Exercises

1. How can a programmer get access to operating system procedures?

2. How many machine instructions are produced by each line of assembler and how many for each line of HLL code?

3. What is Perl, and when would you use it?

4. What are CPU status flags, and how are they used by assembler programs? How do HLL programs use CPU status flags?

5. What three program structures are represented in all computer languages? Give example code fragments from two different languages.

6. What is the current role of assembler level programming?

7. Can a user distinguish between programs coded in HLL and those coded in assembler?

8. List the advantages gained from using an HLL.

9. What jobs does a systems administrator regularly carry out?

A. What is a command line interpreter? Name three different examples.

B. Why does Windows NT make direct access to the hardware so difficult? Are the needs of office workers, systems administrators, application programmers and students of Computer Science all the same?

C. What is the Unix pipe facility, and when might it be useful?

D. List the levels of functionality (virtual machines) for a modern computer. Give examples of functionality which might be found in each of the various levels of a computer system.

E. What does an application package user need to know about a computer before starting the program? What does a HLL programmer need to know about the target system?

F. Describe what aspects of the CPU could be seen as supporting the three software structures SEQ, IT and SEL.

10. Try entering this C program and using the Microsoft Developer Studio debugger's memory window to view the structure of the IEEE floating-point numbers:

```c
int main(void) {
  float a = 1234.5625;
  float b = -3.3125;
  float c = 0.065625;
return 0;
  }
```

Readings

- Wall (1996)

- Aho *et al.* (1988)

- Fire up Netscape and check out the following Web sites:
  http://www.eng.ncat.edu/help/Unix_Tut_Perl.html
  http://www.noinfo.com/technology/perl/index.html
  http://www.nhh.no/geo/unix-dem/awk000.htm
  http://gnu.senet.com.au/gawk-3.0.3/

- Heuring and Jordan (1997), Sections 1.2–1.5: different views of the computer.

- Hennessy and Patterson (1998), Appendix A: discussion about assemblers and linkers.

- The Web sites can be accessed via the Companion Web site for this book at:
  http://www.booksites.net/williams/

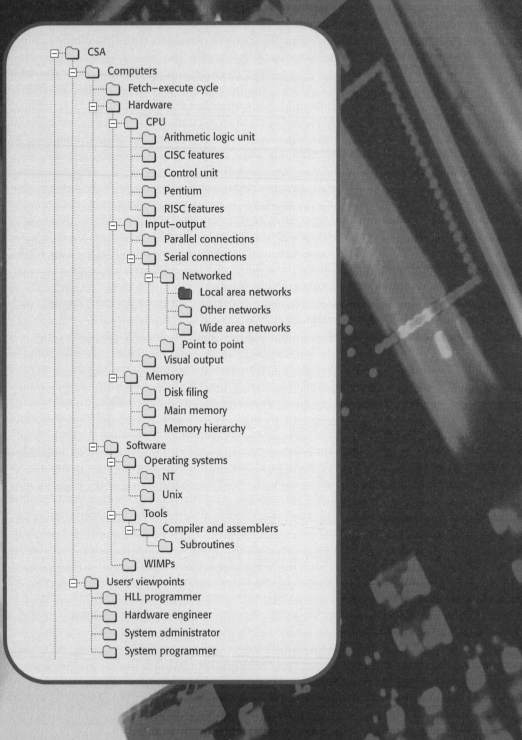

Local area networks

Overview

Local area networks (LANs) became popular because they provided easy communication and resource sharing for microcomputer users. PCs have only needed a network expansion card to be inserted to operate as a LAN station. The Ethernet CSMA/CD scheduling method was successful because of its simplicity. In an attempt to improve data transfer rates, recently the classical bus Ethernet has been displaced by the star switch arrangement. The addressing scheme used for LANs has to be compatible with WANs, and so appears rather complicated. A logical numbering scheme is overlaid on the physical unit numbers to provide more flexibility for the user. Programming the transfer of data across a LAN using the socket facility is introduced.

Reconnecting the users – email, printers and database

The first computing facilities which became available to a wider group of users were provided by **mainframes** (Fig. 14.1). These expensive leviathans were housed in secure air-conditioned premises consuming prodigious quantities of electricity. The installation of water cooling pipes to each of the main CPU units now makes the miniature fans used in PCs seem quite self-effacing. Each processor sometimes served the needs of hundreds of users, and needed the regular care of several technicians to maintain the operation. They were thankfully replaced for most applications by the less avaricious **minicomputers**. These then became the most common provision during the 1960s and 1970s for office and laboratory computing before networks of PCs again altered the computing landscape. The DEC VAX-11 minicomputer was a very popular choice in the role of the 'departmental' computer. Here, a single processor served the needs of between 5 and 50 people. These computers commonly used character-based VDUs, such as DEC VT100 units, individually connected to the host by dedicated serial lines. With these minicomputers, Unix and the Internet were developed. Strangely, in the initial rush of enthusiasm for desktop PCs, the obvious

Fig. 14.1
Evolution of computing provision.

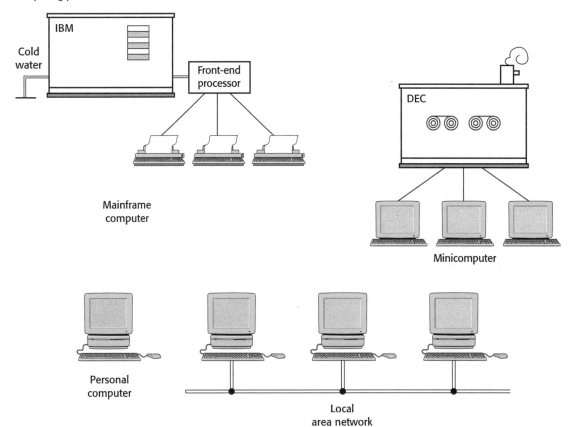

Mainframe computer

Minicomputer

Personal computer

Local area network

need to share files and communicate with others was overlooked, and users found themselves inconveniently isolated from their colleagues. Very soon the widespread installation of **LANs** solved this problem, and now most office PCs and all Unix workstations have LAN interfaces as basic equipment. This allows standardized communication with a variety of other equipment such as printers, gateways and CD-ROM jukeboxes. PCs commonly require the LAN interface on an expansion board which plugs into the PCI extension bus. Several different LAN sockets are provided for connecting to the different types of cable. Sun Unix workstations have always included the LAN interface as original equipment on the motherboard, a decision now being adopted by PC manufacturers. The **LAN interface board**, described more fully in Section 14.2, contains electrical interfacing circuitry, a fast UART, a RAM buffer and a dedicated microprocessor with firmware routines stored in EPROM to manage the low-level data transfer operations. All these items comprise what is commonly referred to as the **MAC** layer (Media Access Layer), and is well below the normal programmer's line of sight. Although for a long time Unix has been supplied with the necessary software to handle networking facilities, it is only recently that Microsoft has considered networking software important enough to integrate into the main operating system. Up until this recent enhancement, Novell has been able to readily exploit the apparent gap in Microsoft's products.

LAN technology can be traced back to the pioneering network established in the 1970s by the University of Hawaii. The university had a particular problem in maintaining communications between the various departments and campus sites scattered around the archipelago, so it was decided to develop a new system based on radio broadcasting. It was hoped to demonstrate that information could be usefully exchanged between the various island campuses by this means, and so reduce the institutional telephone bill. The simple idea was that a data transmitter would first check that the radio band was free, and then start transmitting. All the time the quality of the transmission would be monitored at source, so if another transmitter also started up, in error, the corruption would be noted, and a retransmission attempted. This was the origin of the Ethernet **CSMA/CD** (Carrier Sense, Multiple Access/Collision Detect) scheme, and continues in an improved form in present-day packet radio networks.

Performance displays can reveal the variation in packet traffic along your LAN. In Fig. 14.2, the traffic is being displayed by the Sun `perfmeter` tool. The small blip in the centre is email, while the much larger following surge is due to a large PDF file being transferred across the network to another host.

In the mid-1980s, LANs were widely accepted by business users to regain some of the communal advantages of mainframe computing, which were lost when the personal computer arrived, isolating the users. As the variety of different types of LAN increased, the IEEE started to establish standards, a few of which are listed in Table 14.1. In addition to the LANs there are now several other types of network to take into account. Broadly, these can be classified as **Local**, **Wide** or, recently, **Metro** to distinguish their size, access possibilities and the type of services provided. The term **VAN** (Value Added Network) has been used to emphasize the facilities available through the network, rather than the interconnection technology itself. This chapter deals

Fig. 14.2
Displaying the current
LAN traffic using Sun's
`perfmeter`.

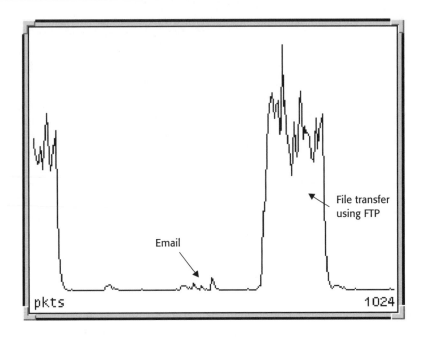

with local area networks (LANs), while Chapter 15 will present the larger Wide Area Networks (WANs).

With the development of office LANs, data sharing and inter-user electronic communication became possible again, and centralized expensive equipment became accessible without the need to walk over to another workstation clutching a floppy disk containing precious data files.

I will deal mainly with the Ethernet LAN running the TCP/IP protocols, although there are other well-established and successful alternatives; Novell NetWare and AppleTalk being the best known. The justification for this choice is that the Internet is based on TCP/IP and that most universities and colleges have access to Unix or Windows NT, both of which offer TCP/IP.

Ethernet was originally configured as a shared media bus, with all the connected devices having equal priority. This unprioritized multiple access arrangement suffered from serious deficiencies when the traffic load surpassed 60%. The very advantage of LAN topology, that there are no point-to-point connections, entails its major weaknesses. Remember that this is a half-duplex **broadcast** scheme, which inherits many of the same problems that radio and television broadcasters have been

Table 14.1
Some of the IEEE 802
Standards Committees.

802.3	CSMA/CD
802.4	Token Bus
802.5	Token Ring
802.6	MAN
802.11	Wireless LAN
802.12	100 Mbps LAN

Fig. 14.3
Traditional office bus
LAN facility.

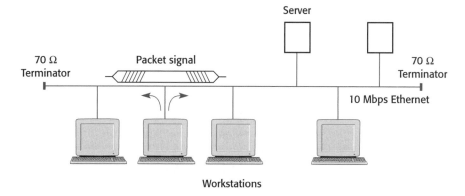

struggling with for many years. Only one transmission per channel can take place at any time or interference will occur, corrupting the message. Security is a significant problem when anyone can listen to any conversation. Allocating the channel fairly among several users who are trying to share the resource becomes a thorny issue too. We will see that some of these difficulties have been dealt with by moving from the bus (Fig. 14.3) to star LANs (Fig. 14.4). Do not think, however, that the star has completely done away with the single channel problem. The dedicated connections to each host can be misinterpreted. A simple **hub** only acts as a central polling station, allowing, yet again, a single transmission at a time and relying on round robin polling to respond to the demands of the attached hosts.

Hubs have between 8 and 24 connection ports for workstations, dedicating each port to a single piece of equipment. The connection is now commonly done not with coaxial cable but with cheaper twisted pair cable. This is known as the **10BaseT** standard. A separate pair of wires is used for transmitting in the two directions, so theoretically full duplex interaction is possible, although this benefit may not be exploited by the software. Hubs still only support a single connection between data ports at any time (Fig. 14.5), but the more sophisticated **Ethernet Switches** are capable of several transfers simultaneously. This really does help to increase the available bandwidth because several conversations between different pairs of ports can be carrying on at the same time. So it is possible for several stations to be communicating independently in parallel: a clear improvement over

Fig. 14.4
Star topology, switched
hub, Ethernet.

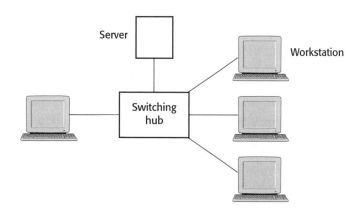

Fig. 14.5
Star topology with
hierarchical hubs.

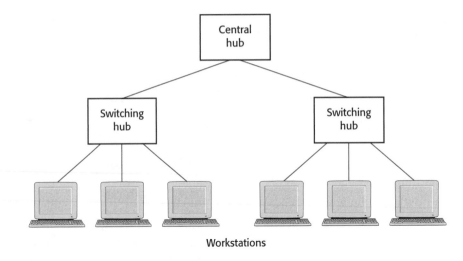

Workstations

the LAN topology. Of course, you are replacing a length of cable with an expensive programmable switch unit, so some progress is to be expected! Hubs can be connected in a hierarchy to take in more hosts than they have ports.

The resource sharing benefits of local area networks have now been fully accepted by computer users. You can retain personal authority over the local processing load, but still have convenient access to other resources. The advantages of fast file transfer, easy email distribution and shared laser printers are clear. But with less use of computer centres' expensive mainframe facilities, the opportunity was seized to reduce the number and skill of technical support staff. The inevitable result of these cutbacks was an increase in the number of network disasters due to poor planning and reduced maintenance. The emerging disadvantages of allowing DIY LAN extensions, unrestricted availability of floppy disk drives and widespread use of Internet browsers, clogging the available bandwidth, still remain to be confronted. Distributed misery is not an uncommon viewpoint of network users. Managing a 100 user central server is probably easier than keeping up with a network of 100 hyperactive PCs! Practical experience with large LANs, using the excellent Sun NFS product to share data and programs transparently across a network, reaffirms the adage 'You never get anything for nothing'. The daily advantages of network interconnectivity can leave the whole system susceptible to single-point failures. This vulnerability can be quite a surprise to regular users when they discover that they are completely dependent on the services of an unheard of computer hidden in a distant cupboard.

14.2   PC network interface – cabling and interface card

The cable commonly used for **Ethernet** bus LAN is known as coax (short for coaxial cable). It is similar to that used to connect your television through to the roof aerial, and has only a single copper core surrounded by a concentric screening braid. This means that Ethernet has to operate in half-duplex mode, there being no separate transmit and receive pathways. Equipment taps into the LAN using **T-piece** connectors, illustrated in Fig. 14.7. But although this is cheap and convenient, it does lead to occasional reliability problems when people disconnect and move equipment without correctly refitting the T-piece connectors. A single break in the LAN stops it all working. Unfortunately it does not then split into two separate, viable networks! Oddly enough, this shortcoming is due to the speed of the electrical signals, which propagate at somewhere near 1/3 the speed of light. Note from Fig. 14.3 the **terminators** at the extreme ends of the LAN. If these 70 Ω resistor stubs are unplugged the network will certainly fail. This is due to the high-speed electrical signals behaving like waves and 'bouncing off' the open cable ends back along the LAN. This interferes with the signals still travelling up the cable, in the same way that water waves, crashing against the harbour wall, are reflected back into the newly approaching wavefronts, creating complex interference patterns. Connecting the terminating stubs allows the electrical energy to be absorbed and converted to heat, though not very much because the Ethernet runs at only 1.4 V!

A positive benefit stemming from this inconvenience is that any reflected signals returning up the cable from an unterminated end can be detected and used by cable testers to locate breaks in the Ethernet. By measuring the time-of-flight, there and back, it is possible to calculate the distance covered by the signal, which travels at around 1/3 the speed of light (1/3 of 3×10^8 m s^{-1}).

The change from coax to multi-core twisted pair cable has meant a change from half-duplex to the potential for full duplex transmissions. One pair can be used to transmit and another to receive. It should be noted that although the hardware may be prepared to support this change, it is quite another thing to get the software to exploit the facility immediately! The move from 10Base2 coax to 10BaseT twisted pair cable has also increased the possibilities of wiring error. Figure 14.6 illustrates the wiring connections to an RJ45 plug. The 10BaseT connections are the two pairs 1 + 2 and 3 + 6. These are termed Pair 2 and Pair 3 in the official documentation.

Although the most obvious aspect of network connections is the cabling between machines, far more significant is the **software** which enables the messages to be passed

Fig. 14.6
Connections to an RJ45
LAN plug.

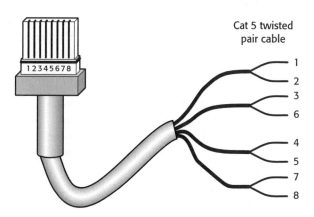

Cat 5 twisted
pair cable

Fig. 14.7
A PC network interface
card with 10Base2 and
10BaseT connectors.

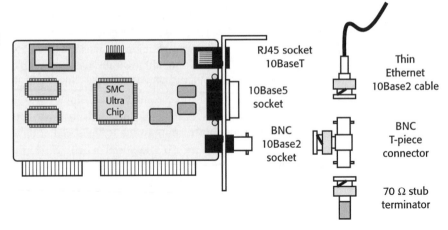

from source to destination without any errors occurring. The most common LAN systems have used **Novell** NetWare for PCs and **TCP/IP** for Unix hosts, but with Windows NT also offering TCP/IP the situation may change. These suites of software have defined **protocols** which means that the messages sent between machines must be structured in a pre-agreed fashion. Communications take place within a tightly specified set of rules, but where two sets of distinct protocols are incompatible, they can interwork over the same network when the correct software is available. The success of TCP/IP as a reliable protocol for WANs and its distribution with the Unix operating system helped it also to become the standard for LANs. This may be surprising, because some of the specially designed alternatives, such as Novell's SPX/ IPX and Xerox's XNS, could have been seen as more suitable for this application area.

Chipsets for LAN interfacing, as shown on the Ethernet card in Fig. 14.7, are readily available from Intel, AMD and Motorola. They are complex dedicated processors, presenting another problem for the low-level programmer to deal with. The 10 Mbit data rate requires more sophisticated hardware than the RS232 UART described earlier in the book. The principal problem is removing the incoming data from the port before it gets overwritten by the following bytes. If this were to be done under interrupt, as with COM1 UARTS, there would be bursts of interrupt activity coming in at 10 MHz. This would simply lock out other CPU activity, even with 500 MHz Pentiums. The solution is to use **local buffering** and then transfer the incoming data from the LAN in blocks using a **DMA** controller. Note that there is no need for modems when connecting to Ethernet because the signalling is done at the original data rate. This is called **Baseband Signalling**, there is no high-frequency 'carrier' to worry about. You might ask why your television cable can handle many channels while Ethernet is limited to a single one. This is because the television signals are all modulated onto higher frequency carrier signals, of which there are many to chose from. It is then possible to transfer several of these high-frequency signals at the same time down the same cable without suffering any mutual interference. Such broadband signalling, using radio frequencies, has been adopted by the cable television networks, which will be further discussed in Section 16.7. It requires all transmitters and

Fig. 14.8
Hardware and software
layers to manage the
LAN interface.

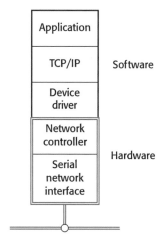

receivers to be equipped with modulators and demodulators, which of course increases the connection cost.

Managing the network interface requires both hardware and software. The traditional way of describing the network interface is in terms of the functional layers. The bottom layers are mediated by hardware and the upper layers by software (Fig. 14.8). This is not necessary in any absolute sense, and may alter in the future. Just as the much slower serial lines can be dealt with entirely by software, so the LAN interface may become a completely hardware-driven facility.

As with the previous discussion concerning RS232 serial data transmission, Ethernet also has to provide solutions to the synchronization and flow control problems. Flow control will be discussed in Chapter 15 because it involves the TCP layer of software, but synchronization can be dealt with here.

In Section 10.2 it was explained that the receiver must have frequency and phase information to capture the value of the bits arriving at its input port correctly. The synchronous method was considered superior but it required sending the transmitter clock signal along with the data so that the receiver has a clear indication of when the middle point of a bit has arrived. This would seem to demand a second wire to carry the clock, but the technique adopted was to logically combine the transmitter clock signal with the data stream and send the combined signal to the receiver. This became known as Manchester encoding and involves using a clock running at twice the bit rate. For the standard Ethernet that would mean 20 MHz, as illustrated in Fig. 14.9.

The data stream of bits waiting to be sent is XORed with the clock signal as it emerges from the transmitter. The resulting transmission code becomes:

rising edge: 0, dropping edge: 1

The receiver has the advantage of always seeing nice edges, so extracting a clock signal is made easier. The frequency of the incoming, extracted, clock and the local oscillator clock are compared (using an XOR gate!) and the 'difference' signal is used to retune the oscillator. It works very reliably. The incoming data can now be

Fig. 14.9
Manchester encoding for
data and clock.

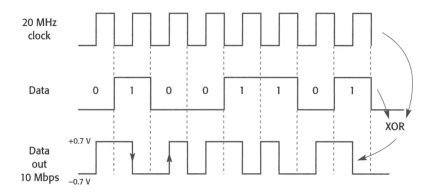

accurately sampled in mid-bit using this clock to time the readings. If Manchester encoding was not employed there would be a problem when the data contained a run of 0s or 1s, because the receiver would have no idea when one bit ended and the next began. It would be as if the transmitter clock had been unplugged. To help the receiver get well synchronized, Ethernet hosts send a sequence of seven special flag bytes before starting to transmit a packet:

10101010 10101010 10101010 101010100 101010100 101010100 10101010

This is known as the **preamble** pattern and the Ethernet receiver has a circuit for detecting the 8 bit flag sequence. As stated in Section 10.2, communications all need synchronization at three levels: bit, byte and message. To cater for the byte level, immediately before the packet starts the preamble is changed to the **SFD** sequence (Start of Frame Delimiter) 10101011. The receiver takes this as a signal that the packet is about to arrive and registers the start of byte point:

10101010 10101010 10101010 10101010 10101011 [Ethernet packet body...]
                                        ↑

The whole operation depends on the reliable detection of a single 'start' bit in the SFD byte. It is a worrying thought! The preamble provides no assistance with byte phase synchronization.

14.3 Ethernet – carrier sense, multiple access/collision detect

When you pick up the telephone handset you expect to hear the dial tone, which is a signal from the local exchange telling you that it is ready and willing to accept instructions. If no dial tone is audible, there would be no point in entering a subscriber number because the exchange is indicating that it is too busy and cannot offer you a connection. (Failure of dial tone can also result from an injudicious application of a

Table 14.2
Various Ethernet media standards.

10Base5	10 Mbps	Thick Ethernet
	500 m segment length	
	minimum tap separation 2.5 m	
	maximum of four repeaters	
	50 Ω coax cable	
	vampire tap (Media Access Unit)	
10Base2	10 Mbps	Thin Ethernet
	200 m (165 m) segment length	
	minimum tap separation 0.5 m	
	maximum of four repeaters	
	70 Ω coax cable	
	BNC T-piece bayonet connection	
10BaseT	10 Mbps	Switched Ethernet
	100 m segment length	
	end-to-end, simplex	
	100 Ω AWG24 twisted pair cable	
	RJ45 telecom jack	
100BaseT	100 Mbps	
	205 m segment length	
	end-to-end, simplex	
	100 Ω AWG24 twisted pair cable	
100BaseF	100 Mbps	Fibre Ethernet
	2000 m segment length	
	end-to-end, simplex	
	optic fibres	

pneumatic drill, causing a physical break in your circuit!) Telephone exchanges are shared resources and rarely have the capacity to deal with all of their subscribers requesting service at the same time. The issue of how to allocate time on a shared facility is also basic to the operation of LANs and is encapsulated in the access protocol, which for Ethernet is known as Carrier Sense, Multiple Access.

The Ethernet network protocol was originally devised by a consortium of three companies: Xerox, DEC and Intel. Although the physical medium has changed since the standards were first published (Table 14.2), the original protocol has been preserved. The access protocol has to work with a simple bus topology, democratically conceived without any master unit. It relies on an ingenious technique to avoid more than one station transmitting at a time: **CSMA/CD** (Carrier Sense, Multiple Access/ Collision Detect). When a computer wants to send packets it first checks whether the line is free. When it is clear of traffic the transmission can begin. But there is still a danger of two stations checking the line and then starting to send data simultaneously, resulting in a corruption of all their transmitted data. To resolve this situation all stations continually monitor the line throughout transmissions and stop ('back off') immediately they detect more than one transmission taking place. Stations even deliberately start transmitting a jamming signal to force other stations to recognize the collision event and respond correctly. They return to transmission only after a random delay period of 10–100 ms. Should the conflict recur the delay range is increased. There is no provision for prioritizing stations or packets, which, although fair to all users, makes the transfer of real-time voice or video traffic unreliable because it will be blocked in an unpredictable way by the transmissions from other stations.

The propagation speed of a signal down the cable and the duration of a packet in transmission are important parameters when reviewing the mechanism of collision detection. The speed of light is 3×10^8 m s^{-1}, while an electrical signal on a wire travels at about 1×10^8 m s^{-1}. Therefore it would take a signal only 25 μs to travel from one end of a 2500 m LAN to the other ($2500/10^8$). The selection of 2500 m for the maximum segment length of Ethernet depends on signal attenuation. The cable is not a perfect conductor and will gradually reduce the voltage as it passes along until it is too small for the receiver to reliably detect it. Repeaters can be inserted to boost the signal, but these then introduce further time delays.

A transmitter must know if its packet has suffered a collision with another one before the last bit has departed. The collision warning must get back to the source before the transmission has completed. After that it would be too late to do anything. This means that when we consider the worst-case scenario for a LAN, concerning stations at extreme ends of the cable, with the maximum length of LAN, allowing a factor of 2 for the return journey of the collision signal back up the LAN, the minimum packet length can be calculated. When other hosts are attached to the LAN, they degrade the quality of the signal, so a maximum segment length of 500 m has been imposed with a maximum number of 4 repeaters to gain the 2500 m reach.

$$T_{\text{packet}} = \frac{500 \times 5 \times 2}{1 \times 10^8} = 50 \, \mu s$$

$$t_{\text{bit}} = 0.1 \, \mu s$$

$$N_{\text{packet}} = \frac{50}{0.1} = 500 \text{ bits}$$

$$N_{\text{bytes}} = \frac{500}{8} = 62.5 \approx 64 \text{ bytes}$$

In practice, this value of 500 bits is rounded up to give 64 bytes as the minimum length of a packet with a maximum length of 10Base5 Ethernet. From Fig. 14.10 you can see that the longer the minimum packet, the better the collision detection margin. The worst situation is illustrated, where the second station starts to transmit just the instant before the first packet bit arrives. Any signal existing on the LAN would of course have inhibited the second station from starting to transmit, so the danger period is the interlude between the launching of a packet and the arrival of the first bit at another station.

Fig. 14.10
Collision detection and
transit times for
Ethernet.

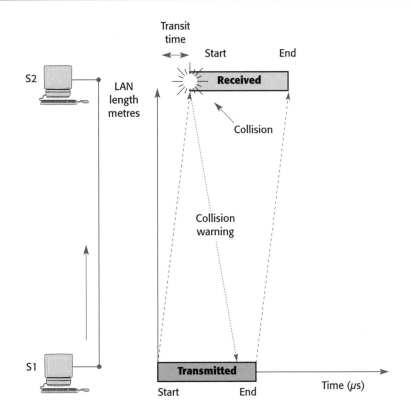

It is during the **transit time** (Fig. 14.10) that a second station may start transmitting and create confusion for the receivers. As soon as the first packet starts to arrive, this second station will realize that the line is not free.

An interesting new standard is 100Base4T which bundles four twisted pairs together in a cable. To reduce the specification of the cable, and so keep the cost down, a category was selected that could not reliably transmit signals faster than 30 Mbps. This posed a problem: how do you squeeze 100 Mbps down a 30 Mbps wire? The solution was to abandon two-level signalling and adopt a three-level code. So we have +0.7 V, 0 and –0.7 V, representing trinary. If we adopt the three digit symbols –, 0 and + for this discussion (see Table 14.3) we can list them in a table against their binary equivalents. If we want to represent any byte (0–255 decimal or 0000_0000–1111_1111 binary) in trinary, it would require 6 trits (trinary bits). This is because $3^5 = 243$, which is less than 256, and the next value is $3^6 = 729$, which is acceptably greater than 256. Thus the number 255 can be expressed by three decimal digits, 8 bits or 6 trits. This numerical encoding is termed 8B6T, which is easy to remember! In Chapter 16 we will encounter the 2B1Q coding scheme used for ISDN transmissions. To further help the receiver, the set of 256 trinary codes does not simply run up from zero, but has been selected to contain at least two voltage transitions. As only 256 patterns from the 729 available patterns are needed, there is scope for selecting the more suitable ones, and leaving the others in the Hamming ditch to assist with error detection. If bemused, you should look back to Section 10.3!

Table 14.3
8B6T coding.

Binary	Trinary
0000 0000	+ − 0 0 + − T
0000 0001	0 + − + − + T
0000 0010	+ − 0 + − 0 T
0000 0011	− 0 + + − 0 T
0000 0100	− 0 + 0 + − T
0000 0101	0 + − − 0 + T
0000 0110	+ − 0 − 0 + T
0000 0111	− 0 + − 0 + T
0000 1000	− + 0 0 + − T
0000 1001	0 − + + − 0 T
0000 1010	− + 0 + − 0 T
0000 1011	+ 0 − + − 0 T
0000 1100	+ 0 − 0 + − T
0000 1101	0 − + − 0 + T
0000 1110	− + 0 − 0 + T
0000 1111	+ 0 − − 0 + T
...	...
1111 1111	+ 0 − + 0 0 T

14.4 LAN addressing – logical and physical schemes

Manufacturers of network interface hardware install a unique 48 bit identifier or address in each unit. This is sometimes referred to as the **MAC** number (Media Access Control). The allocation of blocks of these numbers is supervised by the IEEE Registration Authority. Normally only Ethernet chip or board manufacturers are involved in obtaining new numbers. Although the Ethernet address is usually fixed at the factory, alternative configurable schemes are employed on some systems, whereby the workstation IP number is used to generate part of the Ethernet address. The Ethernet packet header (Fig. 14.11) has three fields, with a trailer field containing a CRC error check number. If the Type field contains 800, the payload will be an IP datagram. In Chapter 15 the structure of an IP packet will be described, explaining how a further pair of IP addresses are also included. The 48 bit MAC destination address is important because it is always used as the next-hop direction. Ethernet receivers read this 48 bit MAC destination address field as the packets pass by. Any packet holding the reader's address (or a broadcast address) will then continue to be read into the input buffer. Such a scheme avoids having to read all the passing packets, and also does not involve the main CPU in any activity at all. However, the manner in which a host discovers the hardware address of another host does raise many problems and complexities.

Fig. 14.11
Internal structure of an
Ethernet data packet.

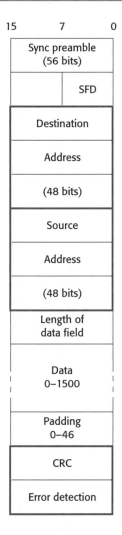

With a small group of workstations connected to a single Ethernet, all their hardware addresses could be written into a reference file manually which would then be copied to each host. If a packet is seen to have a 'foreign' destination address it would either be ignored or redirected to the **gateway** machine which would pass it onto the wider network. However, this solution soon becomes impossible to maintain, due to daily changes and hardware failures. When many LANs are interlinked the simple manual solution fails completely because of the impossibility of achieving reliable routing.

Another problem occurs when addresses are tied to low-level hardware. If an Ethernet interface card needs to be swapped out, the result would be a complete change of the computer's LAN identity, which would be an unacceptable situation. Would people tolerate an arrangement where their telephone number had to change every time the handset failed?

The mechanism adopted to circumvent both the previous problems involved the establishment of a second set of addresses – virtual IDs. These are known as **IP numbers** (Internet Protocol Numbers). Strangely, they were set at only 32 bit, shorter than the physical MAC numbers. IP numbers are usually referred to in dotted-decimal form: 164.11.9.90, where each digit group (0–255) represents 8 bits, while MAC numbers are presented in hex colon format: 08:00:20:8e:86:5f. Every network device is allocated an IP number by the local systems administrator. If the Ethernet hardware ID changes there is no difficulty because the existing IP number will continue to work with the new card.

IP version 4 numbers, such as 164.11.10.206, are functionally divided into four parts. The top few bits specifies the Class of IP number, then comes the site ID, then the so-called subnet identifier; finally, the lower part identifies the actual machine. This separation into fields is important to understand when networks are being configured and ranges of addresses need to be allocated to each LAN segment. Remember, only the lower subnet + host values can be revised by the local administrator; the upper network (domain) part has been allocated to your site by the Internet Assigned Number Authority (NIC).

Figure 14.12 lists the five 'classes' of IP number. The Class B numbers are the most useful, with 256 subnets each capable of attaching 256 hosts. Unfortunately these are mostly used up, so multiple Class C numbers are often allocated to a single organization instead. The site ID is obtained from a central bureau to avoid address clashes. The local system administrator who manages the site network will set the subnet values to distinguish between the local site LANS, with many host machines on each. Whereas the net/user division is specified by the leading bits in the IP number, the subnet/host division is specified by the local 'subnet mask', which has to be installed during system initialization. These details will loom again in Chapter 15, where we discuss Internet routing.

Fig. 14.12
The five forms of IPv4 numbers and their ranges.

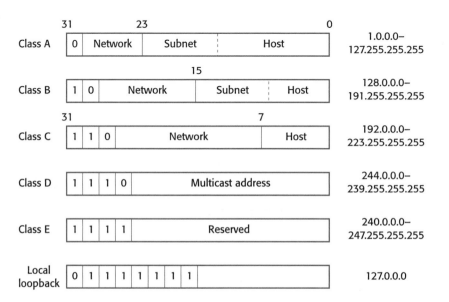

The 'directory enquiries' problem, however, was not solved by the introduction of IP numbers. If anything it was exacerbated by organizing their allocation not by any geographical or topological criteria, but by how many hosts the applicant was likely to acquire! It also doubled the number of identifiers to be managed and introduced the possibility of dynamically changing IP–MAC pairings. Nevertheless, so far the IPv4 scheme has worked reasonably well. Millions of packets are successfully routed every second throughout the worldwide Internet.

For small isolated LANs the mapping from IP address to Ethernet MAC ID can be done statically. A file could be maintained by the system administrator and copied to all the workstations only when a change occurs. When an IP packet needs to be transmitted, the destination IP address can be used to obtain the Ethernet number from this file. Unfortunately, such a straightforward approach would quickly fail in the normal everyday run of events.

The method adopted on many Unix systems is called **ARP** (Address Resolution Protocol). Hosts automatically maintain a lookup table to hold pairs of IP and Ethernet (MAC) numbers. You can inspect this table directly using the `arp -a` command (Fig. 14.13), but you may have to search out the directory where it is hidden on your system. Manual entries can be inserted into the ARP table by the administrator, but it is more common to rely on the ARP process itself to maintain the table. It does this by sending out a query packet when it cannot find a matching MAC number in the ARP table. All the neighbouring hosts on the LAN see this ARP request packet, which contains the unmatched IP number. If any recognize it as their own they will immediately respond with details of their MAC number. The instigator of the ARP exchange can then update the local ARP table with the returned value and dispatch the waiting data packet, now correctly addressed. If no reply is received to an ARP request it will probably result in the data being sent once again to the default gateway!

Fig. 14.13
ARP table, translating IP addresses into MAC numbers.

```
rob@milly [20]/usr/sbin/arp-a
Net to Media Table
Device    IP Addr        Mask          Flags  Phys Addr
---------------------------------------------------------
hme0      lentil    255.255.255.255      00:00:8e:06:07:cf
hme1      pb4       255.255.255.255      00:80:5f:cc:5c:20
hme0      rice      255.255.255.255      00:00:8e:06:07:e9
hme0      beans     255.255.255.255      00:00:8e:06:07:c4
hme1      ivor      255.255.255.255      08:00:20:1a:9d:16
hme0      carrot    255.255.255.255      00:00:8e:06:07:e6
hme1      router8   255.255.255.255      08:00:20:19:1c:9a
hme0      hops      255.255.255.255      00:80:8e:06:07:e3
rob@milly [21]
```

Fig. 14.14
Hosts table: translating
host names into IP
addresses.

```
rob@olveston [20]cat /etc/host

# Internet host table
#
127.0.0.1          localhost
164.11.10.206      olveston        loghost
164.11.8.16        egg ns0
164.11.253.2       sister ns1
164.11.8.99        ada ns2
164.11.10.5        riff ns3

rob@olveston [21]
```

14.5   Host names – another layer of translation

To further promote confusion, following MAC and IP numbers, a third nomencla-ture, using abbreviated names, such as olveston.uwe.ac.uk, was introduced. This was intended to avoid the need for users to remember their 32 bit IP numbers. Once again, some translation was required, this time from acronym to IP number. It was felt that requiring a 32 bit IP number to send email to a colleague would not be very satisfac-tory. (Despite the fact that we have successfully managed 11 digit telephone numbers, equivalent to 77 bits in ASCII, or 37 bits in integer format). Nevertheless, it is far more convenient to remember friendly mnemonics instead. The computer can assist by maintaining a lookup table, called the hosts table, in which IP numbers and host name pairs are stored. When a packet of data is being assembled, the destination address can be obtained from the hosts table using the host name. The hosts table must be regu-larly updated, either manually by the systems administrator (Fig. 14.14), or more likely using the Domain Naming Service (DNS) which provides a remote lookup service over the Internet. This is further explained in Chapter 15.

14.6   Layering and encapsulation – TCP/IP software stack

The **TCP/IP** protocols are a set of rules and definitions which allow computers from a wide variety of vendors to exchange data packets across a network. Because they were originally intended for use within WANs they will be more fully explained in Chapter 15, but we still need to mention them here because they have been very successfully

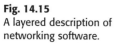
Fig. 14.15
A layered description of networking software.

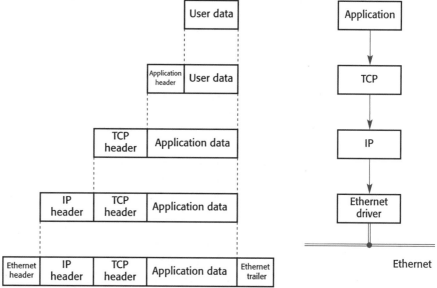

used in the less demanding field of LAN transmissions. The structure of the software responsible for implementing the TCP/IP protocols for data communications is organized in a vertical stack. Each layer administers a specific protocol. The application sits at the top and calls procedures from the layer immediately below. This layer then accepts data from above, repackages it, and passes it on to the lower layers. A similar sequence is employed for incoming data, but it passes upward through the TCP/IP stack, shown in Fig. 14.15. It appears to get progressively unwrapped until the final data payload is revealed and passed to the target application.

14.7 Networked file systems – sharing files across a network

Unix allows users with administrators' permissions to **mount** and unmount file systems onto the root file system. This is the normal way of extending the filing capacity when installing new drives. Most Unix commands will be unable to deal with files held on a new disk drive until the file system is correctly mounted. On Unix, a table holding all the information about the mounted file systems is held in a file called /etc/mnttab.

Sun Microsystems extended this facility by introducing, a scheme known as **NFS**, which allowed Unix hosts, and other networked computers provided with the appropriate software, to access files and directories transparently across the network. The remote mounting scheme was not limited to computers running the Unix operating system, and PC-NFS enabled PC users to integrate their file systems into a wider structure. The action depends on the already existing Remote Procedure Call (RPC) facility which allows a program running on one computer to start up and benefit from a program on another computer, receiving the results back over the network. For systems administrators as well as ordinary users the chance to mount remote file systems for local access was a real boon. It meant that you no longer had to copy files between machines – all that became unnecessary because the files on any connected host could be made visible and accessible without having to employ special transfer instruction, like rcp, uucp or ftp. Your file system can be inspected by the mount command, or more usefully using df, as shown in Fig. 14.16. To mount and unmount file systems does, however, require administrator permissions.

The information from the Unix df (disk free) command concerns the amount of disk space used by file systems. It also reveals where all the parts of a workstation's file system are actually sitting. In this case, Olveston's local hard drive (c0t0d0) holds the root (/), usr, var, tmp, cache and local directories, But you can see that the directory /usr/misc is imported from the host named thalia, while files within tutorials are actually held on milly. Similarly, the file system mail comes from the host mailhub, projects from ada, and so on. This is how NFS makes files available transparently throughout a network.

With Windows NT a similar network facility is obtained through the drive mapping option. This allows a user to nominate some part of a remote file system, if access permission allows, as a virtual drive. This is illustrated in Fig. 14.17, which shows the Windows NT directory Explorer being used to set up a network drive. It is obtained with a right mouse click on the Start button, followed by selecting Explore → Tools → Map Network Drive. Once a directory has been mapped into your machine it behaves much like a local disk drive, except for the longer access times!

Fig. 14.16
Inspecting the state of a Unix file system using df.

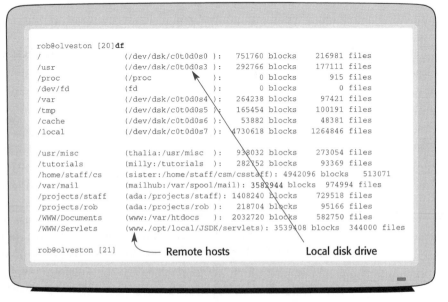

Fig. 14.17
Installing a virtual drive
using Windows NT.

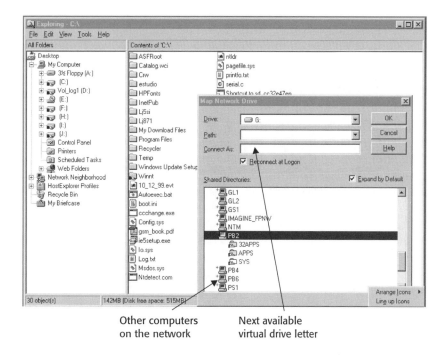

Other computers   Next available
on the network   virtual drive letter

14.8 Interconnecting networks – gateways

LANs are quite frequently connected to other LANs. This can simply mean extending the LAN into another room or building by physically joining the cable. However, when the interconnections become complex, or the combined traffic too heavy, it becomes necessary to partition the network system to maintain the desired level of service. As far as possible the independence of the local segments should be protected to avoid flooding the LAN with unnecessary traffic. It is not ideal to broadcast all the packets over all the networks when most traffic is really destined for a neighbouring host or printer. This partitioning is the role of the **gateway** unit, shown in Fig. 14.18. This is a piece of equipment, or a computer with at least two network ports. Its job is to pass only the properly addressed packets through to the other network. Host computers on the networks know the box as the default gateway which means that when a packet has an IP address that is unknown in the ARP table it will be given the MAC address of the gateway and sent more in hope than knowledge to the gateway box.

14.9 Socket programming – an introduction to WinSock

One of the most useful facilities available on a wide variety of operating systems is the **socket.** This allows programmers to establish communication between processes

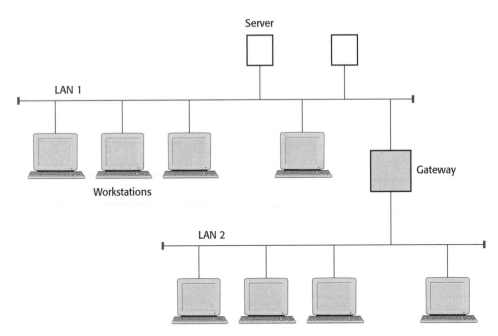

Fig. 14.18
Interconnecting bus
LANs using a
gateway.

running on different computers connected by a TCP/IP network. Because the
protocol is associated with the TCP/IP definition, rather than a proprietary operating
system, it is possible to achieve intercommunication, as in Fig. 14.19, between a
program running on Unix and another program running on Windows NT (or whatever). It provides a common interface which can be relied on. There are two types of
socket which are of concern to programmers. The **datagram** socket allows a computer
to send a single message, while the **stream** socket supports an ongoing data exchange
or conversation between the participating processes.

A socket address has two components: the IP number of the host and a port
number to identify the process involved on that host. The role of the port number will
be further described in Chapter 15.

The programmer deals with the socket very similarly to a file, with special system
calls to initialize and connect the sockets, pass data and finally close down the connection. If the two communicating processes reside on the same Unix machine, the
sockets can be addressed by path name. But if, as is more common, the processes are

Fig. 14.19
Socket communication
between remote
processes on alien
systems.

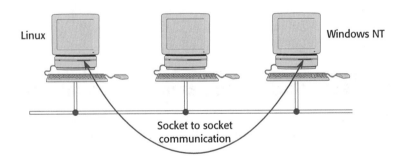

on different machines, the sockets have to be associated with the machine's IP number and a port number. Sockets are closely associated with TCP and UDP ports, which will be introduced in more detail in Chapter 15.

Because there are two processes participating in such communications, it is important to distinguish their roles. One will act as the **Server** and the other the **Client**. The server will wait for a request from a client. The request may be to read or write information, so do not confuse the direction of data flow with which process is responsible for initiating a transaction. The client initiates; the server responds. Data may end up flowing in either direction, depending on the needs of the client and the service

Fig. 14.20
Communication with client–server connection-based (STREAM) sockets.

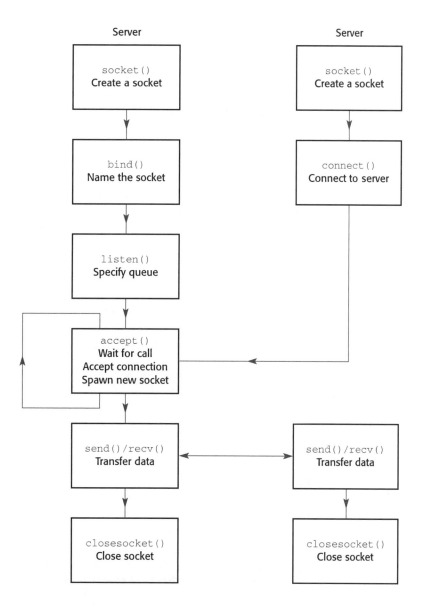

offered by the server. The server has to exist, and be known about, before a client can successfully connect to it and use its facilities.

As illustrated in Fig. 14.20 for a STREAM channel, the server computer creates a public socket using the `socket( )` call. Then, using `bind( )`, the process, local IP number and port number (Section 15.2) are all bound together. This enables a client process to establish a network connection with the server process using the IP and port numbers of the server machine. Once the server has set up the socket it can sit back and wait for a customer to ask for service. The `listen( )` call declares a willingness to accept incoming connections from client processes and optimistically opens up a queue. `Accept( )` blocks the server process until a request arrives. When a client does request service, using the `connect( )` call, the server wakes up and uses `accept( )` to register the client's address. A new socket is spawned, a quick exchange is made between client and server, and the communications channel is established for data trasfer until the session is terminated. The point of spawning a new socket for each client is to free up the publicly known socket for fresh contacts to be made. In addition, it is common to `fork( )` a new process to look after each new socket. This will be further explained in Section 17.7. Windows NT can do the same thing by initiating a new process thread for each new socket. Data can then be exchanged by employing the `send( )` and `recv( )` functions without disturbing other socket activity. The Win32 socket function calls are presented in Fig. 14.21 with their parameter lists. The socket arrangement may seem rather crude when contrasted with the efforts made elsewhere to mask technical detail and offer 'user-friendly' mnemonics.

When building the socket code for Windows NT using the Microsoft Developer Studio, it is essential to include the header file `winsock.h` in the source file, and the library `wsock32.lib` on the link line. This latter operation is achieved by selecting the Developer Studio project options Build → Settings → Object → Libraries, and adding `wsock.lib` at the end of the link list. Do not overlook the online help supplied by Developer Studio or the relevant Unix man pages! Fig. 14.22 illustrates the slightly simpler datagram version of a socket connection where a server accepts single messages without establishing an enduring communications channel. The function calls are more elaborate due to the need to pass a full destination address for each message.

Fig. 14.21
Win32 socket function calls.

```
SOCKET socket(int af, int typesock, int protocol)

int bind(SOCKET mysock, const struct sockaddr *psock, int nlength)

int listen(SOCKET mysock, int qmax)

int connect(SOCKET yoursock, const struct sockaddr *sname, int nlength)

SOCKET accept(SOCKET mysock, struct sockaddr *psock, int *addrlen)

int send(SOCKET yoursock, const char *pdbuff, int dblen, int flags)

int recv(SOCKET mysock, char *pdbuff, int dblen)

int closesocket(SOCKET mysock)
```

Fig. 14.22
Communication with
client–server
connectionless
(datagram) sockets.

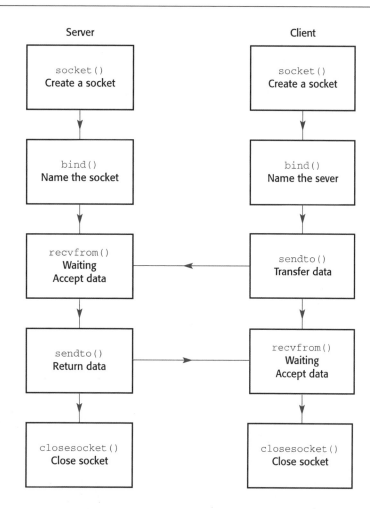

Review

- Local area networks (LANs) have been very successful in reconnecting users of personal workstations so that they can exchange email, benefit from central filing and generally share resources.

- The traditional shared bus LAN topology has given way to a hierarchically organized star or tree configuration in an attempt to increase available bandwidths.

- LANs, including Ethernet, rely on a broadcast routing scheme. Every connected station sees all the packets, but saves only those with the correct destination address.

- PCs still generally require a network interface card to be installed in an ISA or PCI slot for network connection.

- Ethernet adopted the CSMA/CD network allocation strategy. This works well at lower traffic rates, but does not provide high enough bandwidth (10/100 Mbps) for a shared highway. There is also no packet prioritization scheme.

- The inconvenience of using hardware defined numbers is avoided by adopting a second address, the IP number, for packet addressing. However, a translation back to the hardware version still has to be done using the ARP table.

- The TCP/IP network protocols are a set of definitions and rules which allow the interconnection of computers from different suppliers. Originally they were intended for use with WANs.

- The ability to access file systems on remote computers is a very useful network facility. Both Unix and Windows support this.

- LANs are interconnected by units called gateways. These route packets between neighbouring networks.

- Programmers can send data to remote computers across the network by using the socket communication functions.

Practical work

The recommended practical work involves accessing your LAN, initially using the standard utilities (telnet, ftp, nfs), then the more specialist tools (arp, ifconfig) and finally by writing simple socket programs in C. This really gets you into networks from the bottom up.

Exercises

1. List some advantages and disadvantages of connecting PCs to a LAN.

2. What is the transmission bandwidth (bit rate) of Ethernet? If you had a 20 Mbyte image file to transfer, how long might that take? What factors can influence the result?

3. How many bits are there in an IP address? How many bits are there in an Ethernet MAC number? Can you find out the value of these numbers for your workstation?

4. How does the computer translate a host name into an IP address? How does it determine the destination MAC number from the IP address?

5. What is meant by the term 'baseband signalling'? Does this scheme require modem equipment? What are the advantages and disadvantages of baseband signalling?

6. Ethernet employs synchronous transmission because the source station broadcasts clock and data information. How is this possible on 10Base2 when there is only a single wire to use? Is it wise to rely on a single bit to signal the start of a packet?

7. What receiver synchronization techniques are used by Ethernet? What flow control method is used?

8. What is the maximum segment length for 10 Mbps Ethernet? What parameters determine this value and how can it then be calculated?

9. List some of the advantages and disadvantages of the two Ethernet topologies: Bus and Star. Read up on the other arrangement: Ring.

10. Try out and then explain what the following Unix network utilities might be used for. The Unix online manual man can be a starting point.

```
/usr/sbin/arp -a
/usr/sbin/ifconfig -a
telnet
ftp
```

Use the NT command prompt window and try them there (use `ipconfig` not `ifconfig`).

11. Is TCP/IP a suitable protocol for use on LANs? What were the principal reasons for its adoption as a LAN protocol? Will Novell NetWare disappear now that Windows NT offers TCP/IP?

12. What advantages would fibre optics bring to networking? As light travels faster than electricity, does its speed increase the data transfer rate? If not, why does FDDI (Fibre Distributed Data Interface) have a higher bandwidth than other networks? Is the role of high-speed parallel buses being eroded?

13. The IPv4 numbering scheme is described in Fig. 14.12. Class A, Class B and Class C allow for different numbers of hosts within a single IP domain (network). How many does each class provide? What type of organization would each one be suitable for? How will IPv6 divide its vast array of 2^{128} numbers?

14. Use a packet monitor, such as `perfmeter`, and deliberately load up the LAN so that you can see the packet traffic.

15. Sketch the Manchester encoding for the data 0001 1011 0110 1101. Does it matter whether you start as a 0 or a 1?

Readings

- Comer (1999)

- Hodson (1997), a good introductory text.

- Stevens (1994)

- Stevens (1998)

- Some useful introductory pages can be found at:
    http://www.rad.com/networks/1996/fasteth/intro.htm
    http://www.well.com/user/nac/alt-winsock-faq.html

- Heuring and Jordan (1997), Section 10.3: local area networks.

- An interesting introduction by one of the leading equipment suppliers is available:
    http://www-fr.cisco.com/univercd/cc/td/doc/cisintwk/ito_doc/
    introlan.htm

- A full introduction to Unix socket programming is available at:
    http://www.scit.wlv.ac.uk/~jphb/comms/sockets.html#ip

- The Web sites can be accessed via the Companion Web site for this book at:
    http://www.booksites.net/williams/

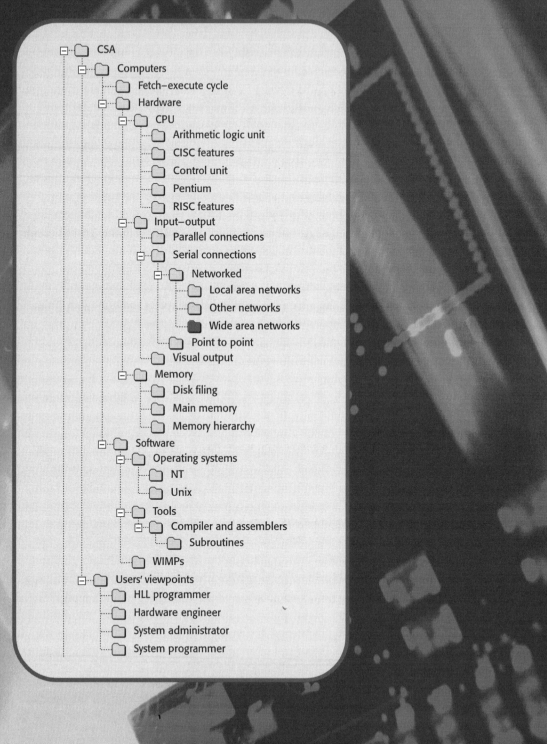

Wide area networks

15

Overview

The development of WANs started in the USA with ARPAnet and NSFnet, but soon encompassed LAN technology and spread out into other areas. The TCP/IP protocols became an essential part of the standardization and promulgation of networking techniques. Unix played a central role because TCP/IP was bundled up in the software releases from a very early stage. Routing packets through an 'unknown' network required the development of dynamic routing schemes, of which a range now exists. The use of a separate naming scheme to reference Internet hosts requires the translation from name to IP number. This is done using a distributed database: DNS. The WWW introduced the Internet to a much wider group of users. The search engines offer an essential indexing and searching facility without which the WWW would be considerably less useful.

15.1   The Internet – origins

The field of wide area networks (**WANs**) has only recently become the centre of intense commercial and technical interest. Governments have recognized the key role to be played by communication facilities through the worldwide **Internet**. This relies on the interconnection of thousands of diverse networks comprising millions of computers. Now, wiring together large numbers of computers requires special software as well as the more obvious hardware links. The outstanding success of the **World Wide Web** in opening up the Internet resources has only just begun to be exploited by individuals and businesses in all manner of ways.

The starting point for all of this was the ARPAnet which was funded by the US Department of Defense for WAN research in the 1960s. At that time, there was great concern in the USA that a nuclear strike would render all traditional communications useless, partly because of the large, vulnerable switching centres that the telephone system relied on. Thus a big research effort was started to construct a decentralized, resilient, self-configuring communication network. Once it was up and running it became a very popular means of exchanging current information and research gossip between academics. Recognizing the potential, the NSF (National Science Foundation) saw the advantages of such a network and instituted the non-military NSFnet in the mid-1970s. This was built up around a fast core network linking six major university computer centres in the USA: Boulder, Champaign, Ithaca, Pittsburgh, Princeton and San Diego. The hardware and communications software was based on the experience gained from operating the ARPAnet. There was a gateway provided at Carnegie Mellon University between the ARPAnet and the NSFnet. However, while the system was government-funded, for the sole purpose of supporting research work, it was not possible for commercial organizations to use it or develop the resources. Thus the basic scheme was again revised to take into account the participation of commercial interests. This led to the present Internet, where large telecomms companies run the main switching hubs and the interconnecting trunk routes on behalf of all the users. Thus a commercially diverse scheme has developed, where several different routes, offered by different organizations, are available between all the major sites. It is stunning to realize that two results from that wretched period of Cold War paranoia and war fever are online pizza purchase and millions of international e-pals. Only the USA could pull off such a magnificent manoeuvre within such a short period of time: a worthy successor to NASA's non-stick frying pan.

The telephone network (**PSTN**), although primarily intended to transmit voice signals, has for some time been used for data transmission. This was achieved by employing modem equipment to convert the digital signals from computers into suitable analogue voltages for the telephone network. This is somewhat inefficient and limits the rate of data communication to fit within the 300–3300 Hz voice bandwidth. Rather oddly, all long-haul trunk lines now use digital transmission techniques in order to share their broadband channels between many callers. However, the data service has not really benefitted from this: modems are still required because the local lines remain analogue. The Unix community had used dial-up telephone connections for data transmission since the late 1970s to pass newsletters between sites and transfer the latest versions of Unix releases. The uucp suite of tools (unix to unix copy) had been written for just such a purpose. The Internet backbone is now supported by dedicated high-capacity links (Fig. 15.1) between the ISPs and major switching centres, so our LANs are linked together by high-capacity trunks using optical fibre in place of the original dial-up telephone lines and modems.

It was intended that the whole of the PSTN, including the local subscriber loops, would become digital to allow a fully integrated data/voice service (ISDN). In the UK, BT has so far offered System-X to achieve this but the newer **DSL** (Digital Subscriber Line) equipment is starting to replace this as a network goal. **ISDN** allows a 64 kbps duplex connection direct to the end-user's terminal equipment, while the more recent DSL technology (see Section 16.6) offers between 1 and 10 Mbps.

In addition to the PSTN a second network solely for data has been established, known as the **PSS** (Packet Switched System). This enables computers and terminals to exchange messages at much higher speed than possible using the PSTN with modems. The messages are split into a number of 128 byte packets for transmission purposes. The Internet, which links computers throughout the world, partly relies on this method to achieve the speed of transmission and flexibility of routing.

Both the costs and the error rates incurred by long-distance data communications can be reduced if the PSS is used instead of the PSTN. The charges levied for accessing the PSS vary from country to country, but you can be billed for installation, rental, local line interconnect time and the amount of data transferred.

The full bandwidth of PSS is often limited by the local connection to the PSS exchange. This may still involve modems and copper telephone wires. For simple 'character' terminal interconnection the packets are assembled and dissembled within minicomputers (**PADs**) situated at the PSS local exchanges. Alternatively, this job can be done on-site by the user's equipment if it has the correct software running.

Fig. 15.1
WANs providing long distance interconnection for LANs.

The UK Government encouraged the development of **JANET** (Joint Academic Network), which was not a full part of the Internet, using the X25 protocols. JANET now provides full TCP/IP services and a gateway to the international network for WWW access, file transfer and mail delivery. The Internet gateway machine for the

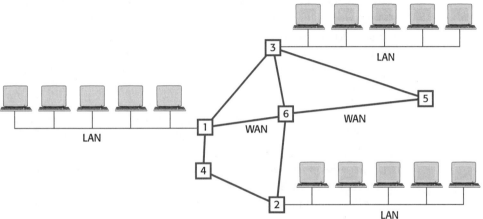

academic domain (.ac.uk) is at ULCC (University of London Computer Centre) and then connected into **LINX** (London Internet Exchange), which is a major data switching centre in the UK.

15.2   TCP/IP – the essential protocols

Communication **protocols** are sets of rules and definitions which provide programmers with sufficient information to produce software which will be able to interact reliably with other products conforming to the same protocols. Issues such as what type to declare variables as, how to initiate a conversation and then gracefully terminate the session, and what to do if an error occurs, are all part of the TCP/IP protocols. When it came to designing software to handle the fast, semi-autonomous communications between computers, the complexity of the problem was tackled in the traditional way of modularization. This resulted in the elegant **layered** structure as shown in Fig. 14.8 and Fig. 15.2. It is often referred to as the **TCP/IP stack**, and has been implemented many times for different systems. It is now possible to buy libraries to build TCP stacks, thus saving a lot of coding effort.

An introductory discussion has to be somewhat selective and limited in scope because the field of networking, and TCP/IP itself, has grown so large. Therefore we will not be dealing as much with UDP, which is an alternative service to TCP. Whereas UDP offers **datagram** delivery, TCP provides a fuller, so-called **virtual circuit**, facility. The choice depends on the data transmission needs. Isolated packets are better sent using UDP, whereas large data streams are better dealt with using TCP. Both UDP and TCP make use of IP services to actually send their data.

A network communication starts by an application program passing some data and the destination address, down to the **TCP** layer. It does this by making the appropriate system call, much like writing data to a file. The TCP layer validates the request, segments the data, wraps it up with headers containing the correct port numbers, sequence count, and passes it down to the IP layer. The TCP software also has the tricky task of dealing with transfer problems. In the event of the failure of a packet to be acknowledged by the intended destination within a preset time, the data has to be sent again. It is the TCP layer that handles the delay timing, acknowledgement discarding and retransmissions when necessary. It may also cut the user data into pieces if it is too big to send in a single packet. The fragments can be as small as 512 bytes, but most modern systems handle packets as large as 8 kbyte without difficulty. Although 64 kbyte packets are theoretically possible, they are not common.

The **IP** layer has the responsibility of finding a route to the destination. It accesses the local routing table and selects the local output port for the best next-hop destination where the packet will be re-routed. The TCP frame is then prefaced by an IP header containing the IP destination and source addresses, and the whole passed to the MAC, or **data link** layer, along with the IP number of the chosen next-hop router.

Fig. 15.2
The TCP/IP stack at work.

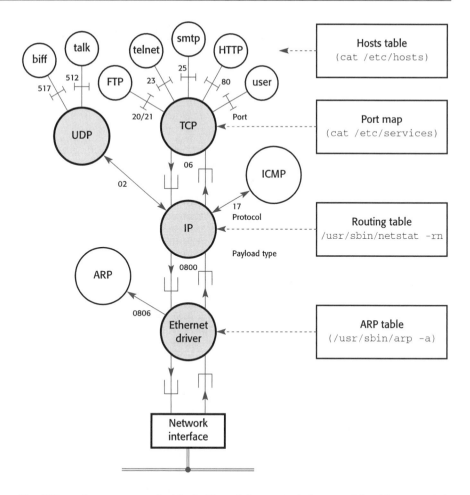

The IP layer is unconcerned with the fate of the transmissions, and for this reason it is regarded as an 'unreliable' service. The data link layer deals with the hardware and device driver routines. It also has to search the ARP table for the 48 bit MAC equivalent of the 32 bit IP address of the intended next-hop, as described in Section 14.4. Finally the packet, with the MAC header inserted at the front, is offered to the Ethernet device driver routine for despatch. Dealing with incoming packets is the reverse process, but is more complex because there can be many processes running on the receiving computer, for only one of which will the incoming data be destined. The lower NI layer will screen out ARP packets and pass valid IP payloads on to the IP process. The IP layer will then look at the Protocol field to determine where to pass its payload on to. The three most common next layer destinations are listed in Table 15.1. If you refer back to Section 14.9 you can understand that UDP is based on datagram sockets and that TCP uses stream sockets. Interlayer data transfers can be put in the context of a full TCP/IP software stack by looking at Fig. 15.2. Furthermore, where the Protocol Number fits within the Ethernet packet can be seen in Fig. 15.3: the 8 bit field is next to 'TTL max hops'.

The action of the TCP/IP software (Fig. 15.2), confusingly referred to as the TCP/IP stack, can be considered along with the packet structure (Fig. 15.3). The internal

Table 15.1
IP field values.

Number	Protocol
02	ICMP
06	TCP
17	UDP

structure of the Ethernet packet header is not too complex. After the synchronization preamble and the SFD start bit, the first 6 bytes contain the destination MAC address. This is followed by a further 6 bytes for the previous host's MAC address. Then follows a 16 bit number which indicates the length of the payload. A further 6 bytes hold constant values, and then comes the 2 byte Payload Type field. If it holds 0800,

Fig. 15.3
Ethernet, IP and TCP encapsulation.

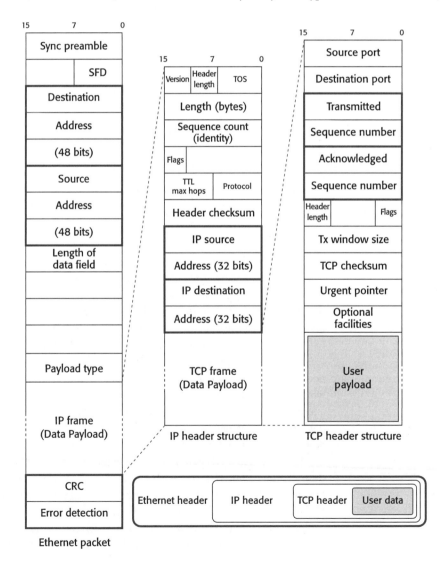

Ethernet packet

the contents of the data frame is an IP packet, while an ARP request is coded with 0806.

If the Ethernet packet contains an IP payload, the description becomes more complex. The Version field indicates whether it is v4 or v6, soon to appear. Next the length of the Header is given as the number of 32 bit words coming before the payload field. Because it is only 4 bits wide, the header is limited to 64 bytes. The TOS (Type of Service) field was intended to offer transmission prioritization, but is not often used. The next 16 bit Length field holds the total IP packet length in number of bytes, thus limiting to a maximum of 65 536 bytes. The maximum size is not often chosen. When fragmentation takes place to reduce the size of the payload, the next Sequence field will be used to reconstruct the message. TTL (Time to Live) is used by routers to discard packets which have travelled too far (64 hops) without arriving at their destination. The original sender will set this field to 16, 32 or 64, and each router will decrement the value by one as the packet passes through. When a packet is thrown away, the router will also send a message back to the source with the bad news. This status information will be in the form of an **ICMP** (Internet Control Message Protocol) code. What particular protocol is used by the payload is contained in the next field (Fig. 15.2). The Header checksum field does not cover the payload, which has to make its own arrangements for error detection. The source and destination IP addresses come next, each occupying 4 bytes. Finally comes the payload frame, with its valuable cargo of data.

After IP, the TCP header will not appear so frightful. The inital fields contain further routing information by way of Port Numbers. These are either **WKP** (Well-Known Ports) or ephemeral, client application ports. As shown in Fig. 15.4, Unix can provide a list of active Port Numbers and their attached services. The WKP are dedicated to named applications, such as mail, ftp and WWW. They have been given numbers between 1 and 255, but now seem to have spilled over up as far as 1024. Above that are the user-available ports, which can be 'borrowed' to set up an application and then returned when no longer required.

A 32 bit sequence number is provided to allow for 'sliding window' flow control at the byte level. This flow control technique was introduced in Section 10.4. The Acknowledged Sequence field is part of the reply handshake, telling the sender what the receiver expects next. Then comes a 4 bit Header length field, referring again to 32 bit words, and six status flags. The Tx window size contains the size in bytes of the available buffer space left at the receiver end. Transmitters can use this to change their maximum packet size parameter. The Urgent pointer, when used, can indicate the start of some urgent data. The data payload completes the TCP field structure.

15.3 TCP – handling errors and flow control

An important responsibility of any communication protocol is enabling the receiver to control the flow of data out from the transmitter. With RS232 this could be done

Fig. 15.4
TCP port numbers and
their services from /
etc/services.

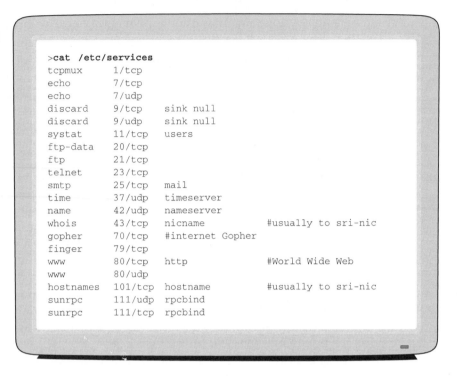

```
>cat /etc/services
tcpmux     1/tcp
echo       7/tcp
echo       7/udp
discard    9/tcp    sink null
discard    9/udp    sink null
systat     11/tcp   users
ftp-data   20/tcp
ftp        21/tcp
telnet     23/tcp
smtp       25/tcp   mail
time       37/udp   timeserver
name       42/udp   nameserver
whois      43/tcp   nicname          #usually to sri-nic
gopher     70/tcp   #internet Gopher
finger     79/tcp
www        80/tcp   http             #World Wide Web
www        80/udp
hostnames  101/tcp  hostname         #usually to sri-nic
sunrpc     111/udp  rpcbind
sunrpc     111/tcp  rpcbind
```

using the CTS/RTS control lines, or by sending the Xoff/Xon codes. Networks have the same problem: senders may talk too fast for receivers, potentially producing data overrun errors in the receive buffers. There are several techniques which might be considered. The simplest is to ignore data when it arrives inconveniently. Some method of repairing the losses will then be subsequently invoked. Or you may insist from the start that only one item of data is sent until a specific acknowledgement is returned to the transmitter by the receiver. This has the added facility of allowing positive rejection of an item if the receiver judges that it is corrupted, but its principal purpose is to regulate the flow of data across the network. The receiver has to be able to positively acknowledge the successful reception of a packet, or send a request for it to be retransmitted, as well as halting incoming transmissions and recommencing them when ready. Special codes are needed for each action. In addition, the danger of a lost packet is ever-present. How does a transmitter respond to an unexpected quiet period? The normal strategy is to use a timer to warn the transmitter when an acknowledgement has not arrived within a fixed period. The transmitter can then repeat the transmission. To avoid confusing the receiver the packets will have to be individually numbered in sequence. Then any inadvertent duplication can easily be detected and rectified. Perhaps surprisingly, flow control activity is vested in the higher TCP layer of software, together with error control. In contrast to TCP, UDP offers no error control, and will simply discard unwanted packets. The underlying IP layer also ignores transmission errors affecting the data and discards undeliverable packets. A useful development of this 'one packet at a time' handshaking arrangement

Fig. 15.5
Flow control using a
four-packet buffer.

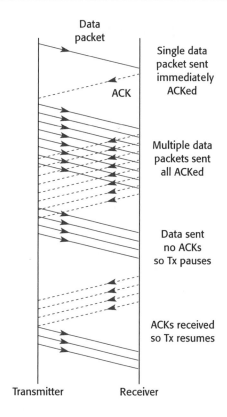

Data
packet

Single data
packet sent
immediately
ACK ACKed

Multiple data
packets sent
all ACKed

Data sent
no ACKs
so Tx pauses

ACKs received
so Tx resumes

Transmitter   Receiver

can be obtained if the transmitter is able to retain local copies of all the recently transmitted packets. Then it is possible for the transmissions to continue for a time, even
when an acknowledgement signal has not been received. A retransmit request can still
be honoured, should it eventually arrive, by looking back through the local buffer for
the affected packet. Only when a packet has been acknowledged as successfully transmitted may the copy held in the transmit buffer be deleted. When an acknowledge
signal is delayed, the transmitter can continue to send packets unless the local buffer is
full of unacknowledged data. Then it must pause to wait for an acknowledge signal.
Such a handshaking scheme is known as **Sliding Windows,** the size of the local transmission buffer determining the window. In Fig. 15.5 you can se the situation of a
single packet successfully sent and acknowledged, followed by an equally successful
transmission burst. Then the receiver fails to ACK the next four packets, making the
transmit buffer fill up with unacknowledged data. The result is a pause in transmission until the delayed ACKs are received. Should a NAK response arrive, the transmitter has only to retransmit the packet. A further elaboration can be incorporated if
the channel is operating in full-duplex mode. Then the ACK/NAK responses may be
'piggy-backed' on data packets passing in the reverse direction, so hardly any bandwidth is taken up with flow control signalling!

15.4   IP routing – how packets find their way

Although the Internet is described as just an interconnection of networks, making it sound like a simple expansion of existing LANs, it involves a completely different approach to delivering information to the intended destinations. Whereas LANs can employ a **broadcast** strategy – shout loudly and the right person will hear you – when the group of possible receivers is worldwide, this approach is not possible. (Note that the BBC still relies on it for its transmissions!) A method of individually routing packets had to be found. Thus the Internet is selective in its routing, more like the Post Office than BBC radio. We saw in Section 14.8 that delivering, or routing, packets on a LAN is quite straightforward if there is only a single default gateway. Any packet with an unknown destination address gets directed to the gateway machine and forgotten about. If, however, there are two or more gateway routes, decisions have to be taken. This is the start of the Internet.

One available method is to allow the originator to specify the complete route, from end to end across the WAN, by inserting a list of IP addresses into the packet header. These addresses would have to specify exactly the journey taken, and if any of the intermediate addresses were wrong the packet would get lost. This option is rarely used because of the complexity and changeability of the Internet structure. The more usual technique leaves the actual route taken to be decided along the way by the gateways or router hosts.

An interesting utility, `traceroute`, is provided by Unix. This sends out probe packets to the named destination and attempts to trace their routes through the Internet. These probe packets are set with a small TTL (Time to Live) value, so error messages will be returned from the intermediate routing hosts when they recognize a 'beyond sell-by date' on the incoming packet.

In the main, data packets trigger fresh routing decisions when they arrive at a gateway. Because long messages are split into several packets for transmission, the actual routes taken by each packet may be different. This leads to the unfortunate result of packets arriving at their destination in the wrong order. The necessary rearrangement of incoming packets to reconstitute the original message is then a responsibility of the TCP layer. The IP layer is unconcerned with such details! Although TCP is referred to as providing a **virtual circuit** service, in this case it does not mean that packets containing TCP frames all follow one another along the same route, only that reordering and retransmission requests are handled transparently by the TCP layer. Both TCP (connection-oriented, virtual circuit) and UDP (connectionless, datagram) packets use the same routing mechanisms and strategies. We will see in Chapter 16 that with ATM networks the term 'virtual circuit' implies something much more predictable.

At the centre of the Internet are the **backbone routers**. These developed from the original NSFnet hosts and maintain complete routing tables for all the connected networks. They do not record individual host numbers, only the network part of their IP address. In principle, any packet getting to them should be directed to the correct gateway and then onward to the destination network. However, if all Internet traffic

Fig. 15.6
Differentiating repeaters,
bridges and routers.

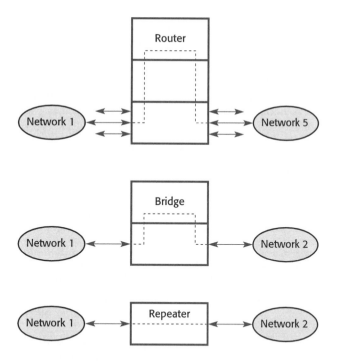

had to go through the backbone routers the system would not be able to sustain the load. It would also be vulnerable to single-point failure, which runs contrary to one of the primary specifications of the ARPAnet. A scheme of localized packet steering was needed. This is carried out with the aid of dynamically updated local **routing tables** which are stored in gateways and hosts.

There are several types of gateway, which perform different functions and carry out different levels of decision making. Roughly these can be layered as dealing with electrical signals, Ethernet packet addressing (MAC) and Internet packet addressing (IP number).

The interconnection schematic presented in Fig. 15.6 indicates the different roles played by the various software layers within the interconnection units.

Repeater – when there is a need for some signal amplification or for electrical isolation of one part of a network from another, a repeater box can be used. It simply copies the signal through, without any understanding or modification of the information carried by the packet. Repeaters can pass data at full LAN operating speed: 10 Mbps for a 10Base2 Ethernet.

Bridge – packets are read and stored for a moment, only to be transferred to the adjoining network if the Ethernet (MAC) destination address is appropriate. Bridges only work between LANs of the same type: Ethernet to Ethernet. They are low-level traffic filters, operating at speeds of around 50 000 packets/s. Most bridges automatically detect the MAC numbers for the hosts connected to the networks directly on either side. They then build up MAC tables to direct the filtering operations, allowing packets through only if the destination MAC number is to be found on the opposite network. This method is known as the **spanning-tree** algorithm.

Router – packets are read and stored for the moment. Unlike the bridge, the IP destination address is used rather than the MAC address. By referencing a local routing table, the router can choose which output port leads to the most suitable network to reach the destination machine. The routing table must be regularly updated to maintain its usefulness. Any computer with more than two Ethernet cards can be running routing programs, and so take on the role of network router. More and more, however, this function is being handed over to dedicated specialized equipment.

As shown in Fig. 15.7, you can look at the routing table in Unix or Windows NT with the **netstat -rn** command. When the routing table specifies a gateway (G flag), rather than a direct host connection (no G flag), the IP number for that gateway is taken and the associated MAC number obtained from the ARP table. It is this Ethernet address that is prefaced to the packet. The original destination IP address is left unaltered. Take care not to misinterpret the H flag: it signifies that the destination address shown is a full IP address (32 bits); otherwise it is only a network address with

Fig. 15.7
Unix `netstat` utility showing the routing table.

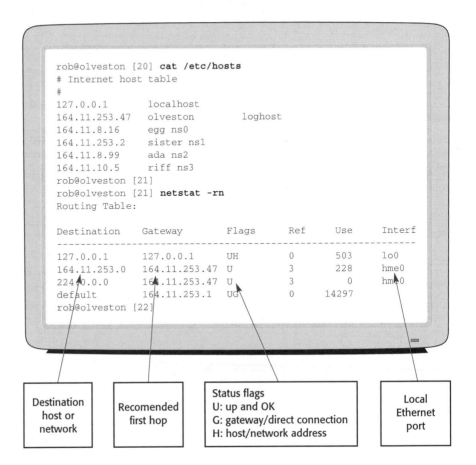

```
rob@olveston [20] cat /etc/hosts
# Internet host table
#
127.0.0.1        localhost
164.11.253.47    olveston         loghost
164.11.8.16      egg ns0
164.11.253.2     sister ns1
164.11.8.99      ada ns2
164.11.10.5      riff ns3
rob@olveston [21]
rob@olveston [21] netstat -rn
Routing Table:

Destination     Gateway          Flags     Ref     Use        Interf
-----------------------------------------------------------------
127.0.0.1       127.0.0.1        UH        0       503        lo0
164.11.253.0    164.11.253.47    U         3       228        hme0
224.0.0.0       164.11.253.47    U         3       0          hme0
default         164.11.253.1     UG        0       14297
rob@olveston [22]
```

| Destination host or network | Recomended first hop | Status flags U: up and OK G: gateway/direct connection H: host/network address | Local Ethernet port |

some trailing zeros in place of the host ID. (The number of zeros will depend on the class of the IP number.) This distinction matters when consulting the table for routing advice because it is first scanned for an exact, full match, indicating a host that is directly accessible. Then the scanning is reduced to match the network part of the address. Finally, in desperation, the default gateway is sought out.

A choice of onward direction may be available because the host is provided with more than one Ethernet port. Alternatively, the LAN to which the single Ethernet port is attached may support more than one gateway. Whichever is the case, the next-hop router must be accessed by MAC address. You can see from Fig. 15.3 that packets contain only the IP number of the final destination and the originator. There is no provision for holding the IP address of the next-hop router. This means that the chosen router must be 'visible' at the MAC level, and accessible by Ethernet number alone. Such a constraint limits the distance of the next-hop router to the same Ethernet segment, or at least only a bridge or two away! The local routing table should contain sufficient information to allow the selection of a temporary MAC address to be used during the packet's next hop.

The maintenance of routing tables is central to the operation of the Internet. There are several options available in this area. The most obvious is to compute and install at boot time a static routing table. This would not need to be enormous because it only has to include local hosts and networks. The default gateway can handle all other packets for the time being. If you look at the screen dump in Fig. 15.7, you will see that the default entry to the routing table is not present in the hosts file. So the default entry has been entered either manually, or more likely dynamically through the action of the routed process. The routing table can easily be updated manually by systems administrators using the utility `route`. Unfortunately this plan would never work. The interconnection environment changes so regularly that it would not be feasible to carry out the necessary manual revisions quickly enough. Another simple strategy is to eliminate routing decisions altogether: broadcast everything, the same as LANs. Every router could blindly copy the incoming packets to all its output ports. Clearly, the communication channels would soon get flooded with packets going nowhere useful. Some would come back to the origin and confuse the situation. From Fig. 15.8 you can see that after five hops, if each router spawns only two packets for each received, there will be $2^5 = 32$ identical packets travelling along, trying to locate the destination host. If the routers had three alternative output ports, the number of packets would have increased to $3^5 = 243$. It is said in support of this strategy that the

Fig. 15.8
Traffic flooding without routing decisions.

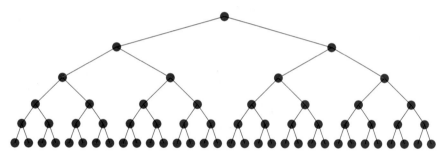

least hops route is bound to be discovered, but with the injection of so much congestion I wonder whether that will always be the quickest! An additional problem occurs when multiple copies of the same item are dispatched. If several versions arrive at the intended destination it has to be able to distinguish them. For this reason, packets must be uniquely numbered so that repeat copies can be discarded by the receiver.

The impact of 'lost' packets passing around the network can be limited by instituting a regime in which they are discarded after a fixed number of 'hops'. Although this is not a panacea for the doomed broadcasting technique, it is still carried out by routers in order to regulate traffic. The **hop number** field, which is included inside every data packet (see Fig. 15.3, IP Header, TTL/max hops count field) gets decremented by each router as it passes through until zero is reached; the packet is then discarded.

For IP numbers, the least significant part is the host identifier, the middle section is the local network identifier (subnet number), and the upper, most significant, portion has the IP domain number – see Fig. 14.12 for more details. All WAN routing is achieved using only the upper, network, part of the 32 bit IP address. This sensibly leaves the final stage of the delivery, requiring only the subnet and host number, to the entry gateway of the IP domain which contains the destination machine. This, as we have seen, may simply broadcast the packet on the LAN, or more likely, pass the packet inwards to a local gateway which is unknown to the outside world. The core domains (Fig. 15.12) are separated under the naming system, not the numbering system. The two distinct uses of the word 'domain' lead to much confusion. This coexistence of distinct IP numbering and domain naming schemes is an historic anomaly. The names are not really necessary, as packets are routed by IP number. However, most users prefer to refer to hosts and users by name. So an online directory to carry out the translation is provided (DNS). But whereas the IPv4 numbers were divided up into classes and allocated according to the number of hosts to be serviced at the applicant's site, a completely different strategy was adopted for names. From the start, the naming system was hierarchical and based on geography or organizational function.

As we stated earlier, routers maintain look-up tables so that when a packet arrives with a foreign network address the table can be consulted for a recommendation. This will take the form of the address of a nearby gateway and then the packet is sent onward to that address for further dispatching. The table lists the IP address of best local gateway for any distant network that has been requested so far. After the initialization at boot time the table has to be regularly updated. **ICMP error messages** coming back from other routers, who have judged that a packet had been badly routed, help in this regard. The ICMP protocols, introduced in Section 15.2, offer such a message facility. When a router accepts a packet and chooses a best route forward using its routing table, and then discovers that it is being returned to the same port that it came in on, it immediately fires off an error message back to the source router. This contains advice on the other route, which may be better.

A method for dynamically maintaining routing tables up-to-date is still used but much criticized, and is based on **RIP** (Routing Information Protocols) packets (Fig. 15.9) and the Unix `routed` (route-demon). On Sun Solaris systems it is included

Fig. 15.9
RIP packet fields.

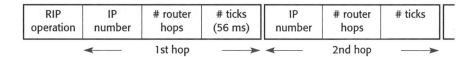

RIP operation	IP number	# router hops	# ticks (56 ms)	IP number	# router hops	# ticks

← ———— 1st hop ————→ ← ———— 2nd hop ————→

within `inetd`. This method appears to have just grown and been accepted because it works. The RIP technique involves **solicitation** and **advertising**. When a router is booted it will send out requests for its neighbouring routers to share their information. If this invokes a response, the new router will then build a table based on this information. Subsequently, it will respond to solicitation requests from other routers and periodically broadcast its routing table, just in case anybody is interested. A somewhat sneaky trick used by routers is to take the evidence from a solicitation request packet to update the routing table as well! Is this a kind of stamp collecting activity, where you peel used stamps off envelopes even if they contain bills?

Entries in routing tables have a limited lifetime. If they have not been updated within the last three minutes they will be marked as invalid and after a short delay completely removed from the table – quite a ruthless policy.

All routers have a duty to give their nearest neighbour routers a copy of their routing table. This can be seen as a scheme to slowly promulgate locally stored information across the Net. Remember that the **directly connected networks** are represented in the routing table as well as some of the distant networks. Thus each router is giving other routers first-hand knowledge of nearby networks, as well as second-hand experience of transit times to distant networks. This latter comes from the stored **hop count**, information which is actually the number of intervening routers encountered when taking that route to the distant network. Using this number, routers can eliminate less efficient routes and install better directions. Criticism of the RIP method arises from its poor settling time after a disturbance, such as a router failure, and the possibility of looped routes appearing in the tables.

An increasing problem is the size of the central routing tables. This has been exacerbated with the allocation of multiple Class C IP numbers to single organizations because of the exhaustion of Class B numbers. As a result of this policy, routing tables may have several entries in numerical sequence, with the same suggested gateway. **CIDR** (Classless Inter-Domain Routing) has been introduced in an attempt to limit the increase in size of these critical routing tables (Table 15.2). The Class C numbers are now issued in a geographically sensible order so that the packet routing becomes easier to carry out. Each country and then region will have groups of numbers reserved, much like the telephone system. Routers will work differently. Instead of checking the upper network part of an IP address, the full 32 bit address will be used, with a specific bit-length mask to indicate the number of relevant bits to be considered. Thus a group of 2048 Class C IP numbers may be allocated to an organization. Therefore A31 down to A11 will all be the same from the router's point of view. A10–A8 are used to distinguish the internal subnets of the organization, while A7–A0 are the regular host numbers, distinguishing the workstations. The CIDR router takes the 32 bit IP number and applies the associated mask: 255.255.248.0.

Table 15.2
CIDR IP number
allocations.

Region	IP numbers reserved
Europe	194.000.000.000–195.255.255.255
North America	198.000.000.000–199.255.255.255
South America	200.000.000.000–201.255.255.255
Pacific Asia	202.000.000.000–203.255.255.255

With the imminent arrival of IPv6, it is interesting to see that a hierarchical, geographically organized DNS scheme has been followed, with blocks of the new 128 bit IP numbers being allocated to countries and to commercial service providers. Perhaps the Internet has learned something from the PSTN experience at last.

15.5 DNS – distributed name database

To transmit a packet of data across the Internet requires several phases of identifier translation to be carried out. These are shown in Fig. 15.10.

The first is a manual look-up to obtain the user and host IDs. This has to be carried out only once before starting the transmission. The other two translations have to be carried out for each transmitted packet.

The 32 bit IP numbers, even when written in dotted decimal format, are not very convenient or memorable, so we generally use alias names instead. The Internet name space is split into seven generic domains – .com, .edu, .org, .mil, .net and .gov – and many national domains: .uk, .fr, .sp etc. The 'most significant', domain portions of the dotted name identifiers are issued by the main domain authority **NIC** (Network Information Center; http://www.nic.com/). Authority is ceded to lesser domain organizers within countries. Network Solutions Inc. currently issues licenses in the USA for the global domains. A company called Nominet (http://www.nic.uk/) oversees the .uk domain, and UKEARA handles requests for names in the gov.ac and ac.uk subdomains. There are repeated disputes over the use of commercial names, which are unprotected by copyright law. Cornering a well-known identifier before it gets recognized has turned into quite a cottage industry.

Finally, the local network administrators have the task of assigning the remaining parts of the names to achieve rational subdivisions of their local domains. In this way the network administrator can decide how many networks (subnets) the site will be split into, and how many individual computers will be addressed on each.

Fig. 15.10
Identifier translation
required for
transmitters.

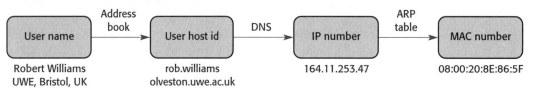

User name	Address book →	User host id	DNS →	IP number	ARP table →	MAC number
Robert Williams UWE, Bristol, UK		rob.williams olveston.uwe.ac.uk		164.11.253.47		08:00:20:8E:86:5F

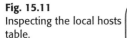

Fig. 15.11
Inspecting the local hosts
table.

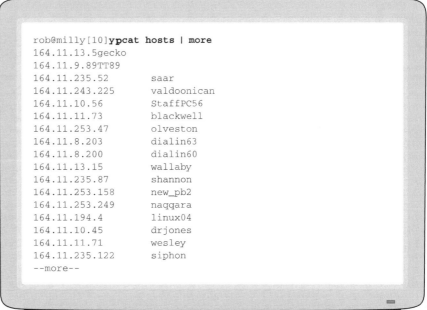

```
rob@milly[10]ypcat hosts | more
164.11.13.5gecko
164.11.9.89TT89
164.11.235.52       saar
164.11.243.225      valdoonican
164.11.10.56        StaffPC56
164.11.11.73        blackwell
164.11.253.47       olveston
164.11.8.203        dialin63
164.11.8.200        dialin60
164.11.13.15        wallaby
164.11.235.87       shannon
164.11.253.158      new_pb2
164.11.253.249      naqqara
164.11.194.4        linux04
164.11.10.45        drjones
164.11.11.71        wesley
164.11.235.122      siphon
--more--
```

It is perhaps worth noting that the host IP numbering system for IPv4 is based on size classes (Fig. 14.12). This is not really convenient for geographical grouping or hierarchical packet routing. In fact, it is a disaster if either of them is required. However, with the host naming scheme a different approach was taken, which allocated names to **domains** either by country or by organizational status. Such an approach facilitates fast searching and would help with network structuring and more effective traffic routing if it were used for that. It is modelled on the old telephone system. For some reason, the **generic** domains use three letters, while the **country** domains are limited to two letters.

Host names, such as my current title, olveston.uwe.ac.uk, can be stored in local host name files for reference, or, more likely, held in a network-accessible database: **DNS** (Domain Name System). DNS is a distributed database offering an online directory service to discover the IP number of any connected host when the network name is available. Each DNS server contains all the names and numbers of machines residing within its own domain. Enquiries which refer elsewhere are passed upward to the root server for that Internet domain. So a hierarchy of nameserver hosts attempt to **resolve** any query within their local domain.

The names, of course, have to be uniquely assigned, and the responsibility falls to the domain organizers. But in the same way that filenames can be shared because they are 'hidden' within a directory, and all reference has to be by the full pathname, so the full net-name distinguishes between all the users called R Williams around the world. It would be different if there were two people in my department named R Williams (which unsurprisingly there are, so we have to resolve the clash by my colleague utilizing his middle name).

Fig. 15.12
Hierarchical naming
domain structure.

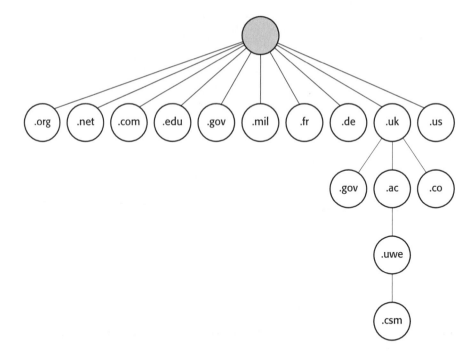

To test the local name server there are the Unix commands `nslookup` and `whois`. The latter does have rather unpredictable results. Both use the DNS name servers to find the IP numbers of domains, nets or hosts. The normal way for a C program to access the name servers is by calling the function `gethostbyname( )`. This will return a record of information, including the IP address, for the nominated host. The local name servers are listed in `/etc/resolv.conf`, so you can see where your queries are going. This is illustrated in Fig. 15.13.

Although the DNS name servers work autonomously, as far as they are able, on one occasion the complete failure of one of the seven core routing hosts in the USA (`herndon.com`) resulted in all the email from other domains intended for the `.com` domain being rejected. For a distributed network, with its origins in 'nuclear proof' communications, this disaster surprised many users.

15.6 World Wide Web – the start

One of the major recent developments in the world has been the growth of the Internet and the **WWW** (World Wide Web). This was spawned from a synthesis of pre-existing technologies, and it took most people by surprise. As we have already said, the Internet is a network of networks and has been growing steadily since the original ARPAnet was funded by the US Department of Defense in the early 1970s. Gradually, at first, more and more networks in different countries from all over the

Fig. 15.13
Using the DNS name
look-up facility.

```
rob@milly [33] cat /etc/resolv.conf
domain csm.uwe.ac.uk
search csm.uwe.ac.uk uwe.ac.uk
nameserver 164.11.8.16
nameserver 164.11.253.2
nameserver 164.11.253.11
nameserver 164.11.8.99

rob@milly [33] c/usr/sbin/nslookup
  Default Server: egg.csm.uwe.ac.uk
  Address: 164.11.8.16

> smilodon.cs.wisc.edu
  Server: egg.csm.uwe.ac.uk
  Address: 164.11.8.16

  Non-authoritative answer:
  Name: smilodon.cs.wisc.edu
  Address: 128.105.11.80

> ^D
rob@milly[35]
```

world have been connected together and the result is the worldwide Internet. Because of this evolutionary approach, the topology of the Internet is irregular, but it still allows computers from all over the world to exchange information.

The World Wide Web was started up by the work of Tim Berners-Lee at CERN. It provides a method of organizing, accessing and searching for information stored in many different computers using a hypertext protocol. Hypertext is text which has embedded in it links, or pointers, to other document files, which may be on the same computer or on another one connected across the network. Accessing a file in this way is no more than an FTP transfer, which had been common for many years before the WWW appeared. The hypertext technique had also been pioneered on Apple Macintosh computers for some years, as an alternative 'user-friendly' database. The WWW allows a network of documents to be generated, usually in some form of loose hierarchy. 'Hypermedia' is the term given to hypertext documents which have been extended to include other forms of media, such as graphics and sound.

The basis of the WWW is the use of **HTML** (Hypertext Markup Language) and the **HTTP** (Hypertext Transmission Protocol). Rather than store and transmit documents in PostScript or PDF, it was decided to use a simpler scheme which was more closely related to Unix's nroff and troff utilities. Text documents are coded in plain ASCII with extra formatting instructions embedded as control sequences. When these are required to be viewed, a browser program will reformat the document, obeying the control codes in a manner appropriate for the display being used. In this way, the hypertext documents are not tied to any particular capability or functionality. In addition, facilities were included which allowed the creator to embed in the document reference pointers to other documents, images, graphics and sounds. The hypertext or hypermedia is stored on a server computer, usually linked into the Internet if you want others to have access to the information. Each document has to be allocated a unique address called a URL – Uniform Resource Locator – and it is the URLs which are used to link the resources together. In fact, the URL is more of an instruction-to-find than a file address. Users of the WWW need to use client software known as Web browsers to decode the hypertext easily. Netscape Navigator and Microsoft Internet Explorer are the best-known products at this moment. (Perhaps, in time, Gnu will offer a Web-compliant emacs!)

A related development, which has had an immediate impact (certainly on Computer Science courses in college), is the Java programming language. This language has so far had a chequered history. Although it was intended as a control language for domestic equipment, in a similar vein to Forth, it has found an enthusiastic welcome from programmers responsible for WWW applications. It is similar to C++, but avoids some of the more dangerous pitfalls. It includes concepts from some other programming languages, but its distinctive feature at the moment is the need for an interpreter – few Java compilers producing native machine code are yet available. However, because the run-time system is small and can easily be ported to other new platforms, its popularity is still increasing. The relevance to the WWW comes from the inclusion of this interpreter inside the latest versions of Netscape Navigator and Internet Explorer. Thus Java code can be downloaded and run as easily as a hypertext document. This provides a simple way of distributing programs across the Internet and gives greater dynamic functionality to static Web pages.

These – and other – developments mean that much of the future of computing is seen as being intimately tied up with networking and distributed computing across the Internet. The architecture of new computers has already been adjusted to meet these new needs. There is a greater emphasis on supporting 'multimedia', which simply means better graphics and high-quality sound output. Most domestic PCs are supplied with telephone access modems simply to connect to the WWW. Networking interfaces are being included on PC motherboards, 25 years after Sun made the same decision for its workstations.

15.7   Browsing the Web – Netscape Navigator

Netscape Navigator is a Web browser, as illustrated in Fig. 15.14. This means that it can be used to view Web page documents and assist with searching out new documents, which can either be obtained from a local disk drive or downloaded from distant servers linked only by a network. To achieve all this, Navigator has several capabilities which are required to interact with other programs, exchange information and then interpret and display the documents they send. To access a Web page the **URL** must be obtained. These are three part specifiers:

```
URL = Protocol identifier/Machine name/file path
```

Fig. 15.14
Netscape Navigator Web
browser.

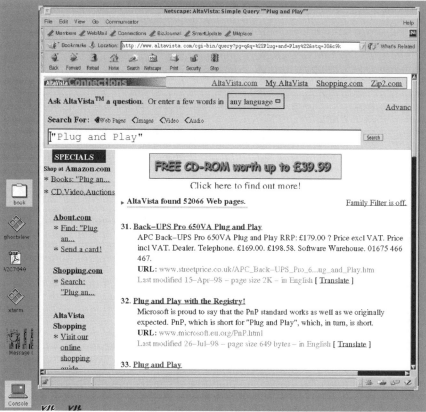

Although they bear a passing likeness to file pathnames they are more than simply the location specifier.

Primarily, the browser has to have an HTML interpreter producing screen images for you to look at. If you have already produced a Web page for display, **HTML** (Hypertext Markup Language) will be familiar to you. It consists of a series of formatting commands, known as HTML **tags**, which can be embedded in the text so that the receiver can reformat the page according to the local conditions. This has the advantage that the viewer can then benefit from the best use of local resources. There may be differences in screen resolution, colour availability or limited font files. Being able to accept the text and display it in a suitable way rather than simply painting an image on the screen provides a much more flexible approach to document distribution than that offered by bitmap image files. The text markup approach to document distribution is more flexible than that offered through PDF files. The most similar scheme is the Unix troff language (in which this book was originally coded). HTML is less powerful and considerably less expressive than PostScript, but is more compact. As languages go, it is easy to learn, but even so many Web authors create their pages using special **WYSIWYG** editors, removing any necessity to view the underlying HTML codes.

Fig. 15.15
Introducing
`world.html` to
Netscape on Unix.

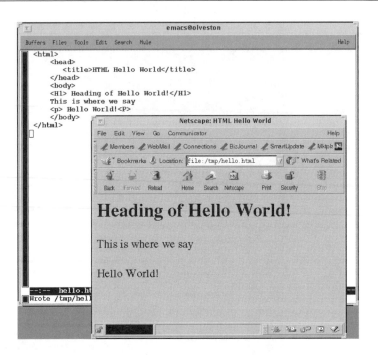

HTML code for the obligatory 'Hello World!' demonstration is displayed in the emacs editor window towards the top of the screen in Fig. 15.15. The file, `world.html`, was then read into Netscape Navigator, which interpreted the format control tags by the salient brackets, '< ... >', carried out the relevant actions, and continued reading the file. Non-tag symbols are simply displayed as text in the Netscape display window. Table 15.3 provides a list of basic HTML document tags.

Hypertext documents have been supplemented with the ability to call up sound and video files. The browser again has to recognize the special tags alerting the arrival of a special kind of data and correctly pass it through to a Sound Blaster audio card or a video display window. But an even more important development was the inclusion of the possibility of interaction. This means that as well as viewing or listening, the user can respond to questions and send data back to the server. This uses either the **CGI** (Common Gateway Interface) or the newer **Java** applets.

15.8　HTTP – another protocol

From Fig. 15.4 you can see that HTTP is allocated a well-known port above the TCP layer. This means that an outside request for a connection to port 80 will be directed to a server demon which is willing to follow commands if they are coded in HTTP format. Now HTTP is an ASCII code, so it can be handled directly from a terminal. You are probably now very familiar with using browsers such as Netscape Navigator

Table 15.3
Starter set of HTML tags.

Tags	Functions
<HTML>...</HTML>	Page delimiters
<HEAD>...</HEAD>	Page heading
<TITLE>...</TITLE>	http title (invisible)
<BODY>...</BODY>	Main text delimiters
<BASEFONT FACE = "Helvetica" SIZE = 12>	Body text font selection
<FONT FACE = "Arial" COLOR = "#800040" SIZE = +2>...</FONT>	Font type, size and colour
<Hx>...</Hx>	Subheading at level x
<B>...</B>	Embolden font
<I>...</I>	Italicize font
<UL>...</UL>	Unordered list
<OL>...</OL>	Ordered list
<MENU>...</MENU>	Menu
<LI>	List start
 	Break text (equivalent to \n in C)
<P>	New paragraph
<HR>	Horizontal line
<PRE>...</PRE>	Preformatted text
<IMG SRC = "...">	Insert image file here
<A HREF = "http://www..." > [Press]</A>	Set up a hyperlink

to send and receive your HTTP commands, but it is possible to do it manually. As in Fig. 15.16, connect to a WWW server using telnet, with the port set to 80. Then request a page using the get command, remembering the HTML release version of your browser. If you already have the same page showing on Netscape in a different window it will be easier for you to recognize the HTML code.

HTTP is a client–server protocol intended for use when retrieving documents from the World Wide Web. Documents are addressed using URLs such as http://vzone.virgin.net/sizzling.jalfrezi/. The HTTP protocol is not extensive, but offers several commands which support a client–server dialogue. Some of them are listed in Table 15.4.

In Fig. 15.16 a connection is made to the http port (80) on www.altavista.com, and using the HTTP get command the root page is requested. The HTML for the welcome page is fairly straightforward, if rather long. The <href> hyperlink button definitions can be seen in a block and you should note that immediately the transaction is completed the connection is broken. Each request has to make a new, fresh connection. This connectionless strategy is being reviewed at the moment, with the intention of improving the performance of page servers.

Fig. 15.16
Attaching to a Web server using telnet for an online session.

```
rob@olveston [50] telnet www.altavista.com 80
Trying 204.152.160.69...
Connected to altavista.com.
Escape character is '^]'.
GET /
- - -
<img src="/av2/gifs/dart.gif" width=8 height=9 hspace=5 vspace=5 align=top><a
<img src="/av2/gifs/dart.gif" width=8 height=9 hspace=5 vspace=5 align=top><a
</font></td></tr></table>
<br>
<table width="100%" cellpadding=0 cellspacing=0 border=0><tr>
<td aligh=center><font size=-2 face="arial,helvetica" color="#003399">
<a href="/av/content/about.htm">About AltaVista</a> |
<a href="/av/content/help.htm">Help</a> |
<a href="/av/content/questions.htm">Feedback</a> |
<a href="http://www.doubleclick.net/advertisers/altavista/">Advertising Info</a> |
<a href="/cgi-bin/query?pg=addurl">Add a Page</a><br>
<a href="/av/content/disclaimer.htm">Disclaimer</a> |
<a href="/av/content/privacy.htm">Privacy</a> |
<a href="http://image.altavista.com/AV_CopyrightPolicy.htm">Copyright</a> |
<a href="/av/content/av_network.html">International<a/> |
<a href="/cgi-bin/query?pg=tmpl&v=pref.html">Set your Preferences</a>
</font></td></tr></table>
</body></html>
Connection closed by foreign host.
```

Table 15.4
Hypertext transmission protocol (HTTP) examples.

http proxy [URL]	The proxy command allows a proxy HTTP server to be defined which will be used in subsequent client commands. Providing a URL argument sets the proxy server. Setting the proxy to an empty string turns the proxy feature off.
http head url	The head command retrieves the HTTP header for the document located at `url`.
http get url file	The `get` command retrieves the document located at the `url`. The body of the document is written to file. The command returns the HTTP header as described for the `http head` command above.
http post url filename_1 filename_2	The `post` command posts the document in `filename_1` to the location URL. The body of the returned document is written to `filename_2`. The command returns the HTTP header as described for the `http head` command above.
http put URL file	The `put` command copies the file into the URL. The command returns the HTTP header as described for the `http head` command above.
http delete URL	The delete command deletes the document at the URL. The command returns HTTP status information.
The %X variables are substituted before a script is evaluated:	
%A	The network address of the client.
%P	The URL path requested by the requestor.
%S	The search path contained in the URL path.

15.9   Search engines – DEC AltaVista

The various search engines are the very heart of the WWW. They really make it all viable. Any large library is rendered practically useless without an effectively indexed catalogue. Nobody is prepared to simply roam around the miles of shelving hoping to hit upon the desired text. The same would be true for the WWW if there were no search engines. Even with the maze of interconnecting hypertext references that the authors insert into their pages, there would be problems with the introduction of new material. It would be as if you could only use the bibliography section of existing books to find other books of interest. The role of AltaVista, Yahoo, Lycos, Infoseek and many others in handling millions of search enquires every day is pivotal to the success of the WWW. A current WWW index file can be as large as 200 Gbyte, and even then is estimated to refer to only 15% of the available material.

Before the Internet was overwhelmed by enthusiasm for images, audio and the WWW, there had been a more sedate epoch of text. ASCII-coded documents were made available at many Internet sites through the mechanism of anonymous **FTP** (File Transfer Protocol). This simply required the systems administrator to change the access permissions on those files so that anybody with the user ID 'anonymous' would be allowed to read them. Executable binary files could also be handled by FTP, but many people preferred to encode them in ASCII, using the Unix utility `uuencode`, for safer transfer. Any computer user could then log onto the server over the Internet, or dial directly using a modem port, inspect a local index file and then request the chosen file to be downloaded to their local computer. To achieve this a copy of `ftp` had to be available on both computers: one would run in server mode while the other ran in client mode. Many university departments considered the provision of anonymous FTP server facilities as part of their duty to disseminate software. There were active sites for PC, Unix, Atari, Macintosh and many other special interest groups. There was little interaction between the sites, save the establishment of some 'mirror' sites in Europe to reduce the need for transatlantic transfers. The problem of locating useful material held on unknown FTP sites was somewhat ameliorated by a database service known as Archie. This offered the first electronic directory, a service which would be taken up by the current search engines.

The AltaVista search engine was designed and built by DEC (Digital Equipment Corporation), which is now part of Compaq. It was intended originally as a public demonstration of the power of the new 64 bit Alpha processor, but quickly assumed a solid position at the centre of the WWW. AltaVista is a networked group of Alpha-based computers, many having multiple CPUs and massive main memories.

The performance that AltaVista has to deliver is quite impressive. Its WWW database in 1999 held information on 140 million Web pages, or 700 Gbyte of text. It responded to about 44 million queries every day, with a peak rate of more than 1000 queries per second. Despite this load it managed to achieve an average response time of better than 0.6 s. The growth of usage by the public is still not decelerating. The size of the operation is difficult to understand, but if the data contained were printed on paper, the AltaVista database would create a pile over 100 miles high. One of the DEC AlphaServer 8400 computers can find any unique word in less than half a second.

The query interface computers accept the initial requests from the Internet and provide the welcome screen at `http://www.altavista.com/`. There are three AlphaStations, each equipped with 1 Gbyte of main memory and accessing a local 6 Gbyte disk, which pass the keyword queries on to the index servers. The WWW has grown so large, and has such a dynamic existence, that only a technical *tour de force* could hope to support an effective online catalogue service. The query engine comprises a network of 16 AlphaServers, each holding 12 Alpha processors, 8 Gbyte of memory and accessing 300 Gbyte of RAID (see Section 19.5) disk. The WWW index is shared across these systems to improve the response to enquiries.

If the AltaVista service was limited to this a problem would remain as to how the database could be updated sufficiently quickly for all the new material which daily appears on the Web. The job of continually updating the index is taken by another computer known as Scooter, although more commonly referred to as the Spider because of its role in wandering about across the Web, searching out changed pages and new material. This technique of actively searching for index material is in contrast to some other sites, which rely on written submissions from page authors. Scooter is provided with 1.5 Gbyte of memory and a 30 Gbyte RAID disk, and spends all its days sending out enquiries to Web sites and scanning the information returned for key subject words which can then be entered into the main index. The index is recompiled and distributed to the query engine array by Vista, a further AlphaServer with twin processors, 2 Gbyte of RAM and 180 Gbyte of RAID disk. There is some anxiety that with increasing indexing activity, the Spiders are having a negative impact on the available Internet bandwidth!

If you have an HTML page that you would like others to share, you really must get it registered with the main search engines. Although there are commercial services to do this, you can manage the operation yourself with little difficulty. Altavista has an 'Add URL' button towards the bottom of its home page (`http://www.altavista.com/`). This displays instructions for registering your URL and specifying the keywords for their index. Yahoo is organized in a different way, but again the instructions for registering are available from their home page under the 'How to suggest a site' button.

It is worth noticing that the 32 bit address limits the Pentium (unlike the Alpha) to 4 Gbyte of main memory. Like DEC, Intel will be moving to 64 bit addressing with their next generation CPU.

15.10   Open Systems Interconnect – an idealized scheme

Communication protocols such as TCP/IP are rules and procedures, often implemented in software, to allow for the transfer of information in a secure and controlled manner.

Fig. 15.17
ISO seven layer OSI
model.

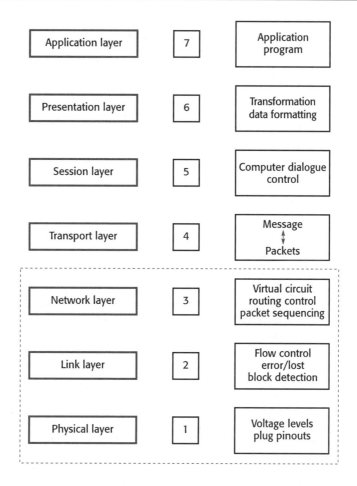

In the early 1980s, the International Organization for Standardization (ISO), part of ITU-T, provided a design framework or model architecture for data communication networks (Fig. 15.17). This is known as the **Seven Layer Model** with each layer responsible for accepting data, processing it and handing it on to the next layer. The layers have clearly defined interfaces with their neighbours, which include data formats, command codes and functional services. It was hoped that the model would help to promote improved compatibility between the different manufacturers' equipment, both hardware and software. In the event the commercial pressures of *de facto* standards have slightly overwhelmed the good intentions. TCP/IP, which does not perfectly fit into this descriptive model (see Fig. 15.18) has succeeded in dominating the WAN market-place. The presence, however, of an internationally recognized specification has subsequently influenced communication software designers, despite its failure to win unanimous commercial adoption. Perhaps the rather bureaucratic approach of organizing a prolonged series of committee meetings to deliberate on abstract structures, while others were already running code, was just doomed to end up as the regular subject of academic examination. It is interesting to look back and

Fig. 15.18
Comparison of TCP/IP
with OSI seven layer
model.

see that the perceived competition to the ISO model in those days was from IBM, with its SNA (Systems Network Architecture) protocols.

The term **peer-to-peer** communication can be used in the context of such a layered model. Consider an arbitrary layer in the transmission stack which receives data and instructions from the layer above. It will carry out the instructions and probably encapsulate the data with some extra information and instruction before passing it down to the next layer. The extra instructions are actually destined to be read and obeyed by the equivalent layer in the receiver stack. It is as if each layer is seizing the opportunity of 'piggy-backing' messages to its partner layer on the destination machine. In fact, the packets often have to pass through intermediate hosts and routers. These, too, will read in the packet, draw it up the input stack to the highest level necessary, and then pass it back down through the output stack. Thus the peer protocol messages are not only read by the destination layers.

Each layer 'talks' to its partner at the other end about error and flow control. Messages are cut into packets which are wrapped with the necessary routing and control information before dispatch. The X25 protocols are used as access rules for the WAN–PSS networks with some success; however, the upper layers are still largely experimental and not usually implemented.

Review

- The development of wide area networks (WANs) started with analogue telephones and was extended for the exchange of data between computers.

- The Internet has been amazingly successful since the introduction of WWW browser tools and search engines.

- The principal protocol used on the Internet and most LANs is TCP/IP. This provides definitions and rules to govern the transmission and reception of data packets.

- The software which implements the TCP/IP rules is organized into a multilayer stack.

- Ethernet uses broadcast to deliver packets on a LAN. For the WAN a different routing strategy was needed. Routing tables are maintained by sending probe packets and by regularly exchanging

■ information about the success or otherwise of packet delivery. The routing mechanism is distributed, not vested in a single master router. Every main router holds tables with all the networks but not all the hosts.

■ Another level of address designation, or naming, was introduced to overlay the IP and MAC layers already present. The allocation of names was governed by geographical location or functional characteristic. The translation from name to IP was carried out by a dynamic distributed database: DNS.

■ IPv4 is running out of numbers, so IPv6 is being introduced to increase the IP number from 32 to 128 bits. At the same time a hierarchical allocation scheme has been introduced to make routing easier.

■ Encoding text documents in a simple markup language (HTML) and distributing them through the Internet using hypertext protocols has been very successful. Image and audio files can be accessed using the same method.

■ The introduction of GUI interfaces to browsers has led to an explosive interest in the World Wide Web. This has been possible not least because of the effectiveness of the search engines, such as AltaVista and Yahoo.

Practical work

The recommended practical work involves programming sockets across the network between diverse operating systems, probably Unix and Windows NT. This allows you to pass data between machines regardless of supplier. It might also be interesting to pursue some research into GSM facilities by sending email to and from a mobile handset. You will need to obtain access to a gateway with Internet connectivity.

Exercises

1. List some advantages and disadvantages of the Internet. What will be its most enduring effects on our lives?

2. Distinguish between the operation of a repeater, a bridge and a router. Which have their own MAC numbers? Which have their own IP numbers?

3. Which layers in the TCP/IP stack use the following facilities?

    (a)   the file /etc/hosts

    (b)   the ARP table

    (c)   the routing table

    (d)   the file /etc/services

4. IPv6 is 128 bits long. In the CIDR scheme, how many numbers are reserved for Europe? Do you think that that is enough? If all domestic appliances in the world were issued with IP numbers at manufacture, would 128 bits be enough?

5. If a single isolated LAN does not need dynamic routing or DNS, does it need to have the TCP/IP stack?

6. What automatic techniques are possible to update the IP routing table? Can it be done manually, too?

7. Is 'client–server' the same as 'peer-to-peer'?

8. You are driving through an unfamiliar foreign land, trying to reach a holiday destination. Compare the following navigational strategies:

    (a) Planning the exact route from a library map before hand. Noting down all the necessary left and right turns on a convenient list which the driver refers to in the car.

    (b) Buying your own map and taking it with you for reference when necessary.

    (c) Taking no map or direction list, but stopping and asking local people as often as necessary.

    (d) Relying completely on the available road signs.

9. Why do some machines have two IP numbers? Do they need two names?

10. Experiment with the `ping` utility. This sends off exploratory packets and asks the destination host to reply to the source.

Readings

- Heuring and Jordan (1997), Section 10.4: introducing the Internet.

- Buchanan (1998), Chapter 36: introduction to TCP/IP and DNS.

- Tanenbaum (1996)

- Stevens (1994)

- The principal site for the WWW Consortium is:
  `http://www.w3.org/`

  Try the protocols section for more information on HTTP.

- All the original specifications (RFCs) for the WWW can be seen at:
  `http://www.FreeSoft.org/CIE/index.htm`

- An authorative historical essay on the Internet can be read at the ACM site:
  `http://www.acm.org/crossroads/xrds2-1/inet-history.html`

- A good introduction to creating html documents is at:
  `http://www.ncsa.uiuc.edu/General/Internet/WWW/index.html`

- Some more WWW information and fun at:
  `http://vzone.virgin.net/sizzling.jalfrezi/`

- The Web sites can be accessed via the Companion Web site for this book at:
  `http://www.booksites.net/williams/`

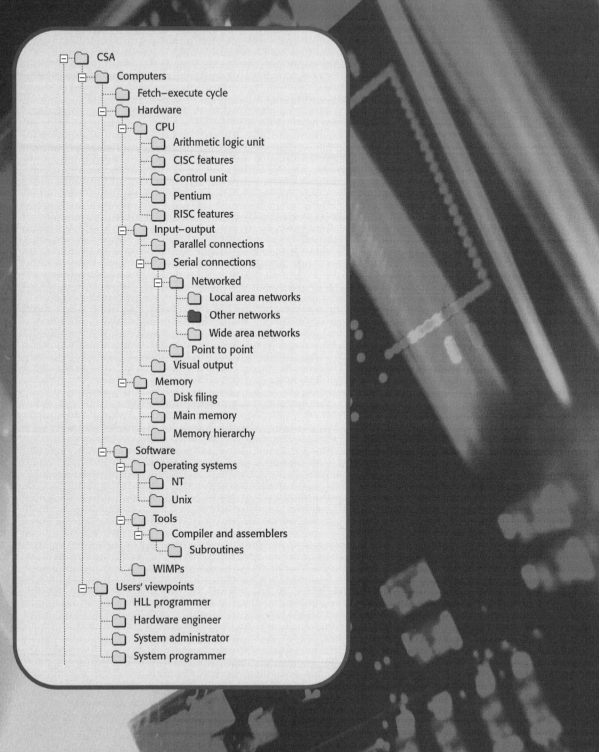

- CSA
  - Computers
    - Fetch–execute cycle
    - Hardware
      - CPU
        - Arithmetic logic unit
        - CISC features
        - Control unit
        - Pentium
        - RISC features
      - Input–output
        - Parallel connections
        - Serial connections
          - Networked
            - Local area networks
            - Other networks
            - Wide area networks
          - Point to point
        - Visual output
      - Memory
        - Disk filing
        - Main memory
        - Memory hierarchy
    - Software
      - Operating systems
        - NT
        - Unix
      - Tools
        - Compiler and assemblers
          - Subroutines
      - WIMPs
  - Users' viewpoints
    - HLL programmer
    - Hardware engineer
    - System administrator
    - System programmer

Other networks

16

Overview

All kinds of different types of networks and computer application areas requiring data communications are now being tested for commercial viability. The traditional fixed line telephone system has provided data communication links between computers for some time, but now specially designed networks are preferable for mobility of operation, increased bandwidth and reduced costs. The new ATM standard attempts to unify data and voice transmission into a single network. Radio networks are no longer reserved for the use of taxis and the emergency services, and have been adapted to incorporate dynamic routing and packet switching technology.

16.1   The PSTN – telephones

Although this is an introductory text for computer science students, there has been a rapid and closely related expansion in the telecommunications industry which relies heavily on software and microprocessor technology. The technological convergence mentioned in Chapter 1 has brought telecommunications and computing closer and closer. This area now presents some exciting career and research opportunities that should not be overlooked by programmers and software engineers. Computer networking provides us all with the means to share information, express opinions to a wider group of readers and seek answers to difficult questions. These have always been important activities for mankind and spawned the first and still largest communication network, the **PSTN** (Public Service Telephone Network). This started over 100 years ago and, as explained in Chapter 15, has become very significant in providing the means for interconnecting computers over long distances. However, because it was based on analogue voltages, modems were needed. For some time, telephone companies, such as BT in the UK, have been keen to offer customers a fully digital service which would then eliminate the need for modem equipment. This would also remove one of the obvious differences between tele-comms and data-comms.

However, the principal distinction remains the nature of the interconnection. When you 'dial' a number and establish a telephone connection, the route along a copper wire, through the exchange equipment and along a trunk line, in spite of its complexity, is dedicated to your conversation, even when you are silent. You are renting a guaranteed circuit from the telephone company. The whole telephone system was designed to provide reliable delivery of voice signals, and the customer is charged for the duration of the call, even when nobody is speaking. This is different from the situation with data WANs, where, after a connection fee, you pay only for the data you transfer. This is possible because you are sharing **bandwidth** with other customers. Your data packets jostle with others for space on the Internet highway. If we all tried to transmit at the same time there would be some queuing delays imposed on our packets. Normally this does not matter because the data will still get through in good time. It does, however, introduce an unpredictability into the transmission which has made the Internet unsuitable for high-quality voice communication. Currently there is much debate as to whether it is possible to raise the bandwidth (bits/sec) of Internet highways sufficiently beyond the level of customer demand to enable voice packets to be routinely transferred across the Internet without suffering traffic hold-ups. If the Internet does begin to carry significant amounts of voice traffic, the PSTNs would need to change dramatically, perhaps offering NANs (Neighbourhood Area Networks) and dedicating all their trunk routes to serving the Internet as WANs.

Telephone networks are based on circuit switching. This requires the exchanges, as in Fig. 16.1, to establish a pathway, when a call is requested, from the initiating telephone through to the destination, with the same pathway maintained for the duration of the call. This **circuit switching** technique started in the era of 'copper pathways' but has been extended to encompass high-bandwidth microwave channels where many

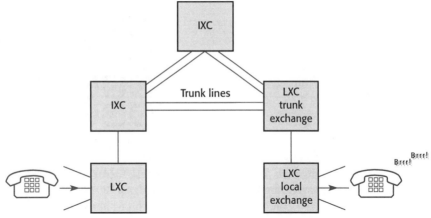

Fig. 16.1
Traditional telephone
interconnection network.
LXC = local exchange
centre; IXC: inter
exchange centre.

calls are multiplexed onto the same path. This is referred to as the establishment of **virtual circuits**, there being no dedicated physical pathway from source to destination. The significant factor to be decided is when the routing decisions are taken. Circuit switching, including virtual circuits, is configured prior to the call starting or the data being sent, while the Internet supports the dynamic rerouting of datagram packets as they progress across the network.

Exchange equipment is often referred to as the **switch**, reflecting this interconnecting activity. Modern exchanges are fully digital in operation and appear more like computer centres than manual switch panels! The whole operation is under the control of **embedded processors** which communicate among each other, setting up circuits to route calls around the world. The transmission of control and status information between exchanges is just as significant as the voice data of which we are all aware. A feature of the PSTN, which has allowed the introduction of many modern facilities, is **common channel signalling**. This is the scheme of separating control and status signals from the voice data channels. This is very different from user 'dialling', where DTMF tones are overlaid on the voice channel. For subscriber lines this is acceptable, but for long distance trunk transmissions separate channels are employed to distribute call setup information. These control and signalling channels have provided the means of passing increasingly sophisticated commands around the telephone network.

The **DTMF**, Dual Tone Multi-Frequency, signalling is termed 'in-band' because it is transmitted openly along the voice channel where it can be heard by the speaker and listener. From Fig. 16.2 it can be seen that each digit is represented by a pair of frequencies. This frequency encoding is similar to that used by modems to transmit binary data, but is more complex because there are 12 symbols to represent, not just two. The receiver has to be equipped with detector circuits which can recognize the tones and select the number which they represent. The advantage of using this in-band scheme is that it can be employed both before the call, to establish the route, and during the call to control user equipment or further routing if desired.

As illustrated in Fig. 16.3, the analogue speech waveform is digitized on the **LIC** (Line Interface Card) as it enters the local exchange. If, however, a fully digital ISDN

Fig. 16.2
DTMF: touch-tone
signalling keypad.

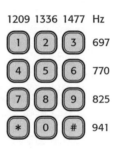

connection is used, the signal is digitized by the terminal equipment in the customer's premises. In either case, a special **ADC** (Analogue to Digital Converter) known as a **Codec** samples the speech voltage signal 8000 times a second and produces a stream of 8 bit numbers, one every 125 μs. This 64 kbps data stream represents a one-way telephone conversation, so a return stream is also required. The codec also compresses the amplitude to improve the perceived quality of the sound at the receiver. The nonlinear compression gives more channel capacity to the quieter sounds and less to the loud sounds. The shape of the compression curve used is slightly different in Europe (A-law) and North America (μ-law), so adjustments have to be made to all trans-Atlantic speech signals. Look at Fig. 16.4 and, using a ruler, mark out on the vertical axis the output for various inputs. Such a scheme fits quite well with the logarithmic sensitivity of the human ear, and reduces the effect that transmission noise has on the quieter passages of the delivered sound. More complex compression techniques are used for cellular telephones because the available bandwidth is more limited. It is useful to note that codecs do not shift the signal frequency band, so they are baseband devices, unlike telephone modems.

The **LXC** (Local Exchange Centre) in Fig. 16.1 directs the call, if necessary, to the nearest **IXC** (Inter or Trunk Exchange Centre) for connection over a long distance trunk line. This pathway will then be reserved solely for that communication and will not vary in route or allocated bandwidth. There are obvious advantages to this plan. After an initial start-up delay, the system transports the data without the need for any recurrent routing information. The clients have a guaranteed level of service once connected, and maintenance of privacy is seemingly certain. When the call is finished the route is broken up and the bandwidth recovered.

The excessive cost of the circuit switched approach, because of the dedicated pathways, which for speech signals are mostly silent, has generated the recent interest in

Fig. 16.3
Digitization of telephone
speech signals.

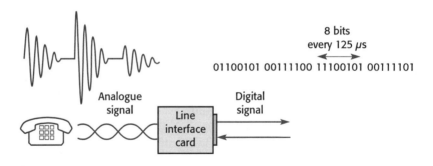

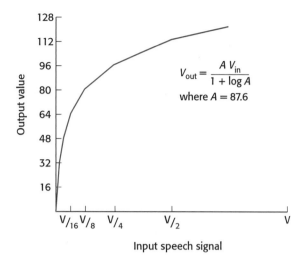

Fig. 16.4
Nonlinear voice
compression for
telephone transmission.

$$V_{out} = \frac{A\,V_{in}}{1 + \log A}$$

where $A = 87.6$

packet switching techniques. Here again the convergence of computer and telecommunications technology is apparent.

The conversion of analogue voice signals to a stream of binary numbers is especially
useful for long distance transmission. This is because trunk lines are not perfect
carriers, so analogue signals would deteriorate noticeably while travelling from, say,
La Rochelle to Bristol. Many signal amplifiers would be required along the length of
the line to boost the power so that it would still be capable of driving the loudspeaker
at the destination. The transmission of binary numbers is simpler because the voltage
representing 1 or 0 can deteriorate to the very point of indistinguishability but still be
recoverable with no subsequent impact on the message quality. However, establishing
a Hamming distance between neighbouring analogue voltages is impossible – all voltages within the permissible range are valid. So binary data has a greater resilience to
noise degradation because there need be no adverse effects until the 1s and 0s become
indistinguishable. Even then, error detection and correction techniques, as described
in Section 10.3, can manage to recover the binary data if the damage is only
intermittent.

Long distance trunk transmission of binary coded voice data normally uses the
TDM (Time Division Multiplex) method which allows 30 conversations to share the
same channel by taking quick turns at transmitting their data, one after the other. This
is possible because the bandwidth of even the slowest trunk line (2.048 Mbps) can
cope with many 64 kbps voice sessions. It is worth noting that:

$$\frac{2.048\ \text{M}}{64\,\text{k}} = \frac{2 \times 10^6}{64 \times 10^3} = \frac{10^3}{32} = 32$$

giving us the possibility of 32 multiplexed channels.

Two channels, C1 and C2, are reserved for signalling information to set up calls and
clear them down. C1 precedes the data while C2 is inserted between voice slot 15 and
16. The others all carry 8 bit digitized voice samples.

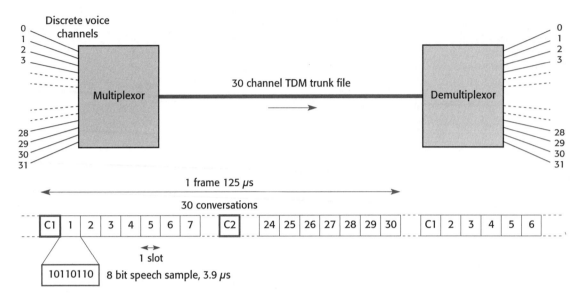

Fig. 16.5
Time division
multiplexing (TDM)
for trunk line sharing.

The construction of simple data multiplexer circuits was discussed in Section 4.3 and digitized voice streams can be handled in an identical manner. Because the binary value representing a voice signal needs to be refreshed and transmitted every 125 μs to reproduce a clear copy of the original speech signal, the TDM channel is switched between the component slots at a rate of 8000 Hz. This is illustrated in Fig. 16.5 for a 2.048 MHz trunk line which uses **TDM/PCM** (Time Division Multiplexed/Pulse Code Modulation) encoding. This can carry 30 independent channels of voice simultaneously. In North America the standard is slightly different, with 24 slots running at 1.54 MHz. But still each voice sample has to be retransmitted 8000 times a second to maintain an undistorted voice link. Clearly a second trunk line is needed in the reverse direction in order to satisfy normal, duplex conversational requirements!

The obvious way to interconnect telephone handsets is through an array of switches. Fig. 16.6 illustrates this technique and demonstrates how a computer can be controlling the whole operation. To make the diagrams simpler, only circuits in one direction are shown. A complete system would need a replica switch to carry data in the return direction. Such a scheme could be constructed to switch either traditional analogue or digitally encoded speech signals, but the latter is now far more common because it does not noticeably degrade the transmitted signal.

Fig. 16.6 shows that the input line 2 has been connected to the output line 0, input line 5 has been connected to output line 8, and the input line 8 has been connected to output line 4. The cross-point switches are all under the control of the embedded processor, which receives instructions as to which inputs to connect to which outputs through the common signal channel. As the voice data has already been converted into digital form a suitable switch element would be very similar in operation to the data flow control gate illustrated in Fig. 4.4. A different approach to the switching problem is found in time division switches. Here it is simply a matter of each input taking turns in sequence to copy their value to a common data bus, and each output

Fig. 16.6
Space division circuit switching with control processor.

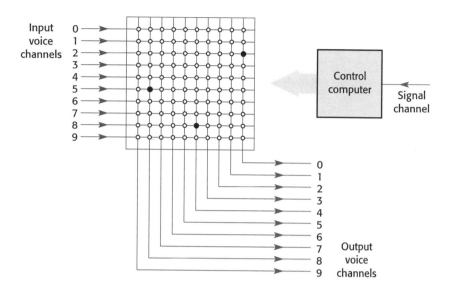

'knowing' when the intended value occupies the bus, and is ready to be read. This switching technique is sometimes referred to as time slot interchanging.

The time division multiplexed bus illustrated in Fig. 16.7 shows the cyclical pattern of frames containing the timed transfer slots. When an input channel is assigned a slot, the controller will arrange to transfer the 8 bit digital value from that channel into the chosen slot, 8000 times a second. Similarly, at the output side the controller will set up the periodic transfer from this timeslot into the destination channel. So an input line is connected through to an output line by arranging for the port to copy data to the TDM bus at the correct moment for it to be read by the output port. Effectively the chosen lines are interconnected for a $3.9 \mu s$ instant when the current voice sample gets transferred across. Figure 16.7 has only two multiplexer cards 'plugged into' the TDM bus, but many more can be inserted, giving a wider chose of routes. Also, several channels can be allocated the same timeslot, which produces a conference call.

Fig. 16.7
Time division circuit switching.

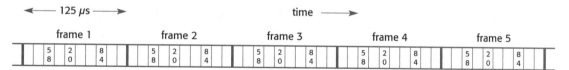

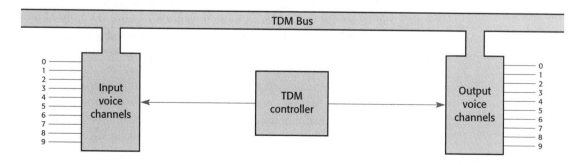

Most telephone switching equipment utilizes both time and space division techniques to establish pathways between caller and called. Often the exchange equipment core is based on a space switch, with the input and output lines being dynamically connected to the core switching matrix by TDM (time division multiplexed) buses. Both the time and space switches are controlled by embedded processors which receive routing signals to direct their actions.

It may strike you that the circuit through a time division switch is not continuously allocated to any one call. Even so, the method is still characterized as maintaining the pathway throughout the duration of the call, like the space division switch. This tricky point makes traditional telephonic circuit switching less different from packet switching than at first we were led to believe. In Section 16.3 we will see that ATM further blurs the distinction between circuit and packet switching methods.

One of the acknowledged achievements of the telephone industry is the establishment and maintenance of agreed, workable standards by **ETSI** (European Telecoms Standards Institute) and the **CCITT** (Comité Consultatif International pour Télégraph et Téléphone) which is now referred to as **ITU-T** (International Telecommunications Union, Telephone Committee).

A quite new network interface option is the PC telephone card, which operates as a telephone exchange/switch for a small office. It also takes and delivers voice messages in place of the traditional answering machine, storing the digitized voice data on disk so that it can be played back later. It appears that because of the large reduction in costs that could be gained from such a scheme, the next generation of telephone switches may be based on standard PC hardware. Microsoft already offers an extension to the Win32 API known as **TAPI**, Telephone Application Programmer's Interface. This can be adopted by telephone card manufacturers to provide a standardized function interface to their products, which makes it easier for programmers to develop software to run on a variety of hardware platforms.

16.2   Cellnets – providers of mobile communications

Cellular telephones have established the possibility of a new type of WAN. It is based partly on short-range radio links and partly on the existing telephone trunk lines. This is another example of the successful convergence of disparate technologies. Designing, implementing and maintaining such systems requires the collaborative efforts of diverse skills: radio and antenna engineering, traffic planning, protocol negotiation, real-time programming for the user handsets and the terrestrial switches, performance simulation and prediction, database management for call routing and charging, and many more. By bringing together mobile, short-range UHF radio transmission, terrestrial trunk line networks, and computer-based call switching, the limitations of the individual technologies can be overcome. Radio communications have always been constrained by the limited bandwidth available. Because cellular

Fig. 16.8
Bands within the
electromagnetic
spectrum.

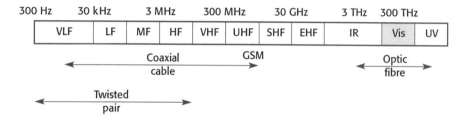

transmissions are only low-power local signals, the radio spectrum can be shared by many callers. This arrangement is possible because the data is carried over the majority of the distance by the traditional terrestrial network, not requiring radio bandwidth. The advantage of caller mobility is delivered by the use of fast call switching which responds to user requests for connection wherever the caller may be positioned, and also to the changes in signal strength as the caller moves about. The radio bandwidth fits into the middle of the electromagnetic spectrum, which spreads from ultra-high-frequency γ-rays down to the very low-frequency long wave radio broadcasts. Figure 16.8 shows some of the names used to refer to the different spectral regions referred to in this chapter and the transmission media.

Transmitting information by radio involves imposing information on the high-frequency (MHz–GHz) radio waves. This applies both to analogue and digital transmissions. The reason that audio frequencies are not directly used for radio broadcasts is the very limited range of such frequencies. So to improve the transmission range of radio broadcasts, a much higher frequency is used, known as the carrier frequency, and the signal to be sent is imposed on it. In Fig. 16.9 the three common ways which are used can be seen. **AM**, Amplitude Modulation, is the technique where the radio waves appear to be 'squeezed' into the shape of the signal to be sent. For a voice channel the radio wave might be oscillating at 100 MHz, while the imposed voice signal is only reaching 3 kHz. Thus the radio wave is made louder and softer in synch with the intended signal. **FM**, Frequency Modulation, involves the radio frequency being varied in sympathy with the signal. If this is only a binary stream, the carrier frequency varies between two values representing the 1s and 0s of the signal to be sent. This can be likened to a violin player bowing a note but at the same time moving a

Fig. 16.9
Radio wave modulation
using amplitude,
frequency and phase
techniques.

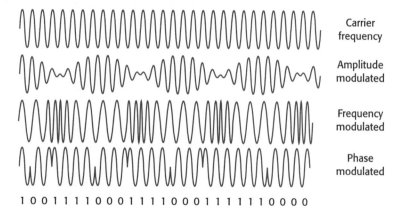

finger up and down to change the tone of the sound. This is the modulation method used for high-quality radio broadcasts (UHF/FM). For GSM cellular digital transmissions, the carrier frequency is held steady but the phase of the sine wave is switched between fixed values representing binary values. The bottom diagram in Fig. 16.9 shows a wave changing in phase by 180° (π rad) which can be detected by the receiver and interpreted as a change in binary value: $1 \rightarrow 0$ or $0 \rightarrow 1$.

As described for modems in Section 10.9, two of the modulation techniques can be used simultaneously to increase the data transmission rate through limited bandwidth radio channels.

The technical details of the original European analogue system, known as TACS/ETACS (Extended Total Access Communication System), were derived from the American AMPS (AT&T, Advanced Mobile Phone System) network. In the UK, the government allocated 1000 channels, around the 900 MHz frequency band, and shared them between the competing organizations, Cellnet and Vodaphone. The success of mobile phones has surpassed all expectations. Around London, within the M25 motorway ring, there has been a rapid saturation of resources, despite extra channels being made available and a reduction of cell size by the introduction of many more radio masts which allow the cell areas to be reduced.

The principal advantage of the cellular scheme is largely one of frequency sharing, sometimes termed 'spectrum reuse'. This enables the same frequency to be used simultaneously, without mutual interference, by a large number of handsets as long as they are not within immediately neighbouring cell areas. It is an example of spatial division multiplexing, in contrast to the frequency division and time division schemes. The radio spectrum is shared by geographically separating those who are using the same parts of the radio band. Signal compression methods are used to reduce the bandwidth needs further. Only 25 kHz is allocated for each conversation. Of the 1000 channels available, 21 are used for signalling and control rather than voice data.

The radio antenna serves an area or cell immediately around it. Neighbouring transmitting antennae may be connected by landline to a local base station and switching centre, as in Fig. 16.10. When a mobile handset is turned on after a period of power-down, it searches out the strongest control channel to lock onto, and registers its presence with the local base station. This information will be relayed by a

Fig. 16.10
Radio cell equipment and interconnection.

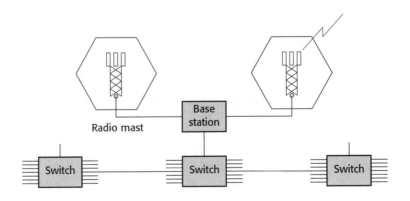

Table 16.1
Utilization of radio
frequency bands.

0.1–0.3 GHz	VHF	Terrestrial television and radio
0.3–1.0 GHz	UHF	Television, GSM mobile (0.9 GHz), packet radio, pagers
1.0–2.0 GHz		Navigation aids, GSM mobile (1.8 GHz)
2.4–2.5 GHz		Short-range radio control (Bluetooth)
3.4–3.5 GHz		Neighbourhood antennae

conventional network to the home base station so that calls may be redirected. If the mobile wishes to initiate a call it will signal through an available control channel, and wait to be allocated a voice channel. A call made to a mobile terminal uses the paging control channel to try to alert the mobile to the incoming call.

Radio bands (Table 16.1) have been oversubscribed for some years. The commercial demand for radio communications has been increasing since the early 1950s and the limited resources are now allocated in the UK to different application areas by band.

In addition to the public service transmitters, the requirement for domestic receive and transmit radio links has expanded rapidly. Due to the massive increase in the market that this has produced and the subsequent improvement in manufacturing capability, the cost of handsets has dropped very quickly.

In Fig. 16.11 you can see that any cell is separated from a cell with the same label by at least two cell widths. This means that the radio band allocated to a Cell 2 can be simultaneously used by all Cell 2s, as long as the transmission power is strictly controlled, preventing any cross-interference. The original 7 hex cell configuration allows a 1000 call band to support 1000/7 = 140 simultaneous calls in every cell with no frequency overlap. Thus, with an area divided into 100 such cells, there would be 14 000 simultaneous calls with minimum mutual interference. With the 4 cell repeat pattern (Fig. 16.12) the economics work out better: 1000/4 = 250, giving 25 000 simultaneous calls. By reducing the repeat factor and cell size the number of calls possible does increase; however, there are also other problems to be considered: the cost of building base stations and antennas, managing the increased rate of 'hand offs' as the mobiles roam from cell to cell, and the increased problem of mutual

Fig. 16.11
Cell arrangement with a
repeat 7 pattern of radio
frequencies.

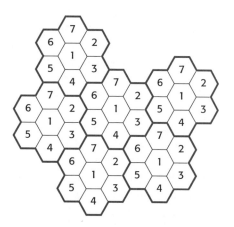

Fig. 16.12
A cell arrangement with
only repeat 4 pattern.

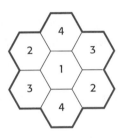

interference between nearby cells using the same frequency band. The result is a compromise, where the 7 cell repeat pattern is most commonly used by operators.

In GSM, the radio channels are structured in an **FDMA/TDMA** (Frequency Division Multiple Access/Time Division Multiple Access) format. This means that the channels are based on a TDMA signal format implemented on multiple frequency bands.

To further reduce mutual interference and conserve battery power, the strength of the handset transmissions is dynamically adjusted to the minimum level sufficient to maintain a satisfactory call. For the ground station transmissions, signal strengths are carefully adjusted to limit the spread of radio signals beyond the immediate cell vicinity. Statistics concerning the quality of service provided are continuously collected in order to respond to the changes which occur in the transmission environment due to the appearance of new buildings and competing radio sources.

The 900 MHz GSM allocation is split into two frequency bands: 890–915 MHz for the uplink (handset to base station) and 935–960 MHz for the downlink. These bands are further subdivided for FDMA into 124 pairs of carriers each spaced by 200 kHz. Every cell has a fixed assignment of up to fifteen frequency bands and the cell size can be anywhere from 1 to 5 km in diameter according to the local geography and user demand. Each of the 200 kHz channels is subdivided into time slots using a fixed TDMA format. This employs a gross rate of 270.833 kbps (bit duration of 3.69 µs), and a time slot carrying 156.25 bits, hence requiring a slot duration of 577 µs. There are eight time slots, forming a 4.615 ms transmission frame. A voice connection is allocated one of these eight time slots to use for the duration of a call.

With mobile radio handsets there are particular problems with varying signal strengths and multiple signals arising from reflections from nearby buildings and objects. The carrier wave frequencies can get Doppler shifted when communicating with fast vehicles, in the same way that train horns change their pitch as they rush past. All these effects are regulated by the equalizer circuits. This technique routinely transmits a known 26 bit test pattern to assist with tuning and optimization adjustments. Although conversations are classified as full duplex, handsets do not actually transmit and receive simultaneously, but alternately. To extract the very weak incoming signal from a relatively powerful outgoing burst would not be easy.

The handsets are of equal interest to the programmer, as they are packed with software to handle the call initiation and request as well as voice compression algorithms. Although the analogue speech signal from the internal microphone is sampled at 13 bits by the codec ADC 8000 times a second, this would be far too high a data rate. It is now compressed to a 13 kbps data stream before it is transmitted. The chosen compression algorithm, and the acceptance threshold of speech quality that users are happy with, are fiercely debated at committee meetings! The codec actually outputs 260 bits of encoded speech every 20 ms. This gives the 13 kbps (260/0.02 bps). To further reduce transmission bandwidth, silent periods are sensed and suppressed. This has the extra benefits of increasing the battery life and reducing radio interference effects. Voice data is heavily error protected by CRC, convolution codes and block interleaving. The 260 bits are subdivided into classes, with the first 182 bits, named class-1 bits, coded, while the other 78, named class-2 bits, are not coded. This is because some bits in the speech samples have a greater influence on the speech quality than others, so the error control is applied selectively to the more significant class. Block interleaving distributes related data across several transmission blocks, thus reducing the impact of burst noise interference. When an error is detected, the common strategy is to substitute the immediately previous speech sample for the damaged item.

In terms of processing needs, the principal demands within a GSM handset arise from the following: radio modem signal reception equalization, data encryption, speech compression encoding for transmission, speech resynthesis on reception, and channel data encoding and decoding. To assist with these very demanding (25 MIPs) real-time processing requirements, the handset has several CPUs, at least one of which is a DSP (Digital Signal Processor) optimized for dealing with speech data. The relationship between the principal units is shown in Fig. 16.13.

The type of modem employed to pass the digital voice and data over the analogue radio link is known as **GMSK** (Gaussian-filtered Minimum Shift Keying). **Roaming**, or 'handing over' of calls, as an active client moves from one cell to another should be done within 300 ms and is achieved through monitoring the signal strength of the neighbouring stations. The terrestrial network then orders the ongoing call to switch channels to another base station when the signal becomes too weak.

Fig. 16.13
GSM handset signal processing schematic (based on Redl *et al.* (1995)).

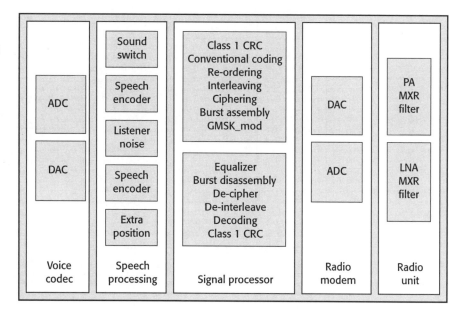

As with all analogue transmissions, the earlier TACS network suffered from loss of signal quality and the possibility of unauthorized eavesdropping. The current generation of cell phones, **GSM** (Groupe Spécial Mobile de Conférence Européene des Administrations des Postes et des Télécommunications), employs all-digital transmission techniques through using the GMSK carrier modulation technique. This gives many more channels, more security, better voice quality through more sophisticated compression techniques, powerful error correction, and simpler data transmission facilities. Thus personal portable fax equipment can be obtained and Internet browser handsets are now widely available. A Short Messaging Service (**SMS**) is already supported by the cellnet providers. This behaves rather like a bidirectional pager, allowing up to 160 bytes of text messages to be quickly transferred using a signalling channel not occupied by the principal voice data. Because of this it is possible to send and receive short text messages while a voice connection is active. When a GSM handset is used in normal 'circuit switched mode' to send and receive faxes or data by connecting to a PC, it is limited to a maximum transmission rate of 9600 bps, which is considerably slower than fixed line telephones. The alternative SMS facility is convenient for short text messages, but cannot be extended for longer file transfers. There are, however, SMS–email gateways which offer a forwarding service, allowing a mobile to send and receive short text emails.

A GSM cellular network comprises three parts: a mobile handset, the base station (BTS) with antenna, and a mobile telephone switching centre (MSC). We are now quite familiar with the mobile handsets, but less so with the other two, which form part of the necessary infrastructure. GSM is defined to allow insertion of a 'Subscriber Identity Module' (SIM) into handsets (see Fig. 16.14), in the form of a smartcard, to increase user security. Any mobile unit may have a new SIM inserted, and the user is then able to make and receive calls immediately. Every base station cell provides an

Fig. 16.14
GSM handset functional modules (based on Redl *et al.* (1995)).

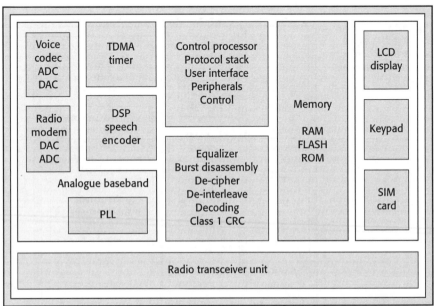

interface between the MSC and the mobile units, through the base station subsystem (BSS). This is composed of the radio transceiver station (BTS) and the base station controller (BSC). Cells are defined by the positioning of the BTS antenna. The Base Station Controller provides management of the radio resources, and the switching between the radio channels and the E1/TDM trunk used to communicate with the local MSC. The MSC controls call signalling and processing, and coordinates the handover of a mobile handset when it moves from one BTS cell to another. The Switching Centres link groups of neighbouring Base Stations using the normal point-to-point trunk lines or microwave channels.

Each MSC is in turn connected to the local public switched telephone network (PSTN or ISDN) to provide connection between the mobile and the fixed telephone users and also the other mobile cellular networks around the world. The MSC can also provide connection to public data networks (PDN), such as the packet switched data networks, so that users can also transmit/receive data through their mobile units.

GSM requires a number of databases which are used to manage handset mobility. This is designed for the convenience of roamers, users who move from one service system to another. The management of intersystem roaming is through two databases: the home location register (HLR) and the visiting location register (VLR). The HLR maintains and updates the mobile subscriber's location and his or her service profile information. The location update assists in routing incoming calls to the mobile. There is logically one HLR per GSM network. The VLR contains selected administrative information from the HLR, necessary for call control and provision of the subscribed services for a roaming subscriber.

To improve the data transmission capabilities of GSM the **GPRS** (General Packet Radio Service) facility has been agreed to provide a bandwidth of 170 kbps by simultaneously using all eight time slots within a frame to carry data (see Fig. 16.15). Such a data rate is capable of supporting mobile, hand-held web browsers, remote email terminals and similar applications. Each GPRS-enabled handset would require an Internet number and name, raising the vexed question of how to route packets efficiently when the destination terminal is allowed to change its position within the network. A new Internet protocol **WAP** (Wireless Application Protocol) has recently been introduced to allow authors of Web pages to specify what part of the page will be presented to a microbrowser running on a mobile telephone. In this way, textual and

Fig. 16.15
Packet structure for GSM voice

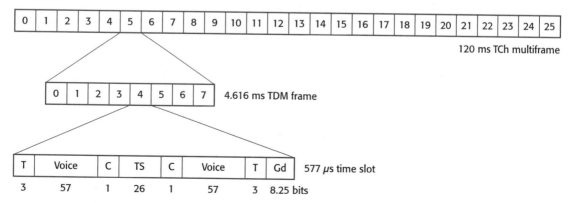

some graphical items will be made available to GSM users who swap over to the new WAP handsets, supplied with somewhat larger LCD screens.

The structure of GSM data and signalling protocols is very complex. The radio spectrum is divided into 200 kHz bands, offering 50 channels within the 10 MHz band. The digital transmissions are sent using a phase modulation technique which allows more than a single bit of data to be represented by a single state.

Each channel offers eight time slots within a repeating frame. The time slots accept 148 bit packets containing 114 bits of voice data. This comes from the speech encoding system used to compress the voice stream down to 13 kbps, which has error correction checksums appended to bring the rate up to 22.8 kbps. So if the 114 bits payload of each packet is to transport the 22.8 kbps data successfully, it must be sent at least every 5 ms ($114/22.8 = 5$). In fact, due to the extra signalling and control information, the delivery is more frequent, with an interval of 4.62 ms. To further improve the survival of signals in noisy conditions, the error correction code block is interleaved over eight frames, spanning 35 ms, which increases the resilience to burst damage.

Notice that the 8 kHz rate specified for the traditional telephone network has been avoided by using a lower bit rate encoding scheme. Each frame has eight time slots, which can operate as four duplex conversations. If slot 0 is allocated to transmit from base station to handset, slot 2 may be used to transmit in the reverse direction. The central 26 bit packet field is used to synchronize the receiver to the transmission and provide a measure of the strength of the current signal. This is especially useful in situations where multiple reflections from nearby structures are disrupting the reception of the principal signal. The encoded voice data is carried in two fields, either side of the synchronization field.

The radio transmissions run at the higher rate of 270.833 kbps, so that eight packets of data can be serially transmitted every 4.6 ms.

Unlike the previous analogue schemes, the standards are internationally agreed, allowing the same handsets to be used throughout Europe. Because of the reduction in manufacturing costs, the handsets have become much more accessible to the general public. This in turn may reduce the pressure on the supply of fixed line telephone connections, which in some countries has limited the availability of telecommunications facilities. Perhaps the 'virtual office' and 'remote information services' will at last become financially viable.

An interesting spin-off from the GSM industry has been the continuing improvement in speech compression techniques developed and refined for use in the small, mobile handsets. As described in Section 16.1, the fixed line digital telephone system adopted the 8 bit PCM scheme, with logarithmic compression (A-law or μ-law), giving a bit stream of 64 kbps. The enhanced parametric codecs used with GSM offer acceptable speech quality at only 16 kbps and even down to 2.4 kbps. The real-time algorithms used to achieve such a large amount of compression are very CPU-intensive, sometimes requiring 20 MIPS of processing power to run fast enough to keep up with human speech data. All this has to be packed into a small battery-powered unit. Specially designed **DSPs** (Digital Signal Processors) are used to speed up the arithmetic operations and carry out more and more speech compression. If you remember that halving the bandwidth required for a telephone conversation goes a long way to doubling the revenue, you can appreciate the resources that telecomms companies are prepared to invest in such programming efforts!

16.3   ATM – asynchronous transfer mode

WANs provide the long-haul connections between the LANs, which all go together to make what is called the Internet. As described in Chapters 14 and 15, the routing methods used by LANs and WANs are very different. LANS rely on broadcast while WANS need routing switches to divert messages to their destinations. There are several network technologies available for supporting WAN traffic. The **PSS** (Packet Switched Service) sevice in Britain, referred to as SMDS (Switched Multimegabit Data Service) in North America, Frame Relay, X25 and, most recently introduced, ATM. Each has advantages and disadvantages, but I will only offer a description of ATM because it is probably the candidate most likely to succeed in the future.

ATM (Asynchronous Transfer Mode), is a true virtual circuit networking technology developed by the telephone industry in response to the growing success of the Internet and the desire to provide a unified and more flexible way of satisfying the rapidly increasing demand for transmission facilities. If a single network could cope with telephone and data, there would be great savings to be gained. Also, it has been predicted that much money could be made by an organization which solves the technical problems which currently prevent viewers downloading full-length feature films through the telephone line rather than making trips to their local video store. The bandwidth limitation of standard domestic telephone lines is a major technical hurdle to be overcome – the replacement costs would be prohibitive in most areas, although organizations offering cable television have justified the expense by simultaneously installing television channels and enhanced telephone connections.

From Fig. 16.16 it can be seen that there is a setup delay in establishing a call through a circuit switched network, which then works more quickly than the datagram packet routing equivalent. This indicates that from the user's point of view, packet networks are suitable for short, occasional communications, where frequent setup costs have to be taken into account.

A different strategy is used for ATM. The communication route, or **Virtual Circuit** is established at the start of the session and remains unchanged, thereby nearly eliminating the routing overhead experienced by TCP/IP data packets. The cells, or minipackets, do not carry full destination addresses but get switched by the ATM routers according to a 24 bit number held in the cell header. To assist with rerouting and the general organization of traffic through the network, the virtual circuits are often grouped together within so called virtual paths. This is more apparent when the cell header is inspected (Fig. 16.17) and the division into two parts called VPI (Virtual Path Indicator) and VCI (Virtual Circuit Indicator) is recognized. During most of the

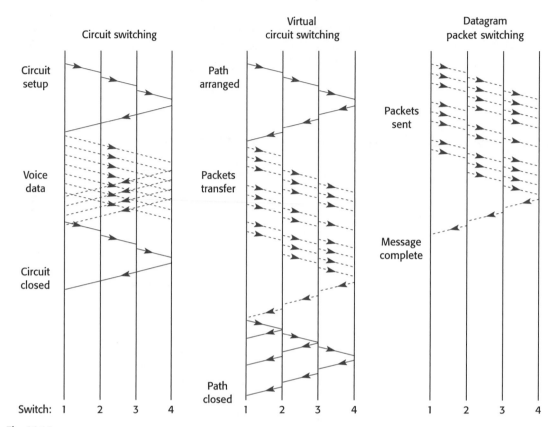

Fig. 16.16
Comparison of circuit
switched and packet
switched message
timing.

data cell's travels through the network, only the upper, VPI, value is used to select the route; however, at the final switch the VCI is used to select the destination line to the client's equipment.

The development of ATM protocols and routing algorithms has been accompanied by a large improvement in line driver circuitry. Differential line driving techniques have enabled the engineers to far exceed the earlier line speed limitations by reducing the impact of electrical noise and cross-channel interference. So, while RS232 serial communications would fail above 19 600 bps, and Ethernet was rated at 10 Mbps, the newer drivers raised the speed for transmission along unscreened twisted pair cabling to 52 Mbps and even 155 Mbps for better quality cable. The same techniques have allowed Ethernet to be upgraded to 100 Mbps. Achieving such high data rates does require some sophisticated coding methods to be used, such as 8B6T, illustrated in Table 14.3.

Fig. 16.17
The ATM frame structure.

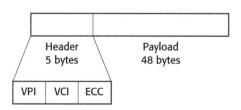

The intention is for ATM networks to carry both constant rate traffic, voice and video, as well as variable rate data traffic. The primary transmission rate is 155 Mbps and may use optical fibre or cheaper twisted pair cable. Despite the fundamentally synchronous nature of voice traffic, the higher speed of the ATM network should be able to transfer the 64 kbps streams as long as busy routes are not permitted to become overloaded. ATM uses hub circuit switches similar to a telephone PABX, but offers a mini-packet delivery service, not circuit leasing.

ATM follows the LAN method of dividing data into packets for transmission, but uses smaller fixed size packets called **cells**. These consist of 53 bytes, of which 48 are data and five are reserved for addressing information in the header. This header is much simpler than the Ethernet and IP equivalents in order to reduce the processing time at routing switches.

The cells carrying a message are all routed along a pre-established route, making ATM a switched virtual circuit, connection-oriented technology. By using virtual circuits the transmission can be established with a guaranteed minimum bandwidth and maximum through delay. A call is established by dispatching a SETUP message and bandwidth is reserved for the duration of the session. Much consideration has gone into dealing with 'bursty' traffic which might occasionally hog the whole route at the expense of other users, while remaining within the agreed maximum traffic ceiling as measured by the average value of cells/second.

ATM switches, as illustrated in Fig. 16.18, come in various sizes, offering from 16 to 1024 ports. The routing is achieved by setting up within the switch a routing table associating each active input port with an output port. The arriving data cell has a code number in the header which is used to select the port pairing, and so route the data cell to an output port. The data cell routing code in the header is not held constant throughout the trip, but modified at each switch ready for the next node. The switching mechanism is made to act as fast as possible, given the requirement to pass data from several input ports, each running at 155 Mbps. This precludes a software-based lookup table approach. Mostly, suppliers are relying more and more on configurable gate arrays, as mentioned in Section 4.4. Besides the basic routing function, from input port to output port, the ATM switch must have a way of dealing with collisions. These happen when two incoming cells simultaneously request the same output port. To cope with this situation, either one cell has to be discarded, or it must be held back for the other to pass. The latter option is more popular!

Fig. 16.18
Schematic ATM router switch.

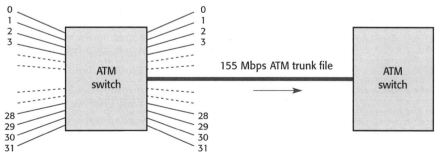

Fig. 16.19

Interconnection inside an ATM Banyan switch.

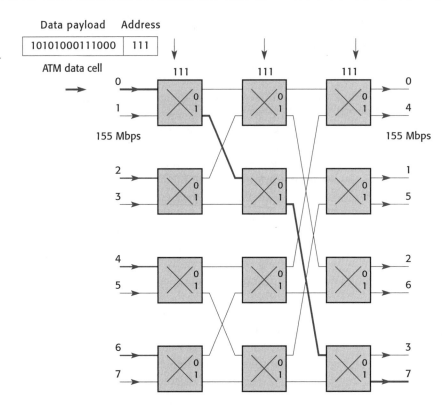

The schematic structure of an 8 × 8 (3 bit address) ATM switch is shown in Fig. 16.19. Switches which handle far more input–output ports are commercially available. This type is known as a Banyan switch because of the complex interconnecting pathways. The whole unit is constructed from 2 × 2 switching elements which are wired in such a way as to provide progressive routing from column to column. The internal routing logic is referred to as the 'fabric', so the Banyan switch is said to offer 'self-routing fabric'. Any of the left-hand inputs can be switched through to any of the right-hand outputs. In each switching element, one output is selected by an address bit value 0, while the other is selected by an address bit value 1. The first column of switches use the most-significant address bit, switches in the middle column are controlled by the middle address bit, and the final, right-hand, column is switched by the least-significant bit.

Follow an imaginary cell arriving with address 7 (111) as its destination. The first switch selects the lower output port, transferring the data cell to the middle column, where again the lower port gets selected by the value of the middle address bit (1). Finally, the lower port is selected in the last switching stage to pass the data out to port 7. Check that this works for each of the eight input ports. Then try some different 3 bit address values.

ATM switches with self-routing fabrics behave in some ways as miniature versions of the Internet. The next-hop destination is determined moment by moment as the

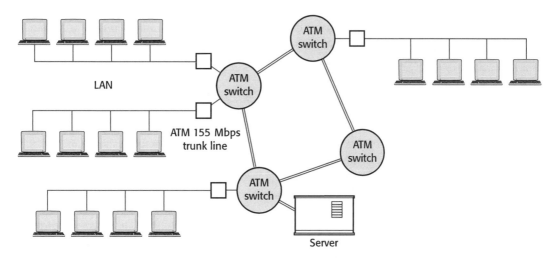

Fig. 16.20
ATM WAN links
joining together
diverse LANs to form
part of the Internet.

data cell progresses through the fabric, in the same way that a datagram is directed by the intermediate router hubs.

If both inputs to a switching element want to go to the same output port, there is a clash. Several remedies can be employed to attempt to resolve this traffic jam. Storage buffers can be provided so that data cells can be held back and routed later. Or the switching rate could be set at double the arrival rate, enabling the two inputs to be polled in turn. To provide an insight into how good these techniques can be in reducing the packet loss rate, it is interesting to note the results of a computer simulation for a large (1024 × 1024) Banyan switch run at full input load. With the internal links running at twice the cell rate (and hence capable of establishing two subsequent paths within one time slot) and a buffer size of five cells in each switching element, as many as 92% of the input cells were safely delivered, compared with about 25% for an unbuffered design.

An ATM network is assembled by interconnecting several ATM switching hubs. When the peripheral LANs and servers are taken into account we can see (Fig. 16.20) how the Internet is formed.

16.4 Messaging – radio paging and packet radio networks

Passing text messages to and from mobile terminals has been a less exciting area of technical development which has not yet caught the public imagination in the same way as voice-oriented cellphones. The original 'beep' pagers, often associated with hospitals, have now been developed to handle numeric codes, alphabetical messages and even short voice recordings. The ability to reach someone, wherever they are, by simply using the ordinary telephone network, is a valuable service and remains much cheaper and more reliable than the cellnet mobile telephone service. Pagers remain a one-way communication medium which has the advantage of not requiring expensive rechargeable batteries, because primary cells can last more than 3 months without replacement. The signalling method commonly used is frequency modulation of the carrier wave. For the international Eurosignal paging system, a sequence of six 100 ms tone bursts are transmitted for each call. The frequencies are chosen from a set of ten discrete tones, so there are a million address values available to address pager units. Calls are separated by 200 ms intervals, giving a maximum call rate of 1.25/s. The more recent digital paging systems use a more complex coding system. The British POCAG (Post Office Code Standardization Advisory Group) protocol has been accepted by the ITU as a standard for international pagers. It uses a 20 bit address packaged into a 32 bit cell, or codeword, with a 10 bit BCH error detection checksum. Each address may also select one out of four actions or displays using a 2 bit function code. For transmission, the codewords are batched into groups of 16, with a preceding 16 bit synchronization header. To send numeric or alphabetic messages, the codewords following the address word will contain data. This is marked by the leading bit, which signifies an address word when 0 and a data word when 1. Messages can be any length, terminating when the next address word arrives. The bandwidth for pager transmissions is very low (1024 bps), but the geographic coverage of the transmitters is very extensive and the error rate relatively low. This is necessary because there is no acknowledgement of the successful receipt of the pager message unless the target user responds with a telephone call. The digital paging word format is shown in Fig. 16.21.

An international alpha messaging standard operates throughout Europe (ERMES) using the 169 MHz band. Service operators offer the possibility of paying only for the calls made, after the pocket pager has been purchased. This reduces the administrative costs as the charges can be collected through the telephone bill of the caller. Pager networks use a multiple frequency FSK system to encode the binary data in much the same way as the previous generation of telephone modems. Where pagers offer more than the basic alert service, a numeric or alphabetic display is required. These are usually multi-character LCD panels with a message store provided by 2 kbyte of static CMOS RAM. A recent development was the marketing of wristwatch pagers with

Fig. 16.21
Digital paging word format.

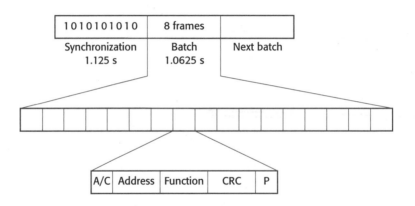

Fig. 16.22
Application of packet
radio data messaging.

LCD displays, and high coverage satellite-based systems are also available which are suitable for certain applications.

An alternative bidirectional messaging service is based on **packet radio**. This has developed in the commercial area to support travelling delivery and service staff, but has now extended into other enterprises, such as on-street car parking (Fig. 16.22) and the direction of emergency vehicles. The technology relates closely to the original experiments in Hawaii with the **Aloha** wireless broadcasts. One operator of packet radio services has divided the allocated radio band into 30 channels, each of which is capable of transferring data at 8 kbps. The message packet size is 512 bytes, which may not be transferred immediately, but stored and transmitted onward at the convenience of the network. This is a text paging service, with the extra facility allowing the mobile receiver to acknowledge and even reply to the message. Communications are private, with any connection to the Internet being the responsibility of the end user. But advances are being made in this area, and portable, fully Internet-compliant email terminals are coming onto the market. These will require their own IP numbers, and the need to route IP packets to mobile hosts is a difficult problem. One solution is to require that all packets have to pass through a central host, which then has the responsibility for tracking the handheld units and forwarding the packets. Such a system is not based on circuit switched cellular technology. The radio bandwidth is shared in the same way that an Ethernet LAN accepts data packets from many sources on a first come, first served schedule. The transmitter/receiver stations serve surrounding areas for about 25 miles, larger than GSM cells.

16.5   ISDN – totally digital

When the PTTs started in the early 1980s to contemplate the wholesale conversion of telephone facilities to fully digital technology, enormous costs and difficulties were anticipated in the change. Interestingly, the introduction of digital technology by the mobile phone companies has rapidly outpaced the traditional fixed line market sector. In Europe, few digital lines are installed to domestic premises. Commercial provision is higher, but still lags far behind the early optimistic predictions. Perhaps the opportunity has now passed, and ISDN for customer connection, direct to the home and office, will be replaced by the more recent, faster technologies offered through cable television networks and DSL modems.

ISDN (Integrated Digital Services Network) was conceived as a means of rationalizing data and voice provision and increasing the end-to-end bandwidth. This aim must be set against the bandwidth limits imposed on traditional telephone lines of only 4 kHz, so promising an increase to 64 kbps was judged impressive. The 4 kHz constraint was originally introduced to reduce mutual electrical interference between neighbouring calls and so allow the maximum utilization of transmission and switching equipment. To achieve the proposed increase to 64 kbps, through the implementation of ISDN, required thorough refurbishment of switching centres and the cooperation of subscribers in the purchase of new handsets and interfacing equipment. For whatever reason, this has not really happened. ISDN handsets are a rare breed. However, the previous acceptance of narrowband analogue telephone lines by domestic subscribers has recently been disturbed by the popularity of the Internet, and a growing impatience with lengthy download times. Although more sophisticated modems allow the transmission of more than one bit for each clock pulse (see Fig. 16.9) the 4 kHz limit remains in place. ISDN still offers a way out of this straitjacket by providing the possibility of subscribers benefiting from two simultaneous 64 kbps voice and data channels.

ISDN comes in two versions: broadband (B-ISDN) and narrowband (N-ISDN). The latter is the service offered to ordinary clients (Fig. 16.23) and is often referred to as 2B-1D ISDN, because it provides two 64 kbps basic voice channels and one 16 kbps data channel. These three channels are full duplex. Interface points to the ISDN network are defined by the ITU and referred to as R, S, T and U. The NT1 network

Fig. 16.23
Narrowband ISDN
defined interfaces.

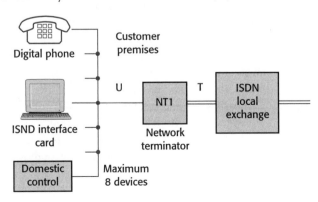

terminator provides the T standard point for customers to connect their ISDN-compliant equipment. Special terminal adaptors also offer the R interface which is a general non-ISDN connection.

N-ISDN transmissions occur as baseband signals, like Ethernet, but are perhaps considered rather slow in comparison with the speeds offered by the recent broadband (carrier modulated) services. B-ISDN (broadband) is normally only used for high capacity trunk lines because it can carry 30 voice channels and 1 common signalling channel. It is now based on ATM technology. This has already been introduced in Section 16.3. Rather surprisingly perhaps, N-ISDN is a circuit switched protocol while B-ISDN is packet switched, although deployed in virtual circuit mode!

Narrowband ISDN was designed in order to use the existing, low grade twisted pair cable from the local exchange to the customer's premises. Within this constraint it can provide two digital voice channels and a third lower rate data channel. If we look back to the origins of ISDN, the technological view was very different. Computer terminals provided only character display and so required serial links of only 1.2 kbps, or 9.6 kbps if you were fortunate. Voice, in comparison, was seen as high-capacity traffic, demanding 64 kbps. The view today is very different. Screens are linked directly to PCs through short, high-bandwidth cables carrying 30 MHz video signals. LANs are being upgraded from 10 to 100 Mbps. This increase in the requirements for transmitting complex image and video streams is set beside the success in compressing voice data down to 16 kbps. The tables have been turned – handling voice traffic is no longer the speed goal to be aimed at. The commercial interest is now focused on the possibility of transmitting full-length video films across the telephone network. ISDN will have to adapt quickly to this change if it is to survive as a useful standard.

The ISDN basic voice channel was set at 64 kbps because of the availability of reliable equipment to handle 8 bit digitization 8000 times a second. Such channels, even operating in tandem, cannot satisfy the current desire for dial-up video. With domestic users able to buy 56 kbps modems, and commercial offices installing 100 Mbps switched Ethernet LANs, the prospect of paying a premium for the upgrade to 64 kbps is not very attractive. Consequently there is a question mark over the continuing development of ISDN. It is now debated whether the newer technologies, such as DSL, have overtaken and will displace 2B-1D ISDN in the role of providing the fixed line connection to clients.

The baseband (non-modulated) transmission technique adopted for the N-ISDN subscriber connection transmits digitally in full duplex mode and is illustrated in Fig. 16.24. This is possible only if the cable is using similar echo cancellation circuits to those employed in the V.32 modem (Section 10.9). To further increase the data rate a multilevel transmission code is used (Fig. 16.25). In Europe this involves three voltage levels (+V, 0, −V) and in the USA, there are four levels (+V/2, +V/4, −V/4, −V/2). This allows four bits of data to be represented by three 'trits', or, in the USA, two bits to be

Fig. 16.24
2B-1D narrowband
ISDN protocol timing.

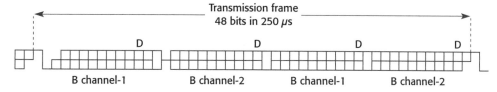

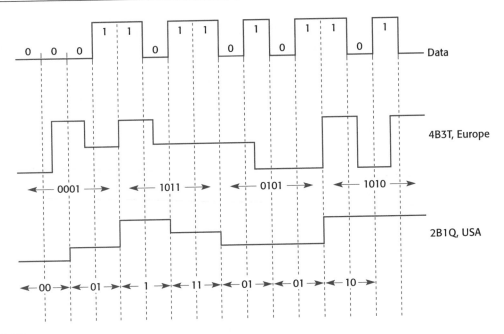

Fig. 16.25
Multi-level baseband
encoding increases
the bit signalling rate.

transmitted with a single 'quat'. Notice how a single frame of data holds two samples
for both the B (voice) channels and similarly for the D (data) channels.

The full set of three-level codes is given in Table 16.2. As there are more possible
codes ($3^3 = 27$) than needed for the 16 numbers to be transmitted, the extra codes are
used to provide alternative values which can be used to maintain the line average at

Table 16.2
Three-level 4B3T
encoding table.

Binary data	3-level codes	
0 0 0 0	+ 0 −	
0 0 0 1	− + 0	
0 0 1 0	0 − +	
0 0 1 1	+ − 0	
0 1 0 0	+ + 0	− − 0
0 1 0 1	0 + +	0 − −
0 1 1 0	+ 0 +	− 0 −
0 1 1 1	+ + +	− − −
1 0 0 0	+ + −	− − +
1 0 0 1	− + +	+ − −
1 0 1 0	+ − +	− + −
1 0 1 1	+ 0 0	− 0 0
1 1 0 0	0 + 0	0 − 0
1 1 0 1	0 0 +	0 0 −
1 1 1 0	0 + −	
1 1 1 1	− 0 +	

zero over the length of a message. This assists the electronic engineers in building their circuits.

16.6   DSL – digital subscriber line

For many years it was believed that the poor quality of the 'local loop' copper wires leading into subscriber premises was the main constraint on telephone line transmission rates. Recently, however, this view has been challenged. The amazing success of the telecomms industry in driving 30 channel PCM trunk lines at 2.048 Mbps using the same type of cable seemed to have passed unnoticed. But now there is a new proposal for a high-speed (1 Mbps) data service to homes and small offices: DSL (Digital Subscriber Line). This retains the analogue voice technology but shares the same line with new high-speed modems as shown in Fig. 16.26. Line sharing is possible by utilizing carrier frequencies for the data transmissions outside the audible range. This also raises the maximum data rate ceiling. To avoid the need to pass the wide bandwidth data through telephone switching equipment, the data and voice signals are split apart at the entry to the local exchange. Voice follows its traditional route, while the data, after being demodulated, is incorporated in an ATM-based network. In this way the subscriber can effectively use the normal dial-up telephone network while simultaneously enjoying immediate access to a data network, as with the office LAN.

Asynchronous Digital Subscriber Line (ADSL) acknowledges the larger demand for fast Internet downloads by unequally dividing up the bandwidth. At top performance, a file download can proceed at 4 Mbps, while the uplink gets by with only 1 Mbps (not forgetting that a telephone call can also take place simultaneously). The allocation of bandwidth by an ADSL modem and splitter is illustrated in Fig. 16.27. This device divides the frequency bandwidth into the 4 kHz voice channel, a data up-channel of 135 kHz and a download channel of 540 kHz. By employing the multilevel encoding schemes described in Section 10.9, the bit rate can again exceed the carrier frequency. So with an eight-level scheme (QAM) we could obtain a 4 Mbps download speed and a 1 Mbps uplink. The generous separation of the three bands allows the data/voice

Fig. 16.26
Digital subscriber line
configuration.

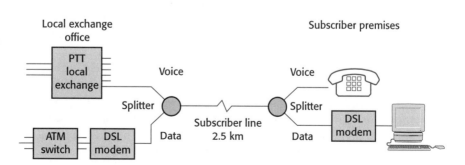

Fig. 16.27
Subscriber line
bandwidth allocation for
ADSL communication.

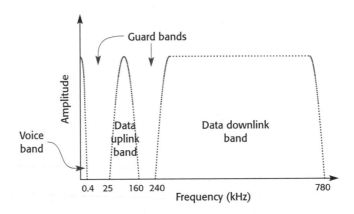

splitting to be achieved by straightforward electronic filtering. This avoids the need
for more sophisticated echo cancellation circuits.

The establishment of a universal standard for DSL is currently being fought over
within the industry. The potential confusion for early customers can be appreciated
from the list of some of the technologies which are in contention: ADSL, ADSL-Lite,
G.Lite, SDSL, HDSL, IDSL and VDSL. Internal PCI modems are now available from
several suppliers, but of course there is no use obtaining one unless the local PTT
supports the DSL service.

16.7   Cable television – facilities for data transmission

Local cable networks were set up to distribute a range of television channels and offer
an alternative source of telephone interconnectivity. In the UK this has mainly been
achieved using a hybrid technology involving fibre optic trunk lines and twinned
coax/twisted pair subscriber links. Whereas the traditional subscriber telephone
required several kilometres of cabling to connect through to the exchange, the cable
operators pushed the first level interface right out onto the neighbourhood streets.
Such interfaces demodulate and demultiplex the high-capacity fibre optic channels,
separating television from telephone, and retransmitting the signals along copper
wires into the subscribers' premises. It is as if some of the exchange equipment had
been relocate to the street kerbside. Figure 16.28 illustrates the organization of this
new design of network. The use of fibre optic, coax and twisted pair cables has generated the descriptive term Hybrid Fibre-Coax (HFC). The benefits of using optical
fibre for local trunk distribution has massively increased the potential bandwidth
available to the subscriber. So far it has been allocated to traditional analogue television broadcasts and analogue telephony, but the changeover to digital encoding is
currently underway. The Headend office brings together the various television signals
from satellite and terrestrial sources. These require frequency shifting to multiplex
them all, together with the modulated telephone signals, onto the light emitter for

Fig. 16.28
Cable network television and telephone distribution scheme.

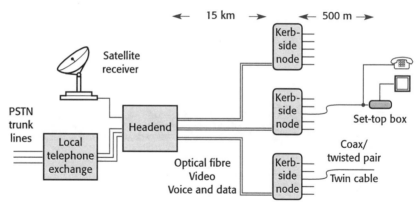

passing down the distribution fibre. At each of the local kerbside boxes, the light signals from a fibre are converted into electrical equivalents for onward transmission to the subscriber's 'set-top box'. It is here that the television and telephone signals are separated and the VHF television channels are sent along the coax part of a twinned cable to the set-top box. Here, the VHF television signal is converted into the UHF band for compatibility with contemporary television receivers and video recorders. The partner side of the twin cable provides several twisted pairs, one of which is used to carry the traditional analogue telephone signal.

The majority of the 745 MHz bandwidth is used to transmit the 59 television channels. Only 12 MHz is committed to telephony! A VHF analogue television signal is employed, modulated onto the PHz (light oscillates at 10^{15} Hz) carrier waves. With the change to digital, this same band is capable of transmitting 700 digitally compressed (MPEG-2) video streams for digital television.

As can be seen from the spectral allocation presented in Fig. 16.29, there are considerable regions set aside for interactive digital communication. Unlike the traditional telephone network, neighbourhood cable is far from saturated.

Internet access will be speeded up with the arrival of high-frequency cable modems. These fulfil the same role as traditional modems, but operate at up to 10 Mbps rather than 56 kbps. It seems that neighbouring subscribers will share a 10 Mbps access channel, providing a LAN-like facility to equal the Ethernet 10Base2 standard as far as the kerbside node. Unfortunately, such a scheme will eventually suffer from the same problem of excess demand, leading to unpredictable traffic delays.

The new standard for passing data over cable is now defined by **DOCSIS** (Data Over Cable Service Interface Specification). Where communications between

Fig. 16.29
Indicative bandwidth allocation for a neighbourhood cable network.

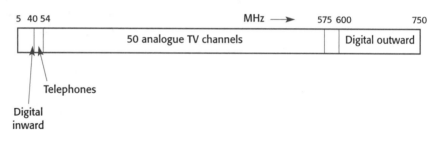

subscribers to services provided by different network operators are concerned, standards are essential.

Review

- The telephone network routes (connects) using circuit switching. This may no longer mean a solid copper pathway from end to end, but does commit, and charge for, bandwidth resource throughout the duration of the call. Data transmissions can be carried out using modem units at both ends.

- Voice signals are digitized for long distance transmission, but local digital connection (ISDN) is still quite rare except for specialist business needs. Trunk lines commonly use 32 channel time division multiplexing (TDM) operating at 2.048 Mbps.

- Interconnection switches (exchanges) may use cross-point switch arrays, time slot shifting or a combination of both to route calls.

- Telephone cards (CTI) can be inserted into ISA/PCI slots to provide fully integrated data/telecomms facilities as required by call centres. The TAPI programmer's interface supports this type of development.

- The GSM mobile phone network is a wireless, land line hybrid scheme which has been very successful. Beyond voice, it offers 'traditional' data transmission using modems, SMS via the low-capacity control channels and 170 kbps GPRS direct digital connection.

- ATM technologies have been adopted for trunk voice and data lines. It provides another example of technological convergence. It uses fixed length packets (cells) and virtual circuit routing.

- The less well-known packet radio system also offers connectionless data transfer for low to medium capacity applications. It could be seen as an extension of bidirectional paging.

- The long-coming ISDN fully digital network looks set to flop. The subscriber version (N-ISDN) costs too much, and the endpoint bandwidth (64 kbps) now appears unimpressive. The performance is limited by baseband subscriber loop transmission and the unmanageable expense of upgrading exchange equipment. The long distance trunk version (B-ISDN) has merged into ATM (155 Mbps).

- DSL offers radio frequency modems from home to exchange, fitting in above the analogue voice band. This potentially offers up to 10 Mbps to the subscriber using existing twisted pair cabling.

- Cable television companies have installed new hybrid optical fibre/coaxial cable infrastructure using revenue from pay-to-view channels. The original analogue transmission scheme will be supplemented by a digital system as equipment becomes available. Bandwidth availability will match ADSL – until all your neighbours get online!

Practical work

The practical session requires some research, using the Internet, for information on the current state of mobile telephony and the plans for the next (UMTS) generation. You may be able to use GSM technology through your mobile phone to test the gateway between the Internet and your telephone network provider.

Exercises

1. What is the normal bandwidth in Hz allocated to an analogue telephone? How many bps does this require after 8 bit digitization? What is the bandwidth of broadcast quality stereo music? How many bps does this require after digitization at 16 bits per sample?

2. Given the rather modest upper frequency limit of an analogue telephone line (3.3 kHz), how can modems transmit at such a high data rate (56 kbps)?

3. What compression techniques can be applied to speech data in order to reduce the bandwidth demands? Which are used by GSM?

4. Draw carrier waves modulated in the three principal ways: AM, FM and PM. Try combinations of the 3 techniques.

5. What are the major differences between LAN, IP and ATM routing methods?

6. Draw out the cell repeat pattern for the 7 hex scheme. Show that the interference between cells allocated the same frequency band is increased with a 4 hex repeat scheme.

7. Why is the current GSM data transmission rate limited to 9600 bps? For GSM, what is the difference between the transmission technique used by SMS and the proposed GPRS?

8. As both the telephone codec and the modem convert signals from analogue to digital and back, what is the difference between them?

9. What is the maximum bit rate offered by N-ISDN? How does this compare with the more recent ADSL standard? Analogue television transmissions require 6 MHz. After digitization and MPEG compression, this reduces to a data stream of 1.5 Mbps. How could this be transmitted to your home?

10. The time division switch needs to pass an 8 bit sample of voice, for every connected line, once every 125 μs. If there are 1000 lines, what is the maximum read–write cycle time allowable? Would you use 60 ns EDO DRAM for the data buffers?

Readings

- Tanenbaum (1996)
- Comer (1999)
- Macario (1997)
- Schiller (1999)

- ATM technology, especially switch design, is presented in:
  `http://www.rad.com/networks/1994/pak-swi/intro.htm`

- For an introduction to GSM technology try:
  `http://ccnga.uwaterloo.ca/~jscouria/GSM/gsmreport.html#3.1`

- This is a useful summary of GPRS:
  `http://www.mobilewap.com/whatiswap.htm`

  Also:
  `http://www.links2mobile.com/`

- A good introduction to ISDN can be found at:
  `http://www.ralphb.net/ISDN/`

- For more technical information on ISDN try:
  `http://www.3com.com/nsc/500606.html`

- For an introduction to the technical issues behind DSL, try:
  `http://www.virata.com/broadband.html`

- A quick summary of the new data techniques can be read at:
  `http://www.cis.ohio-state.edu/~jain/cis788-97/rbb/index.htm#Cable`

- A good introduction to GSM technology can be found in: Redl *et al.* (1995).

- The Web sites can be accessed via the Companion Web site for this book at:
  `http://www.booksites.net/williams/`

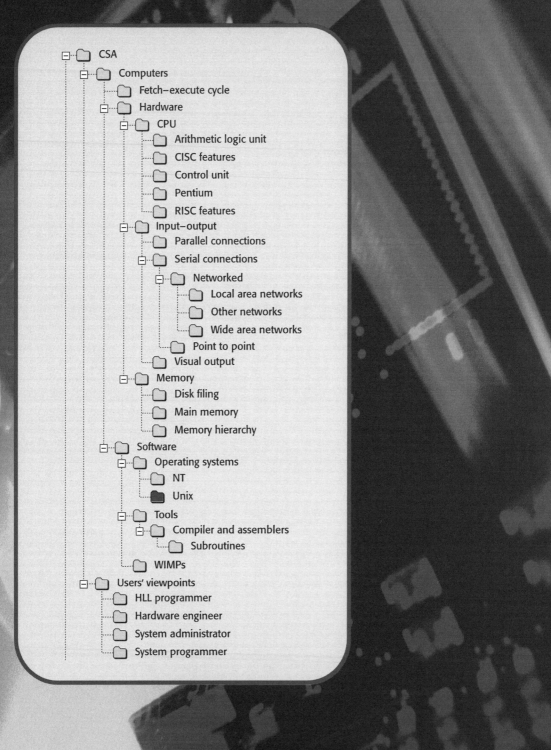

Introduction to operating systems

17

Overview

Operating systems (Unix, Windows 95/98 and NT/ 2000, Linux) are special programs, or groups of programs, designed to help users employ the resources of the computer more securely and efficiently. With multi-user, and even single-user multitasking systems, the allocation, arbitration and control of shared resources are primary functions. When the computer is shared between a number of users, the problem of data security becomes paramount. More and more, the operating system provides convenient access to a network and the Internet beyond. Unix remains an important commercial example, and has also attracted more enthusiasts with the introduction of the Linux version.

17.1   Historic origins – development of basic functions

Some of the major components of the **operating system** have already been introduced in earlier chapters: memory management, networking, WIMP interfaces, IO device drivers. This chapter is an attempt to bring them all together into a unified perspective and understand their interactions. As already stated, the operating system provides the character of the machine more than any other unit of hardware or software. Changing the CPU will probably go undetected, but changing from MS-DOS to Windows, or from VMS to Unix would never pass unnoticed! The operating system resides as a layer between the hardware and the user application code. This situation can facilitate the porting of application code from one hardware platform to another, as long as both platforms run the same operating system, or at least the same API. The **API** (Application Programming Interface) is the set of function calls which an operating system makes available to the applications software. Microsoft has provided a standard API, called WIN32, for all its operating systems: 98, NT, CE and 2000. Unix has a similar range of different functions to encompass all the normal operating system facilities. When porting software, if the original platform and the new platform offer different APIs, the process can be very time-consuming and fraught with hidden difficulties.

Fig. 17.1
Types of computer operating system.

Operating systems can broadly be divided into either **Batch**, **Online** or **Real-Time**, as expressed diagrammatically in Fig. 17.1. Batch systems are now less popular than

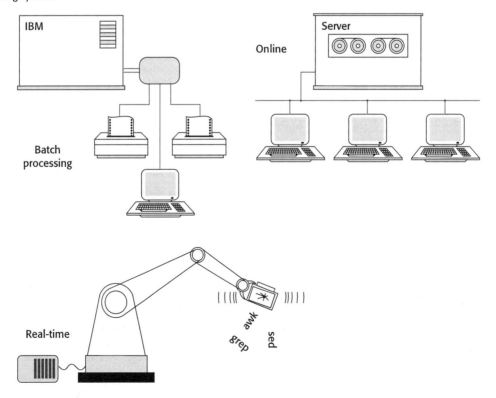

previously, perhaps because they are offered on larger, more expensive computers. In addition, they are not in principle structured to allow executing programs to communicate directly with user terminals. This has never been a popular limitation with programmers. Online, time-sharing, multi-user systems are better for program development and interactive computing. Users can share the CPU and other resources because the system rapidly switches the focus of fetch–execute from one program to another. Online systems can be further divided into time-sharing systems and personal computing. Examples of the former can be seen in travel agencies, where they give access to large central databases of holiday and travel information, or in banks where they update customer account records. The latter type of system can be seen in homes and offices across the land! Finally, real-time systems specialize in applications requiring a rapid response to events in the world. They are often employed in the monitoring and control of apparatus or machines, but this definition is now stretched to include equipment like set-top boxes and data switches. In fact, the three formal categories overlap considerably, as the various available operating systems offer facilities which blur the distinctions. For example, Unix offers a batch queue facility. The **real-time executive** OS-9 has a well-developed file manager and several interactive shells.

Small, embedded microprocessor systems are sometimes developed to run entirely without the support of an operating system. The application programmers take on the responsibility for all the task scheduling, IO handling and memory allocation. If only a constant well-defined functionality is required, this may be successful at the start, and result in a tightly coded, efficient product. But if further developments are later demanded, or the application has to respond to the demands of an unpredictable environment, such an approach will inevitably become unworkable.

It should now be clear that computer hardware cannot do anything until a program has been loaded into main memory. The problem of how to load the first program into a bare memory is known as the bootstrap problem after the 'self lifting' dilemma. Before the mid-1960s, a short routine would have to be 'toggled' by hand into memory using binary front-panel switches. Now, a permanent loader program is available in BIOS PROM, ready to be executed immediately the power is switched on. This begins a complex sequence, outlined in Fig. 17.2, during which hardware is checked and initialized, software is loaded and installed, and finally the multi-user login facility is enabled. In this situation, the **bootstrap loader** loads another more sophisticated loader which then brings in the main operating system program from disk. So an important function of operating system code is to bring itself into memory ready to accept further commands from the user.

Another disadvantage of the early computers was their inability to offer services to more than one user at a time. They were truly **single-user systems**. The pioneering programmers worked with little help beyond primitive monitor software which allowed them to trigger binary core dumps when their programs crashed. Debugging was time-consuming and tedious. Often, even access to IO and auxiliary tape storage was left to the ingenuity of the applications programmer. This duplication of effort was very inefficient and quickly led to the sharing of loader, IO and mathematical routines which had been written and tested by other programmers. To make the

Fig. 17.2
Unix boot sequence.

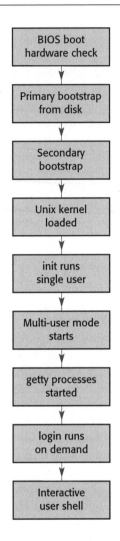

situation worse, it seems that most of the early programming development was done in the middle of the night when computer time was more readily available! Programming involved assembler code because compilers had yet to be invented.

The first operating systems were administered from moment to moment by technicians who manually loaded user programs into a job queue from decks of punched cards. They then watched over them as they ran, one after the other. Most users wrote their own software; there were few 'packages' beyond programmers' tools, so compiling the programs became a major concern. To gain some improvement in throughput, it was usual to organize compiler time. Thus if you wanted to compile a FORTRAN program you waited until Tuesday, when the FORTRAN compiler would be loaded! Perhaps COBOL was Wednesday. This was done because of the excessive length of time it took to load the compiler program from tape. More frustratingly, there was no possibility of any user interaction with their running programs. The input data was read from pre-prepared cards and the output normally sent to a line printer. If a program crashed, as it usually did, an octal core dump was printed out on paper for debugging purposes. Programming, in those days, required as much grim determination as technical skill!

When disk units became larger, users were encouraged to store their data online because it was more reliable. This helped to speed up data processing. But this gave rise to new problems. Writing blocks of data onto your own personal tape was acceptable because any programming error resulted in consequences only for you. However, accessing a shared disk introduced a new calibre of general risk. Also, retaining control over spindle, head, track and sector numbers was far too difficult to contemplate for most programmers. Thus a logical, secure interface was required which protected user data and gave access through filenames rather than a set of numbers. The disk **device driver** routines and **file manager** programs were developed to ensure that all access to disks was strictly regulated and was carried out by trusted routines. So, along with the loader programs, we can see the birth of an operating system.

Mainframe resources were centralized and expensive, so there was a need to use them efficiently, an aim that has practically been abandoned with the arrival of cheap, desktop PCs. But having the CPU waiting around for slow input data was obviously unacceptable when it tied up multi-million dollar machines. The methods developed to mitigate these shortcomings were **multiprocessing** and IO **SPOOL**ing (Simultaneous Peripheral Operation Online). The former allowed many programs to run concurrently, halting when waiting for data and continuing when the data became available. The latter involved decoupling slow output operations from the much faster central processor by buffering output data on disk to avoid holding up the main CPU. A similar technique was developed for input data, as mentioned above. With many programs competing for CPU time, the **scheduling** had to be undertaken automatically. No longer could the human operators decide which program could run next, because the switching could happen hundreds of times every second.

It became clear that the code needed to implement these facilities was not easy to design, write, test and debug. In addition, the number of computer users was growing and they no longer wanted to spend time understanding the more technical aspects of hardware and systems programming. They had other priorities in life. Thus the area of operating systems became a a very specialized skill and fewer programmers became involved.

17.2   Unix – a landmark operating system

Although Unix was by no means the first operating system, having been developed by Ken Thomson and Dennis Ritchie at AT&T Bell Labs in the late 1960s, it marked an important moment in the computing industry. Because it was designed to be portable, and easily recompilable for new architectures, it became the first-choice operating system for developers. All that was needed was a C compiler and lots of

Table 17.1
Some Unix tools.

Tool	Function	Example
awk	text processing language	`cat file	awk '$0 !~ /^$/ {print}'`
cat	opens and concatenates files	`cat header ch_01	groff -petfH > /tmp/tmp.ps`
diff	file comparison	`diff ch_01.a ch_01.b`
echo	repeats argument to stdout	`echo $PATH`
find	file search utility	`find ~ -name "*rob*" -print`
grep	string (reg expr) search	`grep "rob" /etc/passwd`
lpr	print demon	`lpr -Pnts -#25 ~/Sheets/unix_intro`
ls	directory listing	`ls -al`
more	text viewer	`more book.txt`
ps	process listing	`ps -af`
sed	stream editor	`sed 's/r-williams/rob.williams/g' <file1 >file2`
sort	string sorter	`cat file	sort +1 -2`
spell	spell checker	`spell letter.txt`
tr	transpose strings	`tr -cs 'A-Za-z' '\012'`
troff	text formatter	`groff -petfH`
uniq	repeated line detector	`sort	uniq -c	sort -n`
users	network users list	`users > checkfile`
wc	file size	`wc -w assignment.txt`
who	local user list	`who`

enthusiasm. Thus, universities and research groups would prefer to port Unix to new platforms, rather than write completely new operating systems. Popular DEC VAX and IBM machines were equipped with versions of Unix which went on to outshine their proprietary competitors. The continuing interest in Unix has been rekindled lately by the arrival of **Linux**. This has a new version of the Unix kernel rewritten in the early 1990s by Linus Torvalds. Linux is freely available to run on standard PC Pentium hardware. It also runs very well on the older i80486 CPUs! A remarkable feature of the development of Linux is the role that the Internet has played in the rapid dissemination of ideas and bug-fixes. After some initial scepticism (even ridicule), established manufacturers have recognized the value of offering new products with Linux installed. All this has further extended the availability of the Unix tradition and programming tools.

From the start, Unix was a programmer's environment. It was appropriately described as a workbench, on which tools were gathered and used in the correct sequence to carry out a job. Some of the tools which are supplied with Unix are listed in Table 17.1, with an indication of their application.

The elegance of the original vision and the quality of the work carried out at Bell Labs and the subsequent revisions and additions, by Bill Joy at Berkeley, Sun Microsystems and Richard Stallman at GNU, have kept Unix ahead of its competitors in many respects. On the other hand, Microsoft has generated and benefited from a vast collection of business applications, which far outstrips the quantity available for Unix. One lesson worth remembering from the history of Unix, in its struggles to gain wider acceptance in the market-place, is the damage inflicted by a diversity of standards. A minor incompatibility between products which are intended to work together with no problems is very disturbing from the user's point of view. Because of a lack of agreement on standards between the biggest computer suppliers, Unix has suffered. Perhaps freeware Linux will finally resolve these commercial disputes by rendering them irrelevant.

Unix is a multi-user, multitasking, network-enabled, multiprocessor-capable, virtual memory operating system. Each of these 'buzz' words needs to be understood because they really carry substantial information. So we will deal with them one at a time. **Multi-user** means that several different users may logon simultaneously and share the resources. Not all operating systems cater for this – MS-DOS and Windows NT do not. Even with personal workstations, it can be a very useful facility, allowing several users to gain access remotely through the network port without needing to sit down in front of the main screen. In such circumstances, a good password scheme has to be running to ensure adequate security for the user processes and files. **Multitasking** describes the scheduling action of the operating system, whereby it quickly skips between processes, giving each a fraction of a second on the CPU before swapping to another. **Network-enabled** implies ease of connection to a LAN, and then to the Internet. Unix has had TCP/IP software incorporated as 'standard equipment' for many years. **Multiprocessor-capable** refers to the ability of Unix to run cooperatively on multi-CPU platforms, one of the few operating systems which achieves this successfully. **Virtual memory** allows the physical memory (DRAM) to effectively spill over onto the much larger disk space.

Official documentation was one of the original application areas for Unix, and it is of immediate significance to this book, which was written using some of the original text production tools. Others appeared later: emacs, pic, eqn, tbl, groff, ghostview, gs and xv. The raw text and prototype version of this book were prepared and formatted into PostScript on a Sun Ultra-5 workstation. A PDF version was also compiled for transmitting to the publisher.

Unix is now considered a relatively small and efficient operating system when compared with Windows NT. This was not the case in the previous MS-DOS era, when Unix was rejected by many as unacceptably large, requiring 20 Mbyte of disk space and a memory size of 100 kbyte.

17.3 Outline structure – modularization

The operating system software is normally separated into quasi-independent modules to assist the development and maintenance activities. These are frequently

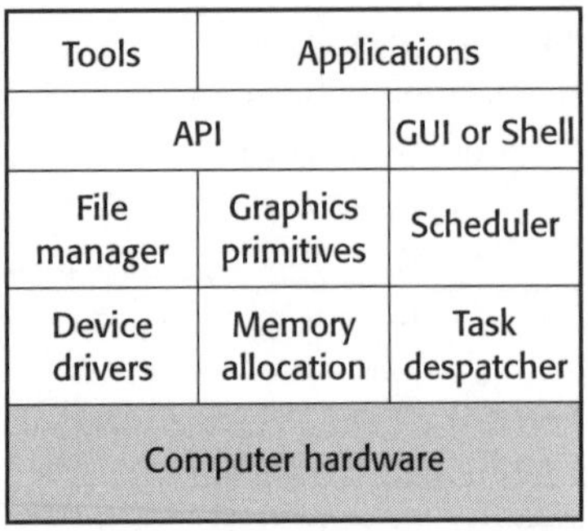

Fig. 17.3
Typical operating system
layered structure.

Tools	Applications	
API		GUI or Shell
File manager	Graphics primitives	Scheduler
Device drivers	Memory allocation	Task despatcher
Computer hardware		

represented in an onion, or layered, diagram such as Fig. 17.3. This encourages the reader to see a hierarchical structure in the design of the operating system. In this way individual modules can be upgraded without needing to reload the whole system. Some operating systems provide for this to be completed live, while others require a complete hardware reboot.

17.4   Process management – initialization and dispatching

All operating systems have a set of common functions, although the emphasis may vary according to the intended field of application. A real-time executive, like Microware's OS-9, has less complex support for interprocess security and disk filing, while a system designed to support corporate data processing, such as Windows NT, has many subtle security features and strong interprocess exclusion.

Processes have often been characterized as programs which are being executed. But there is more to be explained. A program file contains executable codes, but it does not contain space for all the data variables which will be required. Rather, the memory space needed for data is assessed by the compiler and then reserved either when the program is loaded into memory or when the subroutines are actually invoked during the run time of the program. A program has to be registered with the operating system before a process can be fully installed and ready to run. This requires the creation of a task control block. When the operating system decides to hand over control to a user process, it requires some critical process information: location of code in memory, stack pointer value, user ID, access rights, priority value and many more. This data is referred to as the **volatile environment** and is held by the **Task Control Block** (TCB), or Process Control Block. The contents are summarized in Fig. 17.4, but often much more information is also stored there. The TCB holds all the information that the operating system needs to run the process. The Semaphore and Signal ID fields are only used when the process is blocked, waiting for a semaphore, or has an incoming signal queued for action. On some systems there is room within the TCB for saving

Fig. 17.4
Summary contents of a
TCB.

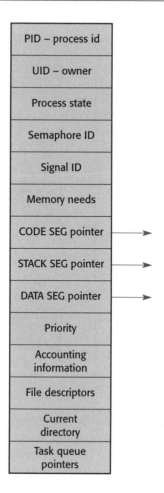

the CPU registers and other values which go to make up the process's volatile environment. These can also be held on the stack for future access. The TCBs are all initialized by the operating system when a process is created, and by using the TCBs the operating system manages all the processes and retains total control of the system.

You may have noticed in Fig. 17.5 that tasks 2 and 3 are sharing the same code block. Such a situation is only possible if the compiler that was used to create the code generated unmodified, **pure code**. This can be achieved through the strict use of relative address referencing and complete separation of data from instructions. Modern compilers and CPUs are planned from the start to support this scheme through the segmentation of memory. In Section 8.6 we have seen how the local variables may be installed onto the stack for use by the current function. This clearly isolates data in the stack segment, allowing access only through the ESP and EBP pointers. Such a system allows many users to share the same program code, without ever knowing it. For a large multi-user Unix computer, dozens of users could all be executing a single copy of the editor code, with their individual text buffers held on separate stacks. To reduce the amount of code loaded into memory even further, most systems provide

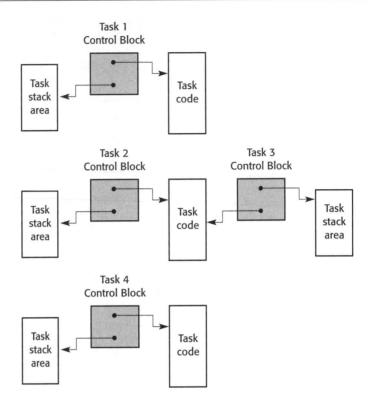

Fig. 17.5
Tasks specified by their control blocks.

mechanisms to share memory-resident subroutine libraries. These routines are not bound into the user programs by the linker, that would simply give every process private copies of the same routines. Instead, the linker can be made aware that there are memory-resident code modules available. These are known as **Dynamic Link Libraries** (DLLs) and are linked to the application code either at load time or later at run time. The linker will satisfy the external references by using stub library routines, whose function is to access the appropriate DLL at run time. In this way, you do not have to be executing exactly the same application as your colleagues to be sharing code, only calling the same DLL subroutines.

Operating systems often set up linked lists, or queues, of the TCBs of all the currently active tasks. Figure 17.6 illustrates this mechanism. Although only a single queue is shown, several of them are needed to maintain the status of a multitasking environment. The queues record which tasks are in which states of completion: Executing, Blocked, Waiting and Ready. Only a single task can be running, or executing, at a time if there is only a single CPU. The Ready queue holds tasks capable of immediately running, were they to be selected by the scheduler. **Blocked** tasks are generally waiting for data to appear on an input channel or disappear on an output channel. There are other causes for blocking, too. Tasks waiting for a semaphore operation, are held on separate queues in a state called **Waiting**. In a similar manner, a task may deliberately execute a 'pause', which will force it into another Waiting queue until a signal arrives to free it. A task may execute for the full duration of its allocated time-slice, in which case the operating system will have to intervene and swap the task

Fig. 17.6
Task control block
queue.

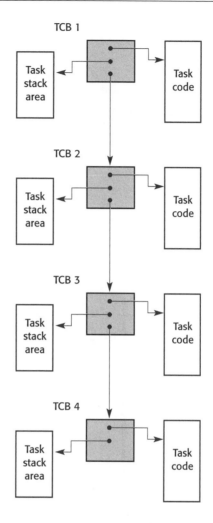

out. Occasionally processes run to completion, or suffer termination and exit. This indicates the final removal of processes from the operating system table. Should the parent process no longer be available to catch this event the child enters the **Zombie** state.

The current state of each of these processes can be described very well using a state diagram (Fig. 17.7). The Executing state is special in that only one process can be in that state at any time (for a single-CPU machine). The other states can be occupied by many processes simultaneously. Interactive processes, such as editors, spend most of their lives in Blocked because the input data is not ready, and the process has to wait for it to appear.

A large time-sharing Unix system may be juggling hundreds of processes at any time. Some of these processes are run by users, but many are owned by the system and are carrying out vital housekeeping duties. At this moment the multiprocessor Sun, running Solaris 5.5, on which this document is being typed has a full process list extending to 450 processes, as shown in Fig. 17.8. Figure 17.9 presents a slightly abbreviated version of the process listing for my Sun workstation, which has 55 processes active.

Fig. 17.7
State diagram showing
the task life cycle.

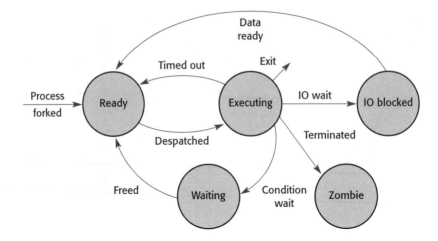

Fig. 17.8
Unix `ps` command to
count running tasks.

```
rob@olveston [100] rlogin milly
  Last login: Wed Mar 29 19:22:33 from
rob@milly [41]
rob@milly [41] ps -A | wc -1
                    450
rob@milly [42]
rob@milly [42] logout
  Connection closed.
rob@olveston [101]
rob@olveston [101] ps -A | wc -1
                    55
rob@olveston [102]
```

The processes or tasks running on a Unix computer can be listed with the `ps` utility. This presents, as shown in Fig. 17.9, all the information concerning the active processes. The meaning of the information in each column is available from the Unix online manual page, part of which is presented in Table 17.2 for your convenience!

17.5 Scheduling decisions – time-slicing, demand preemption or cooperative

A large time-sharing Unix system may be juggling hundreds of processes at any time. The operating system **scheduler** is continuously assessing the relative importance of processes, but it is the **dispatcher** which actually loads a process onto the CPU for

```
rob00lveston [141] ps -AF
   UID        PID    PPID     C    STIME    TTY       TIME    CMD
   root         0       0     0    Mar 16   ?         0:01    sched
   root         1       0     0    Mar 16   ?         0:02    /etc/init —
   root         2       0     0    Mar 16   ?         0:00    pageout
   root         3       0     0    Mar 16   ?         3:39    fsflush
   root       322     297     0    Mar 16   ?       145:37    /usr/openwin/bin/Xsun :0 -noban
   root       122       1     0    Mar 16   ?         0:00    /usr/sbin/inetd -s
   root       318       1     0    Mar 16   ?         0:00    /usr/lib/saf/sac -t 300
   root       102       1     0    Mar 16   ?         0:00    /usr/sbin/rpcbind
   root       112       1     0    Mar 16   ?         0:00    /usr/sbin/kerbd
   root       110       1     0    Mar 16   ?         0:00    /usr/lib/netsvc/yp/ypbind
   root       284       1     0    Mar 16   ?         0:02    /usr/sbin/vold
   root       226       1     0    Mar 16   ?         0:00    /usr/lib/autofs/automountd
   root       240       1     0    Mar 16   ?         0:01    /usr/sbin/cron
   root       230       1     0    Mar 16   ?         0:00    /usr/sbin/syslogd
   root       249       1     0    Mar 16   ?         0:01    /usr/sbin/nscd
   root       259       1     0    Mar 16   ?         0:01    /usr/lib/lpsched
   root       319       1     0    Mar 16   console   0:00    /usr/lib/saf/ttymon -g -h -p olves
   root       274       1     0    Mar 16   ?         0:00    /usr/lib/utmpd
   root       292       1     0    Mar 16   ?         0:00    /usr/lib/sendmail -q15m
   root       321     318     0    Mar 16   ?         0:00    /usr/lib/saf/ttymon
   rwilliam   340     323     0    Mar 16   ?         0:00    /bin/ksh /usr/dt/config/Xsession
   root       325       1     0    Mar 16   ?         0:00    /usr/openwin/bin/fbconsole -d :0
   rwilliam   408     407     0    Mar 16   ?         0:00    olwmslave
   rwilliam   342     340     0    Mar 16   ?         0:00    /bin/ksh /usr/dt/bin/Xsession
   rwilliam   388     378     0    Mar 16   ?         0:00    /bin/ksh /usr/dt/config/Xsession
   rwilliam   412       1     0    Mar 16   ??        0:00    /usr/openwin/bin/cmdtool -Wp 0 0
   rwilliam   378     342     0    Mar 16   ?         0:00    /bin/tcsh -c unsetenv _ PWD;
   rwilliam   389     388     0    Mar 16   ?         0:00    /bin/ksh /home/staff/csm/csstaff/
   rwilliam   407     389     0    Mar 16   ?         0:18    olwm -syncpid 406
   rwilliam 19576     407     0    10:07:01 ??        0:02    /usr/openwin/bin/xterm
   rwilliam   415     412     0    Mar 16   pts/3     0:00    /bin/tcsh
   rwilliam 19949   19577     0    14:04:16 pts/5     0:05    ghostview /tmp/tmp.ps
   rwilliam   469     407     0    Mar 16   ?        10:35    /usr/local/bin/emacs
   rwilliam  1061    1050     0    Mar 16   ?         0:00    (dns helper)
   rwilliam   553     407     0    Mar 16   ?         0:21    /usr/openwin/bin/filemgr
   rwilliam 11510       1     0    Mar 22   ?         4:08    /opt/simeon/bin/simeon.orig -u
   root     20818   19577     1    18:01:46 pts/5     0:00    ps -Af
   rwilliam 20304   19949     0    15:31:45 pts/5     0:06    gs -sDEVICE=xll -dNOPAUSE -dQUIET
   rwilliam  1050     407     0    Mar 16   ?        14:39    /usr/local/netscape/netscape
   rwilliam 12251       1     0    Mar 22   ?         0:17    /usr/local/Acrobat4/Reader/sparcs
   rwilliam 19577   19576     0    10:07:02 pts/5     0:01    tcsh
```

Fig. 17.9
Displaying Unix task
list using `ps`. The
different tasks are
listed below the
diagram.

sched	the OS scheduler; notice the PID value, an important process following boot
init	startup process from boot time; gets all the other Unix processes started
pageout	virtual memory page handler
fsflush	updates the super block and flushes data to disk
Xsun	X Window server
inetd	Internet server daemon; provides remote services such as ftp, telnet, rlogin, talk
sac	port services access controller
rpcbind	address mapper for remote procedure calls
	(continued overleaf)

Fig. 17.9
(Continued)

`kerbd`	source of kerberos unique keys; used for network user authentication
`ypbind`	NIS distributed password system
`vold`	file system (volume) management for CDROMs and floppy disk drives
`automountd`	daemon to handle remote file system mount/unmount requests
`cron`	schedules tasks to run at particular times
`syslogd`	system message handler and router
`nscd`	name service cache daemon
`lpsched`	printer service scheduler
`ttymon`	monitors terminal ports for activity
`utmpd`	user accounting daemon
`sendmail`	Internet mail server
`ttymon`	monitors terminal ports for activity
`ksh`	Korn shell user interface
`fbconsole`	console window
`olmslave`	Open Look X Window manager
`ksh`	second korn shell user interface
`ksh`	third Korn shell user interface
`cmdtool`	command tool window handler
`tcsh`	a tenex shell user interface
`ksh`	fourth Korn shell
`olwm`	Open Look Window Manager
`xterm`	X terminal window
`tcsh`	a tenex shell user interface
`ghostview`	PostScript screen viewer
`emacs`	the best editor!
`dns`	domain naming service for Internet name to IP number conversions
`filemgr`	drag and drop file manager, useful for floppy disks
`simeon`	mail client
`ps`	this produced the process listing!
`gs`	ghostscript translator
`netscape`	Netscape Navigator Web browser
`acroread`	Adobe Acrobat reader for viewing PDF documents
`tcsh`	another user interface shell

execution. This involves recovering the volatile environment from the TCB and restoring all the CPU register values just as they were when the process was swapped out.

Nearly all operating system schedulers can set the hardware to interrupt a process after a preset period to allow the next process from the Ready queue to be swapped in. If a 10 ms **time slice** appears rather short, remember that it could contain a quarter of a million instructions or more! This scheme is effective and reasonably fair, each process inevitably having its turn on the CPU. But it also entails a disadvantage because not all processes are of equal priority, so a simple first come, first served schedule may not supply the performance required. Taking this into account, Unix sorts the Ready queue on the basis of process priority, and implements an 'ageing' technique, where the basic priorities are incremented the longer the process remains in the Ready queue. This attempts to deal with scheduling on a fairer footing. The alternative scheme used by real-time operating systems is termed **preemptive**.

Table 17.2
Information in the ps display, taken from the man page for ps.

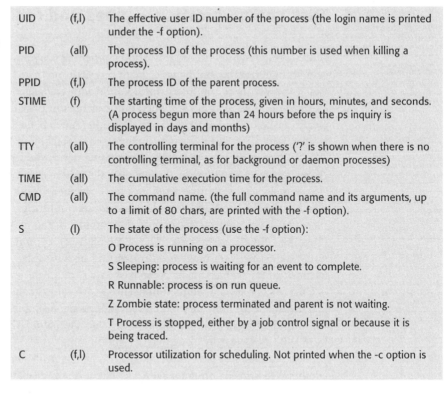

UID	(f,l)	The effective user ID number of the process (the login name is printed under the -f option).
PID	(all)	The process ID of the process (this number is used when killing a process).
PPID	(f,l)	The process ID of the parent process.
STIME	(f)	The starting time of the process, given in hours, minutes, and seconds. (A process begun more than 24 hours before the ps inquiry is displayed in days and months)
TTY	(all)	The controlling terminal for the process ('?' is shown when there is no controlling terminal, as for background or daemon processes)
TIME	(all)	The cumulative execution time for the process.
CMD	(all)	The command name. (the full command name and its arguments, up to a limit of 80 chars, are printed with the -f option).
S	(l)	The state of the process (use the -f option): O Process is running on a processor. S Sleeping: process is waiting for an event to complete. R Runnable: process is on run queue. Z Zombie state: process terminated and parent is not waiting. T Process is stopped, either by a job control signal or because it is being traced.
C	(f,l)	Processor utilization for scheduling. Not printed when the -c option is used.

Although time-slicing does cut into, or preempt, a process's run time, in this context 'preemptive' is reserved for interrupts derived from IO operations. In this way the operating system can respond to the varying needs of the environment, adjusting sympathetically to load changes. On some older systems alternative scheduling strategies were employed, such as **short jobs first**. However, these often required an accurate usage profile for the process to work effectively, and if the loading changed they became inefficient.

When comparing scheduling algorithms, there is a need for some performance criteria to measure and compare. Unfortunately there is no single parameter. System managers like to see the **CPU utilization** percentage as high as possible. This has been considered as a reasonable indicator of an overloaded system, justifying further purchases. **System throughput**, or jobs/min completed, is really only useful in a batch working environment, where a fairly constant mix of jobs can be expected. Any variation of the routine would disrupt this measure. Similarly, **turnaround time**, how long users have to wait for results, is only relevant for compute-bound activities. In real life, turnaround time can depend more on the human link in the chain than the raw processing power of the machine. The amount of wasted **waiting time** that processes suffer while attempting to complete a task can be usefully recorded, but is influenced by a variety of causes. Finally, the mean **response delay** is the principal parameter for most users who spend a lot of time editing or connected to the Internet. Interactive computing has different requirements from batch data processing.

17.6   Task communication – pipes and redirection

Multitasking systems encourage the development of programs which are made up of several concurrently running tasks. With this situation there is a need for facilities to enable the tasks to communicate information without danger of mutual interference. As introduced in Section 13.3, operating systems can provide a **pipe** facility which enables tasks to transfer data between each other much in the same way as they would read or write files. Unix in particular pioneered this technique (Fig. 17.10), and allows all tasks to pass data to other tasks through the standard output and standard input channels, which would normally default to the screen and keyboard devices.

As has already been suggested, pipes can be likened to disk cache buffers set up in memory to hold data blocks from files in readiness for further read requests. On Unix, pipes can be created by the user at the command line or from within executing programs using system calls. The availability of communication pipes makes multitasking programming more interesting because they provide 'data channel' facilities through which one task can pass data to another.

Unix offers a special **redirection** facility which can take the output from one task and stream the data into another task for processing. A simpler alternative is to direct the output into a named file using the '>' character. Similarly, data can be directed from a file into a task by using the '<' symbol.

Some examples of the use of '<' and '>' are given in Fig. 17.11. The first runs another 'hello world!' program, which would normally display its galactic greeting on

Fig. 17.10
Piping data between tasks in Unix.

Fig. 17.11
Redirecting data from tasks and files in Unix.

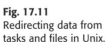

```
rob>   world > hello.txt

rob>   echo "Hello world!" > world.txt

rob>   tr -d "\r" < ch_10.asc > ch_10

rob>   cat header ch_*  > book

rob>   cat > letter << +++
  ?  Dear Craig
  ?  Here is the book that I promised to send
  ?  Rob
  ?  +++
rob>
```

the screen. With the '>' symbol, however, the words are redirected into the named file, hello.txt. The second example in Fig. 17.11 runs the process echo instead of your hello.c program. The third example is using the tr utility to strip away unwanted CR characters from a text file where they were inserted by a foreign word processor. The fourth example is concatenating text files to produce a single big file called book. The final example is weird. It makes a file called letter from immediate keyboard input, making the system behave rather like a micro-editor. This latter technique is referred to as a 'here document' to indicate the immediacy of its appearance.

To enable data piping and redirection to take place, Unix arranges for all processes to have a uniform data interface. Each process is provided with three standard channels, 0, 1 and 2, as shown in Fig. 17.12. These are implemented in the form of 'file descriptors' and allow other processes to 'plug in' their channels and exchange data. To allow such a free exchange of data to take place, there is no data structuring specified by Unix. Whereas other operating systems have recognized all sorts of file types and data record formats, Unix simply offers a simple byte stream. All data structures are left to the application programmer. Without this uniformity, the redirection of data would be practically impossible.

When a new process is created it is normal for channel 0 to be attached to the console keyboard and channel 1 to the console screen; channel 2 is also directed to the screen, but is used for error messages. The normal Unix terminology is to refer to **stdin** 0, **stdout** 1 and **stderr** 2. Although processes start with the three standard IO channels set up as described, the channels can be redirected, and that is exactly what is being done with the '|', '>' and '<' operators. This standard process interface is one of the most useful features of Unix (other operating systems do not offer it); it allows programmers to 'glue' together existing programs and so build up larger processing pipelines.

Redirection of process stdio is accomplished by the shell process responsible for starting the process running. Remember that you type into a shell the command cat hello.c in order to list hello.c code on the screen. However, with the redirection symbol, the shell receiving your instructions will redirect the output to a file: cat hello.c > world.c. This will either create a new file or overwrite the existing world.c. If you really wanted to append your code to the existing file, Unix offers the following: hello.c >> world.c. For cautious programmers redirection may seem to offer too easy a route to disaster. It can quickly and permanently erase valuable data. To guard against this risk, Unix can refuse to redirect to an existing file. To

Fig. 17.12
Standard IO for Unix processes.

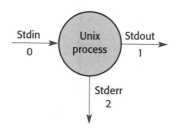

impose this condition you need to type the arcane command `set noclobber` into the shell. Now you are truly advancing into the Unix badlands!

17.7 Exclusion and synchronization – semaphores and signals

The first encounter in this text with the problem of **mutual exclusion** was in Section 9.5. In that case the intervention of an interrupt could risk compromising the integrity of a data structure if a mainline process was at that moment in the middle of updating it. With multitasking systems this problematic scenario is magnified manyfold, because every time the scheduler pre-empts a task, there is an opportunity for so called 'critical data corruption'. The operating system needs a way of knowing when a task is dealing with a shared data structure which could be vulnerable when swapping tasks. This is the role of **semaphores**.

From the point of view of data, semaphores behave like software flags which police task access to data: see Fig. 17.13. They operate in a straightforward manner. When a task needs to control access to an exclusive resource which only one task at a time may use, it is required to call a special operating system function and demand allocation of a semaphore. This will be registered, and from then on any task will be required to call another operating system function `WAIT(sem)`, which checks the designated semaphore flag, before gaining access to the critical data area. On relinquishing the resource, a matching call to `SIGNAL(sem)` must be made. Thus calls to `WAIT` and `SIGNAL` are placed around the critical region like turnstiles at a football stadium.

The origins of semaphore use go back to Dijkstra's work in the 1960s. For some time, wait and signal were referred to as P and V, after the Dutch words meaning wait and increment. The more common way now of using semaphore functionality is to hide the critical data within an object, where it can only be inspected or updated through trusty methods. The wait and signal functions can then be inserted within these access functions. Programming with semaphores has often been considered difficult, but this comes down to checking that all `WAIT( )` calls are paired with a call

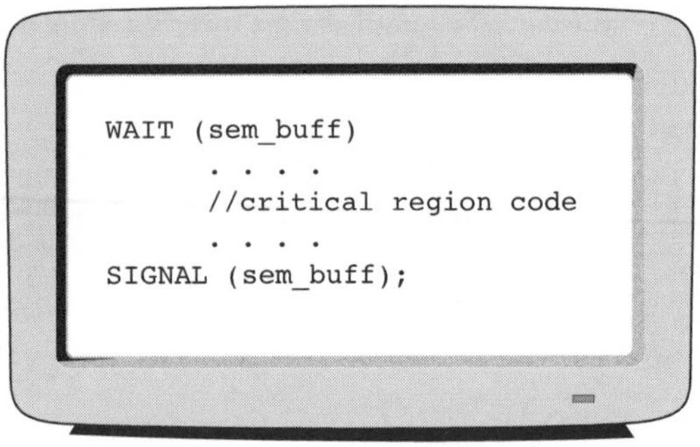

Fig. 17.13
Placement of semaphore operators, `WAIT` and `SIGNAL`.

```
WAIT (sem_buff)
      . . . .
          //critical region code
      . . . .
SIGNAL (sem_buff);
```

Fig. 17.14
Semaphores protecting a
cyclic data buffer.

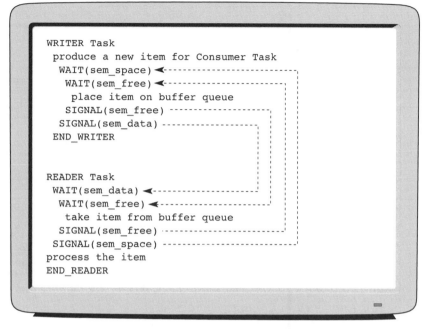

```
WRITER Task
  produce a new item for Consumer Task
    WAIT(sem_space) ◄-------------------------┐
      WAIT(sem_free) ◄----------------------┐ ┊
      place item on buffer queue            ┊ ┊
      SIGNAL(sem_free) ---------------------┘ ┊
    SIGNAL(sem_data) ------------------------┐┊
  END_WRITER                                 ┊┊
                                             ┊┊
                                             ┊┊
  READER Task                                ┊┊
    WAIT(sem_data) ◄-------------------------┘┊
      WAIT(sem_free) ◄-----------------------┐┊
      take item from buffer queue            ┊┊
      SIGNAL(sem_free) ----------------------┘┊
    SIGNAL(sem_space) ------------------------┘
  process the item
  END_READER
```

to SIGNAL( ). So far, the semaphores appear only to be serving the role of 'busy flags', which are raised when the resource is available and lowered when it is taken. This would lead to a wasteful use of CPU time, with the blocked tasks simply spinning in dedicated polling loops, waiting for the flag to rise. But each semaphore also includes a task queue. This is used by the operating system scheduler to park blocked tasks until the associated semaphore indicates that the resource is once again free, and the next task can be moved forward off the semaphore queue. In this way, semaphores can be seen as part of the scheduling mechanism provided by the operating system, rather than a 'busy flag'. The use of interlocked semaphores is illustrated in Fig. 17.14. There is no need to employ three semaphores, but two *are* required. The necessity for two is explained by considering how a deadlock situation could develop if only a single sem_free semaphore were used. If the data buffer were empty and available, a READER task would get accepted, lock the access and prevent a WRITER from depositing an item of data. Similarly, if the data buffer were full and available, a WRITER could acquire the resource and lock out any READERs. The double inter-locking semaphore scheme prevents such deadlocks occurring.

Pseudocode is used in Fig. 17.14, partly because the implementation of semaphores by Unix is very general, flexible and confusing. Check out the man page for semop and see if you disagree with this judgment. On the whole it seems that Unix program-mers prefer signals to semaphores when synchronizing tasks. Operating systems use **signals** to 'nudge' processes to execute a specially designated function, in a similar fashion to interrupts. Signals do not carry much data, usually only offering a minimum self-identification in the form of an integer number. If a programmer intends to direct signals at a process, there has to be a signal handler function installed.

Fig. 17.15
Installing a Unix signal handler to count and display signal hits.

```
/* kbdcnt */
#include <stdio.h>
#include <signal.h>
#define MYSIG 44

/* Signal handler function, evoked by sig 44
   reinstalls after each sig hit, prints number of hits
*/
void getsig(int s)
{
static int count = 0;
printf("signal %d again, %dth time \n", s, ++count);
signal(MYSIG, getsig);
}

/* Process to demonstrate signals, sets up a sig handler to
   count the number of sig hits received. Loops forever.
   Start using "kbdcnt &" and make note of pid value returned
   Recommend to use "kill -44 pid" to send signals
   Remove using "kill -9 pid"
*/
int main(void)
{
signal(MYSIG, getsig);
printf("start counting kbd kills\n");
   while(1) {};
return 0;
}
```

The example in Fig. 17.15 shows the signal handler as a function which has no direct software call. In this regard signals are very like interrupts, each source of interrupt has an ISR (Interrupt Service Routine) similar to a signal handler.

The action of a signal can be demonstrated using the code listed in Fig. 17.15. Here a short program installs a signal handler function, getsig( ), and uses (somewhat arbitrarily) the signal number 44 to invoke it. Before you select a signal number on your Unix system it is worth checking their usage. Look in /usr/include/sys/ signal.h, where you will find a list and the maximum value allowed defined as NSIG.

The installation of a function to catch the signal as it comes into the process is achieved by using the signal( ) system call. Note that it has to be repeated after every signal event because the system resets to the default handler. The signal handler itself receives the incoming signal number as a parameter which may be used within the function to take decisions on what to do. In this way it is possible to have a single function catching all the incoming signals. To send a signal to a process the shell-level command kill can be borrowed. Normally this is used to remove errant processes from the machine, but it can also send less final notifications! Signal number 9 is known for its lethal effectiveness, but here we are using signal number 44, which has

Fig. 17.16
Using a signal to notify a Unix process.

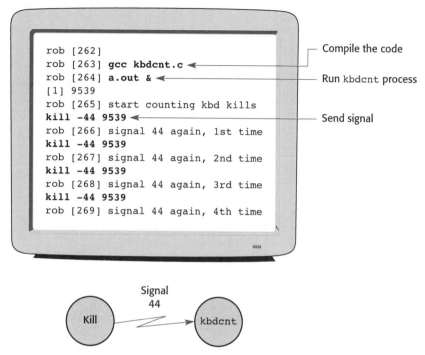

not been otherwise allocated. In Fig. 17.16 the complete compile, run and test sequence is shown.

Notice how the Unix process can be detached from the keyboard and made to run in the background by including an '&' after the command (a.out &). In this example it is not so important (we could always use another window to fire kill -44), but elsewhere it is an essential facility.

The program listed in Fig. 17.17 shows two processes communicating by passing signals. It also demonstrates the way Unix creates new processes by using the fork command to split a single process into two. This duplicates the process environment and data segment, but retains a single code segment. The two resulting processes, parent and child, run the same code but 'know who they are' by inspecting their own PID value (Fig. 17.18). So, after the fork instruction has completed, there will be two nearly identical processes, each executing the same code which comes after the fork instruction. They could continue as cloned processes, or diverge by using their distinct PID values to alter their execution routes. In this example, the cpid variable is used to switch execution into the different sides of an IF-ELSE statement. IF is executed by the child process, while ELSE is taken by the parent process. This appears at first sight to be a strange way to start up a new process, but it does have some advantages when you require the processes to intercommunicate or run synchronously. The fork activity is presented diagrammatically in Fig. 17.19.

The use of fork( ) to duplicate a process does not actually load in a new program. It simply gives the programmer the opportunity to split a program into two processes. Each of these processes will be running the same code, but may decide to

Fig. 17.17
Demonstrating the use of signals by Unix processes.

```c
#include <stdio.h>
#include <signal.h>
#include <errno.h>

#define PSIG 43  /* check the value of NSIG in      */
                 /*    /usr/include/sys/signal.h    */
#define CSIG 42  /* before choosing the signal values*/

int ccount = 0;
int pcount = 0;
char str[] = "error message ";

void psigfunc(int s)
{
     pcount++;
     signal(CSIG, psigfunc);
}

void csigfunc(int s)
{
     ccount++;
     signal(PSIG, csigfunc);
}

main()
{
int ke, tpid, ppid, cpid;

     ppid = getpid();
     cpid = fork();  /* spawn child process */
     if (cpid == -1)
     {
          printf("failed to fork\n");
          exit(1);
     }
     if (cpid == 0 )
     {
     /* Child process executes here */
          signal(PSIG, csigfunc);
          printf("Child started\n");
          while (1) {
            pause();
            printf("Child hit! count = %d\n",ccount);
            sleep(rand()%10);
            if( (kill(ppid, CSIG)) ) perror(str);
            }
     }
     else
     {
     /* Parent process continues execution from here */
          signal(CSIG, psigfunc);
          printf("Parent started\n");
          while (1) {
            sleep(rand()%10);
            if( (kill(cpid, PSIG)) ) perror(str);
            pause();
            printf("Parent hit! count = %d\n",pcount);
          }
     }
}
```

Fig. 17.18
Running the Fig. 17.15
program on Unix.

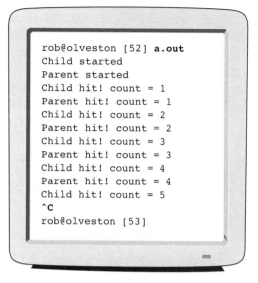

```
rob@olveston [52] a.out
Child started
Parent started
Child hit! count = 1
Parent hit! count = 1
Child hit! count = 2
Parent hit! count = 2
Child hit! count = 3
Parent hit! count = 3
Child hit! count = 4
Parent hit! count = 4
Child hit! count = 5
^C
rob@olveston [53]
```

Fig. 17.19
Unix process creation
using fork( ).

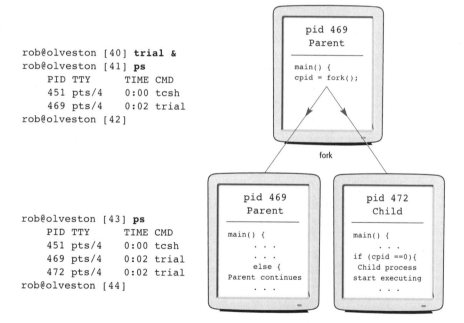

```
rob@olveston [40] trial &
rob@olveston [41] ps
    PID TTY      TIME CMD
    451 pts/4    0:00 tcsh
    469 pts/4    0:02 trial
rob@olveston [42]
```

```
rob@olveston [43] ps
    PID TTY      TIME CMD
    451 pts/4    0:00 tcsh
    469 pts/4    0:02 trial
    472 pts/4    0:02 trial
rob@olveston [44]
```

pid 469
Parent

```
main() {
cpid = fork();
```

fork

pid 469
Parent

```
main() {
  . . .
  . . .
else {
Parent continues
  . . .
```

pid 472
Child

```
main() {
  . . .
if (cpid ==0){
Child process
start executing
  . . .
```

execute different parts by using the difference in PID between parent and child to switch execution thread. If a completely different process is required, Unix offers the exec( ) family of system calls. This would enable the child of a forked process to load in from disk a completely different program to take its place. In this way processes can be spawned in memory and communicate by signalling each other.

On Unix systems it is also still accepted to use **lock files** to protect critical resources. A lock file contains nothing and is only important because it exists, or not! Because the creation and deletion of files was implemented in a unitary manner, not permitting interruption or process rescheduling, it was realized that a file directory entry could behave like a simple semaphore. Although hardly an elegant solution to the exclusive resource problem, it has stood the test of time. On my Sun there is a lock file (`~/.netscape/lock`) created every time I run Netscape Navigator. This serves the purpose of giving a warning of the presence of an existing program to subsequent evocations.

17.8   Memory allocation – `malloc( )` and `free( )`

Because Unix offers a virtual memory environment, programmers are not immediately faced with size limitations. Available virtual memory space, although ideally 4 Gbyte for each segment, is actually fixed by the swap file capacity on disk. When installing an operating system it is normal to allocate to the swap file at least twice the size of main memory, and reserve a disk partition for its use.

The C programmer is usually only aware of memory allocation issues when dealing with dynamic data variables. These are not given a name nor declared at compile time, but requested during run time by using the `malloc( )` system call. `malloc( )` takes as parameter the size of the data area required. Data areas reserved in this fashion cannot be referred to by 'name', because none has been given by the programmer. Instead, the operating system returns an address (pointer) to the beginning of the new data area, and the program has to make do with that. In fact, this has long been a subject of dispute among programmers because of the not uncommon bug that follows this approach to handling data memory. When a dynamically allocated item is no longer required, it remains the responsibility of the programmer to dispose of the space. This can be done by calling `free( )` with the original pointer value as parameter. When this is carried out correctly, the operating system retrieves the data area and can make it available to other users. Unfortunately, given the capricious vicissitudes of software, this simple housekeeping can all too easily get overlooked or bypassed. When this happens another chunk of swap space is rendered unusable until the process exits correctly or the system is rebooted.

As described in Section 12.5, in modern virtual memory systems, a complex address conversion takes place for every memory access (Fig. 17.20). This involves placing the code, data and stack segments within a single, linear address space using segment base registers. Then every process has a page table installed in memory where virtual address format is translated into physical address values. This is accomplished by reading the upper part of the virtual address as a page number, while the lower part is taken as the offset within the page. Using the page table the page numbers are translated into physical frame numbers. The extra memory access which every fetch cycle would require with such a scheme would make the computer unacceptably slow. So special memory management hardware caches the recent page–frame pairs to avoid some of the extra memory accesses demanded by the virtual to physical translation.

Fig. 17.20
Virtual address
translation into physical
address.

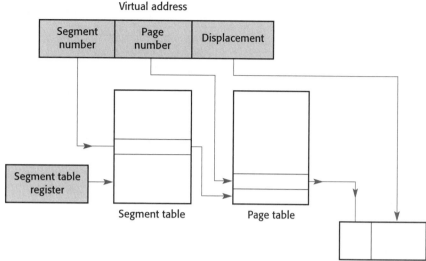

17.9   User interface – GUIs and shells

An important part of any user's experience of an operating system is the command interface. On Unix this is supplied by a so-called **shell**. There are several available for Unix, with variants also ported to other operating systems. The most popular are listed in Table 17.3. A shell is running whenever you login, and it interprets all your keyboard commands, except when you have started an application program, and are communicated directly with that.

When you type a command, such as `ls`, `ps` or `emacs`, into a shell it will result in the shell process forking. The parent shell will wait for the child process, which itself goes on to exec the command program. When the command has completed it will terminate and return an exit value to the waiting parent shell. Besides acting as command line interpreters, dealing interactively with keyboard input as typed by the user, shells can handle command files or scripts. In fact, every time a shell starts it will look for a special start-up file to execute. This can contain initialization instructions to tailor the environment for the job in hand. List the `.cshrc` file or the equivalent stored in your home directory. You will find that it is full of shell instructions. This capability to execute command files makes shells very useful during the system boot phase because they can assume control of the whole procedure. The shells found with Unix are also responsible for managing the redirection of stdin and stdout, as described in Section 17.6, for the child processes which they spawn. Another interesting feature of Unix shells is their ability to negotiate **command substitution**. In this, the output from a Unix command is directed into the position of a shell variable. This can be a very useful facility when building complex processing scripts out of the basic Unix tools.

Examples of command substitution are given in Fig. 17.21. Watch out for the backwards sloping grave accents, `` ` ``, which enclose a command to be evaluated. Do not get them confused with the forwards sloping acute accents, ´´ which can be used to hide

Table 17.3
Interactive shells.

sh	Original shell from Steve Bourne
csh	C shell from Bill Joy
bash	Bourne again shell
tcsh	Tenex shell, my favourite
ksh	Korn shell, very popular

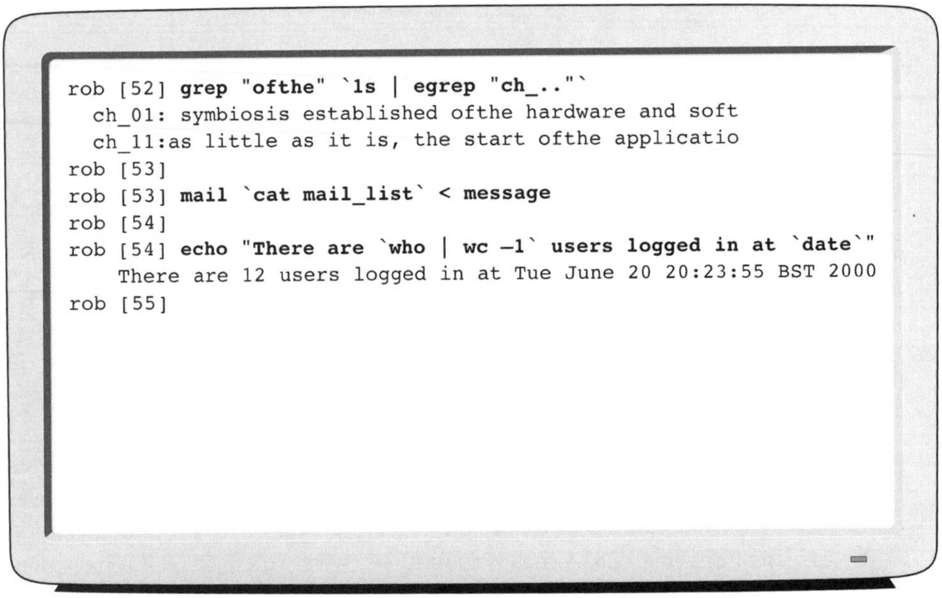

```
rob [52] grep "ofthe" `ls | egrep "ch_.."`
  ch_01: symbiosis established ofthe hardware and soft
  ch_11:as little as it is, the start ofthe applicatio
rob [53]
rob [53] mail `cat mail_list` < message
rob [54]
rob [54] echo "There are `who | wc -l` users logged in at `date`"
    There are 12 users logged in at Tue June 20 20:23:55 BST 2000
rob [55]
```

Fig. 17.21
Examples of shell
command
substitution on Unix.

information from the shell. This can also be explained as 'quoting' the contents, in order that they are treated literally as data items, not signifying anything special to the shell. The double quotation marks, " ", are less violent in their action. They are mostly used to glue strings together.

17.10   Input–output management – device handlers

As we have already noted, one role of an operating system is to hide the complexity and variability of the hardware from the programmer. An additional problem which is central to all IO management is the disparity in speeds between the CPU and the mechanical world of interfaced equipment. Working along these lines, and achieving a supreme ratio-nalization in the structure of Unix, the IO subsystem was absorbed into the file system. Devices were made to look like files. There were block-structured devices, like hard disks, and serial devices, like Ethernet. All this is apparent when you look into the directory /dev, where you will see all sorts of device-related files. The list from my Sun workstation is presented in Fig. 17.22. From the kernel's point of view all files and devices are treated

```
rob@olveston [154] ls /dev

arp        icmp       ptmajor ptyq5  ptyrd      syscon    ttypc  ttyr4
audio      ie         ptmx    ptyq6  ptyre      systty    ttypd  ttyr5
audioctl   ip         pts     ptyq7  ptyrf      tcp       ttype  ttyr6
bdoff      ipd        ptyp0   ptyq8  qe         term      ttypf  ttyr7
be         ipdcm      ptyp1   ptyq9  rawip      ticlts    ttyq0  ttyr8
conslog    ipdptp     ptyp2   ptyqa  rdiskette  ticots    ttyq1  ttyr9
console    isdn       ptyp3   ptyqb  rdiskette0 ticotsord ttyq2  ttyra
cua        kbd        ptyp4   ptyqc  rdsk       tnfctl    ttyq3  ttyrb
diskette   kmem       ptyp5   ptyqd  rfd0       tnfmap    ttyq4  ttyrc
diskette0  kstat      ptyp6   ptyqe  rfd0a      tty       ttyq5  ttyrd
dsk        ksyms      ptyp7   ptyqf  rfd0b      ttya      ttyq6  ttyre
dtremote   le         ptyp8   ptyr0  rfd0c      ttyb      ttyq7  ttyrf
dump       llcl       ptyp9   ptyr1  rmt        ttyp0     ttyq8  udp
ecpp0      log        ptypa   ptyr2  sad        ttyp1     ttyq9  volctl
es         logindmux  ptypb   ptyr3  sehdlc     ttyp2     ttyqa  winlock
fb         m640       ptypc   ptyr4  sehdlc0    ttyp3     ttyqb  wscons
fb0        md         ptypd   ptyr5  sehdlc1    ttyp4     ttyqc  zero
fbs        mem        ptype   ptyr6  sound      ttyp5     ttyqd
fd         mouse      ptypf   ptyr7  sp         ttyp6     ttyqe
fd0        null       ptyq0   ptyr8  spcic      ttyp7     ttyqf
fd0a       openprom   ptyq1   ptyr9  stderr     ttyp8     ttyr0
fd0b       partn      ptyq2   ptyra  stdin      ttyp9     ttyr1
fd0c       printers   ptyq3   ptyrb  stdout     ttypa     ttyr2
hme        profile    ptyq4   ptyrc  swap       ttypb     ttyr3
rob@olveston [155]
```

Fig. 17.22
Unix device drivers in
directory /dev.

identically. To achieve this the devices are represented as 'special files', which can participate in data redirection in the same way as files. This can be demonstrated by starting two xterm windows, discovering their ptty or pts (psuedo-terminal) number using the ps -al command, and then sending text messages between them using:

```
echo "hello other window" > /dev/pts/0
```

The final number specifies which X window to send to 0, 1, 2,....

Each of the entries listed in Fig. 17.22 is a device driver or some related resource. Device drivers are the routines which handle data IO. In Unix they are closely associated with the kernel, and cannot normally be installed dynamically. In other words it is necessary to rebuild the operating system kernel and reboot the whole computer. While this appears a somewhat drastic activity if you are only wanting to swap a printer, it has long been accepted by the Unix fraternity! The large number of device drivers already installed in /dev makes this a rare necessity for most users.

The null entry in /dev is somewhat of a curiosity. It performs the role of 'byte bucket' in process pipes. Should you want to pass a mass of data through a process pipeline, but have no reason to retain the resulting data stream, it can be redirected into the byte bucket using: > /dev/null.

Unix organizes the device drivers in two groups. Block device drivers are indexed from one array, while character devices are indexed from a second array. Devices are identified within the system by which array they belong to and a device number. This can be split into two. The so-called **major number** identifies the correct location within the device driver array, and the minor number specifies the particular hardware unit to be accessed. In this way similar devices can share a device driver but remain distinguished by the system.

If we glance back to Fig. 2.6, you will remember the problem of buffering keyboard input before it is handed on to user programs. This was discussed so early, even though it is a consequence of the operation of a device driver, because every student falls foul of the problem during the first weeks of learning C. So the tty device driver normally buffers user input, allowing single line editing, until the ENTER key is pressed. Alternative modes are available for the programmer to use when required. In earlier, pre-X Window, times the multiplicity of terminal types drove programmers to distraction. In an attempt to overcome the diversity of control codes offering screen editing functions, Unix set up a terminal characteristics database file. This was called termcap and can still be found at /etc/termcap. Inside you can see all the control functions encoded in standard format for hundreds of different terminals from dozens of different suppliers (see Fig. 17.23). By writing software using the termcap meta-controls (Table 17.4), it was possible to rapidly port programs which depended on terminal IO from one VDU to another. The padding characters are needed because terminals are slow compared to the CPU, and even the transmission rate of the interconnected line is faster than the terminal frame rate.

Fig. 17.23
Unix termcap entry for an xterm.

```
rob@olveston [101] more /etc/termcap
        . . .
xterm|vs100|xterm terminal emulator (X Window System):\
    :AL=\E[%dL:DC=\E[%dP:DL=\E[%dM:DO=\E[%dB:IC=\E[%d@:U
    :al=\E[L:am:\
    :bs:cd=\E[J:ce=\E[K:cl=\E[H\E[2J:cm=\E[%i%d;%dH:co#8
    :cs=\E[%i%d;%dr:ct=\E[3k:\
    :dc=\E[P:dl=\E[M:\
    :im=\E[4h:ei=\E[4l:mi:\
    :ho=\E[H:\
    :is=\E[r\E[m\E[2J\E[H\E[?7h\E[?1;3;4;61\E[4l:\
    :rs=\E[r\E[m\E[2J\E[H\E[?7h\E[?1;3;4;61\E[4lE<:\
    :kl=\EOP:k2=\EOQ:k3=\EOR:k4=\EOS:kb=^H:kd=\EOB:ke=\E
    :kl=\EOD:km:kn#4:kr=\EOC:ks=\E[?1h\E=:ku=\EOA:\
    :li#65:md=\E[1m:me=\E[m:mr=\E[7m:ms:nd=\E[C:pt:\
    :sc=\E7:rc=\E8:sf=\n:so=\E[7m:se=\E[m:sr=\EM:\
    :te=\E[2J\E[?47l\E8:ti=\E7\E[?47h:\
    :up=\E[A:us=\E[4m:ue=\E[m:xn:
```

Table 17.4
Some Unix `termcap`
metacodes.

Code	Arg	Padding	Function
al	str	(P*)	add new blank line
am	bool		terminal has automatic margins
bs	bool	(o)	terminal can backspace with ^H
cd	str	(P*)	clear to end of display
ce	str	(P)	clear to end of line
cl	str	(P*)	clear screen and home cursor
cm	str	(NP)	cursor move to row m, column n
cs	str	(NP)	change scroll region to lines m through n
ct	str	(P)	clear all tab stops
dc	str	(P*)	delete character
dl	str	(P*)	delete line
im	str		enter insert mode
ho	str	(P)	home cursor

%d	decimal number starting at 0
%2	same as %2d
%3	same as %3d
%.	ASCII equiv
%+v	adds x then taken as %
%>xy	if value is >x; then add y. No transmission
%r	reverse order of rows/columns
%i	origin is at 1,1 not 0,0
%%	gives a single %
%n	XOR row and column with 0140
%B	BCD format
%D	reverse coding

Review

- Operating systems are large programs, often supplied along with the computer hardware, which are intended to provide the user with enhanced facilities, beyond those possible with bare hardware alone. Unix, Linux and Windows NT are examples of operating systems.

- There are broadly three categories of operating system: batch, online and real-time. Modern systems incorporate aspects of all three.

- Porting application software from one platform to another can be straightforward if both use the same operating system. Otherwise it can be a nightmare!

- Operating systems have evolved from the early days of programmers sharing useful routines to the current situation where the operating system allocates and protects resources.

- Unix remains an important multitasking operating system, for both personal workstations and Internet routers and servers. Multitasking refers to the ability to make the computer swap quickly from one task to another, without the interactive users being aware of it.

- For multitasking systems, there are several different strategies for judging when to swap tasks: time-sliced, preemptive or cooperative. Interrupts are used in all cases to carry out the transfer through to the operating system scheduler. This will then decide which task to run next.

- Communication between tasks is supported and regulated by the operating system facilities. Semaphores, pipes and signals are all offered for the application programs to use.

- An important role for the operating system is to protect access to exclusive resources, making sure that the tasks which share the data do not read corrupted data. Semaphores and signals are the most common methods of achieving this aim.

- Semaphores are software devices which are used to protect critical resources within a multitasking environment. Semaphores offer a 'busy flag', functions to test, clear and set the flag and a task queue where the operating system parks the blocked tasks.

- IO operations are now controlled by the IO subsystem, which is part of the operating system. The operation of passing data into and out from the computer is closely integrated into the task scheduling scheme.

Practical work

The recommended practical work involves the use of Unix tools, building process pipelines and writing small scripts in sh or csh. You will gain some familiarization with Unix as a programmers' and administrators' workbench.

Exercises

1. What role does an operating system perform in a personal workstation?

2. When porting a program to a new platform, what issues would have to be taken into account?

3. What is a TCB (Task Control Block)? What would you expect to find stored in it?

4. What does the symbol '&' signify in the second line of Fig. 17.16? What does the following Unix pipe achieve:

   ```
   cat file | tr ' ' '\n' | sort | uniq -c | sort -n
   ```

   What is the difference between the symbols '|' and '>'?

5. How does a signal handler function communicate with its main process? Is it possible to suffer from a critical region problem?

6. Clearly distinguish semaphores from signals. Amend the code given in Fig. 17.15 to count only the DEL keyboard hits. DEL sends signal #2, and can be caught and diverted. What is special about Ctrl-C?

7.   What is a shell? If you are using the X Window system, do you still need a shell? Name four alternative shells available for Unix.

8.   Explain what spooling is and why it was introduced. Is it still necessary with pre-emptive multitasking operating systems?

9.   What is a device driver? Are they only needed for printer interfacing?

10. One of the most useful Unix tools is `find`. Hide a file called `sardine` deep in your own directory tree. Then relocate it using: `find ~ -name sardine -print`. Read the manual page for `find` and modify the instruction to automatically delete the lost file.

11. Try the following pipe and find out what it does:

```
du -a ~ | sort -n | tail
```

Now find the five biggest files. You may need to use the online manual to look up the `du`, `sort` and `tail` tools.

Readings

- A good introduction can be found in Ritchie (1997).

- A more detailed treatment of operating systems is provided in Silberschatz *et al.* (2000).

- For those curious about Unix, Wang (1997) is a good text.

- Read Unix `man` pages for some of the most useful commands and tools: `ls`, `ps`, `kill`, `grep`, `setenv`, `printenv`, `lp`, `whereis`, `which`, `who`.

- Unfortunately the Windows NT help files are not very technical and rarely provide any useful information.

- A short history of Unix and Linux is available on:
  `http://crackmonkey.org/unix.html`

- Lots of FAQs:
  `http://howto.linuxberg.com/`

- Standardizing Linux:
  `http://linuxunited.org/`

- A European source for Linux:
  `http://src.doc.ic.ac.uk/`

- Information source:
  `http://www.linuxhq.com/`

- Commercial Linux development and support:
  `http//www.redhat.com/`

- The Web sites can be accessed via the Companion Web site for this book at:
  `http://www.booksites.net/williams/`

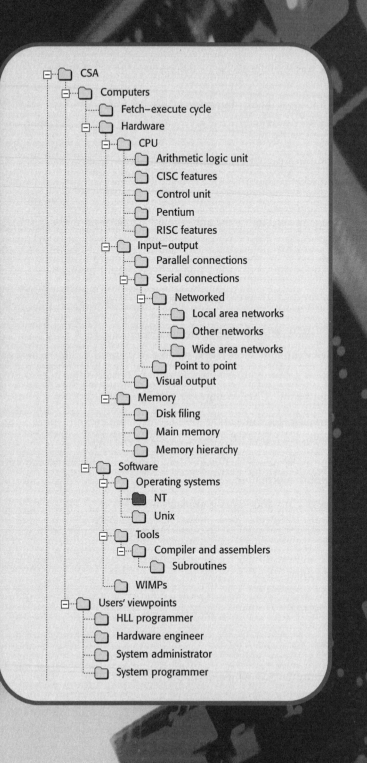

Windows NT

Overview

The Windows operating systems have developed from Windows 3.1 which depended on MS-DOS, through Windows 95 and 98 to Windows NT. This is being displaced by Windows 2000, but most of the discussion of Windows NT in this book also applies to Windows 2000, so we shall use the former name for simplicity. Windows NT is available in server and workstation form, and provides a multitasking environment.

18.1   Windows GUIs – responding to a need

Windows was originally developed by Microsoft to sit on top of MS-DOS to provide a graphical user interface. The final version of the first product was Windows 3.11. With it the DOS command line interface was abandoned, and only the disk handling routines and file manager continued to be used. Windows 95/98 extended this move to the point where MS-DOS was no longer required. Microsoft and IBM had collaborated in the development of the OS/2 multitasking operating system. This was targeted at the PC and included a WIMP interface. In 1988 the partnership was dissolved and Microsoft took the next big step by initiating the development of Windows NT. David Cutler was recruited from DEC, where he had been responsible for the well-respected VMS operating system. (The conspiracists among you will know that the three ASCII characters 'IBM' can be transformed into 'HAL' – the computer in *2001: A Space Odyssey* – by subtracting 1 from each character. But try adding one to 'VMS' in the same manner and you obtain 'WNT'. Such mnemonic arithmetic reminds me with sinking despair of my childish attempts to assist my mother with crossword anagrams.)

Windows NT was developed completely afresh, not as a further rework of the existing Windows 3.x or Windows 95. It was intended to retain the ability to host MS-DOS, OS/2, Windows 3.1/16 bit and POSIX-compliant code. It contained only 32 bit code, offered multi-threading within processes, networking facilities, preemptive as well as time-sliced scheduling and increased file security. The market addressed was the corporate network, with the particular requirements to flexibly control shared file access, and minimize the soaring costs of network administration. It is claimed to have involved the efforts of 250 programmers over a period of five years and comprise 14 million lines of code: a very different provenance from that of Linux.

Windows NT, like Unix, denies user programs direct access to IO ports because of the security risk that this would incur. Instead, all input–output operations have to be handed over to the operating system, which uses its own secure device drivers to carry out the necessary transfers. This change from the more relaxed MS-DOS regime, which had been continued into Windows 95 and 98, caused great problems with expansion card suppliers who sometimes had not understood the complexities involved in writing a new device driver to run under Windows NT. The issue of operating system security was central to the design of Windows NT, partly because that area was always identified as a weakness in Unix, and partly because of the growing demand from banks and insurance companies for secure online computer systems. In addition, there was a clear recognition that the global market required a simpler approach to 'localization', the translation of prompts and menus into the appropriate local language. Microsoft confronted this difficult issue by adopting the 16 bit Unicode character set in place of the limited 8 bit ASCII set.

Microsoft also required Windows NT to be readily portable to other processor architectures. At the start, the principal CPUs to be supported were Intel Pentium, DEC Alpha, IBM PowerPC and MIPS RISC. In the event, the grand plan of hardware independence has rather collapsed, with only the Pentium continuing to host

Windows NT. Nevertheless, the majority of the operating system code that needed to exchange data with the hardware was designed to deal instead with **HAL** (Hardware Abstraction Layer) an interface or buffer layer interposed between the hardware and the operating system. Such a scheme does allow for easier porting to new hardware.

The NT software architecture is divided into user and kernel portions. The executive runs in kernel mode and offers low-level services, including process despatching, memory allocation, and interrupt and IO management. All software in kernel mode benefits from higher privileges, allowing access to the full repertoire of machine instructions and all memory locations. By separating the basic functionality into separate modules, it is possible to build versions of Windows NT which provide different services. This is the way NT Server and NT Workstation are derived from the same set of source code modules.

Many of the functional modules are implemented as DLLs to be linked at run time with the other parts. Thus although the operating system appears to the user as a single monolith of code, it is in fact many distinct semi-autonomous units.

Interestingly, the executive also contains an **Object Manager**. This supports the object-oriented scheme of software implementation within Windows NT. The NT kernel defines a set of built-in classes (object types) for use by the kernel itself, the executive and the subsystems. Windows NT and all of its applications are managed at the kernel level as trusted objects, running in supervisor mode.

As can be seen from Fig. 18.1, HAL, the NT kernel and NT executive execute at supervisor privilege, giving them access to the whole machine. The environmental subsystem executes in user mode and supports a particular API, which is made available to application programs.

The HAL hides the different hardware characteristics by transforming them into a standardized format. It operates as a kernel mode DLL which other operating system processes link to. Rather than referring to specific absolute memory or port addresses, determined by the CPU architecture, generalized calls to HAL functions can be made. The HAL interface even allows the difference in the interrupt structure between

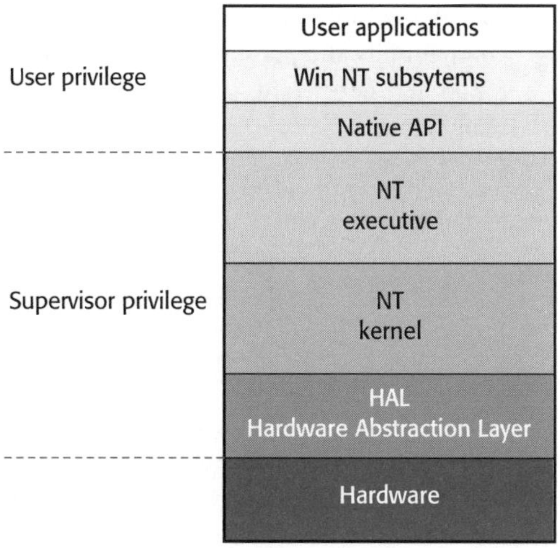

Fig. 18.1
Windows NT structure.

	User applications
User privilege	Win NT subsytems
	Native API
Supervisor privilege	NT executive
	NT kernel
	HAL Hardware Abstraction Layer
	Hardware

Pentium and Alpha to be hidden from the rest of the software. The hardware abstraction layer is a considerable achievement, but it does incur a performance penalty. With the range of available processors nearly reduced to one, the utility of retaining this 'virtual machine' level of translation could be questioned.

18.2   Win32 – the preferred user API

The NT executive communicates with the **Subsystem Layer** which sits above it providing a variety of services suited to different application environments. As mentioned earlier, it is possible to run programs which have been written to the POSIX standard. Another program may expect the OS/2 services to be available, while a third uses Win32. Windows NT will support them all. To ensure backward compatibility with MS-DOS, there is even an MS-DOS subsystem which allows 16 bit MS-DOS programs to execute.

Programmers know operating systems by the functional interface that they provide. These are referred to as **APIs** (Application Programming Interface) and can be quite extensive. Microsoft's API is called Win32 and has been offered with Windows 3.11, 95, 98, NT and 2000. It covers graphical control of the screen, multitasking, data IO and many other important aspects of process activity. A list of Win32 function calls is available at the supporting Web site. Once you have identified the name of the required function, it is best to check the online help system supplied with Microsoft Developer Studio for the exact details of parameters and functionality. I find that this approach is easier than trying to locate the relevant function name if you only have the help browser.

Microsoft offers several alternative APIs, as shown in Fig. 18.2, but Win32 is the preferred, recommended programmers' interface to Windows NT, 98 and even the baby of the family, Windows CE (for handheld computers). There are straightforward compatibility and portability advantages to acknowledging a single interface standard for a range of operating systems. In fact, Unix has achieved such standardization for many years.

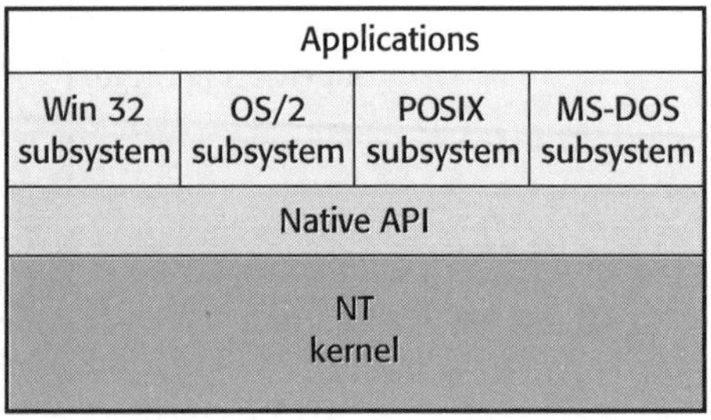

Fig. 18.2
Win32 and the kernel.

Applications			
Win 32 subsystem	OS/2 subsystem	POSIX subsystem	MS-DOS subsystem
Native API			
NT kernel			

18.3   Processes and threads – multitasking

When a program is loaded and registered with the operating system as an executable process it will be allocated the necessary resources and then despatched (allocated time on the CPU) whenever it is selected by the scheduler. Programs can consist of several processes, each of which is independently scheduled by the operating system. For these processes to cooperate in completing a job, they need to exchange data and control information. This can be relatively inefficient because it involves some time-consuming overheads. One way to retain the advantage of multitasking without incurring the overheads of inter-task communication is by using **threads**. These are 'lightweight' processes which share a common execution environment. So a program may be written to execute as several threads, all of which have access to the same data environment and can therefore communicate easily with each other. The Windows NT thread scheduler supports several mechanisms for swapping between threads. These include time-slicing, priority-based multi-level round robin queued, preemptive and cooperative hand-back. On Windows NT, the process time slice is generated from the system clock and is typically 50 ms. Often Servers are set up with longer time slots than Workstations, which need to offer good interactive performance. Windows NT offers 32 process queues, organized in priority order. These are divided into three categories: real-time, variable level and system level. Although Windows NT is not promoted as a real-time operating system, it does support preemptive scheduling based on interrupt-driven IO. However, the interrupt processing is often not carried out immediately but relegated, or deferred, to another process queue. This introduces an uncertain latency in completing the interrupt processing. Nevertheless, such worries about timing issues may appear somewhat academic when 1 GHz processors are being installed!

PCs running Windows have a Task Manager utility (Fig. 18.3) which can be activated by using the CTRL+ALT+DEL key combination, or clicking the right mouse button on the taskbar. This tool displays a list of current tasks (processes) with their memory and CPU usage statistics. It can also be used to kill off a renegade task!

Using multithreaded code raises once again the problem of critical sections (see Section 9.5). This becomes even more tricky to resolve when the multiprocessor facilities of NT are being exploited. In this case, it is necessary to anticipate the situation where execution threads, running on different CPUs, are competing for the same exclusive resource. Windows NT handles the problem by offering kernel-level spinlocks. Such actions are implemented using a Test-and-Set and Bus-Lock machine instructions where possible, but these facilities are seen at the user API level as semaphore Wait and Signal calls.

The NT Executive uses the services of the NT Kernel to implement process management, memory allocation, file management and IO device handling.

Fig. 18.3
Displaying the PC task list using the Task Manager.

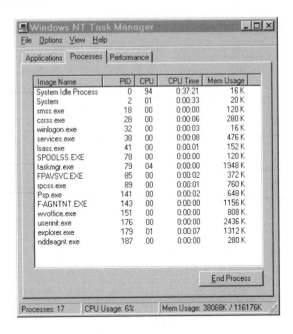

18.4 Memory management – virtual memory implementation

Windows NT is a demand-paged virtual memory operating system. Each process at creation is given 4 Gbyte of virtual address space. This is divided in half: the bottom 2 Gbyte is user space and the top half is shared with the system, allowing DLLs to be mapped into the process's own address space. Room is also reserved within this virtual space for data variables. The allocated part of the process's virtual address space is held on disk within the swap file. As described in Section 12.5, when the code starts running, the MMU (Memory Management Unit) maps pages from the virtual space into a physical address space within the computer's main memory. Thus only the current page of code and data are actually needed in RAM for the process to execute.

18.5 NT Registry – centralized administrative database

The NT Registry is an important information database which holds configuration data about many aspects of the operating environment. It replaces many of the .INI and .PIF files which used to be scattered around earlier PC file systems. The database is stored in two files, USER.DAT and SYSTEM.DAT, which normally reside in the C:\WIN32 or C:\WIN32\SYSTEM directories. A common facility, made possible

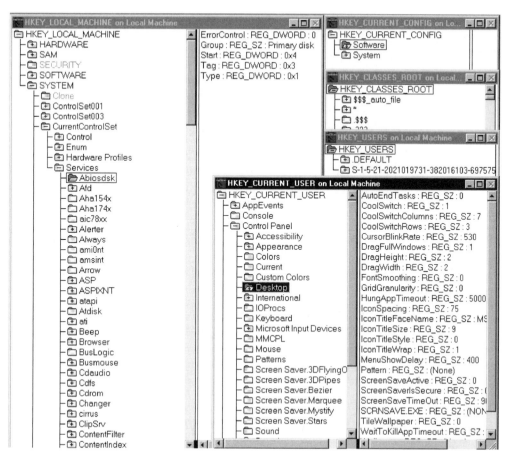

Fig. 18.4
Windows NT Registry Editor windows displayed.

through the Registry, is the automatic identification of the correct application program to fire up when a data file has been selected for reading or editing. The Registry holds the file extension identifiers associated with the specific application, such as .doc being associated with the Microsoft Word word processor. Another useful facility, which can help compensate for the shortage of free interrupt lines in the PC, is the Hardware Profile. This allows the user to select a specific set of device drivers during the boot sequence by responding to a menu. In this way, devices may be stood down and others enrolled to use the free IRQs.

To give access to the information held in the Registry it is best to use the regedt32 program (Fig. 18.4) which acts like a Registry browser. Information is stored in the form of 'keys' and 'values'. Values may be binary or textual. When editing the Registry, great care should be taken to avoid disturbing other entries. The scheme can be exemplified by understanding how an application stores the name of the last file opened before the application was shut down. The key might be called LastDocument, with the associated value holding a list of filenames. Alternatively, and more suitable for other situations, is the hierarchical arrangement where keys hold subkeys which hold further subkeys, until, at the bottom, each subkey has an associated filename.

Table 18.1
Windows NT Registry
top level keys.

HKEY_LOCAL_MACHINE	Holds the hardware configuration, installed device drivers, network protocols, software classes
	Configuration parameters for local computer
	Enum device configuration
	Hardware serial port configuration
	Network user login information
	Security remote administration permissions
	Installed software
	System booting information
HKEY_CURRENT_CONFIG	Holds the current hardware configuration, where options exist
HKEY_CLASSES_ROOT	Holds document types, file associations, shell interface
HKEY_USERS	Holds login users' software preferences and desktop configuration
HKEY_CURRENT_USER	Holds copies of the preferences of the current user

At the top level of the registry are half a dozen principal or Handle keys which act as the roots for information trees. These are displayed in Fig. 18.4 and listed more clearly in Table 18.1.

18.6   NTFS – Windows NT file system

Windows NT offers an alternative to the FAT-based file handling scheme, which is known as **NTFS**. It offers full support for the extensive Windows NT access controls, and is used where data security is an important issue. Significantly, unauthorized users cannot bypass security on the NTFS partition by booting the server from a floppy. The disk space is separated in volumes, which can be taken as equivalent to partitions, but may envelop several partitions, or even drives. Although it is claimed to be a non-FAT system, the data is still divided into clusters and indexed by a single LCN (Logical Cluster Number). To reduce the fragmentation problems that the FAT-16 system ran into, NTFS does not generally use large clusters; in fact, it recommends a 512 byte cluster for volumes (partitions) less than 512 Mbyte. Because the NTFS stores file lengths as 64 bit numbers, the maximum file size is 2^{64} bytes, which is quite big enough for most purposes. The LCN is 32 bits wide, which imposes a maximum volume size of 16 Tbyte with 4 kbyte clusters. It is normal to initialize partitions to use 4 kbyte clusters (the same size as for floppy disks). This matches the page size of virtual memory, which must assist in achieving more efficient memory management.

To improve user convenience, NTFS can handle extended 256 character filenames and supports upper- and lower-case letters. These extended names are truncated for use with FAT-16 file systems. All disk access activities can be logged in the event of a system failure. This means data can be recovered more easily in such circumstances. It does, however increase the processing time.

Although only NT computers can use NTFS files directly, network users can access files on NT Servers whether they are using FAT or Unix file systems. NT presents files to non-NT computers in a form the computers can accept. Unix file systems can also be accessed from Windows NT if the **Samba** file server is installed on the Unix host.

Dual-boot machines offering both Linux and Windows NT require a shared FAT partition to exchange data between the two operating environments. For large amounts of data (greater than 10 Gbyte) and where security is an important issue, it is now thought advisable to forsake the traditional FATs and use NTFS!

A dynamic disk caching scheme is implemented by the Windows NT Cache Manager process. When a file is opened, a substantial block of data, 256 kbyte, will then be temporarily stored in main memory disk cache in case it is referred to again. This facility reduces the amount of disk activity by reading and writing in larger chunks. It effectively memory maps the file while it is in use. The cache manager can also try to anticipate the need for data to be read into the cache before it is required.

18.7 File access – ACLs, permissions and security

As with all operating systems, the basic security of Windows NT relies on a secure password system. This is much more elaborate than the Unix version and involves the **SAM** (Security Access Manager) for that particular **Domain** authorizing the password during the login episode. A Domain is a group of linked, cooperating workstations which support several users who are identified in **Workgroups**. (As always, the nomenclature is a big stumbling block for newcomers.) If the SAM is not resident on the login workstation, there is a security risk involved with transferring the password itself across the network. Windows NT solves this by employing the method of 'challenging'. The local workstation passes all login passwords through an encryption process. Then the plain-text password is deleted. The encryption to all intents and purposes is a 'one way' hashing function, impossible to reverse unless you have some inside information. The Domain Controller, running SAM, will then respond to the login request with a challenge to the workstation. This operates in the same way that banks require you to tell them some weird piece of personal information, such as the middle two digits of your mother's birth date, when you make an enquiry by telephone.

As we are frequently warned by systems administrators, the 'hacker' more often benefits from seeing passwords plainly written on sticky notes and clearly displayed next to the workstation than from subtle algorithmic intelligence. Even guessing passwords can be easy due to our lack of imagination. Frequently they are chosen from car number plates, family names or birthdays, or items of food. With online dictionaries

Fig. 18.5
Setting network shares
and permissions to a
directory.

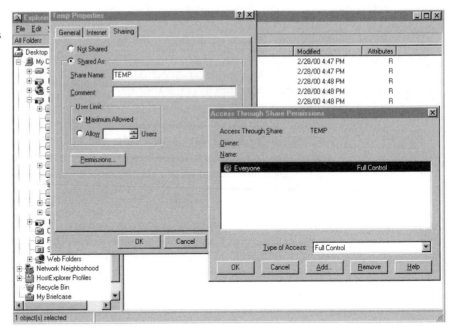

available, it is relatively easy to test out every common word as a password. Do any of your passwords fit into these categories?

To control the access to files and directories within a network, Windows NT offers several features beyond passwords. The owner of a file or directory may set **share permissions** to 'export' the item in a limited manner, but it gets rather more complicated than Unix because there are share-level, directory-level and file-level permissions to be negotiated. This is illustrated in Fig. 18.5 where the Explorer window has been opened (RMB, Start → Explore; RMB = right mouse button) and the desired directory (C:\TEMP) has been RMB selected, which reveals a menu with the 'Sharing...' options available. When this is selected the Properties box will appear which allows the directory to be exported as a named 'share'. The actual permissions offered are set from the Permissions button. The three types of access are: Full Control, No Access, and Read and Change.

The new Share name which an exported directory can be known by throughout the network domain can be up to 12 letters. This draws our attention to the somewhat confused position which Windows NT has adopted with regard to effective string lengths, as outlined in Table 18.2. Adopting a share alias for a directory does not generally seem to be a sensible decision, though. The user groups or individual login names can now be inserted by using the Add button on the Permissions box. Another nice touch is the inclusion of a 'hidden share' facility. You publicly export a directory, but then deliberately make it invisible to those you do not inform of its existence! This is possible by inserting a '$' at the end of the share name. You may have noticed the comment field on the Share Properties box. This affords the opportunity to tag a helpful commentary to every shared directory in order to help users find the correct files.

Table 18.2
Discrepancy in effective
string lengths.

Filename	256 characters
User name	20 characters
Passwords	14 characters
Machine name	15 characters
Workgroup names	15 characters
Share names	12 characters

The obvious meaning of assigning 'Read' access is extended to include the execution of programs and being able to attach to subdirectories. 'Change' also includes the right to add, append and delete items. 'Full Control' is self-explanatory.

A further level of controlling access to individual files and directories, independent of the network sharing facility, is also provided, but only within the NFTS file system. It does not work within FAT-16. Within Explorer or My Computer, the file or directory in question needs to be RMB selected. The Properties box offers 'Permissions' which leads to 'Security'. This is the box which allows the individual access permissions to be set for groups or individual users.

RMB on Filename → Properties → Security → Permissions → Add → Members

This level of file access control is the most powerful and overrides the network share permissions.

From the other end of the operation, a user on a workstation who needs to gain access to a directory on a server, or even a neighbouring workstation, that has been exported using 'shared' permissions, employs the technique illustrated in Fig. 18.6. The directory has to be installed as a virtual drive on the local machine.

RMB, Start → Explore → Tools → Map Network Drive

The browser will reveal all the available network directories which have been made visible through the share option from the domain server and the neighbouring workstations.

18.8 Sharing software components – OLE, DDE and COM

Since the introduction of Windows, Microsoft has been struggling to provide a robust mechanism to enable applications to exchange data. This could be seen as an extension of shared files or data modules. Although Object Linking and Embedding (OLE), was seen only as providing standards for compound documents, it was a first step. Initially this technology was layered on Dynamic Data Exchange (DDE). Unfortunately, this was inadequate when it came to supporting audio and video facilities. The

Fig. 18.6
Installing a shared
directory as a local
virtual drive.

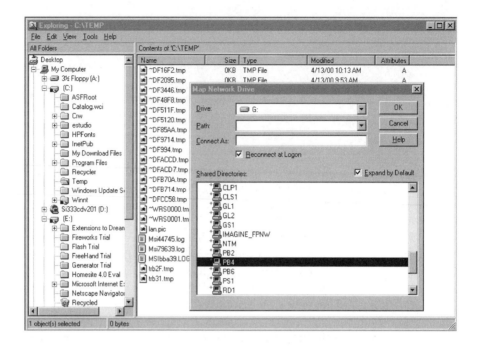

current method is referred to as Component Object Model (COM). COM is now the underlying technology for OLE, ActiveX, ActiveX controls and Microsoft Transaction Server. COM has now been extended to add distributed facilities within the Distributed COM (DCOM). The intention has always been to establish a software component market-place, where software could be bought and sold like chips.

18.9   Windows NT as a mainframe – Winframe terminal server

In a similar manner to Unix X Windows, Windows NT can update windows displayed on remote workstations. This is a scheme that was developed by Citrix and called Winframe. Since then it has been dubbed **thin client**. The apparent aim is to recentralize the processing and filing provision on large, powerful servers within the computer centre. The desktop workstations will only need to offer the minimum screen/keyboard facilities and network access. Because the network traffic would be substantially increased when servicing hundreds, if not thousands, of remote window displays, at least a 10BaseT switched star topology would be needed. For large networks, the advantage to systems administrators is the ability to regulate the users' computing environment more tightly, even going as far as specifying their desktop configuration. If the users are mobile this may benefit them by providing a standard screen and set of tools whenever they logon. But more likely they will become increasingly dissatisfied with such an inflexible regime. When sharing with many other (unknown) users, the unresolvable difficulty is the inability to predict what the response time to a request will be. This was at the core of the frustration which users felt with the earlier mainframes, and this will still remain a problem for Windows NT servers. The LAN transmission rates can never be as fast as the VGA cable between PC and screen, and the central server will never, ever be large enough to satisfy all the users on a Monday morning.

Unfortunately it does seem to be a return to the late 1950s, when users' needs were ignored and computer centres were in open conflict with the departments they were intending to serve. The result, as we have historically witnessed, was the eclipse of centralized computing in favour of local control and greater flexibility. I suspect that as the network staggers under the assault of a multitude of Netscape downloads, users will again demand more autonomy and a greater authority in choosing the computing resources on which they depend.

Review

- Following on from the experience with IBM's OS/2 and DEC's VMS, Windows NT was targeted at large corporate network users.

- Windows NT is a preemptive, multitasking, virtual memory, networked operating system. It is based on a modular object-oriented design. It can be ported to different processors more readily due to the HAL virtual machine layer.

- The modularity allows several APIs to be supported simultaneously, so programs for MS-DOS, Windows 3.1, OS/2 and POSIX may be executed. The recommended interface is the Win32 API.

- A central database called the Registry replaces all the diverse initialization files which had proliferated so much in earlier operating systems.

- Windows NT offers secure networked computing through enhanced password handling and expanded permission facilities.

- An improved filing system, NTFS, can deal with larger files and data distributed across a network. There is better failure recovery built into the file manager.

- Unix hosts can be incorporated into an NT network through X Window servers running on NT workstations and Unix files being exported to Windows NT.

Practical work

The recommended practical work involves the use of the Windows NT operating system. This will include the application of security facilities (Shares and Permissions), and the installation of network virtual drives. Personal passwords and Access Control Lists will be investigated.

Exercises

1. What are the differences in user needs for a desktop facility at home and in the corporate office? How does Windows NT address these differences?

2. What is Unicode? Why did Microsoft decide to abandon ASCII in its favour?

3. How does the structure of Windows NT help when being ported to a new processor? How does it deal with the differences in interrupt provision?

4. The file cache management system aims to reduce disk accesses and so speed up program execution. How could the compiler get involved in this activity?

5. In what way does Windows NT offer cooperation with networked hosts running other operating systems?

6. Win32 is the standard API to Windows NT. Summarize the types of facilities that it offers to programmers.

7. What extra facilities does the Windows NTFS filing system offer which could be helpful when recovering from a disk crash?

8. When NT was revised for release 4, the graphics code which manages the screen was moved into the kernel. This was done to improve speed. Do you foresee any problems with this change?

9. What is the difference between a thread and a process? Under what circumstances might you encounter a critical data problem? How would you resolve such a problem?

10. Because Windows NT is based on object-oriented principles, the efficient passing of messages is critical. What mechanism is provided to carry out this activity?

Readings

- A short introduction to Windows NT can be found at the back of Nutt (1999) and in Silberschatz *et al.* (2000).

- A thorough reference guide, not an introduction, is provided by Pearce (1997).

- Simon *et al.* (1995).

- You should try the extensive MSDN (Microsoft Developer Network) Web site. It contains many articles on COM, OLE and DCOM as well as many other topics:
  `http://msdn.microsoft.com/library/default.asp`

- Try this for a short summary of NT benefits and facilities:
  `http://rncnt1.lbl.gov/NT/rnc_nt_intro/index.htm`

- The Web sites can be accessed via the Companion Web site for this book at:
  `http://www.booksites.net/williams/`

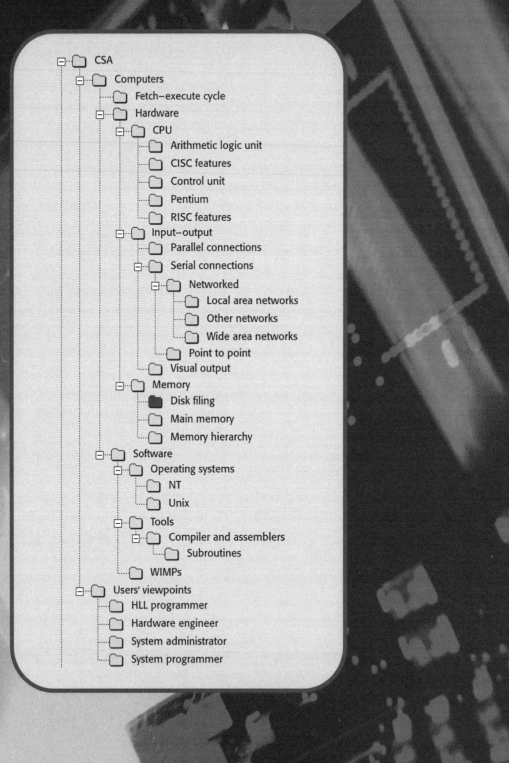

Filing systems

Overview

Filing, which is the ability to organize and store large amounts of data over long periods of time, remains one of the most important services offered by computers. Databases, which offer more flexible access to stored data, are displacing simple files in many applications. By using hard disks it is possible to retain fast, convenient access to any element of the data. Filing systems now have to encompass hard disk, floppy disk, CD-ROM, CD-RW and backup tapes. This range includes any file reachable through the Internet.

19.1   Data storage – file systems and databases

One of the most useful features of nearly all operating systems is disk filing, whereby data and programs can be saved by users and recovered at some time in the future without demanding any deep understanding of the underlying hardware mechanisms.

In Chapter 12 the technical details of how disk drives manage to record and restore vast amounts of binary data were introduced. Here, we are concerned with the methods used by operating systems to effectively hide these complex activities so that users can more conveniently use the facilities offered by disk hardware and other mass storage devices. The data to be filed is sorted into some kind of order and split into blocks before writing them to disk. If you are to avoid the time-consuming search through all of the data blocks comprising a file to find a desired record, some indexing method has to be employed. It would be helpful if the application could itself supply the number of the target data block, and so avoid sequential scanning by steering the read head directly to the correct head, cylinder and sector. This elaboration is termed direct file access. It does in some way effect a partial bypass of the logical file access methods which we have said are so popular with users!

Another way of accessing data records stored in files on disk is known as indexed-sequential. This is where a separate index gives the block number, and so the location on disk, of the target record. The three methods, sequential access, direct access and indexed access, are compared in Table 19.1. In addition, instead of limiting the relationship between data records to a single, linear sequence, it is increasingly popular to use multiply-linked relationships between records. In this case database support is required in order to keep track of the data records and their inter-relationships, and carry out the complex searches requested.

Sequential file organization is the simplest. Data records are stored in key field sequence and every data record is uniquely distinguished by a chosen key field value. Access is by moving sequentially through the records until the target is recognized, a slow process for large files, but suitable when carrying out a batch process, such as quarterly gas bill calculations or monthly salaries.

Table 19.1
Data filing and databases.

Data organization	Application type	Advantages	Disadvantages
Sequential	Batch processing	Simple; efficient	Maintenance; data needs sorting
Indexed-sequential	Batch processing	Sequential and direct access; no data sorting	Index takes up space; less efficient
Direct	Online	No data sorting; fast access	Space inefficient; inconvenient to use
Database	Online	Flexible access	Performance poor; maintenance costs

To speed up this rather slow technique, **Direct Access Files** use the data record key field value to calculate a disk block address. This can then be used to locate the record on disk. It involves a 'many to few' mapping which is often carried out using a **hashing** algorithm. No separate lookup index is needed to operate this scheme. Unix only supports sequential access files, which is considered a disadvantage by some programmers.

The organization of an **indexed-sequential file** merges the two previous approaches. The data is sorted in key field order, but may also be accessed directly using a supplementary index which has to be built at the same time as the file. Data records can be located directly with the help of the index, or sequentially by key field order.

Databases require the data records to include extra fields for link pointers. These implement the logical organization of the relationships between the items of data in storage. They could be considered as cross-references between the data records. Database records are still key field sorted, but also depend on these pointer links to support the more complex SQL query searches that many users demand: 'What is the telephone number of everyone over 40, married, living in Bristol, owning a house with windows, not yet double glazed, and receiving winter gas bills larger than £200?'. To provide fast access to such information requires that complex indexes to all of the data records are built and maintained.

Anybody who have ever used a PC will be familiar with the **hierarchical** filing scheme displayed in the **file browser**, called from 'My Computer' by selecting the File → Explorer pulldown. The browser tool offered by Windows NT 4 and shown in Fig. 19.1 helps you to navigate around the directories and files so that you are better able to organize your own work. You may be able to make out the file `Msdev.exe` in the middle of the right-hand panel. This is the main executable file for Microsoft Developer Studio 5, hidden deep in the directory: `C:\Program Files\Common Files\DevStudio\SharedIDE\bin`. If you do not have a desktop icon set up, the easiest way to start a program is to use the Taskbar Start → Run facility. The later versions of Windows NT integrate the file browser into Internet Explorer to provide a unified 'Resource Browser'. This is another move towards a seamless view of the whole WWW, from your local machine to geographically distant servers. Whether this will genuinely help users is open to debate.

Unix, too, has always arranged its system files in a hierarchy, and offers the same facilities to users. The equivalent file browser on the Sun is called File Manager (Fig. 19.2). (Unix users seem to remain loyal to the old `ls` / `cd` approach in most situations!)

If you have ever worked with a flat file system, where hundreds of files are simply held, without any classification or subgrouping, in a single 'top level' directory, you will know how difficult it is to locate previous work. It is like not having drawers in a filing cabinet, only a single shelf to stack all your papers on. Handling hierarchical directories and files is an important responsibility of the operating system. A secondary advantage to hierarchical filing arrangements is the tolerance of files with identical names. If the same name is used for two files, as must often occur, as long as the files are positioned in different directories the operating system will have no

Fig. 19.1
Windows NT file
browser showing the
file hierarchy.

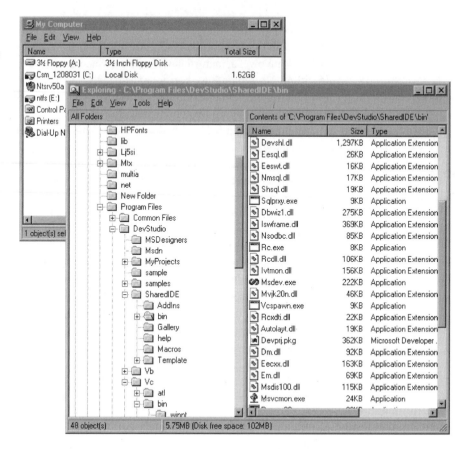

problem in distinguishing them. This is due to the fact that the identifier is not really the *name* of a file but its **path name**. This is the full directory location, such as: /home/users/staff/cs/rwilliam/Book/ch_19. I do have another file, ch_19, held in /projects/rob/uh/book, but this presents no immediate dilemma to the operating system. So to get to the file containing the text for this chapter, I need to type in the full, **absolute path name** to unambiguously tell the operating system which file I require. This would undoubtedly be too inconvenient if it had to be carried through each time you access a file, so there are a number of short cuts provided. The most useful approach is to use a **relative path name**. The shell can recognize an absolute path name because it always begins with a '/' character. Otherwise filenames will have the current working directory path name prefixed to create an absolute format beginning with /. This way of referring to files from your current position is only useful because you can easily change your current directory using the cd command. Another short-cut is to refer to files relative to your own home directory. This is the default directory that you always start in, immediately after login. Unix recognizes the ~ (tilde) symbol to represent the absolute path name for your home directory. This allows me to use the abbreviated reference ~/Book/ch_19.

So it is now normal for file systems to be structured in a hierarchical fashion, which can be likened to the spreading roots of a tree, with a file hanging from each root tip.

Fig. 19.2
Sun File Manager
display with floppy
disk browser.

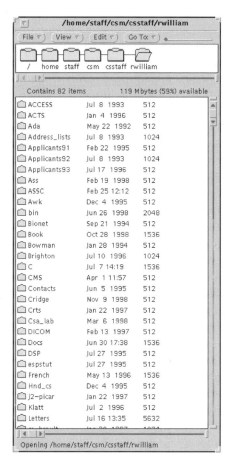

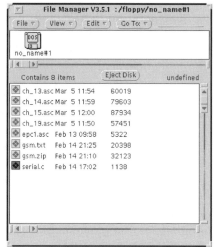

Unix actually calls the topmost point in the file system **root**. The ability to embed subdirectories within directories not only helps users to organize their work but also reduces the time taken by the system to locate files.

The programmer can save and restore data and programs by simply associating unique names with each directory, subdirectory and file. This facility to name files eliminates the need to remember the track and sector numbers for all the blocks of data held on disk. Such a nightmare would make the maintenance of disk-based directories and files very tedious. Operating systems help further by providing functions to open, read, write and close files. They also have to manage the allocation and recovery of disk space as well as offering some access security to ensure that only authorized users can read, write or delete the files. We will return to this subject later.

When writing data to a file, generally, the application program may assume the responsibility of grouping small data items together in a **record** and then make a request to the operating system to write the record to disk. We speak of 'writing a file', but a file is only a grouping of data which can be conveniently accessed through a unique identifier. There is no physical 'wrapper' set around the data ensuring the integrity of a file. The component blocks of data within a file are only linked together by pointers. This gives a lot of flexibility to the file management routines in their space allocation and placement of files on a disk. It was explained in Section 12.7 that data is written to disk tracks in sectors which are commonly 256 or 512 bytes long. These may further be associated together in so called **clusters** of 4 kbyte to help with space allocation difficulties. The disk will now only read or write a minimum block of 4 kbyte. This does lead to some wastage of space because every file will not exactly fill the last 4 kbyte cluster. In fact, on an average statistic, every file will waste half the final cluster. This is not too serious, but it is worth looking into. Using `ls -R | wc -l`, I discovered that I own more than 4800 files on Unix. This results in a cluster lossage of about 10 Mbyte, which is perhaps tolerable when even small disk drives offer 8 Gbyte of space. Thus I have only lost 0.125 % of a single drive.

When a file is made up of several data blocks they do not have to be written in a continuous sequence of contiguous sectors: they can, and often are, scattered all over the disk surface, wherever there is available free space. Such **fragmentation** of the disk space tends to occur over a period of time, during which files are written, deleted and replaced by others. Although it is unavoidable, it is not desirable because it makes reading a file much slower, with the increased amount of head movements required. To maintain disk performance on Windows NT, a defragmentation program can be employed to reorganize scattered file blocks so that they are rewritten into more adjacent positions to reduce the amount of head movement when accessing data. Unix employs a different strategy of limiting the allocation of data blocks to neighbouring cylinders. This is somewhat like establishing a large number of partitions in order to constrain head movement.

In Fig. 19.3 the blocks from a file are shown scattered over a single surface of the top disk. It would require a lot of head movements to read or amend the data. However, if the same data were rewritten onto a single cylinder, as also shown, no head movements would be required once the first block had been located.

Fig. 19.3
Alternative layouts for blocks 1, 2, 3, 4, 5, 6 and 7 to reduce access times (head movement delays).

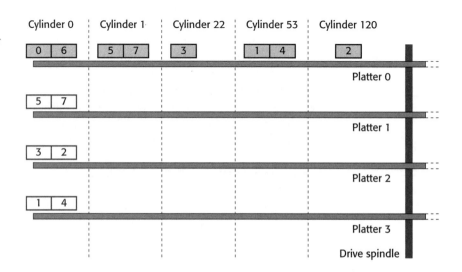

Fig. 19.4
Hard disk with four
partitions.

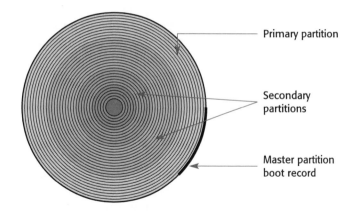

The data to be stored in a file may be in a variety of forms depending on the application: binary integer numbers, complex records, simple ASCII char streams or many other formats. Some operating systems recognize these variations and support them with specialized access functions. Others, like Unix, eschew such complexities and only acknowledge byte streams. All the data formatting then has to be carried out within the user application program, or at least by a dedicated library. There are arguments both ways; Unix started life as a host for text processing tools, so it is not surprising that simple byte-wide data is its principal preoccupation.

The PC utility **fdisk** can group disk cylinders into distinct **partitions** (Fig. 19.4) and lay down **Partition Boot Records** at the start of each partition (Fig. 19.5). fdisk recognizes the undocumented /mbr option to carry out this latter operation. In particular, the **Master Partition Boot Record** (MPBR), which is 512 bytes long, is positioned in the very first sector of the disk drive (Cylinder 0, Head 0, Sector 1). It

Fig. 19.5
PC disk master
partition boot record.

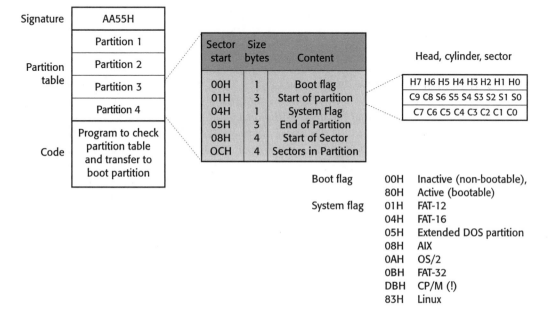

contains the *second* program to run when a PC is turned on. The BIOS PROM clearly runs first of all, loading the MPBR program and then passing execution over. Perhaps it is worth noting that the MPBR has been the target of virus attacks for some years, which result in the failure of transfer from BIOS to the operating system. All operating systems (MS-DOS, OS/2, Windows 3.1, Windows 95/8/NT/2000, Linux, OS-9) that run on the PC recognize and use the same MPBR. It holds important information, principally the start positions of the partitions that are set for that disk, and which of the partitions is to be 'active' and supply operating system code during boot up. Inconveniently, the MPBR provides space for only four partitions. However, each of these may be set to boot up a different operating system. If files are to be exchanged between the different operating systems, it is common to designate one partition for MS-DOS with a FAT-16 file system. This still seems to be recognized by most current operating systems.

With large capacity hard disks, four partitions is certainly not enough when you consider that Windows can handle 24 partitions, represented by the letters C to Z. To get round this limit, when there is a need for more partitions, Primary and Extended partitions are used. The extended partition is then further subdivided into many logical DOS volumes. These are not registered with the MPBR table and so cannot offer booting facilities. Their initial cylinder numbers are held in the individual partition records in linked-list fashion – one partition record points to the next.

Partitions also provide some measure of security in times of head crashes. If one partition is damaged, the others may still remain unaffected and readable when the system is rebooted from CD-ROM or a floppy disk.

Unless you use an interactive Boot Manager utility, such as LiLo, the MPBR will always transfer the boot-up process to the partition assigned as Active. Here will be found another table known as the **Partition Boot Record** which is tabulated in Fig. 19.6. These are positioned at the very start of each of the disk partitions, and contain important parameters. They are installed by the high-level formatter utility: `format`.

As mentioned at the start of this chapter, a facility universally offered by all operating systems is the ability to accept a name as a file identifier. This is the role of the **directory**, which allows the operating system to translate user filenames into a numeric format required by the disk controllers. At the hardware level, all that is really reqiuired are the three numbers **Cylinder**, **Head** and **Sector** (CHS); the controller will then correctly position the appropriate read head and wait for the sector to come round. But only very rarely do we ever have to access a disk using CHS parameters. Even when a file system becomes corrupted the normal intervention would be at the intermediate **Logical Block Number** (LBN) level with the help of a Disk Doctor toolkit such as Norton Utilities. The LBNs are simply the sequence number of the data block, or cluster, as they occur on the disk. The clusters are numbered from the start to the end, each partition having a separate sequence of numbers. Once again, the width of the index number determines the maximum size of storage space possible.

Fig. 19.6
A partition boot record
(non-master).

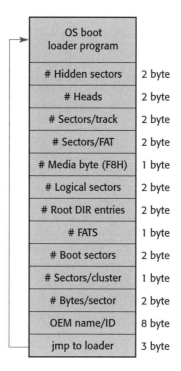

OS boot loader program	
# Hidden sectors	2 byte
# Heads	2 byte
# Sectors/track	2 byte
# Sectors/FAT	2 byte
# Media byte (F8H)	1 byte
# Logical sectors	2 byte
# Root DIR entries	2 byte
# FATS	1 byte
# Boot sectors	2 byte
# Sectors/cluster	1 byte
# Bytes/sector	2 byte
OEM name/ID	8 byte
jmp to loader	3 byte

19.2 The PC file allocation table and the directory

Access to disk data is still achieved fundamentally by telling the disk controller which cylinder, track and sector to access. This is known as cylinder, track, sector accesssing, representing the lowest physical level. But to simplify matters, a logical to physical translation is carried out by the operating system. All the physical sectors on the disk, or within a partition, are numbered sequentially from the outer track inwards. Thus only the single logical sector number is needed to retrieve data. This logical sector number was originally 12 bits and increased to 16, and then 32 bits to deal with larger disks. Physical sectors were 512 bytes, giving the largest volume accessible as 512×2^{16} kbyte = 32 Mbyte. This simply was not adequate and was increased by grouping sectors into 4 kbyte 'logical sectors' or **clusters** for access purposes. This imposed a 4 kbyte minimum file size, but pushed the maximum partition size to 256 Mbyte.

The translation from logical file identifiers into physical data sector locators is carried out when a file is accessed. The operating system manages the **directory** for this purpose. Every file, when it is first created, has an entry set up in the relevant disk partition directory. The principal purpose is to translate the user filename into a numeric disk address which the disk controller can use to locate the blocks of file data. Each disk partition has a separate, independent directory. A directory entry will also hold other important adminstrative details, as listed in Fig. 19.7. By having the owner's ID and the access permission parameters, the operating system can regulate who does what with each file. The file management technique introduced with MS-

Fig. 19.7
Essential information for
directory entries.

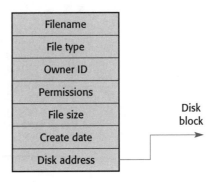

DOS, and still widely used in Windows, is known as the **FAT file system**. It is illustrated in Fig. 19.8. As we have said, users want to access their files by name, but disk
controllers uses Cylinder, Head and Sector (**CHS**) numbers to position the read
heads. An alternate reference strategy uses block or cluster numbers and goes under
the name **LBN** (Logical Block Number). The FAT method uses LBNs, but refers to
them as **cluster numbers**. This means that we end up with a double translation before
we can access file data. The filename is used to obtain the LBN of the first 4 kbyte

Fig. 19.8
FAT-16 directory and
file allocation table.

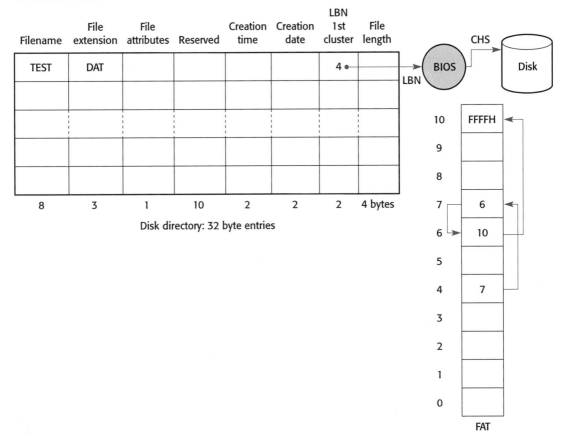

cluster from the directory, and then this LBN is converted to the correct CHS. All of this is done by the operating system with no assistance from the user.

If the FAT file system is to be used, each hard disk partition needs a separate directory and FAT. As illustrated in Fig. 19.8, accessing a file through the DOS FAT scheme involves first locating the filename and extension in the directory table. Here are found the LBNs for the starting cluster of every file held in that partition. The initial LBN can be used to access the first block of data from a file. For subsequent clusters the directory is of no help, and reference has to be made to the **FAT** (File Allocation Table). The FAT holds a linked list for every file which is larger than a single cluster (4 kbyte). When a large file is written to the disk, a chain of cluster numbers is set up within the FAT to link together the separate blocks of data. So a file is 'held together' by a linked list of cluster numbers threading up and down the FAT. In Fig. 19.8, the cluster sequence for the file TEST.DAT is 4–7–6–10, which can be identified in the FAT because the first node is held in the directory. Chains are terminated by the FFFFH marker. The FAT cluster chains can be extended, shortened, have items inserted and deleted in a very flexible manner. When considering the maximum size of file which can be dealt with using such a scheme, both the cluster size and the width of the LBN are relevant. The LBN has steadily increased from 12 to 16 and now to 32 bits, which are referred to as FAT-12, FAT-16 and FAT-32 respectively. The latest revision (32 bit FAT) has enabled the scheme to take on 16 Tbyte disk volumes, which should provide for the time being! Because the FAT is so critical to the filing system, and carries no specific error correction coding, it is duplicated on the disk to provide some gesture of secure intent! When a directory gets corrupted the normal access route to data files is blocked. But much worse, a confused FAT will require hours of patient attention should valuable data need to be recovered from the disk.

Although filenames are limited to 8 characters on MS-DOS and Windows 3.x systems, Windows NT offers a welcome extension to 255 characters. In order to maintain compatibility a clever method of truncation is available which takes the first 6 of the 255 characters and appends a number to ensure a unique identifier. Thus robert_williams.txt would be abbreviated to robert~1.txt. The integer is incremented for other robert_something.txt names.

With the introduction of higher and higher capacity IDE drives (greater than 18 Gbyte) the performance limitation of FAT schemes has been criticized, and part of the motivation for changing to Windows NT is often to use NTFS, which is better suited to large data sets. Nevertheless, it is still common to have at least one FAT partition, and in any case, floppy disks are limited to this technique.

During the initial formatting, any faulty sectors are detected and the corresponding entry in the FAT is marked as unusable. The FAT entry of the last cluster in a chain is set at FFFFH, while unused clusters are marked with a 0000H. As the length of any table is determined by the width of the addressing index, which in this case is 16 bits, the FAT is 65 536 entries long. Thus in this form it can only manage a maximum space of: $64 \text{ k} \times 1 \text{ kbyte} = 64$ Mbyte. This is far too small for contemporary disk drives, which are commonly 8 Gbyte and growing every month. To increase the span to a more useful figure, first the cluster unit was increased, then the cluster index itself was stretched to 32 bits. See Table 19.2 for a summary.

Table 19.2
FAT cluster size and
volume capacity.

Sector size (bytes)	Sectors per cluster	Cluster size (kbyte)	Cluster index size (bits)	Max. volume capacity
512	4	2	16	128 Mbyte
512	16	8	16	512 Mbyte
512	32	16	16	1 Gbyte
512	64	32	16	2 Gbyte
512	16	8	32	32 Tbyte

In summary, to get access to data in a file held within a FAT system, you need to supply the filename. The directory will translate this into the LBN of the first cluster, which will be converted into the Cylinder Head Sector values of the first sector. For subsequent blocks of data the directory is of no use, and reference has to be made to the linked list of LBNs held in the file access table.

19.3   Unix inodes – they do it differently

Unix organizes directories and access to files in a different manner to Windows NT. The superficial layout of its hierarchical file system, though, is much the same. Figure 19.9 shows the file system administrative structure, starting with the Boot Block, which contains the system loader. Next, the Super Block contains information about the file system: maximum size, number of inodes and number of data blocks. It also holds a pointer to the list of free inode blocks for when a new file is created. This gets copied into main memory on boot-up. Unix needs at least one file system to be available at boot time. From then on extra file systems can be added using the **mount** command. Unfortunately this interesting facility is usually restricted to super-user, but try /etc/mount and see.

The Unix file system depends heavily on data structures called **inodes** (index node). Every file, and directory, has a unique identifying inode block which holds pointers to the file data blocks. Typically, an inode is 64 bytes long (Fig. 19.9), containing access control information as well as 10 pointers to data blocks which hold the data for that file. Should more capacity be required for the file, there are two extension indirect pointers, each linking to 10 further inode blocks, which in their turn will be pointing to 100 data blocks. If even then the file capacity is too small, a single doubly indirect pointer is provided which can access 1000 extra data blocks. The structure of an inode block can be seen in the header file /usr/include/sys/stat.h. The C structure stat is presented in Fig. 19.10, and you can see the fields used for accessing the data blocks. The record field st_ino is the most important because it holds the inode value; only through this is it possible to find the first block of data.

```
rob@milly [20]/usr/sbin/mount
/   on  /dev/dsk/c0t0d0s0 read/write/setuid on Mon Jul 19 08:12:44 2000
/usr on /dev/dsk/c0t0d0s3 read/write/setuid on Mon Jul 19 08:12:44 2000
/proc on /proc read/write/setuid on Mon Jul 19 08:12:44 2000
/dev/fd  on   fd read/write/setuid on Mon Jul 19 08:12:44 2000
/var  on  /dev/dsk/c0t0d0s4 read/write/setuid on Mon Jul 19 08:12:44 2000
/cache/cache1 on /dev/dsk/c0t0d0s7 setuid/read/write on Mon Jul 19 08:13:4
/cache/cache2 on /dev/dsk/c0t1d0s7 setuid/read/write on Mon Jul 19 08:13:4
/cache/cache3 on /dev/dsk/c0t2d0s7 setuid/read/write on Mon Jul 19 08:13:4
/cache/cache4 on /dev/dsk/c0t3d0s7 setuid/read/write on Mon Jul 19 08:13:4
/cache/cache5 on /dev/dsk/c0t10d0s7 setuid/read/write on Mon Jul 19 08:13:
/opt on /dev/dsk/c0t0d0s6 setuid/read/write on Mon Jul 19 08:13:45 2000
/tmp on /dev/dsk/c0t0d0s5 setuid/read/write on Mon Jul 19 08:13:45 2000
/tftpboot on /dev/dsk/c0t1d0s0 setuid/read/write on Mon Jul 19 08:13:45 19
/home/student/csm/BSc/CRTS/2 on /dev/dsk/c0t1d0s3 nosuid/read/write/quota
/home/student/csm/BSc/other on /dev/dsk/c0t1d0s4 nosuid/read/write/quota on
/home/student/csm/BA/other on /dev/dsk/c0t1d0s5 nosuid/read/write/quota on
/home/student/csm/PhD on /dev/dsk/c0t1d0s6 nosuid/read/write/quota on Mon
/home/student/csm/BSc/CRTS/2p  on  /dev/dsk/c0t2d0s3 nosuid/read/write/quota
  . . .
```

Fig. 19.9
Unix mount table, showing the file system mounting points.

Programmers can find the inode record for a file by using the function int stat(const char *path, struct stat *buf).

The management of hierarchical directories, and also the facility to use filenames in place of inode numbers, is done through **directory blocks**. These hold a list of inode pointer/filename pairs for a particular directory, allowing the symbolic to numeric translation to be carried out when accessing files. It is important to remember that there are several types of inode block, dealing with data files, directories, devices and pipes. Thus a data file inode has pointers indicating the location of data blocks. The directory inode has pointers which indicate the location of blocks containing inode_pointer/filename pairs.

Starting at the top of the file system, the root directory inode will have its pointers indicating directory blocks, each representing a subdirectory, such as /etc, /bin or /home. The entries in these subdirectory blocks will point on to further directory inodes, which in their turn locate directory blocks... and so on, building up the file system hierarchy. This idea might be better understood looking at Fig. 19.11.

The 512 byte disk sectors can be grouped into blocks for speed of access in the same way as explained in the previous section. The BSD 4.3 version of Unix allows for a variable block size, to reduce the waste of space in the last block of every file. Thus each file is represented by an inode record which holds 10 pointers (32 bit sector numbers) pointing to the data blocks for that file. Should more capacity be required for the file, three more 'indirect' pointers link to further inode blocks, which in their turn may be pointing to data blocks or further inode blocks.

```
struct stat {
        dev_t           st_dev;         /* device holding the relevant directory */
        long            st_pad1[3];     /* reserve for dev expansion, */
        ino_t           st_ino;         /* inode number */
        mode_t          st_mode;
        nlink_t         st_nlink;       /* number of active links to the file */
        uid_t           st_uid;         /* file owner's ID */
        gid_t           st_gid;         /* designated group id */
        dev_t           st_rdev;
        long            st_pad2[2];
        off_t           st_size;        /* file size in bytes */
        long            st_pad3;        /* reserve for future off_t expansion */
        timestruc_t     st_atime;       /* last access time */
        timestruc_t     st_mtime;       /* last write time (modification) */
        timestruc_t     st_ctime;       /* last status change time */
        long            st_blksize;
        long            st_blocks;
        char            st_fstype[_ST_FSTYPSZ];
        long            st_pad4[8];     /* expansion area */
```

Fig. 19.10
Unix file system
inode structure.

Fig. 19.11
Unix inode file access
records.

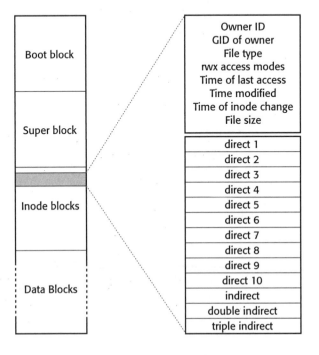

Fig. 19.12
Unix inode pointers indicating a file's data blocks.

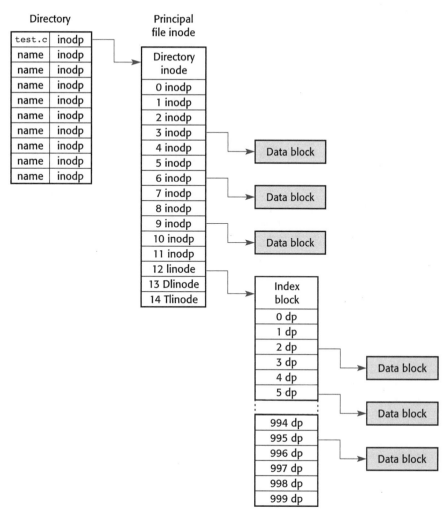

Directories appear as a special type of data file containing filenames and corresponding inode numbers. The utility `fsck` (file system check) will run a thorough check on the file system integrity and attempt to mend any errors.

The directory utility `ls` displays the symbolic names from the current directory block. Using `ls -l` includes some of the inode fields for each file. The directory file in Unix contains a simple list of filenames with their allocated inode numbers. This is all that is needed to access the first block of a file. Figures 19.12 and 19.13 show how inodes identify data blocks and directories.

Unix treats files as linear sequences of bytes. Any internal structuring is the responsibility of the application programmer. IO devices are included as a file type to provide a more unified approach to handling data input–output. Disks, terminals and printers are assigned inodes within the file system directory at /dev. This can be seen as a software map of all the attached devices. In this way they can be treated the same as files;

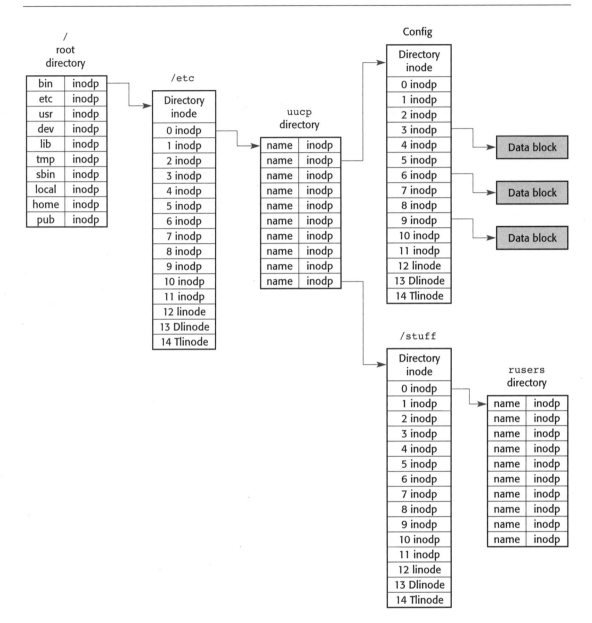

Fig. 19.13
Relating Unix
directories to the
inode blocks.

for example, devices can have data directed to them using the same commands as for a file: `cat device.h test.c > /dev/tty`.

A useful strategy to reduce the problem of disk fragmentation is offered by Unix. Instead of allocating free blocks from a single Super Block pool, this is subdivided into regional pools. In this way blocks are allocated by locality, if possible on the same cylinder as the existing blocks. This would reduce or even eliminate the extra head seek movements that are the undesirable result of disk fragmentation.

19.4   Microsoft NTFS – complexity and security

Microsoft introduced the NTFS file system to replace the extremely well established, but rather limited FAT scheme. This had been designed in the 1970s for the first release of MS-DOS, and was quite closely related to the earlier CP/M operating system. Although FAT-16 had been upgraded to deal with larger disk volumes, and superseded by FAT-32, there were still major shortcomings in the basic structure and function when handling large files. Nevertheless, as so many people remain committed to the FAT file system, it will remain supported for some time to come. There are significant differences between FAT and NTFS, and they are completely incompatible. Using a FAT partition or inserting a FAT floppy will require different software drivers and file managers to be running. Interestingly, the same hardware will cope with either configuration.

As you would expect, NTFS offers a hierarchical file system, as with Unix. Filename identifiers can be up to 256 Unicode characters long. Demanding 500 bytes just for a name, which until now had occupied a frugal 8 bytes, is indicative of the change. Although case sensitivity will eventually become available, at the moment, with the present release of Win32, this is not possible. The maximum file capacity under NTFS is 2^{80} bytes, and all file pointers are 64 bits wide. Drive letters, such as 'C:', are used to refer to disk partitions or drives. As we have seen in Section 19.3, Unix handles this situation by mounting the new volume under root, making it appear unified with the existing file system. NTFS will also offer this facility with the release of version 5.0 of Windows NT. The drive may be partitioned and each partition can contain up to 2^{64} clusters. These are set between 512 bytes and 64 kbyte in size at format time, and remain fixed until the partition is reformatted. This gives the $2^{16} \times 2^{64} = 2^{80}$ value for maximum file size. The **MFT** (Master File Table – Fig. 19.14) plays a similar role to the directory in MS-DOS. Every file and subdirectory has an entry containing names and pointers to the data clusters. The MFT, and a partial copy in case of failure, are held in separate files on disk.

Fig. 19.14
Windows NT master file table.

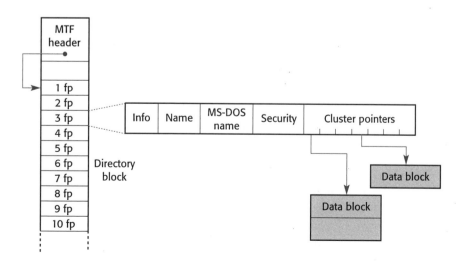

The directory is sensibly positioned towards the centre of the disk to reduce head movements, and small files occupying less than 2 kbyte can actually be stored within their own directory records. To offer more flexible access control, each file and directory can have an **ACL** (Access Control List) associated to provide close control over which users can have what type of access to the item.

Each NTFS file is referenced by the operating system using a unique 64 bit file reference number. This comprises a 48 bit file identifier value, used to index into the MFT, and a 16 bit sequence number. This latter is a check digit which gets incremented every time the MFT entry gets written to. This allows Windows NT to perform consistency checking on recycled positions within the MFT.

To enable data recovery to be carried out in the event of a failure, NTFS has a fault-tolerant capability whereby dual disk packs can be handled in tandem. Thus, if one fails the other is immediately available as a substitute. NTFS also maintains a transaction log file. Using this it is possible to go back over the recent file changes and correct any errors which may have occurred. A curious feature of the specification of the directory entry is the option of storing data from a a small file actually in the pointer block. This reduces the administrative overhead of managing small files. The cluster pointers may point to individual clusters or to a sequence of clusters which are laid out in consecutive positions on the disk. The provision of much tighter security controls was an important requirement for the Windows NT development team. From the start, access control lists were incorporated into the file management.

Data compression and decompression routines are built into the read and write functions so that disk space may be saved, especially when dealing with large image or audio files.

Because of the extra complexity involved with NTFS, it is still faster to access files smaller than 500 Mbyte through the old FAT scheme.

19.5   RAID configuration – more security for the disk subsystem

An interesting technique used on commercial servers is disk mirroring. Two separate drives have partitions twinned so that they receive the same commands from a single controller. Should the primary file system throw an error for some reason, the secondary copy on the alternate disk can be immediately invoked. Ideally, users should be completely unaware of the changeover. Fault tolerance, however, is rather limited because the same controller is used for both drives. **RAID** (Redundant Array of Inexpensive Disks) is a more robust method of protecting the file system from serious system error. This would include a total drive or controller failure, leading to corruption of the data recorded on the disk. RAID works by configuring several drives

Fig. 19.15
RAID 0 configuration.

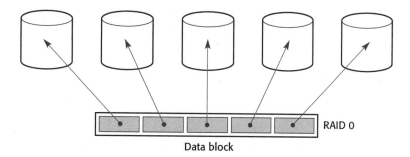

Data block

to work in parallel, each taking responsibility for handling part of the data set. Although, when SCSI drives are used, it is convenient to run the multiple drives from a single controller, this would reduce the system integrity. RAID error detection and correction works by including an **ECC** (Error Correction Code) with each block of written data so that recovery can be achieved. Data is not lost, even if a complete disk drive fails. RAID is sometimes presented as several disks working together as a single 'logical drive'.

This has the added advantage of speeding up access to data because all drives work in parallel to read and write their fraction of the data, thus reducing the data transfer delay. RAID may involve the multiple drives, and separate controllers, in such a way that no single failure will irrevocably lose data. There are six commonly discussed RAID configurations, each suitable for different situations.

If speeding up data transfer is the main issue, rather than fault tolerance, the RAID level 0 technique (Figure 19.15) of writing a block of data across several drives is chosen. This is known as **data striping**. It follows the RAID method of using the disks in parallel, but does not usually include the ECC to save space and increase speed. Single drive failures are dealt with in the same manner as any single disk system. There is no integrity improvement, and the reliability is arithmetically worse due to the greater complexity.

RAID level 1 is disk mirroring, simply doubling up the disk drives to provide backup on failure. There is no performance improvement.

RAID levels 2 and 3 are extensions of RAID 0. A block of data is cut up and distributed to several drives. The difference is that the size of portion is not the sector, but a word or even a byte. This brings with it all sorts of synchronization problems and so is not often attempted. RAID 3 dedicates an extra drive to parity checking. Surprisingly, this application of single-bit parity delivers error correction in addition to error detection, but only if the offending drive 'gives off smoke', telling the system where the error has occurred.

RAID levels 4 and 5 offer full error detection and data recovery by the use of more sophisticated ECCs. The difference between them is the positioning of the check block. RAID 4 maintains all the checksums on a single drive, which can result in a performance bottleneck at that drive. RAID 5 deposits the check block on each of the drives in turn, removing this traffic problem.

Table 19.3
Unix file and directory access control options.

	Read	Write/delete	Execute/attach
Owner	r-- --- ---	-w- --- ---	--x --- ---
Groupees	--- r-- ---	--- -w- ---	--- --x ---
Any user	--- --- r--	--- --- -w-	--- --- --x

19.6   File security – access controls

Both Unix and Windows NT protect their resources using a scheme of personal passwords which have to be entered correctly at login time. On Unix, this password can be changed by the owner using either the `passwd` or `yppasswd` command. Other users can also be given limited access to files when identified as belonging to one of three categories, as listed in Table 19.3.

So access can be allocated at only three different privilege levels: Read, Write/delete and Execute/attach. Each file can be given one of these privilege levels for owner, group and anybody, by using the `chmod` command. The use of this is shown in Fig. 19.16. The READ | WRITE | EXECUTE permission flags are stored as three bits, but represented in decimal format to the user. So '7' (111) gives total access, '0' (000) gives none, while '6' (110) gives READ and WRITE but not EXECUTE.

Fig. 19.16
Setting file access permissions in Unix.

```
rob@olveston [63] ls -al
-rwx------ 1 rob csstaff      280  Sep   5  1998 timezone
-rwx------ 1 rob csstaff       48  Sep  11  1999 tit
-rwx------ 1 rob csstaff      229  Jan  22  1999 to_arthur
-rwx------ 1 rob csstaff    25007  Apr   1  1999 unzipit
-rwx------ 1 rob csstaff      251  Sep   5  1998 vorc
-rwx------ 1 rob csstaff      243  Sep   5  1998 vorcorn
rob@olveston [64] chmod 666 unzip
rob@olveston [65] ls -al unzip
-rw-rw-rw- 1 rob csstaff    25007  Apr   1  1999 unzipit
rob@olveston [66] chmod 000 unzipit
rob@olveston [67] ./unziput
 ./unziput: permission denied.
rob@olveston [68] ls -al unzip
---------- 1 rob csstaff    25007  Apr   1  1999 unzipit
rob@olveston [69] chmod 100 unzipit
rob@olveston [70] ./unzipit
rob@olveston [71]
rob@olveston [71] chmod 711 unzipit
rob@olveston [72] ls -al unzipit
-rwx--x--x 1 rob csstaff    25007  Apr   1  1999 unzipit
rob@olveston [73]
```

You can check which Unix 'group' you are registered with using the `groups` command from the keyboard. (Try `grouprs root` for a more interesting result.) However, to instigate a new 'group' of users requires superuser privilege, which is a real shortcoming of Unix. However, the Sun ACL facility can be manipulated by ordinary users with no special privileges. The commands are `setfacl` and `getfacl`. With these a group of nominated users can have specified access rights (rwx) to a named directory or file. This can be very useful when working in a group. The availability of ACLs was seen as an important improvement over previously available facilities, even though the operating systems MULTICS and PRIMOS offered the same in the 1970s!

The superuser, also known as root, has complete access to everything for administrative purposes. Because it is essential to defend root access, beyond the normal password control, login as root can be prevented from remote terminals and Windows NT strictly denies this option. To some commercial organizations, the straightforward scheme of passwords and permissions appeared too limited. On large sites, with many different types of application user, more fine-grained differentiation and better methods of security were required. To accommodate this demand Microsoft and Sun have introduced Access Control Lists (**ACL**). These are lists of approved users, with their personal access rights, which can be associated with any file or directory. Nevertheless, the original Unix security method has been accepted as satisfactory by professional programmers for many years and will probably endure for some years yet. One development which has been widely adopted is the facility to supply passwords across the network from a central server. This avoids the inconvenience of needing to change your password on every individual workstation.

Sun uses **NIS** (Network Information Services) to manage password verification across a network of hosts. This was originally called `YP` (yellow pages) and it can still be accessed through `yp*` commands such as `yppasswd` to change a user password for all the hosts attached to a network. In this way a central master password file is maintained by the NIS server for distribution to the other local hosts. Any password modification will be sent to the NIS server for checking and registration, before being redistributed around the network.

19.7 CD portable file system – multi-session contents lists

Removable CD-ROMs and CD-RW disks are available with storage capacity (650 Mbyte) much greater than floppy disks (1.4 Mbyte). The issue, as ever, that had to be resolved was inter-system compatibility. How were CD-ROMS to be read by a variety of operating systems which used very different structures and methods? This was tackled during the 1990 conference at Lake Tahoe.

Data on an optical disc may be divided into sessions. A CD-DA (Digital Audio) has no need of more than a single session, but CD-ROMs are partitioned into sessions for convenience of indexing. With CD-RW disks operating to ISO-9660 (High Sierra) standards, each session has to be written continuously, with no pause, and the management overhead for registering each session on the disk is 14 Mbyte! This is suitable for audio tracks, but not very efficient where computer data is involved. A CD-ROM typically has 270 000 blocks, each holding 2 kbyte of data with a header and error correcting code appended. The 16 byte header holds a 12 byte signature, marking the start of the block, and a 4 byte identification. This contains three pairs of BCD numbers: 12–23–45. They indicate the sector, seconds and minutes position of the block. In terms of audio play time, there are 75 sectors to a second, 60 seconds to a minute and 60 (well, actually, 70) minutes to a disk. The fourth byte proclaims whether the Reed–Solomon ECC has been used or not. This is a very effective 288 byte error-detecting and correcting Hamming code.

In 1980 Philips and Sony agreed to certain standards for CD development. Because the conference notes were kept in a red binder, the standard became known as the 'Red Book'. Since then, all the standards have been coloured to distinguish them.

The original 'Red Book' defined a CD-DA recording standard for the music industry. Red Book CDs can have up to 99 music tracks including data on the title and duration of the recordings. The 'Yellow Book' specifies a standard for data, with ISO-9660 specifically covering computer-related issues. The 'Green Book' deals with multimedia, interactive standards which are intended for set-top box equipment. CD-R and CD-RW are dealt with by the 'Orange Book'. There are also some other less well known colours and standards.

The **ISO-9660** internationally agreed standard concerns a special CD data filing system. It is also referred to as the CD Logical Format and is a way of organizing files and directories on a CD so that they can be accessed by any operating system, although native file formats can also be supported if required. While the ISO-9660 standard does offer good compatibility, it is not so good for recording files one at a time, since it was originally designed for a read-only format to be manufactured in a factory rather than written on a PC. Another standard called **UDF** (Universal Disc Format) is becoming popular in CD recording and DVD as it is more convenient for rewritable technologies.

Review

- The capability to organize data into files and store these on dependable media is an essential part of the facilities offered by operating systems.

- Several different ways of logically accessing filed data are provided, including databases.

- The directory provides translation from a logical filename to the disk location of the first data record. To identify further blocks of data needs either a FAT or index blocks.

- The PC directory also holds information about ownership, size and access rights for every file.

- The PC has used FAT-12, FAT-16 and now FAT-32 to extend its failing capability, But Windows NT has another more advanced technique: NTFS.

- Unix uses inodes and index blocks to keep track of data blocks stored on disk and to hold ownership and access rights.

- The Microsoft NTFS scheme was developed to provide better data security in the event of a disk head crash, more flexible access controls and more efficient access to large files.

- To obtain better data security, multiple disk packs can be used in a RAID configuration. By recording redundant information, by way of data repetition or CRC codes, data lost in a system failure can be recovered.

- CD-ROMs need to have a separate file system to allow them to be read on a variety of operating systems. Floppy disks survive by requiring the host computer to recognize their FAT-12 configuration!

Practical work

The recommended practical work involves the use of a disk doctor utility with a floppy disk FAT file system. This allows the recovery of files even when the directory has been lost or corrupted. The same procedures could be used with a hard disk if a FAT system is involved, but incur much greater risk!

Exercises

1. How many pages of word processor text are there in a gigabyte (Gbyte) of data?

2. What are the Norton Utilities? When might you have urgent need of them?

3. List the advantages and disadvantages of the FAT-based file system.

4. What is the effect of the layout of disk data on the performance of an application program such as Microsoft Word?

5. Compare the price in bytes/pound of magnetic disk and semiconductor RAM.

6. Read about the basic system calls to BIOS disk access routines for any microcomputer operating system. What functions are served by the BIOS?

7. Using the Sun Solaris (Unix) ACL facilities, set up a new directory for a group project in which each member has sole write access to a subdirectory for their own work, and the whole group can read everything. Another group write directory allows the software to be brought together for linking. Use `man setfacl` for the commands you need. Do test the access rights!

8. Use the Unix `man yppasswd` command. Would it be possible for the local machine password to be different from the central NIS server version? Why are words such as 'biscuit', 'caterpillar' and 'splendid' not good passwords?

9. When a user deletes a file, is the actual information erased? When would that happen?

10. What difference is there between a RAM disk and a disk cache? Is a RAM disk ever preferable?

Readings

- Heuring and Jordan (1997) give a short description of disk drive hardware in Section 9.1.

- A straightforward introduction to operating systems can be found in Ritchie (1997). Chapters 9 and 10 deal with filing systems.

- Look at PC magazines for disk adverts.

- Try this site:
  ```
  http://www.storagereview.com/guide/?#topics
  ```

- Hex Workshop is a nice FAT sector editor which is available from:
  ```
  http://www.bpsoft.com/
  ```

- An introduction to CD technology and standards is available:
  ```
  http://www.pcguide.com/ref/cd/cdr.htm
  ```

- The Web sites can be accessed via the Companion Web site for this book at:
  ```
  http://www.booksites.net/williams/
  ```

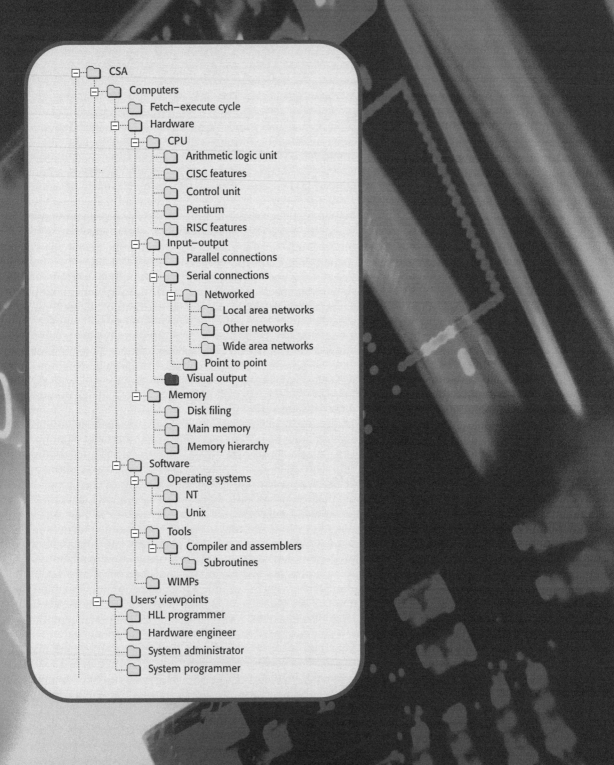

Visual output

Overview

Colour graphics screens and PostScript laser printers provide the routine visual output from contemporary computers. The interfaces required and the various data formats and processing needs for such devices have exerted a strong influence on the PC architecture. The differences between the various manufacturers' equipment, with regard to the low-level interfacing and functional controls, have, for the most part, been hidden from both user and programmer by the layers of operating system software.

20.1   Computers and graphics – capture, storage, processing and redisplay

When we look at something, the lens in each eye focuses an inverted image on the retina at the back of the eyeball. The retina is a curved array of about 130 million light-sensitive cells which fire digital nerve pulses up to the brain in response to light energy. So we start out by detecting the world as a pair of nearly identical two-dimensional image arrays. Feature detection is then carried out by the neural network in the retina and brain so as to identify image edges and surface areas. Eventually we end up seeing a collection of solid objects moving around in a three-dimensional world which we refer to by name and reach out to touch with our hands. Computers similarly have different ways of encoding, processing and displaying images. Most printer and display equipment, whatever their style of input, do operate by presenting a two-dimensional **pixel** array for the eye to view. Such a picture may be in one of several **formats** as listed in Table 20.1.

There are advantages and disadvantages to each of these display formats. Currently I am typing in front of a high-resolution, 21 inch, greyscale monochrome monitor, which is operating in black and white mode because of the limitations of the computer driving it. This does not worry me when using a word processing package; however, it would not be acceptable for graphical modelling and image processing packages. The amount of data required to represent a full colour version of my display would be 24 times larger, which would require an immediate trip to my nearest DRAM supplier. Consequently I am quite happy to forego the pleasure of red spell-check warnings!

Although some early graphics display terminals worked by 'stroking' lines into the screen in a programmed sequence, these **vector** displays have been completely displaced by the **bitmap raster** (television-like) type, which are cheaper to manufacture and deal much more easily with colour images as well as line diagrams.

The **CRT** (cathode ray tube), as illustrated in Fig. 20.1, remains the core of most desktop terminals, despite its size and weight. **LCDs** (liquid crystal displays) have been universally adopted for portable computers, where the extra cost is offset by the advantages of reduced weight, size and power consumption. As LCD technology improves, they will probably displace CRTs from the desktop market, too. But such predictions were made decades ago with regard to the 'new' LED arrays, and CRTs unexpectedly carried on dominating both television and computer terminal markets!

Table 20.1
Data requirements for different display types.

Display	Pixel data	Image file size (display size 1024 ×768 pixels)
Full colour	24 bits	2.25 Mbyte
Reduced-range colour	8 bits	0.75 Mbyte
Greyscale monochrome	8 bits	0.75 Mbyte
Black and white monochrome	1 bit	96 kbyte

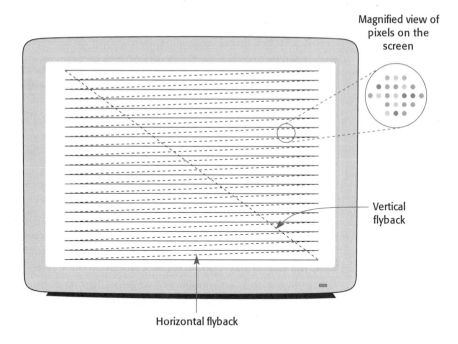

Fig. 20.1
Bitmapped raster
display.

Magnified view of
pixels on the
screen

Vertical
flyback

Horizontal flyback

It is worth looking at the CRT in some detail because the special manner in which
the image data is handled has certainly influenced PC architecture. For the moment,
imagine a large, evacuated glass bottle, coated on the inside of its base with a special
light-emitting paint (**phosphor**), lying on its side. Include a heated wire through the
cap and some big wire coils arranged around the neck, and you have the basics of a
CRT. From Figs. 20.1 and 20.2 you can visualize the beam **scanning** back and forth
inside the display tube. Initially it might surprise you that the beam is not a laser; in
fact, it is not a a light beam at all. This is due to the difficulty of deflecting photons at
such a rate: spinning mirrors were tried, but with only limited success. Free electrons,
however, can easily be created in a vacuum by heating a wire; they can then be
deflected conveniently using magnetic fields from electric coils. If you hold a small
(small!) magnet near to the glass of your television screen you can show that the
picture can be disturbed by a magnetic field. The magnetic field is curving the electron
beams before they strike the inside of the front glass screen. Only when an electron
strikes the inside surface of the screen glass does it cause light to be emitted from the
phosphor coating. This, then, is the light that we see coming from the screen. A television tube works in the same way as a computer screen, but with an overall reduced
performance. For RGB colour tubes there have to be three different phosphors emit-
ting light in three distinct parts of the visible spectrum. There must also be three electron beams carefully targeted at each phosphor. In this way, an appearance of white
can be built up by causing the three phosphors to emit the correct relative amounts of
coloured light. Each pixel includes some red, green and blue phosphor to enable it to
appear any desired colour. The electron beams used to draw out the raster pattern
have to be modulated in intensity (switched on or off) for each pixel on the horizontal

Fig. 20.2
Shadow mask with a single pixel illuminated inside a colour CRT.

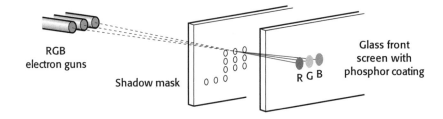

RGB electron guns

Shadow mask

Glass front screen with phosphor coating

R G B

scan lines. Thus an image is built up pixel by pixel, line by line, frame by frame, 60 times every second.

Figure 20.2 indicates how the metal shadow mask stops electrons hitting the wrong colour phosphor dots. The alignment of the shadow mask with the phosphor dots is done using the same type of projection lithography used in the manufacture of silicon chips. It is yet another example of a good concept being made practicable only through the application of even cleverer manufacturing ideas! Using a magnifying lens you can see the separate spots of colour on the screen. However, the human eye does not respond fast enough to changes in light occurring at 60 Hz, and we see the screen as continuously lit, despite the fact that it is dark for a large part of the 16.67 ms cycle for a 60 Hz screen, or 14.9 ms for my 67 Hz display.

The horizontal line sweep rate for domestic television is commonly 15.75 kHz with a 60 Hz frame rate. Computer monitors have to perform much faster (Table 20.2), with both horizontal and vertical scan rates increased to help reduce the flickering effects that computer users often find very distracting, especially in high ambient lighting conditions. Displaying image data at this speed demands high-frequency driver circuits, of the order of 30 MHz for PC monitors. With so many frequency combinations the manufacturers endeavoured to supply a **multi-sync** monitor which successfully locks on to a set of these frequencies. If you are given an old monitor, of excellent quality and superior size, you may find that the standard graphics card will not be able to provide an acceptable synchronization frequency.

Reading the image data out from memory to drive a raster scan display requires high-bandwidth access at a fast enough rate (30 MHz) to keep the three beams

Table 20.2
Normal CRT horizontal and vertical scan rates.

Resolution	Vertical scan rate (Hz)	Horizontal scan rate (kHz)
640 × 480	60	31.5
640 × 480	72	37.8
800 × 600	75	46.9
800 × 600	85	53.7
1024 × 768	75	60.0
1024 × 768	85	68.8
1152 × 864	85	77.6
1280 × 1024	75	80.0
1280 × 1024	85	91.2

supplied with RGB intensity values. It may be useful to preview Figs. 20.7 and 20.8 and Table 20.3 to appreciate the normal configuration of hardware. The time period for writing a single pixel onto the screen can be estimated:

$$\frac{1}{60 \times 1024 \times 768} = 21 \ \ ns/pixel$$

This timing requirement is compatible with SRAMs, and appears initially to be *nearly* compatible with DRAM access times. Using DRAMs would be preferable from the cost point of view. However, it does not take into account several adverse factors. Firstly, DRAM needs to have time allocated for refreshing the stored data, and also the main CPU requires frequent access slots to update the display data. During these accesses, the screen is effectively cut off from the display memory to prevent partially updated images being viewed. This is an example of 'critical data', where a resource needs to be accessed by several processes at the same time, thus requiring protection as discussed in Section 9.5. Finally, DRAM **cycle time** is much longer than the 60 ns **access time**. It is more like 150 ns for most chips, which exposes the full extent of the problem. The solution adopted by video card manufacturers is to interpose a pair of fast line buffers between display memory and the screen driver hardware. These work alternately, one filling while the other empties, turn and turn about. It is another example of the use of caching to speed up consecutive reads. In addition, to overcome memory cycle delay, multiple memory banks are configured so that accesses can be arranged in a sequence which does not refer again to the same chip before it has recharged following the previous read. By employing wide data buses, memory can be organized to supply information for 16 pixels at a time, thus reducing the rate of memory reads required.

As mentioned earlier, portable computers cannot use the CRT due to its weight, size and power consumption. The most popular alternative is the flat LCD screen (Fig. 20.3). This works by sandwiching a thin layer (10 μm deep) of special organic liquid between two glass plates. The liquid has large, polarized molecules which can gather together in a semi-ordered fashion (this is why they are called liquid crystals). The molecules will influence any light passing through, reflecting or transmitting

Fig. 20.3
Liquid crystal panels.

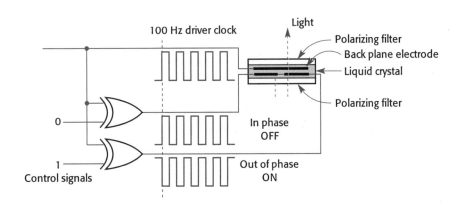

Fig. 20.4
Twisted nematic LCD
panels, showing the
polarized, ribbed
panels.

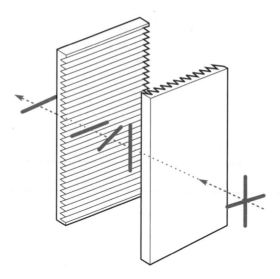

according to their orientation relative to the plane of polarization of the light. Because the molecules are polarized, it is possible to steer them about using an electric field.

To exploit this physical curiosity, a pattern of transparent metallic film electrodes is deposited on the inside of the glass plates so that an electric field can be imposed across the organic liquid. It is also possible to precisely control the alignment of the molecules by physically grooving the surfaces of the container. The alignment of the molecules follows the grooves, so if the grooves are exactly parallel, then the alignment of the molecules also becomes exactly parallel. With the so-called 'twisted nematic panels' the orientation of the ribbing on the front and back glass plates is set at 90°. This forces the molecular pattern through the liquid into a short spiral.

Figure 20.4 shows more details of the physical arrangements. Imagine the light passing through the polarizer, then through the glass, the metallic film and the ribbed surface layer into the liquid. The rays pass through the liquid and return through the opposite wall of the panel to be seen from the opposite side. The scheme relies on the linear **polarization** of light, the same effect used in Polaroid sunglasses. If the molecules in the liquid feel an electric field they align themselves with it. At the same time they affect the light waves passing through, changing the plane of polarization. So if the front and back glass plates are both coated with polarizing films, parallel to the plate ribbing and aligned at 90° to each other, the application or withdrawal of an electric field, will block or transmit light waves passing through. It works like a 'solid-state' shutter. The same principle is used for incident-light or backlit LCD panels. One technical detail is that the electric field needs to be alternating at between 60 and 100 Hz in order to prevent damaging the liquid crystals. So the pixel is controlled by switching the front voltage in or out of phase with that on the back plane. Here is yet another application of XOR gates (Fig. 20.3). The LCD panels are manufactured with each pixel marked out at the intersection of a column and a row, and the complex driver circuits are often supplied as part of the display unit, offering a direct interface to the computer bus. The LCD is basically a digital device which will make interfacing to the computer's memory much simpler once the analogue VGA standard can be completely abandoned.

It can be recognized as a great achievement of modern operating systems and HLLs that the enormous differences between the CRT and LCD are rarely visible at the programmer's level. All the distinguishing aspects are hidden by device drivers and HLL library code so that programmers can, for the most part, ignore any functional differences. If you had to take into account the physical characteristics of the hardware every time you wished to send a character to the screen, software would be much more complex.

But while displays and printers produce bitmap images for people to view, inside the computer there are real disadvantages to maintaining pictures in simple bitmap form. The size of the data sets, even when cleverly compressed, is wasteful of disk space and needs large, expensive RAM buffers on the display interface card. As listed in Table 20.1, a single colour SVGA (Super Video Graphics Adapter) compatible bitmap image, uncompressed, requires 2 Mbyte. Also, different output devices require different bitmap formats, resulting in extensive reprocessing for each new display. If a size change, or zoom feature, is needed, the bitmap is again not very convenient.

So for various reasons it is preferable, whenever possible, to store graphical data in a higher level, **abstract representation**, only regenerating a bitmap for display to humans. We have seen how the monitor screen sweeps out a raster pattern of a bitmap at high speed, painting spots of light as it goes. Laser printers too produce a bitmap which then gets represented on paper. In both cases the original picture might not have been supplied as a bitmap, although, of course, many bitmap files containing, say, photographs are needed. Some common extensions used to identify bitmap pixel image files are .IMG, .RAS, .PIC, .BMP, .GIF and .JPG. If you need to input a real picture, either from a photograph scanner, Web site, or from a video frame grabber, the computer will read it in as a large pixel array, perhaps bundled into such a file format. This is not the case when a line diagram is being read from disk or a Web site. In such circumstances, the picture may be encoded as a series of instructions which, if followed correctly, will regenerate the diagram. Actually, this is exactly the situation for most of the diagrams in this book. They are not held on disk as bit images, but redrawn from a very condensed description script. In fact, we can say that each diagram is a program in its own right. The draft versions were written in a language called `pic`; the final versions are created using the PostScript language.

Scripts in `pic` can be written directly, or produced using a diagram editor like `xfig`. However, they do have to be translated into bitmaps before you can see what they are intended to draw! Fig. 20.5 shows the code which generated the draft of Fig. 20.9. The `pic` program is executed by an interpreter which draws directly into a bitmap array. Once this has been carried out it can be immediately displayed on a screen or sent to a printer for output. (It becomes slightly more complicated in practice because there is an intermediate PostScript stage, but the principle is genuine.) A similar strategy is used by all graphical interfaces, such as Windows NT or the X Window system. The Win32 graphical API will be introduced in Section 20.6, but it

Fig. 20.5
Example pic script for
Fig. 20.9.

```
.PS
define Driver { [line right 0.3 down 0.1
           line left 0.3 down 0.1; line up 0.2]}

Base:     box wid 6 ht 2 invis
          line up 2 from Base.sw
          line up 2 from Base.sw+0.4,0
          line right 0.4 from Base.w+0,0.4
          line right 0.4 from Base.w-0,0.4 """"image""data"below
          circle rad 0.02 at Base.w+0.2,0
          line up 0.5 from last circle; arrow right 2 "color#""" above
Palet:    box wid 1.2 ht 1
          ibox wid 1.2 ht 0.2 with .n at Palet.n "RGB Palette"
          ibox wid 1.2 ht 0.2 with .n at last box.s "table"
          ibox wid 1.2 ht 0.2 with .n at last box.s "R  G    B"
          {move up 0.1; line left 1.2}
          {move down 0.1
          line left 0.4; {line up 0.2}; line left 0.4
           {line up 0.2}; line left 0.4}
          line down 0.7 from Palet.s-0.3,0
          arrow right 1.2 "8 bits" below; [Driver]
           line right 0.2 from last [].e then up 0.25 then right 0.2
          box wid 0.6 ht 0.3 invis with .n at last [].s "DACs"
          line down 0.1 from Palet.s+0.3,0
          arrow right 0.6 "8 bits" below; [Driver]
           line right 0.2 from last [].e; line down 0.25; line right 0.2
          line down 0.4 from Palet.s
          arrow right 0.9 "8 bits" below; [Driver]
           line right 0.4 from last[].e then up 0.07 then right 0.4 then right 0.5 up
          line down 0.6 "CRT  " rjust
          line left 0.5 up 0.2; line left 0.4; line up 0.07
          box wid 0.8 ht 0.2 at Base.w+1.1,0.2 "image base"
          box wid 0.8 ht 0.2 with .n at last box.s-0,0.1 "Y      X"
          {arrow <- right 0.2 from last box.e
            move down 0.1
             for i=1 to 2 do {
                line right 0.1 then up 0.2 then rigt 0.1 then down 0.2
             }
            line right 0.1
          }
          line from last box.n to last box.s
          arrow -> left 0.2 from last box.w
          box wid 0.6 ht 0.4 invis with .n at last box.s "image pointer"\
          "23" at Palet.nw+0,0.2; "0" at Palet.ne+0,0.2
          box wid 0.5 ht 0.3 invis "Memory" with .nw at Base.sw
.PE
```

serves a similar role to the pic interpreter in that it allows programmers to control
the screen display using more convenient high-level commands.

20.2   PC graphics adapter cards – graphics coprocessors

For a short time, the pioneer microprocessor programmers were forced to recycle
scrapped telex terminals (ASR-33) to input program code and print out their results.
This truly juxtaposed the ancient and the modern, relying on the technology of sewing
machines and manual typewriters to access the more subtle power of silicon circuitry!
Such arrangements soon became intolerable and new graphics controller chips were

developed to drive CRT image displays directly. It was quickly realized that they were fast enough for games use, which broadened the user base considerably. To achieve this performance, the memory containing the image data required a high-bandwidth pathway to the video display. The usual RS232 serial cable was nowhere near fast enough to update a screen image. So the decision was taken to couple the display screen closely to the main microcomputer unit. The Commodore PET, Atari ST and Apple Macintosh all included the video circuitry on the computer board, while the Apple II and IBM PC offered a variety of alternative plug-in graphics cards. With the popularity of personal microcomputers, individually equipped with high-resolution colour screens, came the opportunity for extending display graphics into other application areas. A major difficulty when trying to use the mainframe computers of that era was the cryptic command line interface which demanded that the user learn a large number of abbreviated command mnemonics, such as `dir`, `chmod`, `cat` and `pip`. For this reason, **WIMP** (windows, icons, mice and pointers) techniques were developed to support a pictorial style of user interface. But the need to routinely represent information by displaying a wide variety of images, rather than more limited character fonts, put great pressure on the graphics subsystems. If the new Windowing interfaces were to be successful, it was essential that the graphical computations and screen redraws took less than 2 seconds. This was because computer users had grown used to character-based terminals taking about 2 seconds to update.

Technical improvements to the video subsystem made major contributions to advances in the area of interactive computing. Line graphics, bitmap images and text are supported on the graphics adapter. Previously, user interaction relied on character-based instructions keyed into a VDU. These were supplied with only 2 kbyte of display RAM to hold the 1920 (24 lines × 80 characters) ASCII codes which could be presented on a single screen. Compare this with a modern SVGA graphics card with a minimum of 4 Mbyte of dedicated VRAM to handle the display bitmaps, many of which only represent character fonts! VRAM is dual-ported RAM, which supports the two connections, one from the main CPU and the other to the screen, more efficiently.

As mentioned already, the IBM PC was designed with the display interface on a separate card which plugged into the PC/ISA expansion bus. Fig. 20.6 illustrates a

Fig. 20.6
An SVGA graphics adapter card with AGP interface.

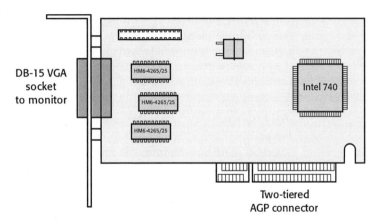

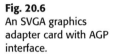

DB-15 VGA
socket
to monitor

Two-tiered
AGP connector

Table 20.3

Evolving range of PC standards for screen display.

Mono	1981	Text-only mode offered by original 8088 PC	
Hercules graphics	1983	First mono graphics card	720 × 348
CGA	1983	First colour (4) graphics card from IBM. Double horizontal resolution if limited to mono	320 × 200
EGA	1984	16 colour graphics	640 × 350
VGA	1987	EGA compatible 16 colour (high resolution) 256 colours 256K colours (18 bits/pixel)	640 × 480 320 × 200 (CGA)
SVGA	1990 1995	256 colours (8 bits/pixel) 24 bit true colour (3 bytes/pixel)	1024 × 768
XGA	1997	32 768 colours (15 bits)	1280 × 1024

modern version of such an adapter card which is plugged into the **AGP** (Accelerated Graphics Port) socket next to the PCI cards. This hardware arrangement, splitting the graphics away from the motherboard, has both advantages and disadvantages. Although graphic facilities could be upgraded relatively easy, the screen performance was originally limited by the slow ISA bus transfer rate (16 Mbyte/s). Only when enough RAM was installed on the graphics adapter cards to contain a full screen image was the bus limitation overcome. To reduce these access limitations further, separate graphics processors have been developed, capable of taking instructions from the main CPU and then following them to draw lines, fill boxes and move chunks of image and other graphical items directly into the screen memory. Such coprocessing greatly benefits the overall system performance because it reduces data transfer delays across the buses and relieves the CPU of routine low-level tasks. The ISA bus bottleneck has also been bypassed, first by the faster PCI bus, and more recently by the AGP slot, which can transfer data between main memory and the graphics card at 266 Mbyte/s. Graphics accelerators come in a wide variety of forms and capabilities. In general there are two markets: commercial machines running Windows and domestic machines running games.

The steady improvement in the performance of graphics hardware is listed in Table 20.3. With the change from digital to analogue signalling, the socket connecting monitors to the graphics adapter card has changed from the older DB-9 to the high-density DB-15. This was to allow 0.7 V analogue signals to pass from the EGA card to the monitor. The earlier cards only offered ON/OFF, 5 V, digital control of the picture, a system which was based on the previous monochrome technology. It is likely, however, that there will be a return to digital graphics display units in the near future.

Cables which convert from DB-9 to DB-15 connectors (Fig. 20.7) are occasionally used to allow a variety of older graphics cards to drive multi-sync VGA monitors. Sometimes special facilities are available by occupying the unassigned pins. In this case the only option is to study the technical manual carefully before trying to plug the

Fig. 20.7
Different monitor
connector standards.

DB-9 CGA Monitor
Socket

DB-15 SVGA Monitor
Socket

Pin	EGA
1	Ground
2	RED-2
3	RED
4	GREEN
5	BLUE
6	Intensity
7	BLUE-2
8	H Sync
9	V Sync

Pin	SVGA
1	RED
2	GREEN
3	BLUE
4	
5	Ground
6	RED rtn
7	GREEN rtn
8	BLUE rtn
9	key-pin
10	SYNC rin
11	
12	Mon id
13	H Sync
14	V Sync
15	

equipment together! The DB-15 (VGA) plugs are sometimes supplied without the unnecessary pins 4, 5, 9 and 11, the common earth connection being connected to the cable screening sheath. With any such high-density connector there is a real danger of bending pins when clumsily inserting the plug, especially with the socket out of sight at the back of the PC. This can escalate from an inconvenience into a minor trauma if the cable is internally connected to the monitor!

The change from digital to analogue monitor control allowed a much wider range of colours and intensities to be provided without having to increase the number of pins beyond reason. Consider how 8 bit RGB colour would require at least 28 pins (RGB: 3 × 8, HSync, VSync, Earth, return), or 52 if individual return lines are required. Such cables are too thick for easy use. In the future, digital monitors, perhaps based on LCD technology, may be connected to the host computer by optical fibre, which can easily provide the 30 MHz bandwidth. An alternative scenario puts the motherboard behind the LCD panel, offering direct interfacing between the bus and the LCD driver circuits.

To get a picture, or character, to appear on the monitor screen requires millions of spots of phosphor to be 'excited' to emit light by the scanning electron beam. Which dots to hit, and which to miss, is determined by the screen data held as a bit image in display memory. As the electron beam is swept across the screen it is turned on and off under the control of the image data. Colour screens need three phosphors and three beams. As each colour gun is controlled by an 8 bit binary number, there is a requirement to store 24 bits per pixel. This is known as a true colour system, offering over 16 million different shades and needing large memories.

Fig. 20.8
Driving a colour screen.

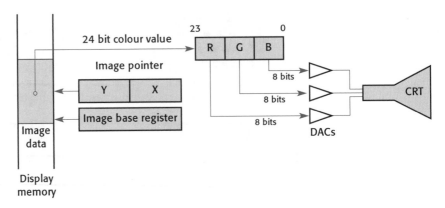

The video hardware is 'told' where the image data is stored in memory through a base register (see Fig. 20.8), normally accessible through a system call. To change the screen display it is only necessary to build a new image in memory and write the base address into this register. The display refresh hardware will inspect the base register during the vertical flyback period, thus avoiding half torn images appearing on the screen.

Often a palette table is used to reduce the size of video memory needed (see Fig. 20.9). Instead of holding 24 bit values for each pixel in the display, only a much shorter number (4 bits) is stored. This is used to index a lookup table where a set of 24 bit RGB numbers are held. Frequently the user is provided with a desktop tool to adjust these RGB values to suit a preference.

The three colour control lines (RGB) carry analogue signals, which are generated by the so-called **RAMDACs**. These circuits rapidly read the next three RGB binary values from graphics memory, convert them to analogue form and transmit the voltages out to the monitor to control the intensity of the electron beams. In this way the brightness and colour of the picture is regulated.

Fig. 20.9
Driving a PC screen using a palette table.

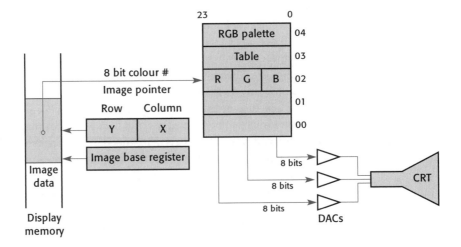

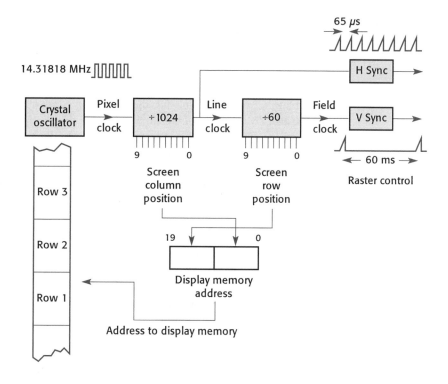

Fig. 20.10
Synchronization of screen raster with accessing display memory.

The position and the intensity of the electron beam are controlled by the graphics interface hardware, not the monitor. This has to steer the beam along the raster pattern and read a value from display memory to set the brightness level of each pixel position. To accomplish such an intricate task, a high-frequency crystal oscillator is used to generate horizontal and vertical synchronization pulses which control the circuits responsible for horizontal and vertical beam movement. The frequency divider/counter chips also provide a parallel read-out which can be used to build the memory address, as shown in Fig. 20.10. The beam position is thus synchronized with the location in display memory which is being accessed for the RGB value assigned to the current pixel. The beam flashes across the screen, taking only 63.5 μs to write the 1000 pixels on each row. The horizontal and vertical flyback strokes are invisible to the viewer because the beam is turned off during those periods. Some graphics controllers supply the computer with signal pulses when the flyback suppression starts. These can be exploited by the CPU to run update routines, such as the movement of cursors or sprites. If this was done during the normal screen drawing period, it would lead to all sorts of fragments and flickering particles appearing on the screen. The PC has IRQ2 reserved for the VBI (Vertical Blanking Interrupt) which happens every 16.7 ms (60 Hz). Not all software drivers use this facility, so another technique has to be used to prevent any flickering effects which occur when the image is changed midway through a screen draw.

20.3   Laser printers – this is mechatronics!

Most printers in current use build up the picture of each letter using a fine matrix of ink dots. Whether this is achieved by pushing inked ribbons against the paper with magnetic pins, blowing fine drops of ink directly onto the paper or using a scanning laser system to electrostatically fix ink dust onto a rotating drum, the principle is the same.

The simplest printers store a few font patterns in lookup PROMs which are read out effectively by using the ASCII codes in a text file as the memory addresses. Other fonts may be downloaded from the host computer into the printer before the text file is sent for printing. Alternatively, bit image files can be sent to the printer to provide for diagram and picture prints.

Laser printers employ a drum (Fig. 20.11) made of light-sensitive semiconductor, possibly selenium or amorphous silicon. The basic physics of the process is identical to that of a photocopier; only the source of light to make an image is different. For the photocopier an image of the original page is projected through lenses onto the drum, while for laser printers a **scanning laser beam** is used to 'draw' an image of the page. The drum is first sprayed with negative electrons which will only escape – leak away – if the surface is exposed to bright light. The laser diode source is modulated (turned on and off) by a signal derived from the bit image of the page to be printed, which has already been built in the local memory. Cheaper laser printers used the main memory of the workstation to save money, but then the print time was much longer and the workstation was locked up for the duration of printing. The black ink powder is fed onto the main drum from the toner hopper using a smaller drum rotating at twice the speed. This drum has a magnet inside which attracts the toner dust, and a magnetized blade helps to distribute it evenly over the surface. As the spreader drum rotates towards the main drum, the toner particles are attracted by electrostatic force onto the

Fig. 20.11
Schematic diagram of a laser printer.

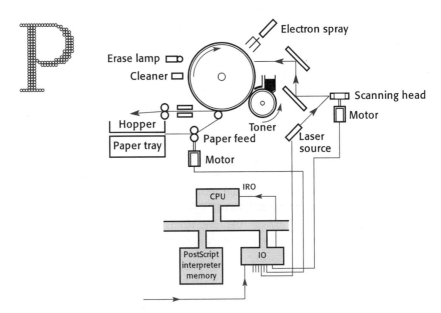

main drum, but only where the laser beam has NOT discharged. There is no direct contact between the two drums. The toner particles are then contact transferred onto the paper, which is heated to fuse the toner permanently into the surface of the paper.

The opposite process, capturing an image from a paper copy, is known as scanning. Image scanners suddenly dropped in price a few years ago, mainly due to the success of mass-produced fax machines. They now generally avoid the expense of rotating optical mirrors, and use an integrated array of light sensors to pick up the pixel values from the paper. This can achieve a resolution of 300–600 dots per inch (dpi). Either the sheet of paper is rolled over the sensor array or, in the case of flat-bed scanners, the paper remains stationary and the array is moved.

Once a bit image of an A4 page (210×297 mm, or 8.27×11.69 inches) is held in memory, compression algorithms can be applied to reduce the size for transmission or disk filing. When only text characters are involved, the data can be analysed by OCR (Optical Character Recognition) software, converting it from image format to ASCII codes. This can dramatically reduce the data size. For a 600 dpi image (allowing for page margins):

$$\text{single A4 page image} = \frac{11 \times 7 \times 600 \times 600}{8} = 3.5 \text{ Mbyte}$$

The same page may be represented by far less data if it is ASCII coded:

$$\text{Maximum number of characters on an A4 page} = 60 \times 100 = 6000 \text{ char}$$

In fact, the average number of characters on a word-processed page is closer to 2500, requiring 2.5 kbyte of ASCII data. Thus, the compression ratio would be:

$$\text{compression ratio} = \frac{2500}{3500000} = 0.0007$$

Such a size reduction is certainly worth achieving, but OCR software has only recently been improved enough to give acceptably fast and accurate performance.

The functions of photocopier, laser printer and fax machine, are now being combined into a single box for office applications. This reduces the space taken up and will introduce users to new functions, such as document scanning, which may help to develop new application areas.

20.4 Adobe PostScript – a page description language

PostScript printers work differently. **PostScript** is a page description language, supplied by Adobe Systems, and widely used in laser printers. Instead of sending bitmap images or ASCII text files to the printer, a program containing a list of drawing commands is dispatched. The printer contains a (substantial) processor and interpreter PROM which can take the PostScript 'program', execute it and produce a bit image for printing. PostScript programs are always interpreted rather than precompiled, which makes for rather slow operation. Not all laser printers have the PostScript facility, but it is now very common. The printer needs at least an MC68030 with 16 Mbyte of RAM, and frequently a RISC processor with 128 Mbyte of RAM. Sometime laser printers have a local hard disk to buffer incoming print jobs and hold the extensive font dictionaries.

An example fragment of PostScript code is presented in Fig. 20.12. It shows the principal distinguishing characteristic of the language: reverse Polish stack notation, where the operands are listed first, followed by the operator. This can be seen in line 2, which moves the drawing point to coordinate position 270,360 on the page. The coordinate scheme used to refer to positions on the page is the normal x,y graph system with 0,0 at bottom left, the x-axis horizontal and the y-axis vertical. The basic unit is the printers' point: 1/72 inch (353 μm). All this can make PostScript code difficult to follow for programmers more familiar with traditional C or Java structures. The Forth programming language uses a similar system, as did the original Hewlett-Packard

Fig. 20.12
Example PostScript development with emacs and Ghostview.

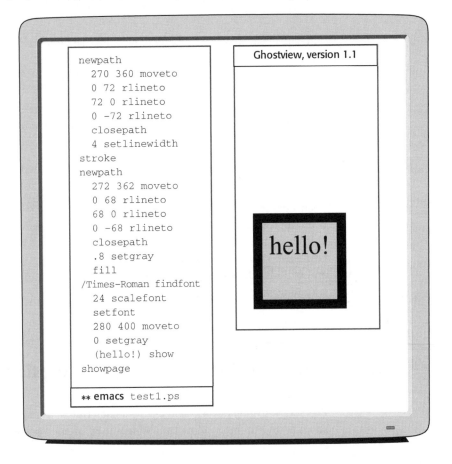

hand calculators. Like Forth, PostScript encourages the use of many nested user-defined procedures. You certainly need to know that to start a new line segment the command `newpath` is required. The command `stroke` is needed to fill in a line, and the final command `showpage` actually renders the image visible. Figure 20.13 offers a more complex example, producing curved graphical images with the `arc` command. Note that `fill` allows the programmer to flood colour into closed shapes.

Writing PostScript routines directly, rather than using a drawing package to produce the code, can be fun if you enjoy the experience of programming backwards. The routines in Figs. 20.12 and 20.13 can be tried out by entering the text into a

Fig. 20.13
More PostScript.

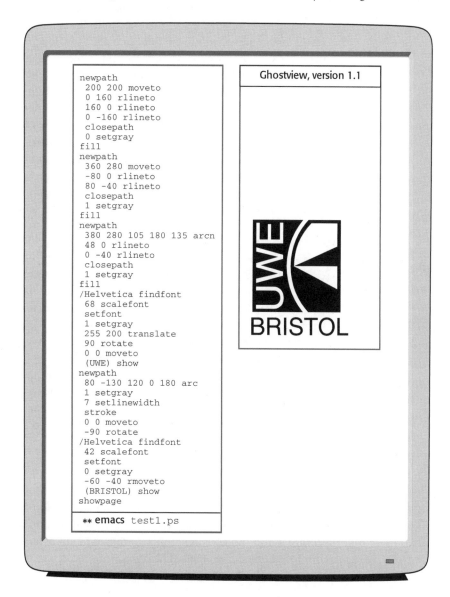

```
newpath
 200 200 moveto
 0 160 rlineto
 160 0 rlineto
 0 -160 rlineto
 closepath
 0 setgray
fill
newpath
 360 280 moveto
 -80 0 rlineto
 80 -40 rlineto
 closepath
 1 setgray
fill
newpath
 380 280 105 180 135 arcn
 48 0 rlineto
 0 -40 rlineto
 closepath
 1 setgray
fill
/Helvetica findfont
 68 scalefont
 setfont
 1 setgray
 255 200 translate
 90 rotate
 0 0 moveto
 (UWE) show
newpath
 80 -130 120 0 180 arc
 1 setgray
 7 setlinewidth
 stroke
 0 0 moveto
 -90 rotate
/Helvetica findfont
 42 scalefont
 setfont
 0 setgray
 -60 -40 rmoveto
 (BRISTOL) show
showpage
```

Ghostview, version 1.1

** emacs test1.ps

file and sending the file directly to a laser printer after inserting the header: `%!PS-Adobe-3.0`. This informs the printer that the following ASCII data represents a PostScript program and may be so interpreted. Or, if you have the Ghostview utility program available, you can look at the results on screen. This has the extra benefit of cheap colour!

Distributing documents as PostScript files, on floppy disk, by email or by FTP, offers a new kind of fax facility. You can print the file on a laser printer, but editing it is inconvenient and difficult: few programmers are willing to wrestle with PostScript code generated by a word processor package.

A common problem with this type of document distribution is the unavailability of identical fonts at the source and destination. Although PostScript is intended to support 'device independence' there are still difficulties with passing the file to a distant unfamiliar environment. For example, if the document is set up to demand a particular style and format of font, and this is not available at the final printer, a substitute has to be found. This may have the wrong widths for some of the letters, so the transmitted document will end up looking quite different to the original. The obvious solution would be to transmit the full font description with each PostScript document, but this could unacceptably enlarge the file by a factor of 20. An additional stimulus was the increasing practice of offering viewable Web documents online. With these in mind, Adobe introduced the Portable Document Format (PDF). PDF is derived from PostScript, but includes the fonts with the text and uses compression techniques to reduce the overall file size. There are several data compression techniques which can be exploited by PDF. Data in the file is subjected to LZW (Lempel–Ziv–Welch) compression. This complex data compression technique has been patented, but is used widely for storing and distributing GIF image files. LZW works by using a 'dictionary' or 'code book' to substitute short code numbers for longer bit sequences found in the raw data. Further JPEG compression methods can be applied to any image arrays within the file to further reduce the size.

As with PostScript, an interpreter is required, so a new viewer, known as Adobe Acrobat, was developed and provided for free by Adobe to assist with reading the PDF documents. Generally, people download the Acrobat reader from the nearest Adobe Web site and then browse the PDF document.

To create a PDF file, Adobe provide the Distiller program, which converts PostScript into PDF. An alternative is to use the gnu Ghostscript program which offers many command line options. The following Unix command line (here split over two lines) changes a PostScript version of 'Chapter 16' into its pdf equivalent:

```
gs -dNOPAUSE -dBATCH -r1200 -sDEVICE=pdfwrite
    -sOutputFile=ch_16.pdf ch_16.ps
```

The change in file size indicated by the numbers in Fig. 20.14 is worth pondering. We start with an ASCII coded file of 42 253 bytes, produced by a PC wordprocessor package in text mode. This grew somewhat to 52114 bytes when it was transfered to Unix for editing under emacs. The PostScript version rose to 1.2 Mbyte, with the PDF file shrinking back to 840 kbyte. Remember: to print a PDF file it has to be converted

Fig. 20.14
Comparing file sizes:
ASCII, PostScript and
PDF.

```
rob[57]cat header ch_16|groff -t -e -p -fH>ch_16.ps
rob[58] gs -dNOPAUSE -dBATCH -r1200 -sDEVICE=pdfwrite -sOutputFile=ch_16.pdf ch_16.ps
....

rob[57]ls -al ch_16*
-rw-------    1 rwilliam csstaff 52114 Jul 1 08:42 ch_16
-rxw------    1 rwilliam csstaff 42253 Jun 28 13:26 ch_16.asc
-rw-------    1 rwilliam csstaff 840398 Jul 1 08:44 ch_16.pdf
-rw-------    1 rwilliam csstaff 1212385 Jul 1 08:43 ch_16.ps
-rw-------    1 rwilliam csstaff 22093 Feb 24 11:07 ch_16d
-rw-------    1 rwilliam csstaff 16437 Nov 5 1998 ch_16d~
-rw-------    1 rwilliam csstaff 23975 Jun 16 16:42 ch_16~
....

rob[58]acroread ch_16.pdf
....

rob[59]ghostview ch_16.ps
....

rob[60]
```

back to PostScript using the Acrobat reader or Ghostscript. Printers do not yet directly accept this format (but it will probably be only a matter of time!). Be warned that PDF code appears much less clear than the equivalent PostScript. Cast your eye over the PDF code listed in Fig. 20.15, which simply prints the usual 'Hello World!' greeting. If you care to enter the text into a file and open it with Adobe Acrobat, the message should be displayed as in Fig. 20.16. Be careful though: Acrobat has zero tolerance, and no concept of helpful error messages.

20.5   WIMPs – remodelling the computer

The way in which users interact with computers has changed radically since the introduction of WIMP facilities. The screen has evolved from a paper-saving device, where full page editing could be carried out more conveniently, into the centre of all human–computer exchanges (see Fig. 20.17). This reliance on the screen for both immediate output and input has spawned new layers of software, dedicated to graphical functions. To track the active window, direct keyboard input correctly and respond appropriately to mouse button clicks has required the development of new event-handling techniques which are only distantly related to hardware interrupts. The model once proposed of the 'virtual desktop' is not adequate to describe the more dynamic interaction that modern windowing software supports. Perhaps it can be compared to the distinction between watching and playing tennis. Such close interaction with the system does seem to alter our perception of the objects involved.

The next step in computer interaction will probably involve ditching the keyboard and relying on voice recognition software. This is already available with a high level of

Fig. 20.15
The 'Hello World!'
example in PDF code.

```
%PDF-1.0

1 0 obj
<<
/Type /Catalog
/Pages 3 0 R
/Outlines 2 0 R
>>
endobj

2 0 obj
<<
/Type /Outlines
Count 0
>>
endobj

3 0 obj
<<
/Type /Pages
/Count 1
/Kids [4 0 R]
>>
endobj

4 0 obj
<<
/Type /Page
/Parent 3 0 R
/Resources <</Font<</F1 7 0 R>>/ProcSet 6 0 R>>
/MediaBox [0 0 612 792]
/Contents 5 0 R
>>
endobj

5 0 obj
<< /Lengtb 44>>
stream
BT
/F1 72 Tf
100 50 Td (Hello World!) Tj
ET
endstream
endobj

6 0 obj
[PDF /Text]
endobj

7 0 obj
<<
/Type /Font
/Subtype /Type1
/Name /F1
/BaseFont /Helvetica
/Encoding /MacRomanEncoding
>>
endobj
xref
0 8
0000000000 65535 f
0000000009 00000 n
0000000074 00000 n
0000000120 00000 n
0000000179 00000 n
0000000322 00000 n
0000000415 00000 n
0000000445 00000 n
trailer
<<
/Size 8
/Root 1 0 R
>>
startxref
553
%%EOF
```

Fig. 20.16
Viewing the PDF File
using Adobe Acrobat.

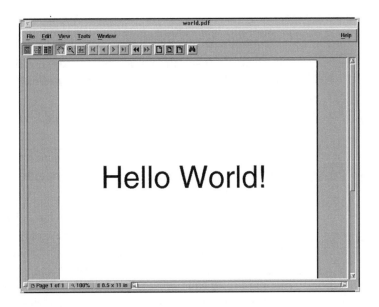

Fig. 20.17
Layout of a typical
window scheme.

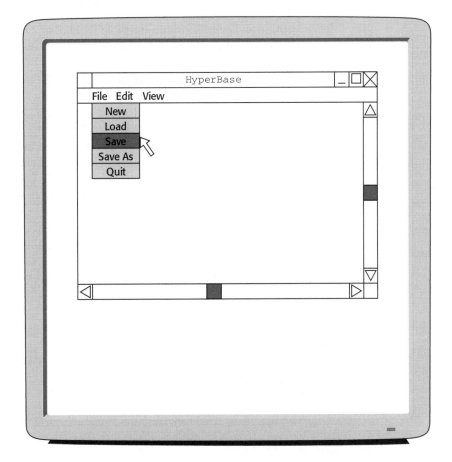

accuracy and functionality, but requires a somewhat protracted setup. Whether the 2D window format, developed for a manual steering device and on-screen pointer, will adapt conveniently to this modality change remains to be seen. Initially it would appear that the previous 'command line' scheme might be more appropriate for voice input of user commands.

20.6   Win32 – graphical API and more

Win32 is an API (Application Programming Interface) supplied as a number of DLLs (Dynamic Link Libraries). The principal purpose of supplying the library was to make Windows programming simpler and uniform, and so more accessible to programmers. The graphical functions have now been extended by a wide range of activities which far exceeds opening and closing a display window. An extensive list of the function names and their actions is provided on the supporting Web site. They are supplied simply as a first access point list. The best way to obtain fuller information about these functions is to use the online help facility which comes with Microsoft Developer Studio. All the parameter lists and operational constraints will then be provided when you need them. A short summary of the range of operating system facilities offered is given in Table 20.4.

You experienced the flavour of programming within the Microsoft Developer Studio in Chapter 7 when using the debugger to inspect the action of code at the CPU register level. Now you need to become more familiar with the libraries and functions offered under C and Win32. The sophisticated facilities offered by such IDEs (Integrated Development Environments) are intended to support much more complex programs than we will be attempting here, but it serves as a good introduction to the more advanced C++ Windows programming which you may wish to take up later in your course. You can now recompile your 'hello world!' program for a Windows display (Fig. 20.18).

As already mentioned, the range of the Win32 library is impressive. Microsoft is gently discouraging the direct use of this library, proposing the object-oriented MFC (Microsoft Foundation Classes) in their place. This throws the programmer fully into object-oriented methods, C++ and Wizard code builders. For the purposes of this introductory course it is wiser to stick with simple C programs and direct Win32 function calls.

20.7   The X Window system – enabling distributed processing

Unix was born long before anybody would have thought that a nice graphical user interface was necessary. Computing was a professional, difficult, technical skill,

Table 20.4
Win32 API facilities.

Graphical device interface (GDI)
Bitmaps, icons and metafiles
Creating windows
Operating windows
On-screen menu handling
Dealing with mouse and keyboard events
Handling dialog boxes
Timer events
Threads and process scheduling
Exception messages
Free memory management
Device handling
Printing and text output
File management
Data interchange through clipboard
OLE/DDE data interchange
System parameter registry management
System information
DLL management functions
Network access routines
Passing and processing messages
Audio data management

Fig. 20.18
Your first Windows application (see the Glossary for an explanation of the unusual message).

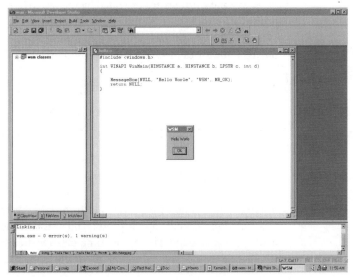

Fig. 20.19
X Windows
programming.

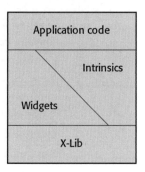

limited to engineers or the rare computer scientist. Society has changed. Computers have evolved into disposable consumer products, and everybody needs one to access the Internet. This massive sea change was brought about by the success of the micro-processor and the WIMP. Unix, too, was retro-fitted with a WIMP interface. In the mid-1980s, researchers at MIT developed the X Window suite of programs. The current (X-11) version has been ported to all manner of systems, not just those running Unix, but it remains of most importance as the principal windowing inter-face to the Unix operating system.

An interesting feature of X Windows is the central importance of an extensive set of communication protocols. These are character-based and convey all the commands necessary to draw the required item on a screen or page. This means that all screens have to be running an X-Interpreter, very similar to the PostScript interpreter. Such an arrangement allows for a very flexible approach to network computing. The real computation or database can be positioned anywhere across the network, exchanging X-protocol instructions with the screen servers running on workstations. This is a thorough client–server arrangement. Even the Window Manager, which is respon-sible for organizing the screen layout, can reside on a distant host!

Programming for X Windows can be done at several levels, as shown in Fig. 20.19. Fundamental routines are provided by the X-Lib library, but these are somewhat too primitive for most uses. At the next level up are the X-Intrinsics and above that the X-Widgets. The Widgets are tailored to particular look-and-feel styles, and are normally obtained for Motif or OpenLook as commercial products.

20.8   MMX technology – assisting graphical calculations

Intel added eight extra 64 bit registers (Fig. 20.20) to the Pentium II to speed up some of the specialist calculations which are widely used in graphical programming. It also inserted some 50 new instructions into the CPU instruction set which were directly targeted at multimedia applications. This was definitely a CISC approach to perfor-mance enhancement! There was some debate whether these changes were useful or whether it would still be better to delegate such specialist computations to the

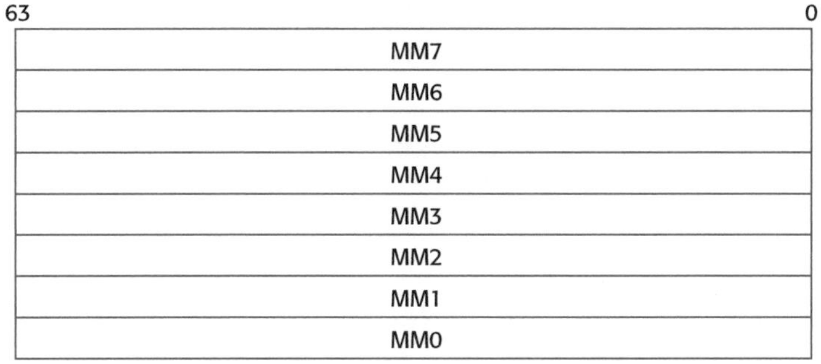

Fig. 20.20
MMX CPU data registers.

coprocessors provided on the more advanced graphics cards. Remember that the image to be processed is actually held in the video RAM on the card, local to the coprocessor, reducing bus activity. The acquisition of a second dedicated processor, capable of operating in parallel with the main CPU, should greatly improve the overall processing throughput.

The extra instructions were designed to assist with operations on matrices: single instructions dealing with multiple elements of data. This is referred to as **SIMD** (Single Instruction Multiple Data) architecture. Because the maths focus was quite obvious, MMX (MultiMedia eXtension) was also termed 'Matrix Math eXtension' by some. The instructions involve integer operands only, but the Pentium FPU (floating point unit) unfortunately becomes involved because the floating point registers are aliased to the MMX set. So it seems that the new MMX instructions should not be intermingled with FPU operations.

To further speed up processing the L1 caches on MMX Pentiums were doubled in size to 16 kbyte and the instruction pipelines extended to six stages. This had to be accompanied by a revision of the decoding circuits, which were speeded up and re-organized to allow more instructions to run in parallel without the access conflicts that had blocked this before.

Review

- Video output from computers involves the presentation of large (1024 × 768) two-dimensional arrays of pixels to the human eye. These are often updated 60 times a second, and each pixel may be represented within the memory by 24 bits of data.

- Currently, PCs need graphic adapter cards to drive the RGB inputs to analogue VDU monitors. With the imminent change to LCD panels, which are basically digital, this may alter.

- To reduce the amount of data stored for each pixel, palette look-up tables are used to hold a limited range of RGB data which is then selected using an index number stored for each pixel.

- Laser printers are raster scan devices like VDUs. They normally include powerful microprocessors which interpret PostScript files to draw the image of the desired page.

- PostScript and PDF are special page description languages used by display devices. They offer flexible image scaling and device independence.

- The Win32 API gives programmers an enormous range of function calls to carry out graphical manipulations and much else besides.

- The X Window system is the Unix windowing system, which also offers a distributed client–server programming facility. This is very helpful when developing networked software.

Practical work

The recommended practical work involves familiarization with the PostScript language. Although the need for direct PostScript programming skills is comparatively rare, understanding the structure of a PostScript program which uses postfix Polish notation with stack-based evaluation makes for an interesting comparison with the more common programming languages.

Exercises

1. What are the advantages and disadvantages of having the PC graphics controller on a separate plug-in card?

2. Produce a PostScript file (file.ps) using a word processor package. This can usually be done by saving the print file to disk rather than sending it to a printer. Look at file.ps in a text editor and then in Ghostview.

3. On Unix, use man gs and look up all the flag options. Explain the PostScript → PDF command line in Section 20.4. Convert your PostScript file into PDF using gs. View it using Acrobat Reader. Compare the sizes of the PostScript and PDF files!

4. Explain how LCD panels function. How does the computer affect the light levels? Are LCD panels analogue or digital? Is the normal VGA monitor interface suitable?

5. Explain the difference between the way a letter is represented in a file in the four situations: ASCII text, PostScript file, PDF file, image file (BMP or IMG). How is a letter drawn on the page by the printer?

6. Consider your CSA textbook. Estimate how many letters of text it contains. How large is the ASCII file containing the book's text? How large would an uncompressed image file be?

7. What is a palette table and what is its value? Does the VGA card use one?

8. What is the display synchronization problem? Why are games programmers concerned with it? How does the PC deal with it?

9. A 15 inch diagonal display is rated at 800×600 pixels. How many dots per inch does it present? What size are the pixels?

10. When a monochrome VDU beam can only be controlled ON/OFF, how can a grey scale be presented?

11. Find how many pages your departmental laser printer manages on a single toner cartridge. Then estimate the amount of toner each page is carrying away with it. How much does this thin layer of soot cost?

Readings

- Adobe Systems (1985)

- A first guide to PostScript:
  `http://www.cs.indiana.edu/docproject/programming/postscript/postscript.html`

- Adobe Systems Web site:
  `http://www.adobe.com/`

- Adobe Solutions Network: Developer Program:
  `http://partners.adobe.com/supportservice/devrelations/nonmember/acrosdk/docs.html`

- For several documents concerning the use of `pic` for diagrams, try:
  `http://www.kohala.com/start/`

- For more on LCD display technology try:
  `http://www.pctechguide.com/07panels.htm`

- For beginners' X Windows programming: Mansfield (1993).

- Advanced X Windows material: X Window System series, Vols. 0–8, O'Reilly & Associates. See `http://unix.oreilly.com/` for details.

- Heuring and Jordan (1997), Section 9.2: visual display units; Section 9.3: printers.

- The Web sites can be accessed via the Companion Web site for this book at:
  `http://www.booksites.net/williams/`

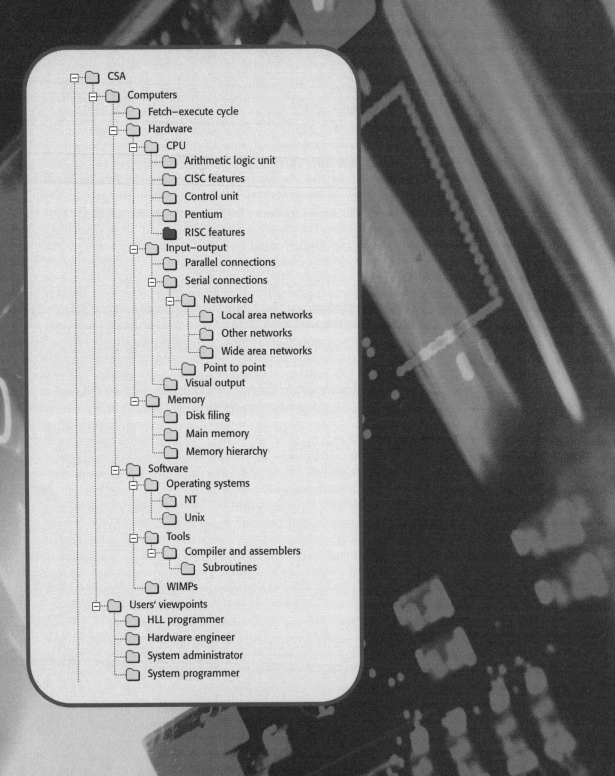

RISC processors

21

Overview

The route that computer systems engineers have pursued for a number of years has recently changed abruptly. A large increase in performance using RISC techniques is possible by implementing a relatively simple processor which executes instructions very efficiently and fast. The improvement in performance happens even though each instruction does not do as much work as a CISC instruction. With these simpler designs, the smaller RISC CU frees space on the CPU chip for other functional units. Special compilers are normally developed to get the best out of the architecture; otherwise there can be some reduction in performance.

21.1   Justifying RISC – increased instruction throughput

The complexity of CISC CPUs increased steadily from the early days of the first computers in the 1950s until the 1980s. It was a generally held view that much could be gained by migrating functionality downwards through the hierarchy towards the faster, more expensive, central resources (Fig. 21.1). It was common to see ideas first tested in application code and then to be assimilated into operating systems routines. From there they were transferred into microcode for increased speed and finally implemented in hardware logic units for ultimate efficiency. This development pattern produced the ultra-sophisticated processors of the super-mini era, such as the DEC VAX-11 or the PRIME-950. Designers followed the improvements in manufacturing technology and added more and more complexity to the ALU and CU. But as HLLs were improved and universally adopted by programmers, it became clear that though much effort was being expended on each new generation of machines, the expected improvements in performance were not always forthcoming. Suspicion arose that simply adding more complex circuitry to the underlying hardware might not be the answer. A good example of this dilemma was the inclusion of an instruction in the DEC VAX instruction set to specifically carry out polynomial evaluations. Whether it was ever executed in a real user's program is debatable. The DEC VAX and Motorola MC68000 families of processors can be seen as close to the apex of CISC development. They were supplied with hundreds of instructions and dozens of addressing modes, together resulting in some very complex instructions which required sophisticated microprogrammed control units.

The drive to improve system throughput by migrating functionality downwards reminds me of a possibly apocryphal tale. Some systems programmers were given the brief to speed up a corporate database. So they spent weeks studying the daily workload and applying the latest instruction set profiling tools. In the end they devised a

Fig. 21.1
Functional hierarchy.

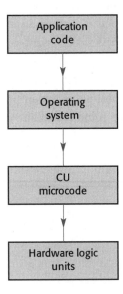

scheme to identify the most wasteful instructions and rewrite the microcode in a more streamlined fashion. Months later, their work having been done, they started up their newly coded CPU. To their alarm there was simply no change. What had gone wrong? Well it seems that deep in the operating system were some WHILE loops which just squandered time, as it happened repeatedly executing the targeted instructions. Selling the concept of efficient burn loops to sceptical customers could be a tricky proposition – a cautionary tale for the technical enthusiast.

During the early 1980s, computer designers began to question this whole approach to computer development. It was established by analysing executable files that compilers rarely used 80% of the available instructions, but their inclusion in the CPU incurred both a cost and performance penalty. It seems odd that a similar survey carried out for Motorola in the 1970s was cited at the time as evidence for the wide-ranging instruction set which was coded into the MC68000! I suppose research can be like that sometimes. Further studies showed that simple RISC architectures can perform at least as well as conventional CISC architectures when provided with well-conditioned programs. Intuitively, one might not have expected to discover that simple instructions ran more slowly in the more complex CPUs, as well as costing a lot more to develop and implement! In retrospect, this drive to offer more and more complex operations in hardware may have been partly due to the sales effect of widely published benchmark performance tables. If performance on one of the artificially constructed benchmark trials could be improved by enhancing an instruction, there was every motivation to carry on with CISC elaboration. Unfortunately for the users, the benchmark trials often bore little relation to the average daily diet of programs that the processor would have to deal with on their desktop.

An alternative approach was called for. For a variety of reasons, which we will inves-tigate in a moment, most manufacturers adopted the RISC approach in the design of their future processors. The radical new architecture which resulted from this investi-gation was called RISC (Reduced Instruction Set Computing; the UltraSPARC II processor shown in Fig. 21.2 is an example) to reflect the reduction in number of machine instructions, but this is not a strict definition. There are only certain guiding principles, as set out in Table 21.1, to distinguish RISC from CISC. Perhaps it is worth remembering that the Pentium is a CISC design with RISC amendments to improve its performance.

The first two principles in Table 21.1 allow the RISC architectures to return to a much smaller and simpler plan of operation. This then delivers several benefits. In the space saved on the CPU chip, other units, such as cache memory, can be installed to gain from the close proximity to the CPU. The functioning of these other units is greatly improved by reducing the transmission delays to and from the CPU. The uniform length imposed on machine codes means that all instructions can be treated identically. It also means that a faster hard-wired decoder would suffice in place of the increasingly unmanageable complexity of microcoding. Perhaps most importantly, the fixed instruction size and decode time enabled the introduction of pipelined parallel decoding techniques. This aspect, more than any other, has accelerated RISC way beyond CISC. It is a way of implementing parallel activity within an essentially sequential environment.

Fig. 21.2
Sun Microsystems'
UltraSPARC II.

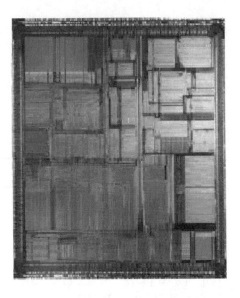

By introducing more registers into the CPU, possible with the space freed from the microcode store, variables can be read into a register and held there for much longer periods before the space has to be conceded to other more deserving variables. Thus the programs have less frequent need to access variables stored in memory, an operation which had been identified as one of the critical system bottlenecks. The research which led up to the RISC revolution had also revealed how non-optimal many CISC compilers were. This lesson has now been learnt, and the RISC designers set about producing customized compilers which made best use of the designated CPU. Once again, assembler-level programming had received its marching orders!

The use of microcoding in the CU was originally encouraged by the situation when ROM memory was much cheaper and faster than magnetic core store. So it was to everyone's advantage to design the computer to minimize program lengths while maximizing the activity of each instruction. This comparison is now reversed. DRAM chips have faster access times than the high-density PROMs used in microcode

Table 21.1
Principal features of RISC
CPUs.

1.	Single length instruction codes
2.	Single clock cycle execution period
3.	Limited arithmetical complexity supported
4.	Extensive supply of CPU registers
5.	Limited repertoire of machine instructions
6.	Only straightforward addressing modes supported
7.	Hardware support for procedure handling
8.	No structured data types recognized
9.	Compiler supplied to support the architecture
10.	Hardware CU, pipelined decoding
11.	Simplified interrupt facilities

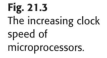

Fig. 21.3
The increasing clock
speed of
microprocessors.

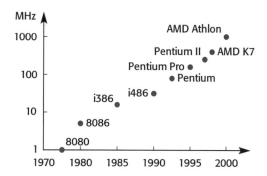

memory. EPLDs and FPGAs are the preferred implementation devices for fast hardware rather than PROMs. RAM is cheap and plentiful.

The speed of modern CPUs (Fig. 21.3) can easily outstrip all but the fastest memory cycle rates. Within 25 years the clock rates have risen from 1 MHz to 1 GHz: an amazing achievement. This could, however, lead to the CPU wasting time by having to insert WAIT states into all memory access bus cycles, effectively stalling the CPU until the next instruction or item of data returns from memory. Faster page- or row-oriented memory access techniques can alleviate this problem by delivering a stream of instructions in a burst, but the CPU then requires an instruction pre-fetch buffer, or local cache. Thus once again the advantage of a small RISC CU is revealed.

On the CPU chip, the physical size of the CU was an important consideration. The relatively large area of silicon used by the microcode PROM excluded other eligible functions from the privileged on-chip position in close proximity to the ALU. It should be recalled that whenever signals leave a chip and descend onto the printed circuit board they incur an extra transmission delay due to the increased capacitance of the PCB tracking. A major advantage of the RISC design philosophy was the reduced area taken by the smaller hard-wired decoder, allowing on-chip cache, MMU and FPU. It is now recognized that the microcoded CUs squandered silicon in supporting complex instructions which were only rarely used in real programs.

Because the cost of DRAM had fallen and their access speed was improving, two of the original motivations for using more PROM and less RAM had disappeared. As microprocessors recapitulated the development path of earlier generations of computers, there was seen to be a need for better performance from the other facilities: cache, MMU and FPU. These could best be achieved by integrating them onto the CPU chip, if space were available.

The common method used by CISC computers to pass parameters to functions used the system stack. In fact, this had been so widely accepted that the alternative methods shown in Fig. 21.4 had been almost forgotten. With the introduction of RISC machines the stack method came under fresh scrutiny because of the amount of time spent PUSHing and POPping parameters and return addresses. Part of the RISC mission was to reduce the frequency of memory accesses, which was clearly in direct conflict with the enthusiasm of modern software for stack operations. Intel has faced this by installing fast L1 data cache, while Sun has provided SPARC CPUs with a dedicated stack cache on the CPU chip. Thus, the convenience and flexibility of stack-oriented processing could continue without incurring the heavy memory access penalty.

Stack passing Parameters are pushing up onto the stack before transferring control (jumping) to the subroutine. The subroutine code shares the same stack and can access the parameters through the stack or frame pointer. Copies of VALUE parameters are simply pushed onto the stack, while reference (VAR) parameters are 32 bit addresses pointing back at data. Stack frame setup overheads and access times to non-local variables within scope are issues.

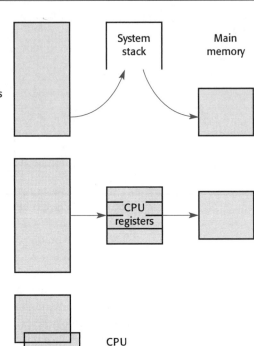

Register passing Using CPU registers to hold the parameters is the fastest method, but is limited by the number and size of registers available. Compilers select this technique only if a couple of simple (integer, char) variables are to be passed IN and for the single OUT return value from functions.

Register windows This is a specialized stack technique used by SPARC processors to reduce the amount of stack PUSHing and POPing. By physically overlapping the stack frames for adjacent procedures, some of the local variables can be visible as parameters with no data copying. To further speed up the process. SPARC CPUs have fast stack caches.

Parameter blockers For machines without stacks, the problem of where to save the return addresses is solved by the CALL instruction inserting the return address at the top of the procedure code before transferring control. The parameters are cunningly inserted in a block immediately after the CALL instruction, thus giving the procedure access by using the return address as a pointer.

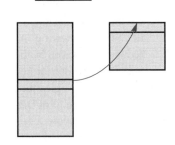

Global access Fortran and BASIC would rely on global data blocks visible to all code. This system of memory parameter blocks has been reinstituted for graphics and Windows programming, where the number of parameters is so great that little else could be suggested.

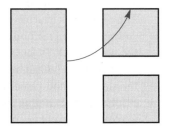

Fig. 21.4
Variety of parameter passing methods to choose from.

21.2   Pipeline techniques – more parallel operations

Parallel, or overlapped, execution of instructions had long been seen as the way to improve performance. But the variable width of the CISC opcodes and the different execution times made such schemes difficult to implement. If you are running several instructions simultaneously and they all complete at different moments, there is a problem of resynchronization to be overcome before the cooperating CPUs can continue executing the program. Several methods were investigated to implement parallel instruction execution, and the most fruitful so far has been the scalar pipeline technique, in which several instructions pass along a multi-stage 'processing line'. On each period of the system clock the execution of an instruction is completed and the code leaves the pipeline. Thus, although the instruction cycle still requires several, say five, phases for completion, it appears as if the fetch–execute cycle is five times faster once the pipeline has been charged up.

A five-stage pipeline is illustrated in Fig. 21.5. It shows the instructions passing along the processing pipeline, and completing after five clock cycles.

Pipeline decoders are not without their own problems. When conditional branch instructions, such as bz and bnz, are encountered, the instruction pre-fetcher has to anticipate which alternative will be taken. The result of the evaluation of the entailed condition may not be available until the instruction has reached the third or fourth

Fig. 21.5
Multi-stage pipeline decoding – parallel processing.

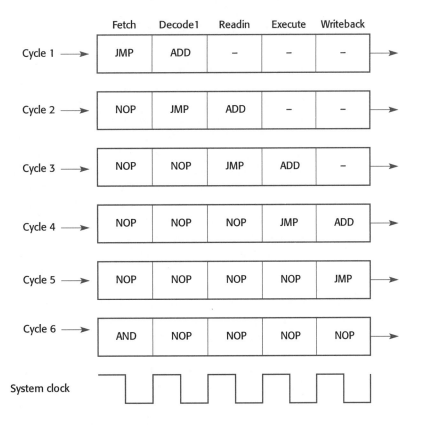

pipeline stage. If one option is then selected the instructions in that arm of code will be valid, but if the alternative arm is selected the current contents of the pipeline will have to be flushed and new memory accesses invoked. The SPARC architecture (see Section 21.7) allows for delayed branching, or pre-execution to assist with this dilemma.

Another difficult problem occurs when neighbouring instructions depend on the same variable. When this happens, the execution of an instruction will stall because the result of a previous instruction has not yet emerged from the pipeline. Such an event throws the decoder into temporary confusion, wasting a lot of time. Some RISC compilers try to avoid such 'pipeline interlock' holdups by inserting NOP instructions to space out the variable references. These appear like WAIT states on the system bus, delaying everything until the slowcoach catches up. A different solution, which is sometimes available, is for the compiler to reorder the instructions in the program to reduce such clashes. But this option is of only limited effectiveness.

A negative effect of the introduction of parallel operations, is the requirement for more than one adder unit. This is necessary because several simultaneous pipeline phases may occasionally need an adder to continue their action unimpeded; for example, during the addition of operands or the calculation of an address pointer.

21.3   Superscalar methods – parallel parallelism

The term **superscalar** is used to describe CPUs which are capable of dealing with more than one instruction during each clock cycle. This can be achieved by equipping the CPU with several independent decoders, usually of the pipelined type. Pentium and SPARC processors are so equipped. Note that there is still only a single instruction stream, but any inherently parallel operations required by the program may be exploited by carrying out several instructions simultaneously on separate hardware units. Although programs are written down as a sequential list of instructions, there is often no logical need to execute the instructions in any particular order. However, running instructions from a single program in parallel is clearly not always possible because they frequently depend on the results from earlier operations. Thus, the superscalar CPU, as with the single pipelined decoder, requires the detection of instruction dependencies within the program in order for the scheme to deliver any performance benefits. This can be assisted by preparatory work carried out by the compiler, but currently depends mostly on the ability of circuits in the CU to detect **Data, Control and Resource Dependences** between neighbouring instructions. Where no mutual dependencies exist there is no reason why several instructions should not execute simultaneously, and this is what superscalar processors aim to accomplish.

Both scalar (pipelined) and superscalar (simultaneous) parallel processing must deal with instruction dependencies. These are classified as listed in Table 21.2. One

Table 21.2
Instruction
dependencies.

Dependency type	Description	Example	Blocked until...
Data	RAW, read after write	MOV EAX,10 ADD EBX,EAX	EAX is loaded
	WAR, write after read	MOV EBX,EAX MOV EAX,10	EAX is read
	WAW, write after write	MUL 100 ADD EAX,10	Sequence correct
Control	The outcome of a previous instruction is essential for an instruction to complete	CMP AL,'q' JZ exit	Z flag set
Resource	Limited availability of hardware resources	Floating point arithmetic	Unit free

way of avoiding the problem is to rely on an enhanced compiler to detect and attempt to avoid such interlocking dependencies by repositioning instructions within the program. Although this seems to be an ideal solution, it does mean acquiring a new compiler and recompiling all executable code for every processor upgrade – a situation that would have prevented Intel from pursuing its policy of binary compatibility throughout the last decades of 80x86 and Pentium developments. Perhaps because of this policy, the Pentium CPU uses a dedicated hardware unit to deal with instruction dependencies.

21.4   Register files – many more CPU registers

With the saving in space gained from the reduction in CU complexity when microcoding was abandoned, it was possible to greatly increase the amount of on-chip storage. This was implemented partly as fast L1 cache and partly as an increase in the number of CPU registers. Both of these changes were intended to reduce the frequency of accesses to main memory. To reflect this intention further, the instruction set of RISC processors was modified and led to the definition of a LOAD–STORE philosphy. Only a limited set of instructions were allowed to access main memory, the 'normal' accesses being directed at CPU registers.

Processors such as the Sun SPARC and Intel Pentium are termed superscalar because they support several parallel pipelines capable of independent decoding and execution. A practical limitation arises from their use of multi-port register files. Currently, it is technically difficult to extend the number of access ports beyond around 20. With each pipeline decoder requiring at least three ports, there is a ceiling imposed on the number of useable pipelines. Comparing Figs. 7.13 and 21.6 clearly illustrates the difference between the scalar and superscalar arrangement for a pipelined processor.

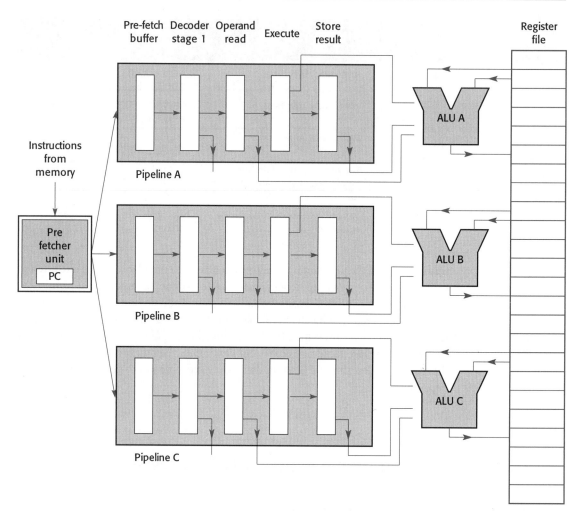

Fig 21.6
Use of register file store with superscalar processors.

Some processors now insert extra buffering at the head of each pipeline. These can be used to delay the progress of any instruction which suffers from a dependency interlock. Such a technique of temporarily deferring instructions is known as **shelving** and is implemented in the Pentium Pro and SPARC64 processors.

A rather surprising register file facility which is exploited by some newer processors (AMD K5 and Pentium Pro) is **register renaming**. This is a technique which allows the compiler, in close collaboration with the CPU, to use temporary registers which are invisible to the programmer to hold variables. This speeds up processing by avoiding some of the mutual ordering constraints which instructions exert on each other. These effects become apparent when several instructions are executed simultaneously, as occurs in scalar pipelines, or superscalar parallel processors. The technique can be applied to WAR and WAW dependencies, as defined in Section 21.3. To clearly understand register renaming it is necessary to translate the more common two-operand instructions into a three-operand format. Thus there are two source

Fig 21.7
Register renaming.

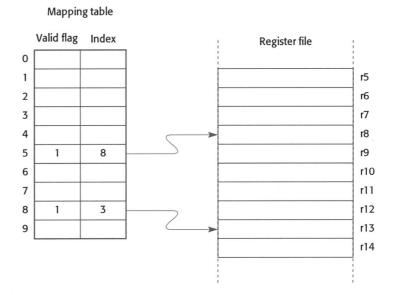

Mapping table

operands and a separate destination, or result, term. Often the result destination will be the same as one of the source operands. In Fig. 21.7 you can see that a reference to a CPU register can be redirected to another register when necessary to avoid over-writing an unsecured variable. This is exactly the situation that arises with the WAW and WAR dependencies. Such a mechanism could be referred to as 'Virtual Register Management' because of its similarity to virtual memory management.

The problem of control dependency (Table 21.2) will be discussed in the next section using the example of a conditional branch instruction.

21.5   Branch prediction methods – maintaining the pipelines

A significant problem associated with the technique of pipeline decoding is how to deal with conditional instructions, such as JZ, JNZ or LOOP. The execution route which follows such an instruction cannot generally be determined by the compiler – it has to be evaluated at run time. With non-pipelined CPUs, where the next instruction is only fetched from memory after the previous instruction has been fully completed, there is little difficulty. The branch decision has already been taken before the next instruction is to be fetched. But with the pipeline decoder, several instructions are held in readiness by the pre-fetcher, and the conditional branch instruction code will have progressed half-way along the decoder pipeline before the uncertainty of the branch route gets resolved. Because of this arrangement, the pre-fetcher needs to know which of the possible branches to fetch from *before* the choice has actually been

Fig. 21.8
Control unit branch
prediction table.

Conditional instruction address	Branch target address	Prediction confidence value

made. Either both branches of instructions need to be fetched, or accept the risk of fetching and partially executing instructions from the wrong branch. If instructions from the wrong branch are pre-fetched, once the conditional instruction has been evaluated the pipeline will have to be flushed, and an execution stall will then occur. Instructions from the correct branch have to be read into the pipeline from memory. Such pipeline stalls have a serious impact on CPU performance.

One option adopted by some compilers to avoid wasteful pipeline flushing and reloading is to reorder the instructions or to stuff no-ops (NOP) instructions into the code immediately following each conditional instruction. This delays the need to fetch from either branch until the decision has been taken and the branch known.

The Pentium uses hardware Branch Prediction Logic (BPL in Fig 7.4) which monitors the outcome of conditional instructions, using the stored result from previous decisions to guess the outcome of subsequent branches. This is termed **speculative execution**, and can work quite effectively in a loop where, for example, a target item is being sought. Most of the time the loop jumps back for another test, only occasionally detecting the target and dropping through. To implement such a strategy requires a fast cache store to track the results of conditional instructions (BTB in Fig. 7.4). The minimum layout is given in Fig. 21.8, where the three column table allows the BPL to check for conditional instruction addresses as they enter the pipeline. If it is the first time of execution within the recent time frame, the address will get entered. Should the instruction be already present in the table, the BPL can use the second entry as a 'best bet' for the branch, and continue fetching from that address. The third column is used to hold a confidence value, based on the outcome of earlier executions of the conditional instructions.

21.6   Compiler support – an essential part of RISC

The HLL compiler is now seen as an essential, associate component of the RISC CPU. Silicon suppliers, such as Sun or Intel, no longer rely on third-party programmers to produce compilers after the microprocessor has been launched. The provision of a specifically developed C compiler is essential to the success of any microprocessor, but especially so for RISC devices. This situation has arisen partly because the 'simplification' of the instruction set has placed greater demands on software libraries, and partly because of the need to precondition software to make the best use of the parallel facilities provided by the RISC CPUs. The important issues discussed in Section 21.3 (data and code dependencies) can be partly resolved at compile time to allow the code to fully exploit the scalar and superscalar parallelisms.

When the CPU offers a decoder pipeline, the compiler can ensure that for unconditional branch instructions, such as CALL or JMP, the pre-fetcher switches its focus to the new target before the pipeline has fully executed the CALL instruction which is actually responsible for switching to the new location. Otherwise the pipeline would be supplied with the instructions immediately following the CALL, which would be useless.

Compilers can also support the effective use of parallel hardware facilities by reordering the original code sequence. This can help to avoid data and code dependencies or simply exploit the available hardware resources more fully.

21.7 Sun SPARC – scalar processor architecture as RISC

The SPARC processor was launched by Sun Microsystems in 1988 as a processor to supersede the MC68030 for the new Sun-4 Unix workstation. There remains some ambiguity over the term 'scalar', which some texts construe as 'scalable'. Sun itself distinguishes 'scalar' processing from other high-performance designs which offer vector processing. The SPARC carries out multiple scalar operations simultaneously on a stream of instructions, while the vector processors operate in a simultaneous, parallel, style. Alternatively, scalable could refer to the planned improvements in manufacturing techniques which enable chip designs to be made smaller and smaller, making them cheaper and faster. Sun has always intended that the basic architecture would support a variety of CPUs, ranging from portable laptop systems to powerful database servers. The enhanced 'SuperScalar' architecture means that more than one instruction pipeline is in operation, leading to the possibility of the completion of more than one instruction per clock cycle.

Where novelty is seen as a key marketing factor, development time-scales are under increasing pressure. The original SPARC chip took only 10 months from design to market and future revisions were made with much less difficulty because there was no complex microcode to negotiate.

Consistent with its 'Open Systems' policy for software, Sun offered licences to other hardware manufacturers to improve the supply and speed up development of other versions. Because of their simpler instruction sets, it is generally considered easier to design and manufacture RISC processors, but achieving high performance will also involve multiprocessor schemes. Sun Microsystems used Fujitsu Gate Arrays to build its first chip, while other licensees use different technologies for manufacturing their CPUs. A wide range of designs have now developed from the Sun original, including the SPARClite range of embedded processors from Fujitsu.

A number of hardware facilities have been incorporated to improve the performance of SPARC processors. The separate FPU is served by a separate floating-point instruction pipeline.

- **Instruction pipelining**
  As we have already observed, modern CPUs can outpace the normally available memories. Various strategies have been tried to avoid the insertion of wasteful WAIT states. Suns use local on-chip SRAM cache, and interleaved DRAM to help avoid the problem. A wide 64 bit bus can fetch four instructions at a time. The SPARC then sorts the instructions into two pipelines, discriminating between integer and floating point operations to allow parallel execution of instructions. Pre-fetching also enables overlapping of CPU activities to further increase performance.

- **Register windowing**
  Access to main memory for the stack is reduced in the SPARC by the use of a stack cache in the CPU. This allows the implementation of a fast parameter-passing mechanism known as **Register Windowing**. The CPU register bank is divided into groups, or windows. A short pointer is used to indicate which window is active. The CPU is provided with a **Current Window Pointer** register (CWP), which can be advanced or withdrawn by the instructions SAVE and RESTORE. There are 24 registers in a window: 8 IN registers, 8 LOCAL registers and 8 OUT registers. At any moment the following situation exists:

IN registers:	incoming parameters
	return address
	returned values
LOCAL registers:	automatic variables (local variables)
OUT registers:	outgoing parameters to subroutine
	return address for subroutine

The advantage of this technique depends on the 'overlapping' of the OUT section of the caller with the IN section of the called when the SAVE and RESTORE instructions are used. The limited size of the CPU register bank will require swapping operations to main memory stack (see Figure 21.9).

21.8 Intel Itanium – the next generation

Since it invented microprocessors in 1971, starting with the Intel 4004, Intel has regularly redefined the performance that users can expect from their processor hardware. This has been accomplished partly by physically shrinking the circuits and partly by incorporating new techniques to speed up the fetch–execute cycle. Now it seems that

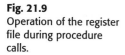

Fig. 21.9
Operation of the register
file during procedure
calls.

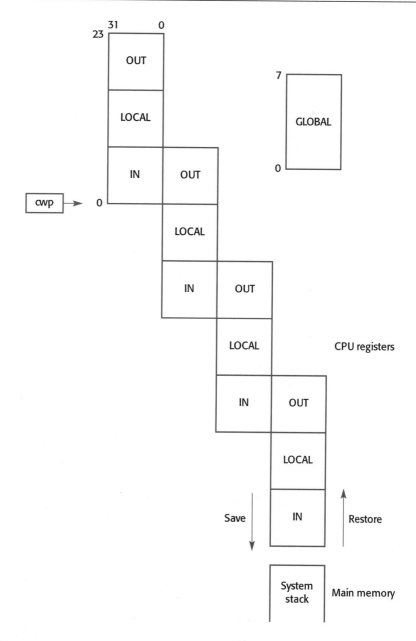

the i80x86 family has reached the end of its time as the flagship of Intel processors. The 32 bit Pentium is to be superseded by the Itanium, formerly called Merced, based on the new IA-64 architecture. Backward binary compatibility with the current IA-32 Pentiums will be retained, but nevertheless a definitive break with the architecture will be instituted because the IA-64 will not be instruction-compatible with its predecessors. The IA-64 specification has emerged from a research collaboration between Hewlett-Packard and Intel which was aimed at establishing an architecture which would fully exploit the lessons which have been learned from recent experience with

RISC processors. Moore's Law has again delivered considerable gains in speed and circuit complexity, and Intel is aiming to manufacture the chips with only 0.18 μm line widths. The space freed on the silicon die when the circuits are shrunk can be used in a number of different ways. Intel has chosen to increase the width of words and lay in more execution pipelines to support **Instruction Level Parallelism**. An instruction length of 32 bits qualifies the Itanium to be categorized as a **LIW** (Long Instruction Word) machine. The benefit of longer instructions stems from the reduction in decoding that the CU has to perform before it can start signalling the required activities. It makes available to the compiler much greater flexibility in choosing combinations of operations which would not previously have been possible. The reason for this lies with the CU decoder. The more it decodes, the less variety of operations are visible to the compiler. Consider a 3 bit instruction offered up to a 3-to-8 line decoder. There are eight code numbers (000, 001, ..., 111) and eight alternative output selections (00000001, 00000010, ..., 10000000). But there are potentially 256 different output patterns available (00000000, ..., 11111110, 11111111). So the compiler is constrained by the decoder to a limited set of actions. If the instruction was widened from three to eight bits, the compiler would gain complete control over the computer.

If the instruction were to grow out to 96 bits it would reach the length of the microcode instructions used within previous CISC processors. Then a very fast decode/execution cycle would be possible and the compiler would be able to specify in exact detail what will happen within each phase of the machine cycle. Also, with a longer, fixed length instruction, the Itanium can supply three execution pipelines working in parallel. In support of this, the instructions are handled in **bundles** of three, as shown in Fig. 21.10. A 128 bit bundle containing three 32 bit instructions, each with an associated 8 bit **predicate value**, also carries a **template code** from the compiler which indicates the instructions readily capable of parallel execution.

The 64 bit Instruction Pointer holds the logical address of the bundle containing the current instruction. Because bundles contain 16 bytes, and this is the minimum unit to be fetched, the four least significant bits of the IP are always zero. Several of the problems which beset pipeline architectures, discussed in Section 21.2, have been specifically addressed. These include the ability to pre-fetch and execute instructions from both arms of an IF-ELSE structure until the condition is tested and decided. This eliminates the need to predict at run time which arm to follow when fetching ahead. The Itanium compiler takes more responsibility for reordering the instructions to avoid any interdependences which would block the parallel execution pipelines. The technique used is termed **Predication**. Predication is a way of reducing the number of conditional branch instructions used to implement a program and so remove the need for the CU to make decisions about instruction reordering. This is

Fig. 21.10
Instruction bundle for
the IA-64 architecture.

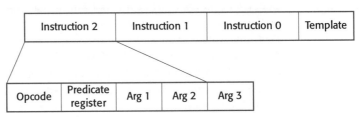

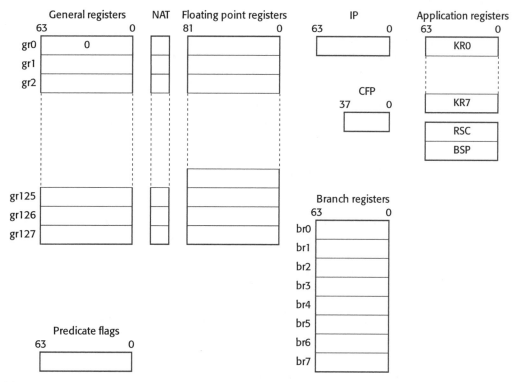

Fig. 21.11
Intel IA-64/Itanium
register set.

achieved by embedding a conditional test in every instruction. Such a facility has been limited in the past to a small number of the instructions. The Pentium has conditional move instructions (CMOV) and the 8 bit Z80 sported conditional CALL and RET (CALLNZ, RETZ). In these instructions the action is governed by the indicated CPU status flag. So the IA-64 scheme effectively expands the role of the CPU Status flags in binding together the traditional pairs of: condition test → flag set followed by the flag test → conditional branch, and extends their scope to affect all instructions. The Itanium contains 64 **Predicate Flags**, shown in Fig. 21.11, which are capable of controlling the outcome of several instructions executing in parallel. The predication technique effectively replaces several conditional branch instructions with the conditional execution of all instructions.

The General Register bank has an associated **Frame Pointer** (CFP) which indicates the position of the current frame, holding local variables and parameters, within the register bank. Registers GR1 to GR31 are reserved for general-purpose data/address activities, while 32–127 can be used for subroutine data frames. By overlapping the *calling* and the *called* frames a method of passing parameters is used which does not involve any data copying. This is similar to the SPARC stack windowing technique. Note that the first register, GR0, will supply a zero when read, and a nice run-time error when written to!

Passing parameters between the higher privilege operating system routines back to a user application is catered for by the **Kernel Registers**. These offer fast secure communications for this special situation.

With a predicated instruction set, it is possible to deal with the two alternative instruction streams arising from an IF-ELSE statement using a single execution pipeline, or by employing two independent units. Rather helpfully, programmers always arrange their code so that the two alternative blocks are quite independent of each other – perfect for parallel execution. Instructions from both arms of an IF-ELSE structure will be passed along the decode–execution pipeline until the conditional clause is evaluated, setting the relevant predicate flags, which will then lead to the results from the instructions in the rejected arm being discarded and the results pending from the accepted arm being confirmed. No pipeline flushing, with the associated delays, is involved. Another important source of the performance advantage which comes from this brinkmanship approach to execution is the more regular and predictable pattern of memory management that is possible. If all paths are to be executed, all relevant cache lines must be read in, a situation that the compiler can easily plan for and implement by marking instructions and data to be moved up the memory hierarchy in anticipation of their imminent need. In the present scheme, any pre-reading may incur a penalty should the wrong conditional path be chosen. However, it may be worrying you that with this design more instructions and data will be moved into cache and from there into the CPU, some of which will turn out to be superfluous to requirements. Although this appears inefficient, the data flow can be arranged by the compiler, which can reduce the number of unexpected memory misses. In any case, executing redundant unnecessary instructions and throwing away the result is not so bad as incurring cache misses or, more seriously, a page fault.

The Pentium processor was equipped with circuits to carry out **instruction re-ordering**. The intention was for the processor to decide, on the fly, whether the order of instructions received from the compiler could be improved for the benefit of parallel (pipeline) execution. Because the Pentium also broke down the more complex instructions into micro-ops for further decoding and execution, the reordering was attempted at this level. Moving instructions 'upstream' to get a better execution flow is termed **hoisting**. An important change with the IA-64 architecture is to commit such decisions to the compiler, which has a better view of the code and is permitted a much longer time to think about the issues.

The IA-64 compilers are also required to look out for opportunities to pre-read data so that operands can be entered into CPU registers before they are needed. This is known as **Speculative Loading**. It clearly could be of a great advantage in circumstances where the use of variables can be accurately predicted at compile time. It should be noted, however, that this could start a large ripple-through effect on cache and virtual memory controllers, which may be triggered into trying to pre-read pages or cache lines, running the risk that a memory exception will occur. This negative side effect is particularly annoying when the memory exceptions and delays may be due to the reading of subsequently unneeded items. To avoid this penalty, the IA-64 architecture has provided the ability to defer the response to memory miss exceptions until a special CHECK instruction is reached. The **NAT** (Not A Thing) flag is used to indicate that the associated data register is waiting for a deferred exception to be honoured and a fresh value to be rolled in from memory. With these facilities, pre-reading can take place without the risk of triggering unnecessary memory exceptions. Whether this exciting new approach delivers performance advantages in all application areas, such as database searching, remains to be seen.

It can be seen that several diverse areas of research have contributed to the development of the IA-64 specification. The design of the CPU circuits, the instruction set and compiler functionality have all been pursued in concert so as to develop the **EPIC** (Explicitly Parallel Instruction Computer) architecture.

There are 256 CPU registers in the Itanium. Such a large number helps to reduce the frequency of memory access cycles required. Of the 256 64-bit registers, 128 are dedicated for general purpose and integer operations, while the remaining 128 are dedicated to floating-point variables.

The EIP, like the other registers, is 64 bits wide, thus extending the maximum length of memory from the current 4 Gbyte to 64 Tbyte. Although the physical memory of desktop PCs is still well short of the 4 Gbyte limit, in the field of file servers and database engines this limit is being approached, with 0.5 Gbyte memories now quite common.

21.9 Future processor design – debate

After discussing several diverse CPUs supplied by different manufacturers, it may be surprising to remark that this is a field within which systems designers have seen their choice diminish over the past two decades. The decision now is constrained by the limited range of commercially available microprocessors. The range on offer is steadily decreasing as the fabrication start-up cost spirals into the hundreds of million of dollars. The ongoing argument about whether the RISC or CISC approach is the best for future computer architectures will not be resolved by academic debate, but once again by the market-place. In the future there will be many radical reversals when technologies change, as has happened in the past. The basic difference between the two camps concerns the architectural level at which system functionality is assigned. RISC designers put the functionality at a higher level than CISC designers, assuming that the language translators will perform an efficient mapping to low-level code. CISC designers build more functionality into the lower level architecture because it is faster.

A peripheral influence which has encouraged the adoption of RISC techniques is the development advantage of working with smaller, simpler units. Currently, the market-place is fashion-conscious: new CPUs are advertised on prime-time television. They have to arrive in the shops just at the correct moment to benefit from the marketing activity. Project experience with the development of complex, microcoded CISC CPUs is not compatible with this fast turn-around philosophy. Shareholders prefer a RISC!

At the moment the problem of the 'semantic gap' is being coped with by the introduction of support tools. Integrated development environments, CASE tools and designer workbenches are all offered to ease the task of transforming the high-level concept into runnable machine code. Perhaps the widening of the semantic gap by the introduction of RISC CPUs has demonstrated that at least one historic difficulty has been overcome. Orthogonality was another target for CISC designers to aim at, which has been abandoned since the RISC architecture has gained supremacy. A recognition that the compiler is an essential part of the design and development of a new microprocessor is in marked contrast to the early 8 bit processors, which were offered with only an untested assembler for support.

Backward compatibility has now become an essential requirement for new processors because of the large investment in software that customers have to protect. It is no longer possible to assume that free software upgrades will be made available to eliminate the problem, With so much 'shrink-wrapped', supermarket software in circulation, it has become a dominant theme.

Review

- The earlier design constraints – expensive slow main memory, assembler coded programming, cheap fast PROM – have changed, and even reversed, over the last decades.

- The CISC principle of migrating more and more complex operations downwards through the functional hierarchy has been challenged. The resources taken up by sophisticated instructions were not justified by their usage.

- CISC expanded the power and flexibility of the processors by introducing a repertoire of addressing modes in support of HLL constructs.

- The RISC philosophy is to keep the CPU as small as possible, reduce the number of instructions and modes, decode rapidly using hard-wired logic and consider alternative ways of accelerating performance.

- Because RISC instructions are simple and of constant length it is possible to decode several simultaneously in a push-through pipeline.

- Parallel pipeline decoders are also possible if the selected instructions do not mutually interfere.

- To reduce the number of time-consuming memory access cycles, RISC CPUs are furnished with increased number of data registers.

- To better exploit the RISC architectures, special customized compilers are supplied. This means that processing can be carried out at compile time rather than execution time.

Practical work

The recommended practical work involves carrying out research into the relative merits of CISC and RISC CPU architectures, and presenting the results in a seminar session. This could be done by choosing and comparing one example of each.

Exercises

1. Draw up a list of the advantages and disadvantages of microcoded CPU architectures: consider the end-user as well as the development phase.

2. Why isn't there a BASIC microcode engine?

3. Discuss the 'code hierarchy' in a digital computer.

4. How would you decide at what level to insert the following new functions:

    block moves of binary data in memory,

    floating point square-root,

    data encodement for fax transmission

    BST ⟷ GMT system clock changeover

5. Explain the phrase: 'Interrupts are only polling in microcode'.

6. What is the principal performance enhancer in RISC processors?

7. Which do you think would be a better way to use up spare area on the processor chip: enlarging the L1 cache or enlarging the CPU register file?

8. What are the advantages of VLIW (Very Long Instruction Word) architectures?

9. Why is instruction pre-fetching advantageous?

10. Why do supporters of RISC advocate giving more responsibility to the compiler?

Readings

- Heuring and Jordan (1997), Section 3.4: introducing the SPARC as a RISC microprocessor.

- Hennessy and Patterson (1998), Chapter 6: pipelining methods.

- Kidder (1981): a good, racy account of microcode development.

- Tabak (1990)

- The Intel Web site containing technical information about the IA-64 architecture is:
  http://developer.intel.com/design/ia-64/

- The main Sun repository is found at:
  http://www.sun.com/microelectronics/whitepapers/

- An article by Bill Joy, co-founder of Sun Microsystems, can be seen at:
  http://www.cs.washington.edu/homes/lazowska/cra/risc.html

- The Web sites can be accessed via the Companion Web site for this book at:
  http://www.booksites.net/williams/

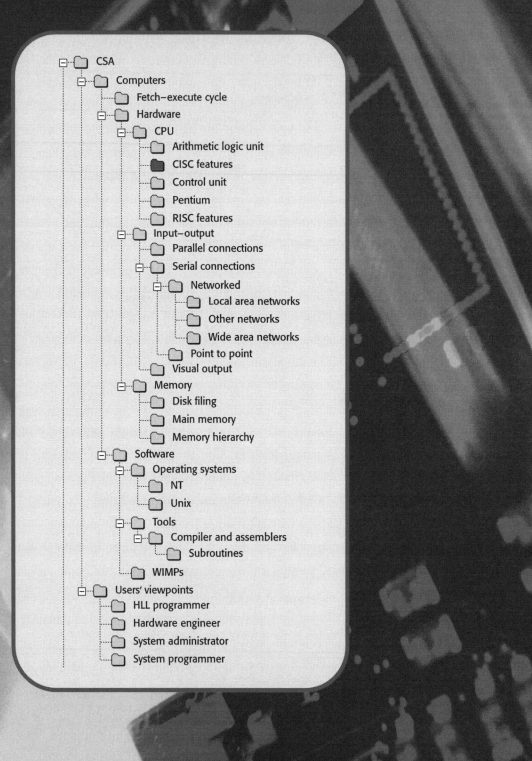

The Motorola MC68300 microcontroller

22

Overview

There is a very large market for microcontrollers and the MC68300 range of devices is our chosen example. It is also a good example of the classical CISC CPU, being based on the well-established MC68000 design. The CPU register set and status register are presented for comparison with the Pentium and SPARC. Although the more varied machine instruction set and addressing modes can be judged more useful to programmers, they are no longer the sole issues to be considered in an assessment. The typical characteristics of a CISC CPU are discussed.

22.1   The MC68300 – an example microcontroller and CISC processor

It is considered preferable to introduce new subjects with simple examples. However, in the case of microprocessors this is becoming quite difficult because they are being built with more and more sophisticated circuits in a never-ending search for improved performance. Rather than use an invented 'idealized' processor I have described the Pentium processor in Chapter 7, and the SPARC in Chapter 21, and here we will be investigating the Motorola MC68000 CPU. This is a good example of a **CISC** processor and even though it is now over 20 years old, the 68k CPU specification is still being widely used in contemporary microcontrollers. With this in mind, it is useful to take this opportunity of introducing microcontrollers through the MC68300 range of devices (not to be confused with the MC68030 CPU). Also, the MC68000 CPU has retained the prestige of being generally considered a 'seminal' example of CISC architecture. Every now and then a product emerges which retains a reputation long after its commercially active life is over. The DEC PDP-11 and the IBM/360 are similarly worthy of historic study.

With the MC68300 microcontroller (Fig. 22.1), the 68000 CPU does not occupy the whole chip. Rather, it fits into one corner, and works alongside a variety of other complex IO circuits dedicated to specific roles in embedded automotive control or domestic appliances. We have already investigated the popular Pentium and SPARC CPUs, but the increasing importance of the less powerful microcontoller devices should not be overlooked. Microcontrollers integrate CPU, memory and IO interface circuits on a single chip of silicon. The original intention was to reduce production costs, but physical miniaturization now appears to be more important than cost if we look at recent developments in cellular telephone handsets. Because an enormous amount of programming effort goes into developing better radio receivers, faster fax

Fig. 22.1
Functional schematic of the MC68300 microcontroller.

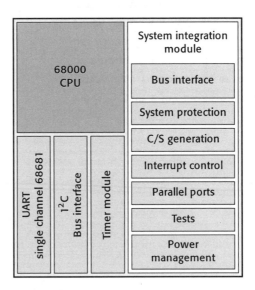

Fig. 22.2
Block diagram of
MC68376
microcontroller.

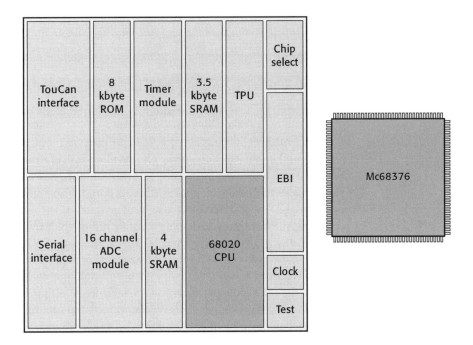

machines, cleverer burglar alarms, and a plethora of other products all intended to satisfy the market for 'intelligent' devices, programmers should no longer ignore this opportunity and abandon it to hardware engineers.

The range of microcontroller devices is expanding rapidly. For example, the MC68736 (Fig. 22.2) is intended for car engine control, having special timing registers and analogue voltage conversion circuits necessary for controlling the spark and fuel injectors. The extra flexibility and accuracy which can be achieved with such programmable controllers helps to regulate engine emissions and improve fuel efficiency. The TouCAN interface, sitting in the top left-hand corner of Fig. 22.2, is a dedicated network interface which has been adopted by several car manufacturers, providing a means of communication between the various subsystems within a car. The ADC (analogue to digital converter) can accept real-world signals from transducers, translating them into binary format suitable for digital processing. Perhaps unsurprisingly in this application, there is quite a lot of hardware support for timing operations which will assist with the fundamental engine management functions.

A new problem for the programmer getting to grips with microcontroller-based developments is the need to understand the activity of **Cross Development**. This arises when the target computer has insufficient resources to support the actual software development. Perhaps it has no screen, or cannot host a compiler. In these circumstances it becomes necessary to use another computer as a development host, and download the code when it is ready to be run and tested. Figure 22.3 illustrates the arrangement with the microcontroller installed on the **SBC** (Single Board Computer). It is the SBC that will be delivered to the customer, not the workstation. Such computers are often referred to as **Embedded Systems** when they are closely coupled with the equipment that they are monitoring or controlling.

Fig. 22.3
Cross development for
microcontroller systems.

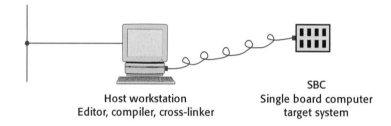

Host workstation
Editor, compiler, cross-linker

SBC
Single board computer
target system

The cable between the host and target provides a path both to download the executable code and to provide debugging information during the testing sessions. If the SBC has been provided with its own Ethernet port, the host and target can communicate over a LAN, which makes the arrangement much more convenient. It can be very confusing, the first time you develop software using a PC/Pentium, to run a compiler on behalf of a completely different CPU. Furthermore, the linking process will need to be much more explicitly visible and is frequently more problematic than linking for a Unix or Windows-based host.

While the MC68300 microcontroller retains its 32 bit processing power, the less romantic roles of washing machine sequencer, central heating controller or knitting machine 'brain' are handled admirably by much simpler 4 bit CPUs. The most successful of these is the Texas Instruments TMS1000, which has been embedded in millions of toys. Thus there is an increasing range of microcontrollers designed to fit into any imaginable application, even parking meters. Undoubtedly, special **DSP** (Digital Signal Processing) microcontrollers will be made available to handle the anticipated demand for voice-operated equipment when the algorithms have proved to be sufficiently reliable – all of which requires exciting creative effort on the part of the programmer!

22.2   MC68000 CPU – the CPU registers and their use

The MC68000 family of microprocessors was a very popular and successful range of 32 bit CPUs and was selected for the Atari ST, Commodore Amiga and Apple Macintosh, as well as the first Sun workstation. Motorola successively issued the 68000, 68008, 68010, 68012, 68020, 68030, 68040 and 68060. It was developed from the simpler 8 bit 6800 and 6809 processors and is considered a typical CISC processor. This classification arises from the range of instruction types, the number of data and address registers and the complex addressing modes available. Some people compare it to the DEC PDP-11 and VAX minicomputers which preceded its development. As described in Section 4.10, CISC CPUs have microcoded CUs in order to deal with the range and complexity of their machine instructions. The proportion of the MC68020 CPU chip taken up with its CU is around 60%, compared with only 10% for the more recent RISC chips, which use CUs equipped with hardware decoders. This is an

Fig. 22.4
MC68000 CPU
registers.

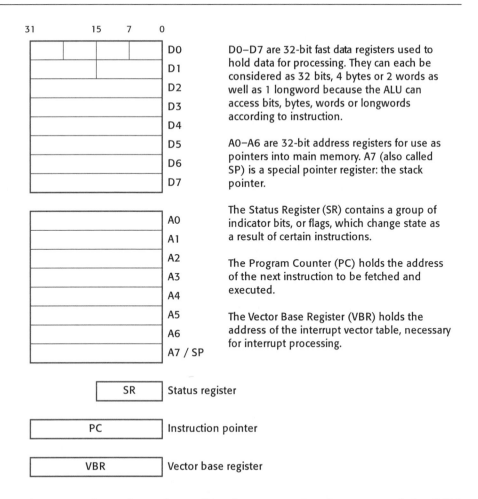

D0–D7 are 32-bit fast data registers used to hold data for processing. They can each be considered as 32 bits, 4 bytes or 2 words as well as 1 longword because the ALU can access bits, bytes, words or longwords according to instruction.

A0–A6 are 32-bit address registers for use as pointers into main memory. A7 (also called SP) is a special pointer register: the stack pointer.

The Status Register (SR) contains a group of indicator bits, or flags, which change state as a result of certain instructions.

The Program Counter (PC) holds the address of the next instruction to be fetched and executed.

The Vector Base Register (VBR) holds the address of the interrupt vector table, necessary for interrupt processing.

important factor in understanding the reasons for the success of the RISC architectures.

The 68000 CPU, like other CISC processors, has a small set of fast data registers associated with the ALU to help improve performance. These are presented in Fig. 22.4. By copying a variable from memory into a CPU register any arithmetic or other manipulation can then be carried out without incurring further memory access delays. Assuming that most activities undertaken with variables will require repeated reading and writing, the time saved by holding a temporary copy of the data in a CPU register can easily be better than 30%. The MC68000 CPU has 16 registers, as shown in Fig. 22.4, for the program to use.

It is quite interesting to compare Fig. 22.4 with the equivalent for the Pentium (Fig. 7.5). Notice how Motorola does not give individual data registers special names, which means, significantly, that they are not assigned distinct roles. Intel prefers to refer to 'the Accumulator' (EAX), 'the Counter' (ECX) and the 'Base Register' (EBX). This is because each can perform a special function when a particular instruction is executed. Often they behave as implied operands, participating in an instruction without being explicitly referenced in the instruction code or the associated assembler mnemonic. Motorola requires all operands to be cited explicitly in the instructions, which is perhaps easier for novice assembler level programmers! For example the equivalent FOR loop instructions are:

```
Pentium: loop start_loop
68000: dbra D0,start_loop
```

The Pentium loop instruction assumes and demands the use of ECX, while the Motorola version gives the programmer the opportunity of choosing any one of the 8 data registers. This is an example of how the MC68000 has greater 'orthogonality' than the Pentium, in that it offers more freedom of choice in associating types of operands with any operation. A similar distinction occurs involving assembler mnemonics when declaring the width of the data item to be handled. While the Intel assembler uses different operand names (AL, AH, AX and EAX) to distinguish between 8, 16 and 32 bit registers, Motorola employs an operator suffix (MOVE.B, MOVE.W or MOVE.L) instead. This is actually insignificant at the machine code level, where instruction sub-fields specify the item width (Fig. 7.7), but it can confuse assembly programmers.

22.3   MC68000 status register – communication flags

As explained in Section 7.5, the flags provide another means of inter-instruction communication. In fact, the simpler the instruction, the more compelling is the need, because any useful action will require several instructions to complete. Linking instructions together is the job of the status flags. This can be compared with short-term memory in humans. When we compare two items we somehow store a representation of the first item, then quickly look at the second item. Any intervening activity may result in the status flag being overwritten, but each instruction affects different flags, and experienced assembler programmers can exploit the differences to produce tight code.

In addition to this role, some of the CPU status bits, shown in Fig. 22.5, are used to indicate the current mode of the CPU. The MC68000 has two major modes: supervisor and user. This allows the CPU to classify all instructions as special privilege supervisor instructions or just ordinary user instructions. The purpose of the S mode flag is to support operating system security measures, protecting the computer system from renegade or malicious programs. Without such an interaction with hardware facilities, it would be very difficult to write operating system software to trap attempts to access data or privileged routines illegally. It is clearly necessary to forbid all user programs from setting the S flag, and so gaining supervisor privilege. The only way to assume supervisor privilege is through an exception event, all of which can be checked for validity before being processed.

Fig. 22.5
MC68000 CPU status
flags.

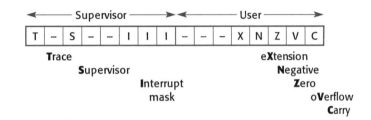

The T mode flag indicates whether the CPU has been set into single-stepping trace mode for a low-level debugging session. This is rarely used, except in extreme circumstances when some awkward run-time error is occurring and a thorough debugging session is demanded. Single-stepping through code, either at the machine code level or the HLL source level, is time-consuming and not always desirable. If you are working in a real-time or multitasking environment, the very process of using such a trace facility will interfere with the normal timing and sequence of your system. For students of computer science, however, such single-stepping activity can be priceless in view of the information that it reveals about the operation of the processor. If you did not follow the advice in Section 7.8 you now have a second chance: get some code and load it into a debugger!

The three I bits are known as the interrupt mask, containing a 3 bit number which represents the minimum priority level of interrupts that are currently being accepted. A zero would allow the CPU to recognize and accept for processing any interrupt signal, whereas a mask value of 7 would lock out all interrupts except those of the very highest priority. This would normally indicate an imminent power failure or other non-recoverable crisis. Interrupt processing for input–output data transfers was described in Chapter 9, but its use has much wider significance for embedded microcontrollers.

The five status flags, X, N, Z, V and C, are set and cleared by the activity of the ALU. As explained in Section 7.5, many machine instructions have an effect on several of the status flags in addition to producing a main data result. The basic set of MC68000 assembler instructions is given in Table 22.1. You can compare them with the Pentium equivalents given in Table 7.3.

22.4 Addressing modes – more power and complexity

The MC68000 has more sophisticated addressing modes than the SPARC or even the Pentium. They are provided to assist when accessing more complex HLL data structures. As described in Section 7.4, all instruction codes are subdivided into bit fields to help the decoder carry out its job quickly and efficiently. The addressing modes which help to build the operands' effective addresses are allocated bit fields within the machine instruction. Table 22.2 lists the Addressing Modes for the MC68000 family.

Table 22.1
Basic 'starter'
instructions for the
MC68000.

MOVE	Copies data from location to location, e.g. register or memory
CLR	Clears a location to zero
LEA	Special way to create an effective address
PEA	Push an address onto the stack, possibly as a subroutine parameter
ADD/ADDQ	Arithmetic addition; the Q version is quicker for small numbers (< 8)
SUB	Arithmetic subtraction for two's complement integers
AND/OR	Logical operators
CMP	Compare two values (really a subtract with no answer)
TST	Test a location to see if it is zero; sets Z flag
BRA	The unconditional jump instruction; uses a relative offset
BEQ/BNE	Conditional relative jump
BSR/RTS	Call and return for subroutines
DBRA	Special loop counting instruction, intended for FOR loops.
TRAP	Software interrupt call to get into an operating system routine

Table 22.2
MC68000 addressing
modes.

Data register direct	000	reg# 0–7
Address register direct	001	reg# 0–7
Address register indirect	010	reg#
Address register indirect, postincrement	011	reg#
Address register indirect, postdecrement	100	reg#
Address register indirect, postdecrement with displacement	101	reg#
Address register indirect with index	110	reg#
Absolute short (16 bits)	111	000
Absolute long (32 bits)	111	001
PC with displacement	111	010
PC with index	111	011
Immediate	111	100

It is often easier to understand what is intended by looking at example code. Remember that Motorola mnemonics use the operands in reverse order to Intel.

Register direct:	MOVE.L D0,D1	Copy the contents of D0 into D1.
Register indirect:	MOVE.L (A0),D0	Copy the contents of the memory location indicated by A0 into D0.
Register indirect with displacement:	MOVE.L 10(A0),D0	Add 10 (offset) to address in A0 before accessing the value in memory; offset is 16-bit value.

...and indexing:	`MOVE.L 10(A0,D1),D0`	Offset + base address + index register to build a pointer address. Index is 16 or 32 bits, offset is only 8 bits.
with autoinc:	`MOVE.L (A0)+,D0`	Pointer register (A0) is incremented after each memory access to advance to next item.
with autodec:	`MOVE.W D0,-(A0)`	Pointer register is first decremented then the memory access is made.
PC relative:	`MOVE.L $10(PC),D0`	Binary relocatable code.
	`MOVE.L 100(PC,D1),D0`	
	`MOVE.L RSYMB(D1),D0`	Common form for assembler translation.
Immediate:	`MOVE.L #100,D0`	Load the value 100 into D0.
	`MOVE.L #number,D1`	Load the value of constant called 'number' into D1.
Absolute (long):	`MOVE.L $107FFC,D0`	Load 4B contents of memory location $107FFC into D0; can access 16M range.
(short):	`MOVE.L $100,D0`	Can access 64K range, 0–7FFF and FF8000–FFFFFF.

After some consideration you will appreciate that addressing modes make the basic instructions (actions) more powerful and flexible, especially when dealing with large data structures, such as arrays or records. In this way the computer architect has planned the machine instruction set to make compilers easier to write and more efficient to use. This is another example of the hardware providing close support for the higher layers of software.

You may notice that Motorola does not offer specific PUSH and POP instructions as found with the Pentium. The programmer has to build them using the autoincrement and autodecrement modes:

```
MOVE.L D0,-(SP) PUSH register D0
MOVE.W (SP)+,A1 POP into register A1
```

Remember, as we pointed out in Section 7.6, that register indirect mode is one of the most efficient ways of reading data from memory, and that Memory Direct is one of the least efficient. Perhaps the fundamental mode for all computers could be identified as register indirect autoincrement, because the fetch–execute cycle relies on it, using PC as an address register, to read instructions from memory.

When classifying processors, the range and sophistication of addressing modes are among the features which distinguish CISC from RISC.

22.5 CISC designs – principal features

As we have already stated, the CISC philosophy for improving performance was based on the migration of functionality down through the computer system hierarchy (see Fig. 21.1) towards the digital hardware. This was driven by the belief that if an operation could be completely carried out by hardware without the intervention of software control, it must necessarily be better. Thus the special string compare, block move, and matrix addition instructions were born. The CISC assumption neglected to take into account the negative impact of implementing complex instruction sequences on alternative acceleration techniques. This turned out to be the central issue in the battle with RISC, especially when it was discovered that the more complex instructions were rarely used by compilers when generating executable code from HLL source.

There is no exact distinction between RISC and CISC; for example, the Pentium is broadly a CISC CPU which has benefited from the inclusion of RISC techniques. But CISC CPUs are generally identified by the group of features and facilities listed in Table 22.3, which conversely RISC CPUs tend to avoid.

The introduction of variable length instructions resulted inevitably from the need to handle different sizes and numbers of operands. Some instructions have no operands, while others have 1, 2 or even 3. To positively exploit this facility, it was often possible to encode the more popular instructions into a shorter format. Of course, this resulted in differing execution periods for the instructions, which made the CU decoder much more involved. It was never considered necessary to provide more than a dozen or so ALU data registers, because these were viewed as temporary processing buffers only. The *proper* place for variables was definitely main memory. So although CISC spawned more and more modes and operations, it did not breed registers! The principal way of supporting HLL code was identifed with CALLing and RETurning from procedures. This involved assisting with stack-based parameters and local variable stack-frame management. When application code was inspected, the need for string manipulations was highlighted. This led to the development of more elaborate machine instructions to handle structured data types (records, arrays, sets). The need to support run-time checks, such as the verification of within bounds array indexing, made further development of instruction decoding necessary. Because many of these CPUs had to administer to the demands of dozens of disk drives and hundreds of terminals, there was a demand for well-developed interrupt response circuits. The only viable technique of dealing with all this variety and complexity was the microcode CU, as outlined in Fig. 4.21.

A significant factor in the demise of CISC architectures may have been the manner in which more and more complex instructions were introduced. It appeared that designers were reluctant to assess the wider issues, neglecting to consider the alternative uses that the silicon could be put to. The enhancements also tended to focus on arithmetic operations, with only limited relevance to general-purpose computing.

It can be seen that CISC philosophy evolved to the point where it had no route to improving performance except by effectively exploiting multiprocessor architectures.

Table 22.3
Principal features of CISC
CPUs.

1.	Variable length instruction codes
2.	Variable execution time instructions
3.	Complex arithmetical operations
4.	Few CPU registers
5.	Extensive range of instructions
6.	Sophisticated memory addressing modes
7.	Instructions to support procedure handling
8.	Instructions to deal with structured data types
9.	Error checking instructions
10.	Microcoded CU
11.	Complex interrupt support facilities

This approach to improving computing has been the subject of intense research for many years, and still fails to deliver easy rewards. The problem centres on the programmer's task. With only a single CPU to deal with, whether RISC or CISC, the code can be planned in a serial fashion. One of the advantages of the RISC approach to parallel processing, through the provision of pipeline decoders within the CPU, has been that the programmer can ignore it and still benefit from improved performance.

With microcode it is possible, without changing any hardware, to offer the ability to execute programs written in different machine instruction sets. Only the CU microcode would have to be changed between program runs. Although this might initially seem like an interesting idea, having a single machine to execute *any* program, it has rarely been exploited with any commercial success. Most cases of (say) running VAX microcode on a Hewlett-Packard minicomputer are traced back to academic or research institutes, where aims and motivations tend to be more speculative! In fact it was soon discovered that writing microcode was more difficult, expensive and error-prone than writing assembler, which you already know is considerably more difficult that writing HLL code! Thus, it was recognized that buying a new CPU which had been specifically designed for a particular instruction set was more efficient than trying to refit the old CPU to the new software. With the introduction of cheap, mass-produced microprocessors, the idea was largely forgotten, and with the adoption of non-microcoded RISC processors the proposal that users might want to modify their own microcode was apparently buried. However, as we saw in Section 2.11, the possibility of reconfiguring hardware is now practicable with the availability of EPLDs (Erasable Programmable Logic Devices). This means that even the hardware decoding circuits used within RISC control units could, theoretically, be made modifiable by the user. This would turn us back towards the days when electronic engineers designed different hardware circuits to carry out different tasks. If such activities could be made as cheap, efficient and flexible as von Neumann's vision of a general-purpose machine capable of doing *anything* by virtue of the running program, the industrial situation might alter radically in the future.

22.6   MC68000 memory – family variations

The maximum memory addressing range is determined by the width of the address bus. But the original MC68000 designers had difficulty in obtaining a package with enough pins to accept all 32 bits of the full address, so the first MC68000 was provided with only 24 address pins. This clearly limited the memory to 16 Mbyte, but that was considered adequate until larger packages with more solder pins became available. With the arrival of the MC68020, the full 32 bit address was revealed, enlarging the memory space to 4 Gbyte.

68000	24 bit	16 Mbyte
68008	20 bit	1 Mbyte, also limited to an 8 bit data bus
68010	24 bit	16 Mbyte
68020	32 bit	4 Gbyte
68040	32 bit	4 Gbyte
68300	24 bit	16 Mbyte

Each byte in memory has its own 32 bit address, but the MC68000 data bus was 16 bits wide which allowed 2 byte words to be read in a single memory access operation. Making the data bus wider can increase the performance of a computer if the CPU is fast enough, which nowadays is generally the case. When dealing with structured data (data items comprising more than single bytes), there must always be a declared policy for the storage arrangements in memory. A word is the simplest form of data structure, comprising two bytes: least significant (LS) and most significant (MS). Motorola adopted the policy of storing words in memory with the MS byte below the LS byte (see Fig. 22.6). Some further confusion arose from the fact that the lower, even, byte emerges on the upper half of the bus.

Fig. 22.6
Byte, word and long
addressing for MC68000.

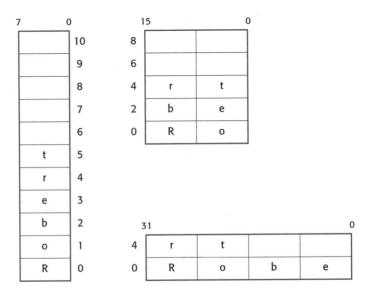

The arrangement of the MS and LS bytes within a word only matters to a programmer in certain special circumstances. Mostly the compiler understands the arrangement and organizes the data correctly. The situation most likely to throw up such a 'byte ordering' problem is when a data file is transferred to a different host computer. Then care has to be taken when re-reading the data in order to retrieve it correctly. Sometimes the simplest approach is to generate a recognizable test file and run a few experiments on it.

Another issue that arises with data items of more than a single byte length is that of 'alignment'. This refers to the constraints imposed on the start point for structured data. The MC68000 did not allow a 2 byte data word to start at an odd address, a constraint that was removed by Motorola when it introduced the MC68020. This need to always start supra-byte variables at even address boundaries is a major source of run-time addressing errors with novice assembler programmers!

In the MC68000, all the IO ports are given individual memory addresses as if they were simply bytes of memory. This scheme, called Memory Mapping, has advantages and disadvantages for programmers and was discussed in Section 6.8. To prevent the IO ports breaking up the continuous sequence of linear memory space, it is common to position all the IO ports together within the top page of memory, but this arrangement does vary from machine to machine. A special instruction, MOVEP is provided on the MC68000 to assist programs accessing sequences of byte-wide IO ports, but there are no special IO port instructions as found with the Pentium.

There is some confusion possible with the use in mnemonic source code of position labels rather than absolute memory addresses. The assembler will read the program source file containing labels and may attempt to replace the references to *logical* labels with *absolute* address values. This can only work if the final position of the executable code in memory is already known. There are two approaches to this issue, and once again Intel and Motorola part company in their chosen solutions! From the start, Motorola intended the MC68000 machine code to be 'position-independent'. This means that the executable file can be loaded anywhere in memory and it will still run without having to make any adjustments to the addresses referenced. This achievement is due to the provision of the 'register indirect with index' addressing mode, and in particular the 'PC indirect with index' mode. This allows any references in CALL or JUMP instructions to be expressed in the relative form:

```
100(PC}                 ; 100 forward from here
-$100(PC)               ; 256 back from here
```

Note that Motorola prefers to mark hex numbers with a leading $, while Intel uses a trailing H. The manner of giving directions: second turning on the right, then first house on the left', is more adaptable than that which contains a specific number: '65 Park Avenue'. Thus, the assembler can replace the user-defined labels with RELATIVE address values:

```
bsr CHECK               ; call the subroutine CHECK
bra error2              ; jump to the exit point
```

In these examples the assembler will replace the labels CHECK and error2 with the offset displacements from the branch instructions to the target position. The assembler has to count forward, or backward, to compute the offset. A similar technique is used to reference data. For security reasons the MC68000 hardware cannot reference data variables by offset from PC, so a different register has to be used. For local variables the stack and frame pointers are used, while for the global data in the heap a special data pointer, often A5, is defined:

```
move.l param1(A6),d0  ; read parameter from stack
addq.w #1,count(A6)   ; adjust a local variable within a subroutine
add.b date(A5),d0     ; access a global variable
```

This capability is only supported by CPUs offering the indexed register indirect addressing mode, and it enables the executable code to be loaded and run anywhere in memory without recompiling and relinking. But when absolute memory references are used (move.b d0,$1234) they will tie the program to a particular position in memory. This position may not always be available because of other programs which have already been loaded.

An alternative approach to this 'relocatability' issue was adopted by Intel for the 8086, and subsequently the Pentium. Special segment registers were included in the CPU: DS, CS, SS and ES. They behave in some ways much the same as the data pointer, A5, in the MC68000 example above. The executable code is loaded into an available area of memory and the CS register set to point to the start of the code. Then DS is set to point to the start of the data area containing the global heap. Similarly, a stack area is allocated and indicated by SS. Because the addresses referred to in the program are always treated as offsets from the base pointers, it appears to the CPU that the program and data are located at address 0. This method is known as segmented addressing and requires that every address going out to memory is added to the appropriate segment pointer before being dispatched. Should you load the program at a different position in memory, only the CS pointer needs to be updated by the operating system loader utility. Segmentation is a rudimentary form of memory management, as discussed in Section 12.5.

Some example assembler code for the MC68000 is listed in Fig. 22.7.

Comparing Fig. 22.7 with Fig. 22.8 (the C equivalent) reminds us of the tremendous advantage that HLL compilers confer, although there are still many pitfalls to avoid when dealing with them.

The small assembler program in Fig. 22.7 just prints the message 'Hello World' on the screen and then waits for the user to hit the Q key before exiting back to the desktop. The C program in Fig. 22.8 achieves the same but with much less effort. The following may help you follow the assembler code: the variable declarations either initialize the space, dc.b "Hello World",0 or reserve empty space by size: ds.b 20.

ASCII strings will require a zero to terminate them. This is the same convention as in C; otherwise the print routines will not know where the end of the string occurs and may continue printing out the whole of memory.

Fig. 22.7
Some example
MC68000 assembler
code.

```
*-------------------------------------------------------------------
* a simple Hello World program
* accessing the UART hardware directly, no O/S support

UART          equ $00FFFF                    base address of UART chip      ⎫
STATUS        equ 1                          UART status register offset    ⎬ constant
DATA          equ 2                          UART data register offset      ⎬ definitions
RXRDY         equ 01                         receive ready status flag      ⎭
TXRDY         equ 02                         transmit ready status flag

              SECTION TEXT
* print a null terminated string
start:        pea welcome                    *pointer to string parameter on stack
              bsr pstring                    *print the char string
              addq.1 #4,sp                   *scrub parameter from stack

* now wait for the quit key
pause:        bsr getchar
              cmp.b 'Q',D0
              bne pause                       *back for another key input?
                                              *reset back to the monitor program
              jmp 0

* subroutines -----------------------------------------------------------

* enter with pointer to null terminated string as a stack parameter
pstring: move.1 (SP)+,d1                      *pop ret address
              move.1 (SP)+,A0                 *pop string pointer
              move.1 d1,-(SP)                 *push ret address back on stack
more:         tst.b (A0)                      *test for null terminator
              beq endos                       *return if end of string
              move.b (A0)+,D0
              bsr putchar
              bra more
endos:        rts

*enter with char in D0, block until send
putchar: btst #2,UART+STATUS *check tx ready
              beq putcha
              move.b D0,UART+DATA *output data
              rts

*block until received char in d0
              getchar: btst #0,UART+STATUS *check for rx char
              beq getchar
              move.b UART+DATA,D0 *input data
              rts

*data variables declaration area -----------------------------------

              SECTION DATA                                             ⎫
              EVEN                                                     ⎬ Variables
                                                                       ⎭
welcome  dc.b "Hello world ! ",13,10,0
*-------------------------------------------------------------------
```

Fig. 22.8
The C equivalent of
Fig. 22.7.

```c
#include <studio.h>
void main()
{
    printf("Hello World\n");
    while ('Q' != getchar()) { };
}
```

Review

- Microcontrollers, which include CPU, memory and IO ports, on a single chip are of increasing commercial importance.

- The MC68300 range of microcontrollers is also an example of a CISC CPU, containing a version of the MC68000 CPU.

- The MC68000 is classified as CISC because it has a microcoded CU, variable length instruction, only 16 CPU registers and complex addressing modes.

- CISC CPUs attempt to improve performance by migrating functionality down from software into hardware.

- This did not really work because better use could be made of the CPU chip area taken up by the microcode needed for less frequently used instructions.

- Complex instructions need complex microcode to carry them out, which resulted in even the simple instructions taking longer.

- The MC68000 CPU, like the Pentium, has progressed through many stages of development, from 68000 to 68060.

Practical work

The end-of-semester review takes place instead of lab work.

Exercises

1. What is the difference between a microcontroller and a microprocessor? Does a microcontroller have to be von Neumann CISC in design? Are there any RISC-based microcontrollers?

2. List the five categories of machine instruction type and then allocate the following MC68000 instructions to the correct category:

   ```
   move.w D0,CCR        movep.b D0,(A0)
   addq.b #1,D0         cmp #10,D0
   bra DONE             bsr DOIT
   trap #10             reset
   ```

3. Why are addressing modes more important for CISC than RISC CPUs? Explain the addressing modes used in this instruction: ADD.L (A0)+,D3. In what circumstances might a compiler utilize this instruction?

4. In what ways are RISC compilers more CPU-specific than CISC compilers?

5. What is the principal advantage to programmers of PC relative addressing? The Pentium does not have such a mode. How does it offer code relocation?

6. Which addressing mode do you consider the fundamental mode? Why?

7. How many addressing modes could be used in the execution of a single MC68000 instruction? Explain the term 'effective address'.

8. What addressing modes are used in the following instructions:

```
move.l d0,d1         add.b #50,d0
cmp.b d0,(a0)        movem.l d0-d3,-(sp)
bsr fred0            move.w count,d6
```

9. Explain the use of the MC68000 `dbra` instruction. If you wanted to loop 10 times, what would be your initial and final loop counter values?

10. Explain the action of the MC68000 `cmp` instruction.

11. What role do the CPU status flags play during program execution? In CISC processors they can be seen as a means of communication between the ALU and the CU. Is it the same in a RISC processor?

Readings

- Heuring and Jordan (1997), Section 3.3: introduces the MC68000 as a CISC microprocessor.

- Any MC68000 assembler book for explanations and examples of assembler routines.

- For those interested in trying out some MC68000 assembler, but without access to the appropriate hardware, there are also several 68k emulator environments which run on PC/Pentiums. Try these sites:

    `http://www2.ncsu.edu/eos/service/ece/project/bsvc/www/`

    `http://winston.fatal-design.com/`

    `http://www.complang.tuwien.ac.at/nino/stonx.html`

    Such software hosted by 200 MHz PC systems can run much faster than the original 16 MHz Atari ST equipment, so playing legacy games can be a real challenge!

- The Web sites can be accessed via the Companion Web site for this book at:

    `http://www.booksites.net/williams/`

Appendix: Microsoft Visual C++ Developer Studio

1 Microsoft Visual C++ Developer Studio – about installation

The CD-ROM included with this text contains a student edition of Microsoft Visual C++ Developer Studio, version 6. The installation takes some time and involves keyboard interaction, so you need to be prepared to watch over it for about 45 minutes. You cannot simply start it off and come back later in the hopeful expectation that it will have successfully completed! The installation demands a minimum of 50 Mbyte of disk space, with a further 150 Mbyte required for the online documentation. More is required if you decide to include all the options.

The online help system is well worth the space, both for novices and experienced programmers. Microsoft have unified all the documentation under the banner of MSDN (Microsoft Developer Network) and made it HTML browser-compatible, so you can read it using Internet Explorer or Netscape Navigator. Further information is provided at the Microsoft Web site: `http://www.microsoft.com/msdn/`.

Before you start the installation make sure you do have enough disk space and that you are logged in with **administrator permissions**. If you do not have sufficient permissions the installation will be blocked from the start. It is highly recommended to distinguish your roles of systems administrator and user/programmer by having two different login IDs and passwords in order to avoid some of the worst accidental disasters.

The CD-ROM will auto-run, so to inspect the contents before running the installation wizard you need to insert the CD-ROM after your system has loaded and then right-click on the CD drive icon. This will then allow you to select the Explore file browser and view the CD-ROM directory (Fig. 1). Note the file `setup.exe` in the top directory of the CD-ROM. This is the installation wizard for Visual C++. However, it does not seem to install the documentation automatically. To make this available on your machine you will need to go into the directory `Msdn_vcb` and run a second `setup.exe`. This can be done at any time after you have installed the Developer Studio.

Fig. 1
Installation CD-ROM
for Microsoft
Developer Studio
v6.0.

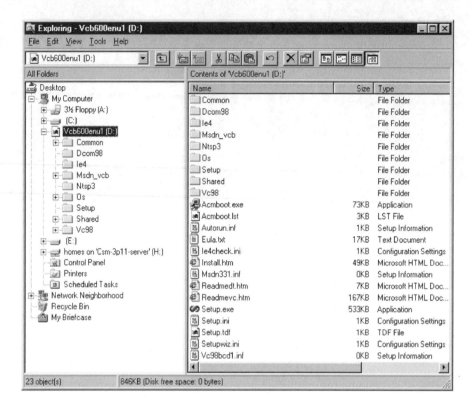

2   Installation

If you are ready, turn on your computer and login as administrator. If necessary, close down all other applications. Insert the CD-ROM in the drive. From the desktop, double click on the 'My Computer' icon and then double click on the CD-ROM icon. The Installation Wizard will start immediately.

1.   Installation Wizard for Visual C++ 6.0 Introductory Offer
      The 'View Readme' button displays some interesting text which is worth looking through when you have time.

2.   End User License Agreement Display
      You have to accept this!

3.   Installation Wizard for Visual C++ 6.0 Introductory Offer
      The Product Number and User Id panel.

4.   Uninstall Developer Studio 97
      If you are reinstalling Visual C++ and you have an earlier version already present on your system, the wizard offers several options. You can delete the previous

software (requiring a system restart), install the new Version 6 software in a different location and so have access to both, or abort the installation.

5.   If you have an earlier version of VC++ and decide to delete it, the system will reboot in order to update the registry. Remember to login in as administrator and leave the CD-ROM in the drive.

6.   Installation Wizard for Visual C++ 6.0 Introductory Offer
     The wizard will take up the installation where it left off if a delete–reboot operation was selected, offering you the possibility of choosing a special destination folder for the installation. The default is `C:\Program Files\ Microsoft\Visual Studio\Common`. It is at this point that the disk space requirement is displayed.

7.   Microsoft Visual C++ Setup
     An information panel flashes up for a moment.

8.   Microsoft Visual C++ Introductory Setup
     A warning panel suggests that all other active applications should be closed down.

9.   Microsoft Visual C++ Introductory Setup
     The individual product 20 digit code is displayed. Make a note of this number and keep it with the disc.

10. Microsoft Visual C++ Introductory Setup
     The wizard offers various levels of installation through the options: **Custom** or **Typical**. Custom allows you to specifically select different software facilities which may be needed for your work.

11. Microsoft Visual C++ Introductory Setup
     Agree to modifying your Environmental Variables setup.

12. Microsoft Visual C++ Information Display
     The file copying now takes place, with a progress bar keeping you informed.

13. Microsoft Visual C++ Introductory Setup
     When debugging code under Windows NT it is useful to have symbols from both your code and the library functions. This can be done if you allow the wizard to copy some extra files at this point. This is not essential, but it is occasionally useful when single-stepping through code.

14. Microsoft Visual C++ Introductory Setup
     The system is now set up.

15. System Restart Request
     Windows NT does require restarting to fully install new software. This can be annoying to those eager to try out their new Developer Studio software! However, now is probably a good time to install the online documentation, before you reboot the system.

16. Return to the My Computer panel and right-click the CD drive. Select Explore and identify the directory msdn_vcb, situated at the top level. Start up the executable setup.exe found inside this folder. This is the documentation installation wizard.

17. Microsoft Visual C++ 6.0 Documentation Setup

18. Microsoft Visual C++ 6.0 Documentation Setup
Your name and organization will be requested, and the registration number previously issued for the software redisplayed.

19. End User License Agreement Display
You have to accept this.

20. Microsoft Visual C++ 6.0 Documentation Setup
The size of the documentation files is displayed (140 Mbyte, minimum)

21. Microsoft Visual C++ 6.0 Documentation Setup
The file copying now takes place, with a progress bar keeping you informed.

22. When the wizard has finished you can remove the CD. Depending on when you actually carried out the software installation you may now need to reboot your system to complete the installation. Otherwise, Developer Studio will be available from Start → Programs → Visual C++ v6 or by clicking on the executable MSDev98.exe held in the folder:

```
C:\Program Files\Visual Studio\Common\MSDev98\bin
```

You can create a useful desktop icon for Developer Studio by click-dragging the MSDev98.exe executable onto the desktop. This will make life easier for you in the future. You can edit the icon text label if you wish.

3   Microsoft Developer Studio – creating simple C programs

The Microsoft Developer Studio is an **IDE** (Integrated Development Environment). It offers more than simply an editor, compiler and linker. It supports large system development through Workspaces and Projects. There is also an inbuilt make facility to assist with compiling and linking. So before starting to write code you must organize some directory space on the hard disk to accept your work. Plan ahead when organizing your directories. Estimate how many projects you will be requiring and think carefully about the titles you are going to use. Never use: test.c, prog.c, final_1.c. Make a note in your lab folder of the location of your work on the hard disk. If you are sharing a directory, it is not unusual to waste time by inadvertently trying to debug someone else's program which has been given the same name as

Fig. 2
Welcome to the
Visual C++ Developer
Studio.

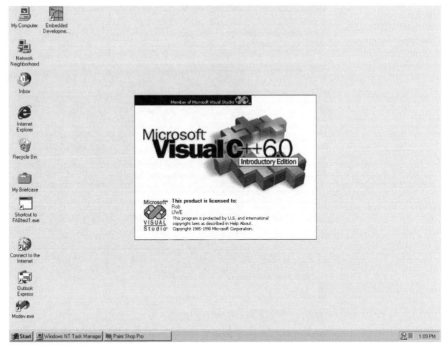

yours. (Indeed, on Unix there is a system program called `test` in the `/bin` directory to further confuse novices!)

To open Developer Studio, click on the desktop icon or select the program name using the Start button menu. The Welcome screen (Fig. 2) will appear while the program is loading.

Be warned that if you are working on a college network, the Developer Studio program may be stored on a central server computer. This will hold all the shared software on a single disk, making administration and maintenance much simpler. In this case the drive might be F: or G: or H: in place of C:.

The opening screen (Fig. 3) is not very exciting, displaying the title bar, pull-down menus and some buttons.

As usual with Microsoft programs, the small icon buttons have associated explanatory names which appear after a couple of seconds if the mouse pointer is positioned above them. Perhaps somewhat annoyingly, the same action can often be selected from the main pull-down menu, a keyboard short-cut, or by clicking on a menu bar icon. It is your choice!

Before you can start typing in C code, a small amount of housekeeping is required to declare your new Project. To start a Project, select File → New from the main Developer Studio menus. Then ensure that the Project tab is uppermost and select Win 32 Console Application . This will allow you to compile and run simple DOS-type applications. To start with, it is better not to venture into the development of full Windows applications because of the extra complexity involved. A few Console options are offered by Developer Studio (Fig. 4). I recommend that you select 'An empty project'

Fig. 3
Microsoft Visual C++
Developer Studio
without a project.

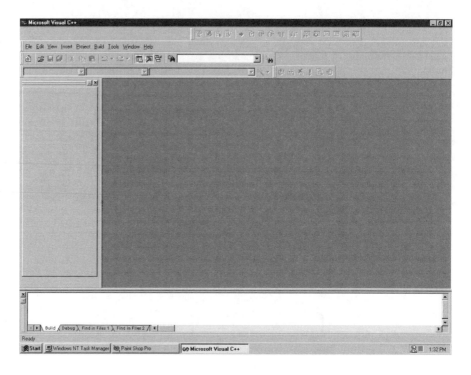

Fig. 4
Console Application
options.

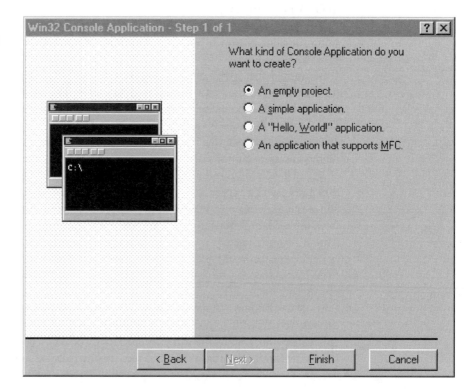

while you are still getting to grips with the environment. The 'Hello, World!' wizard removes all the challenge!

Developer Studio requires that you declare a name for each project that you work on. This becomes an important point of reference, so take some time to think of a distinctive name which will not clash with earlier or subsequent projects. You might plan out your work to use a similar directory structure to that illustrated in Fig. 5. You can see from Fig. 6 that the project name is used to set up a new subdirectory, so make sure that you enter the correct directory/folder location for your new project. It is quite easy to lose your code on an 8 Gbyte disk! There is a default directory, but using this can lead to confusion and muddle.

After you have declared a Project, you can open a new file to receive the code that you will enter into the editor. Select File → New from the main Developer Studio menus and ensure that the File tab is uppermost. Select C++ Source File and make sure that 'Add to project' is set true. Again you must check that the correct location is showing and then enter a name for the program (Fig. 7), with a .c extension. Do not use a .cpp extension unless you will be developing C++ code. A strange linker error will result if you ignore this advice!

Fig. 5
Example hierarchical
project directory.

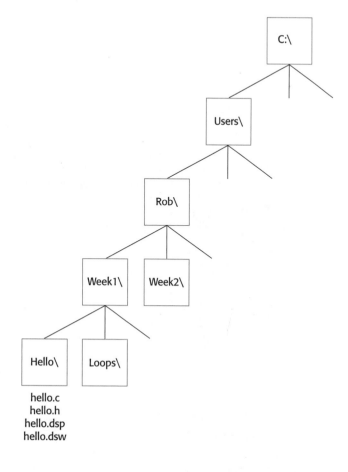

Fig. 6
Starting a new project.

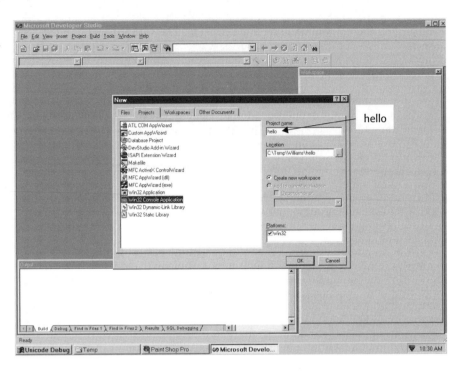

Fig. 7
Starting a new C
program.

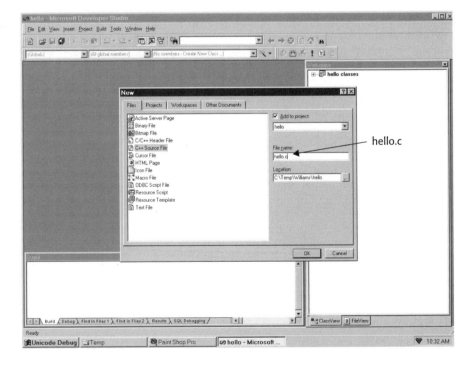

Enter the traditional C program:

```
#include <stdio.h>

int main(void)
  {
    printf("Hello World!\n");
    return 0;
  }
```

Alternatively, in the C++ vein of coding, you could use the equivalent:

```
#include <iostream.h>

int main(void)
  {
    cout << "Bonjour tout le monde\n";
    return 0;
  }
```

But remember to use the .cpp extension when you name the source file.

This editor (Fig. 8) is quite nice (although my favourite editor is still emacs), with help facilities and integrated debugging information available when required. There

Fig. 8
The editor window.

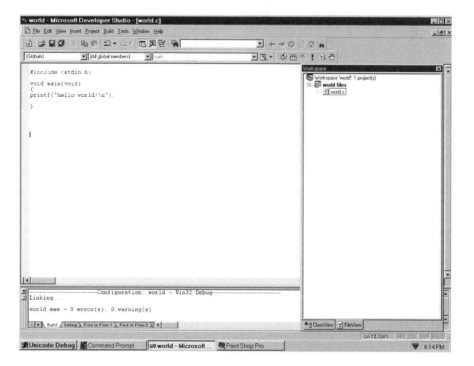

are three main display windows. The code editor window is self-explanatory. To the side is the Viewer window, which can present three different displays: ClassView, FileView or InfoView. The latter provides access to online documentation. ClassView displays your Workspace organized by Classes, which will be useful when you start to use full C++, while FileView displays your Workspace organized as files. Towards the bottom of the screen is the Results window, displaying the output from the compiler and linker. It is also used during debugging sessions.

Note that pressing the Home key takes you to the beginning of a line and End to the end of a line.

Selecting text by swiping with the left mouse button enables the ^X (cut), ^C (copy) and ^V (paste) keyboard options.

The online help facility (Fig. 9) is one of the most impressive features when you first come to use Developer Studio. Placing the cursor on a keyword and pressing the F1 key will immediately display useful information in the information window.

If you simply wish to compile the program in order to check the syntax, you can select the toolbar icon or ^F7. Should an error then be indicated, F4 allows you to return to the Edit window with the cursor positioned on the line containing the next error.

Fig. 9
The Help window.

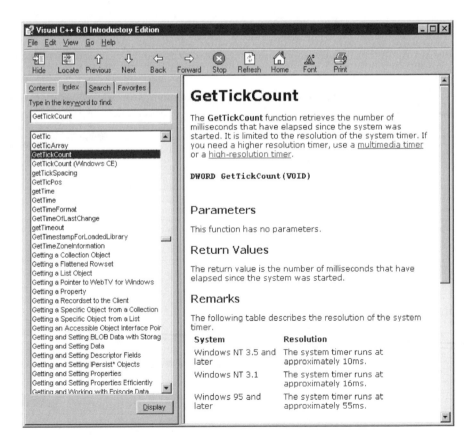

Fig. 10
Building the software.

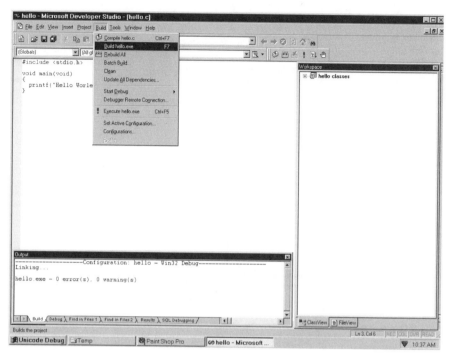

A full compile-and-link, known as a Build (Fig. 10), is again accomplished using a toolbar icon or the keyboard shortcut F7.

To run the code, press ^F5 or select the ! icon; Fig. 11 shows the output.

To get a flavour of Windows programming into the Hello World phase of your programming career, you could attempt the following example. Start a new project:

Fig. 11
Screen output when code in Fig. 10 is executed within Developer Studio.

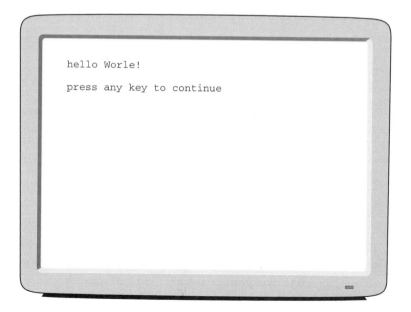

Fig. 12
Your first Windows
application.

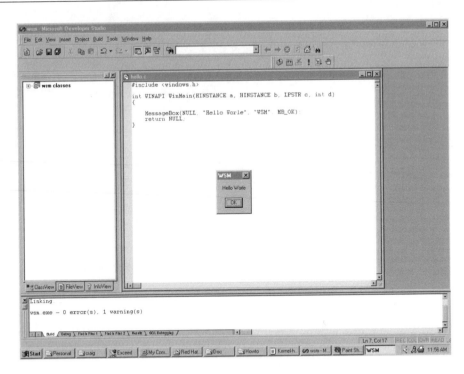

select File → New → Project for Win32 Application. Check the name and location of the project. Then start a new file File → New → File with C++/C Source. Type in the code and Build the program (the output is shown in Fig. 12):

```
#include <windows.h>

int WINAPI WinMain(HINSTANCE a, HINSTANCE b, LPSTR c, int d)
{
  MessageBox(NULL, "Hello Worle!", "WSM", MB_OK);
  return NULL;
}
```

You could also try compiling and linking this from the command line (C: prompt) as an exercise. Obtain a Command Prompt window from the Start button menu. and change directory to your project: cd C:\Temp\Rob\WSM. Check that you can see your source file, hello.c, using the dir command. Then compile and link it using the command:

```
C:\Temp\Rob\WSM > cl hello.c user32.lib
```

Unfortunately, this may not work, because the PATH environment variables may not be set correctly for the compiler and linker. The easiest way to set the environment correctly is to run a provided batch file and then repeat the cl (compile & link) command.

```
C:\Temp\Rob > C:\Program Files\VisualStudio\VC98\bin\vcvars32.bat
```

It is quite usual, in Unix as well as the PC world, to include a header file with related data and function declarations, in anticipation of linking to a library. Thus if the link fails, with an unhelpful **unresolved externals** error message it could be due to several causes:

1.   The correct header file has not been included, e.g.

```
#include <winbase.h>
```

2.   The correct library has not been inserted into the link list, e.g.

```
FABLIB.lib
```

3.   The PATH to the library directory is incorrect, e.g.

```
c:\Program Files\VisualStudio\VC98\lib
```

When you are trying to use a WIN32 system call, such as Sleep( ), you need to know which header file and library to nominate. The simplest way to achieve this is to use the Help → Search facility. Search for the keyword in question, or a related topic, and then left-click on the system call itself when you have it displayed in the title box of the Search/Index panel. This will bring up the InfoViewer Topic page with a short description of the function's action. But much more usefully, click on the Quick Info button! Immediately, and in plain format, you will see the necessary header file and library titles (Fig. 13).

Fig. 13
Getting information about library and header files.

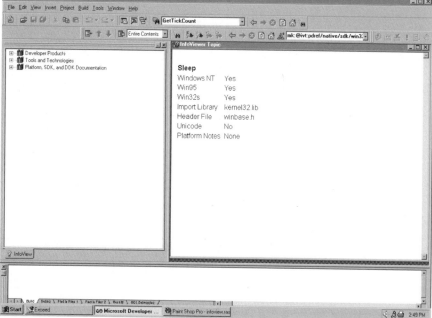

If the program compiles and links without problem, but still does not perform as intended, there is a need for the debugger! Using run-time debuggers always requires the appropriate compiler flags to be set before compiling the code. In Developer Studio this option is the default, but it is worth checking the setup by selecting Build → Config; see Figs. 14–16.

Within Developer Studio, there are various keyboard shortcuts which may take your fancy:

^S   Save file
^F7   Compile file
F4   Go to next error in edit window
F7   Build (compile and link) program
^F5   Run the program

F9   Set breakpoint
F10   Single step over functions
F11   Single step through functions
F1   Get help on marked item

Fig. 14
Switching on debug information.

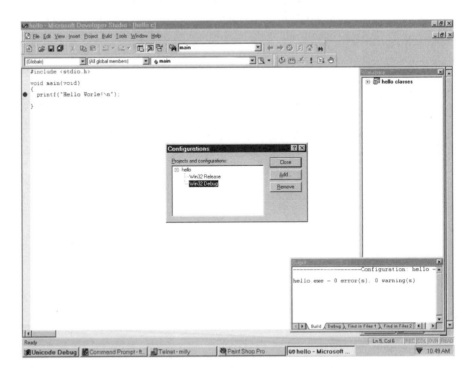

Fig. 15
Starting a debugging
session.

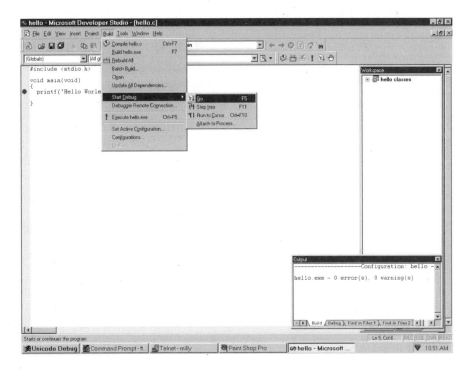

Fig. 16
Visual C++ Developer
Studio debugger.

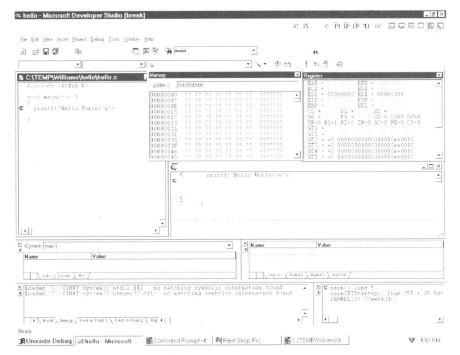

Glossary

10BaseT   The 10 Mbps Ethernet standard which uses a star topology with twinned twisted pair cables and central switches or hubs.

Absolute path name   A fully presented file access address, e.g. `/projects/rob/book/ch_01` or `F:\users\staff\rob\hello.c`.

Access time   The time period required by a storage unit to respond to an access request.

Accumulator   The principal data register in the CPU used for arithmetic and other general manipulation of variables. Known as EAX in the Pentium.

ACL   Access control list: a list of acknowledged users associated with a file or directory. Specific capabilities – read, write, execute – may also be included. All other users are excluded.

Active   The state of the task (process) which is currently being executed by the processor.

ADC   Analogue to digital converter: used to interface analogue signals to digital computers.

Address   A unique name or number identifying a specific memory location inside a computer.

Addressing mode   The method used to form an address to access a data item either in memory or a CPU register.

Address register   A CPU register holding the address of an item in memory in order to access it, e.g. `mov [EDI],0`.

Address unit   The hardware unit within the processor that calculates instruction and data item addresses.

Address width   The number of bits comprising an address.

ALE   Address latch enable: a control bus signal which indicates when the address bus is carrying a valid address.

Algorithm   A sequence of instructions to solve a problem.

ALU   Arithmetic logic unit: hardware circuitry inside the CPU to carry out logical and arithmetic instructions.

AM   Amplitude modulation: a technique of transmitting a signal by superimposing it onto the amplitude (power level) of a carrier wave.

Analogue   The representation of a value using a magnitude from a corresponding system of continuous values; for example, using a voltage to represent the temperature.

API   Application programming interface: a set of library functions made available to application programs to facilitate various activities, e.g. graphics, process scheduling, Internet access.

Application program   A computer program which is executed to perform some task required by a user, but which is not directly concerned with the management of the computer system.

Arithmetic logic unit   *See* ALU.

ASCII   American Standard Code for Information Interchange. Uses 7 bits (sometimes 8) to represent the basic character set.

Assembler   A program that translates an assembly mnemonic language file into the equivalent machine level program made up of binary codes.

Assembly language   A computer language consisting of statements written using mnemonics and labels which have a one-to-one correspondence with machine level instructions.

Associative memory   A memory accessed not by a numerically sequenced address, but by a unique prearranged identifier.

Asynchronous bus   A bus working without a synchronizing master clock.

Asynchronous handshake   A technique of coordinating and controlling the transmission of data using an acknowledgement signal returned by the receiver to the message sender.

Asynchronous transmission   Serial communication without a shared clock. The receiver depends on the occasional signal code to resynchronize (the phase rather than the frequency) its local clock, e.g. a START bit or SFD bit.

ATM   Asynchronous transfer mode: a protocol that transmits data in short, fixed-length packets referred to as cells.

Availability   The proportion of time during which the critical functions of a system are not denied the user due to failure or planned maintenance.

Backward channel   A data channel in the reverse direction to the primary flow. It may employ a much lower rate. It operates in full duplex mode.

Bandwidth   The range of frequencies which a channel can use for transmitting data. Channels have maximum and minimum cut-off frequencies, e.g. 300–3300 Hz for ordinary telephone lines. When dealing with digital channels it is more common to express bandwidth in bps (bits per second) instead of Hz.

Barrel shifter   A circuit used in ALUs to shift and rotate binary patterns sideways.

Base address   The starting address of a data structure, eg. the address of the first item in an array.

Baseband transmission   A system of transmission in which information, encoded into suitable waveforms, is sent directly over a channel without using higher frequency modulation techniques.

Batch file   A file containing shell commands for the operating system.

Batch processing   A traditional method of data processing in which jobs are queued to run with no online user interaction allowed. It can still be found in payroll and billing offices.

Baud rate   The rate at which symbols are sent over a channel.

Beam scanning   Controlling the sideways movement of a beam to draw out a raster on a screen.

Big-endian   The format for multi-byte integers which stores the LSB (Least Significant Byte) at the higher address and the MSB (Most Significant Byte) at the lower position. Used by Motorola and Sun.

Binary   A number system to Base 2, using only the symbols '0' and '1'.

BIOS   Basic input–output system: a set of routines to control the input and output of data. Often found in EPROM, along with the bootstrap routines, on the motherboard.

Bit   A binary digit: 0 or 1. The smallest quantity of information.

Bit pattern   A sequence of bits used to represent a data item or instruction.

Bit rate   The rate at which bits are transferred across a channel. Measured in bits per second (bps).

Block checksum   An error detection method which involves calculating a check number using a block of the original data. The value is recomputed after the period of risk, and should the original check number agree with the later value it is concluded that no error has occurred.

Blocking   The technique, sometimes desirable, used to halt the progress of a program when the required data is not available.

Bootstrap   A program which, when executed, loads a larger, more complex program and then transfers control to that program.

BPL   Branch prediction logic: a technique employed within CPUs to 'guess' which path a conditional branch (IF-ELSE) will follow in order to provide correct instruction pre-fetching.

Bridge   A hardware unit used to link two similar LANs, transferring packets between them.

Broadband signalling   The transmission of data using carrier wave modulation, such as AM, FM or PM or a combination of the three.

Broadcast routing Transmitting data to all listeners, assuming that only the assignee will read the contained data.

Buffer A data area of memory which is used for temporary storage of data items. It may be used to compensate for a difference in speed between the source and destination.

Bundles A 128 bit word containing three 32 bit Itanium instructions, with associated predicate values and compiler template code to organize parallel execution.

Bursting The transferring of several items of data in rapid sequence, thus eliminating the need for separate setup procedures for all the items.

Bus A set of electrical wires used to connect units. The attachment is *common*, not point-to-point.

Byte Eight bits.

Cache Fast local store to speed up memory accesses.

Cache write-through The data caching strategy of rewriting all changed items immediately to primary memory.

Cardinal A positive whole number.

Carrier A continuous, usually sinusoidal, signal sent over a communication channel. Information is imposed on it by varying an intrinsic parameter: frequency, amplitude or phase. On reception the information signal is extracted from the carrier by demodulation.

CCITT International Telecommunications Committee, now referred to as ITU-T.

C flag A CPU condition code indicating that a numeric 'carry out' has occurred in a previous operation.

Cells ATM packets.

Central processing unit CPU: the principal component of any computer, e.g. Pentium, SPARC.

CGI Common gateway interface: a standard for interfacing executable programs into HTML Web pages.

Channel A communication path over which information may be sent.

CHS Cylinder, head, sector: the disk data addressing scheme using physical location numbers.

Circuit switching A technique used in networks whereby a physical pathway is opened up between sender and receiver for the duration of the call. Telephones operate in this way.

CISC Complex instruction set computer, e.g. MC68000.

CLI Command line interface: the program which provides the user interface, e.g. the C shell.

Client the requesting partner in a client–server system.

Client–server A computing paradigm that divides the workload between client software, usually stored on your workstation, and the larger server computer. It started with the X Window system and Unix.

Clock pulse A regularly pulsed signal which is used to synchronize the activities of a number of units.

Cluster A block of data comprising several disk sectors, grouped together for more convenient accessing.

Codec An ADC/DAC used in telephony applications, often including a nonlinear compression function.

COM1, COM2 The PC serial ports.

Combinatorial logic Digital logic circuits which involve no memory devices, e.g. no flip-flops.

Command register The initialization register found in IO chips which determines the actions to be taken.

Common channel A signalling channel shared by several data channels.

Compiler A program which translates a file of HLL instruction codes into the equivalent set of machine instructions.

Conditional branch A jump, or transfer of program control, that depends on the status of one or more condition flags.

Condition codes Single-bit flags that indicate the result or status of an operation.

Control statement A statement that affects the execution path selected by a program, e.g. IF-ELSE.

Control unit CU: an important part of the CPU which carries out the fetch–execute cycle. It coordinates all the activities of the computer.

CPU *See* Central processing unit.

CRC   *See* Cyclic redundancy check.

Critical resource   An item of data or a device which may be used simultaneously by several tasks, or execution threads, thus leading to a possible corruption error.

CRT   Cathode ray tube: the display unit in a television or non-flat-screen monitor.

CSMA/CD   Carrier sense, multiple access/collision detect: the access protocol for Ethernet LAN, which uses no master arbitrator but relies on each attached host respecting the equal priority of all other hosts on the LAN.

CU   *See* Control unit.

Cycle time   The period of time taken to complete a single part of a repetitive sequence.

Cyclic redundancy check   CRC: a checksum technique, using modulo-2 division, which detects errors and which may also identify the bits which have been affected.

Cylinder   In multiple platter disk units, tracks of the same radius are termed a cylinder.

DAC   Digital to analogue converter.

Database   A collection of information organized around a common subject.

Datagram   A packet delivery service which routes each packet as it arrives, with no prior route plan. UDP is such a service.

Data register   A register which is used to hold data. If it is in the CPU, it is temporarily holding variables or intermediate results.

Debugger   A tool to assist with the diagnosis of run-time errors. They normally provide detailed displays of the state of CPU registers and active memory areas.

Decoder   A logic circuit which selects one of its outputs using an input number.

Dedicated polling   The programming technique which commits the code to a tight status-checking loop.

Demand paging   A virtual memory scheme which only reads sections (pages) of code or data from disk into main memory when they are actually needed.

de Morgan's theorem   The rules which allow AND and OR gates to be swapped in a circuit, with adjustments to associated inverters.

DIMM   Dual in-line memory module, a small card with a 168 pin connector carrying several DRAM memory chips. Currently available with up to 128 Mbyte of memory.

Direct addressing   The addressing mode where the effective address is provided explicitly with the instruction.

Directory   A table which links the name of a file to the numeric address which can be used to access the data.

Dirty bit   A status flag indicating that an item of data has been amended.

Disassembly   The method by which binary machine code can be back translated into assembler mnemonics to assist with debugging.

Disk capacity   The quantity of data in bytes that a disk may hold.

DLL   Dynamic link library: object code library modules loaded into memory where they can be used by any running program.

DMA   Direct memory access, whereby data may be transferred along the computer bus directly between one unit and another. Usually it involves data IO. Beyond starting the process off, the central processor does not participate in the transfer.

DNS   Domain naming service: the Internet distributed database service which translates domain names into IP addresses.

Dongle   A small box which plugs into a computer port. It contains a memory device with a code number which is used to verify the licensed status of a program.

Download   Receive information from a remote computer.

DRAM   Dynamic read–write random access memory.

Driver   The software used to interface to a device, usually part of the operating system.

DSL   Digital subscriber line: a new range of higher speed modem equipment capable of transferring data at between 150 kbps and 8 Mbps.

DSP   Digital signal processor: a special design of CPU intended for computational applications dedicated to the analysis of complex waveforms, e.g. speech analysis.

DTMF   Dual tone multi-frequency: telephone keypad signalling standard.

Duplex channel   Two-way simultaneous transmission. Both directions at the same time.

Dynamic linking   The deferral of linking application code to object libraries until run time.

ECC   Error-correcting codes.

Echo   The despatch of received information back to the sender for verification. It also provides a simple means of flow control.

EDO   Extended data output: DRAM which allows the bursting of several adjacent items to speed up average access times.

Effective address   The final address used to access items in memory.

EIDE   Extended integrated drive electronics: the most recent interface standard for hard disks.

emacs   A fully equipped programmer's editor from Richard Stallman's GNU endeavours.

Email   A popular application from the TCP/IP suite. It uses SMTP (simple mail transfer protocol) to route mail between post offices. Popular user front ends include Eudora, Nupop, Elm and PINE.

Embedded processor   A processor dedicated to a particular control task, often physically located within the relevant equipment eg. photocopier, engine control unit, vending machine.

Encryption   The process of security coding messages so that only authorized readers can access the plaintext form of the data.

Environment pointer   The preceding frame base pointer, saved on the stack, which provides access to earlier 'in scope' variables.

EPLD   Erasable programmable logic device: a reconfigurable logic circuit.

Ethernet   The DEC/Intel/Xerox standard for local area networking. It uses CSMA/CD for scheduling accesses.

Ethernet switch   A central hub or switch which interconnects several Ethernet segments, often using 10BaseT cable.

Exception   A general term for a CPU interrupt.

Executable program   A file containing machine instructions which the CU can recognize and carry out.

Executive   A simple form of operating system. Real-time executives are efficient implementations for time-critical applications.

Expansion slot   Slots for extra cards.

Facsimile (fax)   A method of transmitting printed, graphical or other information from a page of a document by scanning the page and coding each point or picture element (pixel). High levels of data compression are used.

Failover   The process of swapping from a failed unit to some alternative piece of equipment.

FAT   *See* File allocation table.

fdisk   MS-DOS disk utility which can partition disks and lay down a Master Partition Boot Record (MPBR). Used before high-level formatting.

FET   Field effect transistor: an electronic switching element, where a small voltage on the gate terminal controls the flow of current between the other two terminals.

Fetch–execute cycle   The sequence of steps, performed continuously by the CPU, by which the next instruction is read back into the CU and obeyed.

FIFO   First in, first out: a data queue

File allocation table (FAT)   An array containing sequences of disk block numbers indicating the blocks allocated to a file. Unallocated blocks are signalled by a NULL entry.

File browser   A utility program which assists with the visualization and organization of directories and general file handling.

Firmware   Programs held in PROM. They often relate to the low-level operations of the hardware.

First come, first served   A very simple scheduling strategy.

Flip-flop   A clocked, synchronous latch which can act as a single-bit memory cell or as a frequency halver.

Floating point   A number scheme used to represent and manipulate numbers that have fractional parts, e.g. 3.123. The accepted format for storing and manipulating floating point numbers is IEEE 754.

Floating point unit   A specialized ALU for floating point arithmetic. It can be part of the CPU or installed separately.

Flow control   The method used by receivers to regulate the transmission of data should it be arriving too rapidly to be processed.

FM   Frequency modulation: a method of transmitting a signal by imposing it on the frequency of a carrier wave.

Forward error correction (FEC)   The correction of errors at the receiver without retransmission. It relies on the original message containing redundant information.

FPU   *See* Floating point unit.

Fragmentation   The undesirable division of available space into units of size too small to be usable.

Frame base pointer   A CPU address register used to indicate the position of the current stack frame holding local variables. The Pentium uses EBP.

FSB   Front side bus: a term derived from the Slot I/II interface but often used to refer to the motherboard clock speed, e.g. 66 or 100 MHz.

FSK   Frequency shift keying: a technique used by modems to transmit binary 1s and 0s represented by distinct acoustic tones.

FTP   File transfer protocol. Part of the TCP/IP suite of applications. FTP is used to download files from remote hosts. Anonymous FTP servers predate the WWW.

Full adder   A three-input, two-output adder circuit.

Functions   Subroutines with a return value.

Garbage collection   A technique used to bring together the fragmented areas of free memory.

Gateway   A hardware unit linking LANs which can make routing decisions using a packet's destination IP address.

Ghostview   A PostScript screen previewer.

Gopher   A menu-based client–server information retrieval system. There are Gopher browsers that connect to Gopher servers. Gopher predates the WWW.

GPRS   General Packet Radio Service: a 170 kbps text transfer facility for cellphones.

Granularity   The size of a subunit.

GSM   Groupe Spécial Mobile de Conférence Européene des Administrations des Postes et des Télécommunications: the digital cellular network.

GUI   Graphical user interface: a WIMP interface.

Half adder   A two-input, two-output adder circuit.

Hamming codes   The use of multiple parity bits to detect errors within a data word and then indicate the position of the affected bit.

Hamming distance   The number of bit positions which need to be changed to obtain another valid number.

Hardware   The electronic circuits or hardware units which form the computer.

Hexadecimal (hex)   An abbreviated representation of four bits. It uses the digits 0–9 and A–F. It is often used to express long binary addresses more conveniently.

High-level language (HLL)   A language designed for problem solving which is independent of the machine architecture, e.g. COBOL, C, C++, Java.

HLL   *See* High-level language.

Host   Another name for a computer.

HTML   Hypertext markup language.

HTTP   Hypertext transfer protocol.

Hub   The central interconnecting unit for Switched Ethernet LAN, probably using 10BaseT cabling.

Hypertext   Text that contains references to other documents through links which start the downloading of the documents across the network from their own hosts. The protocol used is HTTP.

ICMP   Internet Control Message Protocol.

IDC   Insulation displacement connector: a type of ribbon cable connector that does not require soldering.

The connectors have sharp spikes to pierce the plastic insulation and make contact with the copper wires.

IDE   Integrated device electronics: a hard disk interface standard.

IEEE 754   The standard for storage and manipulation of floating point numbers.

Immediate operand   An addressing mode where a constant value is held with the instruction and accessed using the instruction pointer address.

Indexed register addressing   An addressing mode using an address register and offset to access the memory variable.

Indirect addressing   The addressing mode whereby the effective address is already held, often in an address register, pointing to the data in memory.

Initialization   The preliminary phase of processing when devices and data structures are set up.

Input–output (IO)   The interface hardware which is used to connect external devices to the computer bus so that data can be transferred into and out of the computer.

Input–output port   An addressable location at which a hardware device can be accessed, often through a byte-wide latch.

Input port   An addressable location at which a hardware device can be accessed, sometimes through a byte-wide latch.

Instruction   A bit pattern consisting of an operation code and address information used to specify an operation to be performed by the processor.

Instruction hoisting   A compiler technique employed to change the order of program instructions to improve code run time.

Instruction pipeline   The multiple stages of decoding used by modern CUs. A feature of RISC processors.

Instruction pointer   The address register in the CPU that contains the address of the next instruction to be executed. It is known as EIP in the Pentium. Is also referred to as the program counter.

Instruction register   The register in the CPU that holds the instruction which is being executed.

Integer   A number which can have a positive or negative value but no fractional part.

Integrated circuit   Complete electronic circuit, laid out on a sliver of silicon, containing many thousands of miniature transistors.

Interface circuit   A circuit which allows the computer to exchange data with external equipment.

Intermittent polling   The programming technique which enables the code to check a status value at regular intervals.

Internet   A global interconnection of networks.

Interpreter   A program which takes instructions from another file, one at a time, and uses them to select from a repertoire of actions which are available.

Interrupt   A signal which forces the CPU to temporarily abandon the current program and execute a nominated routine (ISR) which relates to the source of interrupt.

Interrupt-driven IO   A programming technique that uses interrupt signals to transfer data into and out from the computer.

Interrupt service routine (ISR)   A subroutine invoked by a hardware interrupt signal or a special software TRAP instruction.

Interrupt vector   An ISR identification number, normally returned by the interrupting device to allow the CPU to select the correct ISR.

IP   Internet Protocol.

IRQ   Interrupt request: the 15 interrupt lines offered by the PC.

ISDN   Integrated Services Digital Network: a standard for totally digital telephone systems.

ISP   Internet service provider: an organization that provides a linkage to the Internet backbone.

ISR   *See* Interrupt service routine.

ITU/TSS   New designation of CCITT.

IVR   Interrupt vector register: register holding an interrupt vector allowing the peripheral to identify its ISR to the CPU.

IVT   Interrupt vector table: memory array (256 entries) holding all the ISR addresses used by the CPU to respond to interrupt requests.

JANET   Joint Academic Network: the UK academic network, which provides Internet access.

Java   The recent object-oriented HLL, of special interest for Internet applications.

Kernel   The very centre of the operating system code. Responsible for process scheduling, interrupt handling and memory management.

Label   A name used to identify an instruction in a program. It is a symbolic address.

LAN   *See* Local area network.

Latch   A storage cell formed by cross-coupling two NOR or NAND gates. Closely related to flip-flops. Sometimes used to refer to a byte-wide device.

LBN   Logical block number: value used to access data blocks on disk.

LCD   Liquid crystal display.

Level 1 cache   The cache memory positioned closest to the CPU.

Level 2 cache   The cache next after Level 1 to the CPU.

Library procedure   A pre-translated procedure held in a library which can be linked to a program to perform some standard unit of processing.

LIC   Line interface card: the circuit which connects to telephone subscriber lines.

LIFO   Last in, first out: a stack data structure.

Linker   The utility program used to bring compiled code together with the required library routines and any external data or ready compiled subroutines.

Linux   A version of Unix written originally by Linus Torvalds and distributed free to enthusiasts. It has now spread to commercial suppliers and is rapidly increasing in popularity.

LINX   London Internet eXchange.

Little-endian   The format for multi-byte integers which stores the MSB (most significant byte) at the higher address and the LSB at the lower position. Used by Intel and IBM.

LIW   Long instruction word: a CU technique used to reduce the decoding delays.

Load address   The address at which a program has been loaded into main memory for execution.

Loader   The system program which loads an executable application program from disk into main memory.

Local area network   LAN, a network extending over distances up to a few kilometres for interconnecting computing and similar equipment, e.g. Ethernet. Typically the routing technique used is that of broadcasting a message with a destination identifier.

Localization   The effect of using parameters to specify the exact action of a subroutine to more closely fit the needs of the caller.

Local variable   An item of data, declared within a function and installed on the stack, which is lost when leaving the function.

Logical address   An address set within an idealized address space which will need to be mapped to physical memory before the program can execute.

Logical block   A unit of data to be written to or read from a disk drive.

Logic gate   A circuit using several transistors to implement a logic function, such as AND, OR or NOT.

Login/logon   A scheme for identifying yourself as a valid user of the system by offering a user ID and password.

LOOK   Local request scheduling algorithm used by hard disk controllers.

Loopback   The technique of routing a channel back on itself for testing purposes.

LRU   Least recently used: a criterion used by operating systems to choose the page or cache line to sacrifice when a new item has to be loaded.

MAC   Media access control: the bottom software layer of the Ethernet interface.

Main memory   The memory containing the executable program and data which the processor accesses during the fetch–execute cycles.

Mainframe   Large, expensive computers, often housed in a secure central location, offering enormous memory and disk storage capacities and often running in batch mode.

make   A utility which assists in the organization and documenting of program building.

makefile   A command file for the make utility.

man pages   A set of online help pages offered by Unix.

Master partition boot record (MPBR)   The first sector of a hard disk containing status information about the disk and its partitions. Written in by `fdisk`.

MC68000   Motorola 68000 32 bit CISC microprocessor.

Memory address register   The address register used to temporarily hold the address of the memory location during a bus transfer.

Memory buffer register   The register into which the data value is copied during a bus transfer.

Memory direct addressing   The addressing mode in which an item in memory is accessed by its address held by the instruction within the program.

Memory management   The planning and implementation of data movements within the computer.

Memory segment   Memory can be divided into characterized blocks for security reasons, e.g. Code Segment, Stack Segment.

Metropolitan area network (MAN)   A network that covers an area the size of a town or city.

Microinstruction   A microprogram instruction held within the CPU used by the CU to decode and action the current machine level instruction.

Microprogram   A program consisting of microinstructions which is used by the CU to perform the actions specified by the machine level instructions which form the processor's instruction set.

Minicomputer   A middle sized computer suitable for a department of about 25 users.

Mnemonic   A short sequence of letters which can be translated into the associated numerical machine code by an assembler.

Modem   Modulator/demodulator: an interface unit for connecting (digital) computers to the (analogue) telephone system in order to transmit data.

Moore's Law   The empirical law formulated by Gordon Moore at Intel, describing the continual increase in VLSI capability.

Motherboard   The large circuit board which holds the CPU, main memory and bus interconnection tracks.

mount   The Unix command used to insert disk storage into a hierarchical file structure. File systems may also be imported using NFS from remote hosts.

Multiplexer   A device which merges several independent channels onto a single higher bandwidth channel.

Multisync monitor   A display monitor which can operate at a range of scanning frequencies.

Nameserver   A means of translating the network name into an IP number. If you use a name/address that your local nameserver does not know, it forwards the request to the next higher level within the domain, until a server is found with the information.

Nesting   The ability to handle several function calls simultaneously, one function calling another.

Network   A group of interconnected computers. The interconnection is usually a common highway, not point to point connections.

Network address   A unique name or number used to identify an attached host in network communications.

NFS   Sun's Network File System. This is a virtual disk system that uses TCP/IP protocol to allow computers on a network to share files and disk space in such a way that it appears to the user as a single seamless file system.

NIC   Network Information Center.

Non-volatile memory   Storage which retains its contents when the electrical power is disconnected. It may use a secondary battery.

NTFS   Windows NT file system.

Object module   A file produced by a compiler which contains executable machine codes, but requires further routines to be linked into it before it can be executed. There may also be address references which need attention.

Offset   The number of bytes that an instruction or data item is displaced from the start of the module or data structure.

Online   The method of accessing a specified computer facility, such as travel enquiries, by logging on remotely to a large host.

Operating system   The software which extends the facilities provided by the hardware in order to assist all users. It is often provided by the original hardware supplier. Examples are Unix and Windows NT.

Operation code (opcode)   A numerical code that indicates the processing to be performed by the CPU.

Optical fibre   A very small-diameter solid glass or plastic tube through which low-powered laser signals may be transmitted for detection at the remote end. Light has a very high frequency ($\sim 10^{27}$ Hz), permitting rapid modulation when used as a carrier.

Order of magnitude   A power of ten. For example: 1000 (10^3) is two orders of magnitude greater than 10 (10^1).

Overflow   The condition where an arithmetic operation gives rise to a result of the wrong sign. For example, the addition of two large positive integers may give a negative result if you are working in a two's complement format.

PABX   Private Automatic Branch Exchange: a customer's telephone switch, routing calls to extension numbers. Commonly computer-controlled and fully digital.

Packet   A block of data with appropriate header information, including destination address and content indicators.

Packet switching   A packet-switched network (PSS) routes data packets without establishing permanent connections. The routing is done on a hop-by-hop basis. At each intermediate node the packet is entirely received and stored before forwarding to the next node.

PADs   Packet assemble and disassemble: the PSS interface unit.

Page   The unit of virtual memory allocation, typically 4 kbyte.

Page table   The look-up table relating physical and logical (virtual) addresses.

Parallel adder   A circuit to add or subtract two binary words.

Parallel port   An IO port, often one byte wide, e.g. the printer port LPT1.

Parallel transmission   The sending of digital information simultaneously over parallel wires, e.g. on a bus.

Parameters   Pre-initialized local variables for subroutines. The caller sets the values for initialization.

Parity bit   An extra redundant bit added to data to ensure that the number is even or odd. This enables a reader to carry out a check for single-bit errors. However, two errors would cancel out and go undetected.

Partition table   The data structure holding information about the layout of information on a disk drive.

Path name   The logical address of a file on disk.

Peer-to-peer   A description of the interaction of software within equivalent strata of a layered system.

Pentium   Intel's last member of the i86 family of CISC processors. It has benefited from the inclusion of RISC features.

Peripheral   External device connected to a computer port, e.g. printer, modem.

Phosphor   Light-emitting chemical used in monitors.

Physical address   The real address of an item in memory.

PIC   Peripheral interrupt controller.

Pipeline processor   A CPU built on RISC lines with multi-stage decoding which effectively supports parallel instruction execution.

Pixel   An isolated single picture element.

Polling   To ask a device to see if it is ready for some action.

Polynomial   The mathematical description of a curve.

POSIX   Portable Operating System Interface: an internationally agreed API or set of operating system calls. It is based on those already provided by Unix rather than Windows. The aim was to offer a programmers' standard which would make the porting of code between different platforms much easier. Unix became the basis for the standard interface because it was not 'owned' by a single supplier. Moreover, because several different variants of Unix existed, there was a strong impetus to develop a set of standard Unix system calls.

PostScript   Page description language developed by Adobe and widely used in laser printers.

Preamble   A sequence of flag bits which precedes a transmission to allow the receiver to synchronize to the transmitter.

Predicate flag   A conditional flag.

Predication   The use of conditional flags to control the execution of all machine instructions.

Pre-fetch buffer   A small on-chip cache to allow instruction read-ahead to keep the CU 100% busy.

Prioritization   Scheduling the execution of routines in priority order.

Procedures   Functions or subroutines.

Process   A program which has been loaded into main memory ready for execution. Also known as a task. It may be running concurrently with other processes.

Process coordination   The ability to synchronize tasks to help them cooperate in some larger activity.

Processor (CPU)   The essential hardware component of a computer system that executes machine level instructions and performs logical and arithmetic operations.

Program counter   Also known as the instruction pointer.

Programmability   The facility to alter the action of a device by loading a new list of commands or a new interconnection schema.

Programmed transfers   The handling of data directly by the CPU under program control, often involving data IO.

PROM   Programmable read-only memory; random access.

Protocols   An agreed set of commands and data formats to facilitate the exchange of data between computers. Rules or conventions governing communications.

PSS   Packet switched system: the data transmission network offered by PTTs.

PSTN   Public switched telephone network: circuit-switched technology.

PTT   Public telephone and telegraph authority, now accepted as a generic term for the local Telephone Operator, e.g. BT, France Telecom, Southern Bell.

QAM   Quadrature phase and amplitude modulation: a high-performance modem technique which combines phase and amplitude modulation methods to enable more data to be transmitted.

Queue   FIFO data structure.

Radix   The number of different digits used in a number system. Decimal notation uses 10 digits (0–9) and therefore is said to have a radix of 10.

RAID   Redundant array of inexpensive disks: configurations to reduce the impact of data errors on stored files.

RAM   Read–write random access memory.

RAMDAC   Digital to analogue conversion circuitry used on graphics cards to drive monitors.

RAM disk   A technique which allows part of main memory to serve as a very fast file store.

Real number   A number which can contain a fractional part. It may be stored in floating point format.

Real-time computing   Processing which is carried out under strict time constraints.

Re-entrant code   Code that is written in such a way that it may be used simultaneously by more than one process. The code is never altered by a process.

Reference parameter   An address parameter.

Refresh cycle   The action required by DRAMs to regenerate the data held on the memory cell capacitors.

Register   A small area of memory, which may be inside the CPU or some other hardware unit.

Register file   The area of memory, usually allocated as stack, which CPU can address rapidly as registers.

Register indirect addressing   The addressing mode that uses an address register to point to a location in memory.

Register window   The area of the register file which is currently active.

Relative path name   The address of a file on disk quoted from the current position.

Repeater   A power amplifier for a large LAN system.

Resource sharing   The need for multitasking systems to equitably and safely use common facilities.

Response delay   The time it takes a unit, such as memory, to return a requested item of data.

Return address   The address used by a subroutine to jump back to the calling code at the end of execution.

RIP   Routing information protocols: used to share Internet routing information.

Ripple-through carry   A situation in which a parallel adder needs to propagate the carry from stage to stage.

RISC   Reduced instruction set computer, e.g. SPARC, ARM.

Roaming   The circumstances where mobile terminals, such as cell phones, can swap over from one base station to another in mid call.

ROM   Read-only random access memory.

root   1. The top level of a hierarchical directory. 2. The administrator on a Unix system.

Rotational latency   The delay incurred while waiting for a disk drive to bring the required data round to the read head.

Router   A network unit which is responsible for rerouting packets to their destination when they are in transit.

Routing table   A dynamic table of information used by routers to forward packets on their journey,

RS232   An Electronics Industry Association standard for slow serial lines, e.g. COM1 and COM2.

SCAN   A hard disk scheduling algorithm.

Scan code   A code that is generated by the keyboard when a key has been pressed or released.

Scheduling   The activity in a computer of deciding which process will run next. The code that actually launches the next process is called the despatcher.

SDRAM   Synchronous burst access DRAM.

Seek time   The average time taken to move a disk drive read head to a new cylinder.

Segments   A unit of data stored on disk, often 512 bytes.

Semantic gap   The yawning chasm between the designer's vision and the capabilities offered by machine instructions.

Semantics   The meaning of something.

Semaphore   An indicating variable which protects shared resources from simultaneous access which may result in data corruption.

Serial communication   Information is sent along a single bit channel, one bit after another.

Server   1. A host computer which offers services of facilities to other systems. 2. The servicing end of the client–server duo.

sh   The original Bourne shell for Unix.

Shell script   A command file intended to be interpreted by a shell, e.g. Perl.

Shortest first   A common scheduling strategy to deal with small jobs first.

Signals   In telephony, signals carry out the call management activities, e.g. call setup, routing and billing.

SIMM   Single in-line memory module, limited to 64 Mbyte on a 72 connector card.

Simulation   The method of running a computer model in order to try out various unknown features of a complex system.

Single stepping   A debugging facility which allows the programmer to slowly execute code, one instruction at a time, observing the results at each step.

Skew   The electronic phenomenon of circuits delaying pulses by unequal times, resulting in parallel buses corrupting the data. It is due to differing propagation characteristics of those channels.

SLIP   Serial line interface protocol: a protocol that lets your computer access the Internet directly via a standard phone line and modem. The point-to-point protocol (PPP) does the same but slightly better.

SMS   The GSM Short Messaging Service, for text messages up to 160 characters long.

Socket   A software structure, used much like a file, giving programs the opportunity to exchange data across a network.

Software interrupts   Interrupts forced by executing an instruction.

Source program   An HLL program that can be translated by a compiler.

Speculative loading   Pre-reading instructions and data in anticipation of the subsequent need.

Spooling   Simultaneous peripheral operation online: the technique of buffering data, for output to a slow printer, on a fast disk. This decoupled the CPU from the time-consuming delays involved in printing.

SRAM   Static RAM.

Stack   A last in, first out data structure (LIFO). The system stack has a dedicated CPU pointer, SP, to speed up the PUSHing and POPping of data items.

Stack frame base pointer   The CPU address register holding the address of the current stack frame containing local variables.

Stack Pointer   The CPU address register holding the address of the top of stack location.

Statement   A unit of instruction in an HLL.

Status register   A register that contains condition flag bits to store the status or result of a previous operation.

Store-and-forward   A transmission technique whereby each node of a network has buffers to hold incoming packets of data.

Subroutine   A collection of instructions which perform a job. It may be invoked many times by different callers.

Swap space   Area reserved on disk to hold any overflow should main memory be too small.

Switch   An exchange. Equipment which physically routes communications traffic.

Symbol table   A table used within a compiler or assembler to hold the names of variables and procedures together with the offset within the module. It is used by the linker.

Synchronous bus   A interconnection highway for several units which all operate following the signal distributed from a central clock.

Synchronous transmission   A form of communication in which receiver and sender share a common clock. Often this is provided by the sender.

Syntax   The grammar of a language, defining legal and illegal combinations of symbols.

System bus   The main bus interconnecting processor, memory and input–output units. It consists of sections dedicated to data, address and control information.

System call   An instruction which causes a transfer of control from the executing process into the operating system so that the requested operation can be carried out.

System clock   The central oscillator used to time and synchronize all the activities in a computer system.

System program   A piece of software used to organize or manage the operation of a computer system.

System throughput   A measure of the work completed by a computer.

Tags   Identifier tokens used in associative cache memories.

TAPI   Telephone Application Programmer's Interface.

Task   *See* Process.

TCP/IP   Transmission Control Protocol/Internet Protocol. This is the communications protocol suite used by the Internet. It is a set of rules and definitions which allow the exchange of information across a network.

TDM   Time division multiplexed: a technique to share a channel by the participants taking periodic turns.

TDM/PCM   Time division multiplexed/pulse code modulation: a telecommunications standard for trunk transmission lines. The subchannels are digitally encoded and time-sliced onto the shared bus.

Technological convergence   A term coined to express the coming together of telephony, computing and television.

Telex   An ancient circuit-switched text-based network for interconnecting 50 bps terminals, consisting of keyboards and printers. The ASR33, of blessed memory, could be pushed up to 110 bps.

Telnet   One of the executable programs included with the TCP/IP software package. It offers remote login and basic terminal emulation services.

Terminator   Electrical resistors inserted at the end points of a LAN to absorb the signal power.

Thrashing   An undesirable condition occurring in overloaded virtual memory systems.

TLB   Translation lookaside buffer: a small, fast buffer holding a translation table for the memory management unit. It speeds up the virtual to physical address translations.

Trap   Software interrupt.

Truth table   A tabular design aid that maps input conditions to required outputs.

TTL   Transistor–transistor logic: the first successful integrated circuit technology from Texas Instruments. Part numbers start with 74, e.g. 74F138.

Two's complement   A representation of positive and negative integers. It allows subtraction to be carried out as addition.

UART   Universal asynchronous receive and transmit: a hardware device (chip), which acts as the interface to RS232 serial lines. It converts parallel data to serial data for transmission, and back for receive. Flow and error control facilities are included.

Unix   A multitasking operating system originally developed by Ken Thompson and then Dennis Ritchie at Bell Labs.

Unresolved external reference   A linker error message indicating that a reference address of a variable or function has not been finalized.

URL   Uniform resource locator: a universal addressing method for accessing sites and services around the Internet, for example `http://www.uwe.ac.uk/`.

Usenet   A worldwide Unix-based network that supports the distribution of messages. It is a 'store-and-forward' protocol and has been largely supplanted by other Internet facilities.

UUCP   Unix to unix copy: an early file transfer utility, intended to connect different Unix systems together.

Value parameter   A parameter which is the value required by the subroutine (not its address).

VAN   Value-added network: a network offering an extra service in order to increase revenue potential.

VHDL   An HLL intended for use by hardware designers; looks superficially like ADA.

Virtual address   An ideal address, starting at zero, which takes no account of physical limitations imposed by the real system.

Virtual circuit   A communication which is established at both ends before the transmission of packets of data starts. TCP and ATM are both said to offer such a service.

Virtual memory   A scheme of extending the main memory address range into a disk area.

VLSI   Very large-scale integrated circuit.

Volatile memory   Memory that loses its contents when the electrical power is removed.

VT100   An ASCII terminal manufactured by Digital Equipment Company (DEC), which became popular during the 1960s and 1970s for use with Unix and other non-IBM systems.

WAN   Wide area network.

Waveform   A repetitive analogue pattern, for example of voltage against time.

Web browser   Software that lets you display text and images stored on Web pages around the Internet, e.g. Netscape Navigator, Mosaic and Microsoft Internet Explorer.

Wideband   Channels capable of high data rates. They employ modulators and demodulators.

WIMP   Windows, icons, menus and pointers. The approach to user interfaces, pioneered by Xerox and Apple, using interactive graphics.

Win32   The standardized Windows API, consisting of hundreds of function calls.

Windows   Microsoft's GUI (graphical user interface).

WinSock   Windows sockets API: a DLL to help create a local TCP socket to link across the network to other processes in different computers.

WKP   Well-known ports: the TCP/IP port numbers for publicly advertised services.

Workspace   The area of memory allocated to a process for its status header, stack and variables.

World Wide Web (WWW)   An enormous set of inter-referring documents, held on diverse computers across the world. They can be downloaded via the Internet and inspected using a Web browser program.

Worle A small suburban excresence of Weston-super-Mare. Local students offer `worle.c` as a good alternative to the better known `world.c`.

WWW *See* World Wide Web.

WYSIWYG What You See Is What You Get: editors with immediate on-screen formatting of the entered text.

X terminal A windowing version of telnet to provide remote system logins.

X Window system Client–server software architecture, intended originally for Unix, which offers a GUI.

Z80 The 8/16 bit microprocessor produced by Zilog, preceding the 8086. It was then the most popular CPU for workstations.

Z flag The CPU condition code which indicates if an operation performed by the ALU resulted in zero.

Answers to end of chapter questions

Chapter 1

1. Understanding the parameters published in adverts can enable you to avoid the hype and select the best buy for your needs. For example, the quoted CPU speed (300–600 MHz) can be misleading because the main board runs at only 100 MHz. If the cache memory is not sufficiently large, this situation will really slow down your CPU. Hard disk access times can also be confusing, but are often the real bottleneck for database applications. Money spent on a bigger screen may be more appreciated by the user than obtaining more DRAM. The raw CPU speed is not really very important for most applications.

2. The name of IBM gave professional users the courage to try out the new concept of a personal computer, which up until then had only been considered fit for hobby use. But many people were looking for a way to escape from the constraints of bureaucratic computer centres. Then the generosity (!) of IBM in publishing its hardware and software interface standards allowed all sorts of third party suppliers to exploit the PC as a platform for their own products. Finally, the platform was expandable through the ISA bus, which allowed the system to evolve in manageable stages: graphics adapters, disc controllers, LAN interfaces and then enhanced processors. Alternative sources of hardware helped to drive down prices. What do you think the next evolutionary step will be for the PC – telephone, television or household control hub?

3. Not really: it is all handled as 64 kbps binary data streams. There is no simple way of distinguishing digitized voice from binary numbers, except by listening to it. Telephone equipment samples and digitizes our voice 8000 times a second, with each sample transmitted as an 8 bit number. IBM used to supply digital telephone exchanges, too.

4. This complex card behaves as a switching centre for audio input and output. It accepts analogue input from a microphone or music source through a 16 bit 44.1 kHz CD-quality ADC and provides the same quality DAC output to low-power analogue loudspeakers or a stereo preamp. It can also accept digitized sound, music or voice, and MIDI-encoded music, which can be played through a multi-voice synthesizer unit. Besides all this, there is a DMA channel to transfer sound data to and from memory or disk, and a joystick port. The DSP facilities can handle compression and decompression to reduce file sizes.

5. The MS-DOS character-based interface also provides a batch file facility which allows you to enter keyboard commands for future playback. A WIMP interface makes this operation difficult to organize, so Windows drops back to a C:> command prompt when required. DOS was originally purchased from Seattle Computer Products as QDOS for $50,000.

6. From home I dial into the University computer. I need a modem for access over telephone lines. University networks have data links through to the Internet backbone without needing to dial up an ISP (Internet service provider).

7. Tim Berners-Lee is seen as the father of the WWW. He developed the first character-based browser while doing research at the European Centre for Nuclear Research (CERN) in Geneva. Have a look at Robert Reid's *Architects of the Web* (Wiley) for a human interest account of Netscape's growth. The Netscape Navigator program was created by Marc Andreessen.

8. A subscription to a commercial Internet service costs around £10 per month. Look in the *Guardian Online* section for free offers. Many companies offer Internet access for free. Hotmail gives remote access to your email from anywhere that an Internet connection is available.

9. Unix was the only operating system that had networking facilities built into the software from a very early stage. This was used first to establish a network of dial-up computers (DEC PDP-11 minicomputers), then a network with dedicated, fast links (DEC Vax-11 super-minis), and finally LANs of workstations (Sun Microsystems). Unix was written by Ken Thompson and Dennis Ritchie at Bell Labs during the early 1970s.

A. MAC/Ethernet number: 42.49.4F.00.20.59 → 48 bits
   IP number: 164.11.9.99 → 4 bytes → 32 bits
   The maximum number of different Internet numbers is: 2^{32} → 4 000 000 000
   Currently there are around 6 000 000 000 people in the world, so 32 bits is not enough, giving only 4 000 000 000 addresses! We are expecting a revision of the IP address up to 128 bits.

B. CompuServe, Demon, Virgin, AOL, LineOne...

C. Gordon Moore, one of the founders of Intel, noticed that the density of circuits on silicon chips was doubling every 18 months. Programmers take notice because the functionality and speed of hardware affects the performance of their software. It is still possible to gamble that in two years' time, when your software will be launched, that RAMs will be big enough and the CPUs fast enough. The fundamental physical limit to this hardware shrinking is set by the Heisenberg uncertainty principle, which states that there is always inaccuracy in locating a particle (electron) which is moving: $\Delta x \Delta v > 10^{-3}$.

D. Technological convergence implies the unification of various facilities, notably telephony, data processing and broadcasting; voice, data and image. Actually the basic common factor is digital processing! If you are a subscriber to cable television you may be able to use a high-bandwidth cable modem to access the Internet.

E. This needs to relate to local circumstances, so get the local guru to check out your sketch. Perhaps email him or her the diagram for a rapid response, but try it out with a friend first: email attachments can be annoying!

F. There are 1000 ms in every second (10^{-3} s)
   There are 1 000 000 μs in every second (10^{-6} s)
   There are 1 000 000 000 ns in every second (10^{-9} s)
   A picosecond is one thousandth of a nanosecond (10^{-12} s)
   A femtosecond is one thousandth of a picosecond (10^{-15} s)
   How much is a Tbyte of DRAM worth? (1 terabyte = 10^{12} bytes)

Chapter 2

0001. A computer is said to 'understand' a program when it can recognize and obey each instruction in the program. It has no other option, it is wired to detect certain binary patterns (instruction codes) and respond by carrying out a fixed sequence of actions. All other patterns will invoke an ERROR! response. Try uploading to your Unix account a PC program from floppy disk. See what happens when you try to run it. Does the operating system intervene? Now try executing a data file to see what happens, on both Unix and Windows NT. (You may have to change the access permissions to get past the operating system controls.)

0010. i80x86/Pentium: Intel/AMD/IBM
MC680X0: Motorola
SPARC: Sun Microsystems
Z80: Zilog
ALPHA: DEC/COMPAQ
PowerPC 601: IBM/Apple/Motorola
6502: Rockwell
TMS1000: Texas Instruments

0011. Human languages are far more expressive and complex than even the latest (Java) inventions. To translate effectively French into English you need to 'understand' the meaning and re-express it in English – word for word substitution will never work well. With computer languages there *is* a direct correspondence between a line of HLL and a sequence of machine instructions – it has been arranged that way! There are Fortran-to-C converter programs which work quite well. Some compilers for new languages actually translate into C so that the C compiler can then be used! Nobody would invent an HLL which incorporates ambiguity or uncertainty, which are regularly found in human languages. We work around the problem in conversation by using redundant (repeated) expression or simply directing the conversation into a more rigorous format to confirm our guesses. HLLs do have a vocabulary and syntax, but these are still tiny constructs alongside the monstrous evolutions that comprise human language.

0100. Assembler: mnemonic representation of machine code. Easier for humans to use than raw binary, or even hex. Needs to be translated into the equivalent binary codes before the computer can 'understand' it.

Binary executable: a file holding a program ready to run – code that has been compiled and linked waiting to be loaded.

Compiling: checking and translating a HLL program into object format for linking with library modules ready to run.

Logging on: identifying yourself to the operating system and setting up a work environment.

Crashing: a fatal failure, due either to hardware malfunction or logical software error. It usually requires a system reboot or at least the manual removal of the offending process.

0101. HLL compilers carry out more checking to trap coding errors. More people can understand HLL programs than the assembler equivalents. It appears that programmers have a practically fixed productivity of 10–20 lines a day, irrespective of the language used! Thus it is sensible to use the most powerful, expressive languages available. We use HLLs because they make us more money. Look at the computing job adverts in your newspaper (often bunched together on Wednesday or Thursday). Draw up a count of all the different HLLs mentioned. Which is currently the most in demand? If you have an historic interest, repeat the exercise with a paper from 10 years ago.

0110. IBM AS/400: corporate database, large business applications in COBOL
Sun: graphical application, Unix workstation, network host
Cray: very large simulation/modelling – weather forecasting, oil exploration
Psion: personal diary, mobile email/fax terminal
PC: general-purpose business/industrial/domestic computer
Can you identify which processors these computers use?

0111. A program is a list of instructions to achieve a goal, or carry out a designated task.
Von Neumann computers have a single bus to interconnect the component units, and a single memory to hold data or programs without distinction. They carry out a repeated cycle of fetching instructions from memory and executing them inside the CPU.
Harvard computers have multiple buses and separate data and program memory.
Harvard architecture, in distinction to von Neumann architecture, is used to refer to computers which separate addressing space into two parts: the main space for programs, and the other for data. Different instructions and addressing modes are used to access the two spaces. Often the data space is smaller. This is not far removed from the separation, within Intel processors, of IO ports from memory. Motorola never adopted such a distinction and required ports to be accessed in the same way as memory. The 8051 microcontroller is an example of Harvard design. This can speed up processing or provide an easier route for implementing embedded systems, such as washing machine controllers – the program is held in PROM chips while the data is in RAM chips. Any instruction trying to write to the PROM should be trapped as an error. The Harvard plan makes this easier.

1000. 'A microcomputer can offer remote windowed access across a 10 million bits per second Ethernet LAN.'
Now try for a nonsense sentence with the same vocabulary:

'The second window is remote as per usual, 10 bits of Ethernet and a micro-LAN will fix it.'

1001. Hex is an abbreviated code for 4 bit numbers. It tells us no more than the binary.

0000	0
0001	1
0010	2
0011	3
0100	4
0101	5
0110	6
0111	7
1000	8
1001	9
1010	A
1011	B
1100	C
1101	D
1110	E
1111	F

As you can see, the first 10 digits are simply the normal decimal figures, with the letters A to F filling in the range from 10 to 15. Hewlett-Packard used to have an alternative set of supra-9 characters which it thought was more distinguishable when displayed on seven-segment LEDs. Before byte-oriented computers and hexadecimal, octal was the preferred 3 bit encoding scheme.

1010.
R	o	b	e	r	t
52H	6fH	62H	65H	72H	74H
1010010	1101111	1100010	1100101	1110010	1110100
82	111	98	101	114	116

0AH – Line feed (LF) – moves cursor to next line down on the page
0DH – Carriage return (CR) – moves cursor to beginning of the line

putchar(7) – you should hear the beep.
putchar('7') – this should print a character 7 on the screen.

Try getting it to sound the beep for 2 seconds continuously, perhaps when nobody else is around. Use `for(i=0; i<100000; i++) { };`. The exact number of zeros depends on your CPU clock speed.

1011. Unicode is the new internationally agreed 16 bit character code. It includes 7 bit ASCII as a subset, but covers most of the world's written languages. Microsoft Visual C++ declares Unicode chars by using the type WCHAR.

1100. Approx 250. The next Intel processor may have fewer because it will be RISC-oriented.

1101. GNU is the mark of the Free Software Foundation, started by Richard Stallman. The FSF supplies excellent quality software under its Copyleft agreement. It started with the emacs editor and C compiler for Unix but has encompassed many other tools, such as gmake, gawk, groff, ghostview. It is all available for Linux and Windows.

1110. A linker is the utility program, often supplied with a compiler, which detects 'unresolved external references' in compiled object files and sets about finding the referenced routines in library files or previously compiled user files. It then sticks all the object modules together in a single run-time file, adjusting all the relative address references as it goes along.

1111. If you are running on a PC, it is worth closing down all other processes. On a departmental Unix box, this is not possible, but you could try running the job in the middle of the night!

   (a) Get a simpler word-processor? See if the main memory is too small resulting in too much page swapping to and from disk. If this is so, buy some more DRAM.
   (b) The algorithm you used is probably at fault or not coded as efficiently as it could be.
   (c) The data structures and relationships might be sub-optimal. Try re-analysing the data and declaring new tables.
   (d) Suppress screen updating on each recalculation. Use indirect cell referencing as more efficient. Reduce the calculation loading in the cell formulae.

Chapter 3

1. CPU, memory and IO unit. They are interconnected by the system bus.

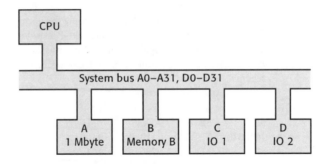

Where do the PCI and ISA buses fit into your diagram?

2. The fetch–execute cycle is the process by which the program instructions are read back into the CPU, one at a time, for decoding and obeying. It is the central activity of the digital computer. It is the 'big idea' of Charles Babbage (or whoever...).

Instruction fetch
Instruction decode
Operand read
Instruction execute
Result write back

What happens if there are two operands to be read from memory, for example an ADD instruction? Most machine instructions have a fixed number of operands: 0, 1, 2 or 3.

3. An interlaced TV frame takes 20 ms to scan 625/2 lines, taking about 65 μs for a line.
The number of 5 ns fetch–execute cycles = 65 000/5 = 13 000. Quite a lot of computing.
An instruction will (roughly) take $1/200\,\mu$s = 5 ns if the code is in the CPU cache already. But the data is not in cache (it is too big), so a DRAM read instruction may take 10 times longer. To check a byte and then loop back if it is not the target will require three instructions (60 ns) and the target will on average be halfway through the memory: $60 \times 10^{-9} \times 1 \times 10^6$ = 60 ms. Such estimates deliver only approximate values because we are ignoring so many other factors.

4. A wide data bus allows more data to be transferred in each bus cycle, which is good. A wide address bus allows access to a larger physical memory, which may be useful when using large programs or accessing databases, but larger memories require more decoding, which slows down each memory access.
The problem of large programs is no longer a serious issue because the size of main memories has grown and virtual memory operating systems provide an overspill area on disk.

5. The bus bottleneck refers to the limitation imposed on the transfer of data around within the computer by the bus interconnection system. Only one item can be on the bus at any time. To overcome this bandwidth limitation wider data buses are being installed, multiple buses are quite common and higher levels of on-chip integration are sought. The system clocks are pushed up to the highest allowed by the circuits in order to increase transfer rates, too, but track capacitance and driver circuit impedance limit this development.

6. The system clock times and sequences all the operations in the computer, including the CPU. The basic clock frequency is divided down to give machine cycles and instruction cycles. Some microprocessors are built so that you can stop the system clock for long periods without losing any information. However, most of them include DRAM-type circuits, requiring regular

refreshing which is driven by the clock tick. If the clock were stopped, information would certainly be lost.

On Pentium systems, it is important to distinguish between the motherboard/system clock and the CPU clock. The former currently operates at 100 MHz and the latter at between 400 and 1000 MHz.

7. Asynchronous buses operate an interlocking handshake between the initiator and the server. A request goes out, and the initiator waits for a reply signal indicating that the command has been obeyed, the initiator will then cancel the request and go on to the next transaction. In this way the minimum length of time is spent on each transaction, even when they might take different lengths of time to complete.

   The synchronous bus scheme assumes that all transactions complete in the same length of time. So all transactions must last as long as the slowest. It is a simpler and faster arrangement if there are no extended transactions to take into account. Should the occasional extended transaction occur, it is possible to arrange for the insertion of a bus WAIT state to stall the initiator while the server gets its act together. It is like playing *The Four Seasons* to customers left on hold.

8. For the 8086, Intel chose to multiplex the address and data buses, and so share the package pins. On every memory access cycle the 8086 would send out first the address and then the data. The disadvantage is the extra time needed in each memory cycle, but because the 8086 would pre-fetch instructions some of this disadvantage was reduced.

9. Electrical signals propagate at 10 cm/ns, so it takes 3 ns to cover 30 cm – about the same as a single logic gate delay. In fact, modern computer circuits have just progressed from being gate-delay limited to being transmission-delay limited.

10. Get the implements
       Get a mixing bowl from shelf
       Get wooden spoon from draw
       Get knife from drawer
       Get beating bowl from shelf
     Set up electric whisk
     Get out scales and weights
     Get a baking tin
     Collect together the ingredients
       Get the flour from the cupboard
       Get eggs from the fridge
       Get sugar from the shelf
       Get sultanas from the cupboard
       Get margarine from the fridge
       Get milk from the fridge
     Line the baking tin with greaseproof paper
     Measure the ingredients
       Weigh margarine into mixing bowl
       Weigh sugar into mixing bowl
       Weigh out sultanas
       Weigh out flour
     Process and mix ingredients
     Crack eggs into beating bowl
     Beat margarine and sugar with wooden spoon
     Whisk eggs into mixing bowl
     Pour flour into mixing bowl

Whisk all together in mixing bowl
Adjust mixture with milk
Continue whisking
Pour sultanas into mixing bowl
Fold in with wooden spoon
Add more sultanas when nobody is looking
Spoon mixture into baking tin
Put tin in oven
Wait 2 hours
Visually check every 30 minutes
Remove tin from oven
Wait 15 minutes
Remove from tin
Wait 15 minutes
Eat cake

It is always surprising how complex our lives have become and how difficult giving basic instructions can be! Think about programming a robot cake maker....

11. A pre-fetch buffer can allow fetching and executing to take place in parallel if the hardware facilities allow it. The Control Unit's decoder can be kept 100% busy until a conditional branch instruction arrives.
    When there is an IF-ELSE or CASE statement the pre-fetcher will not know which route to take. If there are duplicated pre-fetch units, both directions of the IF-ELSE could be serviced until the decision comes in and one side can be aborted.

12. The Level 1 cache holds a small section of the current program and data on-chip in the most privileged position. No faster memory could be provided. Level 2 cache memory runs slightly slower because the electrical signals are driven off CPU chip, down to PCB tracking and back up onto the cache chip. This inevitably involves extra delays due to track capacitance. But Level 2 cache can be bigger: on the PC it is 256 kbyte vs. 16 kbyte of Level 1 cache – 16 times bigger.
    Can you increase the amount of cache on your PC? Try a WWW subject search for 'cache on a stick'.

13. An IO port is a single register like a single location of byte-wide memory, but it is provided with two access routes, one from the system bus and one for the external device. There is 'dual-port RAM', too, often used in graphics cards and called VRAM, which has 'front' and 'back' doors. Output ports are generally latched, meaning that they store the last value written to them. Input ports may not have to be latched.

14. 'Hello World' would appear as the numerical ASCII values representing the letters. The Sun is big-endian, while the PC is little-endian. As chars are written and read in single bytes there will be no problem:

    ```
    0 1 2 3 4 5 6 7 8 9 a
    h e l l o _ w o r l d
    ```

    If, however, the data was read back as integer data the result would be:

Intel integer	0	1	2
	l l e h	o w _ o	d l r
Sun integer	0	1	2
	h e l l	o _ w o	r l d

15. 8 → 16. Much larger programs, mostly generated by using HLLs, widened the repertoire of applications. These needed hard disk storage for volume and load speed. Much more sophisticated graphics cards were developed which allowed the introduction of the first WIMP interfaces to replace command line exchanges. Then network interfaces arrived to reconnect the isolated users and support email and remote filing.

16 → 32. This saw the introduction of a fully multitasking windowed environment in both Unix and Microsoft Windows. No really new applications which would have been previously impossible have yet been forthcoming. In graphics, the major improvements have been taken up in the field of games.

Chapter 4

01. All you need is 10 dual input XOR gates, each comparing one of the user switches with the preset switch value. If the two switch inputs are the same the XOR will deliver a 0. Then the outputs from the 10 XOR gates must be ORed together. An OR gate will give a 0 only if all its inputs are 0. So a 0 from the OR will mean OK, correct code, while a 1 will mean at least one of the switches does not match the preset value.

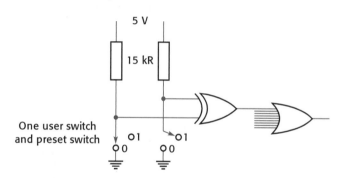

02.

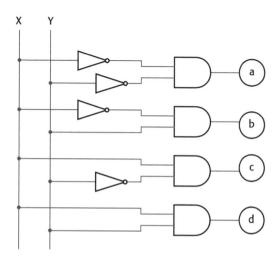

X Y	a b c d
0 0	1 0 0 0
0 1	0 1 0 0
1 0	0 0 1 0
1 1	0 0 0 1

03. A demultiplexer is the opposite of a multiplexer: it takes the output from a shared channel, separates the items and allocates them back to individual channels.

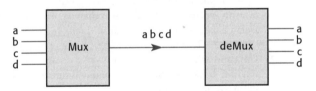

The four input channels to the multiplexer take it in turns to use the common channel through to the far end, where the demultiplexer sorts out the data into the correct channels. Both multiplexer and demultiplexer use a decoder circuit, as in Question 02, to select one channel from the group. For the demultiplexer the input will be the common channel, and the outputs are the four individual channels. The common data is fed into each of the AND gates, which act as data switches. Only one of the AND gates will be enabled, selecting one of the data lines. This acts to effectively steer data into the single output channel.

10. (What number base (radix) are these questions/answers using?)
   I think there are 102 distinct keys, including TAB, SHIFT and CTRL. If we used a single 128 input encoder, which is the opposite of a decoder, you would require at least a 7 bit code number for each key. An alternative, more common, technique for the encoder is to organize a scanned matrix with 10 rows and 11 columns ($11 \times 10 = 110$ keys). Each column is activated in turn through an output port, and the row inputs read through a different port to see if any of the keys are down.

11. Karnaugh maps are popular with textbooks and provide nice diagrams, but in my experience they are not often used in practice. Some people may prefer them to Truth Tables, but I have not yet met an engineer who really uses them in anger. This is because there is rarely an overriding need to minimize gate count. Quite often the real target is to improve performance, or make do with the gates that are actually available.

12. Instead of using seven dual-input XOR gates to generate parity, the 8 bit number can be used as the address input to a 256 bit PROM. The PROM would already be loaded with the correct bits, corresponding to the parity value of the selecting address.

Address	Even parity
1111 1111	0
1111 1110	1
. . .	. . .
. . .	. . .
0000 1001	0
0000 1000	1
0000 0111	1
0000 0110	0
0000 0101	1
0000 0100	1
0000 0011	0
0000 0010	1
0000 0001	1
0000 0000	0

Memory

13. CISC – such as MC68000 or the DEC VAX minicomputer. The Pentium is a hybrid, with microcode as well as RISC decoding features.

20. 1. Draw up the truth table and discover that it is the same as (A XOR B) && C.

21. For a logical XOR, perhaps use the answer from the previous question or

    (A || B) && !(A && B)

22. The dissipation depends on the technology used: bipolar, MOS or CMOS. The cooler CMOS chips still dissipate when switching logic levels, so at high clock rates they still get hot. The Pentium can produce 13 W of heat. It consumes more than 3 A at 3.3 V!

23. The RISC program is longer because it needs more instructions to achieve the same effect. Try recompiling a C test program on different computers and checking the size of executable file generated.

30. 5, and usually a couple of chip select (c/s) inputs too. Get a large sheet of paper, or a fine, sharp pencil, and draw up the truth table.

31. The IR holds the instruction code after it has been fetched from memory, while it is being decoded and executed. The programmer is not offered direct access to the IR, but can deliberately load an instruction into it by forcing the CPU to fetch and execute that value.

32. A 16 bit number has 65 536 different combinations, so the 68k instruction set could be that large.

33. Wire up each of the 20 light sensors to one of the address lines of a 1 Mbyte EPROM. In every location of the EPROM is entered the number that the sensor pattern forming that address most closely matches, or 00000000 if no number pattern is represented. Thus every possible light pattern appears as a 20 bit binary number. Identify by trial and error the sets of code numbers which represent acceptable versions of the scanned digits. Put the numeric values 0–9 into the chosen locations to give the final output.

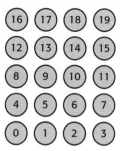

So a number 1, as it passed across the array would activate the sensors serving:

	A0, A4, A8, A12 and A16	→	0001 0001 0001 0001 0001
or	A1, A5, A9, A13 and A17	→	0010 0010 0010 0010 0010
or	A2, A6, A10, A14 and A18	→	0100 0100 0100 0100 0100
or	A3, A7, A11, A15 and A19	→	1000 1000 1000 1000 1000

So at the PROM locations 11111H, 22222H, 44444H and 8888H the number '1' should be stored.

100. The `switch-case` statement.

Chapter 5

1.

AND	OR	NOT
&&	||	!
·	+	−
∩	∪	~

The distinction in C between the logical operations (&&, ||) and the bitwise numerical operations (&, |) is a cause of much confusion. The single versions are used for testing, masking, setting and clearing bit flags. While the double versions are often used to construct TRUE/FALSE evaluation statements in `IF` statements and similar.

2.

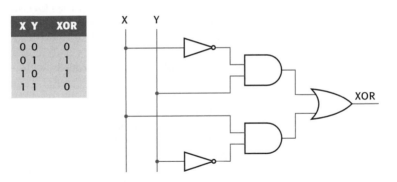

If you were shipwrecked on a desert island with only one type of logic gate, which would you chose? For technical not emotional reasons!

3.   This is a tricky circuit which is not easy to work out. I just remember it.

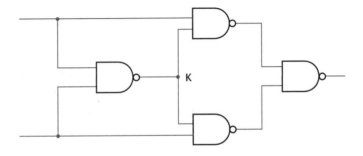

Check it out in a truth table by entering partial result columns for the output from each of the four gates.

Now attach the input to an invert gate at point K. This gives you a circuit with two outputs. What does it do? Draw up the truth table, which will need four columns: two for input and two for output.

4. Yes, INVERT – GATE is not the same as GATE – INVERT. Try it out in hardware and software. Check up the de Morgan equivalences, too.

5. The carry 'ripples' through from LSB to MSB, giving an unpredictable delay in the operation: some additions have no carry overs, while some topple right through. Better adders use carry-look-ahead circuits to remove this uncertainty, even at the cost of extra logic complexity.

6. $2^{32} = 4 \times 10^9$

$$\frac{3 \times 4 \times 10^9}{60 \times 60 \times 24 \times 365} \approx 400 \text{ years}$$

If average luck holds, this will be reduced to only 200 years. Will the petrol stations still be open?

7. Use four quadruple input AND gates to 'look for' the four patterns (1110, 1101, 1011 and 0111) on the input lines. You will only need to look for four of these patterns because the 1111 pattern will be dealt with by the others, and so need not be specifically watched for. Then bring the outputs from the four AND gates into an OR to produce the alarm signal. The logic 1 will need to be amplified to drive a klaxon, though.

8. Texas Instruments produced, and patented, the first integrated circuits. It was very successful with the TTL 7400 range of circuits in the 1960s. Now its expertise is somewhat focused on DSP chips. Look them up on the Web.

9. 64 kbit/s, or 8 bits, 8000 times a second in one direction. So a single page text email (4 kbyte) is data-wise equivalent to 0.5 s of speech!

10. char – 8 bits, long – 32 bits, int – 32 bits (usually), float – 32 bits, double – 64 bits, unsigned char – 8 bits.

11.
```
// shift-subtract demo divide routine 8 bit / 8 bit = 8 bit
#include <stdio.h>

int main(void) {

unsigned short int i,r,d,q;
short int n;

r = 70;
d = 12;
q = 0;

  d <<= 8;

for (i=0; i<8; i++) {
  r <<= 1;
  q <<= 1;
```

```
    n = (r-d);
    if ( n >= 0 ) { q++; r = n ; }
}
printf("a/b = %d\n", q);
return 0;
}
```

Do try this out!

12.

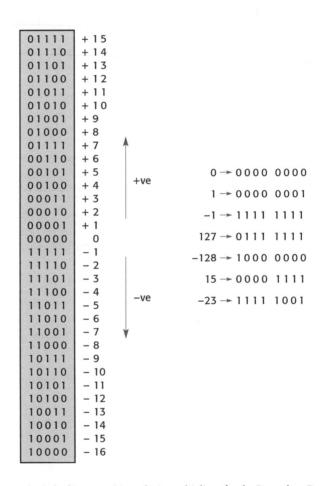

13. Insert XOR gates (switched inverters) into the input bit lines for the B number. Don't forget the extra +1. See the ALU diagram in Section 5.3.

14. int is assumed to be in two's complement format; unsigned int is not! If arithmetic operations take place a difference will show. If sign-extending operations are carried out the difference will also appear.

15. Go on: try it!

Chapter 6

1. Accessing CPU registers is much faster (5 ns) than main memory (60 ns). Also the CPU registers are accessed using different instruction codes from those used to access variables in main memory. Because there are relatively few CPU registers, each one can be referenced by a short number embedded in the instruction code itself. This is not true for memory accesses, where the 32 bit address number is normally found immediately after the instruction code. Another difference is how the compiler allocates registers and memory locations. It is quite free with memory locations, allowing us to give variable names to memory locations with little obvious restrictions. However, compilers keep the CPU registers very much for themselves, only sometimes accepting 'advice' from the programmer as to register usage. Generally the CPU registers are used only as temporary data stores, so that they are available for calculations or algorithmic manipulation. Check up the C declaration:

    ```
    register int n1;
    ```

2. Disaster! If two memory locations both respond to the same address, which is possible when installing new memory or IO cards, the signal on the bus becomes an unpredictable mixture of both values. The result of the read operation coming back to the CPU is rubbish – maybe leading to a crash. In the worst situation one of the memory output drivers may damage the other permanently. If the two locations are erroneously written to, because of the same address decoding error, the outcome will depend on the attached devices.

3. 4 Gbyte. 64 Tbyte (terabytes) – quite big, but powerful database machines, and search engines like AltaVista, already have gigabyte memories installed. Virtual memory for each process has been extended to 64 Tbyte ($T = 2^{40}$ or 10^{12})

4. It is a good idea to remember some binary landmark sizes. I remember:

256	2^8
64K	2^{16}
1M	2^{20}
16M	2^{24}
4G	2^{32}

    Also note that:

    $2^{10} \approx 10^3$, 1000, known as 1K $2^{40} \approx 10^{12}$, 1T (Tera)

    $2^{20} \approx 10^6$, 1 000 000, known as 1M $2^{50} \approx 10^{15}$, 1P (Peta)

    $2^{30} \approx 10^9$, 1 000 000 000, known as 1G $2^{60} \approx 10^{18}$, 1E (Exa)

    If you are amazed that this should be so, and understand logarithms (or have a friend who does) try taking the log of both sides of these identities, bringing down the index on both sides:

    $$\log(2^{10}) \approx \log(10^3)$$

    $$\log(2^{20}) \approx \log(10^6)$$

    $$\log(2^{30}) \approx \log(10^9)$$

    $$10 \times \log(2) \approx 3 \times \log(10)$$

    $$20 \times \log(2) \approx 6 \times \log(10)$$

$$30 \times \log(2) \approx 9 \times \log(10)$$

Divide both sides of the second equation by 2, or the third equation by 3, and you get back the first one. So there you have it: they are the same. What is the next (×4) value? The Tera!

So we need 24 lines for 16 Mbyte and 25 lines for 32 Mbyte. 24 Mbyte is in between, but will require all 25 lines – you cannot have a fraction of an address line!

5. Sorry – trick question. IDE and SCSII don't address data by bytes. Rather they address in 512 byte physical sectors or 32 kbyte logical clusters. A 2 Gbyte disk would be divided into 32 kbyte clusters, with a 16 bit index number for addressing ($2^{15} \times 2^{16} = 2$ Gbyte).

6. 20 address + 1 data + 2 power + 1 c/s = 24 pins. This is a minimum; the real packs will probably have more pins.

7.

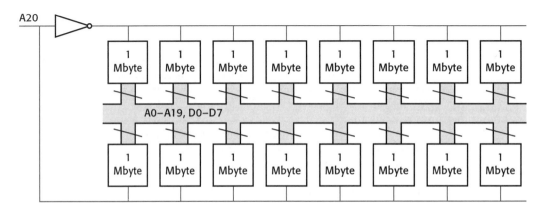

8. A0–A15, or 16 address lines, can address 64 kbyte, so the two banks of ROMs could only contain games programs less than 128 kbyte in size. Compared to the present-day 650 Mbyte CD-ROMs this is a tiny volume. The game Quake runs out at 350 Mbyte, and the Microsoft Encarta encyclopaedia at 650 Mbyte, so clearly this was a mistaken decision by Atari. How big are the Nintendo cartridge ports?

9. 16 Mbyte $= 2^{24}$ and 64 Mbyte $= 2^{26}$, so at least 26 address lines are needed – in fact the SPARC processor has 32.

$$64 \ 2^{64}/2^{26} = 2^{38} = 256 \text{ Gpages}$$

$$32 \ 2^{32}/2^{26} = 2^{6} = 128 \text{ pages}$$

Again, a large difference.

10. The physical memory range can be extended by installing a page register which flips between pages, each one containing the full memory compliment. It works like an extension to the upper end of the IP. The segment registers in the 8086 behaved in the same fashion, extending the 64 kbyte limit of the 8080 by allowing the base address to be repositioned in a larger, 1 Mbyte, physical space. Another technique is to use virtual memory – overflow onto disk.

Does cache extend the size of memory?

11. Access time is the response time to a read (or write) request. It is the latency before the data comes back up the bus. Because DRAMs need to recover from their exertions, there is a longer period to wait before a chip will respond to the next request, called the cycle time. This can be three times longer than the access time, and so is quite important. As programs tend to sequence up through memory, byte after byte, this can be a real problem. The solution is to interleave the chips so that a sequence of addresses actually accesses different chips. This allows each chip to recover before the next access, assuming that the program is content to work its way up through memory in ascending numeric order.

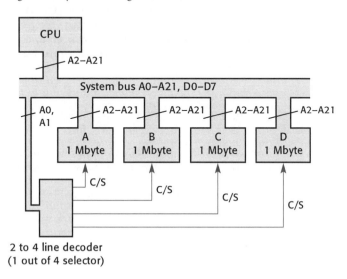

2 to 4 line decoder
(1 out of 4 selector)

12. $\text{cost} = £20 \times 2^{32}/16 \times 10^6$

$= 20 \times 4 \times 10^9/16 \times 10^6$

$= 80 \times 10^3/16$

$= £5000$

This is a very interesting result because, although the current range of motherboards will not accept 64 SIMMS, the cost is not impossibly high. It seems that we are witnessing the beginning of the end for the 32 bit Pentium, in the same way as the Z80's 16 bit address and the 8086's 20 bit address were outgrown in their day.

13. The arguments are repeats of the bus debate: asynchronous is flexible, more complex and 'a good thing', while synchronous is cheaper, and fine as long as everything runs at the same speed. Synchronous RAMs are matched to the system clock so they deliver bursts of data at just the right speed for the cache controller to deal with.

14. DRAMs leak, so they need refilling about 60 times a second. The older PCs used the first DMA channel to carry out the refreshing. Nowadays there is a dedicated refresh controller.

$$n_e = \frac{V \times C}{q_e} = \frac{1.2 \times 20 \times 10^{-15}}{1.6 \times 10^{-19}} = 1.5 \text{ million}$$

There are not very many in the normal course of events; little wonder that they need a regular top-up.

15. $2^{32}/2^{26} = 2^6 = 64$ pages
    So it is 64 DIMMs for bust.

16. The upper two address lines, feeding into a 2 → 4 line decoder, would be the clearest way of selecting the four pages. Or could you produce a logic circuit to do the job?

17. The IO space is still set at 64 kbyte, which can be handled as 32 kword or 16 kquadword if required. This compares to 4 Gbyte of main memory. Separate spaces are liked by hardware designers because it makes planning for the future easier. There are some security advantages because it is easier to control access to ports if a completely different set of instructions are used to get at them. IO ports are often not the most up-to-date technology, and so require slower bus cycles. The introduction of caching and virtual memory makes memory-mapped IO less convenient.

Chapter 7

1. There are EAX, EBX, ECX, EDX, ESI, EDI, EBP all of 32 bits long. But perhaps only EAX, EBX. ECX and EDX would be termed data registers. That makes 4×4 bytes = 16 bytes.

2. The 5 categories of machine instruction are:

1.	data movement (copying)	MOV
2.	data input–output operations	OUT
3.	data manipulation	ADD, CMP
4.	transfer of control	CALL, JMP
5.	machine supervision	INT, HLT

3. ADD EAX, [ESI] involves two arguments; therefore there are two addressing modes. [ESI] is an example of register indirect, while EAX is register direct. This instruction might be used to access an array of data.

4. MOV AX,0   SUB AX,AX   XOR AX,AX

5. With PC-relative addressing it is possible to load and run code anywhere in memory. It is fully relocatable without needing to recompile or relink. This is because there are no absolute address references necessary; all the subroutine entry points are stored as offset values from the current value in the EIP register. With the Pentium this is not possible for data, so the segment pointer is used: DS points through to the base of the data segment, thus allowing relocation of the global data area, or heap, too. The stack variables are always accessed from SP or FP, making them also fully relocatable. The provision of virtual memory management could be said to reduce the need for binary relocatable code because each program can be loaded into an independent segment, with its logical address starting from 0000. The physical addresses then get adjusted by the MMU.

6. Register indirect with post-increment is fundamental to the fetch–execute cycle, so no digital computer could work without it! Consider this expression of the fetch cycle: MOV IR, [EIP]. The address in EIP then needs to be incremented to point to the next instruction in the program.

7. If you exclude the fetch cycle, with two operands you need to specify two addressing modes. The effective address is the address value that gets built by the addressing mode 'calculation'. Mostly it is the operand address in memory or CPU register number, but sometimes you can synthesize an address without immediately using it to access data: `lea ESI,startit`.

8. Two arguments/operands, therefore two addressing modes:

    (i)   Register direct, memory direct
    (ii)   Register direct, immediate (could be called IP indirect post increment)
    (iii) Register direct, register indirect
    (iv)   Register direct, immediate
    (v)   Immediate (IP indirect post increment)
    (vi)   Memory direct, register direct

9. The special Pentium `LOOPZ` instruction carries out a series of operations. It will decrement the ECX register and test the Z flag. A jump back to the start of the loop occurs if the count register is not zero and the Z flag is set to 1.

A. `CMP` (compare) operations simply subtract the two operands, set the CPU status flags and then throw away the result.

B. Both `JZ` and `JNZ` are branch instructions which are governed by the Z flag. If the Z flag is set, indicating that an earlier operation had involved a zero result, the `JZ` will cause a jump back to the target location, while `JNZ` will cause a topple through to the following instruction, out of the loop. Neither instruction affects the Z flag, which will remain the same until another instruction changes it.

C. The CPU status flags are changed by the action of some of the instructions. If a result is zero the Z flag is set to 1. If an overflow occurs the V flag is set. As the instructions often get carried out by the ALU, and the conditional instructions are 'steered' by the CU, it could be said that the status flags are a means of the ALU communicating with the CU. Do all processors use the same group of instructions to set the same flags?

D. There is the `JMP` instruction which force a new address into the EIP achieving a goto. HLLs avoid gotos by planning the change of direction well in advance with an `IF-ELSE` selection or a `DO-WHILE` loop. Having such structures to the language hides the jumps and obviates the worst excesses of spaghetti code.

E. Only the address of the string "`Hello World\n`" is passed to `printf( )`. The count value, although on the stack, is not a parameter: it is held there to save it from corruption during the execution of the `printf( )` code.

   Adding 4 to the stack pointer moves it up the stack. Now any value below the stack pointer position is formally deleted, invisible to the program. When the next `PUSH` occurs it will over-write the remains and it will no longer be visible, even to the debugger.

   The alternative is to `pop eax` and then ignore the value obtained in EAX.

F. `LOOP strout`: this decrements the ECX register, tests to see if the result is still greater than zero, and `jmp`s back to the label `strout` if so. Else it will topple down to the next inline instruction. It is used to implement `FOR` loops.

   `MOV AL,123H`: loads the constant value 123H (291 decimal) into the lowest byte of the accumulator register (EAX).

MOV DX, [count]: takes the 16 bit value from the variable called count and loads it into DX.

PUSH AX: puts the low 16 bits from EAX onto stack.

MOV CX, 0AH: loads the count register with the number 10, possibly to initialize a loop index.

LEA EBX, NAME1: takes the 32 bit address NAME1 and loads it into EBX.

Chapter 8

1. The 'Where did I come from problem?' refers to the decision that has to be taken at the end of a subroutine: where to return to. Because the subroutine may be called from several places within the program, the return address cannot be fixed by the compiler.

    Store subroutine return addresses in a dedicated register, or more commonly, on the stack.

2. They are both held on the stack, and so appear to the function code as much the same. Parameters hold good values from the start, while local variables may not be initialized by the declaration statements. It is said that parameters are simply pre-initialized local variables. Perhaps this should be 'pre-pre-initialized' to distinguish them from the explicitly pre-initialized (int a = 2;) local variables.

3. The stack holds the return address and parameters for all function calls and also the local variables declared within functions. HLL programs rely heavily on procedures/methods to encapsulate functionality. Without a stack it becomes difficult to arrange for nested function calls.

    The Pentium RET n instruction rolls up n bytes from the stack, thus scrubbing the local variables away.

4. The stack pointer is a CPU address register with a special responsibility of indicating the bottom of the stack area in memory. Holding the address in the CPU speeds up stack accesses, which take place for all references to local variables inside functions.

    Holding the actual stack within the CPU would also speed things up, but it is far too big to fit in. In fact, when the stack is active it will be copied into the data cache to speed up accesses. It would seem that the data cache would probably be mostly filled with local variables from the stack. The SPARC CPU has a dedicated cache for the top of the stack.

5. It is normal for the C function return value, often an int, to be placed in the main data register so that the calling program can easily access it. For the Pentium this is EAX.

    For an array to be returned we have problem! If you pass back a pointer in the register *it is vital not to point at a local variable* inside the function. This is a serious error which is all the more serious because it may seem to work – until it finally crashes! The uncertainty arises due to the unpredictability of that area of stack being reused by the next function call.

    The only safe way to pass back an array is to use a reference parameter. In other words, give it an array to work on outside the function so that when the function terminates the array remains valid.

6. If the compiler decides that a particular instruction must be used, and this also requires a special register which is busy, then the contents of that register would be saved on the stack, freeing the register to be 'borrowed'. After the register has been used the original contents will be POPped back down from the stack.

Using the debugger you can see the result of the compiler's translation. It is interesting to see what it does with a `for(;;)` loop.

Alternatively, on Unix try `cc -S test.c`, and look in `test.s` for the assembler output from the compiler. What do the `-o -c` and `-g` compiler flags do? Use `man acc` on Solaris or `man gcc` on Linux and Solaris.

7. Value parameters are copies of variables passed into a subroutine either on the stack or in a CPU data register. The subroutine can then use them in a calculation. The original variable remains unaffected. Value parameters only pass data *into* a subroutine.

A reference parameter is the 32 bit address of a variable. Reference parameters are also passed into a subroutine on the stack or in CPU address registers. But now the subroutine can access the original variable using the address pointer parameter. The original variable can be modified, which can appear as if parameters have passed *out* from a subroutine.

8. Global variables are held in the heap area of data memory, as opposed to the stack area. Global variables are normally accessed using a data pointer with an offset displacement (`mov AL,date(ESI)`), while local variables are accessed using displacements from the frame pointer (`mov AL,date(EBP)`). Things are not much different in C. In Pascal, where local variables are in scope for all contained procedures, accessing higher level variables can be slower due to the multiple pointers.

9. A linker brings together translated object modules and selects the necessary library modules to build an executable module. 'Out-of-module' references to data or functions are resolved by the linker using the symbol table information which is associated with each of the object modules. A start-up module is normally prepended to the code to initialize data structures and handle command-line parameters, should they be present.

A.
```
char letter;          letter: ds.b 1
int number;           number: ds.l 1
char name[10];        name: ds.b 10
char name[] = 'Bob';  name: dc.b "Bob",0
```

These data declarations are not often used directly, but inserted as appropriate by the compiler when it translates the variable declarations.

B. The return address is stored temporarily on the stack. The parameter values are passed on the stack. Local variables are installed on the stack.

When are these entries removed from the stack? Note that this varies with different conventions.

C. Special CPU registers can be reserved to hold the return address and a pointer to a parameter block.

Another technique used by non-stack computers involves reserving the first location of every subroutine as storage for the return address. When a `CALL` occurs, the address of the subroutine, in the `CALL` instruction, actually points to this empty location. The current PC is saved there as a return address, and the subroutine address incremented to point to the first instruction of the subroutine code before it is copied into the PC. At the end of the subroutine is a `JMP` instruction which uses the address stored in the first location, thus achieving a return to the calling program. Any subroutine parameters can be put in a block, immediately after the `CALL` instruction. In this way the subroutine can access them using the return address as a pointer.

Clearly the return address will have to be incremented past the parameter block if the return JMP is to work!

There are several disadvantages to this method. It relies on the code segment being open to write modification, which is now disapproved of. Should you need to deliver a PROM-based system the code will not run. It is also difficult to set up DLL facilities in a multitasking environment, where several processes share the same code. Also the code cannot be recursive (no bad thing in my opinion!).

D.   The normal justification for using another CPU register as a frame pointer is that it needs to remain constant for the lifetime of the subroutine, whereas the stack pointer will change every time another subroutine is called. However, this is not very convincing, as every subroutine invocation will change the frame pointer!

E.   The run-time support software, inserted by the compiler, inserts the parameter count as the first parameter. The subroutine recognizes this number and behaves accordingly. Would it be possible to use a 'terminating sentinel' in the same way that strings are ended by a NULL?

F.   The danger of misapplying a variable name in the middle of a large program will be ever-present. All the variable names will have to be distinct, which is not required when employing local variables. The rather tricky issue of access control is also unavoidable when all code can see all the data. What we need is import/export control, as offered in a few languages.

Chapter 9

1.   Command registers, status registers and data registers. The command registers, sometimes referred to as mode registers, control the operation of the device. Often the required values are written out to the command registers during the initialization phase. Status registers allow the program to monitor IO activities by reading status flags. Data registers are the IO windows to pass data into or out from the system. The program can access IO registers only if it has the necessary permissions. On MS-DOS or Windows 98 systems this is not a problem, but for Unix or Windows NT this is not likely except for special device driver routines which run as part of the operating system.

Mostly the registers would be accessed from C code using pointers. What does the following C fragment achieve?

```
char* pReg = 0xFFFF2;
* pReg = 01;
```

The first line declares a pointer to a `char` variable, which is immediately initialized with a 20 bit value. We can guess that this is an address and will be used to point to a memory location or port register. The second line then writes the value 1 to that location or port.

2.   Polled: Plug-and-Play
      Interrupt: keyboard and mouse, bus or memory failure
      DMA (direct memory access): hard disk data transfers

The DMA controller also uses an interrupt to inform the CPU when the data transfer has completed.

3.   A blocking function means a function that will not return to the caller until the action has been accomplished.

putch( ) would block if the output channel was already full with earlier characters, not yet transferred out.

getchar( ), which fetches characters from the keyboard can be prevented from blocking on a PC by always first testing the keyboard status using kbhit( ). If there is no pending character to read, then do not call getchar( ).

4. Accelerator pedal: 5 Hz, once every 0.2 s
   Inlet manifold: 200 Hz
   Washing machine controls: 1 Hz
   Thermostat: 0.5 Hz
   Barcode scanner: 10 kHz
   Vehicle sensor: 100 Hz

5. Coffee vending: dedicated polling, because the operation is sequential
   LAN: DMA and interrupt
   Fire alarm: intermittent polled (0.2 Hz)
   Credit card scanner: interrupt driven or dedicated polling
   PC mouse: interrupt or intermittent polling

6. The real-time clock interrupt might happen a hundred times a second, and invokes the RTC interrupt service routine. This routine updates the time of day values (ms, s, min, hr) in main memory. The RTC circuit normally has a small battery to maintain its operation at all times.

7. A Real-time Clock interrupt is regularly fired by a hardware oscillator. The RT tick, besides maintaining the TOD, is responsible for process time-sliced scheduling, which most operating systems now carry out. When an RTC tick arrives, the current process status is saved, and the scheduler chooses another process from the queue to take over.

   RTCs may be in the range 50 Hz–1 kHz, depending on the application requirements.

   Look up the GetTickCount( ) in Windows NT's online help. Try writing a clock display program based on a polling loop containing this system call.

8. Flag polling is considered time wasting by the CPU. The reason it is used is the simplicity of implementation, reliability of operation, and the lack of anything else for the processor to do instead! Dedicated, or 'spin' polling would be used on price-sensitive applications, such as domestic equipment, or where the ultimate throughput is required and no DMA facilities are possible.

9. Some compilers offer special library functions, written originally in assembler, which can be used to 'sandwich' an HLL-coded 'interrupt function'. This works well, but is inefficient. It is better to code all ISRs in asembler and link them into your HLL object modules. Some global data will be needed to allow the ISR to communicate with the HLL program, because there are no parameters!

10. The CPU, when responding to an interrupt, can poll all the likely devices to find the active source. But this is an inefficient method which is like replying to an urgent telephone call by writing a letter. The better method is where the IO devices store a self-identifying number (interrupt vector) which the CPU then demands in a broadcast following an interrupt. The source of the interrupt can identify itself by putting the vector number on the data bus.

   The CPU automatically raises the interrupt threshold to stop the same device re-interrupting while it is being serviced. An important job for the ISR is to cancel the source of interrupt before handing back to the main program. The RTS instruction is put at the end of subroutines, while the RTE terminates ISRs. The RTE restores the interrupt threshold and CPU status flags, which have been PUSHed onto the stack during the interrupt processing.

At the start of microprocessor technology, Intel offered a method which allowed the interrupting device to send back a complete instruction as if it were memory responding to a fetch–execute cycle. A likely instruction would be: CALL MY_ISR.

11. PUSH any CPU registers which are used in the ISR onto the stack.
    Identify source of interrupt, if still unknown.
    Cancel source of interrupt
    Carry out required processing, communicating with main program.
    Reinitialize device, if necessary.
    POP the CPU registers from the stack.
    Return and restore flags.

12. A critical region occurs when the ISR and a main program need to write to the same data area. This is especially true if data structures are involved, not just a bit flag. In the latter case special instructions are provided, such as Test-and-Set and Test-and-Clear. These are 'non-interruptible' so will run to completion even when a high-priority interrupt occurs.

    Is there a similar problem for multiprocessor systems using shared memory?

13. DMA = direct memory access.

    The PC uses DMA for transferring data to and from hard disk. It uses one DMA channel to refresh the DRAM chips. The sound card may use DMA to stream audio signals out to the DAC port when it is playing music. The Ethernet interface requires DMA to shift the data packets to and from the network.

    The type qualifier 'volatile' should be used in the variable declaration to ensure that the compiler realizes that the variable is liable to change value without any program intervention. This is necessary in case the compiler decides to 'optimize' your code when it realizes that the array is acting as a constant, never being written to throughout the program. Also the problem of simultaneous access will need to be considered. The DMA controller may demand an update opportunity just when the program is reading the data. This is an example of 'critical data', and requires careful handling in order to prevent data corruption occurring.

14. Unfortunately it collapses big time!

    Input: A CR B CR _ C CR D CR E CR F CR
    Output: A B _ CR CR CR

It never recovers. The reason is that the buffer will always have a residual character left over from the previous entry. In this case it is again the ENTER key, or CR code. Thus the first getchar( ) will pick up the CR, leaving the recent key code (C or D or E in our example) to be gobbled up and forgotten by the second getchar( ). The trailing CR will again be left in the buffer!

Try using scanf( ) instead.

Unfortunately, it too will pick up leading 'whitespace' characters when the format type is %c, otherwise it will helpfully ignore them. However, there is a useful option provided to rescue the situation. if you insert a space before the %c, then scanf( ) will throw away leading whitespace. Try:

```
scanf(" %c%*c", answer);
```

15. Buffering evens out the data rate when it is 'peaky', with periods of quiet interleaved with high-activity bursts. The bursts can overload the receiver, resulting in overrun errors. A good sized buffer will reduce this danger, storing the input data while the computer has time to catch up with the processing.

    The size of buffers varies from machine to machine, which can lead to unexpected failures after years of testing on a different configuration. Output buffers can give the impression that data has been successfully sent, when it is still waiting to get out. Turning off the transmitter in those circumstances requires a full buffer flush beforehand.

Chapter 10

1. Synchronous partners share a bit clock to help the receiver locate the mid-point of the incoming bits. Asynchronous receivers have to provide their own clock which they attempt to phase into the arriving bit stream. Television is asynchronous. Only the occasional synch pulse (one per line and one per field) helps to time the screen drawing at the correct rate. Fax transmissions are asynchronous with headers to synchronize the receiver clock. Ethernet is synchronous, embedding a clock into the data stream. CD-ROMS are synchronous, like the Ethernet.

2. 'A' is 41H – 0 0100 0001

Idle/mark
logic 1/–9 V

3. 14 kbps, but compression is carried out to reduce the amount of data to be transmitted. Run-length coding is suitable for such images.

   $$1142 \times 1728 = 2 \text{ Mbit}; 2 \text{ M}/10 \text{ K} \approx 200 \text{ s} \approx 3.3 \text{ min}$$

   The Huffman run-length encoding compression can reduce the amount of data by a factor of 10 in most normal documents. So we are down to a 20 s transmission. If there was only text on the page, how long would it take to send an email (2.5 kchar/page)? The file would be just 25 kbit: 100 times less than the fax!

4. Digital data transmissions can tolerate more error effects without degrading the information than analogue signals. So digital is more robust in a noisy environment. Digital can be stored conveniently on disk. In networks, digital signals can be switched more cheaply than analogue.

   The disadvantage is the extra bandwidth that the equivalent digitized signals require.

5. CTS (Clear to Send) was the signal that the modem sent to the terminal to inform it that a transmission could commence. RTS (Ready to Send) was the request from the terminal to the modem asking for a transmission.

   Now they are used differently – as a flow control handshake. CTS has to be held low in order for any data to emerge from the transmitter. This is normally done using the RTS output of the receiver but can be done using the RTS output of the transmitter machine if necessary.

   A disadvantage of using the CTS/RTS hardware handshake is the need to obtain a suitable cable, with the correct number of wires. Also there used to be a hardware bug which resulted in repeat transmissions if the CTS was changed in the middle of a character. Furthermore, it is not a suitable flow control method for use with a modem.

6. Flow control is important because, even with input buffering, receivers may be slower at dealing with the information than the transmitters. Then the receiver needs to be able to halt the transmitter for a period so that it can catch up.

7. Our cable television is still analogue. It transmits as a VHF signal, sometimes on copper, sometimes through optical fibre. The set-top box remodulates it to the normal UHF bands that television receivers can deal with.

8. Assume a 56 kbps modem: $2500 \times 10/56000 = 0.45$ s (or 450 ms).

9. 19200 bps → 2400 bytes/s, so this would generate interrupts every three characters (old-fashioned UART) → 800 ips.

10. Add up (in HEX!) the first long row, missing out the S2 header and the final checksum (6BH):

    24 01 04 00 46 FC 26 00 2E 7C 00 08 08 00 61 00 00 5E
    61 00 00 82 61 00 03 3C 46 FC 27 00 23 FC 00 01 06 78

    This comes to 794H (1940 decimal); ignore the leading 7, leaving 94H or 1001_0100 and invert this to 0110_1011 → **6BH**, which is the desired checksum. Hurray!

11.
```
raw data, no parity              Syndrome
 1 0 1 0 1 0 0                    0 0 1
 d d d p d p p

data with even parity bits added
 1 0 1 0 1 0 1                    0 0 0
 d d d p d p p

 ↓ error
 1 1 1 0 1 0 1                    1 1 0   indicates error in position 6
 d d d p d p p
```

12. Each input carries a continuous ASCII representation of the title letter, with the least significant bit first (as happens with serial communications):

    A: 'a' 0 1 0 0 0 0 1 1 0 1
    B: 'b' 0 0 1 0 0 0 1 1 0 1
    C: 'c' 0 1 1 0 0 0 1 1 1 1
    D: 'd' 0 0 0 1 0 0 1 1 0 1

    You should now be able to decode the bit patterns using the ASCII table (Table 2.3). The first 0 is the start bit; then come the 7 ASCII bits, LS bit first, then the odd parity bit, and then finally the stop bit, 1. Now write the binary patterns for capital letters: A, B, C and D.

Chapter 11

1. STROBE, AUTO_FEED, SELECT_INPUT, INIT are control outputs from the computer. ACK, BUSY, OUT_OF_PAPER, SELECT, ERROR are replies from the printer.

   Perhaps only STROBE and ACK (or BUSY) are essential for the data exchange to take place reliably. The transfer operates by the computer checking that the BUSY/PAPER_OUT/ERROR signals are not active, then asserting the STROBE signal after the data lines have settled. The printer responds to the STROBE by reading the data and signals back when this has been done by pulsing the ACK line. The computer can then release the data lines and try for another cycle.

2. The Centronics port can sustain up to 100 kbps transfer rates, much higher than standard serial ports. However, the new USB pushes this up to 1.5 Mbps. The Centronics port is quite simply an 8 bit parallel port with little to go wrong. It does not require a UART. On the PC you may be able to open a connection through to your printer port using the C code below. This is not guaranteed though!

```c
/* Typewriter.c */
#include <stdio.h>
#include <conio.h>

int main(void) {
FILE* fp;
int c;

  if ((fp = fopen("LPT1:", "w")) == NULL) {
    printf("failure to open LPT port\n");
    return 1;
  };

  while ((c=getchar()) != EOF) {fputc( c, fp); fflush(fp);}

  return 0;
}
```

3. Ultra SCSI can handle 15 units and the master controller. The master requests an attached unit to carry out an action, then leaves it to do the job. When finished the unit will inform the master controller. Thus several units can be working simultaneously.

4. Only if a parity bit is sent with the ASCII code. Yes: Unicode is a superset of ASCII, so it is only a question of stripping off the extra byte and sending the ASCII.

5. SCSI has developed a way of offering either synchronous or asynchronous transmission. This is termed Fast SCSI! The units go through an initial agreement phase to decide which to use.

SCSI I	5 Mbps
SCSI II	20 Mbps
Ultra SCSI	40 Mbps

6. IDE does not share a controller: each drive has its own electronics onboard and plugs almost directly into the ISA bus. Each socket can handle two drives, master and slave. Nowadays, PCs usually offer two IDE sockets, allowing for four IDE devices to be connected.

   SCSI master controllers are equipped with a dedicated fast DMA controller which moves the data faster than the PC DMA controller can manage. The SCSI card will also have a larger RAM buffer than that offered by IDE drives.

7. 8 MHz – rather slow by present day standards. 2 bytes/transfer, 16 Mbyte/s; the image is 1 Mbyte, therefore we wait 1/16 s = 63 ms. This is far too long – the same period of time as a complete television frame. What speed does AGP offer?

8. It is the interface chip between the system bus (100 MHz) and the PCI bus (50 MHz). It contains a small buffer which allows the pre-fetching of data in anticipation of the next read.

9. Yes easily: 176.4 kbyte/s, well within the 16 Mbyte/s limit.

10. The ISA bus is now handled as a sub-device of the PCI bus. The PCI bus gateway maps the four PCI interrupt lines (A, B, C and D) onto the existing CPU IRQs as available. The ISA bus still needs to have access to all 15 IRQ lines to retain operational compatibility.

11. Yes, parallel buses have too many limitations and disadvantages. Perhaps we can look forward to optical interfaces built directly into every major component! The area required for a UART circuit and optical transmit/receiver device alongside the CPU will be relatively small.

12. The Plug-and-Play routine in the BIOS sends a request to the known Plug-and-Play port. All the cards respond to this, and a knock-out auction takes place. As each card is isolated it will return its Plug-and-Play code number to BIOS, where it is used to select the correct driver routine.

Chapter 12

1. There are many online sources for RAM prices:

    http://ukram.com/
    http://www.megamemory.com/Prices/PC/PCDT.html

    For disks you could try:

    http://www.streetprices.com/
    http://www.computerprices.co.uk/

2. Intel wanted to increase the size of cache to improve performance. However, the area available on the CPU chip was limited, so it devised the split cache plan, with L1 on-chip and L2 off-chip. If the socket 360 Celeron A, with L2 on-chip, is a success and is able to increase in size, it may signal the end of this arrangement.

3. Because fetch–executes take place in ordered sequences, often in loops, within neighbourhood zones of memory, it is possible to load Lines of the code into faster memory without suffering too many cache misses. Without this feature, caching would not work; neither would virtual memory.

4. Dynamic Random Access Memory (read and write). It is called 'dynamic' because it 'forgets' the written value due to gradual charge leakage from the storage capacitors. So the stored bits need to be refreshed on a regular basis (200 Hz).
    EDO DRAM and SDRAM both access data using bursts which access short sequences of locations. Thus they are not fully random access. In fact, they are behaving more like disks, where the sector start is random access, but all the following block of data is really sequential access. The scheme fits well with the need to load cache memory with lines of instructions and data.

5. The cache data now needs to be written back into main memory before a new cache line can be inserted. For the second method this would double the main memory access delay.

6. Cache memory is used for instructions and data. If both are stored in the same place, collisions may occur, slowing down the CPU. Especially with pipeline decoding, such conflicts may occur due to the different stages imposing demands on memory.

7. Cache misses occur when there are several tasks vying for the CPU. Every time the scheduler swaps the task there may be a cache miss. When a function is called for the first time, or a new area of data in a large array is accessed, then a cache miss would occur. Programmers could group data in cache line friendly units. Data could be structured to reduce the tendency of a program to flit around from location to location at 'random'.

8. A computer system having 64 Mbyte of RAM has hard disks with the following characteristics:

Rotational speed:	5400 r.p.m.
Track capacity:	$266 \times 512 = 136\ 192$ bytes
Heads/cylinder:	4
Head movement time, track to track:	1 ms
Average seek time:	9 ms

How long does it take to dump memory onto disk? Assume the disk is empty.

5400 r.p.m. = 90 r.p.s.

Rotational period = 1/90 s = 1000/90 ms = 11.11 ms $\approx$ 11 ms

Latency = 5.5 ms

Data rate = 136 kbyte/11 ms = 12.38 Mbyte/s

Flow time for 64 Mbyte = 64/12.38 $\approx$ 5.2 s

64 Mbyte needs 64/0.1362 = 470 tracks or 118 cylinders (i.e. 118 head movements)

Total time = head movement (seeks) + rotational delays (latencies) + data flow time

$\qquad$ = $118 \times 9 + 470 \times 5.5 + 5200$ ms

$\qquad$ = 1062 ms + 2585 ms + 5200 ms

$\qquad$ = 8.85 s

9. DVD has smaller bit pits, thus being able to store more data on each disc. It also supports multi-layer and double-sided media. CDs can hold 650 Mbyte, while DVD can go up to 17 Gbyte.

10. $74 \times 60 \times 44\ 100 \times 16 \times 2/8$ bytes $\approx$ 783.2 Mbyte. Most computers can play music from a CD using the Sound Blaster card. There is a special lead supplied to go from the CD drive directly to the Sound Blaster. This allows you to play music while doing the computer science programming assignment.

11. CD-ROMs use laser read–write source/detectors instead of the traditional 'coils' found on magnetic hard disk heads. The laser assemblies are, as yet, larger and heavier than their magnetic counterpart.

Chapter 13

1. There are two routes into operating system facilities:

(i)　using the CLI (command line interpreter) which is now more often accessed from a desktop menu or control panel. The operating system's online help system or an introductory textbook will detail these facilities.

(ii)　using system calls from within a HLL program. You certainly need the programmers' manual as well as the online help which comes with the compiler.

Now print out a list of files in a directory with size and date information from the desktop, and then from within a C program.

2.　Assembler programs contain 'assembler directives' as well as machine instruction mnemonics. So, a line containing ds.b 100 generates no code, it simply reserves space for data variables. Conversely, lines such as mov count,ax will result in a single executable machine instruction.

HLL statements may be translated by the compiler into between 5 and 10 executable statements. It all depends on the language and the processor (RISC or CISC). There is also a dilemma with HLL calls to library routines or the operating system! You could use the disassembler inside the debugger to track the execution path.

3.　Perl is an interpreted scripting language which can be used for systems administration work, or as 'glue' to fit together other programs (tools) to build a new system. It has awk text processing capabilities, Unix socket calls, SQL statements for accessing databases and traditional shell functionality. It is growing in popularity for WWW applications partly because it can run on Unix or NT. Look it up and try it out. You will not be wasting your time!

4.　CPU status flags record part of the result of machine operations, usually from within the ALU. Thus, if an addition overflows, or a compare gives a positive result, or a register goes negative, all of these will set the appropriate CPU flag which can then be used to steer the direction of subsequent conditional operations. These flag bits effectively 'bind together' machine instructions to build more useful operations.

Conditional HLL statements, such as IF-ELSE, rely on the CPU flags for their operation. This is more apparent when looking at the executable code produced by the compiler.

5.　The structures sequence, iteration and selection are supported by all decent programming languages. In C we might have:

```
printf("Do you want 100 copies? "); \* SEQUENCE of instructions *\
choice = tolower(getchar());

if (choice == 'y') { \* SELECTION of possible outcomes *\

  for (i=0; i< LMAX; i++) { \* ITERATION within a loop*\
    printf("\nWelcome Home!");
  }
} else {
  printf("\nNothing requested")
}
```

6.　The use of assembler level programming is now quite limited in commercial circles. Games writers still resort to assembler for optimizing graphics routines, especially where bespoke hardware is involved which compilers might not recognize. Interrupt routines would be written in assembler, but these are always quite short. Device drivers, interfacing the operating system to new hardware, may be written in assembler, though C is preferable. When installing a compiler on a new CPU, there is an opportunity to exploit your assembler skills! But realistically, the realm of assembler is now nearly limited to the academic arena where students gain greater understanding of HLLs and the operation of hardware through low-level programming.

7. End-users of a program would not be able to distinguish the source of the code, unless they start disassembling the executable. Then the recognizable features of compiler-generated code may become visible. Human code cuts corners, does not follow regular templates so often, has 'jokes' and 'clever bits', and even less error checking. Compiler code uses more CPU registers than is strictly necessary because it is following a pattern that was designed to work successfully in all cases.

8. Programming with an HLL is easier to learn. HLLs are intended to assist with the expression of algorithms – solutions to problems. This is sometimes stated by saying that HLLs are better suited to modelling human problems, while assembler code deals with the nitpicking details of how the CPU will carry out the operations. Compilers check syntax, translate code and provide libraries packed with good quality routines. Assemblers do a bit of translation. Compiler error messages can sometimes be helpful. Assembler error messages are rare and fatal.

9. Installing new software packages
   Setting up accounts for new users
   Sorting out the printers (daily!)
   Applying software update patches provided by suppliers
   Checking operational statistics to anticipate serious problems
   Clearing unwanted files
   Reconfiguring the network (weekly)
   Investigating disk error reports, calling in hardware maintenance if needed
   Talking to users occasionally
   Checking that backups are being carried out successfully
   Negotiating for system upgrades

A. The best known Unix command line interpreters are:

   Bourne shell: sh
   C shell: csh
   Korn shell: ksh

   They are programs which accept keyboard input from the user and echo to the screen. They provide key input editing and a history buffer, allowing you to re-invoke previous commands without retyping. Shells can also accept commands stored in files, known as scripts. Windows NT still offers a Command Prompt window.

B. If a user has direct access to the hardware, the provision of security would be compromised. Any user would be able to alter the memory management tables so that they would allow anyone to access any data. Users could switch their privilege to root. Interrupts could be blocked indefinitely. Total anarchy could occur.

   Certainly the needs of office workers, systems administrators, programmers and students are very different. Consider their roles, software needs, access requirements, security risks and computation demands.

C. Unix piping is the facility whereby processes can accept input data directly from the output of another process. The data can be 'streamed' from process to process without needing to open intermediate temporary files. For example the pipe to generate a word list for index generation is:

```
cat ch_* | tr -sc "[A-Za-z}" "\012" | sort | uniq -c | sort -n >
  /tmp/iwords
```

It is a very elegant and useful facility for building larger processing systems from smaller tested units.

D. From the bottom layer upwards we have: logic circuits, coprocessors, microcode interpreters, operating systems, specialist routine libraries and applications code.

Examples of appropriate functionality might be: basic arithmetic/logical operations, primitive screen operations, Windows graphics manipulation, complex text processing operations and handling user interaction sessions.

E. Disk space is now rarely a problem unless you are dealing with image files.

How to use the print facilities, directly or across the network.

Application users need to know how to exit correctly from their package, rather than simply crashing out.

The keystroke repertoire for the package will have to be learnt. Importing and exporting non-standard file formats will be required sooner or later.

Interfacing to the mail system is often required.

Familiarity with the language library.

What operating system is running, equipped with what range of system routines.

Size of user space may be limited.

If there is a network port, how to access TCP/IP services such as sockets and RPCs.

Any port addresses for special hardware interfaces.

F. SEQ – the post-increment address register indirect addressing mode which underpins the fetch cycle: `move.w (PC)+,IR`.

Offering CALL-RET for subroutining assists with organizing SEQ more effectively.

SEL – all facilities assisting with conditional branch instructions: CPU flags, ALU setting CPU flags as a by-product of arithmetic/logical operations, conditional branch with relative addressing (some CPUs have conditional `CALL` instructions, but not the MC68000), address arithmetic could allow `SWITCH-CASE` statements to be implemented more efficiently.

IT – the `dbra` family of instructions supports `FOR` loops.

There are fast INC/DEC instructions (`addq`/`subq`) for bumping index variables. The post-increment address register indirect mode helps with array accessing in a loop.

10. Use the Microsoft Developer Studio debugger.

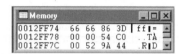

The three floating point numbers are seen in hex representation in their locations on the stack as local variables. They are 32 bits long, so require 4 bytes, or 8 hex digits. Unfortunately the bytes are written left to right across the screen as you go up through memory, down the screen!

1234.5625 Decimal is
0100 0100 1001 1010 0101 0010 0000 0000 Binary or
   44   9A   52   00   Hex

−3.3125 Decimal is
1100 0000 0101 0100 0000 0000 0000 0000 Binary or
   C0   54   00   00   Hex

0.065625 Decimal is
0011 1101 1000 0110 0110 0110 0110 0110 Binary or
   3D   86   66   66   Hex

Chapter 14

1. LAN advantages:

    Connectivity gives the opportunity to establish email contacts
    Allows access to WWW
    Direct queries to departmental databases
    Administrative help with regular file backups
    File overflow areas on central disk prevents your local disk becoming full
    Peripatetic possibilities – you can change workstation and still access your files
    Access to high-quality printer

  LAN disadvantages:

    Waste time reading junk email
    Suffer from the frustrations of the WWW
    Complexity escalation with departmental file structures
    Network crashes affect your independence
    Queuing at a shared printer
    Another source of virus attacks,
    Administrators interfere with your computing preferences
    Builds up a dependency, reducing your ability to work away from the central server

2. Ethernet 10BaseT, 10Base2 and the older 10Base5 operate at 10 Mbps. The newer 100BaseT and 100BaseF have increased to 100 Mbps.

    $20 \times 8/10 = 16$ s

  But it might be compressed to much smaller size (0.1?).

    The time will depend on who else is using the network at the same time because you are sharing it with all other users. Sometimes it appears to be offering little better than a 14 kbps modem connection!

3. 32 bits/IPv4 number. 48 bits/MAC Ethernet number. IPv6 will be 128 bits. On Unix use `/usr/sbin/ifconfig -a`, while on Windows NT try `ipconfig` in the Command Prompt window.

4. The host name → IP number is done by calling up the DNS database using `gethostbyname( )`. IP → MAC translation is done using the ARP table, which is built up from RARP requests and by looking at returning packets.

5. Baseband signalling is where the fundamental rate of the data is used to form the transmission signal. Digital broadcasting will use broadband signalling to gain the maximum bandwidth possible. Broadband requires r.f. modem units.

6. Data and clock are XORed together and transmitted down the same wire. A special PLL (phase locked loop) circuit separates them again at the receiver end. It does seem odd that the Ethernet scheme relies completely on the accurate detection of the single SFD bit which is not covered by any redundancy, error detection or correction.

7. Ethernet does bit synchronization by extracting the clock signal from a Manchester-encoded transmission. A preamble pattern of 62 bits comes before the data packet to allow the receiver to get synchronized. The byte synchronization is carried out by the single SFD bit. Message synchronization is achieved using IP protocols. The TCP protocols handle message fragmentation and reordering.

8. The maximum Ethernet segment length is 500 m. For 10Base2, this value is set by the signal strength. As the voltages are only +0.7 V to −0.7 V, so a small attenuation will disrupt the ability of receivers to detect the bits reliably. The more hosts that are attached to the LAN, the lower will be the signal because each one takes some of the power.

    For the end-to-end 10BaseT, the maximum length is set by the natural degradation of the signal as it passes down the lossy cable, as well as any electrical noise which would interfere with the signal.

9. Bus: simple and cheap. Fair shares to all users. Easy to add extra stations without too much hassle. Incremental expansion, up to a maximum number.

    Star: higher potential throughput. Centralized administrative control. More immune to single-point failure. Easy to reconfigure once the cable points are installed. Incremental expansion, until another hub is required. Better security for data transmissions.

10. If you are using NT, don't forget to cut off the Unix path section from the front of the command. So use arp -a in the NT Command Prompt window. The ifconfig command on Unix appears to have an equivalent: ipconfig on Windows NT.

11. TCP/IP has worked well on bus LANs, but it was intended for the less reliable environment of WANs. It has quite an administrative overhead when sending small amounts of data, such as emails. It was adopted against European government advice and against IBM preferences. Perhaps it was only Unix and the Internet that made it succeed.

    Users of Novell on PC networks are a very loyal band. It is not uncommon for them to prefer to retain NetWare when moving across to Windows NT. They also tend to be suspicious of any Unix influence!

12. Fibre optics offers a much higher bandwidth, if broadband modems are used to benefit from the wider frequency band. They are immune to electrical interference and cannot quickly be tapped into for nefarious purposes, although splicing kits are readily available.

    The higher throughput does not come from faster traffic but rather from more traffic – in other words, bigger lorries rather than faster.

    Yes, the use of parallel buses is being reduced. The interconnection of disks using fibre was a change from the use of SCSI.

13. Class A: 2^{24} = 16M. Large multinational with many subnets.
    Class B: 2^{16} = 65 536. Medium multi-LAN organization with subnets.

Class C: $2^8 = 256$. Small office LAN, possibly no subnets.

IPv6 is subdividing its numbers by geographical location. This is intended to help plan for the routing and switching of traffic in a more organized manner than the present evolutionary arrangements.

15.

Chapter 15

1. The Internet gives easy access to a wide range of information, much of which is of little value to anyone. This is seen by some as an excuse to close traditional libraries. Unfortunately there are no regulations or even guidelines about how long an item has to be maintained on the Web. So, quite often, an important find will have disappeared the following month. It is like using a library with a serious thieving problem! The possibility of paying for information would perhaps be a way around this. Another possibility is the tradition of archiving material for some period after it has been withdrawn.

    Elimination of the telephone network as a separate entity?
    Reduced business travel?
    More active democracy?
    Fewer shops?
    No record companies?
    Personally tailored radio and television?
    Online education for distance learning courses?
    Personal net-ID for life?

2. The repeater simply amplifies the voltage, boosting the signal.
    A bridge filters the packets using the Ethernet MAC address. It has to build up internal tables of the MAC numbers of the hosts attached to the nets on either side.
    Routers work at the IP address level. They reset the MAC address for the next hop.

3. (a) `/etc/hosts` or DNS: Application level.
    (b) ARP table: Data link layer, Ethernet device handler.
    (c) Routing table: IP layer uses the routing table to choose the best next hop destination.
    (d) `/etc/services`: Used by TCP to set up the ports table.

4. 194.000.000.000.000.000.000.000.000.000.000.000.000.000.000
      − 195.255.255.255.255.255.255.255.255.255.255.255.255.255.255

    This gives Europe 2×2^{120} numbers. Should be enough!

5. Yes, for packet handling and internal routing.

6. ICMP rerouting packets. RIP packets from neighbouring routers. Manually using `route` command.

7. Client–server is an interactive session, while peer to peer is a temporary command.

8. (a) A condensed directions list is fast and convenient for the driver to use, but the information source, the library map, would certainly be out of date and eventually demand corrective on-the-spot intervention.

    (b) Looking up the map is time-consuming, but offers good resilience to local routing difficulties. It also offers broad scope, strategic as well as neighbourhood planning decisions. Maps contain a lot of information if you know how to use them!

    (c) This provides up to date information at a local level, but unreliable guidance at the strategic level. It is very time-consuming, but interesting, especially if the dialect is also unfamiliar!

    (d) Depending on how often the signs are revised, this can be quite effective, but an outline strategic route is still necessary to select the correct 'next town'.

9. Computers with two network cards need different IP numbers in order to distinguish the different routes into and out of the machine. If DNS domain names are allocated to these IP numbers, they will have to be distinct. Gateway machines require at least two network cards to perform their function. Not all IP numbers have DNS names associated with them.

10.
```
[rob@zen rob]$ ping src.doc.ic.ac.uk
PING swallow.doc.ic.ac.uk (193.63.255.4) from 164.11.100.4 : 56
data bytes
64 bytes from 193.63.255.4: icmp_seq=0 ttl=248 time=10.2 ms
64 bytes from 193.63.255.4: icmp_seq=1 ttl=248 time=11.8 ms
64 bytes from 193.63.255.4: icmp_seq=2 ttl=248 time=11.6 ms
64 bytes from 193.63.255.4: icmp_seq=3 ttl=248 time=13.5 ms
64 bytes from 193.63.255.4: icmp_seq=4 ttl=248 time=9.9 ms
64 bytes from 193.63.255.4: icmp_seq=5 ttl=248 time=9.7 ms
64 bytes from 193.63.255.4: icmp_seq=6 ttl=248 time=17.9 ms
64 bytes from 193.63.255.4: icmp_seq=7 ttl=248 time=13.6 ms
64 bytes from 193.63.255.4: icmp_seq=8 ttl=248 time=9.6 ms

--- swallow.doc.ic.ac.uk ping statistics ---
9 packets transmitted, 9 packets received, 0% packet loss
round-trip min/avg/max = 9.6/11.9/17.9 ms
[rob@zen rob]$
```

Chapter 16

1. Analogue telephone channels are band limited to between 300 and 3400 Hz. The normal PCM/TDM trunks handle 64 kbps, each way, for a conversation. FM radio is divided into channels which are allocated 30 kHz each. CD-quality recordings are carried out at 16 bits every 44.1 kHz, dual channel for stereo.

2. The raw digital data stream for voice is much more greedy for bandwidth than the analogue version. The latter has, however, been drastically filtered to fit into the 3000 kHz band. The latest modem technology sends more than 1 data bit per carrier cycle as shown in Figs. 10.32 and 10.33. So a 3.5 kHz upper frequency limit could still serve to transmit 56 kbps if 16 bits of data could be successfully encoded into a single carrier period. This is possible by using several amplitude and phase values and data compression techniques.

3. Once the voice signal has been digitized it too can be submitted to a variety of compression techniques. For example, the silences can be detected and no data transmitted. A nonlinear digitization can be applied to optimally use the limited bandwidth available. The binary data could be run-encoded to exploit the similarities exhibited by speech patterns. Sophisticated digital signal processing techniques, such as LPC (linear predictive coding), can be used to generate a limited set of descriptive parameters, which can then be transmitted, in place of the speech signal itself, to allow the speech waveform to be resynthesized at the receiver end.

4. See Figs. 10.32 and 10.33.

5. LAN packets are broadcast with the lowest MAC level address used for the destination. This limits the next destination to a host which is directly connected to the same LAN. All the local stations can 'see' the packet and its contents.

    IP addressing is used to individually route packets through an 'unknown' network. The hop-to-hop routing decisions depending on the destination IP address, are taken 'on the fly', and may vary from packet to packet within a single message.

    ATM sets up a pathway through the network at the start of the session, and arranges for the intermediate routers to always send message cells (packets) the same way. This technique is termed a virtual circuit.

    Telephony has traditionally set up a physical circuit at the start of a call, from source right through to destination.

6. See Table 16.1 and Fig. 16.11.

7. The current allocation for the 160 character SMS packets depends on available bandwidth in the free control channels. It does not use voice channel bandwidth. The 9600 bps digital data facility allocates four voice slots to transfer the data. The new GPRS standard expands this.

8. Codecs devices are dedicated to converting analogue speech into 8 bit samples 8000 times a second, or the reverse operation. A nonlinear mapping is used to expand the quieter signals and compress the louder regions. In this way, codecs are intended to allow analogue voice signals to pass over a digital network. On the other hand, modems are intended to allow a variety of computer data to pass over analogue telephone lines.

9. Narrowband ISDN offers twin duplex 64 kbps voice channels and a single 16 kbps data channel. ADSL is offering a bandwidth matched to the individual line, up to 4 Mbps. Clearly 1.5 Mbps could be handled by the ADSL link, but it goes way beyond the current telephone modems or N-ISDN capability.

10. 1000 accesses every 125 μs means each transfer has to be completed within 125 ns. This must include reading a sample, transferring it and writing it back into the destination buffer. The 60 ns EDO RAM would appear to be adequate for this task.

Chapter 17

1. It looks after file storage and retrieval.
    It provides a GUI interface to the user.
    It offers password management for login security.
    It deals with the network traffic.

Memory allocation and interprocess protection.
Loads and schedules processes.
Takes control of the memory management (cache and virtual).

2. There can be small compiler discrepancies such as integer widths or language extensions which make porting more difficult than anticipated. The new linker/loader may be more limited in flexibility. The new hardware will be constrained by different memory size limits. The new CPU is hardly likely to be less powerful, but other deficiencies may become apparent: floating point arithmetic, relative addressing ranges, access to ports. The main problem often derives from the divergence in operating system facilities. If the new target runs a substantially different version of the operating system, there may need to be serious revisions to the code involving tasking, memory protection, hardware initialization and error handling. The obvious problem of IO mismatch usually appears early on. Terminal device characteristics will probably be different.

3. The Task Control Block holds administrative information about tasks for the operating system. You would expect process ID, owner, priority, data size requirements, volatile storage (or at least a pointer to the storage area) and pointer space so it can be joined into a linked list.

4. The '&' signifies a background job, detached from the keyboard and screen.
    The pipe opens a file and changes all space characters to newlines. This means that every word is on a different line. The words are alphabetically sorted, and then a frequency count is inserted for each word when duplicates are removed. The sort is repeated, but on numerical grounds. Thus it lists the words in order of popularity.
    '|' glues together two processes, piping data from stdout into stdin.
    '>' sends the stdout data to a named file.

5. The signal handler function can only communicate through global variables. This introduces the danger of critical data corruption, because the signal arrives asynchronously, so only very simple data and operations should be used. A semaphore could be contemplated, but only if secure signal queuing facilities are provided.

6. Semaphores are enhanced 'busy flags', with linked access functions and task waiting queues. They are part of the data protection facilities, but serve the scheduling apparatus of the operating system. The linked functions are confusingly called WAIT( ) and SIGNAL( ). The latter has nothing whatsoever to do with the notifier signals which are dispatched by the 'kill' command. These signals operate in a similar vein to interrupts, nudging processes to execute a nominated function. The most common use of signals is to kill errant processes, but they may also be used to synchronize processes within a multitasking application.
    CTRL-C is given special treatment. It sends signal #9 (terminate with severe prejudice). This signal cannot be diverted or ignored.

7. A shell is a command line interpreter. It accepts commands typed in by the user at the keyboard, and either obeys them directly or passes them on to the operating system for action. Shells can often accept input from command or batch files, written in a scripting language. An X Window such as X-term will be hosting a shell such as bash, sh, csh, tcsh, zsh or ksh.

8. Spooling is the technique of storing output data as a file on disk in readiness for when it can be actually output to the slow device. In this way the CPU is decoupled from the very slow printing process. Slow input data can also be prepared offline on disk. However, with efficient multitasking operating systems these arrangements are no longer necessary.

9. A device driver is the software used to interface to equipment that is connected to the computer. Nowadays the device driver is part of the operating system, running in privileged mode. They are often split into two parts, proximal and distal, referring to their position within the system. One part will probably be interrupt-driven, while the other responds to the application calls. All interfaced equipment will require a suitable device driver.

10. Try:

```
find ~ -name sardine -exec rm \{\} \;
```

Be careful to include the backslashes and to position the spaces correctly! A more common use for `find` is to simply print the path of a lost file: `find . -name "complaint*" -print`. It can also list files by time and date.

11. `du` is a utility to present a summary of disk usage, or all the file sizes if the `-a` flag is employed. It displays the number of blocks (512 bytes) used by each file. This is piped into `sort -n` which does a numeric reordering, of which only the last 10 are displayed on the screen. It does include directories as well as files, though. Try this alternative: `ls -Ral ~ | sort -nr +4 -5 | head`.

Chapter 18

1. The importance of simple, straightforward procedures which can be easily understood, and corrected when wrongly carried out is paramount in the domestic environment. For corporate computing, where the technical guru may be on hand to solve such problems, the principal issue is data security and system integrity. Windows NT is not 'simple' to reinstall when something goes wrong, but does offer a complex of security features to protect networked data files from illicit access. This includes export control (shares) and access permissions which can separately reference each file and resolve individual users.

2. The 16 bit Unicode supports many different language alphabets, making it much easier to plan software products for international distribution. ASCII only had 7 bit codes, which were extended to 8 bits to allow it to include European character sets. But this still was nowhere near large enough to encompass all the natural written languages of the world. Microsoft had decided to develop all its products for a world market, and the cost of retrospectively 'localizing' each package for every market would have been too great.

3. Windows NT is constructed on a modular basis. In addition, the hardware is screened by the HAL (Hardware Abstraction Layer) which offers a virtual machine interface to the device drivers and kernel. Porting from one CPU to another involves rewriting the HAL functions, and loading this onto the new CPU. That's the idea, anyway! The Win32 API is common to all versions of Windows, which again makes the programmer's task easier. Even the interrupts can be hidden by virtual interrupts, although this somewhat slows down the response to their request. Device drivers for new hardware interfaces can be installed, with some effort, to deal directly with unusual features.

4. The compiler has a chance to preview the code and so could in some circumstances anticipate what data is required. By inserting pre-read instructions to charge up the cache, the actual reads when they occur will not be faulted. Such planned data handling could be incorporated into the compiler if 'parallel cache loading' is supported by the host. This is usually so, given the availability of DMA channels.

5.   The Windows NT TCP/IP protocol stack offers compatibility with other operating systems which honour the same protocols. Also, files can be exported to and imported from Unix across the network with the aid of SAMBA running on Unix. Windows NT can offer X Window servers, for example from Exceed, and the Citrix Metaframe software enables NT display windows to be exported to foreign operating systems.

6.   Memory management, interprocess communications, graphical interface, process (thread) scheduling control, serial communications, socket communication, keyboard and mouse, file reading and writing functions, inter object message handling, object linking and embedding, printer control, resource allocation, and of course window management.

7.   The NTFS filing system can be configured to support a multi-disk RAID service. This can record duplicate or error-correction codes to reduce the number of data corruptions suffered. A transaction log journal file can be used to rebuild damaged areas of data files or databases. NTFS operates a write–check–commit schedule which reduces the danger of hardware failures resulting in corrupted data. Windows NT supports the operation of a UPS (uninterruptible power supply), too.

8.   The original aim was to separate kernel code from the rest. This clean distinction has been sacrificed with the inclusion of the graphics driver code within the privileged central core of software. The change was justified on performance grounds. Kernel software can run faster and under more predictable conditions than the user modules.

9.   Threads are parts of processes. Processes all have their own data areas and cannot access anyone else's area. Threads share a data pool, which makes for faster communications but gives rise to problems with critical resources. This can be resolved by using semaphores or signals.

10.   The local procedure call mechanism, somewhat like the remote procedure call facility offered by Unix, provides more efficient message passing between processes running on the same computer.

Chapter 19

1. $10^9/2.5 \times 10^3 = 400\ 000$, assuming 2500 characters per page.

2.   The Norton Utilities are a set of PC utility programs which, among other things, provide the means of retrieving data from damaged file systems. HexWorkshop from bpsoft provides similar facilities for FAT-based file system inspection and patching. Generally programmers only resort to such time-consuming data recovery procedures when they are fairly desperate.

3.   FATs are efficient and fast for accessing relatively small files.
      FAT-16 is recognized by several different operating systems.
      Simple to implement and recover after a disk crash.
      No user security as there is no user identification access control, so unsuited to multi-user environment.
      No effective fault tolerance.
      Limited file size capability derived from cluster size and FAT length.
      Imposes a maximum partition size: $2^{16} \times 4$ kbyte = 262 Mbyte.
      Needs regular defragmentation to retain performance.

The fixed format directory limits filename length.
Poor date stamping.

4. The layout of data on disk can make considerable differences to file read time. If the complete file is stored within a single disk cylinder, no head movements will be incurred. On the other hand, if the sectors are scattered all over the platters, the head will be skipping back and forth picking up all the data. To reduce this dispersal effect the Unix file manager attempts to allocate and reserve space within cylinders. Thus the data is held contiguously, reducing the likely access times. FAT-based file systems have to resort to defragging the disks, a time-consuming activity which physically shuffles data around.

5. Today I checked prices and a 20 Gbyte IDE hard drive was offered at £115, while 64 Mbyte PC100 DIMMs were available at £40. So a single byte of disk storage comes in at 0.57 p/Mbyte. The DIMM costs 62.5 p/Mbyte.

6. At boot, the hardware is checked by code held in the BIOS ROM. If Plug-and-Play is active, the BIOS PROM will probe the hardware and register the devices and their interface cards. The operating system loader, held on disk, is loaded itself by a routine in BIOS.

7. Solaris offers the `setfacl` command (set file access control list) which the file owner can employ to restrict access to a limited number of other users:

```
% mkdir group_data
% setfacl -s user::rwx,
group::--x,mask:rwx,other:--x,
default:user::rwx,
default:group::--x,
default:mask:rwx,
default:other:--x group_data
% setfacl -m user:rob:rwx,default:user:rob:rwx group_data
% setfacl -m user:craig:rwx,default:user:craig:rwx group_data
```

The default entry for the directory will apply to subsequent files within that directory, unless overridden by a specific instruction. Now use the `getfacl` command to check the access rights.

8. Yes, it is possible to have different local and network passwords, with different access permissions, but different login names would have to be used. Choosing passwords which are entries in the online dictionary is deprecated! It is a good idea to include at least one non-alphabetic character.

9. No, using `del` or `rm` simply marks the relevant directory entry as available and attaches the data blocks to the free list, from where they may be allocated during a subsequent file write operation. This means that you can recover deleted data, as long as no other data files have been written in the meanwhile.

10. A RAM disk is a software facility which reserves a large area of main memory and makes it behave to the user as if it were a disk volume. A disk cache is simply a large RAM buffer interposed between the system bus and the disk drive. It operates by holding data sectors after the read has been completed, just in case the data is needed again. Both facilities require virtual memory paging to be disabled for the area of memory in use, or no speed advantage would be forthcoming. RAM disks were popular with the previous generation of hobby computers, which often did not have a hard disk, but could have sufficient RAM installed to make a 512

kbyte RAM disk viable. Loading files into RAM disk is under the user control; not so the disk cache, which simply follows the preceding demands on the disk unit.

Chapter 20

1. Having a separate graphics adapter card has enabled the PC to keep up with the hardware developments in display technology. A problem was the bus bottleneck imposed by the 8 MHz ISA bus. This meant that soon the graphics cards started to install large amounts of RAM to avoid the bandwidth limitation when transferring screen image files from main memory to the screen buffer.

   Also, when the PC first came out, the design and development of a new motherboard was considered a large undertaking, whereas currently new designs are appearing every few months.

   The introduction of AGP indicates that the split between main memory and graphics memory may soon be finished. It is not essential, MAC, Atari and Amiga offered a unified memory from the start.

2. Download a PDF file from the WWW. Look at its header in a text editor. Convert it back to PostScript by saving a print file under the Acrobat Reader printer facility. What is the header for this file?

3. The PostScript and PDF versions of the same file are different because the PDF commands are much abbreviated, but the PDF file also includes the font patterns which the PostScript file assumes will be available everywhere.

4. An LCD consists of two polarizing filters with their axes arranged perpendicular (at 90°). This would block all light trying to pass through, and the panel would appear black. But twisted liquid crystals are contained between the polarizers, and these crystals can also affect the polarization of the light waves. The plate that the polarizer is stuck to has finely traced rulings on the underside which 'encourage' the long liquid crystal molecules to line up in an orderly fashion. Therefore light is polarized by the first filter, twisted through 90° by the liquid crystals, finally allowing it to pass readily through the second polarizing filter. But if an electrical voltage is applied across the liquid crystal, the molecules will realign with that. Now it allows the light to pass undisturbed through the liquid, only to be blocked by the second polarizer! Thus, no voltage equals light passing through, while applied voltage equals no light emerging at the other end.

   The LCD operates as a digital device. It would benefit from a fully digital port on the PC, rather than having to reconvert the analogue VGA signals back into digital for use. It has a fixed number of liquid crystal cells and can effectively only offer a single resolution: one cell per pixel. A lower resolution could be organized by using only a proportion of the screen. A 1024×768 panel can display at resolution of 640×480 by using only 66% of the screen. Some LCDs are, however, capable of rescaling lower-resolution images to fill the screen.

   A disadvantage of LCD panels is the irreversible failure of individual pixels. It's possible for one or more cells on the LCD panel to be flawed. On a 1024×768 monitor, there are three cells for each pixel – one each for red, green and blue – which amounts to nearly 2.4 million cells ($1024 \times 768 \times 3 = 2\ 359\ 296$). There is actually only a slim chance that all of these will be perfect. Some may be stuck on, creating a 'bright' defect, while others are stuck off, resulting in a 'dark' defect.

5. ASCII letters are stored as 7/8 bit code numbers, which are used by the printer to look up in PROM the ink dot pattern when it comes to actually printing. PostScript stores letters as subroutine calls to a font library. The fonts are drawn in outline and then filled in. To save time this is only done once per document and the bit image is then reused again and again as long as

the font size and type do not alter. This font library is held locally, so there are problems when the printer libraries differ from the screen viewer libraries. That is why sending PostScript files is a little risky unless you are familiar with the receiver's facilities. To overcome this problem, PDF has the font patterns included, which should make the files much bigger, but they use compressed codes to reduce the overall size. Image files represent the letter as a raw bitmap pattern, which would be used directly by the printer to control the ink density.

6. For a 450 page book with an average of 30 lines, each holding 80 letters, we have a total of $450 \times 30 \times 80 = 1$ Mbyte. Which is not far wrong. At the moment, while I am revising this section, I can still squeeze all the text and `pic` code for the diagrams onto a single 1.4 Mbyte floppy. A file for a single screen dump figure is larger than the whole of the text!

7. Palette tables hold a small number (say 16) of RGB colour numbers (24 bit) which can then be selected by the 4 bit number stored for every pixel. The palette table can be swapped and changed. This gives an extended colour range for the screen without storing the full 24 bits at each pixel.

   The VGA card does use a 256 entry table. When you store 24 bit true-colour for every pixel, the need for memory is increased threefold. Perhaps a fax-like run-length code could be used.

   How would the introduction of random access LCD arrays change the display update problem? Do LCD panels need refreshing?

8. There is a danger when you are updating the display while it is being written onto the screen of partially complete fragments appearing. They will be corrected on the next frame scan, but in game playing, where changes occur very frequently, it would introduce an unacceptable flickering distraction. The PC was provided with an interrupt IRQ2 to indicate when the graphics controller was blanking the beam during fly-back. This is not used now; rather, the graphics card holds at least two screen images. One will be displayed, while the other will be subject to modification by the application code (game). When the modifications are done, the application tells the graphics controller, which remembers to switch display buffers during the next vertical blanking interval. So changes to the screen only occur out of sight.

   There are horizontal blanking periods as well as vertical, which are occasionally exploited by programmers.

9. A 15 inch diagonal has a width of 12 and a height of 9.5 inches. Converting to mm these dimensions become 295×240 mm. So the pixels per inch $= 800/12 = 66$. This is slightly less than the 72 points per inch which printers use as a guideline for human visual acuity. For 800×640, each pixel will be 0.37 mm across (0.35 mm down).

10. The technique used is known as dithering. It involves computing a suitable 'dots per square mm' value for each neighbourhood, and plotting them in a random fashion to achieve this density. From the viewpoint of the human eye, the effect will be a grey area because the individual points are too small to resolve. The same pointillistic technique is used to build up the exact colour required when only red, green and blue are actually available.

11. Our department expects to get a minimum of 15 000 pages of printing from a toner cartridge which costs about £100. Sometimes, depending on the average amount of text involved, four times more pages are printed for each cartridge.

Chapter 21

1. Microcoded CPUs:

    Microcode disadvantages
    A few 'unpopular' complex instructions slow down the whole decoding process.
    Large control memory (PROM) area taken up on CPU chip. Space could be used to more
    advantage for cache or CPU data registers.
    Variable size and execution time instructions make pipelined decoding very tricky.
    Microcoded decoding is slower than hardware-only decoding, so the CPU runs slower.
    Takes longer to develop and bring to market.

    Microcode advantages
    Complex 'meaty' instructions possible to implement useful operations.
    Complex instructions reduce bus traffic.
    Programs are shorter, requiring less disk space, main memory and cache.
    Emulation of alternative machine instruction architectures possible.
    Establishment of an architecture family standard easier.
    Retrospective inclusion of new instructions possible in the field.
    Alternative optimizations offered: database engine, personal workstation etc.
    Separates hardware and microcode development teams.
    Variable length instruction allows for efficient encoding strategies.
    Backward binary compatibility more readily achievable.

2. Perhaps because the BASIC instructions are too complex even for a microcode engine to carry
    out at the single level with no prior translation stages. A complex (expensive) CPU tied up
    running BASIC programs might not have customer appeal.

3. The functional hierarchy can be expressed as: HLL application programs, API functions, oper-
    ating system facilities, CU microcode, hardware logic. Of these, the first four involve code. It
    can be seen as an inverted pyramid, with vast applications relying on only a few kilobytes of
    microcode.

4. Data move: universally required, would benefit from maximum hardware support. I would
    offer DMA or at least special optimized instructions to carry out this action.
        Floating point: rather specialist operations; should not be put in microcode because of the
    adverse impact on other instructions. Supply dedicated FPU hardware, perhaps off-chip if not
    otherwise possible. A software library implementation would be too slow.
        FAX encodement: special software library routine, linked in after compile. Not of general
    interest to other users, but might be eligible for a DLL.
        BST $\leftrightarrow$ GMT: user coding (although Windows appears to have this incorporated into the
    operating system level).

5. An interrupt is a hardware signal to the CPU, asking for immediate attention to be paid to a
    specific device. To implement this facility, microcoded CPUs check the status of interrupt lines
    at the end of every instruction. It is part of the microcoded instruction. In this way it seems to be
    polling at the microcode level.

6. Parallel pipeline decoding is the most significant performance enhancing feature, followed by
    larger on-chip cache memory.

7. This is a tricky issue which depends on the efficiency of the respective addressing modes. Register addressing only requires the operand field to be inspected for a register identifier, and the location can be accessed. When dealing with a memory reference, the address will need to be read and then go through the segmentation and page/frame translations stages before checking the cache for a hit. This must be a slower process. Until we get 'virtual register space', it may be better to increase the number of registers. But alternatively, when any unexpected page fault incurs such a penalty the risk must surely be reduced by increasing the size of cache! A difficult trade-off.

8. By reducing the amount of decoding required by the CU, the compiler can gain fuller control over the sequences and combinations of operations which are carried out during the fetch–execute cycle. The reduced decoding will also speed up the execution.

9. Pre-fetching reduces (prevents) the CPU stalling while it waits for an instruction or data item to arrive from memory. It allows the CU to preview the instructions and possibly reorder them before entering them into the pipeline for decoding. Alternative branches may be fetched and executed until the decision is taken as to which pathway to follow. Complex instructions may be fragmented into simpler microinstructions, thus usefully amalgamating CISC and RISC instruction types.

10. Any decision which is taken by the compiler and not the CU is advantageous because it is only carried out once, and not at run time. Compilers could potentially understand the CPU architecture and choose better ways of executing sequences of actions. Compilers can be easily enhanced and upgraded. Compile-time checking is not so time-constrained.

Chapter 22

1. A microprocessor is an integrated CPU, while a microcontroller includes on-chip program memory (ROM), data memory (RAM) and IO devices (PIO, UART etc.). Microcontrollers often choose to follow alternative design guidelines, such as keeping data and program in separate addressing spaces (Harvard architecture). They do not need to be CISC, and there is a growing RISC microcontroller market sector: ARM.

2.

Data movement	`move.w d0,ccr`
Data manipulation	`cmp #10,d0, addq.b #1,d0`
Data IO	`movep.b d0,(a0)`
Transfer of control	`bra DONE, bsr DOITZ`
Machine supervision	`reset trap #10`

3. CISC CPUs are provided with many addressing modes to give access to memory variables by many different routes. RISC aims to only read and write data items to memory when absolutely necessary, and provides distinct instructions (`LOAD`/`STORE`) for the purpose. As several of the addressing modes are only effective when repeated bursts of accesses to memory are carried out, the need is much less pressing

   `ADD.L (a0)+,d3`: this uses the 'address register indirect, post-increment' mode for the source operand and register direct for the destination operand. A compiler might select such an instruction when accessing an array data structure sequentially.

4. RISC compilers need to know the machine code equivalents for the HLL structures the same as CISC compilers, but also the interlocking problems due to pipelined decoding and instruction pre-fetch have to be anticipated. Reordering of instruction streams can take place at compile time if the compiler knows enough about the interlock problems that occur in the pipeline. Different CPUs have different pipeline constraints.

5. The PC relative addressing mode allows executable code to be completely relocatable. The Pentium uses segment base registers to offset the code within the virtual address space, so all Pentium addressing is relative to the start of the segment. It does not know where the segment has been located within the larger addressing space. At one time Intel demanded a complete reloading operation when changing the position of code, so things are easier now!

6. I think that the 'register indirect, post-increment' is fundamental because it underpins the fetch–execute cycle when applied to the PC (EIP) register.

7. There can be two operands and one instruction, so if you count them all as needing effective addresses, there can be three addressing modes in a single instruction. But mostly people ignore the instruction fetch and only identify the two operands.
    An effective address is an operand address which the CPU builds using the addressing mode and operand address supplied by the instruction.

8. `move.l d0,d1`   register direct, register direct
    `add.b #50,d0`   immediate or PC indirect post-increment, register direct
    `cmp.b d0,(a0)`   register direct, register indirect
    `movem.l d0-d3,-(sp)`   register direct, register indirect pre-decrement
    `bsr fred0`   immediate
    `move.w count,d6`   memory direct, register direct

9. The `dbra dx` instruction is used to implement a FOR loop using any of the eight CPU data registers as the index counter. The instruction is normally positioned at the bottom of the loop. It decrements the count register and `jmps` back if the result is positive or 0 (> -1) When the decrement results in -1 the looping stops and control drops down to the next instruction. Other similar instructions can also test a nominated CPU status flag in addition to the numeric value left in the index register.
    Start with 9 and end with -1.

10. CMP is the same as SUB (subtract) except no result is saved. The only useful effect then is the setting of CPU status flags, such as Z, C or P.

11. CPU status flags record the outcome of an instruction and relay it forward to a later instruction. Often the first part involves the ALU in a logical or arithmetic operation and the second a conditional transfer of control by the CU.
    As RISC processors have several instructions being decoded and executed simultaneously, the situation could be more complex, with status flags referring to different stages of the pipeline.

References

Adobe Systems (1985). *PostScript Language: Tutorial and Cookbook*. Reading, MA: Addison-Wesley.

Aho A. V., Kernighan B. W. and Weinberger P. J. (1988). *The AWK Programming Language*. Reading, MA: Addison-Wesley.

Anderson D. (1997). *Universal Serial Bus System Architecture*. Reading, MA: Addison-Wesley.

Anderson D. and Shanley T. (1995). *Pentium Processor System Architecture*. Reading, MA: Addison-Wesley.

Bourne S. R. (1982). *The Unix System*. Reading, MA: Addison-Wesley.

Buchanan W. (1998). *PC Interfacing: Communications and Windows Programming*. Reading, MA: Addison-Wesley.

Clements A. (1997). *Microprocessor Systems Design: 68000 Hardware, Software, and Interfacing*, 3rd edn. Boston, MA: PWS.

Comer D. E. (1999). *Computer Networks and Internets*, 2nd edn. Upper Saddle River, NJ: Prentice Hall.

Hamacher V. C., Vranesic Z. G. and Zaky S. G. (1996). *Computer Organization*, 4th edn. New York: McGraw-Hill.

Hennessy J. L. and Patterson D. A. (1998). *Computer Organization and Design: The Hardware/Software Interface* 2nd edn. San Francisco, CA: Morgan Kaufmann.

Heuring V. P. and Jordan H. F. (1997). *Computer Systems Design and Architecture*. Menlo Park, CA: Addison-Wesley.

Hodson P. (1997). *Computing: Local Area Networks*. London: Letts Educational.

Intel (1997). *Intel Architecture Software Developer's Manual*, Vol. 1: Basic Architecture. Mt Prospect, IL: Intel Corporation. Also available as a PDF file from: `http://www.intel.co.uk/design/mobile/manuals/243190.htm`.

Irvine K. R. (1999) *Assembly Language for Intel Computers*, 3rd edn. Upper Saddle River, NJ: Prentice Hall.

Jones D. S. (1988). *Assembly Programming and the 8086 Microprocessor*. Oxford: Oxford University Press.

Kernighan B. W. and Pike R. (1984). *The Unix Programming Environment*. Englewood Cliffs, NJ: Prentice Hall.

Kernighan B. W. and Ritchie D. M. (1988). *The C Programming Language*, 2nd edn. Englewood Cliffs, NJ: Prentice Hall.

Kidder T. (1981). *The Soul of a New Machine*. Boston, MA: Little, Brown.

Macario, R. C. V. (1997). *Cellular Radio*. Basingstoke: Macmillan.

Mansfield M. (1993). *The Joy of X: An Overview of the X Window System*. Wokingham: Addison-Wesley.

Messmer H.-P. (1995). *The Indispensable PC Hardware Book*, 2nd edn. Wokingham: Addison-Wesley.

Messmer H.-P. (1995). *The Indispensable Pentium Book*. Wokingham: Addison-Wesley.

Nutt G. (1999). *Operating Systems: A Modern Perspective*, 2nd edn. Reading, MA: Addison-Wesley.

Pearce E. (1997). *Windows NT in a Nutshell*. Sebastopol, CA: O'Reilly.

Redl S. M., Weber M. K. and Oliphant M. W. (1995). *An Introduction to GSM*. Boston, MA: Artech House.

Reid R. H. (1997). *Architects of the Web: 1,000 Days that Built the Future of Business*. New York: John Wiley & Sons.

Ritchie C. (1997). *Computing: Operating Systems: Incorporating Unix and Windows*. London: Letts Educational.

Schiller J. (1999). *Mobile Communications*. Harlow: Addison-Wesley.

Silberschatz A., Galvin P. and Gagne G. (2000). *Applied Operating System Concepts*. New York: John Wiley.

Simon R. J., Gouker M. and Barnes B. (1995). *Windows 95: Win32 Programming API Bible*. Indianapolis, IN: Waite Group.

Stevens W. R. (1994). *TCP/IP Illustrated*, Vol. 1: The Protocols. Reading, MA: Addison-Wesley.

Stevens W. R. (1998). *Unix Network Programming*. Upper Saddle River, NJ: Prentice Hall.

Tabak, D. (1990). *RISC Systems*. Taunton: Research Studies Press.

Tanenbaum A. S. (1996). *Computer Networks*, 3rd edn. Upper Saddle River, NJ: Prentice Hall.

Tanenbaum A. S. (1999). *Structured Computer Organization*, 4th edn. Upper Saddle River, NJ: Prentice Hall.

Texas Instruments (1984). *The TTL Data Book*. Dallas, TX: Texas Instruments, Inc.

Thewlis P. J. and Foxon B. N. T. (1983). *From Logic to Computers*. Oxford: Blackwell Scientific.

Wall L. (1996). *Programming Perl*. Sebastopol, CA: O'Reilly.

Wang P. S. (1997). *Introduction to UNIX with X and the Internet*. Boston, MA: PWS.

Index

C

D

E

H

I

W

X

Y

Z

IMPORTANT: READ CAREFULLY
WARNING: BY OPENING THE PACKAGE YOU AGREE TO BE BOUND BY THE TERMS OF THE LICENCE AGREEMENT BELOW.

This is a legally binding agreement between You (the user or purchaser) and Pearson Education Limited. By retaining this licence, any software media or accompanying written materials or carrying out any of the permitted activities You agree to be bound by the terms of the licence agreement below.

If You do not agree to these terms then promptly return the entire publication (this licence and all software, written materials, packaging and any other components received with it) with Your sales receipt to Your supplier for a full refund.

SINGLE USER LICENCE AGREEMENT

❐ YOU ARE PERMITTED TO:

- Use (load into temporary memory or permanent storage) a single copy of the software on only one computer at a time. If this computer is linked to a network then the software may only be installed in a manner such that it is not accessible to other machines on the network.
- Make one copy of the software solely for backup purposes or copy it to a single hard disk, provided you keep the original solely for back up purposes.
- Transfer the software from one computer to another provided that you only use it on one computer at a time.

❐ YOU MAY NOT:

- Rent or lease the software or any part of the publication.
- Copy any part of the documentation, except where specifically indicated otherwise.
- Make copies of the software, other than for backup purposes.
- Reverse engineer, decompile or disassemble the software.
- Use the software on more than one computer at a time.
- Install the software on any networked computer in a way that could allow access to it from more than one machine on the network.
- Use the software in any way not specified above without the prior written consent of Pearson Education Limited.

ONE COPY ONLY
This licence is for a single user copy of the software

PEARSON EDUCATION LIMITED RESERVES THE RIGHT TO TERMINATE THIS LICENCE BY WRITTEN NOTICE AND TO TAKE ACTION TO RECOVER ANY DAMAGES SUFFERED BY PEARSON EDUCATION LIMITED IF YOU BREACH ANY PROVISION OF THIS AGREEMENT.

Pearson Education Limited owns the software You only own the disk on which the software is supplied.

LIMITED WARRANTY

Pearson Education Limited warrants that the diskette or CD rom on which the software is supplied are free from defects in materials and workmanship under normal use for ninety (90) days from the date You receive them. This warranty is limited to You and is not transferable. Pearson Education Limited does not warrant that the functions of the software meet Your requirements or that the media is compatible with any computer system on which it is used or that the operation of the software will be unlimited or error free.

You assume responsibility for selecting the software to achieve Your intended results and for the installation of, the use of and the results obtained from the software. The entire liability of Pearson Education Limited and its suppliers and your only remedy shall be replacement of the components that do not meet this warranty free of charge.

This limited warranty is void if any damage has resulted from accident, abuse, misapplication, service or modification by someone other than Pearson Education Limited. In no event shall Pearson Education Limited or its suppliers be liable for any damages whatsoever arising out of installation of the software , even if advised of the possibility of such damages. Pearson Education Limited will not be liable for any loss or damage of any nature suffered by any party as a result of reliance upon or reproduction of or any errors in the content of the publication.

Pearson Education Limited does not limit its liability for death or personal injury caused by its negligence.

This licence agreement shall be governed by and interpreted and construed in accordance with English law.